The Public Administration Profession

While many introductory public administration textbooks contain a dedicated chapter on ethics, *The Public Administration Profession* is the first to utilize ethics as a lens for understanding the discipline. Analyses of the ASPA Code of Ethics are deftly woven into each chapter alongside complete coverage of the institutions, processes, concepts, persons, history, and typologies a student needs to gain a thorough grasp of public service as a field of study and practice. Features include:

- A significant focus on "public interests," nonprofit management, hybrid-private organizations, contracting out and collaborations, and public service at state and local levels.
- A careful examination of the role that religion may play in public servants' decision making, as well as the unignorable and growing role that faith-based organizations play in public administration and nonprofit management at large.
- End-of-chapter ethics case studies, key concepts and persons, and dedicated "local community action steps" in each chapter.
- Appendices dedicated to future public administration and nonprofit career management, writing successful papers throughout a student's career, and professional codes of ethics.
- A comprehensive suite of online supplements, including: lecture slides; quizzes and sample for undergraduate and graduate courses containing multiple choice, true-false, identifications, and essay questions; chapter outlines with suggestions for classroom discussion; and suggestions for use of appendices, e.g., how to successfully write a short term paper, a brief policy memo, resume, or a book review.

Providing students with a comprehensive introduction to the subject while offering instructors an elegant new way to bring ethics prominently into the curriculum, *The Public Administration Profession* is an ideal introductory text for public administration and public affairs courses at the undergraduate or graduate level.

Bradley S. Chilton is Professor and Director of the Public Administration Program at the University of Texas at El Paso, USA.

Stephen M. King is Professor and Chair of Government, History, and Criminal Justice at Regent University, USA.

Viviane E. Foyou is Assistant Professor in the Public Administration Program at the University of Texas at El Paso, USA.

J. Scott McDonald is Professor in the Public Administration Program at the University of Texas at El Paso, USA.

"I appreciate the balanced approach of this textbook... the authors have done an impressive job at providing readers with exposure to key thinkers within the discipline. As a professor who is consistently frustrated with introductory PA textbooks that have an unbalanced approach to the levels of government, the structure and foci of this textbook are refreshing. Finally, the authors' decision to ground the contents of the textbook in the ASPA Code of Ethics is exciting, and I think breathes life into a type of textbook that can otherwise come across as muddled and excessively broad."

—**Anthony Campbell**, *Tennessee State University, USA*

"I really like this book... it offers a lot of depth and theoretical background to explain why we 'do' public administration a certain way and where the ideas came from. I also like the focus on ethics, which is a key topic that many texts usually cover at the end and in a manner that is not practical for students. The case studies at the end of each chapter of extremely helpful, as well, and something that I would use. Finally, I am very pleased that there is a chapter on non-profits which is something I have wanted to include in more depth in my course."

—**Chad Kinsella**, *Ball State University, USA*

"... it appears to have a novel approach and in-depth information. I think the book has tremendous strength in terms of its approach and its focus on ethics. Furthermore, the inclusion of topics like 'state and local government administration,' and 'non-profit and faith based organizations' is very important which makes this book more suitable for our students. In addition, the specific sections of each chapter including case study, discussion question, and action steps are very unique and extremely useful in class and outside learning."

—**Suparna Soni**, *SUNY-Buffalo State, USA*

"*The Public Administration Profession* weaves core topics of public administration with essential ethical concepts to create a textbook that is both engaging and practical with chapters that provide case studies highlighting contemporary topics. The material is easily accessible for the traditional student and for the in-practice professional and provides assistance to aid students in developing their writing and critical thinking skills. *The Public Administration Profession* fills a void in current offerings by providing a text that reminds the reader of the importance of incorporating ethics into all aspects of public administration."

—**Cindy Davis**, *Stephen F. Austin State University, USA*

The Public Administration Profession

Policy, Management, and Ethics

BRADLEY S. CHILTON

STEPHEN M. KING

VIVIANE E. FOYOU

J. SCOTT MCDONALD

Routledge
Taylor & Francis Group

NEW YORK AND LONDON

First published 2019
by Routledge
711 Third Avenue, New York, NY 10017

and by Routledge
2 Park Square, Milton Park, Abingdon, Oxon, OX14 4RN

Routledge is an imprint of the Taylor & Francis Group, an informa business

Library of Congress Cataloging-in-Publication Data
Names: Chilton, Bradley Stuart, author. | King, Stephen M. Ph. D., author. |
   Foyou, Viviane E., author. | McDonald, J. Scott, author.
Title: The public administration profession : policy, management, and
   ethics / Bradley S. Chilton, Stephen M. King, Viviane E. Foyou, and
   J. Scott McDonald.
Description: New York, NY : Routledge, 2018. | Includes bibliographical
   references and index.
Identifiers: LCCN 2018011327| ISBN 9780815353430 (hardback :
   alk. paper) | ISBN 9780815353447 (pbk. : alk. paper) | ISBN
   9781351136389 (ebook)
Subjects: LCSH: Public administration—Moral and ethical aspects—Study
   and teaching. | Public administration—Study and teaching.
Classification: LCC JF1525.E8 C54 2018 | DDC 172/.2—dc23
LC record available at https://lccn.loc.gov/2018011327

ISBN: 978-0-8153-5343-0 (hbk)
ISBN: 978-0-8153-5344-7 (pbk)
ISBN: 978-1-351-13638-9 (ebk)

Typeset in Sabon
by Apex CoVantage, LLC

Visit the eResources: www.routledge.com/9780815353447

For Love. BSC
For Debbie, Michelle, and Joshua. SMK
For Irene. VEF
For victims of floods and catastrophes everywhere. JSM

CONTENTS

PREFACE

We present an overview of public administration and policy emphasizing ethics and the public interests, with chapter-by-chapter analysis of the *Code of Ethics* of the American Society for Public Administration. We jump off from current global thinking on the public interests and other concepts congruent with public interests, such as the commons, regime values, the ethics of caring, and moral readings of the Constitution—in new scholarship by economists, philosophers, psychologists, lawyers, and public administrators. This is not your parents' concept of the public interest, which was discarded by skeptics for imposition of the will to power with one right answer to the issues of public goods and services. This is a new pluralistic concept of the public interests emerging from close empirical data that belie the reality of shared meanings of public goods and service, but with varieties of answers.

More pivotal, we address a crisis in public service ethics, particularly in federal public service. The 2017 U.S. Congress Joint Economic Committee reported that "Over the past six months, the Office of Government Ethics has received 39,105 inquiries—up more than 5,000 percent over the comparable period leading up to President Obama's 2012 election and first months in office."[1] While many want change, no one wants to live with corruption, moral myopia or sociopathic upheaval of public bureaucrats. Instead, it is a critical time for public service ethics, empathy, caring, honesty, respect for the commons, and moral readings of the law. These are the *public interests* we expect of the public administration profession—the values embedded in every decision, action, accounting, and leaders' call in public goods and services. The real behaviors of these public values belie shared patterns of moral reasoning. Rather than relegate public service ethics to some obscure narrow professional code of a list of don'ts—or a chapter at the end of the book—we integrate ethics systematically throughout public administration processes, institutions, and roles. Our book recites one precept per chapter from the American Society for Public Administration Code of Ethics. We discuss each Code of Ethics precept fully and with the professional enforcement mechanisms now in place. No other current textbook on the market fully includes the current ASPA Code of Ethics and their enforcement mechanisms, and incorporates these with the traditional overview of public administration institutions, processes and roles. Thus, this book may be useful for pre- and post-integration of ethics in both the introductory course and capstone in helping to produce the public administration profession.

We write this book with hope for a new generation of public administrators with the knowledge, skills, and abilities to administer ethically and in the public interests; to see beyond themselves to each another and their citizenry. Each chapter begins with recitation and discussion of an applied ethical precept from the American Society for Public Administration Code of Ethics, with application and examples from basic topics in a traditional survey of public administration. We survey all the usual topics, concepts, persons, histories, and typologies—in text and boxed inserts—as found in most public administration survey textbooks. In addition, we also feature nonprofits, faith-based organizations, hybrid-private organizations, contracting out and collaborations, and include greater attention to public service in state and local governments as well as in national government. We also include appendices on writing papers and memos in public administration, on personal career management, and professional ethics codes from ASPA, ICMA, the U.S. government, the Department of Defense, and the state of Texas. However, we keep our steady focus on public service ethics and the public interests throughout, such as constitutional duties, democracy and communities, and leadership integrity. Each chapter closes with an applied ethical case study, end-of-chapter lists of key concepts and figures, as well as follow-up activities such as action steps for your local setting.

The text is divided into two parts. Part I introduces the *Foundations of the Public Administration Profession* in history, democratic policymaking, the Constitution and laws, and the public interests. We cover the same introductory concepts, names, and typologies found in most introductory public administration texts. However, we embed within these the three basic ethical perspectives of the study of the public administration profession: virtue, utility, and duty—and how all are linked together in the applied ethical concept of the public interests. The virtue ethical perspective focuses on the good moral character and leadership professionalism of public administrators with their publics and colleagues, attending to ethical virtue theory, with issues such as professional ethics, excessive loyalty, and whistleblowing. This is illustrated by examples of good moral character in the lives of ordinary public administrators, famous leaders, reformers, academics, as well as nonprofit and faith-based participants. Our ethics case study spotlights socialization in children's literature to the public service profession and the character of bureaucrats depicted in Dr. Seuss: superheroes, sociopaths, or detached? The utility ethical perspective focuses on administrators' decision making in calculation of individual preferences or cost/benefits, attending to ethical utilitarian theory, with issues of majoritarianism and democracy. This is placed within the context of democratic institutions and public policy and practices of policy analysts who must balance the commons, public interests, and individual preferences. We closely examine the utility perspective in an ethics case study of the ethics of citizenship in public administration and facilitating democratic policymaking. The duty ethical perspective focuses on the obligations and rules that are weighed upon public administrators, attending to ethical deontology theory, and issues such as rights and duties, equality and discrimination. This is embodied in the Constitution and laws that impose responsibilities upon public administrators. We zoom in on the duty perspective with an ethics case study of information ethics for bureaucrats. We link these virtue, utility, and duty perspectives together in the applied ethical concept of the public interests. We seek meaning from current global scholarship by economists, philosophers, psychologists, and public administrators of concepts that are congruent with public interests, such as the commons, regime values, the ethics of caring, and moral readings of the Constitution. Our ethics case study focuses on the public interest standard in regulation of broadcast media, including radio, television, and now the internet—and the competing demands of the commons, fairness, and integrity.

Part II overviews the *Applications of the Public Administration Profession* (i.e., its functions), with ethical virtue, utility, and duty perspectives in the public interests. Once again, we cover the same introductory concepts, names, and typologies found in most introductory public administration texts on these basic topics. However, we integrate ethics throughout our survey of the practice of these public service applications. First, we check administrative practices of federalism, states, and local communities, such as intergovernmental grants and the constitutional police powers of states, cities, and local government. In this context, we critique the public ethical issues of honesty, evasion, and transparency. Second, we examine public organizations management, including closed and open systems, public management, and entrepreneurial tools of the New Public Service. We critique the ethical issues of loyalty and whistleblowing, especially within public management. Third, we canvass human resources management in the public sector, including historical and current issues of human resources development unions, collective bargaining, and professionalism. We critique the ethical issues of discrimination, affirmative action, and equal opportunity within the public workplace. Fourth, we assay public financial management, including public budgetary politics, public finance, and the management of costs and benefits in the public interests. We critique the ethical issues of corruption within public financial management. Fifth, we analyze nonprofits and faith-based organizations, including the ascendance of the voluntary sector, public service by religious organizations, and current partnerships with public agencies. Our ethics case study critiques contributions and conflicts of faith and religion in public service ethics.

Finally, we close with an *Epilogue* on the public administration profession, including a predictive ethical directional model, as well as aspirations for a more ethical public service in the public interests, and the future of the public administration profession. *Appendices* include primary source materials for professionalism and administrative ethics in the public sector, links for career management and resume-building skills, and comments on information literacy and writing in public administration.

NOTE

1. Senator Martin Heinrich, "The Costs of Corruption to the American Economy" (May 2017), *U.S. Congress Joint Economic Committee*, retrieved from www.jec.senate. gov/public/_cache/files/c6be7b7d-cb39-499a-b6d6-d5b3d65368c8/the-costs-of-corruption-to-the-american-economy-final.pdf. Others go further to marshal evidence that we live under leadership of an entire generation of sociopaths; that our public leaders have boldly flaunted their lack of empathy, narcissism, and disregard for the facts—acting, in other words, as sociopaths. See Bruce Cannon Gibney, *A Generation of Sociopaths: How the Baby Boomers Betrayed America* (New York: Hachette Books, 2017).

SUMMARY TABLE OF CONTENTS

PART I: FOUNDATIONS OF THE PUBLIC ADMINISTRATION PROFESSION

The text is divided into two parts. *Part I* introduces the *Foundations of the Public Administration Profession* in history, democratic policymaking, the Constitution and laws, and the public interests. We cover the same introductory concepts, names, and typologies found in most introductory to public administration texts. However, we embed within these the three basic ethical perspectives of the study of the public administration profession: virtue, utility, and duty—and how all are linked together in the applied ethical concept of the public interests. The virtue ethical perspective focuses on the good moral character and leadership professionalism of public administrators with their publics and colleagues, attending to ethical virtue theory, with issues such as professional ethics, excessive loyalty, and whistleblowing. This is illustrated by examples of good moral character in the lives of ordinary public administrators, famous leaders, reformers, academics, as well as nonprofit and faith-based participants. Our ethics case study spotlights socialization in children's literature to the public service profession and the character of bureaucrats depicted in Dr. Seuss: superheroes, sociopaths, or detached? The utility ethical perspective focuses on administrators' decision making in calculation of individual preferences or cost/benefits, attending to ethical utilitarian theory, with issues of majoritarianism and democracy. This is placed within the context of democratic institutions and public policy and practices of policy analysts who must balance the commons, public interests, and individual preferences. We closely examine the utility perspective in an ethics case study of the ethics of citizenship in public administration and facilitating democratic policymaking. The duty ethical perspective focuses on the obligations and rules that are burdened upon public administrators, attending to ethical deontology theory, and issues such as rights and duties, equality, and discrimination. This is embodied in the Constitution and laws that impose responsibilities upon public administrators. We zoom in on the duty perspective with an ethics case study of information ethics for bureaucrats. We link these virtue, utility, and duty ethical perspectives together with the applied ethical concept of the public interests. We seek meaning from current global scholarship by economists, philosophers, psychologists, and public administrators of concepts that are congruent with public interests, such as the commons, regime values, the ethics of caring, and moral readings of the Constitution. Our ethics case study focuses on the public interest standard in regulation of broadcast media, including radio, television, and now the internet—and the competing demands of the commons, fairness, and integrity.

PART II: APPLICATIONS OF THE PUBLIC ADMINISTRATION PROFESSION

Part II overviews the *Applications of the Public Administration Profession* (i.e., its functions) with ethical virtue, utility, and duty perspectives in the public interests. Once again, we cover the same introductory concepts, names, and typologies found in most introductory public administration texts on these basic topics. However, we integrate ethics throughout our survey of the practice of these public service applications. First, we check administrative practices of federalism, states, and local communities, such as intergovernmental grants and the constitutional police powers of states, cities, and local government. In this context, we critique the public ethical issues of honesty, evasion, and transparency. Second, we examine public organizations management, including closed and open systems, public management, and entrepreneurial tools of the New Public Service. We critique the ethical issues of loyalty and whistleblowing, especially within public management. Third, we canvass human resources management in the public sector, including historical and current issues of human resources development unions, collective bargaining, and professionalism. We critique the ethical issues of discrimination, affirmative action, and equal opportunity within the public workplace. Fourth, we assay public financial management, including public budgetary politics, public finance, and the management of costs and benefits in the public interests. We critique the ethical issues of corruption within public financial management. Fifth, we analyze nonprofits and faith-based organizations, including the ascendance of the voluntary sector, public service by religious organizations, and current partnerships with public agencies. Our ethics case study critiques contributions and conflicts of faith and religion in public service ethics.

Finally, we close with an *Epilogue* on the public administration profession, including a predictive ethical directional model, as well as aspirations for a more ethical public service in the public interests, and the future of the public administration profession. *Appendices* include primary source materials for professionalism and administrative ethics in the public sector, links for career management and resume-building skills, and comments on information literacy and writing in public administration.

ACKNOWLEDGMENTS

It is not possible to name all the persons—our faculty and mentors, colleagues, students, friends, and family—who have directly or indirectly contributed to the development of this book. It would require many more pages, and even then we may miss someone. Please know that you are all dearly appreciated—and you know who you are! We give special thanks to the support of directors, chairs, and administrators at our various academic stations that have supported this project.

The heart of this book came from a dialog on the hope of public administration to share meaning, the commons, and the public interests. We may not have written it all down in these pages, but we stand in responsibility for this book.

Foundations of the Public Administration Profession

The Public Interests[1]

"Advance the Public Interest. Promote the interests of the public and put service to the public above service to oneself."

—(Code of Ethics, American Society for Public Administration, 2013)

BOX 1.1 | CHAPTER OBJECTIVES

1 Introduce yourself to the public administration profession, including the plural concept of the public interests, definitions of public administration, private versus public administration, and professionalism.

2 Define the plural concept of public interests and distinguish between ethical virtue, utility and duty perspectives of the public interests, emphasizing virtue, utilitarian, and deontological ethical theories.

3 Compare public interests perspectives of political philosophers, economists, and public administrators, and their contributions to the development of the concept of the public interests.

4 Critique the public interest standard regulations by the Federal Communications Commission (FCC), with applications today to the internet, social media, and digital knowledge.

INTRODUCTION

We live in a time of crisis in public service ethics. The 2017 U.S. Congress Joint Economic Committee reported that, "Over the past six months, the Office of Government Ethics has received 39,105 inquiries—up more than 5,000 percent over the comparable period leading up to President Obama's 2012 election and first months in office." While many want change, no one wants live with corruption and sociopathic upheaval of public bureaucrats. This book, *The Public Administration Profession*, posits a corrective for public service focused on ethics and public interests prescriptions from the American Society for Public Administration (**ASPA) Code of Ethics**[2] and elsewhere. We focus on the **plural concept of public interests**—including the commons, **regime values**, ethics of caring, and moral readings of the Constitution. This is not your parents' concept of the singular "public interest," which was discarded by skeptics for imposition of the will to power with one right answer to the issues of public goods and services. Instead, this is a return to the etymological root which was always plural for others: *pubes + koinon* (Greek, "to be mature and take care of others").[3] This is also a new pluralistic concept of the public interests emerging from close empirical data that belie the reality of shared meanings of public goods and service, but with varieties of answers. While we may still use the "public interest" here and there as we continue our analysis in this book, we imply a plural meaning, and seek to use "the public interests" (emphasis added) to make our points. Further, we present an overview of public administration featuring ethics woven into its heart. Rather than push ethics into a back corner, we integrate ethics chapter by chapter with all the typical institutions, processes, concepts, persons, history, and typologies as found in most public administration surveys. We prominently feature one precept per chapter from the ASPA Code of Ethics—as well as other ethical sources—with full discussion, examples, self-analysis, and applications with professional enforcement mechanisms. Further, unlike other survey texts, we expand coverage of information technology, nonprofit organizations, faith-based organizations, hybrid-private organizations, contracting out and collaborations, and greater attention to public service at the state and local government levels. We also include end-of-chapter ethics case studies, lists of key concepts and persons, and local community action steps—as well as appendices on writing papers, on personal career management, and professional ethics codes. Thus, our text may be useful for pre- and post-integration of ethics as both an introduction and an exit-capstone in helping shape the future public administration profession.

In contrast to our current era of baby-boomer sociopaths, you may have heard about times or places[4] in America that people came together for a common goal, and put service to the public above service to oneself—as in the ethics precept quoted above from the Code of Ethics of the American Society of Public Administration.[5] Like World War II, when folks gave up metal or rationed gasoline and sugar to fight Nazi fascists? Or after the tragic terrorism events of September 11, 2001? Or perhaps you recall the efforts of police, firefighters, and other first responders who rescued flooded families in New Orleans after Hurricane Katrina, or in New Jersey after Hurricane Sandy? Or members of the U.S. armed service in the global war on terrorism? Or maybe you've seen these united, exhausted but heroic public servants on the streets where you live after that nearby memorable but tragic event, e.g., a tornado, a flood, an earthquake, or other massive tragedy? Do you remember how everyone came to each other and tried to work together, Republican and Democrat, liberal and conservative, Right and Left? Do you remember your feelings in seeing people working together in unity who were former bickering political enemies? Do you remember how people tried to see other people as fellow Americans rather than as competitors in the game of life, or as different in race or ethnicity, or viewpoint?

If you can envision these moments, moments of governance after a crisis or tragedy, you remember administration in the public interests. It is in these moments we see good people overcome the looking-out-for-number-one cult of contemporary American culture. It is often during times of great tragedy that we remember other lessons of our youth—lessons of empathy, goodwill toward others, and caring for one another. In these moments we often witness the best in ourselves and in one another.

Of course, we live in times of criticism and complaint about government— government can't do this or it won't do that. Some of this criticism is on target, but we argue much of this criticism is misplaced or overlooks a bigger picture. And we feel its impact throughout our lives. Let's briefly visit some of how government impacts us daily. Let's start with you lying in bed, your clock radio clicks on to one of your favorite songs—the radio station is federally licensed and must operate to established standards. You lift your head off the pillow—also made to federal standards—pull back the covers and pop off the mattress—made to federal standards. In the bathroom you run some water—provided to you by standards established by the federal government and usually maintained by your local government. Over to the toilet—made to federal, state, and local government standards to be low-flow to use less water. On to breakfast—those food labels are there because of government. And those organic blueberries—they can't be labeled organic unless they meet a set of stringent standards. You catch the weather forecast before leaving for work—that's from the National Weather Service, a part of the federal government. Off to work, drive or take the bus? The bus is usually operated by local government. But today, we'll drive. The roads—potholes and all—government. In fact, just 3.3 percent of the numbers of interstate highways were in unsatisfactory condition in 2014, and the number of traffic fatalities has declined from 51,091 in 1980 to 32,674 in 2014, even though the number of licensed drivers increased from 145 million to 214 million.[6] If you drive an interstate highway—that's the federal and state governments. Your car must meet a boatload of federal standards, from mileage standards to dozens of safety requirements. From windshield wipers to the rearview mirror, to seatbelts and airbags—all required by government. Boring drive to work—check your cell phone for texts—many locales in the **public sector** won't let you do that while driving because, based on federal research that found distracted driving is worse than drunk driving, your local government made driving while texting a crime.

So, what is this public sector? Many think of government jobs when they think of the public sector. We popularly imagine some kind of giant "think tank" where bureaucrats sit at desks all day behind closed doors in neat rows of cubicles, dreaming up things to regulate. The reality is that most **government workers** in the public sector aren't bureaucrats. Steve Ballmer, former CEO of Microsoft, owner of the Los Angeles Clippers and co-owner of USAFacts with his wife (Connie), has found that government workers are really part of a "do tank" involved in direct service to the public. In fact, 90 percent of the 23 million public employees—federal, state, and local governments—are the public servants we come into daily service contact with in hospitals, transportation, parks and recreation, and elsewhere. Nearly half work in education, and roughly 10 percent are active-duty military or involved in police protection.[7] And that doesn't include the millions of other public servants who work in nonprofit organizations, e.g., the Red Cross, the local YWCA, or in hybrid-private organizations that provide public services, e.g., the Medicare-supplement insurance company for your grandmother or other elderly relative.

The intention of our first chapter is to provide a meaningful "big picture" understanding of it all by investigation into the "public" of public administration—the public interests. We will principally examine it through historical and philosophical lenses, while focusing on working definitions, characteristics, and typologies of the public interests, with application to an ethics case study of the **public interest standard** in regulations of the **Federal Communications Commission** (**FCC**). Our summary reflections and implications for the public administration profession take us to the following chapters and applications. But, first, we must overview the meaning of public administration as a concept and as an academic discipline. And distinguish public enterprise from private enterprise.

What is Public Administration?

The many **definitions** of **public administration** are surprisingly diverse. While only some definitions of public administration explicitly include mention of the public interest(s), all include the closely related concept of public. Defining public administration is like the story about six blind men trying to define an elephant. Each touched only a certain part of the elephant, but not the whole. So, the blind man who touched the trunk talked of the elephant as a creature with a huge elongated nose. The blind man who touched the leg talked of the tree-trunk foot. The blind man who touched the tail talked of a snake. So it is with empirical descriptions from an external perspective: no one really sees the big picture—and certainly not from the elephant's perspective!

Definitions of Public Administration   Michael C. Lemay defines public administration as "Whatever governments do to develop and implement public policy."[8] For Nicholas Henry, public administration is a

> broad-ranging and amorphous combination of theory and practice; its purpose is to promote a superior understanding of government and its relationship with the society it governs, as well as to encourage public policies more responsive to social needs and to institute managerial practices attuned to effectiveness, efficiency, and the deeper human requisites of the citizenry.[9]

Richard Stillman describes public bureaucracy as

> The structure and personnel of organizations, rooted in formal laws and informal processes, that collectively function as the core system of U.S. government and that both determine and carry out public policies using a high degree of specialized expertise and technologies.[10]

Melvin J. Dubnick and Barbara S. Romzek define public administration as the "Systematic examination and analysis of the institutions, agents, and processes used in governments' efforts to manage the pursuit of publicly defined societal values."[11] Jay M. Shafritz and E.W. Russell provide eighteen different definitions of public administration, each one including four primary values associated with public administration and affairs: political, managerial, legal, and occupational.[12] George J. Gordon and Michael E. Milakovich define public administration as "All processes, organizations, individuals . . . associated with carrying out laws and other rules adopted or issued by legislatures, executives, and courts."[13] For George Berkley and John Rouse, public administration is "The process of implementing those diverse values in our complex and ever changing society and therefore plays a vital role in the daily lives of all citizens."[14] David H. Rosenbloom posits public administration as "the use of managerial, political, and legal theories and processes to fulfill legislative, executive, and judicial governmental mandates for the provision of regulatory and service functions for the society as a whole or for some segments of it."[15] Robert B. Denhardt defines public administration simply as "the management of public programs."[16] Carl E. Lutrin and Allen K. Settle define public administration as the study of people in organizations, of how these people interact within the organization, and of how the organization relates to the larger political environment, or to that part of the public domain that is primarily concerned with resolving public issues.[17]

David Schuman and Dick W. Olufs III provide no definition.[18] For William C. Johnson, public administration is "simply the activities of government that supply goods and services to the public."[19]

Clearly, scholars do not agree on all aspects of the definition of public administration or all of its key themes. This may be due to the many mini-paradigms of public administration—rather than one dominant academic approach.[20] But it does make a difference for public administrators and it *should* make a difference for scholars and students regarding clarifying a definition and highlighting various themes. And the definition of public administration makes a difference in understanding the public interests. Certainly, American politics and government are linked to an administration of policy, and administration of policy requires fulfilling the public interests as something more than merely the sum of the interests of special client groups or the private market. Or has the recent pursuit of market demands, performance management, and clientele group demands overshadowed the need of the common good, or the public interests? We will examine these dimensions in defining public administration through its evolution within the context of American public administration practices.

Private Versus Public Administration   Another path to definition may be to distinguish **public administration from private**. Are there any differences between Exxon and the Department of Energy, between General Motors and the Department of Transportation, or between Satya Nadella as CEO of Microsoft and Donald J. Trump as President of the United States? On the surface, the answer seems an easy yes. But critics contend that there is such a blurring effect between what is private and public that, perhaps, the obvious answer is not an unequivocal "Yes." For example, both traditional public actors, such as police, and private actors, such as law firms, work to enforce the criminal law and achieve the public interests. If a blurring effect does occur, does this mean we should privatize all government departments and agencies, and nationalize all private firms?[21] We don't think this would be prudent or politically acceptable.

One way to help explain the difference between private and public administration is according to differences between politics and markets, or between government and economics. Robert Dahl (1915–2014) and Charles Lindblom (1917–)[22] argued that the primary reason for the existence of public organizations was due to how governments were formed and why economic market mechanisms worked in the first place. Dahl and Lindblom originally contended in their 1953 work that the complex pluralistic and multi-headed beast that is government, departments, and agencies, which they termed polyarchy, controlled the economics of a society. In their 1976 edition, however, they conceded that various changes over the interim period, both institutionally and procedurally, contributed not so much to a change in the original thesis, but in the dynamic of that relationship; for example, a shift from legislative control over the economy to an imperial presidential control over the economy directly influenced the growth of the public sector, particularly in terms of regulatory nature.

Politics of society regulates human behavior—behavior that is often displayed through economic markets, which is the voluntary buying and selling of goods and services in an open market system, such as in a capitalist state like the United States.[23] It is the responsibility of the government to oversee or correct any problems that arise in the free market system, such as collusion, illegal mergers, depressions and recessions, monopolies and the like. In addition, government uses its taxing power to distribute and redistribute goods and services from those who have to those who have not—a practice that is politically and ideologically divisive. Liberals, for example, call for a greater involvement of the government in the market itself, whereas conservatives generally disfavor unwanted advances by government into the private market.[24] However, after the financial meltdown of the lending, mortgage, and financial institutions in the fall of 2008, future reforms and reformers may seriously rethink how, and to what extent, governments should and will allow the free market their free rein in a democratic society.

Some say that "public" means "people" and "private" means being "deprived of public office or set apart from government as a personal matter."[25] "Public" derives from two Greek words: the first is *pubes*, antecedent to our word "maturity." The Greeks understood that maturity was a moving away from oneself toward an understanding of others. The second word is *koinon*, meaning "common." *Koinon* is also derived from another Greek word, *kom-is*, meaning "to care for others."[26] Thus, both terms imply some kind of relationship, presumably between those who govern and those who are governed. That relationship is not one of self-directedness, but one of public directedness—directed outward, not inward. Public organizations, then, are designed to administer to needs and demands of the public as a whole, not to a select few, thus fulfilling the public interests.

H. George Frederickson (1934–) and others contend, however, that the original meaning of public has been lost, and was replaced with terms like politics and government. Frederickson even argues that the word "public" is now considered frivolous, inadequate, and even meaningless, especially when attached to other words, such as "public good" or "public interests." He argues this transformation is a philosophical one: moving from the original Greek influence to a crass economic one, where, as he notes,

> We are to determine well-being, pleasure, or utility by consequences or
> results—preferably by bureaucratic, technological, or scientific means. There
> is no public, only the sum of atomistic individuals. And there is no public
> interest, except in summing up the aggregate of individual interests.[27]

It is economic bottom-line thinking that Frederickson claims is behind the development of Dahl and Lindblom's politics and markets explanation, thus "judg(ing) consequences or results by the technology of the market" and, by implication, "contribut(ing) to the loss of an ennobling concept of the public."[28]

There are additional distinctions of public organizations and their members. The CEO of the USA (i.e., the President), as opposed to a private corporate CEO (e.g., Satya Nadella), holds an office that is bound by legal authority, usually via a constitution or written contract of some form. Public officials are then bound by oath and affirmation to uphold this legally binding document. They are then empowered to legislate, execute, adjudicate, and administer decisions, such as laws, executive orders, court decisions, and regulations, to the greater public. Public

officials are publicly accountable for their decisions, both in terms of legal authority and at the ballot box. Finally, public officials are empowered to consider the
interests of the whole body or constituency and not just the interests of a few.

According to the atomistic notion of our free market system, private sector
officials and companies are only required to make a profit. Private sector officials,
such as Satya Nadella, are not bound by a constitution or other legally binding
document. Rather they are bound by a pledge to their company's shareholders to
make a profit and return some of that profit to them in the form of stock dividends. Further, Microsoft, for example, is not publicly accountable—at least, not
in the political sense. They are accountable to the buying public of their products
and services. And, last, Satya Nadella's sole concern is to make sure Microsoft's
buying public is satisfied with the products and services he produces, not with
someone who buys an Apple.

However, more and more companies do recognize that they have a larger,
more systemic place and purpose in society today, such as promoting the public
good or the commons, and not one of simply making a profit for themselves. Wal-
Mart and Target stores, for example, work with and in the local communities
they reside in, sponsoring events and movements, from environmental protection
to educational progressivism. There is growing public pressure upon the private
sector, especially with mega-retail companies like Wal-Mart, or power companies
like AES and AIMco, to contribute to the community rather than simply taking from it. Wal-Mart, for example, markets itself as being committed to building community relationships and partnerships through such programs as Kids
Recycling Challenge and Community Grant Programs,[29] while the relatively new
power company AES provides not only electrical power to many customers in
the United States and in twenty-seven nations worldwide, it also helps establish
infrastructure in China, Venezuela, and Qatar, and donates funds for habitable
parkland in Indiana.[30] This pursuit of the public good by many in the private
sector lends credence to the development of the public interests. So, even though
the terms "public" and "private" do have differences in meaning, especially with
regard to philosophical, legal, political, economic, and ethical approaches, there
are indeed practical similarities. Specifically, it seems both private and public
organizations seek ethical control within their respective organizations through
ethical accountability.

Ethics and Professionalism in Public Administration

There has been a rebirth of **moral inquiry** in the social sciences, overcoming old
fears of conformity, intolerance, and idiosyncratic and superstitious approaches
to morality. Social scientists such as James Q. Wilson, Amartya Sen, Robert Bel-
lah, Carol Gilligan, and many others have persuaded social scientists to attend
to the moral aspects of social phenomena. Social sciences such as criminal justice and social work now require competence in philosophical ethics as well as
professional ethics. Much of this has been in response to the perceived need for
accountability. With this comes a choice of morality and ethics over cronyism and
expediency. This rebirth of ethics does not come from a specific religious sect or a
liberal or conservative ideology—or the sectarian bias attached. Instead, it speaks
to all from a humanistic point of view and demonstrates what it means to do the
right thing. Morality is not relegated to the heap of traditionalism and conformity,

for even the liberal belief in individual freedoms is itself a moral belief about state evenhandedness among the competing conceptions of the good life. Fears of an imperialistic and intolerant morality are unfounded. And the dismissal of morality as idiosyncratic, superstitious, and merely the will to power would similarly make all social science impossible and anarchistic; objectivity is as possible and desirable in a moral science as in any other.[31]

The revival of moral inquiry in the social sciences has prospered particularly in the study of public administration.[32] After decades of skepticism in **logical positivism** and behavioralism, a growing group of scholars and practitioners have argued against moral relativism and logical positivism and posited alternatives, including constitutional ethics[33] and moral decision-making models.[34] Not limited to merely some revival of abstract theories or philosophical ethics, these diverse scholars have sought a more systematic understanding of ethics in public administration through the applied ethics concept of the public interests.[35] The Network of Schools of Public Policy, Affairs and Administration (NASPAA), official global accreditors of the professional Master's degree in Public Administration (i.e., the MPA and MPP), requires specified ethical knowledge, skills, and abilities in two of its five basic competencies.[36] The leading academic association of public administration, American Society for Public Administration (ASPA), has proposed and accepted the 2013 ASPA Code of Ethics for practitioners, reflected in the professional ethics precept quote at the beginning of each chapter, and in Appendix A.[37]

The ASPA Code of Ethics also comes with provisions for examination and recommendation of disciplinary action by peer public administrators. The **ASPA Ethics Review Process** was added to the ASPA Code of Ethics in 2014 by the ASPA National Council and ASPA membership approval of the **Ethics and Standards Implementation Committee** (ESI Committee).[38] This ASPA committee has the purpose of providing education about public service ethics, raising awareness of ethical issues and support of a review process for ASPA members. Thus, the ASPA Code of Ethics becomes real because it connects to real behaviors and practices in which each member of the profession is "the keeper of the code."[39] The ASPA **Section on Ethics and Integrity in Governance** (SEIGOV) assists in the education and training of the Ethics Committee. The ASPA Ethics Review Process entails:

1. complaint about a member to the Ethics and Standards Implementation Committee;
2. understanding of the behavior that led to the complaint and determination of this represents a potential violation of the ASPA Code of Ethics;
3. if there is appears to be a violation, the ESI Committee will encourage voluntary corrective action;
4. if the member refuses to comply and the continuing behavior would be a serious violation of the ASPA Code of Ethics, the ESI Committee will investigate the case to confirm the facts of the complaint, with a fact-finding body appointed by the ASPA Executive Director in consultation with the ASPA President;
5. the ESI Committee determines the next step—if the evidence doesn't support the allegation, the complaint is **dismissed.** If the evidence supports the allegation, the ESI Committee may recommend **private censure** communicated only to the member. In more serious circumstances, the

ESI Committee may recommend **public censure** and, in extraordinary circumstances, **removal** from the ASPA. Any sanction made public must first be approved by the ASPA National Council after a confidential hearing in which the member may be present.

6. A complete process for reviewing complaints is provided to protect the due process rights of all members. With this self-monitoring process and reviews, "the Code of Ethics is not just a statement of aspirations that members can decide whether and how to apply themselves."[40]

These processes make the ASPA Code of Ethics real for all members.

Thus, **professionalism** has taken the center stage in today's moral reforms of bureaucracy. We live in an era dominated by the demand that public servants always act properly and professionally toward citizens, clientele, and one another. Doing what is right is demanded, not simply hoped for, and administrators and officials are often criticized for perceived failures to do what is right. Cronyism, illegal diversion of funds, corruption and bribery, abuse of power, and other failures of public service are no longer tolerated. Instead, our society aspires to professionalism and ethics within public service, which has been defined as:

> Professionalism in the public service is an overarching value that determines how its activities will be carried out. It encompasses all other values that guide the public service such as loyalty, neutrality, transparency, diligence, punctuality, effectiveness, impartiality, and other values that may be specific to individual countries. Ethics in the public service are broad norms that delineate how public servants should exercise judgment and discretion in carrying out their official duties. These values and norms are better reinforced if there exists a system of administrative policies, management practices, and oversight agents that provide incentives and penalties to encourage public servants to professionally carry out their duties and observe high standards of conduct.[41]

For example, according to a 2000 survey of the federal executive branch, there were significant relationships between program awareness (i.e., familiarity with professionalism and the Rules of Ethical Conduct program), program usefulness (i.e., in making employees more aware of issues, and in guiding decisions and conduct), and satisfactory outcomes of employee performance. State and municipal ethics studies and surveys show similar findings: for example, with the advent of ethics codes, there has been a greater ethical awareness by citizens and greater degree of compliance by public officials. And overall, public administration scholars find that professionalism and the study and teaching of ethics is on the rise. What does the attention to professionalism mean for administration in the public interests?

Professionalism is fundamentally based in moral conduct, including competence, by persons in a relationship of trust or accountability to others. It is founded in ethics—the systematic and theoretical study of morals touching upon all aspects of human values, not just public affairs. Sociologists may be concerned with comparison of public servants and the social status and behaviors of professionals such as physicians and lawyers.[42] Suffice it to say that public servants are not generally professionals in the sense of licensed physicians or attorneys. Rather, we will acknowledge the status of a developing profession for public service practitioners in general. More importantly, public administration scholars and practitioners have experienced a revival of moral inquiry that has included elements of the traditional professions, such as ethics codes.[43]

THE PUBLIC INTERESTS

Taylor Branch, a Pulitzer Prize-winning author (and MPA graduate), once observed that public service can be divided into two categories: deliver-the-mail and Holy Grail. Public service at times involves performing neutral, mechanical, logistical duties (i.e., deliver the mail). However, Branch argued, even these activities are part of a larger context that always begs the big question and pursuit of the mandate to realize some "grand, moral civilizing goal," i.e., the Holy Grail.[44] The higher order roles and functions the public administrator must consider when carrying out her or his duties include upholding the letter of the law, fulfilling her or his moral compass, and pursuit of the common good, or what we deem the public interests, among others. When these considerations come into conflict, it is the responsibility of the public administrator to carefully examine each perspective and thoughtfully make a decision among competing values. Does the public administrator uphold the law and Constitution? Does she or he maintain professional ties and act according to organizational and professional culture? Can the public administrator make a decision that does not compromise her or his moral beliefs? Should the decision simply be utilitarian—maximize the greatest good for the greatest number? What values and standards should be foundation of informed decision making?

The public interests is a basic ethical concept that is central to public service and administration, much like the concept of justice is basic and central to criminal justice. We seek a more systematic understanding of ethics in public administration by developing the concept of the public interests and applying it to the basic areas of the field, including organization, public management, financial management, personnel management, nonprofits and faith-based initiatives. Can we exercise our discretionary authority in these activities to promote the public interests? First, in Chapters 2–4 we develop applied ethical approaches to public administration from the literature on the history of the public administration profession, democratic policymaking, and the Constitution and laws. Second, from a wide-ranging literature empirically examining ethical behavior and decision making, we apply the ethical public administration to practitioner areas of core concern, including federalism, state and local governance, public organizations management, human resources management, public financial management, nonprofits and faith-based initiatives. Finally, with each application we analyze the predictive quality of patterns of ethical behavior and decision making.

Of course, as with any empirical study of public administration, there are limitations to this approach and in general with research on public sector services. Empirical evidence of the public interests in one public organizational setting constitutes the work product of collaborative efforts and may reflect multiple perspectives on the public interests. Several key decision makers, as well as many managers under their supervision, may have added to or revised specific aspects of a decision to impact on behavior. Mixed perspectives of the public interests are to be expected in such group activities that are designed to promote consensus. Thus, we include a broad spectrum of perspectives on the public interests, including those emphasizing

Norton E. Long's 1991 John Gaus Lecture
BOX 1.2 | Addressing the importance of the public interest

In this excerpt from his speech entitled "Politics, Political Science and the Public Interest," Norton E. Long assessed the influence of the public interest.

It is now over fifty years since Pendleton Herring wrote his *Public Administration and the Public Interest* and the subject remains largely where he left it. In the post war years Glendon Schubert examined the various theories of the public interest and found them empty. Frank Sorauf conceded some value to the notion as a "kind of hair shirt." More recently Richard Flathman has attempted to rehabilitate the concept . . . as an evaluatory expression whose justification can be argued by giving persuasive reasons for its use. However, Flathman's efforts seem to have provoked but a modest response. This is a pity since a normative structure for the study and practice of politics would seem to be of the greatest importance to direct inquiry and to evaluate performance . . . Colleagues refer to the public interest as the Holy Grail for which one might search as if it were the abominable snowman.

If, however, one sees the public interest as a humanly created tool for human purposes, an evaluatory instrument much as Flathman suggests one might devise for judging the worth of motor cars or fountain pens one is in better if less exalted shape. The public interest thus conceived is a standard for appraising the polices and performance of some jurisdiction as it affects the lives of the population of the jurisdiction . . . Developing a clearly articulated standard of the public interest and a process for its actualization in policy and public recognition and debate should be a high priority of students of political science and public administration. ◢

Source: "Addressing the Importance of the Public Interest,"
PS: Political Science and Politics 24 (1991): 670–75.

duty (or deontological rights and obligations), utility (or utilitarian calculus of costs and benefits), and virtue (or analysis of good moral character). These various applied ethical perspectives are detected intersubjectively and necessitate a close empirical research design of qualitative empirical analysis or case studies.

We contend that the most basic responsibility and moral duty of the public analyst or administrator is to uphold and pursue the fulfillment of the public interests.[45] But what are the public interests? Is there a unified or pluralistic definition, or does an adequate definition exist at all? If the public administrator asks the question "Are there identifiable public interests?" then we are essentially questioning if our democracy embraces a shared consensus on key values and the ends most beneficial to civil society. The pluralistic definition of the public interests entails to formulation of the golden-mean balance between the interests of competing stakeholders, each representing a specific public with divergent agendas, plans, and purposes. The public administrator must be adept at identifying the divergent and common values and characteristics of each stakeholder.[46] A key question is whether these values and characteristics apply to everyone at all times in the same way. And, if they do, then doesn't this mean that public administrators simply become robotic automata, not drawing on discretion or intuition or personal moral compass, but simply become facilitators of sorts, lining up all of these values and characteristics according to some predefined positivistic measure of importance, such as utility or performance measurement, and then making the necessary decision? These are compelling and challenging questions that afford no easy answers. In his 1991 John Gaus Lecture, **Norton E. Long (1910–1993)** assessed the influence of the public interests, particularly as it was reflected in governance and politics. Unlike many of his political science and public administration contemporaries, such as Pendleton Herring, Glendon Schubert, and Frank Sorauf, Long did find normative meaning in the term, even highlighting the work of philosopher **Richard Flathman (1934–)**. Long noted, "The public interest thus conceived is a standard for appraising the policies and performance of some jurisdiction as it affects the lives of the population of the jurisdiction . . . Developing a clearly articulated standard of the public interest and a process for its actualization in policy and public recognition and debate should be a high priority of students of political science and public administration."[47] Clearly, Norton Long—who is one of the most well-respected political scientists of the twentieth century—understood and believed that the concept of the public interest was important and worth further investigation.

The Lens of Philosophy: The Public Interests as Political Theory

Walter Lippmann (1889–1974), renowned public philosopher of the twentieth century, described the public interest as "something that is obtainable when men think rationally and logically, while acting in a disinterested and benevolent way."[48] Others claim it is when society maximizes the values of "life, health, and freedom" or when members of society work together to accomplish common goals or purpose.[49] For example, even though the national government reportedly acts on the behalf of the public interests, such as the licensing or regulation of radio, television, and internet media through the authority of the Federal Communications Committee (FCC), the public interests are not directly or necessarily tied to the will of the government but instead to each person in society in this broader definition. Given the absence of a consensus on the elemental definition of the public interests, we need to further examine the broader contextual and historical analysis from the domains of philosophy and ethics, economics, and public administration.

The classical Greek philosophers, such as Plato and Aristotle, wrote of the public interest as an applied concept within the branch of philosophy known as ethics. Ethics is the highly developed philosophical study of morals touching upon all aspects of human values, not just public affairs. The academic discipline of ethics has highly nuanced theories from over 2,400 years ago, and at least 300 canonical names of great philosophers, and parry and thrust arguments that are not so simple to master and cannot be easily summarized in a paragraph or even an entire book. It would be disingenuous of us to pretend to survey and adequately discuss all the myriad aspects of ethics in this single chapter or book, even if we limited ourselves to public administration issues alone. However, the public interest has developed as a useful concept of applied ethics for millennia in a more focused dialog about the morality of public life. The public interests concept does not require that we unpack all of ethics.

The public interest is a concept as old as written political thought. From the times of the early Greek philosophers, the public interest has been many things in the development of political philosophy as a branch of ethics. It was a partial fulfillment of the social contract in the writings of Thomas Hobbes, John Locke, David Hume, and others. It was the embodiment of Jean-Jacques Rousseau's general will. It was in Jeremy Bentham's concept of utility. American Founders addressed it by noting the Constitution was partly established to protect the interests of the majority from the infringement of the minority, and vice versa. Alexis de Tocqueville examined its operation in early America under the priority of customs and manners above the laws. And John Stuart Mill sought it in the protection of individual rights over the interests of the majority. Over the centuries, the public interest became a traditional concept consistently used in political philosophy to denote the common good or commonweal between and among citizens. For example, the protection of individual rights, private property, constitutional heritage, and a variety of other civic, social economic, and religious values are (or have been at one time) at the heart of the public interest. Thus, the public interest cannot be understood or applied without conception and use of political power. This concept of power, whether administrative or political, is the fulcrum for balancing the interests of the state with the common interests, group interests, and the like.[50] Clearly, then, the student of public policy and administration *should* be concerned with a discussion of the public interests.

One of the earliest contemporary discussions of the public interest was by political scientist **E. Pendleton Herring (1903–2004)**[51] in the mid-1930s.[52] In his attempt to unearth the pursuit of the public interest in the work and practice of government agencies, such as the Interstate Commerce Commission, Tariff Commission, Federal Trade Commission, Herring discovered the absence of a uniform definition and meaning of what the public interest is among the agencies he studied. Rather, he determined that, in order to resist the demands of interest groups, there must be an autonomous administrative state. Some even believe that Herring's work might be considered a prototype for the modern state autonomy movement.[53] Herring's thesis and conclusions spawned future scholars to continue and grapple with this elusive concept. Some embraced it as normatively understandable and even plausible—few, though, saw it as empirically operational. Many dismissed it altogether.

By the 1950s, with the advent of the behavioral revolution in the social sciences, and especially political science, the public interest was found to be too normative and theoretical for skeptical empirical scholars. For many, because the public interest had no empirical referent, it was literal non-sense. **Frank Sorauf (1928–2013)**, for example, provided one of the first structured categorizations of the term, finding five basic meanings: 1) rhetorical, 2) elitist, 3) morally pure, 4) balance of individual and social interests, 5) no meaning at all. The only meaning Sorauf found acceptable for the public interest wasn't substantive but only methodological, similar to the concept of substantive due process for constitutional law.[54]

Following Sorauf, political scientist **Glendon Schubert (1918–)** used typological language, where the goal was to provide a working definition and to try and link theory to practice. Schubert provided a three-group definition of administrative decision making in the public interest: (1) Rationalists, who traced the public interest within the rational, logical positivist framework of the decision making process, leaned heavily on the work of Herbert Simon[55] and others for justification; (2) Platonists, who viewed the public interest in a highly moral world, such as Emmette Redford (1904–1998),[56] who argued that administrative decisions are based on the common interests of society, and Paul H. Appleby (1891–1963),[57] who contended that the public interest was greater than the sum of private interests, administrative, political, economic, or even social;[58] and (3) the Realists, who argued that the public administrator is merely a catalyst through which conflict, criticism, and compromise among various interest groups is examined, analyzed, and transmitted into framing the public interest—what is logical and reasonable is given to the parties involved, the question at hand, and the outcomes sought. Thus, Schubert contended that the public interest as a working empirical concept was dead on arrival and effectively a nonentity.[59]

While these skeptical logical positivists discarded the public interest as literal non-sense because its existence cannot be proven with any of the five senses, contemporary empirical researchers discover the operations of patterns that belie the existence and shared meaning of the public interest. These perspectives from economics and public administration take a more radically empirical approach.

The Lens of Economics: The Public Interests as the Commons

Economists such as **Anthony Downs** (1930–) argued that the function of the public interest was to: (1) serve as a barometer for citizens to judge public decisions; (2) placate individuals not otherwise open to the concept, i.e., it is largely a rhetorical and symbolic device, such as the FCC seeks to meet the public interest by limiting what types and how much profanity and nudity can be viewed on network television; and (3) act like a check, again more symbolic than real, on politicians, and to a certain extent public administrators. Downs contends that no "governmental policy is in the public interest if it conflicts with the elements of the minimal value structure that define the society, i.e., the Constitution and traditional democratic values and principles."[60]

The primary contribution of economists is to focus our attention on the public interest—with the inclusion of the commons—to precisely document the diversity of interests in society and overcome the constraints of what is merely popular. The precise calculation of utilities of all affected persons—the commons—gave powerful new tools to policy analysts to make decisions that may not be popular but are in the public's best interests. Under the influence of **Elinor Ostrom (1933–2012)**, winner of the 2009 Nobel Prize in Economics, economists came to refer to the public interests as the commons: a term that is, perhaps, more palatable because it demonstrates a distinction between private and public goods. The commons provide rational benefits to a large number of people, and are paid for by the taxes and efforts of many people. By recognizing the existence of the commons, the economists also establish a **fiduciary trust or duty** where the government or a public servant acts primarily for the benefit of all impacted persons with a precision that may sometimes go against what is popular for those with influence and power.[61] This fiduciary trust relationship suggests an empirical relationship, one that focuses on some type of tangible measureable result. For example, regulatory agencies, like the FCC, are established and instructed to form and implement regulations that provide a good to the public,[62] such as regulating the content of network shows. But today's government agencies, unlike the 1930s world of E. Pendleton Herring, have a clear expectation of public accountability to all citizens and groups.

BOX 1.3 | Elinor Ostrom

Elinor Ostrom was the first and only woman to have won the Nobel Prize in Economics, winning for her analysis of economic governance, especially the commons. Born Elinor Claire Awan, August 7, 1933 in Los Angeles, California, the only child of Leah (Hopkins) Awan and Adrian Awan, she grew up during the depression. Her father was Jewish, her mother was Protestant Christian. She attended Protestant Christian churches and often spent weekends with her aunt (father's sister), who kept a kosher home. Lin graduated from Beverly Hills High School in 1951, describing herself as a "poor kid in a rich kid's school," but active in swimming and the debate team. She worked her way through the University of California at Los Angeles (UCLA) and took a BA with honors in Political Science in 1954. She was awarded the MA and PhD in Political Science in 1962 and 1965, respectively, both from UCLA Department of Political Science. She married fellow political scientist Vincent Ostrom in 1963. The couple went to Indiana University, where Vince Ostrom was offered a faculty position in 1965. Lin was a Visiting Assistant Professor teaching American government in 1965–6, then a tenure-track Assistant Professor and Graduate Advisor from 1966–9. Tenured and promoted to Associate Professor in 1969,

she co-founded the Workshop in Political Theory and Policy Analysis at Indiana University in 1973 with her husband, Vincent Ostrom.

From 1974 to 2012, Lin was Professor in the Department of Political Science at Indiana University, acting as Chair of department from 1980 to 1984 and 1989–90, as well as Founding Director of the *Center for the Study of Institutional Diversity* at Arizona State University, and finally as Distinguished Professor and the Arthur F. Bentley Professor of Political Science at Indiana University. Her research focused on collective action, trust, and cooperation in the management of common pool resources (CPR), with an approach to public policy known as Institutional Analysis and Development (IAD). In addition to her 2009 Nobel Prize, Lin's awards included the 2011 Adam Smith Award, 2009 Sagamore of the Wabash Award, 2008 Galbraith Award, 2006 Cozzarelli Prize, 2006 Membership in American Philosophical Society, 2005 James Madison Award, 1991 Fellow in the American Academy of Arts and Sciences, and many, many other honors. She died on June 12, 2012. ◣

Source: Catherin Rampell, "Elinor Ostrom, Winner of Nobel in Economics, Dies at 78," *New York Times* (June 12, 2012): B20.

Richard Flathman and the Public Interest Universalizability Principle

The 1960s and 1970s saw a breakthrough, both normatively and empirically, in thinking about the public interests. Political philosopher Richard E. Flathman (1934–2015) broke faith with interest group liberalism because, he argued, it did not work empirically in the real-life world of the public administrators' decision making and behavior. Flathman argued that the public interests hold a special place in political discussion, primarily because the concept is logically and rationally acceptable when it constrains and even explains policy issues and administrative actions. As he notes, public interests are used to express evaluations of public policies, and the logic of the concept requires assessment of the consequences of policies for the members of the public. The public interest expresses "public values, such as justice and freedom that are used to evaluate decisions or politics."[63] He found that public administrators ordinarily used the phrase "the public interest" to describe decisions or public policies, such as affirmative action, that are directed to work on behalf of an entire class of affected individuals and not just a select few. Thus, if affirmative action were applied by the U.S. Army to hire only white males to work on construction projects, for example, then this may not be in the public interests.

This thinking led to what he called the **universalizability principle** (UP), which required public servants to take into account the effects of a decision or policy on all affected persons, not just select groups. In other words, what is right or wrong or good or bad for one particular person in a situation must likewise be right or wrong or good or bad *for* another person in a similar or same set of circumstances. The UP is best understood when one compares, for example, public administration as a profession with the practice of law or medicine, because as professionals they share normative values in assessing how effective their peers are in service delivery. The practice of public administration, whether one is a street sweeper or city manager or department head, is not strictly a science or an art, but it is a professionally based and understood craft that requires the practitioner, and the academic as well, to embrace subjective justice interests and objective benefits such as performance-based outcomes of local budgeting practices. More than any other descriptor, the decision-making habit of thinking about others and seeking out the interests of all who are affected characterizes the good public administrator who acts in the public interests. Later on, others like Professor Virginia Held continued Flathman's groundbreaking work. Held studied the Federal Communications Commission (FCC) and found that the public interest meant more than a mere compilation of individual preferences. It was more than a sum of its parts. Instead, it contained significant normative content that was based on constitutional values, such as openness of public discourse regarding regulation of TV and/or radio content.[64]

BOX 1.4 | Richard E. Flathman (1934–2015)

Richard E. Flathman was born on August 6, 1934 in St. Paul, Minnesota, and was married with three kids. He was the George Armstrong Kelly Professor of Political Science at Johns Hopkins University. Along with Brian Barry, David Braybrooke, and Abraham Kaplan, he was best known for pioneering the application of analytic philosophy to key concepts in political science. A graduate of Macalester College, he received his PhD from the University of California-Berkeley in 1962 and taught at the Universities of Washington and Chicago and later at Reed College. He joined the Johns Hopkins political science department in 1975 as a professor. With William E. Connolly, he founded the "Hopkins School" of empirical political theory. He died on September 6, 2015, at age 81.

Flathman embraced the philosophy of liberalism and saw himself as a champion of greater social freedom and a more vigorous individuality in contemporary life. But his acclaimed works are known for lending empirical clarity to important concepts in politics and public life. For example, his highly acclaimed first book, *The Public Interest: An Essay Concerning the Normative Discourse of Politics* (1966), presented an empirical application of contemporary phenomenology, ordinary language philosophy, and pragmatism to analyze how public servants used the phrase "the public interest."

The intellectual emphasis of Richard Flathman, Virginia Held, and Norton Long was on grounding the public interests in more objective constitutional values. This was cogently and persuasively reinforced by the work of **Charles Goodsell (1932–)**. Charles Goodsell posits the public interests as largely symbolic, but that the public interests can be measured along six dimensions, including: (1) legal and moral; (2) political responsiveness; (3) political consensus; (4) concern for logic in policy analysis and the structure of the organization; (5) concern for administration effects, particularly focusing on knowledge, experience, and skills; and (6) an awareness of the policy and administrative agenda.[65] Goodsell explicitly resists the empirical and conceptual relativism in defining the public interest represented in the work of Mark Harmon.[66] In a later work, Goodsell and others explicitly link public administration to the Constitution and the earlier colonial, state, and local governmental frameworks. They make a case that American public administration possesses a long and robust values-based heritage providing an incontrovertible constitutional link for public administration.[67]

Ongoing Elaborations of the Public Interests

The 1980s and 1990s witnessed contrasting understandings of the public interest and the role of normative values that support the study and practice of public administration. Mark Harmon defined the public interest as the product of the ongoing political activity of individuals and interest groups within our democratic governance system. He asserted that the public interest is fluid and highly particularistic given the unique procedural dynamics. In other words, the public interest is only what the proverbial political winds say that it is: during good economic times, tax cuts are in the public interest if you are fiscally conservative; or during challenging times of civil liberties and rights, such as during the 1950s and 1960s, the passage of the Civil Rights Act of 1964 banning discrimination is in the public interest. For Harmon, then, there is no moral, ethical, or constitutional base underpinning the concept itself—it is simply the political outcome of various policy positions.[68]

More recent understandings of the public interests, however, have combined with the study of constitutional law and diverse historical and contemporary moral traditions of American constitutionalism. **The constitutional school of public administration**, for example, has emerged within the discipline of Public Administration, combining elements of traditional doctrinal study of constitutional law with contemporary law, economics approaches, and managerial responsibility.[69] These scholars systematically study public administration by looking at court interpretations, federal statutes, international treaties, and important individuals that have had an impact on public administration in pursuance of the Constitution.[70] In such an inclusive approach, constitutionalism is not merely about the adherence to legal doctrines or deontological duties but also includes the calculation of society-wide needs or utilitarian policies.[71] A more systematic understanding of the public interests must include the diversity of ethical worldview approaches.[72] Taking this inclusive approach to the public interests gives new attention to a merger of constitutionalism and ethics, something we believe has largely been lost or at least misplaced in contemporary public administration.[73]

Contemporary cynics argue that the public interests are nothing more than assertions by public analysts and administrators of their individual preferences—that there are no referents of the public interests to anything that can be seen, heard, touched, smelled, or tasted. In other words, the public interests are nothing more than the will to power of administrators and remains a literal non-sense. If this is true, and we believe it is not, then we raise a question. Can the public interests be refounded, or reconceptualized, to overcome the nihilism of cynical scholars and critics? We believe it can and must.

THE CENTRAL THESIS: VIRTUE, UTILITY, AND DUTY IN THE PUBLIC INTERESTS

Our thesis is that there exists an identifiable public interest entailing both normative and pragmatic elements that should be a foundation concern of every practicing public administrator. In this, the analyst's or administrator's role entails three factors: (1) fiduciary duties to the commons as defined and constrained by constitutional rules; (2) utilities that are calculated in congruence with democratic values, and (3) the **virtue** of non-idiosyncratic good moral character and universal ethics in administrative leadership and decision making. This is the normative role of the public administrator, denoted and explained by duties, utilities, and virtue, and is the day-to-day reality of public administration. This is the Holy Grail quest of what it means to be a public analyst or administrator and to do public administration. These various roles are explored in details in the sections to follow.

Duty and the Public Interests

The role of the public administrator as a neutral, objective, and rational interpreter of pre-existing duties is part of the accepted worldview of constitutionalism in public administration. Conformity of public administrators to pre-existing constitutional duties subordinates personal interests and institutional loyalties to the public good.[74] Current constitutional studies in public administration emphasize a **duty perspective**—or **deontological ethical** duty-bound theory in which bureaucrats learn the rules and make their decisions as the living repositories of such legal rules or duties, declaring the appropriate rule or duty and conforming to these pre-existing constitutional rules or duties. For scholars such as **John Rohr (1934–2011)**, the ideal public administrator is one who can somehow find a constitutionally sound and balanced solution in every case, even with competing legal duties.[75]

For example, the role of the FBI special agent is to rigidly adhere to Fifth Amendment limits when interrogating a criminal suspect, only after giving Miranda warnings. Under this rule-bound approach, the FBI agent cannot simply blurt out the question, "Where did you drop the gun?" We contend, for example, that a more dynamic ethical approach would allow the FBI agent to consider public safety concerns, while balancing the civil rights of the accused, and ask about where the gun was dropped. For example, the focus is to keep a dangerous weapon, dropped somewhere near a school playground, away from kids. The duty perspective and constitutionalism may seem too much like pat answers in which you apply pre-existing constitutional rules to decisions, and the parties are rationally obligated to comply.

Certainly, constitutionalism and the duty perspective provide boundaries within which policy and management issues interact. The determination or mapping of these boundaries contains a high degree of subjectivity and political conflict, but it is the gray middle areas that absorb a great deal of debate and controversy in public administration, as will be discussed more fully in Chapter 4 on law and public interest duty. Constitutionalism and the duty perspective may assume a much higher degree of precision and values agreements than are clearly present. Yet, while constitutional duties seem too much like pat answers, we generally agree that constitutional duties serve as clear bright-line markers to identify boundaries and limits beyond which decisions are clearly not in the public interest.

Utility and the Public Interests

Public policy institutions, processes, and analyses absorb a great deal of the debate and controversy in discerning the public interest by public administrators. This conflict is exacerbated by ambiguous and ill-defined legislation generated by the dynamics of a legislative process that is characterized by compromise given the lack of agreement on cause-and-effect relations among the associated means, ends, and goals. There are many problems and decisions where public analysts and administrators do not, and really cannot, simply discover and apply pre-existing constitutional rules. In these cases, some argue that public analysts and administrators create policy through their decision-making authority by calculating social utilities or preferences. What constrains the utilities decision is their congruence or accountability with our democratic political system and/or democratic values. The public interest **utility perspective** emphasizes an ethical theory of **utilitarianism** where good and bad are defined by balancing or calculating benefits and costs, pleasure and pain, needs versus needs, or individual preferences. It is an applied ethical theory in asserting that there may be no pre-existing duties of the public interest beyond this balancing or calculating of individual interests or utilities. Two common perspectives on the calculation of utilities provide some guidance: **skepticism** and **advocacy**.

Skepticism   One approach to determine or calculate utilities in congruence with the public interest is termed skepticism. John Locke, for example, argued for skepticism that there is no meaning in the concept of the public interest beyond simply the aggregation of multiple personal interests.[76] In this way, scholars such as **James Buchanan (1919–2013)** and Elinor Ostrom refer to the commons in discussions of the public interest as the collective needs of society. By requiring precise measure of the interests of all of society, individual policy analysts will subordinate their personal interests and institutional loyalties to the public good, and treat all persons in society with equal respect, courtesy, in dedication to high standards.

However, many scholars argue that **John Locke's (1632–1704)** skepticism, which also became known as interest-group liberalism, actually results in public policy decisions that may conflict with the public interest or the commons.[77] For example, many publicly funded projects may not be the desire of the public at large but rationally promote the private interests of particular politicians, businesses, or public administrators. These special interest groups rationally promote their self-interests in the stampede to obtain government pork-barrel funding with little outlay and to secure inside information to gain an advantage over

BOX 1.5 | James M. Buchanan

James M. Buchanan, winner of the 1986 Nobel Prize in Economics, was born October 3, 1919, in Murfreesboro, Tennessee, received his BA from Middle Tennessee State College in 1940 and his PhD in political science from the University of Chicago in 1948. He held the Distinguished Professor Emeritus of Economics at George Mason University in Fairfax, Virginia, and Distinguished Professor Emeritus of Economics and Philosophy at Virginia Tech in Blacksburg, Virginia. He is best known for developing the "public choice theory" of economics, which changed the way economists analyze economic and political decision making.

Buchanan's work opened the door for the examination of how politicians' self-interest and non-economic forces affect government economic policy. Along with co-author Gordon Tullock, his highly acclaimed book *The Calculus of Consent: Logical Foundations of Constitutional Democracy* (1962) blended the fields of economics and political science to help create the public choice approach. He died in Blacksburg, Virginia, on January 9, 2013, at age 93.

Source: James M. Buchanan, "What is Public Choice Theory?" *Imprimis* 32 (#3, March 2003): 1–7.

competitors. Thus, local government-bonded building projects—e.g., you may imagine items such as a special children's hospital, skateboard park, or pro-team stadium—have little or no utility for the public at large but promote the rational economic interests of key private individuals.

The incentives and motivations of individual taxpayers to protest are muted given the small aggregate costs of pennies per capita for an individual pork-barrel project. However, the public is aroused when the monetary scale reaches a critical tipping point as occurred in 2008 with the bailout of the banking and financial services industry. For some critics, this means that the public interests have become an unwieldy, cumbersome, and really meaningless jumble of individual preferences. Everyone seeks what is in their rational interest. Thus, the government seeks to make the public administrator accountable or responsible to ensure these individual and oftentimes conflicting interests are somehow met, regardless of how much it costs the taxpayers, both in terms of higher taxes or additional layers of bureaucracy, red tape, and rules and regulations.[78]

Public administrators may seek out these individual personal preferences by means such as community surveys or by public hearings. The administrator's role in this process is to structure and facilitate the input of various citizens or special interest groups and supply the demands or execute the mandates produced. In fact, this skepticism has led to what **Robert Putnam** refers to as **bowling-alone**, contributing to a loss of social capital.[79] Is community a viable, working entity that represents commonly held and practiced social and political values? Is a community merely what citizens define as their individual preferences? Social life—from meeting at the local Hispanic Chamber of Commerce to participating in neighborhood watch groups—loses any sense of commonality or even ethical meaning.

Advocacy   A second approach to calculate utilities in congruence or accountable to the public interest may be termed advocacy.[80] The skepticism perspective that had dominated much of the scholarship on the public interest by economists and political scientists was challenged by critics of the status quo, who claimed that existing theories of the public interests were really just a guise for the preservation of what is popular for established power relationships. Further, by reducing the public interests to a marketplace exchange of private interests, the American political system and the American public have been duped into accepting unwanted excesses of the private market in the public square, such as: (1) the false notion that all marketplace exchanges are politically, legally, and ethically legitimate and equal in meaning and purpose; (2) that the mere opportunity of participation in these processes or markets will yield a defensible theory of the public interest; (3) that the public was duped by faulty causal scientific arguments; or, worse, (4) behind this whole façade of pseudo-science was the operation of will to power and rhetorical ploys to advance the status quo or interests of political elites. The latter has been taken to the extreme. For example, the Nazis in World War II, influenced by the *Übermensch* writings of **Friedrich Nietzsche (1844–1900)**, advocated and justified the Holocaust after designating the Jews, Poles, and others as a defective and dangerous race. If the public interest is mere rhetoric and will to power, what stops this horrible scenario from happening again?[81]

Virtue and the Public Interests

As we noted earlier, Richard E. Flathman presented a theory of the public interest as a social practice of virtue and good moral character in administrative leadership and decision making. It shifts our attention to an empirical focus on the real world of ordinary public servants, their day-to-day concerns, decision, and vision. The attention to the virtue and good moral character of public administrators emphasizes ethical virtue.[82] As a framework for analysis, it promises a means of understanding these complex organizational behaviors and accommodates both the individual and social dimensions of the public interest in a theory based on people's actions. From the empirical observations of Flathman, the public interest criterion may be tested against administrative behavior by non-idiosyncratic, universalized social practices—or habits of the heart—of ethical behavior.[83]

Beyond the skepticism of economic theory or advocacy of will-to-power perspectives came empirical attempts within the social sciences to understand human rights and behavior within a concrete lived world. A social practice, like the practice of medicine or the practice of law, is often used to describe these various approaches to uncover such a character-based virtue.[84] Public administrators and analysts seek personal virtue in a real world filled with political, ethical, and administrative challenges and conflicts. Public administrators and analysts are constantly trying to work out the best solutions of various public issues, such as planning and zoning problems related to where to build a school, or economic development issues associated with rural growth and affordable housing. The virtue of public administrators and analysts is not simply a theory, although they certainly should have a public philosophy about the work they do. They must also act on the behalf of the commons and the public interest and not just for the individualized interest of groups. But how is this done—if at all?

Administration in the public interest illustrates the ethical approach of virtue—not as iron-clad conformity to duties or balancing of precise utilities—but as an aspirational approach to achieve the higher purpose of duties and utilities while maintaining good moral character. By focusing on good moral character that is universalizability, public servants develop a habit of the heart to subordinate their personal interests, legal duties, and citizen utilities to the greater public good. They will also habituate themselves to serve all persons with courtesy, respect, and dedication to high standards. Although critics may still fault a particular public administrator or analyst in a specific decision for imposing their personal preferences, it is clear that administration in the public interest is composed of complex discourse, negotiation, and compromise. It is not universally the imposition of the will of the public administrator or analyst. Changing social forces, politics, laws, human imagination, as well as costs and duration, frustrate any individual public administrator from exercising will to power. In this process, public administrators act as catalysts to direct individuals, groups, agencies, and organizations in a general direction toward this higher purpose, while maintaining the virtue to make it so.

Thus, the virtue ethical perspective of the public interest provides a theory of public administration that preserves attention to pre-existing constitutional duties, insures the congruence of the utilities with larger democratic institutions and populations, and clarifies the normative fiduciary leadership role and good moral character of public administrators. Administration in the public interest is transformed into a discourse between a large number of key decision makers in every situation: from top-level administrators and managers to citizens, politicians, street-level personnel, and nonprofit and faith-based organizations. In so doing, the central question changes from "What about my duty?" or "What about utility interests?" to "What about the public interest?"

ETHICS CASE STUDY | The FCC Public Interest Standard

The Federal Communications Commission (FCC) is entrusted with the Holy Grail of ensuring the public interests in all U.S. radio, television, and other digital media broadcasting. This case study of the FCC public interest standard regulation may also illustrate the activities of other agencies entrusted with the public interests or the commons in policy sectors as diverse as other media,[85] the insurance industry,[86] economic regulation,[87] pharmaceuticals,[88] health care,[89] the environment,[90] gambling,[91] and other arenas. Like these varied policy sectors, FCC public interest regulation has featured development of distinct styles that are both value-based and market-based. The FCC case is illustrative of the perspective that the three elements of the public interests—constitutional duties, utilities calculated in congruence with democratic values, and leadership and decision-making virtue—are present in all major public administration decision areas in a dynamic and shifting balance. The main conflict in the FCC case is between the fiduciary stewardship responsibilities of government in shaping the public interest and the market-based consumerism of the commons approach.

The Public Interest Standard

The FCC was created by Congress under its Commerce Clause powers of Article I of the U.S. Constitution in order to regulate the use of public airwaves. The public interest standard was mandated by Congress in the statute that created the FCC, The Communications Act of 1934 (47 U.S.C. sections 151 and 154). The 1934 Act was based on prior statutes, such as the Radio Act of 1927 (Public Law No. 632), which superseded the Radio Act of 1912 (Public Law No. 264), and in both the assurance of the public interest was of central concern.

The U.S. Supreme Court first upheld the FCC public interest standard in *Nelson Brothers v. FRC* (1933), in which the Federal Radio Commission (FRC) revoked two licenses after evaluating three stations for public interest programming. As stated in the 1934 Act, the "public interest, convenience and necessity" mandate was never defined by consensus and has been a storm center for debates over the FCC's proper regulatory role ever since.[92] But former FCC Chairman Newton Minow believed the 1934 Act—and the role of the FCC—may have been worthless without it.[93] The U.S. Supreme Court again upheld the public interest standard in *FCC v. Pottsville Broadcasting* (1940), and did not require the FCC to consider economic injury to existing stations when considering applications for a new station in *FCC v. Sanders Brothers Radio* (1940). These cases underscore the one major regulatory weapon of the FCC: revocation of operating licenses.

From the 1940s through the 1960s, the FCC was much more aggressive in promoting broadcasting under the public interest standard. In *NBC v. US* (1943), the U.S. Supreme Court upheld the FCC's chain-broadcasting regulations, allowing local network affiliates free of network constraints in their power to select programming to meet the public interest standard. The FCC issued programming guidelines to broadcasters under its public interest standard in the 1946 Blue Book (named for its blue cover), including non-sponsored programs, local live programs, local public issues programs, and elimination of excessive advertising. The Blue Book did not mandate such programs, but merely clarified the FCC's consideration of such public interest programming at renewal time.

The 1960 Programming Policy Statement further clarified the public interest standard with an additional mix of programs that were "usually necessary to the public interest" and considered as evidence that broadcasters were serving the public interest at renewal time. The programming elements included in the 1960 statement were to be locally determined by broadcasters in a series of interviews conducted with community leaders in nineteen FCC-specified categories ranging from agriculture to religion.[94]

The Fairness Doctrine involved a highly rule-bound style of administration introduced in 1949, early during the anti-Communist Red Scare. It was a general FCC policy that both sides of a controversial issue ought to be presented by broadcasters. Congress, however, never explicitly authorized the doctrine.[95] And the equal time rule of the Fairness Doctrine was applied

(*continued*)

only rarely, that is until a 1967 FCC regulation uniformly required it.[96] For example, in *Red Lion Broadcasting v. FCC* (1969), the U.S. Supreme Court upheld both the public interest standard and the Fairness Doctrine of the FCC. Red Lion Broadcasting refused any reply time to Fred J. Cook after a fifteen-minute attack by Rev. Billy Jones Hargis on his Christian Crusade radio show, in which Hargis said Cook was fired from a newspaper for making false charges against city officials, Cook had worked for a communist-affiliated publication, Cook had defended Alger Hiss and attacked J. Edgar Hoover and the CIA, and now Cook had written a book to smear Barry Goldwater (Cook's book was entitled *Goldwater: Extremist on the Right*). Although newspapers could not similarly be required to provide equal time, the Court reasoned that radio and broadcasting were unique because of the limited nature of the public airwave spectrum. The Court decided that

> It is the right of the viewers, not the right of the broadcasters, which is paramount . . . There is nothing in the First Amendment which prevents the Government from requiring a licensee to share his frequency with others and to conduct himself as a fiduciary.[97]

Thus, radio and broadcasting are treated differently than newspapers because "the broadcast media have established a uniquely pervasive presence in the lives of all Americans." Or so the Court reasoned in *FCC v. Pacifica Foundation* (1978), where the Justices affirmed the FCC decision that the late George Carlin's filthy words monologue was indecent. Later, the FCC used the same public interest standard on indecency after Janet Jackson's wardrobe malfunction in a Super Bowl half-time show. As a result, former President George W. Bush signed into law the Broadcast Decency Enforcement Act of 2005, increasing penalties for broadcasters who violated FCC decency standards. And in *FCC v. Fox Television Stations* (2009), the U.S. Supreme Court decided by a 5–4 decision that expletive, nonliteral use of the F-word or the S-word could be legally indecent even if the word is used only once in a broadcast.

Although the Fairness Doctrine was originally enacted to promote pluralism, by the 1970s the FCC and other policy decision makers were concerned that it had the opposite effect. In *CBS v. Democratic National Committee* (1973), the Court warned of the end of the Fairness Doctrine with changes in technology: "Problems of regulation are rendered more difficult because the broadcast industry is dynamic in terms of technological change, solutions adequate a decade ago are not necessarily so now, and those acceptable today may well be outmoded 10 years hence." In *Miami Herald Publishing v. Tornillo* (1974) a unanimous Court decided that "government-enforced right of access inescapably dampens the vigor and limits the variety of public debate." Justice Brennan, writing the Opinion of the Court in *FCC v. League of Women Voters* (1984), wrote that the Fairness Doctrine was "chilling speech." Broadcasters challenged the Fairness Doctrine as promoting censorship instead of diversity and worried that advertising time would be wasted by individuals invoking the equal time rule.

The FCC and the Marketplace Approach

Against this background, the FCC developed a new **marketplace approach** to the public interest standard. By this market-failure approach, public interest regulation only enters in when the marketplace clearly has failed to protect the general interest or the commons. For then-FCC Chairman Mark Fowler (once on Ronald Reagan's campaign staff), that point had not yet occurred in 1982:

> Scarcity, to my mind, is a condition affecting all industries. Land, capital, labor, and oil, they are all scarce. With other scarce goods in society, we tend to allow the marketplace to allocate them. In this Process, consumers' interests and society's interests are well served . . . Put simply, I believe that we are at the end of regulating broadcasting under the trusteeship model. Whether you call it 'paternalism' or "nannyism"—it is "Big Brother," and it must cease. I believe in a marketplace approach to broadcast regulation . . . Under the coming marketplace approach, the Commission should, as far as possible, defer to a broadcaster's judgment about how best to compete for viewers and listeners, because this services the public interest.[98]

In *FCC v. WNCN Listener's Guild* (1983), the Court upheld the FCC's decision not to involve itself in a change of ownership of WNCN and a resulting format change from classical to rock music, reasoning that "marketplace regulation was a constitutionally protected means of implementing the public interest of the act." Further, in 1981 the FCC initiated radio deregulation with the elimination of all requirements for program logs, commercial time limits, required interviews of community leaders, and non-entertainment programming. FCC decision makers reasoned that

> Congress established a mandate for the Commission to act in the public interest. We conceive of that interest to require us to regulate where necessary, to deregulate where warranted, and above all, to assure the maximum service to the public at the lowest cost and the least amount of paperwork.[99]

With the rise of marketplace FCC regulation came also the abolition of the Fairness Doctrine. In *FCC v. League of Women Voters of CA* (1984), the U.S. Supreme Court noted the chilling effect the doctrine had, but refused to find the Fairness Doctrine unconstitutional "without some signal from Congress or the FCC." Finally, the FCC found the Fairness Doctrine to be unconstitutional and abolished it by a vote of 4–0 in its *Syracuse Peace Council* decision in August 1987. The FCC no longer found validity in the

(continued)

spectrum scarcity rationale for the doctrine, or in its effectiveness to insure pluralism:

> the intrusion by government into the content of programming occasioned by the enforcement of [the Fairness Doctrine] restricts the journalistic freedom of broadcasters . . . [and] actually inhibits the presentation of controversial issues of public importance to the detriment of the public and the degradation of the editorial prerogative of broadcast journalists.[100]

Congress tried in a last-ditch effort to preserve the Fairness Doctrine in statutory form in 1987, but former President Reagan vetoed the bill. The threat of a veto by former President George H.W. Bush staved off a 1991 attempt to resurrect the Fairness Doctrine. A 2007 attempt to restore the long-dead Fairness Doctrine was rebuffed by Congress in a 309–115 vote including most Democrats and all Republicans.[101] On August 22, 2011, the FCC formally voted to repeal the language that implemented the Fairness Doctrine, along with removal of more than eighty other rules and regulations following a White House executive order directing a "government-wide review of regulations already on the books," to eliminate unnecessary regulations.[102]

The FCC marketplace approach to regulation continues to reign ascendant with reforms under both Democrat and Republican presidents, as well as bi-partisan efforts in Congress. For example, the Telecommunication Act of 1996 was highly touted as a bi-partisan effort to create a more competitive communications market by removing many media ownership restrictions, distinguishing between information (internet) and communication services, and structuring new cooperation. The 1996 Act promised to deliver a $2 trillion boost to the economy, with up to 1.5 million related jobs, and cost savings to consumers of over $550 million—but instead delivered a $2 trillion loss in the value of the U.S. telecommunication industry, a loss of 500,000 U.S. jobs, and a tremendous upsurge in cable and phone rates. What is worse, say the critics, was the intense media consolidation that resulted, i.e., five companies now controlling 75 percent of all prime-time viewing. Chellie Pingree, President of Common Cause, argued persuasively in 2005 that "Those who advocated the Telecommunications Act of 1996 promised more competition and diversity, but the opposite has happened."[103]

Where does it go from here? Until 2014, the FCC did little to apply the public interest standard to the internet. While radio and television first appeared in a past era of First Amendment concerns and democracy-enriching governance, the internet emerged in an era of 1990s deregulation and exultation of market-driven arbiters of the public interests. The internet and new digital media were born out of governmental massively subsidized research and common carrier regulations, but regulation of the internet has been largely absent, embracing an anti-interventionist role.[104] Until 2014, the FCC only involved itself at the margins of the development of the internet and digital media, such as the regulation of pornography, some provision of internet access to schools and libraries, and incidental services such as broadband access and VoIP telephone use.[105]

In 2015, former President Barack Obama's demands for new and complete regulation of the internet in the public interest were made into law, labeled **net neutrality**. It surprised even the FCC then-Chairman, Thomas E. "Tom" Wheeler, a 2013 Democrat appointee by President Obama.[106] The old Telecommunications Act of 1996 had declared the internet to be an unregulated "information service" by Congress, with the purpose "to preserve the vibrant and competitive free market . . . for the Internet and other interactive computer services unfettered by federal or state regulation."[107] This stood in stark contrast with the extensive regulation of the phone system. The 2015 law was labeled as **Obamanet** by critics who sought continued information-service status under the old Telecommunications Act of 1996. Critical scholars, taking a market approach, argued that the internet would never have been built if its original inventors had been subject to utility-style regulation.[108] The vast expansion of Silicon Valley was due to this freedom to invent: "Silicon Valley could ignore the FCC when the information services category was there, and now they can't."[109] On the other side, Jeff Pulver, VoIP pioneer and co-founder of Vonage, says that all the fears about net neutrality were "bullshit."[110] FCC Chairman Tom Wheeler had insisted that there would be no rate-setting, tariffs, or breakups under net neutrality regulations.[111]

On January 23, 2017, President Trump named Ajit Pai the thirty-fourth Chairman of the FCC. An Indian American growing up in Kansas, Pai was a sitting Commissioner of the FCC; thus, no Senate confirmation was required and he immediately served as the FCC's thirty-fourth Chairman. Pai was a critic of Obama's net neutrality rules. He was also a staunch advocate of deregulation and highly critical of the Democrat's efforts to break up the dominance of the internet's biggest providers, such as AT&T, Verizon, and Comcast. On December 14, 2017, the FCC voted 3–2 along political party lines to repeal Obama-era net neutrality rules. Many protested, and prominent internet companies, such as Amazon, Google, Twitter, and Facebook, posited that the end to net neutrality was bad for consumers and bad for tech business. To his critics, Ajit Pai countered, "It is not going to destroy the internet. It is not going to end the internet as we know it. It is not going to kill democracy. It is not going to stifle free expression online."[112] On January 4, 2018, the FCC officially released its new regulatory text for **Restoring Internet Freedom**. Is the FCC returning to early foundational policy and greater freedoms for the internet industry?

Comparative studies may bear this out in similar regulatory environments. For example, in his analysis of the promotion of media diversity by regulatory agencies in the United Kingdom and Australia in a climate of deregulation and marketplace approaches, Lesley Hitchens concluded that the

(continued)

early foundational policy and regulatory rulings and decisions exert a consideration influence on present-day reforms. To describe these intermeshed approaches of traditional public interest and the commons, he labels the present-day reform tactics "in the public interest*s*" (emphasis added).[113] Is there an emerging global war of **internet governance**?[114]

Discussion

- What is the public interest standard of the FCC?
- What is the fairness doctrine and what ethical perspective is it most congruent with: virtue, utility, or duty?
- What is the marketplace approach and what ethical perspective is it most congruent with: virtue, utility, or duty?
- What should be the impact of the public interest standard on the internet? ▲

CONCLUSION

So, what is the public interest? The surprising reality for those who want one right answer is that our core applied ethical concept takes multiple paths. It's complicated—get used to it! Like the Holy Grail responsibilities found throughout public administration, the definition of the public interests and the commons is central to understanding the day-to-day reality of the FCC and all of public administration. Our brief history of the FCC public interest standard affirms a truth posited by **Barry Bozeman (1947–)** and others: that current microeconomic focus on economic individualism is incomplete and must be supplemented by other public interests approaches.[115] Further, emerging global scholarship points to this plural concept of the public interests in similar regulatory environments, i.e., public agency promotions of media diversity in climate of deregulation and marketplace approaches, which can only be described as "in the public interests."[116] It comes full circle in return to etymological roots which were always plural for the many others: *pubes + koinon* (Greek, *to be mature and take care of others*).

It seems that both the public interests and the commons approaches operate in duality in much of contemporary day-to-day decision making in public administration. The commons approach entails a higher risk of market failure, as was demonstrated with the Telecommunications Act of 1996. Is the marketplace approach ill suited to conducting the more nuanced nature of public interest values? What about the increasing levels of violence and sexuality present in media and its impact on society—should these aspects be analyzed irrespective of public opinion and market demand? Do we need a balanced and ongoing assessment of the public interests by public administrators using all three standards: constitutional duties, the commons utilities congruent with democratic values, and leadership virtue?

Our first precept from the ASPA Code of Ethics—*Advance the Public Interest*—is focused on promotion of the interests of the public above service to oneself. It is a call to aspirations such as:

a. Seek to advance the good of the public as a whole, taking into account current and long-term interests of the society.
b. Exercise discretionary authority to promote the public interest.
c. Be prepared to make decisions that may not be popular but are in the public's best interest.
d. Subordinate personal interests and institutional loyalties to the public good.
e. Serve all persons with courtesy, respect, and dedication to high standards.[117]

However, here at the end of this chapter you may see the many conflicts and limitations in the face of these high expectations and ideals of practice. The public interest is of different consistency for philosophers, economists, and public administrators. In looking at the public interest, different public servants focus on diverse duties, utilities calculations, and virtue of good character to guide their path in their aspiration to do the right thing. Which path is the good public servant to choose? This is our quest for this book—to apply the different perspectives of the public interest to the ordinary work tasks, people, work structures, cultures, issues, conflicts, and problems of public administration so that we can judge within a practical context which path to choose.

Thus, we begin our study of the public interest*s* as the basic plural concept of applied ethics in the public administration profession. From current global thinking, we may interchangeably examine the public interest*s* and other concepts congruent with public interest*s*, such as the commons, regime values, the ethics of caring, and moral readings of the Constitution—in scholarship from economists, philosophers, psychologists, lawyers, and public administrators. This is not your parents' concept of the public interest, which was discarded by skeptics for imposition of the will to power with one right answer to the issues of public goods and services. This is a new pluralistic concept of the public interest*s* emerging from close empirical data that belie the reality of shared meanings of public goods and service, but with varieties of answers. While we may still use "the public interest" here and there as we continue our analysis in this book, we imply a plural meaning, and seek to use "the public interest*s*" (emphasis added) to make our points.

ACTION STEPS

1. How would you define the "public" in public administration? How would you distinguish "private" from public administration? Discuss in small groups your differences defining and distinguishing these concepts. Do you find commonalities? What do these commonalities belie about public administration?
2. Within a small group, or individually, select a contemporary public policy problem. Pick one that an ordinary public administrator, such as a city manager or state agency head, might grapple with. First, articulate the Holy Grail quest for your public policy problem area: what are the public

interests? Second, formulate a workable solution to meets the virtue, utility, and duty perspectives of the public interests. Discuss your responses, thoughts, and strategies.

3. Interview a public servant—ask them what the public interests are, and how their professional duties, utilities calculations, and virtue of good character may fulfill the public interests.

4. After reading the case study of the FCC public interest standard with U.S. Supreme Court decisions, legislation, and administration by the FCC, consider the Holy Grail quest of the public interests in radio, television, and now all digital media. Within a small group, or individually, answer these questions. First, how would you define the public interests to administer radio, television, or internet? Second, how would you measure or know compliance with your definition of the public interests?

KEY CONCEPTS AND NAMES

ASPA Code of Ethics (2013) 3
plural concept of public interest 3
regime values 3
public sector 5
government workers 5
public interest standard 5
Federal Communications Commission (FCC) 5
definitions of public administration 6
private versus public administration 7
moral inquiry 9
ASPA Ethics Review Process 10
ASPA Ethics and Standards Implementation Committee 10
Section on Ethics and Integrity in Governance 10
dismissal 10
private censure 10
public censure 11
removal 11
professionalism 11
Norton E. Long 14
Richard Flathman 14
Walter Lippmann 14
E. Pendleton Herring 15
Frank Sorauf 15
Glendon Schubert 15

Anthony Downs 16
Elinor Ostrom 16
fiduciary trust or duty 16
universalizability principle 18
Charles Goodsell 19
constitutional school of public administration 19
virtue 20
duty perspective 20
deontological ethics 20
John Rohr 20
utility perspective 21
utilitarianism 21
skepticism 21
advocacy 21
James Buchanan 21
John Locke 21
Robert Putnam 22
bowling-alone thesis 22
Friedrich Nietzsche 23
Fairness Doctrine 25
marketplace approach 27
net neutrality 29
Obamanet 29
restoring Internet Freedom 29
internet governance 30
Barry Bozeman 30

NOTES

1 We are indebted to Gary Roberts and the editors of *Administration & Society* for comments and editorial revisions that went into this chapter. See also Stephen King, Bradley Chilton, and Gary Roberts, "Reflections on Defining the Public Interest," *Administration & Society* 41 (2010): 954–78; Bradley Chilton, "Constitutional Conscience: Criminal Justice & Public Interest Ethics," *Criminal Justice Ethics* 17 (1998): 33–41; Bradley Chilton, "Public Interest Ethic," in Allen Kent, ed., *Encyclopedia of Library and Information Science* (New York: Marcel Dekker, 1996), vol. 58, 275–8; and Bradley Chilton, "Managing Information Services in the Public Interest Ethic," *Journal of Information Ethics* 2 (1998): 44–52.

2 James H. Svara, "Who Are the Keepers of the Code? Articulating and Upholding Ethical Standards in the Field of Public Administration," *Public Administration Review* 74 (#5, 2014): 561–9.

3 We may oversimplify this etymology, as there were many influences on the English word "public." Ancient Greek *pubes* referred to "adult population," as did the Latin *pubes*, e.g., Douglas Harper, *Online Etymology Dictionary* (2018), retrieved from www.etymonline.com/word/public. However, Alasdair MacIntyre, in *After Virtue* (Notre Dame: University of Notre Dame Press, 1981), and others have critiqued how modern French and English may be prudish on the influence of sexual maturity to moral maturity. Instead, we envision a moral maturity as natural as sexual maturity.

4 Even fictional places! See, e.g., John P. Thompson, *Without Purpose of Evasion—A Novel: A Story of Conflict, Conscience, and Real-Life Consequences* (Minneapolis, MN: North Loop Books, 2017).

5 American Society for Public Administration, *2013 Code of Ethics*, retrieved from www.aspanet.org/ASPADocs/ASPA%20Code%20of%20Ethics-2013%20with%20 Practices.pdf

6 Steve Ballmer, "I Crunched the Numbers on the U.S. Government—Here's What I Learned: Our Road Are Improving," *Time Magazine* 190 (#5, July 31, 2017): 30.

7 Steve Ballmer, "I Crunched the Numbers on the U.S. Government—Here's What I Learned: Most Government Workers Aren't Bureaucrats," *Time Magazine* 190 (#5, July 31, 2017): 30.

8 Michael C. Lemay, *Public Administration: Clashing Values in the Administration of Public Policy* (Belmont, CA: Wadsworth, 2002), 28.

9 Nicholas Henry, *Public Administration and Public Affairs*, 9th ed. (Upper Saddle River, NJ: Prentice-Hall, 2004), 2.

10 Richard Stillman, *The American Bureaucracy: The Core of Modern Government*, 3rd ed. (Belmont, CA: Wadsworth, 2004), 3.

11 Melvin J. Dubnick and Barbara S. Romzek, *American Public Administration: Politics and the Management of Expectations* (New York: Macmillan, 1991), 12.

12 Jay M. Shafritz and E.W. Russell, *Introducing Public Administration*, 2nd ed. (Reading, MA: Addison Wesley Longman, 2000).

13 George J. Gordon and Michael E. Milakovich, *Public Administration in America*, 6th ed. (New York: St. Martin's Press, 1998), 7.

14 George Berkley and John Rouse, in *The Craft of Public Administration*, 6th ed. (Madison, WI: WCB Brown & Benchmark, 1984), 2.

15 David H. Rosenbloom, *Understanding Management, Politics, and Law in the Public Sector*, 4th ed. (New York: McGraw-Hill, 1998), 6.

16 Robert B. Denhardt, *Public Administration: An Action Orientation*, 3rd ed. (Fort Worth, TX: Harcourt Brace, 1999).

17 Carl E. Lutrin and Allen K. Settle, *American Public Administration: Concepts and Cases*, 3rd ed. (Englewood Cliffs, NJ: Prentice-Hall, 1985), 19.

18 David Schuman and Dick W. Olufs III, *Public Administration in the United States*, 2nd ed. (Lexington, MA: D.C. Heath and Company, 1993).

19 William C. Johnson, *Public Administration: Policy, Politics, and Practice* (Guilford, CT: Dishkin Publishing, 1992), 4.

20 Robert Golembiewski. *Public Administration as a Developing Discipline, Vol. 1, Perspectives on Past and Present* (New York: Routledge, 1977).

21 Hal G. Rainey, *Managing Public Organizations*, 3rd ed. (San Francisco: Jossey-Bass, 2003), 62.

22 Robert A. Dahl and Charles E. Lindblom, *Politics, Economics, and Welfare* (Chicago: University of Chicago Press, 1953; reprint, 1976).

23 Hal G. Rainey, *Managing Public Organizations*, 3rd ed. (San Francisco: Jossey-Bass, 2003), 63.

24 Robert A. Dahl and Charles E. Lindblom, *Politics, Economics, and Welfare* (Chicago: University of Chicago Press, 1953; reprint, 1976).

25 Hal G. Rainey, *Managing Public Organizations*, 3rd ed. (San Francisco: Jossey-Bass, 2003), 65.

26 The following discussion of the Greek words for "public" and their interpretation is taken from H. George Frederickson, *The Spirit of Public Administration* (San Francisco: Jossey-Bass, 1997), 20.

27 H. George Frederickson, *The Spirit of Public Administration* (San Francisco: Jossey-Bass, 1997), 22. Frederickson also cites W.A.R. Leys, *Ethics for Policy Decisions* (New York: Prentice Hall, 1952), 13–32.

28 H. George Frederickson, *The Spirit of Public Administration* (San Francisco: Jossey-Bass, 1997), 22.

29 Wal-Mart Stores, "Community" (2005), retrieved from http://walmartstores.com/GlobalWMStoresWeb/navigate.do?catg=216

30 AES Corporation, http://www.aes.com

31 Alan Wolfe, "The revival of moral inquiry in the social sciences," *Chronicle of Higher Education* 46 (#2, 1999): B4.

32 For example, Willa Bruce, *Classics of Administrative Ethics* (Boulder, CO: Westview Press, 2001); Terry Cooper, *Handbook of Administrative Ethics*, 2nd ed. (Boca Raton, FL: CRC Press, 2000); James Svara, *The Ethics Primer for Public Administrators in Government and Nonprofit Organizations*, 2nd ed. (Burlington, MA: Jones & Bartlett, 2015).

33 For example, John Rohr, *Ethics For Bureaucrats*, 2nd ed. (New York: Marcel Dekker, 1989); David H. Rosenbloom, James D. Carroll, and Jonathan D. Carroll, *Constitutional Competence for Public Managers: Cases and Commentary* (Itasca, IL: Peacock, 2000).

34 For example, Terry L. Cooper, *The Responsible Administrator: An Approach to Ethics for the Administrative Role,* 3rd ed. (San Francisco: Jossey-Bass, 1990).

35 For example, Charles W. Anderson, *Statecraft: An Introduction to Political Choice and Judgment* (New York: John Wiley & Sons, 1977); Barry Bozeman, *Public Values and Public Interest: Counterbalancing Economic Individualism* (Washington, DC: Georgetown University Press, 2007); John Rohr, *Public Service, Ethics and Constitutional Practice* (Lawrence: University of Kansas Press, 1999).

36 See http://accreditation.naspaa.org/

37 See www.aspanet.org/public/ASPA/About_ASPA/Code_of_Ethics/

38 Ethics and Standards Implementation Committee, "ASPA Ethics Review Process," 24–5, in *Implementing the ASPA Code of Ethics: Workbook and Assessment Guide* (Washington: American Society for Public Administration, 2015), retrieved from www.aspanet.org/ASPADocs/Resources/Ethics_Assessment_Guide.pdf

39 William E. Mosher, "Public Administration: The Profession of Public Service," *American Political Science Review* 32 (1938): 333. William Mosher was the first President of the American Society for Public Administration in 1939.

40 Quoted from Mylon Winn, in Donald C. Menzel, *Ethics Moments in Government: Cases and Controversies* (Boca Raton: CRC Press, 2010), 210.

41 United Nations, *Professionalism and Ethics in the Public Service: Issues and Practices in Selected Regions* (New York: United Nations Division of Public Economics and Public Administration, 2000), 1.

42 For example, Robert Dingwall and Philip Lewis, *The Sociology of the Professions: Doctors, Lawyers, and Others* (New Orleans, LA: Quid Pro Books, 2014); Elliot Freidson, *Professionalism: The Third Logic* (New York: John Wiley & Sons, 2013); Magali Sarffati Larson, *The Rise of Professionalism: A Sociological Study* (Berkeley: University of California Press, 1977).

43 Terry Cooper, *Handbook of Administrative Ethics*, 2nd ed. (Boca Raton, FL: CRC Press, 2000).

44 Taylor Branch, "The Culture of Bureaucracy: We're All Working for the Penn Central," *Washington Monthly* (November 1970): 8.

45 Norton E. Long, "Conceptual Notes on the Public Interest for Public Administration and Policy Analysts," *Administration and Society* 22 (1990): 170–81.

46 John Dewey, *The Public and Its Problems: An Essay on Political Inquiry* (University Park: Penn State University Press, 2012 edition of 1930 original).

47 Norton E. Long, "The 1991 John Gaus Lecture: Politics, Political Science and the Public Interest," *PS: Political Science and Politics* 24 (#4, 1991): 674.

48 Walter Lippmann, *The Public Philosophy* (New York: Mentor Books, 1955), 40.

49 Norton E. Long, "Public Administration, Cognitive Competence, and the Public Interest," *Administration and Society* 20 (#3, 1988): 341.

50 Norton E. Long, "Power and Administration," *Public Administration Review* 9 (#4, 1949): 257–64; see especially pages 260–1.

51 For an excellent biographical sketch of Pendleton Herring, his life, and contributions, see Fred I. Greenstein and Austin Ranney, "Pendleton Herring: Biographical Memoirs," *Proceedings of the American Philosophical Society* 150 (#3, 2006): 488–92.

52 See Marshall E. Dimock's review of Herring's book, *Public Administration and the Public Interest* (New York: McGraw-Hill, 1936), in *Public Opinion Quarterly* 1 (#2, 1937): 153–7. Dimock sings Herring's praises in his conception of the role of public administration in fostering the public interest. Dimock argues that "public administration in a democracy cannot expect to be concerned solely with efficiency. It must not lose touch with group interests and citizen attitudes and desires" (153). Herring's understanding of the role of pressure groups is largely based on their influence on the regulatory role of executive agencies.

53 Gabriel A. Almond, "The Return to the State," *American Political Science Review* 82 (#3, September 1988): 853–74; Pendleton Herring, *Public Administration and the Public Interest* (New York: McGraw-Hill, 1936); Norton E. Long, "Bureaucracy and Constitutionalism," *American Political Science Review* 46 (#3, September 1952): 808–18.

54 For example, Frank J. Sorauf, "The Public Interest Reconsidered," *Journal of Politics* 19 (#4, 1957): 616–39.

55 Herbert Simon, *Administrative Behavior* (New York: Macmillan, 1947).

56 Emmette S. Redford, "The Protection of the Public Interest with Special Reference to Administrative Regulation," *American Political Science Review* 48 (#4, 1954): 1103–13.

57 Paul Appleby, *Morality and Administration in Democratic Government* (Baton Rouge: Louisiana State University Press, 1952).

58 But see Frederich C. Mosher, *Democracy and the Public Service* (New York: Oxford University Press, 1982); Mosher doubted whether Platonism was an adequate theory of the reality of public administration (97–8), even when adding a touch of pluralism in the Barnard-Appleby-Bailey construct (229–40).

59 Glendon Schubert, *The Public Interest: A Critique of the Theory of a Political Concept* (Glencoe, IL: The Free Press, 1960).

60 Anthony Downs, "The Public Interest: Its Meaning in a Democracy," *Social Research* 29 (#2, 1962): 1–36.

61 For more on the theory of the commons, see: Terry L. Anderson and Randy T. Simmons, eds., *The Political Economy of Customs and Culture: Information Solutions to the Commons Problem*, 2nd ed. (Lanham, MD: Rowman & Littlefield, 1998); John A. Baden and Douglas Noonan, eds., *Managing the Commons* (Bloomington: Indiana University Press, 1992); Elinor Ostrom, *Governing the Commons: The*

Evolution of Institutions for Collective Action (Cambridge: Cambridge University Press, 1990).

62 Other applied economic research on the public interest/commons looks at the regulatory process from the eyes of the regulators themselves, as well as the perspective of producers and consumers, e.g., Joel D. Aberbach and Bert A. Rockman, "Administrator's Beliefs about the Role of the Public: The Case of American Federal Executives," *Western Political Quarterly* 31 (1978): 502–22; Robert D. Eckert, "The Life Cycle of Regulatory Commissioners," *Journal of Law and Economics* 24 (1981): 113–20; Achon Fung, "Putting the Public Back into Governance: The Challenges of Citizen Participation and Its Future," *Public Administration Review* 75 (July–August 2015): 513–22.

63 Richard J. Flathman, *The Public Interest: An Essay Concerning the Normative Discourse of Politics* (New York: John Wiley and Sons, 1966), 8–9.

64 Virginia Held, *The Public Interest and Individual Interests* (Oxford: Oxford University Press, 1970); see also Michael Feintuck, *The Public Interest in Regulation* (New York: Basic Books, 2004); Michael Feintuck and M. Varney, *Media Regulation, Public Interest and the Law* (Edinburgh: Edinburgh University Press, 2006).

65 Charles T. Goodsell, "Public Administration and the Public Interest," in Gary L. Wamsley and R.N. Bacher, eds., *Refounding Public Administration* (Newbury Park, CA: Sage, 1990), 96–113.

66 Mark Harmon, "Administrative Policy Formulation and the Public Interest," in Robert B. Denhardt and B.R. Hammond, eds., *Public Administration in Action: Readings, Profiles, and Cases* (Pacific Grove, CA: Brooks/Cole, 1992), 49–57.

67 J.C. Beach, E.D. Carter, M.J. Dede, C.T. Goodsell, R. Guignard, and W.M. Haraway, "State Administration and the Founding Fathers During the Critical Period," *Administration & Society* 28 (1997): 511–30.

68 Mark Harmon, "Administrative Policy Formulation and the Public Interest," in Robert Denhardt and B. Hammond, eds., *Public Administration in Action: Readings, Profiles, and Cases* (Pacific Grove, CA: Brooks/Cole, 1992).

69 For example, Stephanie P. Newbold, "Toward a Constitutional School for American Public Administration," *Public Administration Review* 70 (#4, 2010): 538–46; Stephanie P. Newbold and David Rosenbloom, eds., *The Constitutional School of American Public Administration* (New York: Routledge, 2016).

70 For example, David H. Rosenbloom, James D. Carroll, and Jonathan D. Carroll, *Constitutional Competence for Public Managers: Cases and Commentary* (Itasca, IL: Peacock, 2000).

71 For example, Bradley S. Chilton and James A. Woods, "Moral Justifications on the Rehnquist Court: Hercules, Herbert, and Druggies under the Fourth Amendment," *Criminal Justice Policy Review* 17 (2006): 343–61.

72 For example, A.M. Bertelli and L.E. Lynn, *Madison's Managers: Public Administration and the Constitution* (Baltimore, MD: Johns Hopkins University Press, 2006); M.W. Spicer, *The Founders, the Constitution, and Public Administration: A Conflict in World Views* (Washington, DC: Georgetown University Press, 2007).

73 For example, B.J. Cook, "The Representative Function of Bureaucracy: Public Administration in Constitutive Perspective," *Administration & Society* 23 (1992): 403–29; Richard Green, "A Constitutional Jurisprudence: Reviving Praxis in Public Administration," *Administration & Society* 24 (1992): 3–21; H. Jefferson Powell, *The Moral Tradition of American Constitutionalism: A Theological Interpretation* (Durham, NC: Duke University Press, 1993); John Rohr, *To Run a Constitution: The Legitimacy of the Administrative State* (Lawrence: University of Kansas Press, 1986); John Rohr, *Public Service, Ethics and Constitutional Practice* (Lawrence: University of Kansas Press, 1999); David H. Rosenbloom and R.S. Kravchuk, *Public Administration: Understanding Management, Politics, and Law in the Public Sector*, 6th ed. (Boston: McGraw-Hill, 2005); Gary Wamsley and James Wolf, *Refounding Democratic Public Administration: Modern Paradoxes, Postmodern Challenges* (Thousand Oaks, CA: Sage, 1997).

74 M.W. Spicer, *The Founders, the Constitution, and Public Administration: A Conflict in World Views* (Washington, DC: Georgetown University Press, 2007).

75 John A. Rohr, *Public Service, Ethics and Constitutional Practice* (Lawrence: University Press of Kansas, 1999); John A. Rohr, *Civil Servants and Their Constitutions* (Lawrence: University Press of Kansas, 2002).

76 Nicholas Jolley, *Locke: His Philosophical Thought* (Cambridge: Oxford University Press, 1999); Michael Ayers, *Locke: Epistemology and Ontology* (New York: Routledge, 1994); Patrick Riley, *Will and Political Legitimacy: A Critical Exposition of Social Contract Theory in Hobbes, Locke, Rousseau, Kant, and Hegel* (Cambridge: Harvard University Press, 1982).

77 P.S. Landau, "Dividing the Commons: Politics, Policy, and Culture in Botswana," *International Journal of African Historical Studies* 29 (1996): 384–6; M. Somma, "Institutions, Ideology, and the Tragedy of the Commons: West Texas Groundwater Policy," *Publius* 27 (1997): 1–13.

78 Elinor Ostrom, *Governing the Commons: The Evolution of Institutions for Collective Action* (London: Cambridge University Press, 1990).

79 Robert Putnam, *Bowling Alone: The Collapse and Revival of American Community* (New York: Simon and Schuster, 2000).

80 M. Barakso and B.F. Schaffner, "Exit, Voice, and Interest Group Governance," *American Politics Research* 36 (2008): 186–209; W.D. Coleman, "Analysing the Associative Action of Business: Policy Advocacy and Policy Participation, *Administration Publique du Canada* 28 (1985): 413–33; P. Nedergaard, "The Reform of the 2003 Common Agricultural Policy: An Advocacy Coalition Explanation," *Policy Studies* 29 (2008): 179–95.

81 For example, Eugene P. Dvorin and Robert H. Simmons, *From Amoral to Humane Bureaucracy* (San Francisco: Canfield Press, 1972).

82 Richard E. Flathman, *The Public Interest: An Essay Concerning the Normative Discourse of Politics* (New York: John Wiley and Sons, 1966). For an excellent discussion of Flathman's ordinary language philosophy, particularly as it applies to public administration and policy analysis, see Norton E. Long's "Conceptual Notes on the Public Interest for Public Administration and Policy Analysts," *Administration and Society* 22 (#2, August 1990): 170–81.

83 For example, Charles W. Anderson, *Statecraft: An Introduction to Political Choice and Judgment* (New York: John Wiley & Sons, 1977): chapter 2, "Role and Responsibility."

84 Lon Fuller, *The Morality of Law* (New Haven, CT: Yale University Press, 1969).

85 Michael Feintuck, *The Public Interest in Regulation* (New York: Basic Books, 2004); Michael Feintuck and M. Varney, *Media Regulation, Public Interest and the Law* (Edinburgh: Edinburgh University Press, 2006).

86 S.E. Harrington, *Insurance Deregulation and the Public Interest* (Washington: AEI-Brookings Joint Center for Regulatory Studies, 2000).

87 For example, A. Stone, *Economic Regulation and the Public Interest: The Federal Trade Commission in Theory and Practice* (Ithaca, NY: Cornell University Press, 1977).

88 For example, P. Davies, *Contested Ground: Public Purpose and Private Interest in the Regulation of Prescription Drugs* (New York: Oxford University Press, 1996).

89 For example, J.P. Geyman, *The Corporate Transformation of Health Care: Can the Public Interest Still Be Served?* (New York: Springer, 2004).

90 For example, W. Freedman, *Federal Statutes on Environmental Protection: Regulation in the Public Interest* (New York: Quorum Books, 1987).

91 For example, P. Collins, *Gambling and the Public Interest* (Westport, CN: Praeger Books, 2003).

92 G.O. Robinson, "Title I, the Federal Communications Act: An Essay on Origins and Regulatory Purpose," in M. Paglin, ed., *A Legislative History of the Communications Act of 1934* (New York: Oxford University Press, 1989), 3–24.

93 Newton N. Minow, *Equal Time: The Private Broadcaster and the Public Interest* (New York: Atheneum, 1964).

94 T.G. Krattenmaker and L.A. Powe, *Regulating Broadcast Programming* (Washington: American Enterprise Institute, 1994).

95 Louis Fisher, *American Constitutional Law*, 2nd ed. (New York: McGraw-Hill, 1995).

96 D.P. Mullally, "The Fairness Doctrine: Benefits and Costs," *Public Opinion Quarterly* 33 (1970): 577–82.

97 Fred W. Friendly, *The Good Guys, the Bad Guys and the First Amendment: Free Speech vs. Fairness in Broadcasting* (New York: Random House, 1976).

98 E.G. Krasnow, "The 'Public Interest' Standard: The Elusive Search for the Holy Grail," briefing for the Advisory Committee on Public Interest Obligations of Digital Television Broadcasters, retrieved from http://govinfo.library.unt.edu/piac/octmtg/Krasnow.htm

99 Federal Communications Commission, *In Re Deregulation of Radio*, 84 *FCC 2nd* 978 (1981).

100 *Syracuse Peace Council*, 1987, 145.

101 J. Garruso, "Back to Muzak? Congress and Un-Fairness Doctrine," *Webmemo*, Heritage Foundation # 1472 (May 23, 2007).

102 Brooks Boliek, "FCC Finally Kills Off Fairness Doctrine," *POLITICO* (August 22, 2011).

103 Common Cause Education Fund, "The Fallout from the Telecommunications Act of 1996: Unintended Consequences and Lessons Learned." Retrieved from www.commoncause.org/

104 Lawrence Lessig, *Free Culture: How Big Media Uses Technology and the Law to Lock Down Culture and Control Creativity* (New York: Penguin Press, 2004).

105 Anthony Varona, "Toward A Broadband Public Interest Standard," *Administrative Law Review* 61 (2009): 1–137.

106 Ryan Knutson, "FCC Chairman Says Obama's Net Neutrality Statement Influenced Rule," *Wall Street Journal* (March 17, 2015), A1.

107 *Telecommunication Act of 1996*, retrieved from https://transition.fcc.gov/telecom.html

108 For example, Geoffrey Manne, "ICLE and Leading Academics File Amicus Brief Urging the Court to Overturn the FCC's Illegal Net Neutrality Order," *Truth on the Market* (blog, August 7, 2015), http://truthonthemarket.com/tag/professor-gus-hurwitz/

109 Daniel Berninger, "Net Neutrality Versus New Telecosm," *Voice Communication Exchange Committee* (blog, August 2015), http://vcxc.org/blog.html

110 Juliana Reyes, "Vonage Cofounder Says Net Neutrality Fears Are 'bullshit,'" *Philly Technical.ly* (ejournal, October 21, 2014), http://technical.ly/philly/2014/10/20/jeff-pulver-net-neutrality-title-ii/

111 Chris Moran, "FCC Chairman Tom Wheeler Promises No 'Utility Style Regulation' of Broadband," *Consumerist* (June 26, 2015), http://consumerist.com/2015/06/26/fcc-chair-tom-wheeler-promises-no-utility-style-regulation-of-broadband/

112 Mark Wigfield, "FCC Acts to Restore Internet Freedom," FCC News from the Federal Communications Commission (December 14, 2017), https://transition.fcc.gov/Daily_Releases/Daily_Business/2017/db1214/DOC-348261A1.pdf

113 Lesley Hitchens, *Broadcasting Pluralism and Diversity: A Comparative Study of Policy and Regulation* (Portland, OR: Hart, 2006).

114 Laura DeNardus, *The Global War for Internet Governance* (New Haven, CT: Yale University Press, 2014).

115 Barry Bozeman, *Public Values and Public Interest: Counterbalancing Economic Individualism* (Washington: Georgetown University Press, 2007).

116 Lesley Hitchens, *Broadcasting Pluralism and Diversity: A Comparative Study of Policy and Regulation* (Portland, OR: Hart, 2006).

117 American Society for Public Administration, *2013 Code of Ethics*, retrieved from www.aspanet.org/ASPADocs/ASPA%20Code%20of%20Ethics-2013%20with%20Practices.pdf

Virtue of Public Administrators

"Demonstrate personal integrity. Adhere to the highest standards of conduct to inspire public confidence and trust in public service."
— (Code of Ethics, American Society for Public Administration, 2013)

> ### BOX 2.1 | CHAPTER OBJECTIVES
>
> 1 Understand the public administration profession and ethics within historical context.
> 2 Recognize figures, scholars, and practitioners who contributed to public administration's evolution.
> 3 Distinguish the virtues among public administration professionals as lived by leaders, figures, scholars.
> 4 Critique virtue ethical theory and the perspectives of good moral character in our ethics case study of socialization to the profession by Dr. Seuss's public servant—are they benevolent? competent?

For many readers, the questions "What is public administration?" or "what is administration in the public interests?"—are really a question of "Who are **good public administrators**?" And the ethical concept of virtue is the key to each and every answer. In this chapter we seek a systematic understanding of the real world of public administrators and the variety of human experiences with public goods and services, A to Z, from the **administration** of criminal justice to Zantrex dietary supplement testing by the FDA. We present this through a current history of public administrators. There is a rich and growing scholarly literature on the history of administrators and managers in both the private and public realms. Some focus on great or famous men—and women—such as George Washington, Thomas Jefferson, Alexander Hamilton, Andrew Jackson, Abraham Lincoln, Jane Addams, Franklin Delano Roosevelt, Elinor Ostrom, and others. Other histories focus on ordinary lives of individuals, groups, and their organizations and institutions. Still others place people, whether great or ordinary, within the context of schools of thought by scholars as shorthand that gives meaning to the real-world experiences of millions. All seek a big picture of public administration through history that may be more meaningful because it focuses on people and the world they live and work in.

This examination of the real world of the history of public administrators allows us to focus attention on the **virtue ethics** perspective, emphasizing an applied ethics of **good moral character**. History has always focused on the real world of people, about human practices in the meanings, conflicts, and resolutions within an empirical reality. This focus on the actual real-life-world of persons fulfills a human need to judge the person and the context of a character, not just some generic disembodied behaviors. Of course, it is a matter of degree, and any good history also includes aspects of the ethical perspective of duty, such as to the Constitution and laws, and ethics of utility, such as the utilitarian calculations of majoritarianism and political compromises people create. Further, history has for so long been so much about his-story that new feminist perspectives are compelled to posit her-story as well.[1] So, what does it mean to be a good public administrator?

The virtue ethical perspective is a good starting point in our study of the public administration profession because it is ordinary, common, and practical in its simplicity. TV, movies, novels, the internet, and the stories of family and friends—all ordinarily present narratives of people and assess their character, motives, and judgments. You know, who's the good one or the bad one— who's wearing the white hat or the black hat? Even children's books ordinarily depict the character of public servants. Highly influential authors like **Dr. Seuss** (Theodore Seuss Geisel) often depict **public servants** as less-than-benevolent and less-than-competent. May this explain why we view bureaucrats as we do?[2] We commonly judge who is a good person by their virtue or character, defined as a "fixed disposition, habit, or trait to do what is morally commendable."[3] We often call these moral character habits using such descriptions as courage, compassion, benevolence, optimism, truthful, honest, honorable, responsible, incorruptible, nonpartisan, and, of course, virtuous. The virtue ethical perspective answers the question "What ought I do?" with practical simplicity—be true-to-yourself[4]— rather than some detailed list of actions. This practical simplicity may also be popularly expressed by emulating a person, whether it be the imitation of a hero (e.g., Spider-Man), a great historical figure (e.g., **George Washington**), or with a WWJD bracelet (i.e., "What would Jesus do?").[5]

In Chapter 2 we do three things. First, we overview ethical theories—particularly virtue ethics, and its application to the public administration profession. Second, we provide a brief historical overview of the real world of American public administrators, including individuals, political groups, and scholarly schools of thought. Third, within this history we provide examples of virtue ethical perspective, as well as vices. We end the chapter with a critique of virtue ethical theory in our ethics case study of socialization of children to the profession with Dr. Seuss's depictions of public servants—as benevolent? as **competent**?

VIRTUE AND ETHICAL THEORIES

The ethics of the public administration profession are founded upon ethical philosophies, including virtue, utilitarianism, deontology, and ethical egoism. Each ethical philosophy has a long history over the millennia, but we will only briefly cover each with many examples in this chapter (with virtue) and the next two chapters (with utilitarianism and deontology, respectively). Table 2.1

TABLE 2.1

Summary of Ethical Theories and Philosophers, Ideas, and Critiques

Virtue	Deontology	Ethical Egoism	Utilitarianism
• good moral character • teleological	• moral formalism • non-teleological	• subjectivism/relativism • situationalism • sociopath • looking out for number one • teleological	• maximum happiness • pleasure vs. pain • costs and benefits • preferences • teleological
• Plato • Aristotle • Alasdair MacIntyre	• Immanuel Kant • John Rohr	• Friedrich Nietzsche • Joseph Fletcher • Kai Nielsen • Ayn Rand	• Jeremy Bentham • John Stuart Mill • John Rawls • Terry Cooper
For example: • Plato and Aristotle's virtue ethics of character • Christian virtues of love, hope, and faith	For example: • Immanuel Kant's categorical imperative • Rohr's constitutional regime values	For example: • Nietzsche's will-to-power ethics and the Ubermensch • the egocentric or sociopathic	For example: • Bentham and Mill's utilitarian calculation of pleasure-pain, happiness • benefit-cost analysis
• virtue ideas • right and wrong are defined by moral character; being, long-term traits, and personhood	• deontology ideas • right and wrong are defined by proscribed behaviors; duties and rightful acts	• ethical egoism ideas • right and wrong defined as merely personal-cultural preferences or will to power	• utilitarianism ideas • right and wrong defined by pain-pleasure calculus of each act (act utilitarianism) or a predictive rule-of-thumb (rule utilitarianism)
Guided by character traits or examples of good persons and beings, e.g., leaders of religions, states, or other institutions	Guided by universal moral rules or obligations, e.g., behaviors proscribed by family, legal, or religious sources	Guided by one's own egoism or preferences and cultural mores, e.g., what you prefer based on what you desire or were taught to desire	Guided by the greatest good for greatest number, e.g., cost-benefit analysis or pain and pleasure
Virtue Critique *Con* difficult to apply or measure in ordinary life and being	*Deontology Critique* *Con* less concerned with consequences of behaviors	*Ethical Egoism Critique* *Con* dismisses all moral truth, whether universal or majority-supported; can egoism ever be taught?	*Utilitarianism Critique* *Con* neglects the value of intent and aspiration by actors; is anything ever intrinsically good in itself?
Pro extensively urged by our greatest ethical leaders, from Christ to Abraham to Muhammed	Pro firmly rooted in specific proscribed behavior; does not give moral ground due to ambiguity	Pro scapegoat for explaining the negative side of other views	Pro equal recognition of others and precise measurement of good and harm/costs

Sources: James Svara, The Ethics Primer for Public Administrators in Government and Nonprofit Organizations, 2nd ed. (Burlington, MA: Jones & Bartlett, 2015); John R. Walton, James M. Stearns, and Charles T. Crespy, "Integrating Ethics into the Public Administration Curriculum: A Three-Step Process," Journal of Policy Analysis and Management 16 (#3, 1997): 470–483.

describes each with summaries of philosophies and philosophers, their ideas and critiques.

Some people may trash all ethics, to their detriment, usually out of a theory of ethical egoism. Ethical egoism is the philosophy which argues that the only valid moral standard is the obligation to promote your own well-being above all others. It is often associated with popular notions of egoistic behavior that it is natural to look out for number one or sociopathic.[6] Ethical egoism is a normative theory that advocates selfishness in all moral activity, and cynically asserts that all other moral talk is merely the will to power. Ethical egoism asserts that, no matter what people may argue, they are really acting for the sake of their personal well-being only. For example, 1960s radicals claimed that even when new attempts were made to represent minorities and women in public affairs, the decisions and actions continued to reflect old status quo notions, duping the American public by depicting their decisions as the operation of a marketplace exchange of private interests.[7] Behind the façade of pseudo-science was the operation of a will to power and rhetorical ploys to advance the status quo or private interests of political elites.[8] Critics argued this was no different than Nazi Germany of World War II, that made the will-to-power philosophy and Friedrich Nietzsche the official philosopher and depicted laws as the operation of an exchange of private interests: to advocate and justify the holocaust of the Jews. Even more despairing may be the related attitude of moral relativism, the perspective that all normative values and moral beliefs are relative to an individual or culture; the belief that all basic value-judgments of individuals or cultures are so different and conflicting that no one's values may apply to the conduct of others. In its extreme and most cynical form, moral relativism casts aside all value statements, including ethics, the public interests, even ethical egoism, as complete non-sense—and closes the mind to the possibility of dialog and meaningful exchange of ideas.[9]

However, even if moral standards are not 100 percent absolute across all cultures all the time does not mean there are no moral standards at all; moral standards do not have to be absolute in human terms in order to exist.[10] Further, close study reveals empirical patterns of moral development in all individuals, genders, and across cultures throughout the world—even among public administrators.[11] Rushworth Kidder, the founder of the Institute for Global Ethics, believes there is evidence of universal ethics that all people everywhere, including public administrators, should strive to achieve including love, truthfulness, fairness, freedom, unity, tolerance, responsibility, respect for life, as well as courage, wisdom, hospitality, obedience, peace, and stability.[12]

We disagree with cynics who discard ethics and public interests as literal nonsense because their existence cannot be proven with any of the five senses. We believe such reasoning would trash other valued concepts like God, love, justice, and hope. These cynics throw out the baby with the bathwater; in their hard-nosed pursuit of scientific truth, they betray the very scientific principles of empiricism they purport to defend. We believe the reality of public administration clearly demonstrates that when you get closely empirical, follow people around, and ask what they are doing, you find the public interests within ordinary experiences, commonly shared meanings, and practical outcomes. Like so many of the important meanings in our lives, we find the public interests are heart-felt and understood in context.

Chapter 4, on the Constitution and laws, focuses on deontology, an ethical theory about doing the right thing, action, or decision. The term *deontology* is derived from two Greek words—*deon*, binding duty; and -*ology*, the study of—to focus on the ethics of following duties, promises, and other obligations to define what is good and bad. Deontologists deny that the balance of good over evil consequences (teleology) is the deciding factor in determining what is right or wrong. Instead, the goal of deontology is non-teleological and consists of universal, valid means of behavior or activities that are applied fairly and without bias—even if dutifully following the rules should result in mischief, injustice, or tragic ending for a particular person or group. In deontology, one is judged by doing the right act, not by good (or bad) consequences of their acts. Deontology is critical of other virtue and utilitarian ethics theories because we don't ordinarily have the capacity to predict or control the consequences of our actions, but we can perform our duty with the right intent. Further, the duty perspective doesn't simply look at the roles of benefactor-beneficiary, but includes the diverse roles and corresponding duties, such as fiduciary-entrusted, principle-agent, supervisor-supervisee, bureaucrat-citizen, promisor-promisee, lawyer-client, physician-patient, parent-child, and many other roles. Deontology gives consideration to the past as an indicator of the good; past precedents may create obligations in the present.[13]

Chapter 3, on democratic policymaking, focuses on utilitarianism, which holds that the sole ultimate standard or criterion of rightness and wrongness is the principle of utility—or the greatest good for the greatest number. It was promoted by Jeremy Bentham (1748–1842), John Stuart Mill (1806–1873), and federal judge Richard Posner (1939–), and is associated with the identification of the single act (act-utilitarianism) or rule-of-thumb (rule-utilitarianism) that will produce the greatest good for the greatest number. It mandates an additional level of recognition, respect, and accounting to the preferences of each and every person affected by a moral decision. In utilitarianism, rights and wrongs are determined by calculation of benefits and costs; or happiness, pleasure and pain, individual preferences; and other measures of human needs of intrinsic value to produce a maximal value. The thing of intrinsic value itself is not the thing of moral value; rather, "Actions are right in proportion as they tend to promote happiness, wrong as they tend to produce the reverse of happiness."[14] Utilitarianism is not based on the discovery of pre-existing or universal rules or duties (non-teleological), but is skeptical of the value of such rules or duties without specific empirical reference to the consequences to all who are involved (teleology). Utilitarianism emphasizes the ends or consequences of moral decisions (teleology) and the actual production of things of intrinsic value, rather than following the rules for their own sake. Utilitarianism may be hedonistic in focusing on pleasure or happiness or pluralistic with the inclusion of values beyond hedonism, but the trend is to take a third approach of aggregating individual preferences into benefits/costs, especially in applied administrative ethics.[15]

This chapter focuses on virtue ethics with applications in the history of the public administration profession. Although it is difficult to precisely know and measure in day-to-day public administration, we commonly judge who is a good person by their virtue or good moral character, defined as a "fixed disposition, habit, or trait to do what is morally commendable."[16] TV, movies, novels, the internet, and the stories of family and friends—all ordinarily present narratives of people—and assess their character, motives, and judgments. Even children's books and media ordinarily depict public servants, and authors like Dr. Seuss often depicted public servants as less than benevolent, and detached.[17] Rather than some list of detailed behaviors, virtue ethics gives answers to ethical questions with practical simplicity—"be a good citizen"[18]—or by emulating a person or hero.[19] It dominated all Western ethical philosophy from 400 BCE until the Enlightenment, had setbacks in the nineteenth century, but re-emerged in the 1950s.[20]

To be clear, virtue is not just a character trait—defined as temporary dispositions or behavioral tendencies that may not be deeply ingrained in a person. Character traits are not innate; people are not born with them. Instead, character traits are singular dispositions freely selected by people as they mature and develop. We are not born liars, but we may become so if we chose to repeatedly lie or seek to tell the truth. By contrast, virtue is multi-track. For example, a character trait to tell the truth is singular in doing one action for particular reasons; a virtue of honesty includes many actions, emotions, values, choices, desires, perceptions, attitudes, interests, expectations over time in a complex mindset.[21] This is what makes virtue ethics teleological, or concerned with the consequences for one's entire moral character, not just a singular action. Thus, it is reckless to attribute a virtue to a person on the basis of a single action, such as the children's story of *George Washington and the Cherry Tree* attributing the virtue of honesty. And, because a virtue is so multi-track, possessing a virtue is a matter of degree.[22]

The virtues have changed in emphasis over the millennia. Plato (426–347 BCE) prized the virtues of prudence, courage, temperance, and justice in defining a virtuous person as "wise, courageous, moderate and just." His student, Aristotle (384–322 BCE), in *Nicomachean Ethics*, opened the list of virtues with the concept of the golden mean: virtue is the mean between extremes or vices of too much and too little of a particular character quality. For example, generosity is the mean between prodigality and stinginess; moderation, a mean between self-indulgence and insensibility. Contemporary virtue theorists still follow Aristotle's basic elements of virtue: (1) Arete, or excellent moral character, multi-tracks well-entrenched in its possessor; (2) Phronesis, or practical wisdom, from much experience with life to know some situations and the best paths to take; and (3) Eudaimonia, or general well-being, for a flourishing of being and happiness to make for an excellent life.[23] The revolutionary teachings and being of Jesus focused on the virtue of love: "You shall love the Lord your God with all your heart and with all your soul and with all your mind and with all your strength . . . Love your neighbor as yourself" (Mark 12: 30–31). Thomas Aquinas (1225–1274) followed with "The things that we love tell us what we are."

Contemporary ethicists have countered the cynics who dismissed virtue as too vague or difficult to apply. G.E.M. Anscombe (1919–2001) admitted character virtues were vague, but she argued that vice-terms may help us know their opposite virtue anonyms, e.g., lazy, irresponsible, feckless, inconsiderate, harsh, uncooperative, intolerant, selfish, mercenary, indiscreet, tactless, arrogant, unsympathetic, cold, rule, incautious, unenterprising, presumptuous, grudging, brutal, and disloyal. Martha Nussbaum (1947–) admitted that cultural relativism challenged virtue theory, but posited that, while cultures may disagree about local meanings and priority-ranking of the virtues, the virtues themselves are not relative to cultures, but are found within all known cultures.[24] The popular ethical egoism philosopher Ayn Rand (1905–1982) argued that all virtue was really just egoism: the virtuous are really doing just what they want to do; thus, a virtue of selfishness.[25] However, virtue theory is all about motives and intentionality, and reading egoism into a public servant's act of kindness may assume knowledge you don't have. Can you assume what is being cooked just by looking at a grocery store list—rather than asking the intent of the shopper? Yet problems remain for virtue theory, such as what to do when virtues conflict (for example, mercy may prompt you to kill a dying person who is better off dead): justice forbids it, and honesty may require telling truths that could harm another, but compassion would require us to remain silent or even lie to prevent harm. Philosopher Alasdair MacIntyre (1925–) has tangled with these issues and others, and advocates a return to virtue ethics in public affairs.[26]

Washington, Hamilton, Madison, Jefferson, and other founders understood a vision of public service through virtue ethics. Plato and Aristotle posited that our unique reason capacity can help us find our arete (moral excellence), and the mere pursuit of pleasure was a life fit for cattle. The founders were deeply influenced by the ancient Greeks and sought to found a system of arete, as well as magnificence, dignity, cheerfulness, and reason gave us the practical wisdom to make it so. Yet the virtue ethics of the founders were criticized for the lack of obligations and specific legal duties owed by these "philosopher-kings" to the people they served. A more recent remedy proposed by the Blacksburg scholars was to dovetail the biographical study of the virtue ethics of the founders with specific details of their limitations under constitutional laws and values.[27]

So, how do we apply the insights of virtue ethical philosophy to the development of the public administration profession? Our application begins with the etymology and meanings of concepts, such as administration and **management**. We traverse over 200 years of American history of public service, with applications of virtue as extolled by presidents, leading administrators, scholars, and social reform **movements**. Finally, we closely examine current issues in the recruitment of a new generation of public servants and the impact of socialization by children's literature depictions of public servants' characters. What impact may depictions of public servants as less-than-benevolent or less-than-competent have?

EVOLUTION OF AMERICAN PUBLIC ADMINISTRATION

Administration has been with us probably longer than recorded history. Anytime people, materials, and services were moved or rendered, there was a need for administration. Ancient civilizations, such as those found in China, Egypt, sub-Saharan Africa, Byzantium, Rome, Greece, and Babylonia,[28] required the administration of people to build cities, aqueducts, irrigation systems, and roads; fight wars; process information; protect their cities from outside invasion; police themselves; judge those charged with a crime, regulate business and civic matters; educate their children; plan and provide for natural disasters; and care for the needy. From communities to nations the need for administration is ever-present. It is a natural state and process. People are by nature social creatures, and therefore when we engage and cooperate in various activities the need to plan, organize, staff, direct, coordinate, report, and budget (i.e., alluding to Gulick's POSDCORB acrostic; see also Chapter 6) is ever-present.

Management as a concept has a more recent origin in human affairs. The word *manage* arose from the French word *ménage*, involving the care and training of animals, especially horses. The *menagerie* was a small dog and pony show that traveled across Europe. In the nineteenth century, the term *manage* moved from its rural setting to the newly emerging industrial world, referring in part to the *managerial* European industries and economies. Management became the modern task of segmenting processes to manipulate the efficiency of human workers and to increase productivity. With this concept there also came a more behavioral approach to oversight and direction of human organizations.[29] Management was simply added into the much more ancient and larger concept of administration, which dated back to the very beginnings of human society. So, the concept of management was attached to administration in the late nineteenth and early twentieth centuries, spurred on or stimulated by the Industrial Revolution, Progressive reforms, the administrative state, and its backroom politics.

When forced to pinpoint its origins, scholars agree that the modern academic discipline of public administration began toward the end of the nineteenth century, when an obscure professor at Johns Hopkins University named Woodrow Wilson (1856–1924; later, a U.S. President) wrote his now famous article, "The Study of Administration," in 1887.[30] Wilson's article delineated what he considered the stark differences between the science of administration and the art of politics, with the latter inferior to the former. Wilson, and those he influenced—such as Frank Goodnow,[31] Leonard White,[32] W. F. Willoughby,[33] Luther Gulick and Lyndall Urwick,[34] among others—argued that there is and should be a science of public administration, where there is no influence or confusion between it and politics, or a politics/administration dichotomy. Politics, they argued, ought to be concerned with policy development, while public administration should to be concerned with policy implementation. Public administration evolved to encompass both.

Period 1: Founding Period of Public Administration (1789–1829)

When President George Washington (1732–1799) exited public life in 1796, he left a mark on the presidency—that the office of the president was to play an important role in the development and implementation of public policy. Although it is true that the administration of public affairs was generally in the hands of locally elected and patronage positions, statesmen such as Washington and Alexander Hamilton recognized the need for central government direction in the formulation, development, and implementation of public policy initiatives. No formal personnel system was in place, although Washington advocated selection from the educated elite of men of character (sorry, he was gender-specific). This clearly emphasized a virtue ethical theory in which we govern by deferring to elite gentlemen the determination and implementation of the public interests. The office of the presidency was in its infancy, but with the efforts and vision of individuals like Hamilton, it was apparent that important facets of society such as the economy and public finances should be usually directed by this elite group of gentlemen within the national government.

Of course, other founders such as Thomas Jefferson (1743–1826) and James Madison (1751–1836), both later presidents, concluded that too much centralized control impeded the life and vision of the citizens. Still other founders, such as William Livingston, George Mason, John Hancock, Richard Henry Lee, and

TABLE 2.2

Presidential Movements within Modern Public Administration in the United States

Movements in PA	Description	Time Period	Major Figures and Scholars
1 Founding Period	The First American Administrative State	1789–1829	George Washington, Alexander Hamilton, Thomas Jefferson, James Madison
2 Pre-Civil War Period	Jackson's Democracy through the Second American Revolution	1829–1876	Andrew Jackson, Abraham Lincoln, Major General Montgomery C. Meigs (Lincoln's quartermaster general)
3 Post-Civil War Period	The Second American Administrative State	1876–1887	Grover Cleveland, Civil Service Commission (1883)
4 Pre-Classical Period	The Beginnings of Modern Administration	1887–1900	Dorman B. Eaton (1879), Richard T. Ely's autobiography (1938), Woodrow Wilson (1887 article)
5 Classical Period	Intellectualizing the Politics-Administration Dichotomy	1900–1926	Theodore Roosevelt, Frank Goodnow (1900), Frederick Taylor (1911), William H. Taft Commission (1912–1913), Bureau of Budget Act (1920), Leonard White (1926), Mary Parker Follett (1923)
6 The Principles Approach	Principles Approach of Scientific Management	1926–1937	Franklin D. Roosevelt, W.F. Willoughby (1927); Luther Gulick and Lyndall Urwick (1937), Henri Fayol (1930)
7 Behavioral Revolution	Behavioral Challenge to the Principles Approach	1938–1948	Harry Truman, Chester Barnard (1938), Fritz Morstein Marx (1946), Herbert Simon (1947), Dwight Waldo (1948)
8 Public Administration and Political Science	The Effect of Political Science upon Public Administration	1950–1969	Dwight Eisenhower, David Easton (1953), Glendon Schubert (1957), Frederick Mosher (1968), Emmette Redford (1969)
9 Administrative Management	Decision-Making as Theme	1956–1967	John F. Kennedy, March and Simon (1958), McGregor (1960), Katz and Kahn (1966), Dwight Waldo (1956)
10 Reform Management	New Public Management	1968–1979	Jimmy Carter, Marini (1971), Downs (1967), Wildavsky (1964)
11 Public Choice	Economic Theory and Public Administration	1970s–1980s	Richard M. Nixon, Buchanan (1969), Tullock (1970), Ostrom and Ostrom (1971), Elinor Ostrom (1990/2015)
12 Privatization of Government	Privatization and Reinvention	1980s to present	Ronald Reagan, Savas (1987), Osborne and Gaebler (1992)
13 Performance Management	Enhancing Performance of Public Agencies	Mid-1980s to 1990s	William Clinton, Ingraham, Joyce, and Donahue (2003)

(*continued*)

TABLE 2.2 *Continued*

Movements in PA	Description	Time Period	Major Figures and Scholars
14 Re-founding Constitutional Public Administration	Re-emphasis of the Normative, Legal and Philosophical in PA	1990s–present	William Clinton, George W. Bush and Barack Obama, Wamsley (1996), Rohr (1994), Rosenbloom (1997)
15 Waves of Change	PA Revolution of Who is Included: NGOs, FBOs, Postmodernism, Feminism	1990s–present	George W. Bush and Barack Obama, Denhardt and Denhardt (2011), Salamon, (2003); Fox and Miller (2007), Elinor Ostrom (1990, 2015), Stivers (2000), Fountain (2001)

John Witherspoon, were no less passionate about public service and the cause of American liberty than their more famous compatriots.[35] Lynton Caldwell contends that Jefferson's experience in France as ambassador and minister to the court of France only reinforced his disdain for centralized bureaucracy. Caldwell quotes from a letter that Jefferson wrote to Madison: "Never was there a country where the practice of governing too much had taken deeper root and done more mischief."[36] Obviously Jefferson was fearful that such an outcome was close to reality in the new United States under the direction of Hamilton, particularly in the establishment of a central banking system.

Alexander Hamilton (1757–1804), in contrast, favored rule by an educated elite. Jefferson argued for greater civic input by the citizenry. In spite of their differences, both advocated virtue ethics emphasizing governance and administration by gentlemen of **good character**. The difference was a matter of degree as to how many were to be included: Hamilton tended to be more **exclusive,** Jefferson favored broader civic input. Hamilton argued—and Washington agreed—that politicians must direct administrators. He also called for the determination of the public interests by the educated elite through greater centralization of authority, respect for constitutional duties, and above all a strong, central leader—the president. In this way, Hamilton's perspective of **virtue** was most like—indeed, inspired by—the **philosopher-kings** urged by classical Greek philosophers Plato and Aristotle, who should rule because they possessed greater knowledge, judgment, and skill.[37] By contrast, Jefferson promoted more broad-based civic input in virtuous administrative leadership to fulfill his popular political predispositions. This included fostering a culture of decentralization of authority, encouraging harmony among the branches of government, promoting simplicity in governing, being flexible with change, and advocating greater responsiveness of civil servants and government to citizens. Jefferson theoretically disagreed with Hamilton's insistence on strong centralization of authority in the executive branch, but at a practical level Jefferson advocated governance by educated elite gentlemen and, as president, embraced strong central executive leadership.[38] Washington, Hamilton, Madison, Jefferson, and other founders understood a vision of the public interests as described by classical Greek philosophers and virtue ethics theorists over the millennia.

Plato (426–347 BCE) and Aristotle (384–322 BCE) taught that human nature posits a moral function and well-being defined by the unique human capacity of reason. Merely pursuing pleasure was only a life fit for cattle. Our function was **arete**, a Greek word meaning "moral excellence," as well as "magnificence, dignity, cheerfulness," and in the practical wisdom to make it so. Aristotle's *Nicomachean Ethics* detailed a practical wisdom of learning to avoid two extremes in moral decisions: excess (too much) and defect (too little). For example, the virtue of courage is the mean between foolhardiness (excess) and fear (defect).[39]

However, the founders' classical liberal arts education in Plato and Aristotle also may be faulted for fostering **a gentleman's code of ethics** and public interests with few obligations, duties or limits. The result was a polity dominated by elite, white, male property owners. Washington, Hamilton, and others were criticized for creating a strong national government where the public interests were determined by **guardian-kings** who were busy pursuing excellence, but with few or no limits on their actions. What about accountability to the people? What about responsibility to laws?

Period 2: Pre-Civil War Through Reconstruction (1829–1876)

In response came a half-century of public administration characterized by debating, political wrangling, and **administrative spoils**. It was largely initiated by President Andrew Jackson (1767–1845) and his philosophy to emphasize populist political responsiveness. **Jacksonianism** was characterized by a redirected emphasis away from a more centralized executive to a much more free-wheeling democracy. **The era of gentlemen** had passed, and Jackson and his Democrats were not of the educated elite backgrounds of that bygone era. Instead they pursued a utility perspective to the public interests that favored populism, a more radical **egalitarianism** toward men *and women*, and the promotion of the people's voice—evidenced by Jackson's relationship with his wife, Rachel, and rejection of a national bank.[40]

Of course, the pivotal figure in this transformation of the second American administration state was President **Abraham Lincoln** (1809–1865). Lincoln was said to have led the **"Second American Revolution"** with his victory in the Civil War, including freeing millions of African-American slaves, overthrowing the social and political order of the South, and setting new precedents of executive branch leadership and power. As a leader, commander-in-chief and head of the Republican Party, Lincoln set the pace for a revolution of constitutional administration as well. It may be that we all now live in the land of Lincoln.[41] Lincoln promoted his generals less on family ties and social status and more on performance—a definite populist approach. But Lincoln was also the first Republican President—a conservative revolutionary whose goal was to conserve the Union as the revolutionary heritage of the founders. Lincoln was a brilliant strategist and war leader who was responsible for the unconditional Union victory.[42] And he had a brilliant self-taught mind, and had memorized all eight volumes of Euclid's *Geometry* by the age of 12. But, while Lincoln was a student of virtue ethics, he was honest in his humble origins and lack of formal education, akin to Andrew Jackson. Both men shunned ostentation and recognized that virtue and leadership may come from a more egalitarian pool and from many walks of life. Lincoln's observations on virtue ethics made this humility clear in a humorous way: for example, "It has been my experience that folks who have no vices have very few virtues."[43]

During this interim, managing and financing the massive Civil War effort also contributed much to the development and understanding of civil service and the necessary administrative apparatus. Staffs, organization, and procedure were the order of the day. Major General Montgomery C. Meigs, for example, who was President Lincoln's quartermaster general, established the first unified logistical organization in wartime, which helped contribute to the North's ability to develop a sound and systematic organizational apparatus, leading to the South's defeat.[44] National organizations that were patterned after and promoted administrative detail were formed, including The U.S. Government Printing Office and the National Academy of Sciences. National, state, and local government took a greater role in the economy with successes in better managing the monopolies, railroads, agricultural markets, and the police powers (health, safety, morals, welfare, and education of its citizens).[45] According to Paul Van Riper, personnel reform was an issue both before and after the Civil War, and in 1871 Senator Lyman Trumbull of Illinois was successful in getting a rider attached to an appropriations bill that authorized the president to regulate various personnel procedures, with President Ulysses S. Grant (1842–1885) forming the first civil service organization in 1871. Even though it died in 1875 due to lack of funding, it set the course for what would later become the passage of the Pendleton Act in 1883, which created the first permanent Civil Service Commission.[46]

Jacksonian democracy and the Second American Revolution perspectives of the Civil War prevailed to present a more egalitarian approach to the public interests, including the preferences of those who were not part of the educated elite of the era of gentlemen. This marked a shift from classical virtue theory, in which elite guardians determined the public interests, toward more utilitarian calculation of the preferences of a more inclusive list (but still, unfortunately, excluding women, blacks, non-property owners, and others). Yet, virtue in public service was still recognized as dedication beyond obligations, and excellence above and beyond the call of duty, e.g., Generals Lee, Grant, and Meigs.[47]

Period 3: Pre-Classical Period (1876–1900)

Public administration historian Paul Van Riper argues that the four decades after the conclusion of the Civil War marked the beginning of the Second American administrative state. However, this transition may not have actually occurred until after the passage and implementation of the **Pendleton Act in 1883**. This short interlude marked the aftermath of the Civil War, with the period of Reconstruction taxing the nation's attention. Reconstruction marked a significant period in U.S. administrative history, one that highlighted the engineering, construction, financing, and coordination of major building projects throughout the war-ravaged South. In addition to the reconstruction efforts, major attempts were made at passing civil rights amendments, including the Civil Rights Act of 1875, which was designed to eliminate racial discrimination in public places.[48] It failed, but the attempt nonetheless raised the bar for reigniting the Federal Government's role in state affairs—a move that was not only political in nature, but also administrative.

The passage of the Pendleton Act of 1883, forming the first national-level **Civil Service Commission**, was the administrative highlight of this period. President Chester A. Arthur signed into law a bill titled "A Bill to Regulate and

Improve the Civil Service of the United States," which included several key provisions toward establishing a modern public administration system, including: 1) competitive exams, 2) open civil service, and 3) initially no higher educational requirement, although this was modified by the 1930s, with a move toward professionalizing civil service, and 4) the Pendleton Act did not establish a broad administrative hierarchy, such as existed in England at the time, but left the top positions open to executive appointment.[49] Clearly, the Pendleton Act did diverge somewhat from the parallel British model, particularly with regard to the practical aspect of administering competitive exams and, especially, the ability to enter the civil service at a variety of levels, whereas the British model entailed entry-level selection only. In addition, the president was to be de facto head of the civil service, given that the Pendleton Act provided the president with power to 1) appoint and remove members of the Civil Service Commission, and 2) approve the making of the rules of the Civil Service Commission.[50]

In addition to political action being taken at the national level to make more orderly and equitable civil service policy, there were rumblings at the state and local levels. New York and Massachusetts passed civil service legislation in the mid-1880s, and later, between 1900 and 1920, several other states did as well, including California, New Jersey, Ohio, and Wisconsin. Some historians entitle this time period the **Government by the Good**, because it included the groundwork for what would become the **birth of modern public administration**.[51] That groundwork, for example, came in the form of **Woodrow Wilson**'s 1887 article titled **"The Study of Administration."**

Wilson's primary thesis was that politics and administration are and must remain separate, because politics was grounded in what Wilson called the "devilishness" of partisan persuasion, while administration was rigorous and scientific, guided by principles of administration and management. Interestingly enough,

---

> ### ▶ BOX 2.2 | Establishment of the Civil Service Commission
>
> Following the assassination of President James A. Garfield by a disgruntled job seeker, Congress passed the Pendleton Act in January of 1883. The act was steered through Congress by longtime reformer Senator George Hunt Pendleton of Ohio. The Act was signed into law by President Chester A. Arthur, who had become an ardent reformer after Garfield's assassination. The Pendleton Act provided that Federal Government jobs are awarded on the basis of merit and those government employees are selected through competitive exams. The Act also made it unlawful to fire or demote for political reasons employees who were covered by the law. The law further forbids requiring employees to give political service or contributions. The Civil Service Commission was established to enforce this act. The Pendleton Act transformed the nature of public service. Today many well-educated and well-trained professionals have found a rewarding career in federal service. When the Pendleton Act went into effect, only 10 percent of the Government's 132,000 employees were covered. Today, more than 90 percent of the 2.7 million federal civilian employees are covered. ◣
>
> Source: Our Documents, "Pendleton Act (1883)," retrieved from www.ourdocuments.gov/doc.php?doc=48

BOX 2.3 | Woodrow Wilson

Woodrow Wilson (1856–1924) was born in Staunton, VA, to the Reverend Dr. Joseph Ruggles and Janet Woodrow Wilson. Both were of Scottish descent, with his mother immigrating to America from Europe. Raised in a pious and academic household, Wilson had a love of learning and Reformed religious beliefs ingrained in him at an early age.

He received his BA in 1879 from Princeton, his JD from the University of Virginia in 1883 and his PhD in governmental studies from Johns Hopkins University in 1886. After an early and unsuccessful attempt at pursuing a law career, he turned to intellectual endeavors and eventually landed on the Princeton faculty in 1890, where he spent over a decade lecturing, teaching, and writing on history and government. In 1902 he assumed the presidency of Princeton and imposed "democratic" processes—

eliminating the influence of "social clubs" and re-emphasizing academics. His reform tendencies led the Democratic Party machine of New Jersey to seek him out as gubernatorial candidate. He later accepted the Democratic national nomination for President in 1912, leading the country through a series of turbulent economic and social times at home, and, of course, through the end of World War I and the failed attempt at securing his beloved League of Nations through negotiations of the treaty of Versailles. He succumbed to a major stroke in 1919 and later died in 1924. ◣

Sources: Nobel Foundation, "Woodrow Wilson: The Nobel Peace Prize 1919," retrieved from http://nobelprize. org/nobel_prizes/peace/laureates/1919/wilson-bio.html; and "The White House: Biography of Woodrow Wilson," retrieved from www.whitehouse.gov/history/presidents/ ww28.html

---

though, the supposed influence of Wilson's groundbreaking article did not take place in the developmental years of the era of scientific management or the principles. According to Paul Van Riper, "an examination of major political and social science works of the period between 1890 and World War I showed no citation whatever of the essay in any of these volumes."[52] Wilson was not cited until the 1930s, and finally in the 1950s significant importance was placed upon his essay. Wilson set the stage for encouraging the systematic and rigorous study of public administration.

This period marked a return to the virtue ethical perspective, although not of the classical Greek virtue theory of the era of gentlemen. Virtue in the life of the individual public servant was redefined in a more bourgeois concept of merit, and attempts were made to scientifically measure merit. To be sure, those of merit governed a larger and growing bureaucracy. But merit was defined more equitably, without the founders' emphasis on elite class background, education, or aspirations. The pre-classical period may be labeled a bourgeois or **middle-class reform** era, focused on bourgeois competence notions in public service, yet avoiding the excesses of elite gentlemen and defects of populist spoils.[53]

Period 4: Classical Period (1900–1937)

Jeff Greene posits that besides the carrying over of Wilson's dichotomy into the rapidly changing political and economic society at the beginning of the twentieth century, this time period was marked by two distinct models of power fighting for supremacy in American democracy.

BOX 2.4 | Jane Addams

Jane Addams (1860–1935) was born in Illinois in 1860, graduated *Phi Beta Kappa* from Rockford Female Seminary (now Rockford University) in 1881, and worked much of her life in Chicago, Illinois, as a widely admired social reformer who viewed government as "housekeeping on a large scale." She urged the contribution and role of women in governance with a type of feminism that was rarely perceived as threatening. She established Hull House in Chicago in 1889 to house immigrant children and families, which later became the base of campaigns for the women's suffrage movement, in which she served as vice-president, from 1911 to 1914, of the National American Woman Suffrage Association, and after World War I headed the Women's Peace Party and the first Women's Peace Congress at the Hague, Netherlands. She sought to control all violence and posited that the equality of women was essential: as long as men were able to physically dominate and control women, violence would continue on a local, national, and international scale.

Addams was also an avid writer, speech-maker, and public intellectual, regarded as the first woman who was a prominent philosopher in the history of the US. She was a leading pragmatic philosopher—although she supported feminists, pacifists, and socialists, Addams refused to be labeled and insisted she was a pragmatist, not an ideologist. With her college friend and co-founder of Hull House, Ellen Gates Starr (1859–1940), Addams developed three ethical principles: "to teach by example, to practice cooperation, and to practice social democracy, that is, egalitarian, or democratic, social relations across class lines." In 1920, she was a co-founder of the American Civil Liberties Union (ACLU). She is recognized as the founder of the profession of Social Work. In 1931, she was the first American woman to be awarded the Nobel Peace Prize.

Sources: Jean Bethke Elshtain, *Jane Addams and the Dream of American Democracy: A Life* (New York: Basic Books, 2002); Patricia M. Shields, "Jane Addams' Theory of Democracy and Social Ethics: Incorporating a Feminist Perspective," in Maria J. D'Agostino & Helisse Levine, eds., *Women in Public Administration: Theory and Practice* (Salisbury, MD: Jones & Bartlett Learning, 2011), 15–34; Lisa Tutle, *Encyclopedia of Feminism* (New York: Facts on File, 1986), 11.

The first was reform of the rule by factions and gangs, highlighted in the party machines and the control of urban politics, to be replaced by equal rights and social justice for all. For example, Jane Addams (1860–1935) was an internationally admired social reformer who sought the control of violence by men that characterized urban politics, as well as growing numbers of violent events in national and international governance with the advent of World War I.

The second was the ascendance of a **public interest model**, which reflected the dreams of political and administrative reformers, one that highlighted reforms on the local level. For example, the New York Bureau of Municipal Research (1906) established the nation's first school of public administration in 1911. Under the leadership of Charles Beard (1874–1948), the school's mission was to train and educate local administrative personnel. By 1924, the school moved to Syracuse University and became what is now the **Maxwell School of Citizenship and Public Affairs**. These reformers embraced the assumption "that politics should not be mixed with management and that management can be studied scientifically."[54]

Economic depression and recovery was the historical context of the Classical Period of public administration, including recovery from the depression of 1895, World War I scarcity, the 1920–1921 depression, 1920–1933 agricultural

George Holmes Maxwell was a successful Boston patent attorney, financier, inventor, and shoe manufacturer, and a steadfast defender of democracy, education, and the American Way, as it was defined in New England in 1900.

Although distressed with American politics as it was practiced in that era, Maxwell retained his optimism about the nation's future. He helped create a fund of $500,000 for Syracuse to establish a School of American Citizenship. He noted at the time of the School's founding that:

The primary object of this school is to teach good citizenship . . . to cull from every source those principles, facts, and elements which, combined, make up our rights and duties and our value and distinctiveness as United States citizens. This involves the diffusion of good citizenship throughout the entire student body.

Thus the school would focus on civics. But Frederick Morgan Davenport, a former educator and politician who had signed on as a consultant to the new college, argued for a school that also would graduate trained practitioners in public affairs—young people who could instantly enter government and immediately effect a change. The name of the school—the Maxwell School of Citizenship and Public Affairs—reflected the coexistence of these two, often diverse, curricular directions, both of which were represented in the same school, thus making Maxwell a singular experiment in higher education in the United States.

Source: Reproduced from the Maxwell School of Syracuse University, "Maxwell History," retrieved from www.maxwell.syr.edu/deans/history.asp

dust bowls, and the Great Depression of the 1930s. The stock market crashed on Black Tuesday, October 29, 1929, marking the end of the Roaring Twenties and ushering in America's most severe economic downturn. President Herbert Hoover believed government had little or no role to play in recovery. By 1932, the country had slid into bleak times with more than 25 percent national unemployment, with the unemployment reaching as high as 80 and 90 percent in some communities. Thomas (Tip) P. O'Neill, Jr., former Speaker of the House, condemned the selfishness and greed that had allowed this country to waste away: "No society can exist on a public philosophy of I GOT MINE; FORGET THE OTHERS" (emphasis in the original).[55] He described 1930s life as it was for the poor and elderly:

This country is a desperate place. Half the people live in poverty. Twenty-five percent of the work force is unemployed . . . If you become sick, your world collapses. For most people, health insurance is out of the question . . . Life for the elderly is filled with uncertainty, dependency, and horror. When you get old, you are without income, without hope. Only the lucky few . . . have pensions. Social security does not exist, and only three percent have health insurance . . . This land I describe is not some third world nation in Africa. It is the United States of America, the America of the 1930s, the America I knew when I first entered public life.[56]

President Franklin Delano Roosevelt (1882–1945) defeated Hoover's bid for re-election, taking office in 1933. In his first 100 days in office, Roosevelt working with Congress, reorganized the banking industry, repealed Prohibition (again making it legal in some states to consume alcoholic beverages), authorized the

Tennessee Valley Authority to develop the least developed and hard-pressed region in the South, established price supports and conservation measures for farmers, gave workers the right to unionize, established the Public Works Administration to make jobs by way of public projects, created supports to assist in industrial recovery, along with a dozen more major programs. These and later programs began the turnaround and set the stage for the Classical Period of public administration, putting to work the magnificent ideas and theories of **Frank Goodnow**, Frederick Taylor, Leonard White, W.F. Willoughby, Charles Beard, **Luther Gulick**, **Lyndall Urwick**, and others.

Frank Goodnow   A quarter of a century earlier, with the publication of Frank Goodnow's *Politics and Administration* (1900), the intellectualization of public administration began in earnest. Even though Woodrow Wilson came first, we concur with Paul Van Riper's belief that it was Frank J. Goodnow (1859–1939) who spawned the new era of public administration.[57] Goodnow argued that there were two different functions of government: politics and administration. Politics, led by the legislative branch, dealt with the idealisms and values of the public good; while administration, led by the executive branch, dealt with the implementation of that good. Both were necessary to the fulfillment of governmental duties and the public good, but they were not the same. In fact, Goodnow considered administration the superior, given its aspiration to be objective and unbiased in the pursuit of the public good.

This scholarly enthusiasm and practical application of **Scientific Management** was spurred on by the scientific revolution that swept Europe, especially Germany and Great Britain, requiring people to recognize the meaning and merit of machines and the relationship between the two, and the ability to apply this relationship to the administration of organizations. Thus, it was the Scientific Management movement, led by such luminaries as Frederick Taylor and Henri Fayol, which spawned government commissions and reports touting the need for improving governmental economy and efficiency, such as the **Taft Commission on Economy and Efficiency** in Government (1912–1913) and legislative acts, such as the **Bureau of Budget Act of 1920**. The latter, for example, was not only intended to provide the executive branch with much needed input in to the budget-making scenario, but was to show that government was to function more businesslike, meaning it should embrace the values of economy and efficiency.[58] Leonard D. White (1891–1958) wrote his textbook on public administration, *Introduction to the Study of Public Administration* (1926)—the first full-length treatise on public administration as a discipline, reflecting the belief that public administration was a science that strived to be unbiased.

A second major component of the Classical Period was the development of scientific principles for application in administrative areas. Both private industry and government sought scientific principles of management that could be universally applied. In other words, administration was administration and management was management, regardless of the venue.[59] These were not the pre-existing rights or duty perspective of the public interests found in the values of the Constitution or other deeply rooted sources. Rather, these were scientific principles glossed from an overview of military history and the Industrial Revolution—where the primary focus was to produce as many widgets as possible—and other operational similarities in bureaucratic implementation of public policy. The goal of the

Scientific Management process was to discover and apply these operational principles to any number of government functions and operations, with the anticipated result being greater efficiency, effectiveness, and economy of administration. Several questions remained. What were these principles? How did one discover them? How were they applied?

William F. Willoughby's (1867–1960) *Principles of Public Administration* was published in 1927 as the second major text in the academic discipline of public administration. Willoughby furthered the argument that public sector organizations, like private organizations, could achieve outcomes of efficiency, effectiveness, and economy when properly administered, using techniques gathered from the business world, overseeing such functions as data gathering, personnel, finance, organizational staffing, and others. Along with notables such as Frederick A. Cleveland, Frank Goodnow, historian Charles Beard, and management genius Luther Gulick, Willoughby was a member of the 1912–1913 Taft Commission to reform the national bureaucracy. This experience contributed to his basic thesis that **government be run like a business.**[60]

POSDCORB

It was not until the late 1930s that the use of scientific principles was seriously applied by the national government. Both Luther Gulick (1892–1993) and Lyndall Urwick (1891–1983) were friends of President Roosevelt and were tapped to give scholarly legitimacy to his plan to create what may have been an imperial executive branch. Their book, *Papers on the Science of Administration* (1937), was part of a broader report to the President's Committee on Administrative Science, whose primary task was to accept the principles as academically valid and as administratively practical. Whether building a bridge, manning a tank or sweeping city streets, the need for POSDCORB was readily apparent. The management principles of Gulick and Urwick were summarized in the form of the acronym **POSDCORB:**

- Planning: envision and strategize for the future
- Organizing: plan and systematically align and categorize
- Staffing: meet all personnel and human resource needs
- Directing: develop sound leadership and managerial skills
- COordinating: bring together all resources for fulfillment of organization goals
- Reporting: develop sound communication means and technology
- Budgeting: control the organization through fiscal planning and accounting.[61]

Period 5: The Behavioral Revolution (1937–1960)

By World War II, a new wind was blowing through the Ivy Tower, and would soon be replicated in the public workplace. The **behavioralists** challenged the doctrines of the politics-administration dichotomy and scientific principles of administration. The result was a revolution in public administration—both parts of the classical school's theoretical framework were eventually discarded. The behavioralists' first attack: the politics/administration dichotomy was flawed as illogical. Fritz Morstein Marx (1900–1969), for example, argued that no administrative-based decision was ever completely free of politics, simply because by definition an administrative decision involved personal and political aspects. Was it ever possible to discern the difference? Was the underpinning of the politics/administration dichotomy in public administration, at best, naïve?[62] The general answer by academics at the time was "yes." If the dichotomy could be challenged, then what was the reality of the nearly sacrosanct scientific principles of administration? Some had stood for millennia and were widely accepted. Could they be challenged, as well? The answer, too, was a resounding "yes!"

The students of the behavioral revolution did not simply accept statements or ideas or even principles without subjecting them to rigorous empirical testing. At the very least they should undergo strict tests of reason and logic. This is what the behavioral revolutionaries did: they subjected the normative values and application of the principles of public administration to the rigors of reason and empiricism. From their perspective, these principles were found wanting.

Barnard and Simon   The first challenge did not come from the academic community, but from the pen of **Chester I. Barnard** (1886–1961), former president of New Jersey Bell Telephone. Barnard did not look at organizations as functionalist bureaucracies; he saw them as cooperative systems, where the functions of the executive were to balance the work of the employers, particularly in the area of creating and maintaining more effective forms and types of communication.[63] But it was the work of a brilliant University of Chicago Political Science PhD student named **Herbert A. Simon** (1916–2001) that revolutionized the study of public administration—and in particular the decision-making process—that formed the second and most formidable challenge.[64]

It is interesting to note that the young, twentysomething Simon, who took a position at the University of California-Berkeley before his dissertation at Chicago was complete, had never held an administrative position in either the private or public sector. So, how could he critique the classical era figures before him who had vast executive experiences? What could he say that they didn't already know? The first question is answered by Simon himself. In his autobiography, *Models of My Life*, Simon indicated that he read Barnard's book with great care, and drew from Barnard many of the ideas that formed the basis for his *Administrative Behavior*, including the "zone of indifference," the "equilibrium of inducements and contributions," and "bounded rationality."[65] As for the second question, he said that pioneers before him did not accomplish a theoretical and systematic approach to explaining decisions and decision making. This was the primary task that Simon assumed.

Simon was convinced that the scientific principles of administration were more contradictory than practical. For example, since the days of classical Greece, the principle of span of control required a small number (i.e., a span of six to eight) who were directly under the control of a superior in order for communication to be effective and to achieve greater efficiency. If the span of control is small under each supervisor, then the hierarchy of the larger pyramid-shaped organizations increases in size and height. Yet another principle states that messages within the organization are better communicated or maximized in a flatter hierarchy. Simon argued that both principles could be correct: the principle of a small span of control (thus, a taller hierarchy) contradicts the principle of better communication through a flatter organizational structure. It was the contradictory, illogical

BOX 2.6 | Herbert A. Simon

Herbert Alexander Simon was born June 15, 1916, in Milwaukee, Wisconsin, and was a social scientist known for his contributions in public administration, psychology, mathematics, economics, computer science, statistics, and operations research—all of which he synthesized into a key theory that earned him the 1978 Nobel Prize for Economics. Simon and his longtime collaborator Allen Newell also won the 1975 A.M. Turing Award, the highest honor in computer science, for their "basic contributions to artificial intelligence, the psychology of human cognition, and list processing."

Simon graduated from the University of Chicago in 1936 and earned a doctorate in political science there in 1943. After holding various posts in political science, he became a professor of administration and psychology at the Carnegie Institute of Technology (now Carnegie Mellon University) in 1949, later becoming the Richard King Mellon University Professor. He is best known for his work on the theory of corporate decision making known as "behaviorism." In his book *Administrative Behavior* (1947), Simon sought to replace the highly simplified classical approach to economic modeling—based on a concept of the single decision-

making, profit-maximizing entrepreneur—with an approach that recognized multiple factors that contribute to decision making. According to Simon, this theoretical framework provides a more realistic understanding of a world in which decision making can affect prices and outputs. Crucial to this theory is the concept of satisficing behavior—achieving acceptable economic objectives while minimizing complications and risks—as contrasted with the traditional emphasis on maximizing profits. Simon's theory thus offers a way to consider the psychological aspects of decision making that classical economists have tended to ignore. His lifetime of work on administrative decision making was applauded with the award of the 1978 Nobel Award in Economics.

Later in his career, Simon pursued means of creating artificial intelligence through computer technology. He wrote several books on computers, economics, and management, and in 1986 he won the U.S. National Medal of Science. He died on February 9, 2001. ◢

Source: reprinted from *Encyclopaedia Brittanica*, retrieved from www.britannica.com/biography/Herbert-A-Simon

nature of the principles that revealed them to be unscientific, or, as he wrote in 1946, mere proverbs.[66] Proverbs are fine for poems and songs, Simon argued, but not for administrative decision making. Instead, he urged more academic attention that required testing, reasoning, and empirical verification.

Simon, like many other scholars in the behavioral revolution of the twentieth century, explicitly applied the radical skepticism of logical positivism to the study of public administration he called behaviorism. Simon cited the logical positivist A.J. Ayer (1910–1989), who taught that empirical science was the sole source of knowledge. Logical positivists formulated the verification principle, requiring empirical evidence from the senses for any proposition to be meaningful—or referential. Otherwise, it was literally hot air, merely expression of one's desires or will to power. Simon judged all the classical principles of administration to be wanting by this empirical verification standard and, thus, mere proverbs. So, too, was the concept of the public interest discarded as literal nonsense by his criteria. Instead, he sought a value-free approach—free from proverbs and the hot air of public interests.[67]

However, Simon and most behavioralists did not go to the extreme of ethical egoism of Friedrich Nietzsche, the Nazis, Ayn Rand, and others in a world in which the only valid moral standard was the obligation to promote your will to power above all others. Instead, Simon's new scientific approach to administrative behavior applied new formulations of micro-economic concepts such as **satisficing, equilibrium** of inducements and contributions, and **bounded rationality**—for which he was awarded the 1978 Nobel Prize in Economics. His approach to values and public service emphasize the utility perspective or utilitarian ethical theory, but did not embrace the cynical will to power of ethical egoism. For Simon, the public interests were only the sum of its parts—calculations of individual preferences.[68]

Somehow during this time of intense skepticism by academics, public administration continued on and prospered at the national, state, and local levels; perhaps even in spite of these earlier revelations. Perhaps the trust in public administrators was spurred on by the practical successes of bureaucrats in World War II and the postwar economic boom. Perhaps it was the trust in public servants who people knew personally, like the local cop, city manager, or soldiers who came home. Or perhaps the radical skepticism of academics was assessed by most Americans as false-to-life and a bit hair-brained. Contracts were made, business was conducted, and people usually made things work even without empirical verification of every proposition. The fact that all propositions could not be empirically verified, or that people sometimes disagreed, or perhaps even that they did not care, did not mean that there was a complete lack of meaning or mere will to power. Things continued to work in spite of these damning academic criticisms. But this academic venom seemed to close the door to further study of public administration for Simon, who left the study of public administration to spend most of his life seeking a workable approach to artificial intelligence.[69]

Period 6: Management Emphasis (1960–1968)

Within academe, the study of public administration became for many an orphan in a brave new world. It had no home it could call its own; it did not fit within most political science departments after the behavioral revolution. It did not fit into other social science disciplines. So, public administration took up residence in many colleges of business administration during the 1970s. A teaching and research emphasis placed on case studies and the inauguration of comparative public administration during the late 1950s, 1960s, and 1970s helped to balance some of the cynical poison coming forth from the dominant behavioral approach to political science.[70] In addition, the center of epistemological attention became the government bureaucracy. This led to both normative questions of legitimacy, civic pride, and democratic values, and to a new interest in management. Was public administration up to the challenge of embracing management studies, particularly as management research was coming out of business schools and departments of industrial psychology, sociology, and others?

In the real world, the 1960s held a new fascination with management and corporate life, improving the decision-making capabilities of managers, as well as examining the process of making decisions.[71] Popular culture celebrated the rise of American management culture, such as the 1952 book *How to Succeed in Business Without Really Trying*, turned into a 1961 Broadway musical, then into a 1967 film. The movers and shakers for a new **"management is management" movement** came into academe by way of new colleges of business administration. The curricula for new MBA programs displayed many of the same courses that public administration schools had tried to fit within political science departments without success. Classes such as organization theory, personnel management, and budgeting and finance were all about management, and management was all about people and systems. Both were necessary, and both were affected by management principles and ideas: the majority of public administrators believed that there was no difference, or at least little difference, between public and private management.

But public administration scholars came to ask: If this was the case, then why is the term *public* used in public administration and *business* used in business administration? Obviously there must be something different between the two. Those who believed that the two disciplines were similar examined the world instrumentally or in parts; they didn't study the organization as a whole or the environment or nature in which it existed. There really was no need. Surely there must be something different between public and private management, public and private personnel systems, private and public budgeting and finance systems, and so forth?

Public administration scholars were also distanced from political science by examining new areas of public policy that merged with the sciences, such as criminal justice and the environment. Political scientists at the University of California at Berkeley had begun in 1911 to study and teach forensics, police administration, and police law at the Berkeley, California, municipal police department. They eventually offered a major in Police Science by 1920, as did political science programs at Harvard University, the University of Chicago, and elsewhere. By the 1960s, this policy interest grew into one of the largest organized sections of the American Society for Public Administration (ASPA)—the Section on Criminal Justice Administration. By 1984, criminal justice had moved up to become an academic discipline of its own, with separate department status at colleges and universities—yet about 30 percent of criminal justice faculty held their doctorates in public administration.[72] Political scientist Lynton P. Caldwell launched the new field of environmental policy studies with his 1963 article "Environment: A New Focus for Public Policy?"[73] During the 1960s he was the principal architect of the National Environmental Policy Act, the first of its kind in any nation. And he was the catalyst in founding the School of Public and Environmental Affairs (SPEA) at Indiana University, which **separated from political science** in 1972.[74]

Public administration incorporated other distinguished scientific theories, such as operations research and the ideas of Douglas McGregor, Robert Blake and Jane Mouton, and Chris Argyris.[75] These and other scholars broadly influenced many social scientists in adapting cybernetic theory from biology and developing theories of open vs. closed organizational systems. These influences and other scientific theories shifted the focus of public administration scholars toward setting themselves apart from historic skeptical philosophical roots of political science. The result of this era was that most public administration graduate programs were no longer taught within political science departments.

Period 7: The New Public Administration (1968–1984)

The 1960s were a radical era in politics and culture—and in public administration, too. Searching for a renewed public administration, Professor Dwight Waldo (1913–2000) convened the 1968 Minnowbrook conference, made up primarily of younger scholars. The focus and eventual outcome of the conference was known as the New Public Administration. What was new about it? The newness was in the focus. Instead of going over and over the how and why of achieving greater efficiency, economy, and effectiveness—often called the Big E's—a fourth E was presented: social equity.[76] Public bureaucracies were still the locus of their study, but their focus was entirely redirected toward developing a softer side, one that was more normative and ideological and less behaviorist, more socially activist and less functional, more directed toward meeting the needs of clients, and even creating not only the opportunity for social change but creating social change itself.[77]

New Public Administration scholars criticized the behavioral revolution and Herbert Simon specifically for their hidden status-quo-conservativism. In contrast, the New Public Administration openly promoted normative, ideological, activist, and client-oriented social change. To criticize Simon, New Public Administration scholars turned the positivist assumptions of the behavioral revolution upon itself. Logical positivism, underlying the behavioral revolution, cynically asserted that all non-empirical talk is merely the imposition of the will to power or "hot air." Positivism was closely tied to ethical egoism, which asserted that, no matter what people may say, they were really acting for the sake of their personal well-being only. Thus, these 1960s critics claimed that even when the behavioral revolution attempted to include new voices and ideas to the public forum, the decisions and actions by policymakers continued to reflect old status quo notions. Further, the behavioral revolution duped the American public by depicting public policy decisions as the operation of empirically verifiable markets and political processes.[78] So, for these 1960s critics, the behavioral revolution was a façade of pseudo-science that disguised the actual operation of a will to power and rhetorical ploys to advance the status quo or private interests of political elites.[79]

> ### BOX 2.7 | Dwight Waldo
>
> Dwight Waldo, who died on October 27, 2000, was a major figure in the intellectual development of public administration.
> He was a Midwesterner at heart. Born in DeWitt, Nebraska, he did not earn his BA at a prestigious Ivy League school. Rather he attended and graduated from Nebraska State Teachers College. He did receive his PhD from Yale University, and later worked at the Office of Personnel Administration and the Office of the President in Washington, DC. He moved into academic circles, beginning with the University of California-Berkeley in 1946 and then moving to the Maxwell School at Syracuse University in 1967, where he stayed until his retirement in 1979. He served as editor-in-chief for the *Public Administration Review* for 11 years. His lasting, major contribution to the field of public administration was *The Administrative State* (1948).
>
> Source: based on Waldo's meeting and interview with Stephen King.

Their criticism of the behavioral revolution stuck, but the New Public Administration quickly ran out of gas. Their detractors argued that public administration had to accomplish something tangible; it had to focus on outputs, outcomes, and more concrete public interests. Dwight Waldo, H. George Frederickson, and the **Minnowbrook I** (1968) and **Minnowbrook II** (1988) **conference** crowds argued for social equity and social justice to be dispensed by agency bureaucrats. But **Vincent** and **Elinor Ostrom**, James Buchanan, and Gordon Tullock, among others, contended that the theories of micro-economics included in public choice theory should instead be applied to public bureaucracies.[80] Anthony Downs theorized that economics as a whole would go much further toward explaining bureaucratic behavior. Aaron Wildavsky laid the groundwork for budgetary incrementalism. Peter Drucker argued that public administration needed to adopt business principles, strongly suggesting that by adopting them it would enhance the business end of public administration.[81] All of these micro-changes sowed the seed for the later 1980s **privatization**, the 1990s re-engineering and **reinvention**, and later the 2000s version of **performance management**. It also balanced the utility perspective of the public interests—utilitarian benefits/costs analysis—against excesses of justice, equity, and ambiguous philosophical perspectives of the public interests by the New Public Administration.

Period 8: The Re-Founding of Constitutional Public Administration (1984–present)

Gary Wamsley and others from the Virginia Polytechnic Institute and State University (or Virginia Tech), located in Blacksburg, Virginia, published what is now referred to as the **Blacksburg Manifesto** and its various iterations.[82] The Manifesto is an inherently normative prescription for the problems of public administration within the current democratic and political environment, largely focusing on the founding regime values, specifically those values that framed the Constitution. Conceptually, the Blacksburg scholars desired to re-conceptualize public administration from an organizational concept to "The Public Administration"—the institution of government. The focus is not on whether there should be a government or even how to reduce whatever level of government there is, but on what form of governmental intervention is most effective in the real world. The Blacksburg scholars attended to the duty perspective of the public interests as central in defining public administration. But, unlike the ambiguous concept of equity, the Blacksburg scholars focused on exacting pre-existing duties such as freedom of speech, press and religion, property rights, equal protection, and due process of law as written and interpreted by authoritative cases involving the U.S. Constitution and enduring laws.

The Manifesto was a normative statement advocating an enhanced and more complex role for the re-founding of Public Administration: "to run a Constitution" (quoted from Woodrow Wilson). The disjuncture between what is good government and good management increases the likelihood of damning the former and praising the latter, without realizing (or wanting to realize anyway) that both are necessary to run a Constitution. The Blacksburg scholars did public administration a great service by redirecting the focus of the public administration practitioner and scholar toward greater awareness and appreciation of the role of the public interests within a constitutional system as envisioned by the constitutional founders.[83]

In conjunction with the Public Administration came a movement self-titled "The Constitutional School of Public Administration," combining elements of traditional doctrinal study of constitutional law with contemporary law and economics approaches, and managerial ethical responsibility.[84] These scholars systematically study public administration by looking at court interpretations, federal statutes, international treaties, and important individuals that have had an impact on public administration in pursuance of the Constitution.[85] In such an inclusive approach, constitutionalism is not merely about the adherence to legal doctrines or deontological duties but also includes the calculation of society-wide needs or utilitarian ethics.[86] The virtue ethical perspective was cast to include the diversity of ethical and moral worldviews.[87] Taking this inclusive perspective of the public interests gives new attention to a merger of constitutionalism and ethics, something these scholars felt had been lost: or at least misplaced, in contemporary public administration.[88]

What about virtue and moral character in the legalistic, rule-bound world of constitutional ethics? Could virtue be more primary or basic to our sense of what is right and wrong than duty? Does it have greater moral worth? Philippa Foot has argued, "The man who acts charitably out of a sense of duty is not to be undervalued, but it is the other who most shows virtue and therefore to the other that most moral worth is attributed."[89] While narratives of good moral character seem deeply rooted in the human experience, these may not seem sufficient evidence to prove virtue ethics to be primary or more basic than ethics based on the perspectives of duties or utilities. Instead, both perspectives seem to be complementary: for every duty or utility, there is a corresponding virtue. Is virtue merely the mirror image of duties and utilities of the public interests?

The application of constitutional duties to the virtue ethical perspective in the Blacksburg Manifesto follows the injunction that "traits without principles are blind."[90] Students of the Blacksburg School have greatly enriched our understanding of ethical virtue in the lives of great American administrators, such as Alexander Hamilton, Thomas Jefferson, and others.[91] Yet the Blacksburg scholars went beyond biographies of the virtues of great administrators to analyze their applications of specific constitutional doctrines. Without these specific constitutional duties, how can a virtue ethics theory of good moral character determine the rightness or wrongness of particular, specific actions? When virtuous founders committed evil, such as the 1804 duel in which Aaron Burr killed Alexander Hamilton, did we simply call it a moment of weakness in an otherwise good life and turn a blind eye? No, even Burr, who initially was without seemingly any remorse for his evil deed, was later indicted and remembered in infamy.[92]

Rather, virtue of the administrator was not distinct from the means or behaviors in public interests activities, but virtue was always focused on the special moral value of these ends of excellence in character. The goal of the virtue ethical perspective was to provide the opportunity for, and development of, moral excellence of the person. The law and other public interests duties are not the only model of wisdom on human worth—virtue focuses on moral values of greater aspirations beyond mere legal duties.[93] As John Rawls argued in what he called the Aristotelian principle: "The virtues are excellences . . . The lack of them will tend to undermine both our self-esteem and the esteem that our associates have for us."[94] The Blacksburg scholars called much-needed attention to the importance of close ties between virtue and moral duty.

Period 9: Waves of Change (1992–present)

Several other contemporary approaches to public administration seek greater inclusiveness in defining who and what is a part of public administration. After all, implementing the public interests involves more than civil service employees. These contemporary approaches give greater attention to the role of private and nonprofit organizations, faith-based initiatives, postmodern perspectives, feminist perspectives, and digital information shared by all with individual citizens. With such diversity of perspectives, contemporary waves of change greatly expand who is included as a stakeholder, and more closely tie the virtue, utility, and duty perspectives of the public interests.

E.S. Savas promulgated the privatization thesis, which argued that various aspects and components of public administration or public organizations would be more efficient and economical if they were farmed out to the private sector.[95] The Reagan Revolution spurred this type of thinking, given that President Ronald Reagan said that big government was the enemy of the American people and the freedom they love. Instead of government cleaning the streets, guarding the prisoners, and picking up the trash, the privatization scholars urged that we turn these and many other tasks over to the private sector. They argued that the private sector was more efficient and frugal with its funds and the spending of those funds; it was more effective in putting together people, management, and processes that it only seemed right to privatize.

Privatization evolved into reinvention by the late 1980s and early 1990s. David Osborne (1951–) and Ted Gaebler (1941–) and Peter Plastrik (1952–) argued that it wasn't enough to privatize or re-engineer government; it was necessary to reinvent it.[96] Transform it from the inside out. Changing the focus and the locus of public administration was not even the primary ingredient to success (however one defines success). Osborne and Gaebler studied dozens of local governments, talked to many city, town, and county managers, and interviewed many line and staff personnel, who worked in local organizations that engaged in the process of reinventing themselves, all the while redefining their purpose for even existing. The notion was to assume a risk-taking outlook and sport an entrepreneurial spirit that was to enhance the bottom line of public service.

Performance management blossomed in the mid- to late 1990s and continues to the present. Calling for strict guidelines on spending, financial, and output measures, the clarion call among like-minded public administration scholars is one of performance output and performance enhancement, striving to enhance and improve the bottom-line performance of public agencies without engaging in privatization techniques.[97]

Nonprofit organizations and faith-based initiatives play a significantly important and influential role in government service delivery. Robert B. Denhardt and Joseph W. Grubbs pointed out that the importance of nongovernmental organizational (NGOs) was multifold: "NGOs must be considered not only for their part in implementing public programs, but also their growing influence in raising issues to the public agenda, lobbying for particular policy alternatives, and guiding political and administrative decision making."[98] Nonprofit organizations filled roles and functions in society that many governmental organizations, departments, or agencies cannot do as well as nonprofit organizations. A nonprofit organization is defined as an independent or third-sector of the nation or state's economic, social, political, and religious makeup. The Johns Hopkins University

Center for Civil Society Studies found that U.S. nonprofits had 9.4 million paid workers (or 7.6 percent of all paid employment in the US) and another 4.7 million full-time equivalent volunteers, for a total workforce of 14.1 million (as of mid-2004). Nonprofits do make a profit—or else they could not stay in business—but they do not transfer those profits to shareholders. Whatever profit is used (which of course is tax-exempt) must, according to their *501 (c) 3* status, return to the organization itself.[99]

What is the purpose of nonprofits in public administration? How do they help deliver public services? Lester Salamon (1943–), a longtime researcher and advocate of nonprofit organizations, argued that nonprofits were a "special class of entities dedicated to mobilizing private initiative for the common good."[100] Furthermore, nonprofits have a substantial stake in affecting, directing, and ultimately administering public policy. Given the fact, for example, that approximately half of all tax-deductible nonprofits are related to the health and human services industry, it is easy to agree with Brookings Institution scholar Jeffrey M. Berry that "They [nonprofits] have an enormous stake in what government does."[101]

Although scholars are just beginning to examine their impact within traditional public administration, faith-based initiatives are beginning to assume a much more powerful role in the shaping of public policy, especially in the areas of health and human services. Although faith-based solutions to thorny human services problems, such as poverty and homelessness, are not new to the fabric of American caring and compassion, President George W. Bush made them the corner piece of his supposedly compassionate conservatism agenda.

Other challenges to behaviorism or modernism in public administration come from streams of thought within **postmodernism** and **feminist perspectives**. Following one stream of postmodernism within contemporary sociology and philosophy, scholars believe that modern symbols and language in public administration may be deconstructed in order to get at the truth of social and cultural phenomena.

BOX 2.8 | Faith-Based Initiatives

The White House Office of Faith-Based and Community Initiatives, originally headed by Jim Towey, spearheaded a multi-prong federal effort for expanding the "charitable choice" provision of the 1996 Welfare Reform Act. Substantial negative attention was paid to the government's advocacy and use of faith-based initiatives through the federal grants process, largely because of disagreements over the nature and extent of church-state separation. Under President Obama it was renamed the Office of Faith-Based and Neighborhood Partnerships, and was located within the Domestic Policy Council. The purpose of the renamed and reformed organization was "to form partnerships between the Federal Government, and faith-based and neighborhood organizations to more effectively serve Americans in need." Melissa Rogers led the organization from 2013 to 2017. As of February 2018, no successor has been named by President Trump. ◣

Source: Ira Lupu and Robert W. Tuttle, "Freedom from Religion Foundation, Inc (and others) v. Jim Towey, Director of White House Office of Faith-Based and Community Initiatives," retrieved from www.Religionsandsocialpolicy.org/legal/legal update.display.cfm?id=32

For example, feminist public administration scholar Camilla Stivers persuasively argues that the discipline failed to problematize the exclusion of women from public administration, requiring a feminist perspective on knowledge, role, ideals, and discretion.[102] Leading postmodern public administration scholars Charles Fox and Hugh Miller argued for moving beyond the hierarchical bureaucracy that dominates organizations under modernism, because this concept does not truly represent the reality of organizations. Hierarchical bureaucracy is a modernist social construct that we may break down by use of new word construction, puns, etymology, and other wordplay.[103] Similarly, postmodernist David Farmer believes that reflective interpretation can make us more sensitive in how use of language alters our understanding of what public administration is and what it can do.[104] Postmodern public policy scholar Pauline Marie Rosenau suggests the difficulty in categorizing feminists or all postmodernism is that there may be as many forms of postmodernism as there are postmodernists. She has suggested affirmative and skeptical groupings of postmodernism. Skeptical postmodernism is generally more negative, pessimistic, and gloomy in assessing public administration, emphasizing alienation, fragmentation, disintegration, malaise, meaninglessness, and amorality.[105] For example, environmental devastation is the catastrophe awaiting all attempts in environmental policy reform.[106] Affirmative postmodernism offers a more positive, optimistic, hopeful view of public administration, open to positive political action and non-dogmatic or non-ideological normative ethics, faith initiatives, and reforms in public policy.[107] For example, Lynton K. Caldwell (1913–2006), principal architect of the 1969 National Environmental Policy Act and guru of environmental policy at Indiana University School of Public & Environmental Affairs for many decades, took an affirmative postmodern stance to reject environmental policy "how to do it" information, or advocate a "mission" or "mandate," as "obsolete" for "self-serving bureaucrats." Instead, Caldwell sought "foresight, initiative, flexibility, sensitivity and new forms of knowledge" that are not truth claims, but "interactive and synergistic" environmental policy alternatives.[108] Scholars of these postmodern streams and feminist perspectives generally posit that our concept and application of public administration are hindered because of cultural and societal constructs that frame our understanding. Once these constructs (e.g., hierarchy) are reduced, then will it be possible for all persons to realize our dependency upon each other, and not upon false ideas of organization and order.[109]

A final wave of change may come by way of the high-tech information technology revolution that aspires to allow every individual to be informed and participate in public administration through transparency reforms, such as e-governance, Wiki-governance, or collaborative virtual administration. Technological innovations in government, especially in the area of enhanced communication between citizen and the state, are nothing new, and in fact have a rich history.[110] What is new is the speed and transparency with which these technological innovations are changing, or least requiring recognition and responses to the innovations: the way public administration operates, such as the use of **e-government**, web portals, and the Internet. As one scholar notes, "The promise of e-government is not, as some suppose, putting existing paper-based processes of bureaucracy into digital form. Rather, the promise is really nothing less than a profound transformation of the way the government does business."[111]

According to some scholars, building the virtual state[112] is not simply technologically different, but it requires an institutional theoretical framework to help explain the changes that are underway. This theory is important, especially for public administrators, because it questions the way government officials at all levels of government do business *or can do* business within a technologically and virtually enhanced state of affairs.

E-government, *e-citizens*, and even *e-democracy* are terms that did not exist 15 years ago, but are now becoming ingrained in our language, culture, and consciences. With the use of web portals or websites, for example, citizens at all levels of government can not only download and print forms, pay tax bills, renew driver license registrations, and see a digital map of their downtown through Geographical Information Systems (GIS) technology, but may also engage in an e-forum via streaming video, go online and chat with the city manager, town mayor, or county commissioner, or register their disapproval (or approval) of a specific policy decision. The computer, internet, and digital technology are changing the way citizens and public officials interact and the way government actions are made.[113]

What does this revolution mean, especially in terms of legal duties and political accountability of the public administration profession? Who becomes the more important figure in agenda setting, for example: the mayor or the CIO (chief information officer)? Does it mean that if a citizen does not have access to, or cannot afford, a computer or a fast internet hookup that they have fewer citizen rights than others who can? Does increased e-government capacity reduce the number of government officials needed, thus having a negative effect upon personnel retention? Or does e-government increase the number of officials, as citizens expect instant responses to their queries? On a more positive note, we need to ask about the impact of e-governments (even e-governance) upon outsourcing, contracting, performance measurement, and the impact upon the third sector of society: nonprofits.

| ETHICS CASE STUDY | **Virtue and Public Servants in Dr. Seuss—Benevolent? Competent?** |

With each recent generation in America there has come a call to rebuild, revitalize, or re-engage the public sector. For example, in 1988, Chairman of the Federal Reserve System Paul Volcker led the Volcker Commission to rebuild the public sector in recruiting the best-of the Boomers, but the problem was in the denigrating *affect* of a negative public perception of the vices of government service.[114] Paul Volcker once again was Chairman in 2003 and led the National Commission on the Public Service, seeking to revitalize the federal civil service by recruiting the best-of the Gen-Xers, but once again found the issue was a negative public perception of government service vices.[115] We now seem to be gearing-up for yet another national commission[116]—as well as global rebuilding of the public service[117]—to re-engage the public sector with recruitment of the best-of the Millennials, and find the same negative public perceptions of the lack of virtues in government service.

(continued)

Why are Americans, even the young, so negative in their perception of the virtue of public servants? Public Administration scholars Samatha Durst and Charldean Newell concluded in a 2017 article that the media are the message; negative images of the lack of virtues in governmental service are the message of media—children's, civil education, news media, and social media.[118] In contrast, Charles T. Goodsell argues in *The Case for Bureaucracy*[119] that American public servants and institutions are among the best in the world. Yet, each of our recent generations appears to have profoundly negative perceptions of public service.

For some, it is a question of the need for ethical self-reflection by public administrators, much like the Tin Man in *The Wizard of Oz* who mourns, "If I only had a heart!" Thus, the negative public perception of public administrators was documented in the classic book by public administration scholar **Victor A. Thompson**, *Without Sympathy or Enthusiasm*.[120] Thompson demonstrated how public administration norms of impersonal objectivity, rationality, and efficiency worked to alienate the public and foster negative perceptions of public administrators. He posited the need to recognize and satisfy exceptional, individual demands—the need for organizational compassion. Is this negative perception of the virtue of public servants due to the lack of communicating compassion?

For others, it is nothing less than the souls of public administrators at stake. Do the norms of impersonal objectivity, rationality, efficiency, and the politics/administration dichotomy dictate mindless obedience to the political orders of others, even when you know it is wrong? Do such norms of public administration limit our discussion of ethics to a so-called neutral fashion in which we never mention such subjects as administrative evil? Does this reflect a modernistic heart of darkness used to justify and mask the **administrative evil** done by bureaucrats—hidden to the public and themselves?[121] For example, in response to the horrors of World War II and Nazi concentration camps came the **Nuremberg Defense**—"I was just following orders"—in which ordinary city managers, judges, police administrators, and others, knew at the time of their wrongdoing in complying with Nazi laws and sending Jews, Poles, and others to the Nazi concentration camps to be executed. Yet they complied with these political orders objectively, rationally, and efficiently.[122] Similarly, allegations against public servants of just following orders may be found in social movements today, such as #BlackLivesMatter and #MeToo.[123] Is the negative perception of the virtue of public servants due to the masking of administrative evil?

Yet, political psychology posits as a truism that from early childhood Americans see mostly positive depictions of public servants in children's literature and media. In fact, depictions of public authorities and public servants as godlike or superheroes in benevolence and competence are longstanding traditions in children's literature.[124] Scholarly studies of a representative cross-section of children's literature and media have found that public servants were usually depicted as lone individuals engaged in benevolent and protective actions,[125] leading one scholar to conclude that "America's child-oriented mass-media produce an overwhelmingly favorable portrait of the public sector for America's youth."[126] Timothy Cook and others have contested this conclusion,[127] objecting to any study by a random sampling of children's materials—the methodology is critical because the most popular children's authors, L. Frank Baum and Dr. Seuss, didn't conform to such idealized portrayals. Thus, we shouldn't assume children always learn a rosy depiction of the public service. This case study was a content analysis by two independent coders of all the children's books written by Dr. Seuss, alias Theodor Seuss Geisel (1904–1991), coding the frequency and character of public servants depicted.[128]

Public Service in Dr. Seuss

Dr. Seuss depicted public servants at about the same frequency as other children's materials: about 9.2 percent of the Dr. Seuss major characters had public service roles, compared to the 10 percent of public service roles in Marshall's cross-section of all children's literature.[129] Like other children's materials, Dr. Seuss featured law enforcement roles (police, sheriffs), as well as many other public service roles: mayors, firefighters, zoo keepers, and the military. Symbols of public sectors were also depicted, such as flags, signs, buildings, zoos, parks, schools, firefighting, and wars. Public sector symbols or characters were found in nearly 50 percent of Dr. Seuss's books. However, Dr. Seuss rarely shows public sector politics or administration in action, i.e., legislation, court processes, bureaucratic decision making, regulation, voting, volunteering, lobbying, and so forth. The only inside look at public decision making involved royalty, not a more democratic governmental process.

Benevolence

Established scholars of political socialization have postulated that public service characters in American children's materials are overwhelmingly depicted as benevolent, with random sampling of children's materials depicting the benevolent character of public servants in at least 50 percent of the sample[130]—about the same level of benevolence ascribed to depictions of parents, relatives, neighbors, and others. However, when coding the frequency of soothing, reassuring, or comforting verbal or nonverbal communication toward another character, only 39 percent of public servants displayed some sort of **benevolence in Dr. Seuss**. Further, public service characters in Dr. Seuss were decidedly less likely to act out of benevolence to protect others from harm and in self-sacrificing behavior. In random samples, 35 percent of characters in public service roles actually protected others from harm, while only 21 percent of those in public service roles in Dr. Seuss displayed the same behavior. Only 12 percent of the Dr. Seuss public service characters displayed self-sacrificing behavior, compared to about 16 percent in random samples of children's materials. In Dr. Seuss, public servants are more likely to talk than to act benevolently.[131]

(continued)

ETHICS CASE STUDY | *Continued*

To be fair, Dr. Seuss also had a very low frequency of depicting the benevolence of parents, relatives, friends, and those immediate and familiar to the child reader. Self-sacrificing roles were seldom depicted by Dr. Seuss—only about 5 percent of these non-governmental roles. The stories of Dr. Seuss seem curiously devoid of demonstrations of love and those emotions that would require greater benevolence of the parents, relatives, friends, and other familiar characters. Perhaps the message from Dr. Seuss, like the criticisms of egoism in American public life,[132] is that it is natural for people to think of themselves first in times of trouble, not to demonstrate benevolence under such circumstances.

Competence

Established scholars of political socialization have also theorized that public service characters in children's materials were overwhelmingly depicted as competent.[133] Their claim is that American children are raised to think that public servants know what they are doing and can carry out their roles successfully, e.g., teachers know how to teach, firefighters can arrest fires. In analyzing depictions of competence in Dr. Seuss, we examined the frequency of successful problem-solving and reliability of major characters. We first identified when a major character in Dr. Seuss had a problem to solve and whether it was wholly solved, partly solved, or not solved at all (failed). In many Dr. Seuss books, it was not clear whether or not the major characters had any problems to solve, e.g., the ABC books. The percentage of Dr. Seuss books which were "unclear" as to whether or not the major character had any problems was unusually high. Only 6 of the 27 characters in public service roles clearly had problems to solve, which was much lower than in random samples of all children's materials.[134] America is a pragmatic, practical nation and storylines usually reflect the American work ethic by presenting characters that solve problems. Dr. Seuss presents an unusually large number of public service characters that have no worries, no problems to solve.

The few problem-solving characters in public service roles were more often successful than failures in Dr. Seuss. As in random samples of children's materials, Dr. Seuss rarely depicted failure in solving a problem by characters in public service roles. However, Dr. Seuss did depict a very serious public sector failure in *The Butter Battle Book*, but he never ended the story. This lack of ending strongly implies that the public services have failed to resolve the butter battle and destroyed the world in the end. However, Dr. Seuss never explicitly depicted this outcome. Because there are so few instances of any problem solving by government characters, and with the strongly implied failure in *The Butter Battle Book*, we conclude that Dr. Seuss did not depict characters in public service roles as particularly competent in resolving problems.

We also analyzed depictions of competence by assessing the frequency with which major characters demonstrated personal reliability, urged or demonstrated tidiness, or exhibited punctuality or timeliness. Random sampling studies of children's materials found that characters in governmental roles exhibited more of these measures of competence than those in nongovernmental roles. The frequencies of governmental roles were about the same in Dr. Seuss as in the random samples, with about 12 percent of governmental roles demonstrating reliability, tidiness, punctuality, or timeliness.

Finally, we analyzed the lack of competence displayed by major characters who accidentally cause damage or harm to objects or persons. As in random samples of children's materials, Dr. Seuss's major characters in either governmental or nongovernmental roles had a very low frequency of accident-prone behavior. Only about 12 percent of those in governmental roles accidently caused damage or harm. Accident-prone behavior is rare for any characters in Dr. Seuss.

Going Forward

The analysis suggests three findings. First, public sector symbols, programs, service, and servants are often depicted in the children's materials of Dr. Seuss. As a result, children exposed to these popular works are familiar with many aspects of the public service before starting school and in their grade school years. Second, when the public service is depicted in Dr. Seuss, public servants are usually not acting in a benevolent manner. Unlike the random sampling studies of children's materials, Dr. Seuss characters in public roles are less likely to display self-sacrificing behavior or protect others from harm. To be sure, other characters in Dr. Seuss also do not usually communicate benevolence. Dr. Seuss tends to depict all characters as decidedly selfish or less than benevolent. While governmental roles are more often depicted as benevolent than nongovernmental roles, neither includes a majority of benevolent characters. Third, the frequency with which major characters in governmental roles in Dr. Seuss are depicted as competent is very low. Of course, Dr. Seuss depicts few characters of any type as competent in problem-solving. However, when governmental roles appear, Dr. Seuss usually depicts them as having nothing to do, no problems to solve. Further, he strongly implies the ultimate failure of the public servants in a destruction of the world, e.g., *The Butter Battle Book*. We must conclude that the children's materials produced by Dr. Seuss generally depict a less than competent public sector. These conclusions have been proven again in replications of this study,[135] and in comparisons of American and British children's literature: British children's literature presents more benevolent and competent adult characters than American literature, especially with public service figures.[136]

How can we respond to the influence of these popular media? How can public administrators escape the norms of impersonal objectivity, rationality, and efficiency, and begin to communicate empathy or compassion, as critiqued in Victor I. Thompson's *Without Sympathy or Enthusiasm*?[137] Public Administration scholar Kim Viborg Anderson suggests that we

(*continued*)

ETHICS CASE STUDY | *Continued*

re-engineer the organizational culture of the public sector to a more consumer-centric approach, at both the face-to-face and digital e-government points of contact.[138] Similarly, D. Belanche Garcia urges rebuilding public trust in government administrators through e-government actions, transparency, and creatively reaching out to touch citizens through new digital information technology.[139] Michael Baker, retired from the federal civil service and an adjunct university professor in public administration, suggests finding new ways to appeal to the Boomer, Gen-Xer, and Millennial generations on beliefs that government regulations do more good than harm, whether the government controls too much of our daily lives, and whether public administration should focus on domestic rather than international policy.[140] Whatever the means, the path will be challenging, and perhaps more compassionate.

While dismissed by some as "insistently funny,"[141] the writings of Dr. Seuss may have had a profound impact on the nature and origins of current public attitudes toward public service virtues—and vices. His distrust and suspicion of government rose up against a tradition in children's literature that depicted government as god-like or superheroes in benevolence and omni-competence. Whether praised or cursed, the little Dr. Seuss books may have shaped the political socialization or recent, very skeptical generations that have challenged the public service like no other generation before them.

Discussion

- Do Boomers, Gen-Xers, and Millennials perceive government servants negatively?
- What influence may children's literature and media have on children's perceptions of government servants?
- How are public servants depicted in the popular Dr. Seuss books and media?
- How can we respond to the influence of these popular children's media? ◣

CONCLUSION

This history of public administrators presented the real-life-world of the people in public service. Some of our history is focused on great persons, such as Jane Addams, Thomas Jefferson, and Alexander Hamilton. Other attention was given to more ordinary lives of individuals, organizations, institutions, and scholars. All were placed within the evolving schools of thought in public administration through history that may be more meaningful because we focused on people, on the lived world.

Public administration is anything but a static process. It is a dynamic lived world of people in organizations changing with the cultural, political, economic, social, and even psychological winds—winds that come from both academe and the offices of practitioners. It is not so remarkable that change occurs, but it is somewhat disconcerting to note that the changes were often made in order for public administration to find its place in academe. Was public administration a multidiscipline with political science, business, management schools, economics, social psychology, or perhaps—as the Blacksburg scholars hint—even in history or philosophy? Does its academic station make a difference?

This examination of the historical lived world of public administration allowed us to focus on the virtue ethical perspective to ask the fundamental question: What does it mean to be a good public administrator? The virtue perspective is commonly found in the ordinary narrative and storytelling of oral traditions, literature, broadcast, and digital media. We ordinarily make judgments as to who is a good person, and make practical moral decisions by seeking to adopt good traits, imitate our heroes, and be virtuous. The virtue perspective complements utility; and duty perspectives; the public interests, new waves of change, and greater workplace diversity in public, nonprofit, and faith-based sectors.

However, there are criticisms of the virtue ethical perspective. First, as we have seen in our brief history of public administrators, we are not clear on exactly what good moral character is. But there are many useful vice-terms as antonyms to help understand ethical virtues. For example, we have seen the vice-terms of *lazy, irresponsible, feckless, inconsiderate, uncooperative, harsh, intolerant, selfish, mercenary, indiscreet, tactless, arrogant, unsympathetic, cold, incautious, unenterprising, feeble, presumptuous, rude, brutal,* and *disloyal.* Second, do virtuous public administrators have any political accountability and legal duties, or do they just spend all day pursuing excellence? Aristotle and the founders seemed to live by a gentlemen's code which failed to express limits upon philosopher-kings. How can you be ethical without any limits and duties? How can you claim moral excellence or virtue, yet have little or no accountability? In its defense, the virtue ethical perspective was never so fully divorced from the real world of political utility, legal duty, and service to others. But the virtue ethical perspective disputes the idea that law and legal duties constitute the only model of wisdom in valuing moral worth. The virtue ethical perspective focuses on the higher ends of human aspirations, not just dutiful performance of duties or conformity to political utility. And we can all recognize the difference in moral worth between a labor of love and mere duty. Third, how does the virtue ethical perspective propose to determine the rightness or wrongness of actions? While good moral character of public servants is deeply rooted in the narrative of human history, it does not seem to be primary but rather complementary to other perspective on ethics. For every virtue, is there a corresponding duty or utility?

ACTION STEPS

1. Discuss the role of history in the public administration profession by reading the U.S. Supreme Court case of *Winter v. Natural Resources Defense Council*, 555 U.S. 7 (2008). The case included an injunction to stop the Navy's use of sonar that may have caused serious injuries to marine mammals and their habitats. The Court found that "the balance of equities and the public interest . . . tip strongly in favor of the Navy." Do you believe

the Supreme Court treated the Navy bureaucracy differently in past eras of public administration? Would public interests have been similar or different in past eras?

2. In small groups or individually, pinpoint the ethical virtues and public interests values favored by a particular historical period of public administration. For example, what ethical values were expressed by the following statement: "Business administration principles were expected to be translated into public values, particularly in the fulfillment of agency performance." Refer to Peter Drucker's *Management: Tasks, Responsibilities, and Practices* on business values in public administration.[142]

3. What is the Re-Founding movement of public administration by Gary Wamsley and other scholars? Why is it significant to our understanding of the public interests in public administration? What are its underlying assumptions and reactions to pre-existing historical periods of public administration?

4. Discuss your childhood socialization to the public administration profession. What favorite books or movies depicted public servants? How were public servants depicted: benevolent or competent? How may this have influenced your interests in a career with public service?

KEY CONCEPTS AND NAMES

good public administrators 39
administration 39
virtue ethics 40
good moral character 40
Dr. Seuss 40
public servants 40
George Washington 40
management 45
movements 45
Alexander Hamilton 48
good character 48
exclusive 48
virtue 48
philosopher-kings 48
gentleman's code of ethics 49
guardian-kings 49
administrative spoils 49
Jacksonianism 49
era of gentlemen 49
egalitarianism 49
Abraham Lincoln 49
Second American Revolution 49

Pendleton Act in 1883 50
Civil Service Commission 50
Government by the Good 51
birth of modern public administration 51
Woodrow Wilson 51
The Study of Administration 51
middle-class reform 52
public interest model 53
Maxwell School of Citizenship and Public Affairs 53
Frank Goodnow 55
Luther Gulick 55
Lyndall Urwick 55
Taft Commission on Economy and Efficiency 55
Bureau of Budget Act of 1920 55
POSDCORB 56
behaviorism 56
Chester I. Barnard 57
Herbert A. Simon 57
logical positivism 58
satisficing 59

NOTES

1. David K. Hart, "Administration and the Ethics of Virtue: In All Things Choose First for Good Character and Then for Technical Expertise," in Terry L. Cooper, ed., *Handbook of Administrative Ethics,* 2nd ed. (New York: Marcel Dekker, 2000): 131–50.

2. Bradley S. Chilton and Lisa M. Chilton, "Rebuilding the Public Service: Research the Origins of Public Perceptions of the Public Service in Children's Literature," *Review of Public Personnel Administration* 12 (1993): 7278.

3. Tom L. Beauchamp, *Philosophical Ethics: An Introduction to Moral Philosophy,* 3rd ed. (New York: McGraw-Hill, 2001): 150.

4. Terry L. Cooper, *An Ethic of Citizenship for Public Administration* (Englewood Cliffs, NJ: Prentice-Hall, 1991); Camilla Stivers, "Citizenship Ethics in Public Administration," in Terry L. Cooper, *Handbook of Administrative Ethics* (New York: Marcel Dekker, 2000): 583–602.

5. For example, Richard T. Green, "Character Ethics and Public Administration," *International Journal of Public Administration* 17 (1994): 2137–64; Larry Hubbell, "The Relevance of Heroic Myths to Public Servants," *American Review of Public Administration* 20 (1990): 139–54.

6. Bruce Cannon Gibney, *A Generation of Sociopaths: How the Baby Boomers Betrayed America* (New York: Hachette Book Group, 2017).

7. Eugene P. Dvorin and Robert H. Simmons, *From Amoral to Humane Bureaucracy* (San Francisco, CA: Canfield Press, 1972).

8. Ibid., 19–26; Theodore J. Lowi, *The End of Liberalism: Ideology, Policy, and the Crisis of Public Authority* (New York: W.W. Norton, 1969): 85–92.

9. For example, Allan Bloom, *The Closing of the American Mind: How Higher Education Has Failed Democracy and Impoverished the Souls of Today's Students* (New York: Simon & Schuster, 1987); Richard B. Brandt, *Ethical Theory* (Englewood Cliffs, NJ: Prentice-Hall, 1959): chapter 11, "Ethical Relativism"; John Ladd, ed., *Ethical Relativism* (Belmont, CA: Wadsworth, 1973).

10. For example, Walter T. Stace, *The Concept of Morals* (New York: Macmillan, 1965): chapter 1, "Ethical Relativity and Ethical Absolutism."

11. Debra W. Stewart, Norman W. Sprinthall, and David M. Shafer, "Moral Development in Public Administration," in Terry L. Cooper, ed., *Handbook of Administrative Ethics* (New York: Marcel Dekker, 2000): 457–80.

12 Rushworth M. Kidder, "Universal Human Values: Finding an Ethical Common Ground," *Public Management* 77 (#6, 1995): 4–9.

13 Ralph Clark Chandler, "Deontological Dimensions of Administrative Ethics," in Terry L. Cooper, ed., *Handbook of Administrative Ethics*, 2nd ed. (New York: Marcel Dekker, 2000): 179–94.

14 John Stuart Mill, *Utilitarianism* (London: Longmans, Green & Co., 1863): chapter 2.

15 Gerald M. Pops, "A Teleological Approach to Administrative Ethics," in Terry L. Cooper, ed., *Handbook of Administrative Ethics*, 2nd ed. (New York: Marcel Dekker, 2000): 195–206.

16 Tom L. Beauchamp, *Philosophical Ethics: An Introduction to Moral Philosophy*, 3rd ed. (New York: McGraw-Hill, 2001): 150.

17 Bradley S. Chilton and Lisa M. Chilton, "Rebuilding the Public Service: Research the Origins of Public Perceptions of the Public Service in Children's Literature," *Review of Public Personnel Administration* 12 (1993): 72–8.

18 Terry L. Cooper, *An Ethic of Citizenship for Public Administration* (Englewood Cliffs, NJ: Prentice-Hall, 1991); Camilla Stivers, "Citizenship Ethics in Public Administration," in Terry L. Cooper, *Handbook of Administrative Ethics* (New York: Marcel Dekker, 2000): 583–602.

19 For example, Richard T. Green, "Character Ethics and Public Administration," *International Journal of Public Administration* 17 (1994): 2137–2164; Larry Hubbell, "The Relevance of Heroic Myths to Public Servants," *American Review of Public Administration* 20 (1990): 139–54.

20 For example, Tom L. Beauchamp, *Philosophical Ethics: An Introduction to Moral Philosophy* (New York: McGraw-Hill, 1982); William K. Frankena, *Ethics*, 2nd ed. (Englewood Cliffs, NJ: Prentice-Hall, 1973); Alasdair MacIntyre, *After Virtue: A Study in Moral Theory* (Notre Dame, IN: University of Notre Dame Press, 1981).

21 For example, Brian C. O'Connor, *Explorations in Indexing and Abstracting: Pointing, Virtue, and Power* (Santa Barbara, CA: Libraries Unlimited, 1996).

22 Rosalind Hursthouse and Glen Pettigrove, "Virtue Ethics," in Edward N. Zalta, ed., *The Stanford Encyclopedia of Philosophy* (Winter 2016 Edition), retrieved from https://plato.stanford.edu/archives/win2016/entries/ethics-virtue/

23 Ibid.

24 For example, Martha Nussbaum and Amartya Sen, eds., *The Quality of Life* (New York: Oxford University Press, 1993).

25 Ayn Rand, *The Virtue of Selfishness: A New Concept of Egoism* (New York: Signet Books, 1964).

26 For example, Alasdair MacIntyre, *After Virtue: A Study In Moral Theory*, 3rd ed. (Notre Dame, IN: University of Notre Dame Press, 2007); William D. Richardson, J. Michael Martinez, and Kerry R. Stewart, eds., *Ethics and Character: The Pursuit of Democratic Virtues* (Durham, NC: Carolina Academic Press, 1998).

27 For example, Richard T. Green, "Alexander Hamilton and the Study of Public Administration," *Public Administration Quarterly* 13 (#4, Winter 1990): 494–519.

28 For example, William R. Gallagher, *Sennacherib's Campaign to Judah: New Studies* (Vienna, Austria: Brill, 1999).

29 John L. Anderson and Craig Curtis, "A Developmental Analysis of the Term 'Management' and Its Role in Public Administration Thinking," *Administrative Theory & Praxis* 17 (#2, 1995): 62–73.

30 Woodrow Wilson, "The Study of Administration," *Political Science Quarterly* 56 (#4, 1887): 481–506.

31 Frank J. Goodnow, *Politics and Administration* (New York, NY: Macmillan, 1900).

32 Leonard D. White, *Introduction to the Study of Public Administration*, 4th ed. (New York, NY: Macmillan, 1955).

33 William F. Willoughby, *Principles of Public Administration* (Baltimore, MD: Johns Hopkins University Press, 1927).

34 Luther H. Gulick and Lyndall F. Urwick, *Papers on the Science of Administration,* (New York, NY: Institute of Public Administration, 1937).

35 Daniel L. Dreisbach, "Founders Famous and Forgotten," *The Intercollegiate Review* 42 (#2, Fall 2007): 6.

36 Lynton K. Caldwell, "Alexander Hamilton: Advocate of Executive Leadership," in Claude E. Hawley and Ruth G. Weintraub, eds., *Administrative Questions and Political Answers* (Princeton, NY: D. Van Nostrand, 1966).

37 Richard T. Green, "Alexander Hamilton: Founder of the American Public Administration," *Administration & Society* 34 (2002): 541–562; Richard T. Green, "Oracle at Weehawken: Alexander Hamilton and the Development of the Administrative State," doctoral dissertation, Virginia Polytechnic Institute & State University, Blacksburg, 1987.

38 Leonard White, *The Jeffersonians: A Study in Administrative History, 1801–1829* (New York: Macmillan, 1959).

39 Henry T. Edmondson, "Teaching Administrative Ethics with Help from Jefferson," *PS: Political Science and Politics* 28 (1995): 226–9; David K. Hart, "A Dream of What We Could Be: The Founding Values, the Oath, and *Homo virtutis americanus,*" in Terry L. Cooper, ed., *Handbook of Administrative Ethics* (New York: Marcel Dekker, 2000): 207–25.

40 Leonard D. White, *The Jacksonians: A Study in Administrative History, 1829–1861* (New York, NY: Macmillan Company, 1954).

41 Akhil R. Ahmar, *The Law of the Land: A Grand Tour of Our Constitutional Republic* (New York, NY: Basic Books, 2015); Akhil R. Amar, *America's Constitution: A Biography* (New York: Random House, 2005); George P. Fletcher, *Our Secret Constitution, How Lincoln Redefined American Democracy* (New York, NY: Oxford University Press, 2001); Harry V. Jaffa, *A New Birth of Freedom: Abraham Lincoln and the Coming of the Civil War* (Lanham, MD: Rowman & Littlefield, 2000).

42 James M. McPhearson, *Abraham Lincoln and the Second American Revolution,* reprint ed. (New York, NY: Oxford University Press, 1992); James M. McPhearson, *Tried by War: Abraham Lincoln as Commander In Chief* (New York: Penguin Books, 1992). See also David H. Donald, *Lincoln* (New York: Simon and Schuster, 1996); Doris H. Goodwin, *A Team of Rivals: The Political Genius of Abraham Lincoln* (Simon and Schuster, 2006).

43 Bob Blaisdell, ed., *The Wit and Wisdom of Abraham Lincoln: A Book of Quotations* (Mineola, NY: Dover Publications, 2005).

44 David W. Miller, *Second Only to Grant: Quartermaster General Montgomery C. Meigs* (Shippensburg, PA: White Maine Books, 2000); Mark R. Wilson, *The Business of Civil War: Military Mobilization and the State, 1861–1865* (Baltimore, MD: Johns Hopkins University Press, 2006).

45 Loren P. Beth, *Development of the American Constitution, 1877–1917* (New York: HarperCollins, 1972); John E. Semonche, *Charting the Future: The Supreme Court Responds to a Changing Society, 1890–1920* (Santa Barbara, CA: Praeger, 1978).

46 Paul Van Riper, "The American Administrative State: Wilson and the Founders," in Ralph C. Chandler, ed., *A Centennial History of the American Administrative State* (New York, NY: The Free Press, 1987): 13–14.

47 Jeffrey S. Luke and David W. Hart, "Character and Conducting the Public Service: A Review of Historical Perspectives," in Terry L. Cooper, ed., *Handbook of Administrative Ethics,* 2nd ed. (New York, NY: Marcel Dekker, 2000): 529–53.

48 David M. O'Brien, *Constitutional Law and Politics: Civil Rights and Civil Liberties,* 2nd ed. (New York, NY: W.W. Norton, 1995).

49 Nicholas Henry, in *Public Administration and Public Affairs*, 9th ed. (Upper Saddle River, NJ: Prentice-Hall, 2004), 251–2.

50 Paul Van Riper, *History of the United States Civil Service* (Evanston, IL: Row, Peterson & Co., 1958), 110.

51 Frederick Mosher, *Democracy and the Public Service* (New York, NY: Oxford University Press, 1968); see also Daniel P. Carpenter, *Forging of Bureaucratic Autonomy: Reputations, Networks, and Policy Innovation in Executive Agencies, 1862–1928* (Princeton, NJ: Princeton University Press, 2001).

52 Paul Van Riper, "The American Administrative State: Wilson and the Founders," in Ralph C. Chandler, ed., *A Centennial History of the American Administrative State* (New York, NY: The Free Press, 1987), 9.

53 Frederick Mosher, *Democracy and the Public Service* (New York, NY: Oxford University Press, 1968).

54 Jeffrey D. Greene, *Public Administration in the New Century: A Concise Introduction* (Belmont, CA: Thomson-Wadsworth, 2005), 51–2.

55 Thomas P. O'Neill, Jr., "Half a Century of American Achievement," Landon Lecture at Kansas State University, April 22, 1985, retrieved from http://ome.ksu.edu/lectures/landon/trans/oneill85.html

56 Ibid.; see also Thomas P. O'Neill, Jr., and William Novak, *Man of the House: The Life and Political Memoirs of Speaker Tip O'Neill* (New York, NY: Random House, 1987).

57 Paul Van Riper, "The American Administrative State: Wilson and the Founders," in Ralph C. Chandler, ed., *A Centennial History of the American Administrative State* (New York, NY: The Free Press, 1987), 21.

58 Ibid., 17.

59 Jeffrey D. Greene, *Public Administration in the New Century: A Concise Introduction* (Belmont, CA: Thomson-Wadsworth, 2005), 53.

60 Nicholas Henry, in *Public Administration and Public Affairs*, 9th ed. (Upper Saddle River, NJ: Prentice-Hall, 2004), 32–3.

61 Ibid., 33.

62 Fritz Morstein Marx, ed., *Elements of Public Administration* (New York, NY: Prentice Hall, 1949).

63 Chester I. Barnard, *Functions of the Executive*, 30th anniversary ed. (Cambridge, MA: Harvard University Press, 1968), 10.

64 Gary S. Marshall, "Public Administration in a Time of Fractured Meaning: Beyond the Legacy of Herbert Simon," doctoral dissertation, Virginia Polytechnic Institute & State University, Blacksburg, VA, 1993.

65 Herbert Simon, *Models of My Life* (Cambridge, MA: MIT Press, 1996).

66 Jay M. Shafritz, Albert C. Hyde, and Sandra J. Parkes, *Classics of Public Administration* (Belmont, CA: Wadsworth, 2004), 136.

67 Herbert Simon, *Administrative Behavior: A Study of Decision Making Processes in Administrative Organization*, 3rd ed. (New York, NY: The Free Press, 1976 [original pub. 1947]).

68 Herbert Simon, *Models of My Life* (Cambridge, MA: MIT Press, 1996).

69 For example, Herbert Simon, "Designing Organizations for an Information-Rich World," in Martin Greenberger, ed., *Computers, Communications, and the Public Interest* (Baltimore, MD: Johns Hopkins University Press, 1971), 37–72.

70 Jay M. Shafritz, Albert C. Hyde, and Sandra J. Parkes, *Classics of Public Administration* (Belmont, CA: Wadsworth, 2004), 38.

71 Peter F. Drucker, *Management: Tasks, Responsibilities, Practices* (New York, NY: HarperBusiness, original pub. 1973; HarperBusiness edition pub. 1993).

72 Richard H. Ward and Vincent J. Webb, *Quest for Quality: A Publication of the Joint Commission on Criminology and Criminal Justice Education and Standards* (New York, NY: University Publications, 1984).

73 Lynton K. Caldwell, "Environment: A New Focus for Public Policy?" *Public Administration Review* 23 (September 1963): 1329.

74 Wendy Read Wertz, "Lynton Keith Caldwell (1913–2006): His Pathbreaking Work in Environmental Policy and Continuing Impact on Environmental Professionals," *Environmental Practice* 8 (December 2006): 208–11.

75 Chris Argyris, *Organization and Innovation* (Homewood, IL: Richard D. Irwin Publishers, 1965); Robert R. Blake and Jane S. Mouton, *The Managerial Grid* (Houston, TX: Gulf Publishing, 1964); and Douglas McGregor, *The Human Side of Enterprise* (New York, NY: McGraw-Hill, 1960).

76 Frank Marini, ed., *Toward a New Public Administration: The Minnowbrook Perspective* (New York, NY: Chandler Publishing, 1971).

77 H. George Frederickson, *New Public Administration* (University, AL: University of Alabama Press, 1980).

78 E. Dvorin and R. Simmons, *From Amoral to Humane Bureaucracy* (San Francisco, CA: Canfield Press, 1972).

79 Ibid.

80 James M. Buchanan, *Cost and Choice: An Inquiry in Economic Theory* (Chicago, IL: Markaham, 1969); Vincent Ostrom and Elinor Ostrom, "Public Choice: A Different Approach to the Study of Public Administration," *Public Administration Review* 31 (1969): 203–16; and Gordon Tullock, *Private Wants, Public Means: An Economic Analysis of the Desirable Scope of Government* (New York, NY: Basic Books, 1970). Compare to Elinor Ostrom, *Governing the Commons: The Evolution of Institutions for Collective Action* (New York: Cambridge University Press, 1990, 2015).

81 Anthony Downs, *Inside Bureaucracy* (Glenview, IL: Scott, Foresman and Company, 1967); Peter Drucker, *Concept of the Corporation*, revised ed. (New York, NY: John Day, 1972); Aaron Wildavsky, *The New Politics of the Budgetary Process* (Glenview, IL: Scott, Foresman and Company, 1988).

82 Gary Wamsley and James Wolf, eds., *Re-founding Democratic Public Administration: Modern Paradoxes, Postmodern Challenges* (Thousand Oaks, CA: Sage Publications, 1996).

83 Charles T. Goodsell, "Public Administration and the Public Interest," in Gary Wamsley et al., *Refounding Public Administration* (Newbury Park, NJ: Sage Publications, 1990).

84 See Stephanie P. Newbold, "Toward a Constitutional School for American Public Administration," *Public Administration Review* 70 (#4, 2010): 538–46; Stephanie P. Newbold and David Rosenbloom, eds., *The Constitutional School of American Public Administration* (New York: Routledge, 2016).

85 For example, David H. Rosenbloom, James D. Carroll, and Jonathan D. Carroll, *Constitutional Competence for Public Managers: Cases and Commentary* (Itasca, IL: Peacock, 2000).

86 For example, Bradley S. Chilton and James A. Woods, "Moral Justifications on the Rehnquist Court: Hercules, Herbert, and Druggies under the Fourth Amendment," *Criminal Justice Policy Review* 17 (2006): 343–61.

87 M.W. Spicer, *The Founders, the Constitution, and Public Administration: A Conflict in World Views* (Washington, DC: Georgetown University Press, 2007).

88 For example, B.J. Cook, "The Representative Function of Bureaucracy: Public Administration in Constitutive Perspective," *Administration & Society* 23 (1992): 403–29; Richard Green, "A Constitutional Jurisprudence: Reviving Praxis in Public Administration," *Administration & Society* 24 (1992): 3–21; H. Jefferson Powell, *The Moral Tradition of American Constitutionalism: A Theological Interpretation* (Durham, NC: Duke University Press, 1993); John Rohr, *To Run a Constitution: The Legitimacy of the Administrative State* (Lawrence: University of Kansas Press, 1986); John Rohr, *Public Service, Ethics and Constitutional Practice* (Lawrence: University of Kansas Press, 1999); David H. Rosenbloom and R.S. Kravchuk, *Public Administration: Understanding Management, Politics, and Law in the Public Sector*, 6th ed. (Boston, MA: McGraw-Hill, 2005); Gary Wamsley and James Wolf, *Refounding Democratic Public Administration: Modern Paradoxes, Postmodern Challenges* (Thousand Oaks, CA: Sage, 1997).

89 Philippa Foot, *Virtues and Vices* (Oxford, UK: Basil Blackwell, 1978), 12.

90 William E. Frankena, *Ethics*, 3rd ed. (Englewood Cliffs, NJ: Prentice-Hall, 1973), 65.

91 For example, Richard Green, "Alexander Hamilton: Founder of the American Public Administration," *Administration & Society* 34 (2002): 541–62; Stephanie Newbold, "Statesmanship and Ethics: The Case of Thomas Jefferson's Dirty Hands," *Public Administration Review* 65 (2005): 669–77.

92 Ron Chernow, *Alexander Hamilton* (New York, NY: Penguin Press, 2004), 716–20.

93 Lon Fuller, *The Morality of Law*, revised ed. (New Haven, CN: Yale University Press, 1969).

94 John Rawls, *A Theory of Justice* (Cambridge, MA: Harvard University Press, 1971), 443, 445.

95 E.S. Savas, *Privatization: The Key to Better Government* (New York, NY: Chandler Publishing, 1987).

96 David Osborne and Ted Gaebler, *Reinventing Government: How the Entrepreneurial Spirit is Transforming the Public Sector* (Reading, MA: Addison-Wesley, 1992); David Osborne and Peter Plastrik, *Banishing of Bureaucracy: The Five Strategies for Reinventing Government* (Reading, MA: Addison-Wesley, 1997).

97 National Partnership for Reinventing Government, *Performance-Based Organizations* (Washington, DC: National Partnership for Reinventing Government, 1998).

98 Robert B. Denhardt and Joseph W. Grubbs, *Public Administration: An Action Orientation*, 4th ed. (Belmont, CA: Thomson-Wadsworth, 2004), 106.

99 Ibid., 46; see also Janet Denhardt and Robert B. Denhardt, *The New Public Service: Serving, Not Steering*, 3rd ed. (New York, NY: Routledge, 2011).

100 Lester M. Salamon, *The Resilient Sector: The State of Nonprofit America* (Washington, DC: Brookings Institution, 2003), 2.

101 Jeffrey M. Berry with David F. Arons, *A Voice for Nonprofits* (Washington, DC: Brookings Institution, 2003), 6.

102 Camilla Stivers, "Toward a Feminist Perspective in Public Administration Theory," *Women & Politics* 10 (#4, 1991): 49–65; see also DeLysa Burnier, "Bringing Gender into View," *Administrative Theory and Praxis* 27 (#2, 2005): 394–400; Janet R. Hutchison and Hollie S. Mann, "Feminist Praxis: Administering for a Multicultural, Multigendered Public," *Administrative Theory and Praxis* 26 (#1, 2004): 79–95; Camilla Stivers, *Bureau Men, Settlement Women: Constructing Public Administration in the Progressive Era* (Lawrence: University of Kansas Press, 2000); Camilla Stivers, *Gender Images in Public Administration: Legitimacy and the Administrative State* (Thousand Oaks, CA: Sage, 2002).

103 Charles Fox and Hugh Miller, *Postmodern Public Administration*, revised ed. (New York, NY: Routledge, 2007).

104 David John Farmer, *The Language of Public Administration: Bureaucracy, Modernity, and Postmodernity* (Tuscaloosa: University of Alabama Press, 1995).

105 Pauline Marie Rosenau, *Post-Modernism and the Social Sciences: Insights, Inroads, and Intrusions* (Princeton, NJ: Princeton University Press, 1992), 14–17.

106 For example, Robert Costanza, "Four Visions of the Century Ahead: Will it Be Star Trek, Ecotopia, Big Government, or Mad Max?" in Robert Chaires and Bradley Chilton, eds., *Star Trek Visions of Law & Justice* (Denton, TX: University of North Texas Press, 2005).

107 Pauline Marie Rosenau, *Post-Modernism and the Social Sciences: Insights, Inroads, and Intrusions* (Princeton, NJ: Princeton University Press, 1992), 14–17.

108 For example, Lynton K. Caldwell, "Managing the Transition to Post-Modern Society," *Public Administration Review* 35 (1975): 567–72.

109 For example, H. George Frederickson and Kevin B. Smith, *The Public Administration Theory Primer* (Boulder, CO: Westview, 2003), 168–70.

110 Harold C. Relyea and Henry B. Hogue, "A Brief History of the Emergence of Digital Government in the United States," in Alexei Pavlichev and G. David Garson, eds., *Digital Government: Principles and Best Practices* (Hershey, PA: Idea Group Publishing, 2004), 16–33.

111 G. David Garson, "The Promise of Digital Government," in Alexei Pavlichev and G. David Garson, eds., *Digital Government: Principles and Best Practices* (Hershey, PA: Idea Group Publishing, 2004), 2.

112 For example, Cass Sunstein, *Republic.com* (Princeton, NJ: Princeton University Press, 2001); Jane E. Fountain, *Building the Virtual State: Information Technology and Institutional Change* (Washington, DC: Brookings Institution, 2001).

113 Mark A. Abramson and Therese L. Morin, *E-Government 2003* (Lanham, MA: Rowman and Littlefield, 2003); Gregory G. Curtain, Michael H. Sommer, and Veronika Vis-Sommer, eds., *The World of E-Government* (New York, NY: Haworth, 2003); and R.W. Greene, *Open Access: GIS in E-Government* (Redlands, CA: ESRI Press, 2001).

114 Paul A. Volcker [Chairman], *Leadership for America: Rebuilding the Public Service: The Report of the National Commission on the Public Service* (Lanham, MD: Lexington Books, 1990).

115 Paul A. Volker [Chairman], *Urgent Business for America: Revitalizing the Federal Government for the 21st Century* (Washington, DC: National Commission on the Public Service, 2003).

116 For example, John Palguta, "Rebuilding and Re-Engaging a Battered Public Sector Workforce," *The Public Manager* (March 2014), retrieved from www.td.org/Publications/Magazines/The-Public-Manager/Archives/2014/Spring/

117 For example, Kim Viborg Anderson, *E-government and Public Sector Process Rebuilding (PPR): Dilettantes, Wheelbarrows, and Diamonds* (Boston: Kluwer Academic Publishers, 2004); D. Belanche Garcia, "Rebuilding the Public Trust in Government Administrations Through E-government Actions," *ESIC* (2014), retrieved from https://doi.org/10.1016/j.reimke.2014.07.001

118 Samantha L. Durst and Charldean Newell, "Two Thumbs Up: The Media Are the Message," *Public Voices* 3 (#3, 2017): 29–43.

119 Charles T. Goodsell, *The Case for Bureaucracy: A Public Administration Polemic* (Washington, DC: CQ Press, 2004).

120 Victor A. Thompson, *Without Sympathy or Enthusiasm: The Problem of Administrative Compassion* (Tuscaloosa: University of Alabama Press, 1975).

121 Guy B. Adams and Danny L. Balfour, *Unmasking Administrative Evil*, revised ed. (Armonk, NY: M.E. Sharpe, 2004); Gerson Moreno-Riano, "The Etiology of

Administrative Evil: Eric Voegelin and the Unconsciousness of Modernity," *American Review of Public Administration* 31 (#3, 2001): 296–312.

122   See, Hannah Arendt, *Eichman in Jerusalem: A Report on the Banality of Evil* (New York, NY: Penguin Classics, 1963 [2006 reprint]).

123   See, for example, https://blacklivesmatter.com/about/, www.nytimes.com/series/metoo-moment

124   For example, Fred Greenstein, "The Benevolent Leader: Children's Images of Political Authority," *American Political Science Review* 54 (1960): 934–43; Fred Greenstein, "The Benevolent Leader Revisited: Children's Images of Leaders in Three Democracies," *American Political Science Review* 69 (1975): 1371–1398; Thomas R. Marshall, "The Benevolent Bureaucrat: Political Authority in Children's Literature and Television," *Western Political Quarterly* 34 (1981): 389–98.

125   Christopher Cooper and Marc Schwerdt, "Depictions of Public Service in Children's Literature: Revisiting an Understudied Aspect of Political Socialization," *Social Science Quarterly* 82 (#3, 2001): 614–630; Fred Greenstein, "The Benevolent Leader: Children's Images of Political Authority," *American Political Science Review* 54 (1960): 934–43; Fred Greenstein, "The Benevolent Leader Revisited: Children's Images of Leaders in Three Democracies," *American Political Science Review* 69 (1975): 1371–98; Thomas R. Marshall, "The Benevolent Bureaucrat: Political Authority in Children's Literature and Television," *Western Political Quarterly* 34 (1981): 389–98.

126   Thomas R. Marshall, "The Benevolent Bureaucrat: Political Authority in Children's Literature and Television," *Western Political Quarterly* 34 (1981): 397.

127   Timothy E. Cook, "Another Perspective on Political Authority in Children's Literature: The Fallible Leader in L. Frank Baum and Dr. Seuss," *Western Political Quarterly* 36 (1983): 326–336; Christopher Cooper and Marc Schwerdt, "Depictions of Public Service in Children's Literature: Revisiting an Understudied Aspect of Political Socialization," *Social Science Quarterly* 82 (#3, 2001): 614–30.

128   Bradley S. Chilton and Lisa M. Chilton, "Rebuilding the Public Service: Researching the Origins of Public Perceptions of the Public Service in Children's Literature," *Review of Public Personnel Administration* 13 (#4, 1993): 72–8.

129   Thomas R. Marshall, "The Benevolent Bureaucrat: Political Authority in Children's Literature and Television," *Western Political Quarterly* 34 (1981): 389–98, esp. 391–2.

130   Ibid., 393.

131   Ibid., 394.

132   For example, Bruce Cannon Gibney, *A Generation of Sociopath: How the Baby Boomers Betrayed America* (New York, NY: Hatchette Books, 2017).

133   Fred Greenstein, "The Benevolent Leader: Children's Images of Political Authority," *American Political Science Review* 54 (1960): 934–43; Fred Greenstein, "The Benevolent Leader Revisited: Children's Images of Leaders in Three Democracies," *American Political Science Review* 69 (1975): 1371–98; R. Hess and David Easton, "The Child's Changing Image of the President," *Public Opinion Quarterly* 24 (1960): 632–644; Thomas R. Marshall, "The Benevolent Bureaucrat: Political Authority in Children's Literature and Television," *Western Political Quarterly* 34 (1981): 389–98, esp. 390.

134   For example, Thomas R. Marshall, "The Benevolent Bureaucrat: Political Authority in Children's Literature and Television," *Western Political Quarterly* 34 (1981): 395.

135   Christopher Cooper and Marc Schwerdt, "Depictions of Public Service in Children's Literature: Revisiting an Understudied Aspect of Political Socialization," *Social Science Quarterly* 82 (#3, 2001): 614–30.

136 Marc Schwerdt, "Stores of Service: Public Service in the Children's Literature of the United States and Great Britain," *Politics & Policy* 31 (#2, June 2003): 195–214.

137 Victor I. Thompson, *Without Sympathy or Enthusiasm: The Problem of Administrative Compassion* (Tuscaloosa: University of Alabama Press, 1975).

138 For example, Kim Viborg Anderson, *E-government and Public Sector Process Rebuilding (PPR): Dilettantes*, Wheelbarrows, and Diamonds (Boston, MA: Kluwer Academic Publishers, 2004).

139 D. Belanche Garcia, "Rebuilding the Public Trust in Government Administrations Through E-government Actions," *ESIC* (2014), retrieved from https://doi.org/10.1016/j.reimke.2014.07.001

140 Michael Baker, "Generational Perspectives on American Public Administration in the Deep South for Law Enforcement Policy and Community Relations at the Local, State and National Levels," *PA Times* (2017, July 21), retrieved from http://patimes.org/

141 R.K. MacDonald, *Dr. Seuss* (New York, NY: Twayne, 1988), 9.

142 Peter F. Drucker, *Management: Tasks, Responsibilities, and Practices*, revised ed. (New York, NY: HarperBusiness, 2008).

Utility and Democratic Policymaking

"Promote democratic participation. Inform the public and encourage active engagement in governance. Be open, transparent and responsive, and respect and assist all persons in their dealings with public organizations."
— (Code of Ethics, American Society for Public Administration, 2013)

BOX 3.1 | CHAPTER OBJECTIVES

1 Define the nature of democracy in America, citizenship ethics for public administrators, and utility.

2 Survey the democratic policymaking process, its actors and institutions, and its shortcomings.

3 Overview policy analysis, community survey, program evaluation, case study and public policy methods.

4 Discuss the many roles of the policy analyst and their impact on policymaking in the public interests.

5 Critique utilitarian ethical theory in our ethics case study of the issues and conflicts when public administrators promote utility through citizen participation in democratic policymaking.

Our overview of democratic policymaking gives us opportunity to examine the participation and the balancing of citizens and interests, compromises and operations of **democratic institutions,** and of policymaking within our constitutional federalist democratic republic. We also examine utilitarianism and public interest perspectives in which public administrators are ethically obligated to calculate the greatest good for the greatest number (utility). **Utility** is about the radically democratic calculation of the needs, preferences, and resources of all who are involved or affected by the decisions of public administration. And the majority decision rules. As a result, public administration within democratic policymaking may require an additional level of recognition, respect, and accounting to the people. Public interests utility, as an applied ethical concept, is similar to utilitarian ethical theory, in which right and wrong are determined by calculation of pleasure and pain, benefits-costs, and other measures of human needs or preferences of intrinsic value to produce maximal value. The public interests or moral values are not in the things of intrinsic value in itself (e.g., inmates want to eat delicious food), rather: "Actions are right in proportion as they tend to promote happiness, wrong as they tend to produce the reverse of happiness."[1] Thus, the utility perspective and utilitarian ethical theory is not based on the discovery of pre-existing or universal ethical rules or duties, but is skeptical of the value of such ethical rules or duties without specific empirical reference to and calculation of the pleasure, happiness, or individual preferences of all who are involved. Utilitarianism emphasizes the **teleology**—or the ends and consequences of ethical decisions. It is focused upon the achievement of desires, justice, and avoidance of tragedy and pain, rather than following the rules for their own sake. Utilitarianism may be hedonistic in focusing on pleasure or happinesss, or pluralistic with the inclusion of values beyond hedonism, but scholars and administrators tend to take a third approach of aggregating individual preferences. Of course, as with all applied ethics concepts, it is a matter of degree and all three public interests perspectives—virtue, utility, and duty—may be found within these democratic policymaking processes.[2]

The utility perspective of the public interests focuses ethical attention of public administrators to promote the democratic participation of the people. Thus, ethical public administrators must respect and assist all persons in a democracy, along with the trustworthy calculations of the democratic preferences of the people. The utility perspective of the public interests requires public administrators to be open and transparent while protecting the privacy rights of individuals, as well as national security interests. Because some individuals may not have experience or knowledge in dealing with public organizations, ethical public administrators must involve the public in participation in the development, implementation, and assessment of democratically authorized policies and public programs. This may involve additional ethical burdens in communicating clearly, completely and in easy-to-understand language in dealings with the public—perhaps in Spanish and languages other than English.[3] The timely, transparent, and complete flow of public information is crucial to the ethical success of the public administrator under the utility perspective.[4]

Democratic policymaking, institutions and analyses are altogether a complex system involving not only the best-known political players—for example, presidents and legislators—but also many millions of public administrators as well as private organizations, nonprofits and faith-based organizations, and hundreds of millions of citizens. Other participants also include other branches of the public sector, such as judges and courts, as well as officials and bureaucrats from states and community governments. From the private sector, **public policy** participants may include corporate CEOs, corporate lawyers, the media, interest groups, and citizens. In addition, the nonprofit sector travels more often and with greater influence in public policy circles, including faith-based organizations.

The chapter discusses the concepts of **democratic policymaking,** including the institutions, processes, and analysis of public policy. First, we review democracy, the ethic of citizenship for public administrators, and utilitarianism theory. Second, we scrutinize public policy processes and institutions. Third, we analyze the application of policy analysis to public policies in the variety of methods and approaches commonly used today. Fourth, we analyze the different roles of the public servant as **policy analyst** in promoting democracy, facilitating citizen engagement, and calculating utility. Finally, we critique the ethical issues and conflicts when public administrators promote democracy and citizenship through voting and other democratic participation. Throughout the chapter we also illustrate and discuss the meanings, strengths, and weaknesses of the utility perspective or utilitarian ethical theory.

DEMOCRACY, CITIZENSHIP, AND UTILITY

America is a **democracy**; specifically, a **constitutional federalist democratic republic**.[5] Ultimate political authority is from the people—like all democracies—but is exercised by representatives at states and national levels who are responsible to the people, and limited under constitutional rule of law. The word *democracy* is derived from the Greek *demos* (the people) and *kratos* (authority). Democracy may be direct, as found in ancient Athens and in some New England town meetings, but U.S. democracy today is more indirect, representative, constitutionally limited, and exercised by interest groups, legislators, officials, and others in complex bargaining policymaking. Governmental systems may be contrasted by:

- number of **rulers,** e.g., a monarchy is governed by one, an oligarchy is governed by few, a democracy is governed by many;
- distribution of **power**, e.g., a confederation is a loose union of states with limited central government (former Confederate States of America), a unitary state vests all power in one central government (France), federations vest power in both states and a central government (Canada, Mexico, US);
- **religion/state** relations, e.g., a theocracy unifies the head of a religion and the state (Vatican), neutral states govern without protections or regard for religious beliefs (Cuba, former USSR), religious freedom states govern with protections for religious beliefs and support religious institutions by multiple-establishment of all religions (Australia, United Kingdom) or modified separation (US);
- **executive/legislature** relations, e.g., parliamentary government selects the prime minister and executives/ministers from the legislature (Australia, United Kingdom), presidential government allows the people to select and directly empower the chief executive separate from the legislature (Germany, Mexico, US).

Most Americans think of their nation as democratic, yet the term does not appear in the 1776 Declaration of Independence or the 1789 U.S. Constitution. This may be due to the influence of ancient philosophers, such as Plato and Aristotle, who argued democracy was dangerous and impossible as a governing theory; it was mob rule empowering the vulgar masses, made a virtue of the ignorance, sloth, incompetence, mediocrity, and sham covetous takings by the undeserving. Many centuries of history had proven this critique and distaste for democracy, until the success of the American and French revolutions in the late 1700s, when democracy swept the world. Countries around the globe still struggle to achieve greater democracy, especially in Asia and Africa today. The American experiment has inspired many, by overcoming the unsuccessful **1781–1789 Articles of**

Confederation of a weak central government with no power to tax and pay Revolutionary War debts or veterans, 13 squabbling states each with their own currency, and law enforcement too puny to control mob rule in Shay's rebellion. It was the success of achieving the **1789 U.S. Constitution**, the **1792 Bill of Rights**, and implementation of a constitutional federalist democratic republic that inspired new democracies around the globe to this day. The Constitution's preamble and Article VII made clear this democratic revolution. "We the people" in 1788–1789 ratified the new 1789 Constitution by popular vote in all 13 states, rendering the Articles of Confederation and Declaration of Independence to the status of historical documents without legal power. The framers of the Constitution were, after all, a much more conservative, propertied, legally trained group than the revolutionaries who signed the Declaration of Independence and Articles of Confederation. While many constitutional framers owned plantations, only one was, indeed, a farmer—William Few, a chicken farmer from Georgia. Half the framers were lawyers by training who feared Shay's Rebellion (1786) and other mob-rule taking properties of others. They provided for strong central government with power to tax and adequately defend against foreign invasion, for rule of law and law enforcement protections. In the social contract they explicitly created, they seemed willing to exchange much of their wealth for these protections. Given the tough social contract created by the Constitution, James Madison, called "the father of the Constitution," and other framers seem influenced by the tough security-oriented **social contract urged by Thomas Hobbes (1588–1679)** or David Hume (1711–1776) in contrast to the genteel **social contract of John Locke (1632–1704)**.[6] However, while the Constitution may have been Hobbesian or Humean, the 1792 Bill of Rights were Lockean, limiting government and personal liberties and property rights protections.[7] Further, seven of the 17 Amendments following the Bill of Rights focused on expanding **citizenship** and popular democratic participation.

At about 8,700 words, the U.S. Constitution is the shortest national constitution in the world, including a Preamble, seven Articles on basic political institutions, and 27 Amendments. The Preamble expressly designates the Constitution as a living document to be changed over time by Amendments, interpretations, and custom/usage. The Constitution created three branches of government—legislative, executive, and judicial—each with its own powers, shared powers, and checks and balances, so that no one branch would reign supreme. The legislative branch consists of Congress with a Senate (upper chamber, two votes per state) and House of Representatives (lower chamber, votes apportioned by population). Congress has the sole authority to make federal laws, levy national taxes, declare war, and print money, among other powers. Congress also controls the federal budget.

The executive branch consists of the President and Vice President, as well as the military and civilian bureaucracy who execute, enforce, and administer federal laws. The president is selected every four years by the Electoral College and is also the commander-in-chief of the armed forces and has the power to conduct foreign relations. The Executive Office of the President is supervised by the President's Chief of Staff, and provides support to the President for executive decisions, including U.S. trade interests around the world and national security. There are 15 departments within the executive bureaucratic branch, including the Department of State, the Department of Labor, the Department of Homeland

Security, the Department of Education, and others. These are cabinet-level offices headed up by a secretary who is appointed by the President and confirmed by the Senate. Each of these departments also oversees a number of lower government agencies, such as the Federal Bureau of Investigation (FBI) and the Food and Drug Administration (FDA). Independent executive agencies perform specialized functions, and are independent from executive control, e.g., the Central Intelligence Agency (CIA), which protects the US from global threats. Independent regulatory agencies are independent from executive influence and administer laws and regulate key industries and businesses that affect the public, e.g., the Environmental Protection Agency (EPA), which protects human health and the natural environment, and the Federal Trade Commission (FTC), which regulates business practices and monopolies. Government corporations are private/for-profit organizations created by the U.S. government to be completely independent and provide public service, e.g., Amtrak and the U.S. Postal Service.

The judicial branch includes the U.S. Supreme Court, U.S. Circuit Courts of Appeal, and U.S. District Courts—each with justices or judges appointed for life on good behavior by the President with the approval of the Senate. These constitutional courts and other federal courts interpret and apply laws through cases brought before them under jurisdiction rules of the power of a court to hear and decide the cases. All courts exercise constitutional judicial review to ensure legal compliance with the U.S. Constitution. The Supreme Court is the highest judicial authority in the country.

Congress and the Presidency are actually filled by political parties and elections. Political parties are groups joined together to win political offices and control the government. First Amendment Freedom of Association permits a two-party system to exist in the US, Democrat and Republican, with some third or independent party candidates. The President, members of Congress, state governors, and many state, local, and city office holders, must campaign for their positions in elections. Elections are staged by political parties in the US and occur at the local, state, and federal levels—with some differences by locality and state political parties. But, with citizen apathy, voter turnout is very low, with a high of about 50 percent for some Presidential elections and as low as 5 percent for some local elections. The President is selected by the Electoral College, consisting of state political party members elected by the winning popular vote in each state, selected variously from state to state, who have pledged to vote in the Electoral College for their political party candidate for President. Interest groups are organizations of people who share a specified common interest and work together to promote that interest through government by lobbying or grassroots activities. Interest groups also give voice to people outside of elections, and can sometimes skew government policy. The media consists of the private organizations that keep citizens informed about politics and current events through newspapers, magazines, television, radio, internet, social media, and other digital media. The media also keep the government under scrutiny and may influence the government by its coverage.[8]

Citizenship is not explained in the 1789 U.S. Constitution, but it does mention "citizens of the States" and "citizen of the United States." In practice, all citizens of the states were U.S. citizens. Further, all states and the U.S. courts practiced common law—inherited from England—and accepted the rule of *jus soli* (Latin, "law of the soil") or **citizenship** by place of birth. The states and U.S.

law also recognized the rule of *jus sanguinis* (Latin, "law of blood") or citizenship by blood relationship, and included this in U.S. statutes by 1790. Thus, early Americans were citizens by residing as state citizens, or by birth on the soil of the US and territories or by birth from either parent who was a U.S. citizen. Therein lays the rub, as the states defined citizenship differently, excluding non-whites, women, those without property ownership, and recent immigrants. Half of Americans were women, who were not citizens. Nearly one-half of white men did not own property and were not citizens. About one-fourth the total U.S. population was African American (i.e., 570,000 of 2.5 million in 1776)—but only 40,000 were free persons of color, with about 10,000 as citizens. Americans had targeted Africans for slavery and perceived them as soulless, less than human, mere chattel (movable property). By the 1860 Civil War, over two million African Americans were in the US as non-citizens. Their only human right was a ban on unseemly cruelty (as with cattle), but slave owners ignored the law with impunity.

The 1789 Constitution recognized and protected the slave trade to 1808, the continuation of slavery thereafter, and gave lesser human worth to slaves. *Dred Scot v. Sanford (1857)* declared that slaves were not citizens and had no rights.[9] In 1865, the **Thirteenth (13th) Amendment** banned slavery, the 1868 **Fourteenth (14th) Amendment** gave citizenship to former slaves, as well as all persons born or naturalized in the US, and the 1870 **Fifteenth (15th) Amendment** prohibited any denial or abridgement of citizenship on account of race, color, or former slavery. The 14th Amendment incorporated *jus soli* and *jus sanquinis*,[10] and provided naturalization for recent immigrants. **Naturalization** is the exchange of citizenship in another country for citizenship in the US. The federal **Immigration and Naturalization Act**, first passed in 1952 and reauthorized in 2015, established policy regulating the flow of immigration into the United States, and establishes rules regarding how immigrants can become naturalized citizens. The law was passed by Congress, signed into law and implemented by the executive branch, and over the years adjudicated by the federal court system. Yet, with the continuous flow of immigrants into Southwestern Border states, some states such as Arizona have passed their own laws to control the flood of irregularly documented immigrants. This has ignited a firestorm of political opposition, including various organizations, interest groups, political parties and grassroots public opinion to challenge the legality of such laws. Thus, federalism is not only the legal division of constitutional powers; it also provides a way for ongoing citizen involvement in democratic policymaking. Other amendments have enlarged the scope and number of citizens participating to include women (the 19th Amendment), voters in the District of Columbia (the 23rd Amendment), to eliminate poll taxes (the 24th Amendment), and to adults aged 18–21 (the 26th Amendment). Obviously, democratic citizenship participation is important!

Ethics of Citizenship

Professor **Terry L. Cooper (1938–)** posits citizenship as the foundation of ethics for public administrators. He reasons that:

> In searching for the source of legitimacy for the public administrator
> in a democratic society I conclude that it is to be found in the role of
> citizen. Public administrators are "professional citizens," or "citizen

> **BOX 3.2 | The Fourteenth (14th) Amendment, Section 1**

The first constitutional written explanation of American citizenship was included in the 1868 Fourteenth (14th) Amendment to the U.S. Constitution. Section 1 of this amendment declares that "All persons born or naturalized in the United States, and subject to the jurisdiction thereof, are citizens of the United States and of the State wherein they reside." ◣

administrators"; they are fiduciaries who are employed by the citizenry to work on their behalf . . . [P]ublic administrators are to be understood as "citizens in lieu of the rest of us." With this role definition in mind, I argue that the ethical obligations of the public administrator are to be derived from the obligations of citizenship in a democratic political community. These obligations include responsibility for establishing and maintaining horizontal relationships of authority with one's fellow citizens, seeking "power with" rather than "power over" the citizenry. This attitude on the part of public administrators calls for engaging in activities which amounts to an ongoing renewal and reaffirmation of the "social contract."[11]

Cooper's basic ethic of citizenship theory is that our constitutional federalist democratic republic has established a framework for democratic policymaking by citizens. Yet, because their participation is not required (except in jury duty), citizens become passive and focus on other roles involving the continuous pursuit of private interests and the eclipse of citizenship. This necessitates a restoration of the **ethic of citizenship for public administrators.** Public servants become professional citizens as fiduciaries employed by the citizenry to work on their behalf. Thus, the public servants' ethical obligations are derived from obligations of citizens in a democracy. These moral obligations include a responsibility to establish and maintain relationships with the citizens, seeking to partner and represent the citizenry in a democracy. This ethic of citizenship for public administrators renews and reaffirms the social contract of democratic policymaking. The application of this democratic social contract and ethic of citizenship is a fiduciary role for public servants **representing citizens in the policy process,** through policy analysis methods, and as policy analysts for the public interests.[12]

Cooper further develops the application and steps of the ethics of citizenship in his book, *The Responsible Administrator* (see Box 3.3). Cooper frames the ethics of citizenship within an administrative responsibility model hearkening back to Chester Barnard's "The Nature of Executive Responsibility" in his 1938 classic, *The Functions of the Executive.*[13] Cooper uses "rational and comprehensive" ethical decision making, much like Simon's "satisficing" model in his 1947 classic, *Administrative Behavior*—where an administrator will examine as much of the problem as possible, formulate alternative responses, and make an ethical choice or decision.[14] Of course, administrators are human and may respond emotionally, creatively, or philosophically. But a variety of ethical responses should be available, depending on the situation or decision. The public administrator should use his or her creative talents in combination with some basic and guiding moral principles to make a decision. A public administrator may examine broad philosophical or

BOX 3.3 | Terry L. Cooper (1938–)

Terry Cooper is a Professor in the Department of Policy, Planning and Development at the University of Southern California. His research focuses on citizen participation and administrative and governmental ethics. He is one of the co-principal investigators in the USC Neighborhood Participation Project that is researching the role of neighborhood organizations in the governance process of the City of Los Angeles. He was a member of the National Academy of Public Administration during the early to mid-1990s, where he assisted in the development of a decision-making process to encourage intergenerational equity in the management of hazardous wastes by the U.S. Department of Energy. He serves on the Los Angeles Police Department's Professional Advisory Committee and is President of the International Institute for Public Ethics. His primary works on administrative ethics include *An Ethic of Citizenship for Public Administrators* (1991) and *The Responsible Administrator: An Approach to Ethics for the Administrative Role*, 4th ed. (2001).

Source: See USC College of Letters, Arts and Sciences, Faculty, "Terry Cooper," retrieved from www.usc.edu/schools/college/faculty/faculty1003181.html

religious guidelines before deciding. Cooper posits that this process must be fluid within a **rationalist-comprehensive framework**—assessing a variety of variables, situations, and dilemmas to make a decision.[15] In positing the ethic of citizenship for public administrators, Cooper hearkens back to the days of the citizen-democracy of ancient Athens, and the virtues of democratic participation. Yet, by delegating citizen democratic participation to professional public administrators as fiduciary representatives, he creates a utilitarian obligation of quantitative and qualitative competent technical representation of the utilities of citizens. In a sense, the ethical citizen-fiduciary is now virtuous to the degree that calculations of utilities of the represented citizens are precisely correct. The virtue of the ethical obligation of citizen-fiduciaries becomes a mechanical instrumental virtue, and perhaps someday may be replaced with an artificially intelligent expert shell software that directly registers the utilities of the citizens, calculates them precisely correct, and reports them to policymaking elites or key decision makers. Wasn't this science fiction future the dream and vision of Herbert Simon (see Chapter 2): to exactly model administrative decision making to someday replace administrators with expert shell artificially intelligent software? Is an instrumental and technical virtue of representing the utilities of others the sort of ethics we should aspire to in public service? Further, as we also noted in the previous chapter, this has led to what Robert Putnam refers to as bowling-alone, contributing to a loss of social capital.[16] Is community a viable, working entity that represents commonly held and practiced social and political values? Or is community merely what citizens define as their individual preferences? If so, social life—from meeting at the local Hispanic Chamber of Commerce to participating in neighborhood watch groups—loses any sense of commonality or even ethical meaning. We are merely bowling-alone.

However, Cooper's ethic of citizenship, citizen-driven administration, and citizen-centered collaborative public management has been widely imitated around the world.[17] Other related academic disciplines have also caught the spirit and applied the ethic of citizenship—e.g., planners now represent their citizens' utilities in quality of life city plans and designs[18]—not only for its embrace of democratic values, but for elevating utilitarianism to the highest throne of the variety of ethical approaches in public administration. Utilitarianism has long been the darling of public policy analysis and the economists who dominate the field, but Cooper's ethic of citizenship gives legitimacy to the representative republican role of this policy analyst role for the utilities of the many. And Cooper's representative fiduciary logic fits neatly with the neoliberal economic and political theories of current policy analysis, warming hopes of a new type of "invisible hand" to replace the failures of capitalist marketplaces in calculation, accounting, and allocation of the utilities of participant citizens.[19] Cooper's critique of other approaches, such as John Rohr's constitutional regime values, easily wins the popular vote among a positivist dominated discipline.[20] The economists, utility-crunchers, and cost-benefit calculators are thereby canonized as the ethical approach for public administrators. Of course, Cooper is not a complete utilitarian in his approach to ethics and makes strong headway in collaboration with John Rohr and others toward a broader theory of ethics for public administrators.[21] But his proposal for an ethic of citizenship legitimizes the delegation of citizen democratic participation to professional public administrators as fiduciary representatives, and a utilitarian obligation of giving voice to citizens.

Utilitarianism

The ethical philosophy of utilitarianism holds that the sole ultimate standard or criterion of rightness and wrongness is the principle of utility—or the greatest good for the greatest number. For the ancient philosopher **Epicurus (341–270 BCE)**, the measurement of utility was pleasure and pain: "Our highest good is pleasure . . . When confronted by evil the soul is weak, but not when faced with good; for pleasures make the soul secure but pains ruin it." **Jeremy Bentham (1748–1842)** measured utility by pain and pleasure, which he also defined as misery and happiness: "Nature has placed mankind under the governance of two sovereign masters, pain and pleasure . . . Create all the happiness you are able to create; remove all the misery you are able to remove." **John Stuart Mill (1806–1873)** measured utility by units of happiness: "Actions are right in proportion as they tend to promote happiness, wrong as they tend to produce the reverse of happiness." Mill believed Christian theology was based in utilitarianism: "In the Golden Rule of Jesus of Nazareth, we read . . . the ethics of utility. To do as one would be done by, and to love one's neighbor as oneself, constitute the ideal perfections of utilitarian morality." Contemporary spokesperson **John Rawls (1921–2002)** measured utility by its just results: "The fundamental criterion for judging any procedure is the justice of its likely result . . . A just society is a society that if you knew everything about it, you'd be willing to enter it in a random place."[22]

The first element of utilitarianism is **teleology**, where the consequences of moral decisions are the deciding factor in their goodness. Thus, for some, utilitarianism is the sports ethic of Coach Vince Lombardi (1913–1970): "Winning isn't everything, it's the only thing!" But all of consequentialism is not merely utilitarianism,[23] for Chapter 2 detailed the teleological consequentialism of virtue ethics, concerned with the consequences for your entire moral character. Utilitarianism is not based on the discovery of pre-existing or universal rules or duties, but is skeptical of the value of such rules or duties without specific empirical reference to the consequences to all who are involved. Second, utilitarianism is radically **egalitarian** and mandates an equal level of recognition, respect, and accounting to the preferences of each and every person affected by a moral decision. In utilitarianism, right and wrong are determined by calculation of benefits and costs, happiness, pleasure and pain, individual preferences, or other measures of human needs of intrinsic value to produce a maximal value. The thing of intrinsic value itself is not the thing of moral value; rather, "Actions are right in proportion as they tend to promote happiness, wrong as they tend to produce the reverse of happiness."[24] Third, utilitarianism is **scientific** in its inspiration from the Enlightenment successes with sciences. It seeks a unified and uniformly equal metric of moral right or wrong with utility—the greatest good for the greatest number.

In the real world of public service, do we have the time to calculate the utility of our actions or decisions? What about human rights? Maximizing utility doesn't make it right to sell some into human slavery—isn't it simply wrong to harm some in order to make the majority happy? John Rawls (1921–2002) and others have questioned **act-utilitarianism**, or the ordinary approach to utilitarianism by calculating the greatest good for the greatest number in a single act. Rawls concluded that we don't have to do calculations in most cases: we can apply subordinate rules of thumb to guide our utility. Subordinate rules of thumb are commonsense morality we can internalize and follow, subordinate to the basic moral metric of utility. And some acts should simply be absolutely prohibited, such as human slavery. Rawls believed act-utilitarian calculations were impractical or undesirable, but he didn't want to throw away all of utilitarianism, so instead he proposed **rule-utilitarianism,** or rule-of-thumb guidelines, to produce the greatest good for the greatest number. Rule-utilitarianism is the trend in public affairs: aggregating individual preferences into benefits and costs, especially in applied administrative ethics.[25]

However, the definition of public interests as utilities or a calculation of individual preferences has been used by majorities in the US to legitimate morally unacceptable results, such as slavery, racial segregation, torture in prisons and mental institutions, interrogating criminal suspects to the third degree, and other abuses. Under a utility perspective of the public interests, calculations of individual preferences or benefits and costs have been used to justify and mask the administrative evil done by bureaucrats—hidden to the public and to themselves.[26] How can abuses of minorities ever be in the public interests, or moral? Some lay the fault of all administrative evil upon the rise of utilitarian rationality and modernity in the Enlightenment and its unconsciousness, urging a return to virtue ethics in public affairs.[27] In its defense, utilitarian calculations today are supplemented by justice rules of thumb to prevent abuses of minorities, such as rules from the 14th Amendment and Bill of Rights. And some scholars of utilitarianism argue that these levels of harm are of such disvalue that they far outweigh any benefit or vote, when properly calculated or by application of rule-utilitarianism. Yet, the criticisms of abuses to minorities stick to utilitarianism and many remain uneasy about the lack of built-in safeguards to protect against the excesses of majoritarianism.[28] Is anything ever intrinsically wrong?[29]

Our constitutional federalist democratic republic establishes the framework for democratic policymaking. Yet, because their participation is not required (except in jury duty), citizens become passive and focus on other roles involving the continuous pursuit of private interests and the eclipse of citizenship. This necessitates a restoration of the ethic of citizenship for public administrators. Public servants become professional citizens as fiduciaries employed by the citizenry to work on their behalf. Thus, the public servants' ethical obligations are derived from obligations of citizens in a democracy. These moral obligations include a responsibility to establish and maintain relationships with the citizens, seeking to partner and represent the citizenry in a democracy. This ethic of citizenship for public administrators renews and reaffirms the social contract of democratic policymaking. The application of this democracy and ethic of citizenship creates and legitimizes a fiduciary role for public servants representing citizens in the policy process, through policy analysis methods, and as policy analysts who give voice to the public interests. In the next section, we outline democratic policymaking, the definition of public policy, describe theories of policymaking processes, and highlight the ethic of citizenship of public administrators in the public interests.

PUBLIC POLICY

Public policy is the study of the substance of policies implemented by the government, i.e. economic, social, or foreign, and also the process of how these policies are implemented. Public policy is affected by and affects public administration; public policy is the intended courses of action, while public administration is policy in action. For example, when we ask "What is the U.S. policy in Syria?" this raises numerous scenarios regarding substantive policy positions. The official government policy as expressed by President Donald Trump is that the bombing in Syria, for example, is necessary to stop Isis terrorism on its home turf, and in particular prevent it from further negatively affecting America's national interests, including providing for national security and ensuring freedom, both home and abroad. Another policy position holds that because there is no link between Isis and acts of terrorism within the US, the bombing of civilians in Syria was unethical. This position holds, among other things, that the war is about personal revenge or property, and that it is simply an unnecessary, immoral war. Some even go so far as to proclaim the advent of conspiracy theories, directing their anger at President Trump personally, claiming that he and/or his administration knew that the tragic deaths of many innocent Syrian civilians could and might happen, but went ahead without a plan to prevent it.

Public Policy and Public Interests

Important to our consideration of public policy is the effect it has upon the public interests.[30] Although formulating, adopting, implementing, and evaluating public policy is not as simple and linear as it may sound, it is also not a technically or technologically difficult process. What we have found, however, is that public policymaking is incredibly diverse, affecting one or many individuals, depending upon the establishment of values, who holds these values, and how elected and administrative officials respond to the distribution, redistribution, and regulation of those values. We contend that public policy making should be made in the public interests. But how is this possible? How, for example, can public policy be made and administered with regard to socially divisive issues, such as abortion, euthanasia, or national security interests such as fighting the war on terror, and still fulfill the public interests? At the very least, doesn't fulfilling the public interests mean that all individuals, groups, and organizations get what they want at the same time? Because this is impossible, this must mean that either there is no such thing as the public interests or the definition is so ambiguous and/or convoluted that it essentially means nothing. We don't believe either extreme is accurate. For a better explanation of public policy influencing the public interests we first turn to a description of various theories of public policy.

Theories of Public Policy

Since post-World War II political scientists have developed (or borrowed) from other social sciences (such as economics, psychology, and sociology) various theories for trying to explain how policy makers make policy. Theory is needed in any academic endeavor; it is the roadmap, so to speak, for understanding not only how to get to the destination, but what happens along the way. Theory building is all about developing and massaging terms, concepts, and ideas that ostensibly aid both the professional researcher and student in learning and comprehending the depth and nuances of public policymaking. Both the academic and practitioner benefit from this type of inquiry, because for the academic researcher it clarifies concepts and strengthens theory building, and for the practitioner it assists in applying the concepts and variables to professional situations and circumstances. For our discussion we will consider three basic theories that help explain both the substance and process of public policy, including systems, group or pluralism, and elitism.

Systems Theory Systems theory is one of the oldest and most reliable theories of public policy. Originally defined and applied in biology as cybernetics, it was applied to the social sciences, such as political science and public policy.[31] It is linear in its image of policy action and interaction, and because of this is probably less helpful to understanding policy reality. Experience teaches a dear lesson that the policy world is anything but linear. But the systems approach does help explain some components within the overall policy world, including environment, institutions, demands and supports, and decisions made.

The policy environment reflects the political, economic, social, cultural, legal, and even religious context in which policies are framed, adopted, implemented, and to a lesser extent evaluated (see Figure 3.1). Demands and supports represent inputs into the political system itself; that is, various inputs, such as interests of interest groups, individuals, and other organizations putting pressure upon the system to respond to a policy problem, such as abortion or the war in Syria. Second, the political system, sometimes also referred to as the black box, represents just that: the political system, which is composed of the institutions, such as constitutions, laws, rules, regulations, among others. This is the government, at whatever level the issue is at (national defense is at the national level, whereas filling potholes in a city street is at the municipal level), and it is the government's responsibility to respond to the demands and supports placed upon it by these various entities. Third, the outputs—such as the making of laws, passing of rules and regulations, issuing of executive orders, providing judicial decrees, expending money—represent official political system reaction to the demands and supports place upon it. In

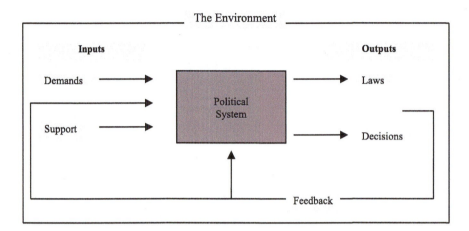

FIGURE 3.1
The Systems Model

Source: James E. Anderson, *Public Policymaking*, 6th ed. (Boston, MA: Houghton Mifflin Company, 2006), 19.

other words, the system, i.e., the government, has to respond and so the response(s) are many and varied, depending upon the institution involved, the issue at hand, and other similar factors. Fourth, there is some type of reaction or feedback by, and to, the system responses (such as protests, letter writing campaigns) by interested constituents or groups. These responses provide the needed insight and reactions to the decisions made; meaning the reaction may be supportive or the reaction may be non-supportive. For example, *Roe v. Wade* (1972) resulted in unfavorable feedback by the public to the court and Congress from the pro-life community, but supportive feedback from the pro-choice community perspective.

Group Theory Group theory or pluralist theory "states that public policy is the product of the group struggle."[32] Philosophers and social scientists, such as David Truman, have contended that pressure groups, or what the Founders called factions, have considerable influence in the policymaking or governmental process.[33] The focus is the interaction and struggle between various groups, such as between pro-life and pro-choice. The issue or central value is choosing between life and choice, requiring lawmakers and judicial referees to decide whose value set is more politically viable or (supposedly) constitutionally valid.

Elite Theory Elite theory is somewhat more controversial (and in many people's minds less directed toward pursuit of the public interest) and perhaps even less documented and accepted academically. Some scholars, such as Thomas Dye, have made a career out of defining and defending such a model. The basic argument is that, based largely upon access and use of political power, economic authority, and even legal force, elite individuals actually influence the making of policy. These elites are defined as the "few who have power versus the many who do not."[34]

Traditional and Non-traditional Actors in the Policy Environment

When we discuss policymakers (and influences) and their environments, especially as they impact policymaking in the public interests, we are talking about a version that reaches far beyond the traditional processes (i.e., constitutional and institutional). So, what is the nature of policy environments and the major traditional and non-traditional actors found in public policy in the public interests?[35]

The policy environment affects public policymaking largely through **political culture**, loosely defined as the transmission of political values, beliefs, and attitudes on what governments should do. Political culture influences policymaking by shaping political behavior. For example, the Bureau of the Budget (BOB), and later the Office of Management and Budget (OMB), played a central role in Federal Government organizational and fiscal policymaking, setting the political culture for a political economy.

Social factors have also influenced and been influenced by both national and sub-national changes and positions in public policymaking—for example, increases in educational levels of workers, continuing expansion of civil rights including affirmative action, reduction of poverty, decrease in crime, major welfare reforms, and the advent of nonprofit and faith-based organizations.

Religion plays a significant role in the formation of public policymaking.[36] Religion has always been a major force in American history and civic culture, ever since the founding period and even before, but in recent years it is receiving significant political and administrative attention. For example, many of the arguments against abortion are made in terms of Christian faith. Contemporary faith-based initiatives have taken a place in the public service. We will examine the faith-based initiatives approach in more detail in Chapter 9.

Traditional institutional policymakers—constitutionally defined policymakers —are key actors in the policy environment. The Constitution defines legislative, executive, and judicial actors by specific and general policy domains. The U.S. Congress has generally delegated-away and given policy ground to executive branch agencies and the President.[37] The President has become the center of policymaking attention and thus has a substantial impact upon the public interests.[38] And, although the judiciary received little attention in the Constitution as

---

> ### BOX 3.4 | The Rooms of Public Policy

- **Living Rooms**: where the public at large forms public opinion in front of the television, etc.
- **Boardrooms**: where corporate and market actors form public policies for their economic interests
- **Courtrooms**: where judicial actors and processes form public policies under rights and legal mandates
- **Cloakrooms**: where legislators and lobbyists form public policies into statutes and budgets

- **Oval Rooms**: where the President, governors, and executives form public policies by executive orders
- **File Rooms**: where bureaucrats form public policies within their discretion domains ◣

Source: Carl E. VanHorn, Donald D. Baumer, and William T. Gormley, Jr., *Politics & Public Policy*, 2nd ed. (Congressional Quarterly, 1992).

a policymaker, the U.S. Supreme Court has used its constitutional judicial review powers to act as the final interpreter of the meaning of the Constitution to make substantial policies in a variety of areas, e.g., *Griswold v. Connecticut* (1965), *Roe v. Wade* (1972), and *Obergefell v. Hodges* (2015). Finally, though not specified in the Constitution at all, the bureaucracy plays an essential role in the implementation and evaluation of policymaking.[39]

Non-Traditional Policymakers—non-governmental actors in policymaking processes—may include citizens on referendums, school board or city council speakers, and interest groups representing others united by common cause or interests. Their influence seems especially important at the state and local levels.[40] While political parties traditionally had little impact at the national level, at the local and state level political parties seem to have much more clout, mobilizing and influencing voters and politicians along a number of issues. Broadcast TV and digital media, newspapers, talk radio, and nonprofit organizations, including faith-based organizations,[41] have influences on public policy.

Policy Process: Focusing on the Stages or Cycle of Public Policy

So, how does public policy come to be? Illustrations of stages of public policy or the policy cycle may help to survey democratic policymaking.[42] For example, consider James Anderson's stages and policy cycle (see Figure 3.2).

1. Agenda setting is the stage where individuals and especially interest groups are working to get a substantive issue, such as civil rights violations, on the political agenda of the key policy makers.
2. Policy formulation, or policy adoption, is the second stage. This is where formal laws, such as civil rights legislation like the Civil Rights Act of 1964, and other types of executive orders (affirmative action) or judicial decisions (Brown v. Board of Education, 1954), are made regarding a specific issue.
3. Policy implementation, or the administrative or bureaucratic side of policymaking, is where the public administrators who work in agencies devoted to specific policy areas, such as the Equal Employment Opportunity Commission, make specific rules and regulations in order to put into operation the laws and decisions passed by the elected officials.
4. Policy evaluation involves research organizations, universities, think tanks, and even the implementing agencies themselves. Their job is to systematically and critically examine how well the implemented policy met its original goals and objectives.

FIGURE 3.2

Stages of Public Policy

Source: James E. Anderson, *Public Policymaking*, 6th ed. (Boston, MA: Houghton Mifflin Company, 2006), 3–5.

FIGURE 3.3
The Policy Cycle

Source: James E. Anderson, *Public Policymaking*, 6th ed. (Boston, MA: Houghton Mifflin Company, 2006), 90.

Of course, we can't forget the two things no one wants to see made: sausages and public policy! Even though actual policymaking may be more complex, the stages and policy cycle models are helpful in visualizing how public policy is made, and how to analyze administrative and policy effectiveness. We include six stages of the policy cycle, to include a more complete model of democratic policymaking (see Figure 3.3).

Stage 1 **Problem identification** entails the identification of what needs to be addressed with a public policy. A policy problem involves a clash between individuals or groups of individuals over some value in which a government entity is required to settle the dispute. For example, Howard Stern, America's infamous shock jock, disagreed with the Federal Communications Commission (FCC) over what language he used on broadcast radio. He wanted to say anything at any time, but the FCC had rules against such language. The FCC won. Stern left the public radio waves controlled by the FCC and entered into a multi-million-dollar agreement with Sirius Radio. What was the problem? One of the primary problems was public airwaves indecency, which is defined by the FCC as "language or material that, in context, depicts or describes, in terms patently offensive as measured by contemporary community standards for the broadcast medium, sexual or excretory organs or activities."[43] The FCC was responding to laws that disallowed public airwaves indecency offensive toward the public interests.

Stage 2 **Agenda setting** is the stage that shows when an issue finally makes it to the government's agenda. No political or administrative action can take place until it is on the government's agenda. How does an issue make it to the government's agenda?[44] One of the more persuasive theories for explaining agenda setting is **John Kingdon's streams metaphor**.[45] The three streams include: (1) the politics stream (i.e., political and public opinion), (2) the policy stream (i.e., possible solutions to a public problem), and (3) the problem stream (i.e., the defining attributes and characteristics of a problem and whether and how the problem is solvable—usually by public administrators). Once these streams merge, they pass through a window of opportunity, a point in time in which the effects and resources of all three streams and the presiding governmental entities come together to offer the best possible solution. For example, the 1964 Civil Rights Act came about as the result of favorable politics, such as President Johnson's intention to memorialize President Kennedy's work on civil rights.

Stage 3 **Policy formulation** is an incremental process. The U.S. Supreme Court did not simply announce one day a full and completed policy on affirmative action. Instead, it developed the nuance of affirmative action policy over decades of resolving real-life legal disputes and doing justice one case at a time. Thus, affirmative action developed by application over decades to current distinctions between quota-style affirmative action in *de jure discrimination* (explicit discriminatory policies) and non-quota-style affirmative action in *de facto discrimination* (no explicit policy, but discrimination in fact).

Stage 4 **Policy adoption** requires some action on the part of the traditional or institutional policymakers, meaning congressmen, presidents, governors, city councilmen, county managers, and other public administrators, who will translate a policy issue into a formal governmental action, such as a law, executive order, judicial decree, or administrative rule and regulation. Policymakers are usually confronted with a large number of policy options, as former President Clinton was with regard to the Don't Ask, Don't Tell policy (see Box 3.5) on homosexuals in the military: keep the policy the same, eliminate the status quo and institute any range of alternatives, or find some type of compromise. The key to the adoption stage is how the policymaker makes a decision, but the decision outcome is also of importance, particularly when the public interests are at stake.

Stage 5 **Implementation** is the crux of public policy for the public administrator, because it is here they actually put into effect or implement the law, executive order, or judicial decree. It is also the phase in which public administrators dominate, where their professional expertise and knowledge of procedures, techniques, and regulations are most needed to affect and influence the public

---

BOX 3.5 | Don't Ask, Don't Tell

In 1993, President Clinton ordered the U.S. military abandon its policy of not allowing homosexuals into the military. However, opposition came from many sectors, including the military, Republican senators and representatives, conservative interest groups, and the general public. As a compromise, President Clinton issued an executive order for the Don't Ask, Don't Tell policy. The goal of the Don't Ask, Don't Tell policy was more pragmatic than idealistic. The military would not seek to find out the sexual orientation of incoming recruits or other military personnel, but neither would military personnel or recruits reveal their sexual orientation. Don't Ask, Don't Tell officially ended in July 2011, when President Obama repealed the controversial executive order. Formulating policy in a conflicted political environment is difficult at best, and requires ample and diverse political, policy, and knowledge-based resources to bring about some semblance of success.

Source: U.S. Department of Defense Directive 1304.26 (1993–2011).

interests. According to John Kingdon, implementation requires organization, interpretation, and application of statutory, regulatory, and judicial decree.[46] Organization is the role of the administrative agencies, or bureaucracies that actually put the law, executive order or judicial decree into action. Interpretation of law requires public administrators to know the intention (or assume the intention) of the decision-making body when it framed its decision. Application of the law is the determination of rules, regulations, procedures, and processes necessary to implement public policy and is accomplished through rule-making, adjudication, and bureaucratic precedent.

Stage 6 Evaluation is where public administrators determine the effectiveness of a policy program and make recommendations for alterations to the program itself. Implementation and evaluation are linked.[47] Quite often the bureaucratic agency that implements a program, such as the Department of Education implementing the No Child Left Behind Act (NCLB), is also the same agency that will evaluate its effectiveness. More specifically, evaluation is dedicated to data collection, interpretation of results, and reporting of those results. In addition, though, evaluation is connected to the political and policy goals and objectives set forth by the original policymakers, even during the early stages of the policy formulation stage—which, of course, affects the public interests.

POLICY ANALYSIS

Policy analysis is not a stage per se in the policy process; it is a process through which public servants as observers of the policy process examine and evaluate the various alternative solutions, policies, and/or programs and offer assistance in solving a public problem. At a fundamental level, policy analysis methods are means by which public administrators exercise the ethic of citizenship, gathering up the preferences of the citizens they represent in democratic policymaking. We will highlight three points in this section: (1) we introduce basic concepts within policy analysis: basic, applied, and analysis-centered policy analysis; (2) we outline the various steps traditionally used in policy analysis—the suggested steps are broad in their application but specific enough for us to describe their importance and applicability to a specific policy area, such as immigration; and (3) we overview research strategies in policy analysis, e.g., case study, policy evaluation, and managerial analysis.

Basic policy analysis is more theoretical and original in nature; it is designed to improve or add to an existing body of knowledge. It is generally focused on original data collection methods, and consists largely of quantitative methodology. The results are usually for academics and are therefore generally displayed in academic outlets, such as journal articles or academic books. Applied policy analysis is not as theoretical or original in nature; it is a synthesis and evaluation of existing data sources. It relies on the development of sound policy arguments. It is usually, but not always, methodologically qualitative in nature, e.g., using personal observation and interview. The results are for use by government agencies, citizen groups, nonprofit organizations, and the like, and is therefore displayed in short policy papers, memos, or issue briefs (Table 3.1).

Applied policy analysis is more conducive to the work of public officials, especially public administrators, because, although it does not include a comprehensive

> **TABLE 3.1**
> **Two Kinds of Policy Analyses**
>
> | Characteristics | Basic Policy Research | Applied Policy Research |
> |---|---|---|
> | Origin of Problems | University colleagues | Governmental clients and citizens |
> | Typical Methods | Quantitative | Development of sound arguments Qualitative |
> | Type of Research | Original data collection | Synthesis and evaluation of existing data |
> | Primary Aim | Improve theory | Improve practice (policy) |
> | Communications Media | Article or book | Policy memo or issue paper (to public official; online outlet) |
> | Source of Incentives | University departments | Government agencies, citizen groups, nonprofit organizations, etc. |
>
> Source: William N. Dunn, *Introduction to Policy Analysis*, 3rd ed. (Upper Saddle River, NJ: Prentice Hall, 2004), 437.

scope and in-depth approach to the study of some type of policy problem, it does provide the public administrator with basic information and tools for understanding the problem, basic alternatives or solutions to the problem, and highlights the consequences of those alternatives for future decision making. Busy public administrators and other public officials do not have the time or inclination to read through lengthy academic pieces; they need basic facts, statement of the problem, possible solutions to the problem, and the consequences and/or implications of one possible solution over another. Thus, whether the problem is how state public educational officials are to deal with the fiscal imbalances regarding the financial needs of special education students,[48] or whether elected public officials must decide if and how to implement mandatory government provided preschool programs,[49] the need for solid, well researched, well-written, and relatively unbiased policy reports is critical to aiding them to make sound public decisions.

Another analysis style is the analysis-centered approach, focused on technical analysis rather than political or policy analysis. It is rooted in the rational theory of decision making and is generally confined to technical academic and professional areas, such as engineering, operations and systems research, and applied mathematics.[50] Most basic policy analysis studies that are theoretical follow this approach. However, many applied policy studies are analysis-centered in design, particularly micro-based policy analysis focused on the impact related to individuals, groups, and organizations rather than macro-level stakeholders, such as cities, counties, states, and regions. The analysis-centered approach is less concerned with a multi-disciplinary approach to policy analysis, and "tends to preclude or restrict concerns with political, social, and administrative aspects of public policy . . . concerns with the political feasibility of alternatives or their implications for democratic processes."[51] This approach is usually technical in nature, relying on quantitative research methods.

Steps in Doing Policy Analysis

There are a wide variety of models for describing the **steps in policy analysis**, but most share commonalities. The following steps are "common to most of the social sciences and professions, and to human problem solving generally" and sufficient for our purposes in describing the how-to of policy analysis.[52] In addition, the following steps correspond with the stages in the policy cycle discussed above. This is not coincidental, given that policy analysis is a process, too. In addition, the steps highlight the approaches discussed above: the basic, applied, and analysis-centered approaches, with basic providing the structure, and applied contributing to the political, policy, and administrative aspects. We introduce each step, briefly define it, and then provide a brief description of its characteristics and how it is understood or applied to a policy issue (see Table 3.2).

Step 1: Problem Definition (Problem Structuring)   Here the analyst must determine what the problem to be solved is. It is critical that the policy analyst correctly define the problem, collect as much information as is possible, particularly within institutional and organizational resource constraints, assess the validity and use of that information, largely by communicating with other analysts and outside organizations, and formulate a statement about the problem. Policy analysts, for example, who focus on addressing the problem of illegal immigration realize that this a large problem area and it is important to be clear just what part of this broad problem is under investigation (e.g., economics, education and social services delivery to illegal immigrants).

Step 2: Prediction of Policy Alternatives (Forecasting)   This step requires the analyst to assess or predict the possible alternatives or solutions to the stated problem. Choosing possible alternatives is largely an incremental process—meaning the analyst is determining past decisions made and building upon those successes and staying away from past failures. However, a rational process that focuses on resource allocation, such as human and financial in order to achieve the largest possible benefit, is also a possibility. For example, when assessing the problem of irregular-documented migration into the US, the analyst must look back over history and learn what worked in various states, such as Texas and Arizona, and what did not work in other states, such as New Mexico and California. Or the analyst can assess what type of impact, both negative and positive, the surge of border migration has upon state and local economies, particularly in farming, lawn care, retail, fast food, and other industries that may attract illegal and legal immigrants. Choosing and tailoring various possible solutions becomes a difficult task, and the analyst is aided by a variety of quantitative methods, such as time-series analysis, where the focus is on examining numerical data that reflects statistical time-based trends in illegal immigration, and qualitative methods, such as theoretical forecasting, that allow the analyst to map and/or model specific

TABLE 3.2

Policy Stages/Cycle and the Policy Analysis Process

Policy Information	Policy Cycle	Policy Analysis Process
Policy problem: "unrealized value or opportunity for improvement which, however, identified, may be attained through public action."	*Problem Identification* Identifying the specific problem; differentiating it from the policy issue	Defining the problem (problem structuring)
Expected Policy Outcome "probable consequence of a policy designed to solve a problem" (i.e., need information about circumstances that gave rise to the problem initially)	*Agenda Setting* (or Policy Formulation) Problems that receive serious attention of public officials	Predicting outcomes (policy forecasting)
Preferred Policy "potential solution to a problem" (i.e., obviously to select a preferred policy analyst needs information about "expected policy outcomes")	*Adoption* Development of support for a specific proposal so a policy can be legitimized or made authoritative	Prescribing various preferred policies; criteria (recommendation)
Observed Policy Outcome "past or present consequence of implementing a preferred policy" (i.e., consequences are generally not stated or known in advance, nor anticipated, making information both ex ante and ex post)	*Implementation* Application of policy by bureaucratic organization	Describing observed outcomes (monitoring)
Policy performance: "degree to which an observed policy outcome contributes to the attainment of values, goals, or objectives" (i.e., in reality, problems are rarely solved; instead they are managed)	*Evaluation* To determine whether the policy met its intended goals	Appraising the value of the observed outcomes (evaluation)

Source: William N. Dunn, *Introduction to Policy Analysis*, 3rd ed. (Upper Saddle River, NJ: Prentice Hall, 2004).

elements or trends related to border migration that might prove helpful to the policymaker when selecting policy alternatives.

Step 3: Prescribing the Best Policy Alternative (Recommendation)   This third step details the possible alternatives that are *best* able to solve the policy problem. Here the analyst must examine alternatives that are actionable, prospective, value-dependent, and ethically complex.[53] First, how realistic or actionable is the policy alternative? For example, if the United States wishes to stop or slow down the initial flow of border migrants from physically crossing into the US, the question arises: Is President Trump's proposed construction of an actual 12-foot-high 3,000-mile fence the best alternative—at about $25 million per mile? Or is the best alternative, proposed by U.S. Representative Will Hurd (R-TX) and others, for a "Smart-Wall" composed of many actual 12-foot walls and fences, as well as radar, lidar (light-detecting radar), sensors, drones, and cameras—at about $0.5 million per mile?[54] Second, prescriptive claims are prospective; that is, they occur *before* the time any policy action is taken. The policy analyst prescribes possible actions before they actually are selected. Third, the policy analyst does not eliminate the need for group, individual, or even societal values when prescribing possible policy claims, such as considering how a 12-foot-high 2,000-mile fence across multiple borders and property lines be considered by a variety of stakeholders. And fourth, analysts must examine the ethical component of any prescriptive claim, such as the ethical impact of turning away U.S. border migrants and forcing them to return to less than desirable economic, social, and living conditions.

Step 4: Describing the Prescribed Alternative (Monitoring)   The fourth step in the policy analytic process is describing the conditions of the selected solution or "monitoring policy actions after they have occurred."[55] Monitoring is the step that produces information about the causes and consequences of various public policies. Monitoring takes different forms, such as auditing and accounting, but the key component of this step is information gathering at various points in time and is of considerable cost to governments. The primary focus of this stage is to monitor both the **policy outputs**, or the measurable part of the policy solution (i.e., what is the cost of building material for the 12-foot-high, 2,000-mile U.S. border fence), and the **policy outcomes**, or the changes in behavior or attitude toward the policy solution (i.e. assessing public reaction to the fence itself).[56] Monitoring depends upon thorough review of facts, statistics, trends, and other measurable and quantifiable indices.

Step 5: Appraising the Worth of Selected Policy Alternative (Evaluation)   The fifth stage is assessment of the value of the policy solution chosen. If, for example, we are to examine the worth (or value)—which by the way necessarily implies the ethics of a decision, discussed above, of raising a 12-foot-high, 2,000-mile-long fence along our southwestern border with Mexico, then the natural question is: Did this solution work? Whereas the monitoring stage audited and accounted for changes in the recently implemented decision to erect the fence—appraising its action status, so to speak—the evaluation stage now tries to determine whether or not the original goal of restricting illegal immigration was met. How was it met? What are the results, both in terms of policy performance and value (ethical) achievement? To answer these questions the policy analyst must do two things: establish a policy analysis research design and conduct specific types of assessments. Let's examine three common research design approaches to policy analysis, including the case study, program evaluation (including community survey), and managerial analysis. There may be overlap in the application of these research designs, with adoption of all in many policy analysis research designs.

Case Study Method

The **case study method** is the most commonly applied policy analysis research design in public administration, both in the real-world and in academia. Noted studies of administrative organizations, processes, and persons have featured the organizational behavior case study method and demonstrate its empirical utility in the study of contemporary phenomena in a real-life context. Other case studies focus on case notes or legal dispute processing by courts, public administrators, and legal professionals. These and other successful applications of the case study method demonstrate its potential for illumination and not simply description: "the essence of a case study, the central tendency among all types of case study, is that it tries to illuminate a decision or set of decisions: why they were taken, how they were implemented, and with what result."[57] The case study method as applied in public administration is similar to clinical studies in medicine and psychology. Both study the subject as embedded in and relative to their particular personal, social, intellectual, and historical conditions. Furthermore, both applications feature quantitative and qualitative evidence gathered about the subject in a variety of data collection efforts. Finally, both applications require the researcher to reconstruct and interpret this evidence in a systematic presentation about the subject that is true to life.

Case studies can serve a variety of functions: (1) to generate hypotheses; (2) to test a theory; or (3) to generalize about behavior. Heuristic case studies are used to explore theoretical solutions to a problem and to generate hypotheses that could be tested by other methods. Hypotheses from this grounded theory may be tested by quantitative or qualitative methods. Case studies are also used to test theory; to verify or disprove prior logico-deductive theory. For example, Graham Allison (1940–) illuminated the decisions made in the Cuban Missile Crisis by matching actual decision-making behavior patterns with one of three different organization theory patterns.[58] Finally, case studies can be nomothetic in generalizing to behavior in other cases. This study of either comparable cases or the hard case may enable researchers to generalize to similar or deviant behavior.

Although the case study method is often criticized as a weaker sibling among empirical research methods, many criticisms stem from a confusion of the case study method with teaching tools and other research strategies. The case study as a teaching tool does not render empirically generalizable explanations. Nor is it subject to the same level of rigorous analysis or comprehensiveness as in research. Criticisms of the case study method also confuse that research approach with ethnographies and qualitative methods. These methods limit empirical research to certain kinds of data—case studies can and do include quantitative collection and analysis.

The case study method is more importantly criticized as not suitably rigorous, generalizable, or quick and easy. Do case studies suffer from a lack of rigor? Yes, when researcher bias and inaccuracies creep into the retrospective reports. But this potential for bias exists in many research designs, e.g., survey construction and experimental designs can be undermined by subjective bias that distorts the researcher's findings. The answer is not to eliminate all of these methods, but to incorporate measures to ensure that the approach is systematic and rigorous.

Do case studies lack generalizability? The non-comparable or atypical case obviously may not be generalizable to theoretical propositions, whether case study, survey, or experiment. But case studies, like experiments, may be generalizable to theoretical propositions, if not populations or universes. A case study may verify or disprove a theory in specific contexts, or it may be used to generate grounded theory to be tested against a larger population for greater generalizability.

Are case studies expensive and difficult? Perhaps the bottom-line criticism of the case study method is simply that it is costly. It takes considerable ingenuity and sometimes luck to gain access to the necessary archives and documents, as well as time to read and scrutinize the evidence. However, it is important to note that the case study method does not require massive archives or participant observations per se. Other data collection methods can provide sufficient information. Use of these alternative methods will not necessarily make the case study easier, but time and cost may be cut.

Program Evaluation

Program evaluation is a rather recent approach to managing social programs, especially after the Great Society Programs of the 1960s under Presidents Kennedy and Johnson. It involves collection of qualitative and quantitative empirical data, rigorous analysis, and provides a systematic understanding and assessment of social programs to determine need, process, and results. Typically the program evaluator(s) work closely with stakeholders and policymakers to produce and analyze the result. Both intended and unintended outcomes are relevant for evaluation. Program evaluation provides assessment of specific programs using one or more of the following criteria: evaluation of need, evaluation of process, and/or evaluation of results.

Evaluation of Need   The purpose of the **needs assessment** is to develop accurate estimates of the amount, distribution, and nature of a given problem. Public concerns or needs are often identified by survey methods, i.e., a **community survey** of all or a representative sample of the public with fixed-response or open-ended questions given by social media, email, internet websites, mailings, in-person interviews, and other methods. Once a public concern or problem is identified, it often presents a complexity of related concerns. The public seeks maximum return on its investment and public administrators are often called upon to evaluate the amount, distribution, and nature of a problem to assess the effective or efficient approach to mediate a problem. Here you will be responsible to develop and implement a method to collect, collate, and assess specific data on the problem in question to help program planners make specific choices in the determination of the appropriate design and mix of program interventions.

Evaluation of Process   The purpose of the **process evaluation** is to monitor a program to assess its implementation, both as a process and in achieving results. A primary concern of policymakers is that established programs are properly implemented as intended. Even the most well-designed program, if not properly implemented, will not have positive effects on the targeted population. On the other hand, even well-intended individual program administrators may end up with a poorly designed program in need of changes to assure satisfactory results. The purpose of process evaluation is generally to develop and implement a method to help program managers and/or external stakeholders assess program coverage of target populations, program coherence, and fiscal accountability.

Evaluation of Results   The purpose of the **outcome evaluation** is to assess the overall effectiveness of a program in reaching its stated goals and objectives. From time to time during the lifecycle of a program, a manager or other stakeholders may wish to have an assessment of program accomplishments. This can be on an ad hoc basis or pre-designed by self-planned change or the mandates of a funding source. The purpose of outcome evaluation is to develop and implement a method to assess program outcomes (intended or unintended) for management or specific stakeholders. Key to this type of evaluation will be to establish a logic model as a means to guide the assessment of program outcomes.

Program evaluation studies are of two kinds: quantitative and qualitative. Quantitative policy evaluation studies include the use of many of the same techniques and methodologies used at the other stages, including cost-benefit analysis, cost-effectiveness analysis, time-series and regression analysis, and many others. Each is designed, as we determined, to quantitatively measure whether or not various numerical and statistical changes occurred, and if so to what degree these changes merited positive or negative association with the desired goals. Qualitative policy evaluation studies are most pertinent and useful for the applied researcher—and the type of report that most public administrator and other policymakers will most likely refer to. These include on-site and indirect observation, personal interviewing, archival research, and extensive reading.[59] The policy evaluator takes a much more hands-on approach than is used in most quantitative techniques. They are interested in personal observations by the participants involved in the policy decision—from border patrol agents to state governors to Homeland Security agents to, perhaps, the U.S. border migrants themselves. What is the impact of the implemented policy? Sometimes simply running regression analysis does not capture the most complete picture of the policy itself and the influence it has or does not have on the policy problem.

Program evaluation studies often include experimental and quasi-experimental research designs. Experimental research designs are most noted for their use in laboratory sciences, such as chemistry, physics, and biological sciences. They are also widely used in psychology and education. The key characteristics of an experimental design include: (1) control over the experimental treatment (i.e., stimuli) to the subject; (2) use of control versus experimental groups; and (3) random assignment of subjects to either the control or experimental groups. Experimental research designs work exceptionally well for controlled environments, such as the inside of a Petri dish or test tube, but they are not extremely reliable for use in a political environment—thus the need for something less rigid, but still reliable.[60]

Quasi-experimental research designs are the ticket for policy analysts. Why? Because they provide the conceptual framework of an experimental design but are adaptable to the highly charged political environment of the policy world. The use of quasi-experiments extends back to the 1930s. Since then, quasi-experiments have been used in a number of policy areas, including social welfare policy, micro- and macro-economic policy, highway safety, and a number of other areas. The methodological key to both experimental and quasi-experimental designs is **internal validity**: the greater the internal validity, the more confident the policy analyst is that the policy outputs are indeed the result of the policy inputs. Reducing the threats to internal validity, such as time-series instability (i.e. the threat of random error throwing off potential policy outcomes) or instrumentation (i.e. when members of a tested group know they are being tested or react differently because they know they are being tested).[61]

BOX 3.6 | Program Evaluation and the No Child Left Behind (NCLB) Act

Should we do evaluation of the evaluators themselves? Each has a political axe to grind. For example, the Bush administration wanted to see the NCLB succeed and their evaluation may not have been as unbiased and complete as possible. On the other hand, outside policy evaluating agencies, even though they purport to be unbiased and nonpartisan, may very well elicit ideological bias toward or against the program under review. For example, the liberal-leaning Brookings Institution was somewhat biased against the NCLB Act and its purported goal of instituting accountability standards for students, teachers, administrators, and teachers' unions. On the other hand, more conservative-leaning think tanks, such as the American Enterprise Institute and libertarian Cato Institute, were somewhat more positive toward the NCLB Act, because it provided incentives, economic and otherwise, for all parties involved to reach learning goals. Do policy evaluations merely reflect evaluator biases? ▸

In conducting a program evaluation, the program evaluator must first set up a program evaluation design using experimental, quasi-experimental, and/or other research designs. In research design, the policy analyst is concerned with establishing validity, both internal and external.[62] Internal validity seeks to determine whether what was intended to be measured was in fact measured. If the analyst wanted to determine whether or not the presence of the wall was significant in deterring would-be illegal immigrants from crossing the border, then it would be necessary to develop a research design that met that qualification. **External validity**, however, reaches beyond the immediate policy question and asks whether or not it is applicable to broader and more general situations and circumstances. In other words, does this particular study have merit or worth beyond the current situation? If so, then we contend it is externally valid.

Managerial Analysis

A **managerial analysis** provides an in-depth assessment of organizational-level strengths and weaknesses. Two types of managerial analysis are distinguished: (1) a general managerial analysis, with a general overview of multiple organizational functions and the interrelations between them; or (2) in-depth managerial analysis, focused on one organizational function. The purpose of the managerial policy analysis is to assess the functioning of managerial or organizational-level phenomena as applied to the policy process of the unit. It is essential that the administrative analysis be grounded in the public administration literature. This is commonly employed by management consultants who are brought in from the outside to study, assess, and make recommendations to improve the operation of an administrative unit. The managerial analysis systematically considers administrative functions in one or more of the following autonomous areas: organizational formal structure, organizational culture, budgeting and finance, personnel and human resources development, and planning and strategic design. While there is no set range for the size and scope of the organization, it must be sufficiently large to provide autonomous operations of the above areas.

Managerial analysis is most often the focus of policy analysis when the key conflict, problem, or situation is of an organizational nature. There does not need to be a crisis, but there must be an organizational lesson to be learned in the analysis. Often these analyses are part of an organizational development approach (see Chapter 6) to help improve decision making in the unit.

Accountability and Responsibility

So, we've overviewed the nature of public policy, policy processes and institutions, and the utility perspective of democratic policymaking. But the real ethical concerns over public policy focus on *how* to make public servants accountable to the utilitarian processes of democratic policymaking—not just the substantive policies themselves, but the values of public policy, such as the ethics of citizenship for public administrators, who should recognize what input on public policy, what degree of input and specificity should be detailed and proscribed, how policies should be implemented and by whom, and what audit and evaluation should be, and who should do it and how. At least two types of accountability emerge. The first refers to hierarchical linkages and accountability in the organization to ensure that policies are fulfilled, while the second focuses primarily upon individual self-initiative and responsibility to fulfill democratic policymaking.[63] Both concepts of accountability and responsibility are related.

Accountability may be defined as "those methods and relationships that determine which expectations will be reflected in the work of public administration."[64] This definition is vague, to say the least. Others argue that "the premise of bureaucratic accountability holds that public administrators in a democracy are safely constrained by a welter of restraints from making decisions and policies that are anti-democratic, unfair, or unethical."[65] Others claim that accountability is a "primary concept in public sector performance measurement and performance management reforms."[66] For example, the Administration on Aging, which is located in the Department of Health and Human Services, is approximately 67 percent accountable through a Program Assessment Rating Tool (PART), a methodological tool for empirically measuring agency accountability found in the 1993 Government Performance and Results Act. Bureaucratic accountability—keeping administrators duty-bound—is a critical task of government. How is accountability accomplished? How is it in the public interests?

How do we ensure that public administrators actually understand and act in the public interests? In their 2004 book *Unmasking Administrative Evil*, Guy Adams and Danny Balfour posit that both externally enforced professional standards and individual conscience must be included in any framework for administrative ethics—and to avoid administrative evil.[67] They revisit a classic debate within public administration on responsibility versus accountability between **Carl Friedrich (1901–1984)** and **Herman Finer (1898–1969)** in the early 1940s. Carl Friedrich, a University of Heidelberg PhD and professor of political science at Harvard, argued that **internal controls** of individual professional **responsibility** would ensure compliance of public administrative behavior with the public interests.[68] Herman Finer, a PhD from the London School of Economics and also professor of political science at the University of Chicago, argued that only the **external control** of administrators and **accountability** to political superiors could ensure compliance with the public interests.[69] So, which would you prefer: external controls of accountability or internal controls of responsibility?

Carl Friedrich argued that bureaucratic control is best achieved through enhanced means of administrative professional responsibility in which all bureaucrats would achieve high levels of professional expertise and technical knowledge to self-supervise their work in a professional manner—internal controls. Herman Finer, on the other hand, was more dubious of such a self-directing system of professional codes and mores, and argued that bureaucrats must be made accountable, and this could only be attained through external political will-to-power means—external controls. Bureaucrats must be made to answer to their political overseers.[70] In other words, bureaucrats should not be allowed to exercise greater amounts of administrative discretion than is profitable or acceptable in a pluralistic democracy. In the history since this debate, some contend that Friedrich won the debate because empirical studies by political scientists posit that the high levels of discretion in the modern bureaucratic state better match Friedrich's position. But other scholars dispute this and urge that the administrative discretion of bureaucrats should be limited and made directly accountable to external political controls. Which of these two positions—internal and external controls—do you believe best promotes the public interests in democratic policymaking?

Thus, accountability and responsibility focus on a public servant's stewardship or entrusted relationship with the public, whether this is carried out by strict oversight supervision—external controls—or left to the professional socialization and individual conscience—internal controls. Many of the Founders of the U.S. Constitution did not consider necessary a discussion of professional ethics in federal public service. Instead, they established a government of checks and balances, separation of powers, and federalism, all designed to prevent illegal and unethical

---

BOX 3.7 | Carl J. Friedrich (1901–1984)

Carl Joachim Friedrich was a political scientist, political advisor, and educator. For many years he was the Eaton Professor of the Science of Government at Harvard. He was educated at the Universities of Marburg, Frankfurt, and Vienna, and eventually received his doctorate in history and economics from the University of Heidelberg in 1930. While studying in America, he met and later married Lenore Pelham in 1924, and in 1926 was appointed as lecturer at Harvard University, later as professor in 1936, until retiring in 1971—also visiting the University of Heidelberg and other universities. His main areas of interest before World War II were the history of modern political thought, problems of leadership and bureaucracy in government, and public administration, and his early works included *Responsible Bureaucracy* (1932) and *Constitutional Government and Politics* (1937). He also engaged in advisory work, e.g., assisted in reconstruction of post-World War II Germany, served as constitutional advisor to Puerto Rico and U.S. Virgin Islands, and in the European Ad Hoc Assembly. He was American Political Science Association President in 1962, and a member of the American Society for Public Administration. ◣

Source: Harvard University Library, "Biographical Note," retrieved from http://oasis.lib.harvard.edu/oasis/deliver/1hua27003

actions by the close control of public servants by citizens, legislators, executive officers, judges, and other institutional participants. For example, James Madison, in *The Federalist Papers # 51* (1788), argued for governance with a division of political powers and checks and balances between the various executive, legislative, and judicial powers. Over the centuries, additional checks and balances have emerged as external controls of public servants with the rise of interest groups, political parties, and electioneering. Further, internal checks and balances were developed through professionalization and higher education of public servants with the merit system. And expansion of bureaucracy with additional hierarchy seems to deliver accountability with more external oversight control, as well as professional ethics codes.[71] How may accountability and responsibility—external and internal controls—be applied to the variety of roles for policy analysts?

There are at least six patterns or **roles of policy analysts,** including rationalism, pragmatism, protectionism, transferalism, brokerism, and egoism. Each policy analyst role is founded upon a different set of underlying assumptions of ethics and human nature, various approaches to **accountability** or responsibility controls, analysis activities, and criticisms or problems which may emerge

BOX 3.8 | Herman Finer (1898–1969)

Herman Finer (1898–1969) was born in Hertza, Romania, the eldest son to Max Finer (1966/7–1945) and Fanny Weiner (1872/3–1945). His parents were Jewish and immigrated from Romania to England before WWII and engaged in commerce as market traders and as owners of a drapery shop in London. His parents were both killed at their drapery shop in Chapel Street market, Islington, on January 1945 by a Nazi V-2 rocket. Herman studied at Hugh Myddleton School (1910–13), City of London College (1913–16), and took his degrees at London School Economics, including Bachelor of Science (1919), Master of Science (1922), and Doctor of Science (D.Sci., 1924). At London School of Economics he joined their Fabian Society, known for advancing democratic socialism by gradualist reform and not revolution. He was a Lecturer and Reader in public administration at the London School of Economics and University of London from 1920–1942, and special consultant on Post War Reconstruction to the British International Labor Organisation from 1942–1944. He also served in the US during this time as Director of research into administration at the Tennessee Valley Authority during 1937–1938. After WWII, Finer immigrated to the US as Research professor at Yale University Institute of International Studies in 1943, and as Visiting Professor at Harvard University from 1944–1946, where he first met Carl Friedrich. He was Professor in the Department of Political Science at the University of Chicago from 1946 until his death in 1969, and also served as Director of the Kellogg Nursing Research project, 1951. He had married Sophie Paul in 1926, and his daughter, Cherry Paulette, came to the US in 1944 and naturalized in 1951. Herman Finer was the eldest brother of Samuel Edward Finer, who was a professor at Oxford University and instrumental in advancing political science as an academic discipline. Herman Finer was a member of the American Society for Public Administration and American Political Science Association. ◣

Source: "Herman Finer," retrieved from https://prabook. com/web/herman.finer/1086137 in democratic policymaking.[72] Which policy analyst role do you believe is most congruent with utilitarian democratic policymaking and our dominant ethic of citizenship for public administrators? (See Table 3.3.)

Rationalism is an ancient perspective that policy bureaucrats should simply obey the dictates of democratic policymaking and mechanically follow the commands

TABLE 3.3			
Policy Analysts' Roles/Assumptions, Accountability/Responsibility, Actions, and Criticisms			
Roles and Ethical Assumptions	**Accountability/ Responsibility**	**Actions of Analysts**	**Criticisms**
Rationalism: bureaucrats obey and follow the directives of politicians (e.g., Taylor)	Policies are rationally obeyed; Hume, Locke, Weber, Simon; rational obedience to policy	As obedient conduits of public will; positivist and objective policy	Cold-blooded? Value of life or intangibles?
Pragmatism: policy experts are on tap to solve problems determined by the public; "if if works, do it" (e.g., Dewey)	Policy are general mandate to fix public problems, with the discretion to make it so; not philosopher-guardians	As problem-solvers with discretion to fix general mandates as public dictates	Blind leading the blind? How do we pretend all are experts
Protectionism: philosopher king bureaucrats determine and administer all policy; sometimes just stern guardians (e.g., Banfield)	Policies are protective of the people from themselves and each other; the average person isn't capable of knowing what to do, only the experts	As supreme policy experts who know what is best for the public; administrators are expert-trained	Do philosopher kings know all? Isn't this really just conceit?
Transferalism: take from Transferalism: take from the have-nots (e.g., the New Public Administration)	Policies exist to redistribute from the rich to the poor; it doesn't really hurt the rich anyway	As channels to redistribute wealth from the rich to the poor	Isn't the public accountability more than just redistribution?
Brokerism: pluralism and interest group liberalism in aggregating private interests (e.g., Lowi, 1969; Sorauf, 1957)	Policies precisely reflect the inputs of interest groups and aggregation of preferences in the policy process	As promoters of inputs from interest groups and participation in the policy process	Is this just the invisible-hand myth to justify the status quo?
Egoism: bureaucrats are only out for themselves at all times; self-interest (e.g., Downs, 1967)	Policies merely reflect the personal preferences or whims of bureaucrats and will to power	As self-promoters of their careers and personal survival	Isn't public accountability more than self-interest?

Source: adapted form Barry Bozeman, *Policy Analysis and Public Administration* (Belmont, CA: Wadsworth, 1979), 134.

of policymakers. For example, Frederick Taylor assumes that workers would simply follow the commands of their employers as acting within the best interests of the organization, the workers, and society at large—such as efficiency changes in shoveling coal ordered by the time-and-motion managerial consultant for Big Dumb Schmidt.[73] Rationalism in public policy has a long historical basis within Modernism, since the 1500s Renaissance, positing that all persons are rational creatures and can be relied upon for obedience to policy mandates. The accountability role of the manager or policy analyst in public policy is to be a conduit of the public will, in positivist accordance with the expressed desires of the public. The criticisms of rationalism have to do with the unrealistic cold-blooded, mechanical nature of obedience and conduit that does not seem true to life. Does any manager or worker really follow and obey so completely? And don't other values trump such obedience, such as the value of life or intangibles such as love, justice, and aesthetics?

Pragmatism is said to be the American contribution to the literature on public policy, with a unique perspective on public policy as defining problems, and policy analysis as fixing or making policies work. Thus, with the pragmatic perspective, policymakers simply provide general mandates to fix public problems, giving policy bureaucrats with expertise the discretionary authority to solve these problems as listed. For example, American philosopher John Dewey summed it up with the short maxim, "If it works, do it."[74] To be sure, pragmatism does *not* grant to expert-policy-bureaucrats the discretion to act as some sort of philosopher-king in doing whatever they wish. But, rather, managers act as problem-solvers with limited discretion to solve general problems as stated by policymakers. Managers are firefighters—putting out fires, but not generally running the city. The criticisms of pragmatism focus on a skepticism about the expert policy bureaucrats: do they really know what to do any better than the general public? Are they just the blind leading the blind?

Protectionism is a name given the accountability perspective of the philosopher-king since the time of Plato and Aristotle in the 4th century BCE. In this perspective, the manager is the supreme policy expert who determines and administers all policy, rather than the public or its representatives. It is based on an empirical skepticism that the average person simply isn't capable of knowing what is best.[75] Of course, the critique is whether any philosopher-king can actually have such a capacity of knowledge and whether this is simply a type of conceit.

Transferalism is the accountability perspective focused on the redistribution of wealth from the haves to the have-nots as a type of social justice. For example, the New Public Administration of the 1960s was focused on the social justice of redistribution of power and wealth within American public administration.[76] From this perspective, public policy exists as a mandate for the redistribution of wealth and power from the rich to the poor, and public policy analysts and managers exist to serve as channel for this redistribution. Critics question whether accountability is more than merely redistributing wealth.

Brokerism as the accountability perspective focused on the pluralism of politics and interest group liberalism as a means of aggregating private interests and desires of individuals in a society. Public Policy is merely a function of the inputs of interest groups and the aggregation of individual preferences—policy analysts and managers as promoters of this interest group process to more fully aggregate all private interests. Critics question whether this is simply a justification of the status quo by using the invisible hand of the interest group process to justify the result of winner-takes-all, and a pattern of losses to minorities that may belie arbitrary discrimination based on race, gender, or other.[77]

Egoism is the cynical accountability perspective that public policy bureaucrats are only out for themselves and, thus, are not really accountable to anyone except themselves. The content of public policy that is implemented consists of merely the personal desires and whims of individual bureaucrats, who act as self-promoters of their career and survival.[78] Of course, the critique of egoism in accountability is found earlier in this chapter, with empirical questions on whether people always act in their own self-interests at all—or even if they are truly capable of such egoism.

ETHICS CASE STUDY | Voting, Hybrids, and the Ethics of Citizenship

Our ethics case study is a case note, as lawyers call it. Case notes follow a lawsuit in its origins, processes, dispute resolution through appeal, aftermath, and implications. Case notes focus on landmark judicial decisions of greater impact by the U.S. Supreme Court as the highest judicial authority. Our case note focuses on the judicial notice of **hybrid organizations**, or quasi-governmental organizations that increasingly administer governmental functions and are funded with public monies, such as utility boards, oversight commissions, nonprofits, and religious initiatives. In *Northwest Austin Municipal Util. Dist. No. One v. Holder* (2009), the Supreme Court ruled that a hybrid utility organization in Austin, Texas, may bail out on the Voting Rights Act of 1965 requirements for federal preclearance of their changes in local election procedures. The 8–1 decision featured a calculation of benefits-costs, and ruled to continue the duty of federal approval preclearance of all **voting** procedure changes in jurisdictions with a history of voting discrimination (nine states and portions of others). In so doing, the Court gave **judicial notice** of (i.e., officially recognized) the legitimacy and power of hybrid organizations as local political subdivisions of the states, e.g., entitlement to the same bail-outs and other voter practices as county and parish local governments. *NAMUDNO v. Holder* (2009) also questioned the continuing constitutionality of Section 5 of the Voting Rights Act of 1965, but left this issue undecided to this day.

Hybrid organizations form what scholars refer to as quasi-governments. Similarly, the United Kingdom refers to such as "quangos," or quasi-autonomous non-governmental organizations.[79] These bureaucratic creatures are characterized by both public and private features and are a growing part of the governing structure in many democracies today, e.g., US, UK, The Netherlands, Wales, Ireland, Sweden, and Germany.[80] Hybrids range from the international World Intellectual Property Organization, to national (Fannie

(*continued*)

ETHICS CASE STUDY | *Continued*

Mae and Freddie Mac), to research developments, and to thousands of local fire and water districts, utility districts, airports, and electoral districts.[81]

Northwest Austin Municipal Utility District Number One (NAMUDNO) is a hybrid-private utility district with an elected board that sought bail-out on federal preclearance requirements to change its election site. Even though the district didn't register voters in Travis County, Texas, and had no record of voter discrimination, NAMUDNO was responsible for its own elections and for regular public elections in Travis County. The district was considered a political subdivision and so believed it was eligible to apply for bail-out on preclearance requirements, since there was no historical evidence of voter discrimination.

The background origins of the case is found in the 1870 Fifteenth (15th) Amendment, in which the right to vote could not be "denied or abridged" by the national or state governments based on "race, color, or previous condition of servitude." By the 1890s, however, state laws sought to nullify the voting rights of minorities with poll taxes or tests for literacy, morality, and education. Ninety-five years after ratification of the 15th Amendment, President Lyndon B. Johnson signed into law the Voting Rights Act of 1965 to guarantee the right to vote for minorities. The statute applied to covered jurisdictions which had a test or device in place in 1964 that denied the right to vote to minorities (e.g., poll tax). Initially, covered jurisdictions included Alabama, Georgia, Louisiana, Mississippi, 39 of North Carolina's 100 counties, South Carolina, Virginia, and one county in Arizona. Congress amended the Act in 1975 and brought in new minorities (i.e., Native Americans, Asian Americans, Native Alaskans, and Hispanics) and new covered jurisdictions, i.e., all of Texas, Alaska, Arizona, and various counties in California, Colorado, New York, North Carolina, South Dakota, and two townships in Michigan.[82]

Section 5 of the Voting Rights Act was a temporary five-year restraint against covered jurisdictions from making any changes in their voting systems without preclearance. The covered jurisdiction states and their political subdivisions could apply to either the U.S. Attorney General or the U.S. District Court for the District of Columbia to preclear these changes in voting. Congress has extended Section 5 of the Voting Rights Act in 1970 for five years, in 1975 for seven years, in 1982 for 25 years, and in 2006 for 25 more years. In their 1982 and 2006 extensions, Congress specifically allowed the states and their political subdivisions the right to bail out upon proof that they had not actually engaged in discrimination and had worked to end any past discrimination. Many counties and cities have bailed out successfully. The U.S. Supreme Court has upheld the constitutionality of the Voting Rights Act and its extensions by Congress in other cases, including *South Carolina v. Katzenbach* (1966), *Georgia v. US* (1973), *City of Rome v. US* (1980), and *Lopez v. Monterey County* (1999).

The National Association for the Advancement of Colored People (NAACP) and other civil rights interest groups claimed the Voting Rights

Act is the most successful civil rights legislation in history. [83] However, many conservatives believe in removing Section 5 as a cause, faulting the statute for deep intrusion into the sovereign powers of the states and federalism violations. Anthony A. Peacock labeled the Voting Rights Act a "draconian" measure that "effectively put states into 'administrative receivership,' undermining principles of federalism at their most fundamental level."[84] Other scholars consider such claims to be some sort of political identity chest-beating, as "federalism is no longer an operative principle in the United States."[85] While issues of federalism and the constitutionality of Section 5 preclearance requirements were argued in *NAMUDNO v. Holder* (2009), the Court exercised its constitutional avoidance and made no decision on these issues; it left that question for another day. Instead, the decision in *NAMUDNO v. Holder* (2009) was based on case facts and a technical reading of the statute. Does the Voting Rights Act permit hybrid organizations like NAMUDNO to seek bail-out?

The Dispute

NAMUDNO was created in 1987 to serve about 3,500 residents in a portion of Travis County, Texas, and deliver city services such as water, sewer, trash collection, streetlights, parks, pools, and to enforce violations of deed restrictions. It's operated by a private corporation, Crossroads Utility Services Company; it's a hybrid organization with both government and private sector legal characteristics; it's governed by a five-member-board elected to staggered terms of four years who set property tax rates, utility rates, enforce deed restrictions, and make district budget decisions. Even though NAMUDNO is legally responsible for its own elections, it does not register voters. This wealthy, mostly white, newer suburban district had no history of racial discrimination, but was subject to the Voting Rights Act because it's located in Texas—a covered jurisdiction. NAMUDNO sought to move board member elections from private homes and garages to a public location (a local elementary school) to go with the county elections. Ten days after former President George W. Bush signed into law the extension of the Voting Rights Act on July 27, 2006, NAMUDNO filed this lawsuit against the U.S. Attorney General at the District Court, asking to bail out from Section 5 preclearance requirements for these election changes. In its briefs, NAMUDNO stated it had never engaged in voter discrimination, had never been sued in an election case, and had the approval of the U.S. Department of Justice for a bail-out from preclearance requirements of Section 5 of the Voting Rights Act. In addition, NAMUDNO argued that Section 5 was an unconstitutional violation of federalism.

The U.S. District Court decision in *Northwest Austin Municipal Utility District No. One v. Mukasey* (08–322) 573 F. Supp. 2d 221 (DDC 2008) decided against the local utility hybrid organization on both arguments.[86] First, this special three-judge district court interpreted the statute narrowly. It ruled that bail-out from preclearance may be granted only to a state or

(continued)

ETHICS CASE STUDY | *Continued*

political subdivision. NAMUDNO was not a political subdivision, because it was not identified among counties, parishes, and voter-registering sub-units as defined by the state of Texas. Second, extension of Section 5 for 25 years by Congress (and signed by the President) was constitutional because "Congress . . . rationally concluded that extending [section] 5 was necessary to protect minorities from continued racial discrimination in voting."

The case went directly from the three-judge US District Court to the U.S. Supreme Court by special statutory jurisdiction under the Voting Rights Act. Appeals briefs were filed as jurisdictional statements (not *certiorari* discretionary hearing); a dismissal could only be made summarily and without comment by a majority vote of five of the nine justices. Thus, legal briefs were filed by the litigants, as well as interest groups as *amicus curiae* (friends of the Court). A total of 25 *amicus* briefs were filed, representing over 100 interested individuals, organizations, legal foundations, members of Congress, and states and other interest groups such as the Texas NAACP and People for the American Way. During this process, former President Barack Obama was elected and NAMUDNO's reply brief stressed this point to argue that the Voting Rights Act was no longer needed: "The America that has elected Barack Obama as the first African-American president is far different than when Section 5 was first enacted in 1965 . . . Congress cannot distort the federalist structure by wielding the biggest stick at its disposal." Opposing, the U.S. Solicitor General and other *amicus* briefs argued that Congress had collected extensive evidence showing that minority voters continued to face discrimination and Section 5 remained an effective means to remedy this problem. Oral arguments were scheduled on the last day of the court's term, April 21, 2009, and debated contrasting moral principles (e.g., right to vote) against benefits-cost (e.g. impact).

Decision

The Court's decision was announced June 22, 2009, with an 8–1 vote to exercise constitutional avoidance to not decide the constitutionality of Section 5, and a unanimous vote to broaden the concept of political subdivisions to include hybrids like NAMUDNO that may seek bail-out from preclearance provisions of Section 5.[87] The official Opinion of the Court (majority opinion) in *NAMUDNO v. Holder* (2009) was authored by Chief Justice John Roberts and joined by all other justices, enlarging the concept of political subdivisions. The Opinion of the Court begins with discussion of the historic accomplishments of the Voting Rights Act, yet "intrusion into areas of state and local responsibility that is otherwise unfamiliar to our federal system." Using the doctrine of constitutional avoidance, Roberts and the majority reasoned that they should defer to the Congress on the constitutionality of Section 5 of the Voting Rights Act, because Congress had compiled a sizable record documenting continuing racial discrimination in voting and that Section 5 deterred any discriminatory changes. Roberts defined the doctrine of constitutional avoidance by reference to Alexander Hamilton's *The Federalist No. 78*, by which "normally the Court will not decide a constitutional question if there is some other ground upon which to dispose of the case." Much of the opinion of the Court is technical statutory interpretation to broaden the concept of political subdivision in Section 5 of the Voting Rights Act to include hybrid organizations like NAMUDNO and judicial notice of the legitimacy of hybrid organizations. Section 5 seems to define the political subdivision of a state as one that "conducts registration for voting." But the majority reasoned that once a state has been designated as one that "conducts registration for voting," then that language has no further "operative significance" in determining the reach of Section 5 to other political subdivisions (whether they register voters or not). Though admittedly interpretive, to read the statute otherwise would render it a nullity, thus Chief Justice Roberts and the majority take this broad reading of Section 5. Justice Clarence Thomas filed a separate opinion dissenting in part and concurring in part. Thomas agreed with the majority's reading of Section 5 and a broad meaning of the concept of political subdivision of a state to include hybrid organizations like NAMUDNO. However, he disagreed passionately about the use of constitutional avoidance and decried the intrusion of Section 5 of the Voting Rights Act into the sovereignty of state power and the unconstitutional federalism violations.

When the Court's decision was announced, both sides declared a moral, if not a political, victory. NAMUDNO claimed a "complete victory" in getting everything they wanted: principally, a bail-out from the preclearance limits of Section 5. The Texas NAACP celebrated that the "effort failed" by conservatives attempting to scuttle Section 5 and the Voting Rights Act. The U.S. Department of Justice, U.S. Attorney General, and NAMUDNO went on to arrive at a consent decree, signed on November 5, 2009, by judges of the U.S. District Court for the District of Columbia. With a consent decree giving them a bail-out from Section 5, there would be no further challenges to Section 5 by NAMUDNO. Most scholars seemed unsurprised by the compromise decision and constitutional avoidance as the big decision that did not happen. It was assumed that the Supreme Court is ideologically split with prior decision making that suggests they will continue to take a long-term approach with similar strategic compromises to incrementally move the law toward their preferred result.[88]

Implications

First, *NAMUDNO v. Holder* is a landmark decision because the Court granted lawful recognition and legitimacy to hybrid organizations as public, accountable organizations. The case understates this; the Court seems vague as to the details of accountability of hybrid organizations in the American system of governance. The accountability of public agencies within local, state, and national government include much more fully worked-out details in court, legislative, and executive decisions. Second, the Court seems to

(continued)

have signaled a dilution of the constitutional value of voting rights with the use of utilitarian ethical reasoning to bail out hybrid organizations. As we'll see in Chapter 4, on duty to the Constitution and laws, minority civil rights are usually treated as absolute rules and not subject to the variations of utility for the greatest good for the greatest number. Further, when local public agencies ask to bail out of preclearance approval of election changes, there are elections to hold local officials accountable to the voters, administrative procedures to be followed, and legislative checks and balances. Hybrid organizations don't usually have these external controls of democratic governance as a check on the discretion of private actors who lead. While *NAMUDNO v. Holder* (2009) recognizes the legitimacy of hybrid organizations, and posits they are entitled to the same bail-out and other voter practices as traditional county and parish local governments where voters are registered, it does not detail the external or internal controls and accountability to make hybrids democratic.

Discussion

- What is a case note? How does a case note focus closely on empirical data?
- What is a hybrid organization? How do public servants in a hybrid organization exercise the "ethic of citizenship" representing its public?
- What does it mean for the Court to give judicial notice to hybrid organizations?
- What external controls and internal controls may be lacking in the democratic accountability or responsibility of hybrid organizations? ◤

CONCLUSION

The examples from democratic policymaking throughout this chapter give meaning to the accountability of public servants to the public interests utility perspective and the attendant utilitarian ethical theory. Democratic calculations of the needs, desires, and resources of all who are affected seem to characterize the decisions of many public administrators. As in utilitarian ethical theory, public administrators are held accountable to the public interests by democratic institutions, policy process, and policy analysis practices to determine desirable and undesirable utilities by calculation of benefits-costs and other measures of human needs, desires, or resources. However, sometimes entitlements, unfunded mandates, and deregulation of states by national policymakers may impose duties upon public administrators. But public administrators seem to respond with skepticism of the long-term value of such duties—they seem to be just another majoritarian utility calculation that will come and go; or perhaps because they are held to measurable utilitarian values when evaluated in their personal job performance. Ultimately, nothing is forever in this utilitarian world of never-ending majoritarian calculations, and public servants simply seek out the next democratic utility calculation, such as a political referendum, initiative, or other ballot box voting. This is made all the more confounding with the expansion of public administration to include hybrid-private organizations that do not often feature the external controls, internal controls, and accountability measure as imposed upon public agencies.

With the multiple layers and roles of accountability to democratic policymaking, is the job of a policy analyst easy? It is challenging, yes, and even rewarding—but easy, no. The public administrator and the policy analyst operate in a real-politic administering, managing, and analyzing the effects and outcomes of public policy. Sometimes the two are one and the same, although usually policy analysts are specialists who work under supervising public administrators in the various national, state, local agencies—and nonprofits and religious organizations. The making of public policy is not left to one traditional or non-traditional actor alone; it is a complex, interrelated network of individuals, groups, organizations, and even institutions that combine to devise and implement public policy. The basic role of the public administrator in policy analysis is to evaluate the implemented policy and determine—through quantitative or qualitative analysis, or both—the effectiveness of the policy and whether or not it has achieved its stated goals and objectives. Clearly, though, we contend that the study of the democratic institutions, public policy processes, and the practice of policy analysis are and should be done in full appreciation and acknowledgment of the ethics of public administration and the public interests.

ACTION STEPS

1. Contact a public administrator and ask them how they understand democratic policymaking, as it relates to their job; and how they believe they are held accountable in what they do in public policy.

2. Search online for a report of policy analysis conducted with a public organization. Is the policy analysis you examine of a basic or applied type? Is it analysis-centered? What steps did the policy analysis take, as described in the report you obtained? What type of policy analysis research design was taken: the case study method, policy evaluation, or managerial analysis?

3. How may the courts and law make policy analysts accountable? Consider the deference the U.S. Supreme Court gives to economic analysis in the case of *Kelo v. City of New London*, 545 U.S. 469 (2005), where New London, Connecticut, was upheld in taking private property and homes to make way for private corporate development. Consider the backlash against *Kelo* and what this suggests in state and federal legislative attempts to make policy analysts accountable to property rights of others.

KEY CONCEPTS AND NAMES

democratic institutions 84
Utility 84
Utilitarianism 85

teleology 85
public policy 85
democratic policymaking 85

NOTES

1   John Stuart Mill, *Utilitarianism* (London: Longmans, Green & Co., 1863), chapter 2.
2   Gerald M. Pops, "A Teleological Approach to Administrative Ethics," in Terry L. Cooper, ed., *Handbook of Administrative Ethics*, 2nd ed. (New York: Marcel Dekker, 2000), 195–206.
3   J. Scott McDonald et al., "In English and *en Espanol*? Language Accessibility of County Websites," *International Journal of Public Administration* 34 (#13, 2011): 837–42.
4   Jonathan Riley, "Utilitarian Ethics and Democratic Governance," *Ethics* 100 (#2, 1990): 335–48.

5   See also Karen O'Connor, Larry Sabato, and Alixandra Yanus. *American Government*, 12th ed. (New York, NY: Pearson, 2014); Thomas E. Patterson, *We the People: An Introduction to American Government*, 11th ed. (New York, NY: McGraw Hill, 2014); James Q. Wilson, John J. DiIulio, Jr., and Meena Bose, *American Government: Institutions and Policies*, 14th ed. (Cengage, NY: Wadsworth Publishing, 2014); Peter Woll, *American Government: Readings and Cases*, 19th ed. (New York, NY: Pearson, 2011).

6   Indeed, Brad Chilton has read James Madison's bachelor's thesis on Thomas Hobbes and his hand-written notes in the margins of the six-volume set of *Hobbes Works* in the personal library of James Madison. See also Mary G. Dietz, ed., *Thomas Hobbes and Political Theory* (Lawrence: University of Kansas Press, 1990); Ralph Ketcham, *James Madison: A Biography* (Charlottesville: University of Virginia Press, 1990); George Mace, *Locke, Hobbes, and the Federalist Papers: An Essay on the Genesis of the American Political Heritage* (Carbondale: Southern Illinois University Press, 1979); Gary L. McDowell, "Private Conscience & Public Order: Hobbes & The Federalist," *Polity* 25 (#3, 1993): 421–43; Thomas R. Pope, *Social Contract Theory in American Jurisprudence: Too Much Liberty and Too Much Authority* (New York, NY: Routledge, 2013); Dennis F. Thompson, "The Education of a Founding Father: The Reading List of John Witherspoon's Course in Political Theory as Taken By James Madison," *Political Theory* 4 (#4, 1976): 523–9.

7   For example, Akhil Reed Amar, *The Bill of Rights: Creation and Reconstruction* (New Haven, CN: Yale University Press, 1998); Louis Hartz, *The Liberal Tradition in America* (New York, NY: Harcourt, Brace, 1955); Vincent Ostrom, *The Intellectual Crisis in Public Administration* (Tuscaloosa: University of Alabama Press, 1973).

8   See also Karen O'Connor, Larry Sabato, and Alixandra Yanus, *American Government*, 12th ed. (New York, NY: Pearson, 2014); Thomas E. Patterson, *We the People: An Introduction to American Government*, 11th ed. (New York, NY: McGraw Hill, 2014); James Q. Wilson, John J. DiIulio, Jr., and Meena Bose. *American Government: Institutions and Policies*, 14th ed. (Cengage, NY: Wadsworth Publishing, 2014); Peter Woll, *American Government: Readings and Cases*, 19th ed. (New York, NY: Pearson, 2011).

9   Michelle Alexander, *The New Jim Crow: Mass Incarceration in the Age of Colorblindness* (New York, NY: The New Press, 2012).

10 Thus, President Trump's 2017 tweeted promises to revoke citizenship by *jus soli* would require passage of an Amendment to revoke this portion of the 14th Amendment.

11 Terry L. Cooper and Luther Gulick, "Citizenship and Professionalism in Public Administration," *Public Administration Review* 44 (1984): 143–51, esp. 143–4.

12 Terry L. Cooper, *An Ethic of Citizenship for Public Administrators* (Upper Saddle River, NJ: Prentice Hall, 1991).

13 Compare Cooper's responsible administrator approach with Chester I. Barnard, "The Nature of Executive Responsibility," in *The Functions of the Executive* (Cambridge, MA: Harvard University Press, 1938), 258–84. Barnard's *The Functions of the Executive* is still often ranked on lists of the top management books today.

14 Compare Cooper's "rational and comprehensive" ethical decision making with Herbert Simon's "satisficing" model in his 1947 classic, *Administrative Behavior: A Study of Decision Making Processes in Administrative Organizations*, 4th sub ed. (New York, NY: The Free Press, 1997).

15 Terry L. Cooper, *The Responsible Administrator: An Approach to Ethics for the Administrative Role,* 4th ed. (San Francisco, CA: Jossey-Bass Publishers, 2006).

16 Robert Putnam, *Bowling Alone: The Collapse and Revival of American Community* (New York, NY: Simon and Schuster, 2000).

17 For example, Terry L. Cooper, T.A. Bryer, and J.W. Meek, "Citizen-Centered Collaborative Public Management," *Public Administration Review* 66 (2006): 76–88;

T.L. Cooper, "Citizen Driven Administration: Civic Engagement in the United States," in D. Menzel and H. White, eds., *The State of Public Administration: Issues, Challenges, and Opportunities* (Armonk, NY: M.E. Sharpe, 2011); Terry L. Cooper and T. Bryer, "George Frederickson and the Dialogue on Citizenship in Public Administration," *Public Administration Review* 72 (2012): 108–18; W. Wang, H. Li, and T.L. Cooper, "From Subjects to Citizens: How Homeowners' Participation Transforms Local Governance in Beijing," *Administration & Society* 49 (2017): 851–827.

18 For example, Jennifer S. Evans-Cowley and Maria M. Conroy, eds., *E-government and Planning: Key Citizen Participation Issues and Applications* (Columbus, OH: John Glenn Institute for Public Service and Public Policy, 2005), retrieved from http://hdl.handle.net/1811/519

19 For example, Bruce Cannon Gibney, *A Generation of Sociopaths: How the Baby Boomers Betrayed America* (New York, NY: Hachette Books, 2017), 193–214.

20 For example, Terry L. Cooper, *Handbook of Administrative Ethics*, 2nd ed. (Amonk, NY: M.E. Sharpe, 2001); Kathryn G. Denhardt, *The Ethics of Public Service: Resolving Moral Dilemmas in Organizations* (Westport, CN: Greenwood Publishing, 1988), 16–26.

21 For example, Terry L. Cooper, "Big Questions in Administrative Ethics: A Need for Focused, Collaborative Effort," *Public Administration Review* 64 (2004): 395–407.

22 John Rawls, *A Theory of Justice* (Cambridge, MA: Belknap Press/Harvard University Press, 1971).

23 Contrary to Jay S. Albanese, *Professional Ethics in Criminal Justice: Being Ethical When No One is Looking*, 3rd ed. (New York: Prentice Hall, 2012), 36–46.

24 John Stuart Mill, *Utilitarianism* (London: Longmans, Green & Co., 1863), chapter 2.

25 Gerald M. Pops, "A Teleological Approach to Administrative Ethics," in Terry L. Cooper, ed., *Handbook of Administrative Ethics*, 2nd ed. (New York: Marcel Dekker, 2000), 195–206.

26 Guy B. Adams and Danny L. Balfour, *Unmasking Administrative Evil*, revised ed. (Armonk, NY: M.E. Sharpe, 2004).

27 For example, Moreno-Riano, Gerson, "The Etiology of Administrative Evil: Eric Voegelin and the Unconsciousness of Modernity," *American Review of Public Administration* 31 (#3, 2001): 296–312.

28 For example, Tom L. Beauchamp, "The Moral Adequacy of Cost-Benefit Analysis as the Basis for Government Regulation of Research," in Denis G. Arnold, Tom L. Beauchamp, and Norman L. Bowie, eds., *Ethical Theory and Business*, 9th ed. (New York, NY: Pearson, 2012), 163–75.

29 For example, Michael J. Zimmerman, "Intrinsic vs. Extrinsic Value," in Edward N. Zalta, ed., *The Stanford Encyclopedia of Philosophy* (Spring 2015 edition), retrieved from https://plato.stanford.edu/archives/spr2015/entries/value-intrinsic-extrinsic/

30 Anderson is a political scientist who believes, first, that the public interest exists, and second, that it has some meaning relative to public policymaking. For example, he writes that "The task of government, it is often proclaimed, is to serve or promote the public interest. Statutes sometimes include the public interest as a guide for agency action, as when the Federal Communication Commission is directed license broadcasters for the public interest, convenience, and necessity. In this section, this rather elusive normative concept and its usefulness as a criterion for decision-making will be discussed," James E. Anderson, *Public Policymaking*, 6th ed. (Boston, MA: Houghton Mifflin, 2006), 137.

31 David Easton, *The Political System: An Inquiry into the State of Political Science* (New York, NY: Alfred A. Knopf, 1953).

32 James E. Anderson, *Public Policymaking*, 6th ed. (Boston, MA: Houghton Mifflin, 2006), 20.

33 See David Truman's magnum opus *The Governmental Process: Political Interests and Public Opinion* (New York, NY: Alfred A. Knopf, 1951).

34 Anderson quotes from Thomas Dye and Harmon Zeigler's conceptualization of elitist theory. See Thomas Dye and Harmon Zeigler, *The Irony of Democracy*, 10th ed. (Belmont, CA: Wadsworth, 1996), 4–5, here p. 22.

35 See, for example, B. Guy Peters' *The Future of Governing: Four Emerging Models* (Lawrence: Kansas University Press, 1996).

36 The rate of growth of texts and trade books focusing on the relationship between religion and politics is nearly exponential. A popular text that is replete with examples, illustrations, and additional references is Robert Booth Fowler, Allen D. Hertzke, and Laura R. Olson's *Religion and Politics in America: Faith, Culture, and Strategic Choices*, 2nd ed. (Boulder, CO: Westview, 1999). An excellent reader on the topic is Hugh Heclo and Wilfred M. McClay, eds., *Religion Returns to the Public Square* (Washington, DC: Woodrow Wilson Center Press, 2003).

37 An excellent historical overview of Arthur Schlesinger's concept is found in Sidney M. Milikis and Michael Nelson's *The American Presidency: Origins and Development 1776–2002*, 4th ed. (Washington, DC: CQ Press, 2003).

38 See Charles W. Dunn, *The Seven Laws of Presidential Leadership: An Introduction to the American Presidency* (Upper Saddle River, NJ: Pearson-Prentice Hall, 2007).

39 Kenneth J. Meier and John Bohte, *Politics and the Bureaucracy: Policymaking in the Fourth Branch of Government*, 5th ed. (Belmont, CA: Wadsworth, 2007).

40 Larry N. Gerston, *Public Policymaking in a Democratic Society: A Guide to Civic Engagement* (Armonk, NY: M.E. Sharpe, 2002).

41 See Lester M. Salamon, *Partners in Public Service: Government-Nonprofit Relations in the Modern Welfare State* (Baltimore, MD: Johns Hopkins University Press, 1995).

42 Ibid., 86–9.

43 *Stern v. Marshall*, 564 U.S. 462 (2011), at 462.

44 Roger W. Cobb and Charles D. Elder, *Participation in American Politics: The Dynamics of Agenda-Building*, 2nd ed. (Baltimore, MD: Johns Hopkins University Press, 1983).

45 John W. Kingdon, *Agendas, Alternatives, and Public Policies*, 2nd ed. (New York: HarperCollins, 1995).

46 Ibid., 200–2.

47 Ibid., xv.

48 Susan L. Aud, "The Fiscal Impact of a Tuition Assistance Grant for Virginia's Special Education Students," *Issues in the State* (April 2007): 1–21.

49 Amy K. Frantz, "For the Children? No, for the Politicians!" *Policy Study*, no. 07-1 (August 2007): 1–18.

50 William N. Dunn, *Introduction to Policy Analysis*, 3rd ed. (Upper Saddle River, NJ: Prentice Hall, 2004), 41–3.

51 Ibid., 41.

52 Ibid.; David Weimer and Aidan Vining, *Policy Analysis: Concepts and Practice*, 4th ed. (Upper Saddle River, NJ: Prentice-Hall, 2005), 23–38.

53 William N. Dunn, *Introduction to Policy Analysis*, 3rd ed. (Upper Saddle River, NJ: Prentice Hall, 2004), 216–17.

54 Bill Lambrecht, "Border Congressmen Propose 'Smart Wall,'" *San Antonio Express* (2017, July 27), retrieved from www.expressnews.com/news/local/article/Border-congressman-propose-smart-wall-11532258.php

55 William N. Dunn, *Introduction to Policy Analysis*, 3rd ed. (Upper Saddle River, NJ: Prentice Hall, 2004), 276.

56 Ibid., 280.

57 Robert K. Yin, *The Case Study Method* (Thousand Oaks, CA: Sage Publications, 1984), 22–3.

58 Graham Allison, *Essence of Decision: Explaining the Cuban Missile Decision*, 2nd ed. (New York, NY: Pearson, 1999).

59 William N. Dunn, *Introduction to Policy Analysis*, 3rd ed. (Upper Saddle River, NJ: Prentice Hall, 2004).

60 See Robert B. Denhardt and Joseph W. Grubbs, *Public Administration: An Action Orientation*, 4th ed. (Belmont, CA: Wadsworth, 2003), 292–3; William N. Dunn, *Introduction to Policy Analysis*, 3rd ed. (Upper Saddle River, NJ: Prentice Hall, 2004); and for a comprehensive discussion of experimental and quasi-experimental designs, see Donald T. Campbell and Julian C. Stanley, *Experimental and Quasi-experimental Designs for Research* (Chicago, IL: Rand McNally, 1966).

61 Donald T. Campbell and Julian C. Stanley, *Experimental and Quasi-experimental Designs for Research* (Chicago, IL: Rand McNally, 1966).

62 Robert B. Denhardt and Joseph W. Grubbs, *Public Administration: An Action Orientation*. 4th ed. (Belmont, CA: Wadsworth, 2003), 286.

63 Harold F. Gortner, *Ethics for Public Managers* (New York: Greenwood, 1991), 19, 21.

64 Melvin J. Dubnick and Barbara S. Romzek, *American Public Administration: Politics and the Management of Expectations* (New York, NY: Macmillan, 1991), 76.

65 Nicholas Henry, *Public Administration & Public Affairs*, 12th ed. (New York, NY: Routledge, 2012), 436.

66 H. George Frederickson, "Accountability: The Word That Ate Public Administration," *Public Administration Times* 28 (#11, November 2005): 11.

67 Guy B. Adams and Danny L. Balfour, *Unmasking Administrative Evil* (Armonk, NY: M.E. Sharpe, 2004).

68 Carl J. Friedrich, "Public Policy and the Nature of Administrative Responsibility," in Carl J. Friedrich, ed., *Public Policy* (Cambridge: Harvard University Press, 1940), 1–24.

69 Herman Finer, "Administrative Responsibility in Democratic Government," *Public Administration Review* 1 (Summer 1941): 335–50.

70 Debra W. Stewart, "Professionalism vs. Democracy: Friedrich vs. Finer Revisited," in Robert B. Denhardt and Barry R. Hammond, eds., *Public Administration in Action: Readings, Profiles, and Cases,* (Pacific Grove, CA: Brooks Cole, 1992), 156.

71 Debra W. Stewart, "Professionalism vs. Democracy: Friedrich vs. Finer Revisited," *Public Administration Quarterly* 9 (1985): 13-25, at 20–21.

72 Barry Bozeman, *Policy Analysis and Public Administration* (Belmont, CA: Wadsworth, 1979); Robert Heineman, William Bluhm, Edward Kearny, and Steven Peterson, *The World of the Policy Analyst: Rationality, Values, & Politics*, 3rd ed. (Washington, DC: CQ Press, 2001); Robert Nelson, "Confessions of a Policy Analyst," in George De Martino and Diedre McCloskey, eds., *The Oxford Handbook of Professional Economic Ethics* (New York, NY: Oxford University Press, 2016); Deborah A. Stone, *Policy Paradox and Political Reason* (New York, NY: HarperCollins, 1988).

73 Frederick W. Taylor, *The Principles of Scientific Management* (New York: Harper and Brothers, 1911).

74 John Dewey, *The Public and Its Problems: An Essay in Political Inquiry* (University Park, PA: Penn State University Press, 2012 [orig. pub. 1930]).

75 For example, Edward C. Banfield, *The Unheavenly City: The Nature and the Future of Our Urban Crisis* (Boston: Little Brown, 1970); Edward C. Banfield, *The Unheavenly City Revisited* (Waveland, IN: Waveland Press, 1990).

76 For example, H. George Frederickson, *New Public Administration* (Tuscaloosa: University of Alabama Press, 1980).

77 For example, Theodore J. Lowi, *The End of Liberalism: Ideology, Policy, and the Crisis of Public Authority* (Chicago, IL: Norton, 1969).

78 For example, Anthony Downs, *An Economic Theory of Democracy* (New York, NY: Harper and Row, 1957).

79 Harold Seidman, "The Quasi World of the Federal Government," *Brookings Review* 6 (#3, 1988): 23–7.

80 Michael Cole, "Quangos: The Debate of the 1970s in Britain," *Contemporary British History* 19 (#3, 2005): 321–52; Michael Cole, "Asymmetrical Public Accountability: The National Assembly for Wales, Questions and Quangos," *Political Quarterly* 77 (#1, 2006): 98–106; Carsten Greve, Matthew Flinders, and Sandra Van Thiel, "Quangos—What's in a Name: Defining Quangos from a Comparative Perspective," *Governance: An International Journal of Policy and Administration* 12 (#2, 2000): 129–46.

81 Mark Emmert and Michael M. Crow, "Public-Private Cooperation and Hybrid Organizations," *Journal of Management* 13 (#1, 1987): 55–67; Mark Emmert and Michael M. Crow, "Public, Private and Hybrid Organizations: An Empirical Examination of the Role of Publicness," *Administration and Society* 20 (#2, 2001): 216–44; Kevin R. Kosar, "CRS Report for Congress: The Quasi Government: Hybrid Organizations with Both Government and Private Sector Legal Characteristics," updated 1/31/2008, retrieved from www.fas.org/sgp/crs/mics/RL30533.pdf; Jonathan G.S. Koppell, "Hybrid Organizations and the Alignment of Interests: The Case of Fannie Mae and Freddie Mac," *Public Administration Review* 61 (#4, 2001): 468–82; Jonathan G.S. Koppell, *The Politics of Quasi-Government: Hybrid Organizations and the Dynamics of Bureaucratic Control* (Cambridge: Cambridge University Press, 2003); Ronald C. Moe, "The Emerging Federal Quasi Government: Issues of Management and Accountability," *Public Administration Review* 61 (#3, 2001): 290–312.

82 Howard Ball, Dale Krane, and Thomas P. Lauth, *Compromised Compliance: Implementation of 1965 Voting Rights Act* (Westport, CN: Greenwood Press, 1982).

83 Brennan Center, *Brennan Center for Justice: NAMUDNO v. Holder* (2009), retrieved from www.brennancenter.org/content/resource/namudno_v_gonzales

84 Anthony A. Peacock, *Deconstructing the Republic: Voting Rights, the Supreme Court, and the Founders' Republicanism Reconsidered* (Washington, DC: AEI Press, 2008), 10.

85 Malcolm M. Feeley and Edward Rubin, *Federalism: Political Identity and Tragic Compromise* (Ann Arbor: University of Michigan Press, 2008), ix.

86 All quotes in this section from *Northwest Austin Municipal Utility District No. One v. Mukasey* 573 F. Supp. 2d 221 (DDC 2008).

87 All quotes in this section from *NAMUDNO v. Holder*, 557 U.S. 193 (2009).

88 Joshua A. Douglas, "The Voting Rights Act Through the Justices' Eyes: NAMUDNO and Beyond," *Texas Law Review* 88 (#1, 2009): 1–32.

Duty to the Constitution and Law

"Uphold the Constitution and the Law. Respect and support government constitutions and laws, while seeking to improve laws and policies to promote the public good."

—(Code of Ethics, American Society for Public Administration, 2013)

> ### BOX 4.1 | CHAPTER OBJECTIVES
>
> 1 Overview the rule of law, hierarchy of laws, deontology, and the duty perspective of public interests.
>
> 2 Summarize the constitutional foundations of public governance, freedom, property, and equality.
>
> 3 Specifically relate due process of law to administrative law and the public administration profession.
>
> 4 Critique deontological ethical theory and the duty perspective in our ethics case study of information ethics for bureaucrats and the ethical issues with emerging digital information technology.

Recall from our last chapter the classic debate within public administration on accountability versus responsibility, external versus internal controls, between **Carl Friedrich (1901–1984)** and **Herman Finer (1898–1964)** in the early 1940s. Carl Friedrich, a PhD from the University of Heidelberg and professor of political science at Harvard University, argued that **internal controls** and individual professional responsibility would work to ensure compliance of public administrative behavior with the public interests.[1] Herman Finer, a DSci from the London School of Economics and professor of political science at the University of Chicago, argued that only the **external control** of administrators by political oversight and supervision could ensure compliance with the public interests.[2] So, which would you choose: internal controls of responsibility or external controls of accountability?

Or both? The **duty ethical perspective** of the public interests may resolve these debates, incorporating both internal and external controls. It may also address problems with traditional perspectives on ethics, such as a tendency to indoctrinate the moral values of a particular religious sect or adopt a conservative or liberal ideology; and address issues with other contemporary approaches which discuss ethics in a so-called neutral fashion, and never mention such subjects as administrative evil. You see, both traditional and contemporary ethical theory give little attention to the internal conscientizing (moral socialization) of public administrators, or provide for adequate external control. Though ethics training now abounds for public servants, it is everywhere in the chains of understanding that either take an abstruse high road, a mundane low road, or at best an incomplete middle road.

HIGH ROAD, LOW ROAD, MIDDLE ROAD

To understand the place of the duty perspective of the public interests, we hearken back to John Rohr's landmark book, *Ethics for Bureaucrats,* and his discussion of the high road, low road, and middle road.[3] The high road offers the wonderfully rich literature of philosophy, humanistic psychology, and the social sciences on ethics. Building logically upon centuries of sustained inquiry, it can render a systematic understanding of current moral conscientizing through contemporary phenomenology, ordinary language philosophy, pragmatism, and other currents of thought. And it can overcome the abuses of indoctrination or indifference in moral inquiry. Although this literature enriches all inquiry into ethics, it is an overwhelming challenge to practitioners, or even scholars, to master. The complaint is that these highly general materials are too difficult to understand and apply. The high road may be easier to travel for those with more background or reading in ethical philosophy.[4] But requiring an extensive background or some sequence of several courses in philosophy, humanistic psychology, and so forth would be unlikely to be accepted as position requirements in most public sector jobs. But the rigors of the high road demand a background in philosophical ethics related to broad understandings of metaphysics, epistemology, logic, linguistics, psychology, and social and political theory. This is what makes the high road both wonderful and frustrating. It is imprudent, however, to demand such a broad prerequisite understanding from all—or a vast majority of—public servants. Thus, we must provide some other foundation for the basic course in ethics for public administrator practitioners.

The low road, by contrast, is composed of rather unsystematic micro-level case studies of particular decisions to be taken in particular circumstances. Traveled with increasing frequency in agency ethics training programs, the low road avoids the frustrating complexities of abstract ethical theory by focusing exclusively on developing a moral sense for the right decision in particular circumstances. Typically, freeform training discussions lead to a consensus on the right answers to all these particular moral dilemmas. In contrast with the high road, the low road is readily teachable because it does not require lengthy and difficult prerequisite reading or understanding of abstract ethical theory. In fact, agency trainers who embrace the low road often abandon the available ethics materials in the area as too difficult and instead use non-text instruction on the subject that they view as more exciting and less academic. Further, many dramatic media resources, such as feature movies, are available to bring these ethical case studies into training sessions.[5]

The problem with unsystematic micro-level case studies is that the values involved in ethical problems are not easily discernible from a consideration of individual cases. We cannot anticipate all the great variety of moral dilemmas that may face all persons, and the low road may therefore leave students unprepared for many eventualities. Further, the unsystematic nature of many collections of case studies provides no ethical literacy; students confronted with a novel moral dilemma are left without anything to fall back on. In addition, agency trainers we have observed using the low road tend to give inordinate attention to the easily answered cases of corruption, bribery, or lying featured in popular TV or movies. Or they consider marginally significant problems, such as the non-official use of an office phone or email. Thus, ethics on the low road comes to be a laundry list of pat answers to a smattering of moral case studies. It offers no cultural literacy or knowledge to fall back on in coping with the many unanticipated moral dilemmas that practitioners will confront. Although case studies are important, the low road trivializes all ethical dilemmas by reducing them to particular decisions to be taken in particular circumstances. But the recurring patterns of ethical decision making among practitioners belie the workings of moral values that are generalizable beyond the individual micro-case level. Ethical theory can give us the necessary shorthand explanation of the operation of these values.

The **middle road** is usually represented by the professional ethics paradigm, which bridges the gap between the excesses of abstract theory and mundane case studies. It is considered successful in the public administration ethics context precisely because its applied ethics framework, though systematic, avoids the abstruse mystery of the high road. Due perhaps to a number of influential sociologists, the middle road has borrowed heavily from the sociology of traditional professions and focused on the development of a code of ethics, problems of professional autonomy and discretion, and other imitations of the legal and medical professions. The professional ethics framework effectively applies practical duties in a systematic, teachable manner to public administration ethics topics, such as the limits of discretion and the need for accountability. Other thinkers along the middle road, most notably Professor James H. Svara,[6] argue by a three-prong approach to professional ethics that public administrators are not professionals in the classical sense, but may nevertheless base their moral instruction on a commitment to professionalism. Professor Svara was honored by the American Society for Public Administration for heading-up the committee to produce its 2013 ASPA Code of Ethics. Indeed, most other texts focus more often on the middle road of professional ethics or professionalism.[7]

However, the professional ethics middle road and its success have also come under challenge. We err if we adopt wholesale the professional ethics frameworks of the traditional professions of law and medicine. In particular, the application of a traditional professional ethics model to public administrators creates its own ethical dilemmas because the professional ethics framework conceals the true nature of the clientele of public service, may allow for too much individual discretion for many, provides for too much autonomy for many public administrators, can lead to noncompliance with the public interests, and seem unlimited. However, should all public bureaucrats be viewed like autonomous physicians or lawyers? Or should they be viewed as public agents within representative bureaucracies with clear constitutional duties? We believe public servants must be more fully obligated to democratic values than professionals in most other fields.

CONSTITUTIONAL SCHOOL OF PUBLIC ADMINISTRATION

The **Constitutional School of Public Administration** proposes a middle path that is founded upon identifiable and enduring constitutional values, recognizes these duties, and is subject to external controls and review by judges, executives, legislative bodies, and citizens. It is grounded in constitutional law, and possesses two advantages over the middle road. First, it recognizes that public administration practitioners are not pure professionals in the sense that physicians and lawyers are; they are bound to the public interests in a way that the latter are not. Second, although it avoids the sterility of a so-called neutral approach to teaching administrative ethics, a constitutional public interest places normative boundaries (that is, constitutional morality) on practitioner decision making. This then overcomes the problems of personal, idiosyncratic moral judgments that are not subject to external control or review. Further, these expectations of public accountability are made clear in public administration by the symbols of public employment—for example, the required **oath of office** to uphold and defend the Constitution. Similarly, the formal organizational mission of public agencies clearly establishes a clear fiduciary duty to the public. In such public organizations, authority is granted (ultimately by citizens) to the agency by governmental authority.[8]

As detailed in Chapters 1 and 2, scholars in the Constitutional School of Public Administration have renewed the importance of study of the U.S. Constitution and enduring laws as a way of understanding the public interests within public administration. It is focused on the recurring constitutional values that public servants appeal to when they use the phrase *in the public interests*. They have been joined by scholars from law schools, political science, and other legal studies of the moral reading of law and ethical traditions within American constitutional law.[9] To avoid dogmatic constitutional meanings and to reflect the wide variety of constitutional interpretations, these scholars have analyzed the wide variety of U.S. Supreme Court interpretations ordinarily used by public servants. Such analyses begin with a rejection of positivist theories of law that falsely separate ethics from law. Like logical positivism theories that posit public administrators as mere producers of public order in an objective or neutral fashion, positivist theories of law generally view all governance as neutral service and obedience to political power. But public actors ordinarily judge themselves against the aspirations or ethical values that undergird constitutional law; they do not conceive of law merely as the use of political power to require specific minimum behaviors. On this understanding, public servants must discover the Constitution as a document and understand its official interpretations by the U.S. Supreme Court if they are to know the basic ethics, morals, and values that should guide their exercise of discretion in decision making, policymaking, and behavior. Such morals or values are "beliefs, passions, and duties that have been held for several generations by the overwhelming majority of the American people." Thus, the public interests may be said to involve praxis of a dialogic relation of enduring constitutional values and duties to the changing circumstances of public administration.[10]

The Constitution and laws pursuant to the Constitution give us a real-world empirical expression of values, problems, and resolutions within public administration. Further, through case law, judges give meaning to these dilemmas by converting whatever is submitted to them for decisions into claims of right or accusations of fault.[11] Popular culture depictions of public administration have come to focus on these expressions of values in the Constitution, laws, and cases.[12] Many scholars have come to focus on the Constitution and laws as meaningful empirical expressions of the values, disputes, and issues of public administration, such as Rosemary O'Leary, David Rosenbloom, Philip Cooper, the Blacksburg scholars, and many others in the Constitutional School of Public Administration.[13] The law is a powerful vehicle for these public interests duties and ethical values. It is the nature of legal rights to retain the moral dialog of the disputes as presented before the law. For over a century, legal scholars have recognized that the operation of legal rights does not mean automatic resolution of these disputes with a mechanical jurisprudence—in which the judge simply declares the applicable law to the dispute and the litigants comply.[14] Rights illuminate the successful paths taken by judges, administrators, officials, and others to use the law to resolve these disputes over values. Rights in the US are typically founded in the U.S. Constitution and its amendments, as well as statutes, local ordinances, case law interpretations, and common law.

The Constitutional School does not replace professional ethics in public service, but instead qualifies it with law, interpretation, and biography of the Constitution. This is because there are many issues in administrative ethics that are not covered by the U.S. Supreme Court and identifiable constitutional law values. For example, bureaucratic deception, the resort to union action by public service workers, the acceptance of gratuities, the formation of practitioner subcultures, and the limits of discretion are, for the most part, only tangentially connected to constitutional values. As a corrective qualification to professional ethics or professionalism in public service, the Constitution School set the direction and tone of complex moral decisions from the foundation of a public fiduciary duty under the Constitution. But it is not a complete source for all ethics.

In addition, public administrators work within the larger context of law, not just constitutional law. Public agencies, nonprofits and other public sector actors face daily legal concerns that are typical of all enterprises. For example, every day a public administrator somewhere encounters situations such as graft and corruption that involve **criminal law**, or public wrongs that are subject to criminal sanctions and punishment by government. Negligence, or the unintentional wrongdoing of persons, may involve the law of torts, also known as private wrongs that may require compensation for damages. Torts may also include intentional behaviors for which there is civil liability. Public administrators routinely are involved in making mutual promises with other persons, oral or in writing, which may be enforceable under the law of **contracts**. In recent decades, privatization involves contracting out public services from public agencies to nonprofits or private organizations. The **law of property** not only protects private parties from governmental action against their property interests but limits the use of properties owned or operated by the government. **Corporate law** not only specifies the relations of persons within a business, but also limits the interaction of government with the corporation, directing government contact to the top executives entrusted with corporate authority. And of course, constitutional law provides the underlying basis of all law in the US, limiting administrative agencies as well as nonprofits and private parties in their behavior toward others.

This chapter is designed to examine **deontology** and the duty perspective of the public interests, including sources such as the Constitution, administrative law, civil and criminal law, and issues of diversity in public affairs. First, the chapter will explore the basis of law in the US—the Constitution. We will define constitutionalism, examine its roots, and provide the historical and legal basis for the role that a written constitution plays in the governance and administrative structures of public administrators. Second, we examine the three basic legal contexts of freedom, property, and equality, highlighting several policy and administrative issue areas that impact the role of the public administrator in the public interests. Third, we overview the limitations of due process of law, administrative law, information control, and other legal limitations within the U.S. system of governance. Finally, we end the chapter with an ethics case study of *information* ethics for bureaucrats and the ethical issues with our emerging, dominant digital information technology.

DEONTOLOGY

Our study of the U.S. Constitution and laws allows us the chance to focus on the duty perspective of the public interests and the attending deontological, or rights and duties, theory of ethics. When we think of the Constitution and the laws, we think of duties—such as the duty to "do the right thing," no matter what the outcome may be. Following the Constitution and laws requires following your duties, not abandoning them to achieve a desired consequence.[15] Further, deontology preserves the past to indicate morality in the present. Past precedents may create present duties for justice over time. A city manager's deal to get water to Sue's business yesterday may create a duty to get water to Fred, too.[16]

The duty perspective of the public interests attends to deontological ethical theory, which focuses on the "binding duty" (Greek, *deont*) in the study of (Greek, *ology*) human affairs to define what is good and bad. The goal of deontology consists of universal, valid means of behavior or activities that are applied fairly and without bias—even if dutifully following the rules should result in mischief, injustice, or tragic ending for a particular person or group. Deontological ethics are featured in much of Judeo-Christian-Islamic roots in the *Torah*, such as the Decalogue or 10 Commandments. Deontological ethical arguments were featured by ancient philosophers such as Plato (about 427–348 BCE). In Plato's *Crito*, Socrates argues with a friend on his obligation by **social contract** to his city-state, Athens, to accept the jury's guilty verdict against him and drink the hemlock for his crimes. His friend protests and offers to help Socrates flee Athens, but finally comes to accept Socrates' moral argument of obligation:

> if we leave here without the city's permission, are we mistreating people
> whom we should least mistreat? . . . [D]o you think it possible for a city not
> to be destroyed if the verdicts of its courts have no force but are nullified
> and set at naught by private individuals?[17]

While philosophers at least since the time of Plato have discussed the intrinsic good of following one's duties, the term *deontology* was not invented as a label for this ethical theory until 1930.[18] In the applied ethics of the duty perspective of the public interests, public administrators are not judged by good (or bad) consequences of their behaviors, or teleology. Rather, they are judged by doing the right behaviors, or non-teleological. The goodness or badness of ethical behavior is intrinsic to the behavior, or non-consequential. Or, as the old sports adage quotes: "It doesn't matter if you win or lose it's how you play the game." Deontology and the duty perspective have long influenced American public life, as the U.S. Constitution was explicitly framed as a social contract of the sort envisioned by philosophers like **Thomas Hobbes** (1588–1679) in which atomistic and materialistic individuals were willing to give up everything they had to form a social contract to avoid a return to the state of nature of every man against every man—with some exceptions, such as no bills of attainder or ex post facto laws. And the Bill of Rights (Amendments 1–10) amended the Constitution with limitations on governmental powers in order to protect individual freedoms and property rights, as envisioned by **John Locke** (1632–1704). As an illustration, President Truman dropped the A-bomb in Japan to save many lives by ending World War II quickly. Does the consequence of saving many lives make his decision moral? Or is it simply wrong to use such a weapon of mass destruction on civilian children, women, and men? Teleology ethical theorists would approve the consequences, while deontologists would declare the act immoral.

Deontology makes a practical argument that people don't ordinarily have the capacity to predict or control the consequences of their actions, but they can control their intent. The perspectives of virtue and utilitarianism may distort the reality of public administrators into the false belief they have the capacity or choice to select what consequences they want in their moral behaviors. By contrast, deontology focuses on the practical control each person has over their intent to do good. Of course, people who take a deontological approach hope for good consequences to their actions, but they simply don't control all possible consequences. For this reason deontology is sometimes called intuitionism or formalism, because the criterion to do good is intuited in, or within, each person and their intent to do good. It is formalism in that principles for determining good duties are purely formal abstractions, like math, with a self-sufficient logic—not external and dependent on a calculation of the empirical consequences of one's actions. This means that the good or bad moral value is determined in phenomenal reality—"between the ears"—rather than a noumenal reality of the outside world. For example, if you believe in the Ten Commandments, you intuit your good intent to do good by following them, and self-evaluation of moral goodness isn't focused on empirical calculations of the consequences of your actions. Thus, it's motives, not consequences, which determine moral goodness (or badness) for the deontologist.

Immanuel Kant (1724–1804) was the philosopher who famously drew the distinctions between noumenal reality (the world out there) and phenomenal reality (the world our mind interprets). In this phenomenal reality, the mind must rationally create purely formal abstract ethical principles—like math—that were universal in application. His ideas were highly influential in America: we saw previously how President Abraham Lincoln sought to create moral arguments against slavery that were universally rational, like the mathematical formulas he had memorized as a child. For Kant, goodwill was the one good thing in itself, and his categorical imperative formulated it into a universal ethical principle: "Act as if the maxim of your action were to become through your will a universal law of nature."[19]

Contemporary approaches to deontology tend to argue that absolute rules to follow a duty may be destructive. For example, Francis Kamm, JFK School of Government Professor at Harvard University, has argued that one may morally harm another in order to save life.[20] Philosopher W.D. Ross (1877–1971) posited not one universal duty, but several *prima facie* duties (primary on-the-face duties) and that one should weigh or balance several primary duties in each situation to determine which duty to follow as the Actual Duty. The *prima facie* duties are self-evident rules of conduct, including fidelity, reparation, gratitude, non-maleficence, justice, beneficence, and self-improvement.[21] And many billions around the globe today apply the deontology of divine commands from the Ten Commandments, 613–620 Mitzvahs, Shari'a law, or other spiritual revelations—even practicing bureaucrats and judges.[22]

How is deontology applied to ambiguous understandings of intuition, faith, and conscience that may enter into public interests duties? While this chapter answers this with many illustrations, we must consider how judges, officials, administrators, and others may reasonably disagree on ambiguous constitutional language. Indeed, the U.S. Supreme Court has been accused of legislating their will to power in creating individual constitutional rights in areas such as racial discrimination, the death penalty, and sexual freedom.[23] To these critics, Justice William O. Douglas (1898–1980) once stated, "The Supreme Court is really the keeper of the conscience. And the conscience is the Constitution."[24] Douglas argued that many constitutional law values are not clearly expressed as rules of prohibition, but as values of conscience. This attends to **act deontology**, the ethical theory that holds that particular judgments, rather than rules, are basic in many moral decisions. Individual intuitions, faith, conscience, love, and existential choice have each been proposed as a standard for act deontology. With each, a public servant faced with a decision will take a moment to somehow grasp or intuit or observe their conscience on what should be done, when the rules are ambiguous—or even in disobedience of orders.[25] For example, in his decision to allow litigation to reform the Georgia State Prison, U.S. District Judge Anthony Alaimo found one morning that he simply couldn't look at himself in the mirror if he didn't allow the prison reforms. It was obedience to conscience, not to vague rules of civil procedure and jurisdiction, which compelled his decision and ultimately produced the first accredited, constitutional prison in the US.[26] Yet, how could you argue that a jailer acted wrongly in disciplining an inmate with a whipping if duty was based only on intuition, faith, or conscience? How would we ever prefer one act over another if there were no proscribed behaviors with express rules? Act deontology gives attention to the moral worth of intentions in our actions by focusing on intuition, faith, conscience, love, and choice, but we may need something more than these ambiguous notions in deontology.

Thus, deontology and the duty perspective present an administrative reality that seems more bound by rules, law, and duties you are required to follow. It also includes many diverse roles and corresponding duties of public administrators, such as fiduciary-entrustor, principle-agent, supervisor-supervisee, bureaucrat-citizen, promisor-promisee, lawyer-client, physician-patient, parent-child, and many other roles. The many rules and duties of the duty perspective and deontology may be criticized as non-systematic, too pluralistic, a laundry list of morality that fails to provide some unified moral goal. Virtue ethics focuses on arete or excellence; utilitarian ethics focus on benefits/costs or a unified moral goal of utlity. This may also be the strength of deontology and the duty perspective with a very broad view of the moral issues, roles, and relations of people. To help work such a long list of deontological duties, we will briefly summarize constitutional rights by the protection of freedom and property, with extended sections on equality and due process and, of course, the Constitution and laws include perspectives other than simply duty. It is a matter of degree and all three perspectives of the public interests may be found within the Constitution and laws imposed upon public administration—virtue, utility, and duty. Contemporary legal scholars posit a variety of ethical perspectives of law and legal dispute resolution that includes the moral reading of law for pre-existing deontological duties.[27] But other scholars also include the economic analysis of law for utilitarian calculus of benefits/costs,[28] as well as judicial biographies, critical race theory, and other virtue analyses of character of legal participants.[29]

THE U.S. CONSTITUTION

While the Constitution forms the basic rules of the game for all law in the US, the historical roots of the Constitution help us to understand the nature of law and public administration in America today. Our constitutional rules of the game came out of the colonial charters and activities, the Declaration of Independence, the Articles of Confederation, and other prior legal experiences, such as Spanish codes. For example, each of the colonies began with a written charter that specified institutions of governance, as well as a political economy of mercantilism against which we revolted. And the **Declaration of Independence** of 1776 declared our human rights and the necessity of revolution. This was the beginning of a responsibilities perspective or deontological ethical theory of governance, rejecting the virtue of King George III of England and instead placing trust in a more universal set of rules. Our first try at a set of rules of the game began with the failed **Articles of Confederation**. From 1781 to 1789, the 13 states grew further apart, the national government and defense grew weak, and the public order declined with Shay's Rebellion of 1786 and other revolts against the rule of law by debtors and so forth. From this background came the impetus to create a new nation by a new Constitution.[30]

The **1787 Constitutional Convention** brought together 55 delegates in Philadelphia, sent by 12 states for the original purpose of reforming the Articles of Confederation. These "Framers" who attended were mostly lawyers who feared threats to their property interests from covetous grumbling populists, the weak national defense, and potent foreign invaders. The revolutionaries, such as Thomas Paine, Patrick Henry, John Adams, Sam Adams, and Thomas Jefferson, were not there. Neither were there any women, black, or Native American representatives. General George Washington was elected to preside and it soon became clear that most delegates wanted to scrap the Articles and start over, quickly producing an entirely new plan for a strong national government to protect property and national security. And, in ratification, the people of the several states also seemed eager to approve the new Constitution and create a strong national government.

The Constitution of 1789, followed by its 27 Amendments, is relatively short. Its 8,700 words, which outline governmental institutions, roles and duties, take about a half-hour to read—you might want to read it sometime! Australia, Liberia, the former USSR, and other nations used it as a model for their own constitutions. Its simplicity in what it leaves out is what belies the compromises that went into it—and how it succeeded in creating a strong national government in an individualistic, revolutionary world. It outlines powers and duties of legislative, executive, and judicial branches without spouting political theory (i.e., no talk of Montesquieu's separation of powers, for example). It recognizes the states without specifying the exact limits of the powers of national or state governments.

It posits the Constitution as the supreme law without detailing how to deal with conflicts of law. It asserts human rights and processes of governance without itemizing how to administer such rights and processes—instead leaving these details to succeeding generations of Americans.

The Constitution was a social contract of the sort envisioned by philosophers of deontological ethical theory. For example, the original body of the Constitution created a strong central government to secure the people, similar to the social contract urged by Thomas Hobbes (1588–1679) in the *Leviathan* (1651), in which atomistic and materialistic individuals were willing to give up everything they had, forming a social contract to avoid a return to the state of nature of every man against every man. The Bill of Rights (Amendments 1–10) amended the 1789 U.S. Constitution with limitations on the governmental powers of this strong central government, in order to protect individual freedoms and property rights, as envisioned by John Locke (1632–1704) in *The Second Treatise on Government* (1690).

Most important, the Constitution establishes itself as the supreme law of the land by direct power from the people. Article VI of the 1789 U.S. Constitution expressly establishes a hierarchy of laws in the US, with the U.S. Constitution as the "supreme law of the land." Other federal statutes and treaties that comport with the U.S. Constitution are also part of this supreme law of the land. Any lower levels of law that do not comport with the U.S. Constitution (and complying federal statutes and treaties) are unconstitutional and null and void, with no legal power.

Law and Equity

There is the law and there is justice. The U.S. Constitution brought together these two separate legal systems, common law and equity, into one judicial system, and now are basic to the American legal order—under the Constitution.[31] Common law really began with the conquest of England in 1066 by William the Conqueror.

BOX 4.2 | Fast Facts on the U.S. Constitution

The U.S. Constitution was written in the same Pennsylvania State House where the Declaration of Independence was signed and where George Washington received his commission as General of the Continental Army. Now called Independence Hall, the building is on Independence Mall in Philadelphia, directly across from the National Constitution Center. Of the 55 delegates attending the Constitutional Convention, 39 signed and 3 delegates dissented. Established on November 26, 1789, the first national Thanksgiving Day was originally created by George Washington as a way of giving thanks for the Constitution. Some of the Founders and many voters in the state ratifying conventions were very troubled that the 1789 Constitution lacked a description of individual rights. In 1791, a proposed list of rights to the Constitution was proposed. The first 10 amendments ratified became known as the Bill of Rights. Of the written national constitutions, the U.S. Constitution is the oldest and shortest, and an original copy is on display at the National Archives in Washington, DC, where it is stored in an underground vault. When the Japanese bombed Pearl Harbor, it was moved to Fort Knox for safekeeping. ◣

William recorded the common customs of England in order to tax and control. By 1087, his priests had assembled a Domesday Book (and the Little Domesday Book for East Anglia) that recorded ownership and customs of property. By the reign of his great-grandson, King Henry II in 1178, England had a uniform law of common customs of the English and royal courts of common pleas created by the King to present cases before a judge or jury of 12 (akin to the 12 Apostles) in adversary proceedings (like the trial by battle). Soon thereafter, the Magna Carta of 1215 also established legal traditions such as the right to presumption of innocence and due process of law before conviction. The common law was born—also called Latin jurisdiction, as all court records and writing were in Latin. These courts of common pleas featured pleas—short legal arguments in law-Latin phrases. We still use old pleas such as guilty or nolo contendere. But courts of common pleas were excessively rigid or pigeonholed: if there was no existing legal-Latin plea to state your case, the courts of common law could not help you resolve your legal dispute. For example, there was no legal-Latin plea to argue that the court order the builder to finish your stable, but only to get your contract money back.

Equity was born out of the limits and rigid pigeonholing of courts of common pleas. Originally, individuals simply came to the King for a special writ (written order) to resolve legal disputes the courts of common pleas could not remedy, e.g., order the builder back to finish the job. As special requests grew, the King created a Chancellor as assistant to handle all such special requests. Eventually, an entire court system emerged under the Chancellor called chancery courts. These courts had no common law jurisdiction but practiced equity, a set of agreed-upon principles of justice, morals, and natural rights. Unlike the Latin pleas and rigid set of legal actions in the courts of common pleas, equity included wide-ranging discussions in English of the maxims (principles) of justice, and resulted in writs that ordered actions, but not monetary damages. The most popular of these maxims was from Jesus Christ: "Do unto others as you would have them do unto you." Chancery courts developed to a high point with the sixteenth-century Star Chamber, when equity was used by the King to control the excesses of judges and decisions of the courts of common pleas. The courts of common pleas and chancery even went to war, but not a drop of blood was spilled. And, since that time, the two court systems have adopted rules to live together in peace, e.g., the equity maxim of "When the Law fails, Equity prevails" reminds litigants that chancery courts have equity jurisdiction only in those cases that cannot be resolved in the courts of common pleas. By the 1950s, all states had combined law and equity (except Mississippi, Arkansas, and Delaware).

Article III of the Constitution announced the merger of law with equity in all federal courts. Courts of law were formerly constrained to rather ineffective remedies such as the Writ of Mandamus to obtain a document. Injunctions today are used in the courts to obtain broad, sweeping changes of behavior and effect large-scale organizational changes in behavior to conform to the requirements of law. An injunction is a remedy awarded by a judge to order a party to stop doing a particular act or activity. It may also order specific action by a party, although this was traditionally known as a Writ of Specific Performance. The significance of injunctions for America today is their widespread use—from domestic violence injunctions to prevent harassment, to prior restraint injunctions against newspapers or internet websites in publishing a story that may be false or injurious.

The practice of injunctions in federal courts has come to focus on prejudgment use, final injunctions, and sanctions for violating injunctions. The preliminary injunction and temporary restraining order (TRO) are the most often used injunctions, designed to preserve the status quo and prevent further harm until a judge can hear and resolve the dispute. They may be called preliminary injunctions or interlocutory injunctions because they are granted at some early point in a lawsuit and are temporary until a later judicial resolution of the dispute. By contrast, the final injunction is granted after a judicial process has determined the rights of the parties to a dispute and orders a permanent change in activities. Federal judges today often label these as the final order in a case. The conventional sanction for violating an injunction is the contempt citation, designed by the judge to include fines, jail time, or whatever is necessary to bring parties into compliance. To implement injunctions, judges have used special masters, monitors, ombudsmen, receivers, human rights committees, and expert panels, who inspect, report, recommend action, and even close down or take over public organizations.

The Supreme Court in *Brown v. Board of Education* (1954) allowed federal courts to issue injunctions to remedy and end the segregation of public schools. With increasing judicial involvement in the administration of public organizations, traditional remedies at law were regarded as ineffective. Monetary damages to individual plaintiffs had little effect on improving these constitutional conditions. Judges have increasingly turned instead to the injunction at a structural, institution-wide level to create a more constitutional society. A wide range of remedies is permitted in volume 42 of the United States Code section 1983 (42 U.S.C. 1983); once a federal civil rights violation is established, the violator is liable "in an action at law, suit in equity, or other proper proceeding for redress." Liability at law may result in monetary damages awards that are nominal, compensatory, or punitive. Liability in equity focuses on injunctive relief to change action. Following the Supreme Court's lead in *Swann v. Charlotte-Mecklenburg Board of Education* (1971), federal district courts have successfully constructed broad and flexible injunctions to redress institution-wide problems in schools, prisons, public housing, and other large-scale public organizations.[32] *Missouri v. Jenkins* (1990) further expanded equitable power to uphold a "power of the purse" for federal judges to issue injunctions that order local and state governments to levy their tax increases to pay for court-ordered constitutional institution-wide changes.

Congress, President, and Court

The Constitution outlines national government powers that are allocated to legislative, executive, and judicial branches. **Separation of powers** is the label often attached to discussions of these concerns, but the reality is inter-branch relations, cooperation, and duplication of power. Separation of powers is never expressly stated in the Constitution. The Framers did not seek to separate or obstruct government, but to improve upon the discredited Articles of Confederation, which had only a national legislature. Combinations and overlapping powers, not separations, are featured in the Constitution. For example, the budget is proposed by the President, subject to approval by Congress (although this was modified in some ways with passage of the Budget and Accounting Act of 1921). The President may veto legislation, subject to a two-thirds override vote of Congress. The Senate must confirm appointments by the President, and approve his treaties.

Executive and judicial officers may be impeached by the House of Representatives leading to trial in the Senate. Over the last two centuries, administrators in the executive branch have increasingly been the focus of combination and overlapping power between branches of the national government.

Some features of administrative governance were not expressly mentioned in the Constitution, but developed over time and by custom. First is the delegation of authority by Congress to executive branch agencies that has worked to combine government efforts. Except for some instances of excessive delegation by Congress without clear standards in the 1920s and 1930s, the Court has allowed the delegation of congressional powers to create the massive national bureaucracy that exists today—from the U.S. Sentencing Commission, to the U.S. Post Office, and beyond. And after *INS v. Chadha* (1983), the Court no longer allows the Congress to take back its delegated powers in piecemeal fashion for some later legislative review of individual agency decisions.[33]

Second is the practice of constitutional judicial review. The Constitution is not explicit about who is to review the constitutionality of government activities. At least since *Marbury v. Madison* (1803), the U.S. Supreme Court has asserted that it is the proper role of the judicial branch to have the final say on the constitutionality of government activities. After all, judicial review has existed as long as recorded human history, with the judicial interpretation of conformity to laws by parties. **Constitutional judicial review** expands on this traditional role of courts to allow judges also to interpret and check the conformity of public actors with the supreme law of the land, the Constitution. Constitutional judicial review has been used by all levels of courts to check the constitutionality of individuals as well as organizations, such as shipping and railroad monopolies in the nineteenth century, and with schools, prisons, jails, police, mental institutions, public housing, and others in recent times. Constitutional judicial review is said to have created a partnership between judges and the public service.[34]

BOX 4.3 | *INS v. Chadha*, 462 U.S. 919 (1983)

- *Facts:* the Immigration and Nationality Act authorized either body of Congress to veto the deportation rulings of the U.S. Attorney General. Dr. Chadha had overstayed his visa and was ordered to leave the country. The House of Representatives vetoed the deportation ruling.
- *Issue:* Did the Immigration and Nationality Act, which allowed a one-House veto of actions delegated to the executive branch, violate the separation of powers doctrine?

- *Reasons:* (7–2) The Immigration and Nationality Act violated the Constitution in allowing a one-House veto. Chief Justice Burger recounting the debates of the Constitution Convention over issues of bicameralism and separation of powers, and reasoned that, even though the Act would have enhanced governmental efficiency, it violated explicit constitutional standards regarding lawmaking and congressional authority: no one-House legislative veto of delegated powers. ◢

BOX 4.4 | Civil Liability and the Varieties of Immunity

- *Civil liability* is legal liability imposed under civil laws and civil process that places a duty or obligation on the person, as distinguished from criminal laws. Criminal liability is imposed under criminal laws and by means of criminal prosecution.
- *Absolute (sovereign) immunity* is the waiver of liability from all personal civil legal liability without limits or conditions; the absolute immunity of a sovereign government (as a state) from being sued. For an action to be brought against a state or the Federal Government, sovereign immunity must be waived.
- *Executive immunity* is granted to officers of the executive branch of government from personal civil liability for tortious acts or omissions done in the course of carrying out their duties. While the President's executive immunity is absolute, the immunity of other federal executive officials is qualified.
- *Legislative immunity* is absolute immunity from civil liability that is granted to

legislators for tortious acts or omissions done in the course of legislative activities.
- *Judicial immunity* is absolute immunity from civil liability that is granted to judges and other court officers (as prosecutors and grand juries) and quasi-judicial officials for tortious acts or omissions done within the scope of their jurisdiction or authority.
- *Qualified immunity* shields public officials from damages for civil liability so long as they did not violate an individual's "clearly established" statutory or constitutional rights. The immunity is available to state or federal employees, including law enforcement officers, who are performing their jobs. As a result, if a state or federal employee violates an individual's federal constitutional rights, that employee is protected from liability if he or she did not violate rights spelled out by a "clearly established" law. ◢

Source: Findlaw Legal Dictionary, "Liability," "Immunity," retrieved from http://dictionary.findlaw.com/definition/

Constitutional judicial review has also created new civil liability of public administrators in lawsuits for money damages for violating the constitutional rights of individuals or groups they serve. Traditionally, a government and its administrators had absolute (sovereign) immunity and could not be sued for monetary damages for the unconstitutional wrongs it committed against a person, e.g., police racial profiling to harass minorities. An individual or group could ask for an injunction to change government procedures, but public administrators and officials had immunity. However, since the 1970s the courts have developed a new doctrine of qualified immunity in which public administrators may be liable in creating regulations and managing existing laws, e.g., racial discrimination in a hiring decision. Yet, public administrators remain immune for liability in their adjudicatory functions, e.g., deciding not to issue a license after failing the driving test. Nobody wants to be sued for liability; thus, public administrators have obtained liability insurance, or quit the public service to work in the private sector, or avoid such decisions to duck the liability. Qualified immunity laws may also compel lawmakers to compromise and adopt more ambiguous language in laws on controversial matters that may incur personal liability.

FREEDOM, PROPERTY, AND EQUALITY

Constitutionalism shaped the institutions of U.S. public administration, but for most people the law of civil rights and liberties defines ordinary, day-to-day experience with government. Civil liberties were traditionally known as individual freedoms that limited government intrusion by law, as found in the Bill of Rights (Amendments 1–10 of the Constitution). Civil rights were laws of empowerment, as found in the 14th Amendment of the Constitution, by which government helped individuals overcome public and private unconstitutional acts against them. Today, when we claim "I've got my rights!" we usually include both civil liberties *and* civil rights as constitutional rights.

Constitutional rights are limited to public action, and do not extend to wholly private relations. For example, if you are babysitting your nephew and tell him to go to sleep, it makes no sense for him to refuse and argue, "I've got my constitutional rights!" While the Bill of Rights and other constitutional rights originally applied only to the national government, the incorporation of the concepts of most of the Bill of Rights were interpreted by the U.S. Supreme Court into the 14th Amendment due process of law requirements, thus making them uniformly applicable to states and localities as well.[35] With ever-expanding concepts of public action over the past century, constitutional rights have become extremely important limitations imposing civil liabilities on the decision/behavior of many public actors.

This section of the chapter begins to survey the duty perspective of the public interests that attends to **rule deontology**. Rule deontologists, like act deontologists, deny that the balance of good over evil consequences is the deciding factor in determining what is in the public interests. However, rule deontologists focus on the conformity of actions with one or more duties or rules to determine if they are right or wrong. Rules are the measure of moral worth and of the public interests. Some rule deontologists hold that there is only one duty or rule, such as divine command theory in which conformity to the commands of God is the criterion of right and wrong.[36] Immanuel Kant (1724–1804) based rule deontology on one duty he called the categorical imperative: "act only on that maxim which you can at the same time will to be a universal law."[37] Other rule deontologists hold that there are two or more basic rules in morality, such as W.D. Ross's six prima facie duties, or basic moral duties that are apparent on-their-face: nonmalfeasance, self-improvement, beneficence, justice, gratitude, and duties that rest on previous acts of our own (e.g., duties of reparation and fidelity).[38] Many people believe that there are some things that are just plain wrong—not for any single reason, action, rule, or duty. The ordinary commonsense morality many public administrators apply to determine what is in the public interests is often of this type.

Freedom

The most historic of constitutional rights have been those associated with freedoms of religion, expression, and privacy, i.e., found in the **First (1st) Amendment**. First, the **freedom of religion** was of primary importance to the Founders of the Constitution. While most Americans have sought the free exercise of their religious beliefs, or freedom *of* religion, others have pursued freedom *from* religion or prohibitions on the establishment of religion. Our Constitution includes both conflicting protections. For example, when you allow an employee to wear a highly visible cross on their person while they work in an area with much contact with the general public, you also make an official place for Christianity at the public workplace.[39] Generally, in such conflicts, the courts have favored the free exercise of religious beliefs because of other protections, e.g., free speech. The Lemon Test prohibits national, state, or community bureaucracies from benefiting or establishing any religious institution or practice unless the benefit statute has a secular legislative purpose; the primary effect neither advances nor inhibits religion, and does not result in excessive government entanglement.[40] The courts seem to favor the non-establishment of religion when the religious belief is expressed in a way that is dominating a public space or function with a particular religious perspective not open to other perspectives, e.g., a large Ten Commandments statue in the courthouse foyer.[41] So, too, religious activities are not protected when they excessively interfere with public goods or service provision.[42]

Second, the **freedom of expression** includes constitutional rights to free speech and press, petition/redress freedoms, and freedom of association. The 1st Amendment right to free speech and press may include protection of the discussion, teaching, or even advocacy of the revolution against the U.S. Government, to commit a crime, or to illegally discriminate against others. Of course, once that person does something in furtherance of this discussion, teaching or advocacy, they may be charged and found guilty of conspiracy to commit an unlawful act. Or if their expression is obscene, defamatory, or would imminently incite a reasonable person to respond with a crime or unlawful act, there is no protection of free speech or press. But the right to free speech and press is one of the most protected of all freedoms today. For example, in *Brandenburg v. Ohio* (1969), the Supreme Court protected the right of the Ku Klux Klan to march in the state capitol square. *Rankin v. McPherson* (1987) ruled that a public employee's right to free speech in a non-public area, regardless of how inflammatory it may seem to others (e.g., after hearing of an attempt on the President's life, remarking, "if they go for him again, I hope they get him"), is protected speech. Yet, *Garcetti v. Ceballos* (2006) ruled that when a public employee makes a statement, they are not speaking as citizens and thus the Constitution does not protect their speech from employer sanction. Most controversial is *Citizens United v. FEC* (2010), which ruled that corporations have personhood and, thus, the right to use of free speech and political money. As a result, the corrosive use of political money is so entrenched and pervasive that the Court

---

BOX 4.5 | First Amendment, U.S. Constitution (1792)

Congress shall make no law respecting an establishment of religion, or prohibiting the free exercise thereof; or abridging the freedom of speech, or of the press; or the right of the people peaceably to assemble, and to petition the government for a redress of grievances.

may now be unable to even *define* corruption of public officials—what is brib-ery and what is business as usual?[43]

Third, the **right (freedom) of privacy**, though not explicit in the Constitution or Amendments, is found in the meanings of the Bill of Rights. Administration in the public interests is most often focused on respect for autonomy and con-cerned with privacy of information. Clients, charges, the public, and even public employees have a right to keep primarily personal information private, such as their personal medical records. Yet, psychological, polygraph, background checks, and drug testing may be required of public employees. The identification of cer-tain personnel may be kept private to avoid jeopardizing operations, such as with undercover police, CIA field operatives, or the Secret Service. Other privacy rights generally involve bodily matters of sex, reproduction, and end of life. For exam-ple, administration in the public interests must respect the right of adults to pos-sess pornographic materials in the privacy of their own home, the right of married or single persons to obtain contraceptives, the right of women to obtain abortions in certain circumstances, the right to plan one's family, the right to direct termina-tion of life-maintenance medical devices, and other privacy concerns.

A series of high-profile right to privacy cases, based in the 4th Amendment and other provisions of the Bill of Rights, includes: *Stanley v. Georgia* (1969), which upheld the right to private possession of obscene material; *Griswold v. Connecti-cut* (1965), which upheld the right of married couples to use contraceptives; *Roe v. Wade* (1973), which upheld a woman's right to terminate her pregnancy over unconstitutional states' anti-abortion statutes. But in *Cruzan v. Director, Mis-souri Department of Health* (1990), the Supreme Court ruled against the "right to die" rights of parental legal guardians of a terminal patient in a vegetative state, who wanted to stop her life support to let her die. More controversial are the intrusions on privacy rights which have been upheld under the 2001 Patriot Act and amendments, up through the 2015 USA Freedom Act, including warrantless searches, intrusive requests for information, and new secrecy procedures in "anti-terrorism." Even after Edward Snowden and others revealed the abuses of privacy rights by the CIA, NSA, and the security state, even after Ground Zero has gone back to just being another urban shopping mall, the Patriot Act continues on.[44]

Property

The protection of property rights was a major motivation of the Founders, includ-ing constitutional provisions limiting the power of government under the com-merce power, the **taxing** and spending clause, the contract clause, the taking clause, and the concept of substantive **due process**.[45] Continuity of interpretation of these property rights belies the meaningfulness of deontological duties against the criticisms of logical positivists who belittle these concepts as nonsense. Does the Court merely assert its preferences, its will to power? Many scholars still repeat the myth by 1930s Progressive historians who sought to justify the New Deal with a tale of an out-of-control laissez-faire U.S. Supreme Court from the 1870s to 1937.[46] Using examples like *Lochner v. New York* (1905), the Progres-sives argued that the Court of "nine old men" merely asserted their preferences for protection of individual property rights and struck down as unconstitutional any attempt by states or national government to interfere with property rights. But later Revisionist historians and scholars who counted the cases found that nearly all of the hundreds of similar decisions by the Court during that time upheld and allowed the state or national intrusions upon property rights.[47] The congruence of meaning from these early property rights cases to current interpretation helps to lend validity to deontology ethics.

Property rights have never been about freedom *from* government, but rather, *which* government is supreme in regulating property rights. Indeed, the commerce clause, found in Article I, Section 8 of the Constitution, has been interpreted since *Cooley v. Board of Wardens* (1852), to give the national government supreme power over interstate commerce in any area in which Congress displaces state or local laws. So, too, the power to tax has been vested in the national government as the supreme law of the land under the taxing and spending clause of Article I, Section 8, as well as the 16th Amendment of the Constitution. The Constitution also provides specific limitations on the power of state or national governments from impairing the Obligation of Contracts (the **Contract Clause,** Article I, Section 10), from taking property for public use, without just compensation (the **Takings Clause**, 5th Amendment), or from taking property without due process of law (the Substantive Due Process Clause, 5th and 14th Amendments). Yet, the courts have repeatedly allowed state and national governments to impair the obligation of contracts (e.g., requiring a higher standard of coal for industrial smokestacks), to take property for public use with questionable or unfair compensation (e.g., assessing compensation value long after eminent domain proceedings have lowered the land value), and to take property without due process of law (e.g., requiring all pharmacies to be mostly owned by in-state residents, to keep out pharmacy chains). Property rights under the Constitution have been about uniformity

---

BOX 4.6 | Property Rights and the U.S. Constitution

The Congress shall have Power ... To lay and collect Taxes, Duties, Imposts and Excises, to pay the Debts and provide for the common Defense and general Welfare of the United States; but all Duties, Imposts and Excises shall be uniform throughout the United States.
(U.S. Constitution, Article I, Section 8, Clause 1 [1789])

nor be deprived of life, liberty, or property, without due process of law; nor shall private property be taken for public use, without just compensation.
(U.S. Constitution, 5th Amendment)

The Congress shall have power to lay and collect taxes on incomes, from whatever source derived, without apportionment among the several states, and without regard to any census or enumeration.
(U.S. Constitution, 16th Amendment [1913])

No State shall enter into any ... Law impairing the Obligation of Contracts.
(U.S. Constitution, Article I, Section 10)

nor shall any state deprive any person of life, liberty, or property, without due process of law.
(U.S. Constitution, 14th Amendment, Section 1)

under national supremacy, not about the freedom *from* government. Like nearly all governments in Western history, property rights in America have been subject to the will of the sovereign, and the power to tax or impose this will has also been the power to destroy, in whole or in part. Administration in the public interests promises no free lunch!

But disagreement remains over deontology duties and may spur reflection on these rights and duties by a new generation of public administrators. For example, *Kelo v. New London* (2005) permitted condemnation and use of eminent domain by the city of New London, Connecticut, to take homes from individuals and give the property to corporate developers as permissible "public use" under the Takings Clause of the 5th Amendment. The broad public outcry against the case and perceived abuse of property rights power by state and local administrators has forced many to rethink these duties. For example, Freeport, Texas, city administrators faced overwhelming public opposition and were condemned for greed in their attempt to bulldoze a family-owned shrimping business to make way for corporate oceanfront developers.[48] What about the morality of the common use of long delays in land-use planning and eminent domain procedures to "lock up" private lands and homes from other resale—and drive down their "fair market value," promote foreclosures by homeowners, and otherwise obtain these lands more cheaply for proposed roadways and public improvements?

Equality

The equal protection of the laws has been guaranteed in the Fourteenth Amendment and many other aspects of the Constitution, national and state laws, and regulations. These constitutional duties are closely based on deontological ethical ideas on the respect and dignity of all persons. Not to be confused with Equity (the court system of maxims of justice, injunctions, etc.), equality in America has been more about equality of opportunity than the equality of distribution found in socialist or Communist nations. U.S. equal protection laws also distinguish between favored and less-favored categories of persons, or tiers of protection, so that racial/ethnic minorities receive the highest degree of empowerment, women and the poor are protected at lesser levels from arbitrary discrimination.

By the 1970s, the U.S. Supreme Court formulated three tiers of equal protection classification. Since the 14th Amendment (1868), the Court had used a rational basis test to determine if a law or public action was unconstitutional in its arbitrary discrimination, later to be labeled minimal scrutiny. The law/action was lawful and valid if the purpose behind the differentiation was a legitimate one and it was rational (articulable).[49] For example, national and state financial aid programs for college students may lawfully discriminate between students on the basis of wealth or income because it is rational to posit that wealthier students are better able to pay their own way. With *Korematsu v. US* (1944), the Court created a new tier of protection and treated all forms of racial discrimination with strict scrutiny. That is, discrimination by race/ethnicity is lawful only if the classification by race/ethnicity is necessary to achieve a compelling state interest. For example, a national health program for sickle cell anemia that affects only specific race/ethnicity groups may thereby discriminate in order to serve only those groups. In the 1970s, with issues of gender discrimination, the Court developed a middle tier, or intermediate scrutiny that applied to discrimination by gender.[50] That is, discrimination

BOX 4.7 | The Framework of Equal Protection

Minimal Scrutiny	Intermediate Scrutiny	Strict Scrutiny
(e.g., wealth)	(e.g., gender)	(e.g., race/ethnicity) ▶

between genders was lawful if it substantially related to the achievement of an important state interest. For example, the military service draft could be male-only because men had greater upper body strength and other abilities required to fight at the frontlines of battle.

Equality issues in American public affairs includes discrimination along a continuum of behaviors that ranges from the most serious and violent hate crimes, through to many ordinary discriminations (e.g., employment discrimination), all the way down to microaggressions (e.g., small inequalities/slights) that may not be actionable at law or litigation. Under federal practice leadership, the U.S. Government and all 50 states collect data on criminal hate crime and civil discrimination incidents by six categories: race, ethnicity, gender, religion, sexual orientation, and disabilities. We will consider each in our ethics case study at the end of Chapter 7, on human resources management. For now, however, we will overview the constitutional basis of laws against discrimination in America.

Race/Ethnicity   America is known around the world for its equality issues with race, embedded in centuries of a deeply racist form of slavery. On July 4, 1776, about one-fourth of the total U.S. population were African Americans (570,000 of 2.5 million)—and only 40,000 were free persons of color. America had targeted African slaves who were perceived as soulless—less than human, mere chattel (moveable property). There were over two million African-American slaves just before the Civil War. The only human right provided to slaves was a ban on unseemly cruelty, but slave owners ignored the law with impunity. The 1789 Constitution recognized and protected the continuation of slavery, and gave lesser human worth to slaves. *Dred Scot v. Sanford* (1857) declared that slaves were not citizens and had no rights.[51]

The Civil War marked the defeat of the forces of the enslavement of African Americans. President Abraham Lincoln freed the slaves in 1863 and the 13th, 14th, and 15th Amendments gave citizenship, human rights, and the right to vote to the former slaves. Congress passed seven different Civil Rights Acts from 1866 to 1875 to protect the rights of African Americans, but enforcement of these rights quickly dissipated. Jim Crow laws (named for a minstrel show character) were passed throughout the US, enforcing an official racial segregation in travel, housing, education, parks, drinking fountains, parks, toilets, and so forth. In *Plessy v. Ferguson* (1896), the U.S. Supreme Court legitimized these laws, and we continue to live with the impact of Jim Crow to the present day.

Official segregation legally ended when the U.S. Supreme Court reversed itself in *Brown v. Board of Education* (1954), declaring that "separate is . . . inherently unequal." Over the past decades many courageous public administrators, judges,

BOX 4.8 | Post-Civil War Amendments

Neither slaver nor involuntary servitude, except as a punishment for crime whereof the party shall have been duly convicted, shall exist with the United States, or any place subject to their jurisdiction.

(13th Amendment, Section 1, U.S. Constitution, 1865)

All persons born or naturalized in the United States, and subject to the jurisdiction thereof, are citizens of the United States and of the State wherein they reside. No State shall make or enforce any law which shall abridge the privileges or immunities of citizens of the United States; nor shall any State deprive any person of life, liberty, or property, without due process of law; nor deny to any person within its jurisdiction the *equal protection of the laws.*

(14th Amendment, Section 1, U.S. Constitution, 1868)

The rights of citizens of the United States to vote shall not be denied or abridged by the United States or by any State on account of race, color, or previous condition of servitude.

(15th Amendment, Section 1, U.S. Constitution, 1870)

officials, civil rights activists, and citizens have upended and set out to reverse a long history of slavery, chattel, segregation, discrimination, hatred, and noncompliance with new laws for equality in public life, including housing, jobs, schools, prisons, and such.

Is the American public affairs system inherently racist? Racism, or a belief in the superiority of one race/ethnic background, was institutionalized in the past by colonial and U.S. slavery, Jim Crow laws, and the cultural values in American expressions like the "white man's burden." Does the evidence of history reveal an overwhelming racism in America? Or is racism no longer systemic; the system is not racist, only individuals? Should all police, for example, be criticized and liable for the sins of a few police who went beyond their authority to commit crimes? The 1988 movie *Mississippi Burning* depicted a racist system of public affairs in 1964 Mississippi. The state couldn't obtain convictions against 3 cops and 15 citizens who killed civil rights workers. So, in *US v. Price* (1966), federal criminal sanctions were brought against these individuals under 18 U.S.C. sections 241 and 242. Congress later increased the punishment to life imprisonment for causing death under these statutes. Later, new enforcement of civil remedies (money damages) were used in *Tennessee v. Garner* (1985) to penalize the Memphis Police Department for the liability of one officer's use of deadly force to apprehend a fleeing felon and killing a 15-year-old black kid. And the 1992 Rodney King case featured both federal criminal sanctions under 18 U.S.C. sections 241 and 242, as well as civil remedies to sanction the Los Angeles Police Department after an amateur filmed cops beating Mr. King in 1991.

The image of Lady Justice, with blinded eyes, suggests a colorblind approach for keeping racism and bigotry out of justice and public affairs. But should justice be blind to past discrimination? For centuries the American system shortchanged minorities. Should the courts ignore the impact of a long history of racist American slavery, Jim Crow, the genocide of Native Americans, and cultural disdain for the status, education, and well-being of non-whites? Should there be some sort of remuneration for past injustices? For example, should large corporations benefiting from slavery, discrimination, or segregation pay a tax or fee—past or present? After all, treaties with Native Americans have included reparation of property, money and apology for genocide, and independent tribal reservations. These and other issues of racism and ethnic bigotry are developed much more fully in our extended ethics case study in Chapter 7, on human resources management. For now, we will only summarize these concerns of racism and bigotry, as well as other issues of equality in the American constitutional system.

Gender   Women for most of Western history were considered chattel, like slaves and cattle, treated as property and often listed on the property deeds. The common law doctrine of coverture did not allow a woman, singularly, to own real property, but her ownership was covered by a husband, father, son, brother, or other male. With the 19th Amendment, ratified in 1920, women gained the right to vote and citizenship, as well as increasing property rights. However, gender discrimination still exists, often as sexual harassment at the workplace. Sexual harassment may be either quid pro quo (trading), sexual favoritism (for favored status at work), or hostile work environment (abusive or sexually charged workplace). In *Pennsylvania State Police v. Suders* (2004), the Court allowed a more streamlined path to the federal courts for a victim of sexual harassment while working with the Pennsylvania State Police. The Court reasoned because Nancy Drew Suders could prove a hostile working environment so intolerable that quitting qualified as a fitting response that she could proceed directly to federal court and ignore the many administrative hearings required by the agency in sexual harassment complaints. Most controversial, women still only get paid 76–78 percent of what men in America get paid, women remain underrepresented in government, where 19.4 percent of Congress was female and one-third Supreme Court justices are women. Where is the equality?[52]

Religion   Religious discrimination is often expressed by hate crimes, such as vandalism of synagogues, mosques, or churches, as well as discrimination in the public or private workplace. Yet, religious discrimination also occurs daily by public administrators in the name of neutrality. *Employment Division v. Smith* (1990) is the leading case for the Court's neutrality doctrine today, which ruled that states may criminalize peyote use under uniform and evenly applied drug laws, even if it is part of a sincere religious ritual of the Native American Church. Congress responded to the Smith decision with the *Religious Freedom Restoration Act of 1993* (RFRA) and other statutes protecting Native American religions to give greater protections against religious discrimination. But in *City of Boerne v. Flores* (1997), the Court struck down portions of the RFRA as unconstitutional and allowed a City Historic Landmark Commission the power to rule against a local Roman Catholic church which sought to build an addition to their church building. Similarly, the Court in *McCreary County v. ACLU* (2005) ruled that courtroom displays of the Ten Commandments were unconstitutional establishment of religion, because Kentucky legislators discussed sectarian purposes for erecting the statutes, not just a proscribed neutral and secular purpose. What was in the public interest?

Sexuality   Throughout Western history, homosexuality has been persecuted as an abomination to God, as were other sexual orientations that differed from heterosexuality under a marriage covenant. While many homosexuals made great contributions to Western society, heavy stigma attached to homosexual activities. For example, the American Psychiatric Association did not "un-list" homosexuality as a psychiatric disorder until 1974. In the US in 1961, all 50 states and the District of Columbia criminalized homosexual sodomy. But over recent decades homosexuals have become more accepted, so that in *Lawrence v. Texas* (2003) the Court struck down a Texas statute as unconstitutional for focusing only on male homosexuality in criminalizing sodomy. Further, in *Oncale v. Sundowner Offshore Services* (1997) the Court ruled that sexual harassment at the workplace was NOT limited to rights violations of women by men, but may include homosexual harassment between men. The U.S. military and many other public affairs agencies have taken a "Don't Ask, Don't Tell" policy to avoid sexual orientation discrimination at the workplace. Yet, cases such as *Hurley v. Irish-American GLIB* (1995) and *Boy Scouts v. Dale* (2000) have ruled that homosexuals and those of various sexual orientations may not violate the Free Speech rights of others who voice their disapproval of their sexual orientation, or force their way into associations or forums by private groups who disapprove of their sexual orientation.

Mental and Physical Disabilities   Over 43 million Americans today have one or more mental or physical disabilities protected by constitutional rights. Significant congressional legislation has sought to address the injustices and issues of the disabled, including: Age Discrimination in Employment Act of 1967 (ADEA) sought to end age discrimination in employment; Architectural Barriers Act of 1968 required greater access to public buildings; Rehabilitation Act of 1973 prohibits employment discrimination against people with disabilities; Comprehensive Employment and Training Act of 1973 (CETA) created jobs and job training programs for the disabled; Rehabilitation Education Act of 1976 (REA) developed affirmative action for the disabled; Americans with Disabilities Act of 1990 (ADA) required the reasonable accommodation of the disabled. Disability law in the administration of the public interest tends to focus on the ADEA and the ADA. Issues of mental disability typically involve either some type of mental illness or mental retardation, while issues of physical disability often focus on bodily challenges and age discrimination. For example, in *Smith v. City of Jackson* (2005), the Court ruled that city police officers alleging age discrimination in a new pay scheme had a valid claim, were not limited by state sovereignty, and could proceed in the federal court to prove either disparate treatment (age discrimination by policy) or disparate impact (age discrimination as practiced).

DUE PROCESS AND ADMINISTRATIVE LAW

Administrative law is the law governing the powers and processes of administrative agencies. Since the 1940s, law school scholars have distinguished the body of administrative law by the rulemaking, adjudication, and informal decision-making issues addressed in the Administrative Procedure Act of 1946, and similar state acts. In the US, federal and state governments are intended to maintain a tripartite balance of powers (legislative, executive, and judiciary). It also deals with the creation, by statute or executive order authorized by statutes, of independent agencies (e.g., Federal Aviation Administration) or executive branch agencies (e.g., the FBI of the U.S. Department of Justice). Thus, American administrative law deals primarily with the grant of power by a legislature to an agency, the assumption of power by executive branch agencies not originally envisioned as exercising them, and with judicial reviews of administrative agency regulations, decisions, and actions.[53]

By contrast, regulation or **regulatory law** is the law developed by administrative agencies in the course of their operation. In reaction to the great expansion of agency activity, the Federal Register Act of 1935 required executive agencies to record all rulemaking, actions, and procedures in the *Federal Register*. Thus, since the Code of Federal Regulations began, similar collections of state and local agency regulations have also developed. Professor Lief Carter contrasts the definition of regulatory law with administrative law as: "Regulatory law includes such things as antitrust statutes and environmental protection policy . . . Administrative law by contrast states procedures for controlling that power. Administrative law regulates the regulators."[54]

Due Process

The constitutional foundations of administrative law and regulation in America date back to 1789, with the founding of the Constitution. The 5th and 14th Amendments prohibited the national government (5th) and states (14th) from taking "life, liberty or property without due process of law." Early legislation by Congress to interpret the meaning of due process by administrative processes included customs laws, regulation of sea-going vessels, and payment of pensions to veterans of the Revolutionary War. But administrative law and regulation grew substantially in the late nineteenth century, with the growth of public transportation (e.g., railroads) and public utilities. Passage of the Interstate Commerce Act and establishment of the Interstate Commerce Commission in 1887 mark the start of administrative law and regulation as we know it today.

Commerce Power   The **Commerce Power** of the U.S. Constitution, Article I, Section 8, Clause 2 provided the U.S. Congress with the power to regulate commerce "between the several states and the Indian tribes." The commerce power has been

---

BOX 4.9 | Due Process and the U.S. Constitution

nor be deprived of life, liberty, or property, without due process of law; nor shall private property be taken for public use, without just compensation.
  (U.S. Constitution, 5th Amendment)

nor shall any state deprive any person of life, liberty, or property, without due process of law.
  (U.S. Constitution, 14th Amendment, Section 1)

Congress shall have the power . . . to regulate Commerce with foreign Nations, and among the several States, and with the Indian Tribes.
  (U.S. Constitution, Article I, Section 8, Clause 2)

delegated to create administrative agencies that would undertake these economic regulatory operations of Congress. In *Gibbons v. Ogden* (1824), the Supreme Court ruled that Congress had supreme authority to regulate interstate commerce under the Constitution's Commerce Power. Any laws conflicting with Congress's interstate commerce regulations were null and void.

But what is interstate? What is local? The Supreme Court has gone back and forth in defining these limits. Under the 10th Amendment to the Constitution, local police powers were reserved to the states and to the people. Since ancient times, police powers were granted to local authorities to regulate the health, safety, welfare, morality, and education of the people. Thus, under the Constitution, the states had local police powers to regulate misdemeanor and felony crimes, for example, and create law enforcement agencies (later called police) to make it so. So, in *Carter v. Carter Coal* (1935), the Court decided that Congress could not regulate the health and working conditions of coal miners because it was not interstate commerce, but local and under the Reserved Powers of the states. President Franklin Delano Roosevelt was so outraged that he threatened to pack the Supreme Court with six additional justices (from 9 to 15) that he would appoint to vote his way against the "nine old men" on the U.S. Supreme Court. Rather than face public humiliation of the Court in this way, two Justices agreed with President Roosevelt to arbitrarily switch their votes to uphold such interstate laws ("the switch in time that saved nine"). But these debates continue. For example, in *U.S. v. Lopez* (1995), the Court decided that Congress could not regulate the sale of guns near schools because it was not interstate commerce, but was reserved to the states. Are there any real limits to the Commerce Power of the national government?

Delegation Doctrine   Under our Constitution, the sovereignty of all government ultimately resides in the people. In ratifying the Constitution and continuing to make it so, the people have delegated to Congress the power to make all laws on their behalf. Since the time of classical Rome, legislators lived by a maxim of law: *delegatus non potest delegare* (Latin, "a delegate cannot delegate"). It was because in classical Rome (and contemporary Britain) the parliamentary legislature appointed a chief executive from its body and controls the bureaucracy and military directly. So, by tradition and under common law, Congress should not delegate the powers that have been delegated to it by the people.[55] And it makes sense. For example, who would want Congress to delegate to the Pentagon its power to declare war? And how could you maintain checks and balances of power if Congress gave away all its powers? But how do you make this work in a system of a separate President and Congress, rather than a parliament?

Thus, we the people have steadily built up an incredible, almost countless, list of daily concerns that we have entrusted to government to take care of our lives, the lives of our family members, even the lives of people we may never know. Congress is simply incapable of making the countless governmental decisions we have entrusted to it, from academic standards to zoo standards of care for animals, and so much more. And we separately elect and empower Congress and the President.

American administrative law has developed a way of coping with these awesome pressures and respecting the **delegation doctrine** by having the U.S. Congress set the primary standards and delegating to agencies only the power to fill in the gaps.[56] Authorization is limited to allowing administrative agencies to fill in the details of the general laws of Congress. For example, Congress authorized the Federal Communications Commission (FCC) to regulate the broadcasting industry in the public interest.[57] FCC professionals, who are experienced and expert in the workings of various broadcast media, make rules that govern, for example, the licensing of stations. As the delegated agent of Congress, these FCC professionals make regulations that are just as binding on broadcasters as if Congress itself had enacted them. Without this system, Congress would have to abandon any attempt to regulate this high-tech and quickly changing technical industry. For example, in *FCC v. Pacifica Foundation* (1978), the Court ruled that the 1st Amendment does *not* deny the government, in this case the FCC, the power to restrict a public broadcast that contains indecent language. In this example, concerning comedian George Carlin's monologue "Filthy Words," the Court famously stated: "When the Commission finds that a pig has entered the parlor, the exercise of its regulatory power does not depend on proof that the pig is obscene." This illustrates the discretionary power of public administrators to fulfill public interests.

Are there any real **limits of the delegation doctrine today**? Of course! First, with the enabling statute that creates an administrative agency, Congress writes the primary standards and delegates that the agency to fill in the gaps. Thus, the agency may be successfully challenged and limited for exceeding its authorization language. Second, the delegation doctrine today limits the excessive delegation of authority by congressional language that is too vague in defining the limits and primary standards of the agency. The enabling statute and all delegations by Congress to agencies must clearly limit the boundaries on delegated authority. Third, the Constitution itself sets important limits on the procedures and substantive areas of agency authority. For example, just as Congress cannot force people to go to church, neither can an agency require church attendance as a condition for receiving public assistance. Finally, some argue that state and local legislatures are largely limited by the traditional delegation doctrine and cannot delegate what has been delegated to them by the people.[58] Since most governance is at the state and local levels, the delegation doctrine is alive and well!

Congress and Administrative Law While administrative law developed within the larger context of private and public law, under changing delegation doctrines and interstate commerce powers, the real story is the congressional takeover and continued domination of administrative law today. The year 1946 was a banner year for public administrators governing according to administrative rules and regulations: Congress enacted the **Administrative Procedure Act (APA)**, Employment Act, and Legislative Reorganization Act (LRA) that included the Federal Tort Claims Act and General Bridge Act, among other laws.

After the tremendous growth of the U.S. bureaucracy under President Roosevelt's New Deal programs and the international scope of World War II, members of Congress felt themselves antiquated—compared to the rapidly expanded and dynamic executive branch agencies. The U.S. civil service bureaucracy had grown to become many large-scale organizations, and the military was assembling new branches and a Pentagon. Administrators were central to government, quoted in the media, lobbied by industry, and held the status once reserved for senators and representatives. To keep up with the demands of the New Deal and World War II, Congress had delegated legislative authority to agencies on an unprecedented scale, with little thought to oversight, evaluation, or control. This concerned some in Congress. Representative Estes Kefauver (Democrat-Tennessee) was alarmed: "Is Congress Necessary?"[59] And Senator Robert M. LaFollette, Jr. (Progressive-Wisconsin) claimed there was "widespread congressional and public belief that a grave constitutional crisis exists."[60]

Congress asserted itself as the source of powers delegated to agencies and made clear that U.S. administrators served as extensions of Congress. For example, Senator William Fulbright (Democrat-Arkansas) warned that old procedures and old rules may not work to control the burgeoning bureaucracy, its regulations, or the budgetary costs. Congress first debated the Walter-Logan Act of 1940, in which they agreed to return to traditional delegation doctrine (i.e., a delegate cannot delegate) and condemn the broad delegation of congressional power to executive branch agencies. President Franklin D. Roosevelt vetoed the bill successfully. And then World War II rocked the world and, by 1946, Congress came to accept what had been done in the name of delegation during the New Deal and World War II. But was there a way to compel a massive bureaucracy to honor and uphold the values of the people as expressed through their representatives, the U.S. Congress?

ADMINISTRATIVE PROCEDURE ACT

The Administrative Procedure Act of 1946 (APA) and other laws (see above) passed in the same year proved significant for Congress and the exertion of public administrators over quasi-legislative and judicial powers. First, even though much of the delegation was already in place, Congress revisited it all through passage of the APA. With the APA, Congress asserted that the complexity of modern public policy, civil administration, and national security required the use of agencies as extensions of itself to carry out legislative functions. Representative Francis Walter (Democrat-Pennsylvania) made the point clearly:

> Day by day, Congress takes account of the interests and desires of the people in framing legislation; and there is no reason why administrative agencies should not do so when they exercise legislative functions which the Congress has delegated to them.[61]

Thus, agency rulemaking procedures were made standard and required public hearings, responses, and more representative input. The APA and follow-up statutes required greater transparency of agency information to the public. Excessive intrusion and heavy regulatory burden on business by agency activities was curbed. And procedures were streamlined for agencies to be more responsive to demands and their responsibilities, such as Federal Tort Claims Act of 1946 (FTC) allowing agencies to settle claims against the government without congressional bills.[62]

Second, Congress reasserted its role in the oversight, evaluation, and control of agencies. In the Legislative Reorganization Act of 1946 (LRA) Congress reinserted itself back into the daily life of U.S. bureaucracy by reforming both the House and Senate committee structures to more closely parallel and follow the structure of the U.S. bureaucracy. The number of standing committees was reduced and, for the first time in history, was given responsibility for exercising "continuous watchfulness"[63] over their list of agencies. The LRA authorized hiring of professional specialized experts (not just clerical staff) to assist committees in oversight, including the Legislative Reference Service, Congressional Research Service, Inspector General Act, and the General Accounting Office.[64] But the LRA failed in an attempt to place the budgetary process more squarely within close legislative control; however, this was later accomplished with the 1974 Congressional Budget and Impoundment Control Act. Other later acts further empowered Congress to the original goals of the 1946 LRA—for example, the Legislative Reorganization Act of 1970 bolstered the power and staff of legislative committees to oversee agencies, and the 1993 Government Performance and Results Act required agencies to consult with Congress in adopting strategic plans and objectives.

Third, Congress reasserted its interests in public works projects and other benefits to their constituents and district. The Employment Act of 1946 put Congress in control of public works projects—often the pork-barrel extras that bring crucial development, jobs, and federal monies to a state or district. Through this control, it was clear that your local member of Congress—not some federal agency administrator—was owed for the largess of the new hydroelectric dam, park-building project, or other public works employment and monies.[65] This helped representatives and senators in retaining their tenure; pork was now controlled by the Congress, and those with a longer tenure in office would get the most goodies. Thus, the length of tenure of members of Congress went up significantly as both office-holders and their constituents realized the benefits in pork for the district and other expertise in casework to help constituents.[66]

So, what is in the 1946 Administrative Procedure Act and its important statutory amendments? You can gather this outlined content easily by looking over this brief document online (we like the version from the U.S. Archives online). The original APA became effective as law on June 11, 1946, and included 11 outlined sections (see Table 4.1).

Significant amendments to the APA include four statutory additions, as well as numerous judicial interpretative revisions. First, as to information transparency, the original APA was designed to increase access to agency information by allowing the public to participate in agencies' decision-making processes. In 1966, Congress enacted the **Freedom of Information Act**, Pub. L. No. 89–487, 80 Stat. 250 (amended to 5 U.S.C. Section 552), which greatly increased the amount of government information that is available to the public. Congress later enacted similar laws designed to make governmental decisions open to the public, including the Privacy Act of 1974, Pub. L. No. 93–579, 88 Stat. 1896 (amended to 5 U.S.C. Section 552(a)), as well as the Government in the Sunshine Act of 1976, Pub. L. No. 94–409, 90 Stat. 1241 (codified as amended to 5 U.S.C. Section 552 (b)), and the Electronic Freedom of Information Act of 1996, Pub. L. No. 104– 231, 110 Stat. 2422 (amended to 5 U.S.C. Section 552).

After the 1946 APA, it took time for senators and representatives to learn the agencies and all their complexity. Only an experienced senator or representative could match the bureaucratic games of long-term civil service employees. The 1946 LRA further helped to develop this long-term expertise by eventually creating high-level assistants to help senators and representatives solve casework issues for constituents, as well as a retirement system for members of Congress.

TABLE 4.1
The Administrative Procedure Act (APA)

- 5 U.S.C. Section 551: Introductions and definitions of special legal terms, such as agency action (a rule, order, license, sanction, relief, or its equivalent or denial thereof).
- 5 U.S.C. Section 552: special legal definitions of public information; agency rules, opinions, orders, records, and proceedings—with application for the transparency or distribution of information from public agencies. This was later amended with the Freedom of Information Act of 1966 (FOIA) for further requirements in making information public, and is discussed below.
- 5 U.S.C. Section 552 (a): legal definitions of specific individual records, and details on their release to the individual, to others in various relations with the individual, to their guardians, and other limits of release to protect individual privacy rights. Also spelled out is a variety of civil law and criminal remedies to protect individual privacy rights from government.
- 5 U.S.C. Section 552 (b): Open meetings laws and their requirements, including specific notices of when, where, what—as well as details on discussions excluded from open meetings requirements, e.g., national security, trade secrets, criminal accusations, purely personnel rules.
- 5 U.S.C. Section 553: Rulemaking procedures by administrative agencies, including notice as to the time, place, and nature of rulemaking procedures, legal authority and description of the rule. This brief section also specifies the 30-day publication of notice requirement.
- 5 U.S.C. Section 554: Adjudication procedures by administrative agencies, including notice as to time, place, and nature of adjudication procedure, legal authority and factual summary of case. This brief section also exempts some hearings, such as those for inspections, tests or elections, military or foreign affairs functions, and other special adjudication functions.
- 5 U.S.C. Section 555: Ancillary matters, including the right to counsel in agency hearings, the right to subpoenas to obtain documents, and process served on others to appear as witnesses.
- 5 U.S.C. Section 556: Hearings procedures by administrative agencies, including the presiding employees, agency powers and duties, the burden of proof, evidence rules, and a formal written record as basis of decision.
- 5 U.S.C. Section 557: Decisions in adjudication by administrative agencies, including any initial decisions, conclusiveness of decisions, review of decisions by agency, submissions by parties in decisions, contents of decisions, record of decisions.
- 5 U.S.C. Section 558: Sanctions imposed by administrative agencies, including determination of applications for licenses, suspension, revocation, and expiration of licenses.
- 5 U.S.C. Section 559: Legal effect of this Act on other laws, including the legal effect of subsequent statutes and amendments.

Of course, much of the pork and self-serving benefits did little to do contribute to controlling the bureaucracy in the name of the people, but in a totality of the circumstances the 1946 statutes and lengthened congressional careers helped to foster a more democratic and constitutional control of the U.S. bureaucracy.[67] The original 1946 APA and its many statutory amendments and augmentations over the decades principally focused on three major concerns: (1) public information and the provisions of agency information; (2) adjudication, rulemaking, and other agency operations; and (3) judicial review of administrative agencies.

First, the original 1946 APA did little in defining public information beyond previous statutes that required agencies to publicize information about their organization, opinions, orders, and public records in the *Federal Register* since the 1930s. Since the original 1946 APA, the Freedom of Information Act of 1966 amended the APA and required agencies to make available their records and documents to any person requesting them, except under certain exemptions of the statute or other laws. For example, you can't request the medical records of a federal employee (unless it's your personal medical record). The Privacy Act of 1974 protects the right to privacy of individuals, prohibiting agencies from releasing records concerning individuals without their consent, preventing the collection of information that is not relevant and necessary, and allowing individuals to review and seek to correct agency records on themselves. The Government in the Sunshine Act of 1976 requires open meetings by federal agencies, commissions, and boards under most circumstances.

Second, the original 1946 APA focused most of its sections in dealing with agency operations, including adjudication and rulemaking. The concern was with agency abuse in rulemaking, adjudication, and other enforcement of their powers:

> the Constitution of the United States has divided the powers of our Government into three coordinate branches, the legislative, executive and judicial. These have been swallowed up by some administrators and their staffs who apparently believed that they were omnipotent. These have exercised all of the powers of government, arrogating to themselves more power than ever belonged to any man, or group. This has made necessary the enactment of such legislation as is now in the process of passage.[68]

In agency rulemaking, the APA required notice and comment of the public preceding any actions by agencies in most instances. Before the APA, cases such as *BiMetallic Investment Co. V. State Board of Equalization* (1915) deferred to agencies in rulemaking, allowing complete discretion in making law—like the deference given to Congress. But informal **rulemaking** under the APA required agencies to publish a notice of the proposed rule in the *Federal Register*, and to receive and consider comment from all interested parties. Any agency-proposed procedures to make or interpret rules must similarly be published in the *Federal Register*. In some instances, the APA provided for rulemaking on-the-record, also known as formal rulemaking, and specified by the statute that created the agency. But these variants of federal rulemaking proceedings are relatively rare today under the APA.

In agency adjudication, the APA required various levels of due process in agency hearings. These due process standards are designed to promote procedural regularity, fairness, and reasoned decisions by agencies. For example, hearings are presided over by administrative law judges (a title adopted by the APA in 1972), who must be independent of the agency hierarchy. Administrative law judges make decisions over policies, benefits, or budgets that may conflict with their agency director. This has been called judicialization of the federal administrative process.[69] The high-water mark of the judicialization of agency hearings was in the Court's decision in *Goldberg v. Kelly* (1970), in which a disabled police officer was cut off public assistance. The **"Goldberg 10"** required procedural protections before particular public services were cut off: timely adequate notice, right to a hearing, right to an impartial judge, right to a reasoned decision, right to judicial review, right to an attorney, right to cross-exam, right to disclosure, opportunity to obtain witnesses, and right to decision on the record. Formal adjudication with all Goldberg 10 exists under the APA only when an authorizing statute of Congress requires a hearing and decision determined on the record in that situation.

Finally, the original 1946 APA provided for a limited scope of judicial review of agencies. The courts may review the substantive rules or actions of an agency, agency information activity, agency adjudication procedures, agency rulemaking procedures, and even alternative dispute resolution processes by agencies. But the intensity of judicial review may vary from 0 to 100 percent, depending on the deference to agency decisions required by the law. For example, APA Section 706(2) (E) states judicial review must defer to all agency fact-finding except if it is unsupported by substantial evidence. On the other hand, if an administrator's decision clashes with the agency's own rules, judicial review will not defer to the agency's factual, legal or discretionary decisions because the decision was "arbitrary, capricious, an abuse of discretion, or otherwise not in accordance with the law."[70] The case-law interpreting the APA and law of constitutional judicial review of administrative agencies is extensive.

ETHICAL CASE STUDY | Information Ethics for Bureaucrats

What are the **ethics of managing (often high-tech) information technology**, such as the internet, for the public administration profession? The title of this ethics case study, **"Information Ethics for Bureaucrats,"** was inspired by the title of John Rohr's classic book, *Ethics for Bureaucrats*, to emphasize that our approach is to apply to public information technology John Rohr's method of analyzing Court decisions on **regime values**. Like other aspects of public service, the **ethical use of information technology** involves constitutional values in protection of freedoms and privacy, property rights, and due process of law.[71] The unethical and criminal use of the internet and email by public servants, and of public servants, for stalking, cybercrime, encryption, surveillance, and recent scandals, have called attention to the **ethical use of information technology**.[72]

What are the applications of ethical theory to our use of high-tech information technology, such as the internet? Moral decisions with high-tech information technology may be clarified with ordinary morality or general ethical concepts, administrative ethics concepts, professional **codes of ethics for information technology** and computing practitioners, rights concepts associated with information technology, and emerging ethical issues. A number of scholarly journals have come to focus exclusively on these issues, including *Journal of Information Ethics, Ethics and Information Technology, Journal of Information Technology and Privacy Law*, and others. With this information overload, the past decade has produced far too many excellent books, journal articles, and materials to list them all.

Ordinary Morality

Many moral decisions involving information technology may be informed by ordinary morality or ethical theories more generally, such as utilitarianism, deontology, and virtue.[73] For example, a moral decision to copy software for a friend may be clarified by more general ethical theories on the quandary between loyalty to a friend and keeping your contractual obligations by not being an info-pirate.[74]

Ethical Management of Information Technology

The ethical theories that generally guide management practices of public agencies, nonprofit organizations, faith-based organizations, and hybrid private organizations have been revisited in their application to new information technologies.[75] For example, the management of transparent website designs for e-business, e-government, and e-organizations must balance the needs of the organization with the needs of consumers, citizens, or users. Managing information technology in the public interests requires clarification of the larger interests of others, equity and fairness in addressing these interests, and implementation that complies with the regime values of a given society.[76]

Professional Codes of Ethics

The information technology field has no universal professional code of ethics, no enforcement of existing voluntary codes, and no governing body to make it so. To be sure, there are dozens of associations and organizations with substantial codes of ethics for computing and information technology, as listed online at the website of the Center for the Study of Ethics in the Professions at Illinois Institute of Technology.[77] Some information ethics codes are global in scope (e.g., Zimbabwe Computer Society)[78] and others reflect longstanding efforts to develop professional ethics codes (e.g., Association of Information Technology Professionals—developing ever since 1951).[79] Most ethics codes read like commandments, such as the Ten Commandments of Computer Ethics created in 1992 by the Computer Ethics Institute, including "Thou shalt not use a computer to harm other people."[80] As such, they provide little guidance for the many hard decisions involving conflicting commandments. Further, all ethics codes for information technology

(continued)

professionals are voluntary at this time and most practitioners in the field don't seem to be aware of their existence. Even the Enron Corporation in the midst of ethical breakdown had a substantial code of ethics that was carefully implemented, educating workers on their expectations. The lack of coming together and producing a universal code of ethics and a governing body seems due to the very nature of computing and information technology: it's everywhere and in everything. Thus, some scholars predict that computer ethics will transform into global ethics or completely disappear as a focal point for ethics.[81]

Regime Values and Information Technology

Like our discussion at the beginning of this chapter on the high, low and middle roads, an emerging trend posits a source of information technology ethics with the regime values of the Constitution and laws and court decisions pursuant to the Constitution.[82] From the cybercrimes of hackers and cyberstalkers, to the ordinary copying of software or music, contemporary ethical dilemmas in the use of information technology have given rise to litigation to resolve these ethical disputes. Courts give meaning to these ethical dilemmas and conflicts by converting whatever is submitted to them for decisions into claims of right or accusations of fault. Most scholarly and popular analyses of information technology and ethical theories have come to focus on legal dispute case resolutions as a source of regime values on information ethics.[83] Clearly, it is in the nature of rights to retain the conflicts presented; rights do not automatically resolve these ethical dilemmas with clear-cut rules. But rights do illuminate the path taken by others to resolve these ethical conflicts and legal disputes. Rights are typically founded in the U.S. Constitution and its amendments as the Supreme Law of the Land, as well as federal and state statutes, case-law interpretation, and customary or common law. Discussion of rights and information technology most often concerns the regime values of freedom (i.e., free speech, privacy), property (i.e., proprietary rights to information), and due process of law.

Freedom

Free speech rights are founded in the 1st Amendment of the U.S. Constitution and protect expressions and symbolic materials from public censure, even if they are considered hateful, obscene, or seditious. These rights uphold the moral principle of an open discussion of ideas within society, but sometimes with limits. For example, while France would not allow an online auction of Nazi memorabilia, a California appeals court upheld the right of Yahoo.com to do so in 2001.[84] While free speech rights protect most allegedly obscene materials, *US v. American Library Association* (2003) held that all libraries receiving federal funds can be required to filter the internet. And kiddie porn is not protected free speech.[85] Further, while *New York Times v. US* (1971) upheld publishing the *Pentagon Papers* and criticizing Vietnam, the *2001 USA Patriot Act* criminalized any research used by international terrorists.[86] However, free speech rights were upheld by a U.S. Court of Appeals to protect the free speech right of a professor to post the source code of his encryption software, and the U.S. Government has modified export control statutes to continue permitting such internet postings.[87]

Unlike free speech rights, privacy rights are not specified in the U.S. Constitution, but flow from prohibitions of unreasonable search and seizure and other legal precepts to uphold the moral principle of the right to be left alone. Common law privacy rights prohibit the public disclosure of highly private facts, misappropriation of your name or likeness, and intrusion on your seclusion. Privacy rights have been used to challenge widely used techniques for data mining, such as cookies, credit card purchase information, and shopping club card data. As discussed previously in this chapter, the U.S. Government and all states have statutes which protect the privacy of public employees from the release of personal information, such as medical records. Yet, in *NASA v. Nelson* (2011), the U.S. Supreme Court decided that Federal Government employees (civil service or contracted out) do not have a right to information privacy in the employment process of background checks—as long as the information is not released to the public. The European Union has taken a leading role as privacy cop to the world, requiring significant protections for individual privacy rights, including all data mining—by private, public, or nonprofit organizations—give full notice, consumer choice, onward transfer, consumer access, security, integrity, and enforcement powers.[88] Yet, protection of the personal identification information of public employees remains a critical problem. For example, the gunman who ambushed and killed three police (wounding three others) in Baton Rouge in 2016 was also tracking down their home addresses on city websites.[89] The U.S. Government and states have yet to settle on a protection of personal identifiable information of public employees.[90]

Property

Proprietary rights in the area of high-tech information technology focus on copyright, patent, domain name, and trademark laws. These rights uphold moral principles of property ownership and due process of law in taking property for public use or other private uses. While these rights may seem wispy, they trump all competing 1st Amendment free speech rights, e.g., you can't satirize the Dallas Cowboys and use their copyrighted materials without consent. Copyrights and patents are exclusively enforced by the national government under the U.S. Constitution. The power of Congress to indefinitely extend copyrights under the **1998 Digital Millennium Copyright Act** was upheld in *Eldred v. Ashcroft* (2003). The fair use doctrine permits copying of copyrighted material if it is minimal, benefits an

(continued)

educational/nonprofit purpose, and has no negative market effect on the use of the copyrighted work, and is in the public interest. Under these rights, The 9th Circuit U.S. Court of Appeals found that Napster was liable for user copyright infringement of MP3 data files.[91] Similarly, the 2nd Circuit U.S. Court of Appeals ordered DeCSS to desist in making available their DVD decryption program.[92] A related administrative ethics issue may be: who will police the pirate-hunters? Similar to copyright protections, domain name and trademark rights safeguard identifiers of the source of goods or services, and prevent fraud or loss of a good name. But fair use allows free speech criticisms (e.g., "Lucentsucks.com")[93] or the use of trademarks or domain names that have become generic (e.g., "playboy").[94]

Due Process of Law

The U.S. Government and states are required to provide **due process of law** before taking "life, liberty or property" under the 5th and 14th Amendments to the Constitution, respectively. Procedural due process requires a specified proper course of action in such dealings with individuals, while substantive due process protects individual rights such as privacy and security, the prohibition of vague laws, and the regulation and licensure of the professions. With the internet and other information technology usage, due process is a frequent legal issue in rights to privacy and security regarding online communications. A coalition of privacy advocates, online businesses, and think tanks called **Digital Due Process**[95] seeks amendments to the **1986 Electronic Communications Privacy Act (ECPA)**[96] dealing with information technology, patterns means of communication, and the sheer volume of data that were unforeseen when the Act was created in 1986. The 1986 ECPA Act was originally passed to update and amend the **Wiretap Act of 1968**, applying to both government and private uses of electronic communications, protecting the storage as well as the transit of electronic communications. With the great changes in electronic communications since, the 1986 ECPA was amended by the 1994 Communications Assistance to Law Enforcement Act (CALEA), by the 2001 USA PATRIOT Act and by the 2006 USA PATRIOT Act Reauthorization Act. Yet, changes have come even more quickly since, including social networks, cloud computing, and Bit Data mining, and the Internet of Things (IoT), among others. The potential for due process of law violations in online privacy and security has grown exponentially. Digital surveillance technologies have advanced exponentially, triggering the protest online publications of **Edward Snowden**, a former CIA contractor who leaked classified information of the National Security Agency (NSA) in 2013 on global surveillance of many millions of ordinary citizens as well as terrorists. He has been variously labeled a traitor and a patriot, a whistleblower and a dissident—and has deeply influenced popular culture beliefs about global digital surveillance, while in asylum in Moscow, Russia, from 2013 to the present.[97] Others continue on with this mission, such as the coalition known as the Digital Due Process, who seek

> To simplify, clarify, and unify the ECPA standards, providing stronger privacy protections for communications and associated data in response to changes in technology and new services and usage patterns, while preserving the legal tools necessary for government agencies to enforce the laws, respond to emergency circumstances and protect the public.[98]

Big Data presents important current legal issues of information technology and due process of law. Big Data is defined by the use of algorithms to gather and mine our online behaviors and decisions, such as our internet searches, favorites, repeat browsing, purchases, reading, watching, click patterns, GPS locations, and other data we generate online into predictions and ratings of who we are individually and by social groupings. We're usually unaware that we are being scored by Big Data information technology. But who scores the scorers? Who oversees the scoring algorithms that define and label us? Is it fair that we are scored without our knowledge and without our input? Is this due process of law? For example, the U.S. Transportation Security Administration (TSA) and others generate a "no-fly" list based on secret scoring of internet use by individuals, along with other information. Private companies use Big Data algorithms to score individuals as "poor candidates" or "depression inclined" or "potentially pregnant," releasing reports used by hiring managers to determine hiring decisions. Public personnel managers—as well as college admissions decision makers—use Big Data from Facebook and other social media to find evidence of drug abuse, alcoholism, and other wrong-doing of personnel.[99] Exercising its unfairness authority, the **Federal Trade Commission in 2008 ruled against CompuCredit**—which sold credit cards to people with low credit ratings—for use of Big Data analyses to reduce credit limits for customers whom they scored negative for charges such as pool halls, pawn shops, and counseling visits. The CompuCredit customers didn't even know they were being scored, or what the criteria were.[100] Do we need some sort of digital due process? Should we require impartial experts, like the IRS does with taxes, to periodically examine and review the algorithms used in Big Data analyses of our lives?

The rise of the **Internet of Things (IoT)** presents another quandary of due process of law. The Internet of Things (IoT) refers to the increasingly interconnected cyber-physical-biological nature of digital data, devices, systems, and people. For example, increasing numbers of drivers on the road use GPS systems for directions from their location to some destination. Who's responsible when the GPS insists that the driver keep proceeding straight ahead over the depicted bridge over a lake, when the bridge has not been built and the driver and vehicle end up in the lake? While IoT

(*continued*)

technology opens wonderful new potential for opportunities and efficiency, it may also yield undesirable or unsafe behavior, unintended consequences, and intrusiveness. Just as the defining technology of the industrial revolution required new approaches of law and governance to regulate workplace safety, labor conditions, and product liability, so, too, does the new information age require new laws and governance of the defining digital information technology.[101] We must develop governance principles for public administration professionals to answer at least two basic questions. First, as autonomous information systems replace human decision makers, who is responsible or accountable for their behaviors? For example, we now hold manufacturers liable if their anti-lock brakes fail, but who should be liable if their self-driving smart car gets into an auto accident? What if the accident is based on AI calculation of the least potential injury in an unavoidable accident? And second, who will control the ethical use of IoT autonomous technology? Isaac Asimov proposed basic laws to govern the ethical use of robotics, focused on: robots must not harm humans, and robots cannot allow humans to be harmed.[102] However, how would we enforce such ethical use of IoT technology? Would we require some sort of mandatory artificial-intelligence-ethics programming into all automated systems to channel their good and bad decision making?[103] If so, whose ethics do we apply in these automated systems?[104]

Beyond Regime Values

Obviously, many of these and other important ethical dilemmas in information technology take us well beyond the realm of regime values. Perhaps this is because they have not taken the form of rights talk, litigation, and preserved regime values in their conflict resolution—because they have not been presented to the courts or because the law is mute on the subject. More pointedly, where is the *equality* in information ethics for bureaucrats? Why is there such a *lack* of rights talk, litigation, and regime values on the issues of equal access to information in the digital age? Is there a digital divide of haves and have-nots in access to computers and the internet? Or does everyone have access? What about Spanish-language access to e-government websites and other public information?[105] Should access to the internet be as basic to constitutional rights as the right to make a telephone call when arrested?[106] What moral issues arise from the impact of computers and social media on the public workplace, family, church, and other institutions?[107] Should we prohibit bad information technology?

For example, what is the moral status and nature of ethics presented by artificial intelligence? Are machines moral, or are we moral machines?[108] What is our moral relationship with high-tech information technology—what obligations are owed to one another? Can hackers and other deviant users of information technology be ethical, to be a "Certified Ethical Hacker"?[109] These and many other applications of ethical theory to information technology have emerged and do not seem to fade away, as with many other technologies in the past century of technology. Perhaps because high-tech information technology is so closely imitative of our sense of being, it presents lingering doubts about pat answers to complex moral questions. And that is the virtue of it all.

Discussion

- What is the regime values approach to the study of ethics in information?
- How may ethical philosophy and specialty codes of ethics inform public servants on the ethics of high-tech information technology?
- What are the regime values of freedom, property, and due process of law with public high-tech information technology?
- What important ethical issues remain beyond regime values with Big Data, Internet of Things, and equality issues with information technology? ◣

CONCLUSION

Constitutional duties, such as due process of law, have given the public interests real meaning in the world of public administration. The Constitution and laws pursuant to the Constitution give public administrators real-world rights and duties to express ethical values, problems, and resolutions within public administration. Administration in the public interests exists within the larger context of these rights and duties, including the Constitution, constitutional rights to freedom, property and equality, and the provision of due process of law through administrative law. The Constitution has provided an institutional structure for administration in the public interests, such as legislative, executive, and judicial branches, the delegation of authority by Congress to public agencies, and judicial review and the legal liability of agencies and public administrators. Constitutional rights and duties of the freedoms, property, and equality of persons, continue to expand and define many of the day-to-day ordinary interactions with public administration. Finally, due process of law and administrative law are highly specific in protecting individuals through procedural limitations on governance and the public.

This overview of the U.S. Constitution and administrative law also focused on the duty perspective of the public interests and the attending deontological theory of ethics. Following the Constitution means dutifully obeying rules or other ways to grasp the meaning of these laws applied fairly and without bias. The duty perspective or deontology may be criticized, first, for dutiful obedience even though it may result in mischief, injustice, or tragic ending for a particular person or group. Of course, in their defense, people who apply deontology duties as the criterion for determining the public interests are affected by the outcomes or end results of their actions and respond accordingly. From the duty perspective, one may argue that, while people ordinarily don't have the capacity to predict or control the consequences of their actions, they can act with the right intent. The duty perspective may present an administrative reality that seems bounded by rules, law, and duties that you are required to follow—but with a belief that you can act with good intent and achieve greater moral worth. Second, the duty perspective may be criticized for its pluralism, lack of unity, and non-systematic long lists of issues, roles, and topics. In its defense, individuals who apply the duty perspective don't simply ignore all arete-excellence or benefits-costs relations, but may include these diverse ethical perspectives in rules such as fiduciary-entrustor, principle-agent, supervisor-supervisee, bureaucrat-citizen, promisor-promisee, lawyer-client, physician-patient, parent-child, and others. Finally, the duty perspective to the public interests gives consideration to the past as an indicator of the good; past precedents may create duties in the present and ensure fairness over time. Of course, the Constitution and administrative law include perspectives other than just the public interests duty perspective. As with all applied ethics concepts, it is a matter of degree, and all three public interests perspectives may be found within the Constitution and administrative law: virtue, utility, and duty.

The many issues of information ethics for bureaucrats illustrate the interplay, conflict, and development of constitutional values. The case examples of ordinary conflicts in the application of information technology involve public administrators, citizens, customers, and other organizations and illustrate the pursuit of duty and its attendant deontological ethics. The framing of the Constitution has been a most important task, yet it is in the *governing* of the Constitution in which public administrators may take a leadership role with these developing information technologies—not only in resolving conflicts of these disputes, but also in anticipating technological advances and problems to come. Thus, the information ethics cases may illustrate how it is not the law that directs the public interests, but rather the public interests which direct the law.

ACTION STEPS

1. Contact or inquire through the web with a federal or state attorney general's office, or a municipal counsel's office. Inquire about select cases decided in their jurisdiction that deal with public interests. How are public interests defined and operationalized by the legal agency? Compare your findings with others. Is there a difference between how the federal, state, and city officials view the public interests?

2. Why do checks and balances and other limits on power seem necessary in the duty perspective of administration in the public interests? Articulate your reasoning by reading and applying the U.S. Supreme Court case *INS v. Chada* (1983), in which the Court no longer allows the Congress to take back its delegated powers in piecemeal fashion for legislative review of agency decisions. How does the concept of separation of powers prevent the abuse of administration in the public interests?

3. Reflect on *Goldberg v. Kelly* (1970), in which injured NYPD police officer Kelly was cut off the public welfare assistance given to disabled officers. The "Goldberg 10" requires procedural protections before public assistance can be cut off: timely adequate notice, right to a hearing, right

to an impartial judge, right to a reasoned decision, right to judicial review, right to an attorney, right to cross-exam, right to disclosure, opportunity to obtain witnesses, and right to decision on the record. Is the concept of public welfare assistance like a property right that NYPD officer Kelly possessed?

4. Should the exponential growth in digital surveillance be checked by experts, citizens, the law, or some other authority? Break into small groups and debate the controversial dissemination of classified NSA documents on global surveillance by Edward Snowden. Was he a hero? A patriot or a traitor? A whistleblower or a dissident?

KEY CONCEPTS AND NAMES

NOTES

1 Carl J. Friedrich, "Public Policy and the Nature of Administrative Responsibility," in Carl J. Friedrich, ed., *Public Policy* (Cambridge: Harvard University Press 1940), 1–24.
2 Herman Finer, "Administrative Responsibility in Democratic Government," *Public Administration Review* 1 (Summer 1941): 335–50.
3 John Rohr, *Ethics for Bureaucrats: An Essay in Law and Values*, 2nd ed. (New York: Marcel Dekker, 1989).
4 For example, William D. Richardson, James M. Martinez, and Kerry R. Stewart, *Ethics and Character: The Pursuit of Democratic Values* (Durham, NC: Carolina Academic Press, 1998); Patrick J. Sheeran, *Ethics in Public Administration: A Philosophical Approach* (Westport, CT: Praeger, 1993).
5 For example, Dean Geuras and Charles Garofalo, *Practical Ethics in Public Administration*, 3rd ed. (Vienna, VA: Management Concepts, 2011); William N. Thompson and Jaems E. Leidlein, *Ethics in City Hall: Discussion and Analysis for Public Administration* (Boston: Jones & Bartlett Learning, 2008).
6 James H. Svara, "Who Are the Keepers of the Code? Articulating and Upholding Ethical Standards in the Field of Public Administration," *Public Administration Review* 74 (#5, 2014): 561–9.
7 Dennis L. Dresang, *The Public Administration Workbook*, 7th ed. (Routledge, 2011); Liza Irene-Saban, "Understanding the Obligations of Codes of Ethics," in James L. Perry and Robert K. Christensen, *Handbook of Public Administration* (San Francisco, CA: Jossey-Bass, 2015), 598–615; J. Michael Martinez, *Public Administration Ethics for the 21st Century* (Westport, CT: Praeger, 2009); Jeremy F. Plant, "Using Codes of Ethics in Teaching Public Administration," in James S. Bowman and Donald C. Menzel, eds., *Teaching Ethics and Values in Public Administration Programs: Innovations, Strategies, and Issues* (Albany, NY: SUNY Press, 1997); James H. Svara, *The Ethics Primer for Public Administrators in Government and Nonprofit Organizations*, 2nd ed. (Boston: Jones & Bartlett, 2014).
8 See, Stephanie P. Newbold, "Toward a Constitutional School for American Public Administration," *Public Administration Review* 70 (#4, 2010): 538–46; Stephanie P. Newbold and David Rosenbloom, eds.,*The Constitutional School of American Public Administration* (New York: Routledge, 2016).
9 For example, Sortirios A. Barber and James E. Fleming, *Constitutional Interpretation: The Basic Questions* (New York: Oxford University Press, 2007); Bradley S. Chilton, "Constitutional Conscience: Criminal Justice and Public Interest Ethics," *Criminal Justice Ethics* 17 (1998): 33–41; Ronald Dworkin, *Freedom's Law: The Moral Reading of the Constitution* (New York, NY: Oxford University Press, 1996); Michael J. Perry, *Morality, Politics, and Law* (New York, NY: Oxford University Press, 1990); H. Jefferson Powell, *Constitutional Conscience: The Moral Dimensions of Judicial Decisions* (Chicago, IL: University of Chicago Press, 2008); H. Jefferson Powell, *The Moral Tradition of American Constitutionalism: A Theological Interpretation* (Durham, NC: Duke University Press, 1993).
10 Richard T. Green, "Constitutional Jurisprudence: Reviving Praxis in Public Administration," *Administration & Society* 24 (1992): 3–21.

11 Lon Fuller, "The Forms and Limits of Adjudication," *Harvard Law Review* 92 (1978): 1–33.

12 Robert H. Chaires and Bradley S. Chilton, eds., *Star Trek Visions of Law & Justice* (Dallas, TX: Adios Press/University of North Texas Press, 2003).

13 For example, Philip J. Cooper, "Understanding How Public Law Reinforces Administrative Responsibility," in James L. Perry and Robert K. Christensen, eds. *Handbook of Public Administration* (Jossey-Bass, 2015), 77–96; John Rohr, *Ethics For Bureaucrats: An Essay in Law and Values*, 2nd ed. (New York, NY: Marcel Dekker, 1989); Richard Green, "A Constitutional Jurisprudence: Reviving Praxis in Public Administration," *Administration and Society* 24 (#1, 1992): 3–21; Yong Lee, David Rosenbloom, and Rosemary O'Leary, *A Reasonable Public Servant: Constitutional Foundations of Administrative Conduct in the United States* (Armonk, NY: M.E. Sharpe, 2005); David Rosenbloom and Robert Kravchuk, *Public Administration: Understanding Management, Politics, and Law in the Public Sector*, 6th ed. (Boston, MA: McGraw-Hill Company, 2005); Philip Cooper, *Public Law and Public Administration*, 4th ed. (St. Paul, MN: Wadsworth, 2006). Note: at the 2008 American Political Science Association meetings, the "Constitutional School of Public Administration" debuted as an ascendant approach to the study of public administration.

14 For example, Walter F. Murphy, C. Herman Pritchett, and Lee Epstein, *Courts, Judges, & Politics: An Introduction to the Judicial Process*, 5th ed. (Boston, MA: McGraw-Hill Company, 2002); Ronald Dworkin, *Taking Rights Seriously* (Cambridge, MA: Harvard University Press, 1978); Lief H. Carter and Thomas F. Burke, *Reason in Law*, 7th ed. (New York: Longman's, 2004).

15 Charles W. Anderson, *Statecraft: An Introduction to Political Choice and Judgment* (New York, NY: John Wiley & Sons, 1977), chapter 3.

16 Ralph Clark Chandler, "Deontological Dimensions of Administrative Ethics," in Terry L. Cooper, ed., *Handbook of Administrative Ethics*, 2nd ed. (New York: Marcel Dekker, 2000), 179–94.

17 *Crito*, from Plato, *Euthyphro. Apology. Crito. Phaedo. Phaedrus*, trans. Harold North Fowler, *Loeb Classical Library* (Book 36) (Cambridge, MA: Harvard University Press, 1999 [reprint of 1904 ed.]).

18 Charlie D. Broad, *Five Types of Ethical Theory* (London: Routledge & Kegan, 1930), chapter 5; Tom L. Beauchamp, *Philosophical Ethics: An Introduction to Moral Philosophy*, 3rd ed. (New York: McGraw-Hill, 2001), 109.

19 Immanuel Kant, *Grounding for the Metaphysics of Morals* (1785) (Indianapolis, IN: Hackett Publishing, 1993), 24.

20 Francis Kamm, *Intricate Ethics: Rights, Responsibilities, and Permissible Harm* (New York, NY: Oxford University Press, 2006).

21 William David Ross, *The Right and the Good* (1930), Philip Stratton-Lake reprint (Oxford: Oxford University Press, 2002).

22 For example, Michael J. Perry, *Morality, Politics & Law* (New York, NY: Oxford University Press, 1990).

23 For example, Larry Yackle, *Regulatory Rights: Supreme Court Activism, The Public Interest, and the Making of Constitutional Law* (Chicago, IL: University of Chicago Press, 2007).

24 This 1972 interview comment is quoted in John Arthur, *The Unfinished Constitution: Philosophy and Constitutional Practice* (Belmont, CA: Wadsworth, 1989), 1.

25 For example, Hannah Arendt, *Eichman in Jerusalem: A Report on the Banality of Evil* (New York: Penguin Classics, 2006 [reprint of 1963 ed.]).

26 Bradley Chilton, *Prisons Under the Gavel: The Federal Court Takeover of Georgia Prisons* (Columbus: Ohio State University Press, 1991).

27 For example, Ronald Dworkin, *Freedom's Law: The Moral Reading of the American Constitution* (Cambridge, MA: Harvard University Press, 1996).

28 For example, Richard A. Posner, *Economic Analysis of Law*, 7th ed. (New York: Aspen Publishers, 2007); Francesco Parisi, ed., *The Economic Structure of Law: The Collected Economic Essays of Richard A. Posner*, 3 vols. (Northampton, MA: Edward Elgar Publishing, Inc., 2001).

29 For example, "Symposium: National Conference on Judicial Biography," *New York University Law Review* 70 (1995): 485; J. Woodward Howard, Jr, "Alpheus T. Mason and the Art of Judicial Biography," *Constitutional Commentary* 8 (1991): 41; Kimberlé Crenshaw, ed., *Critical Race Theory: The Key Writings that Formed the Movement* (New York, NY: New Press, 1995); Richard Delgado, *Critical Race Theory: The Cutting Edge* (Philadelphia, PA: Temple University Press, 1995); Colin Farrelly and Lawrence B. Solum, eds., *Virtue Jurisprudence* (Hampshire, UK: Palgrave Macmillan, 2007).

30 David Schuman, *American Government: The Rules of the Game* (New York, NY: Random House, 1984), 1–33.

31 See, Bradley Chilton, *Prisons Under the Gavel: The Federal Court Takeover of Georgia Prisons* (Columbus: Ohio State University Press, 1991); Owen Fiss, *The Civil Rights Injunction* (Bloomington: Indiana University Press, 1978).

32 See, for example, Bradley Chilton and Paul Chwialkowski, "The Court Versus Consent Decrees? Schools, Horne v. Flores and Judicial Strategies of Institutional Reform Litigation," *Education and Urban Society* 46 (#1, 2014): 88–108.

33 For various critiques of the case, both liberal and conservative, see Elizabeth A. Martin, "Informational Theory of the Legislative Veto," *Journal of Law, Economics, and Organization* 13 (#2, October 1997): 319–43; Louis Fisher, "Judicial Misjudgments About the Lawmaking Process: The Legislative Veto Case," *Public Administration Review* 45 (November 1985): 705–11; John C. Fortier, "Executive Branch Overhaul Due," *Washington Times*, February 11, 2002, retrieved from www.aei.org/include/pub_print.asp?pubID=13600

34 David. H. Rosenbloom, "Public Administrators and the Judiciary: The 'New Partnership,'" *Public Administration Review* 47 (1987): 75–83.

35 Some of the more important "incorporation" cases in the first 10 amendments are *Gitlow v. People of New York*, 268 U.S. 652 (1925) ["free speech" of the First Amendment], *Cantwell v. Connecticut*, 310 U.S. 296 (1940) ["religious freedom," specifically the Free Exercise clause of the 1st Amendment], *Everson v. Board of Education*, 330 U.S. 1 (1947) ["religious freedom," specifically the Establishment clause of the 1st Amendment], and *Powell v. Alabama*, 287 U.S. 45 (1932) ["right to counsel" in the 5th Amendment].

36 A classic Judeo-Christian example of such "Natural Law" theories may be found in Russell Kirk, *The Roots of American Order* (Malibu, CA: Pepperdine University Press, 1974). An Islamic example may be found in Noel J. Coulson, *Conflicts and Tensions in Islamic Jurisprudence* (Chicago, IL: University of Chicago Press, 1969).

37 Immanuel Kant, *Groundwork on the Metaphysics of Morals*, trans. H.J. Paton (New York, NY: Harper Torchbooks, 1964).

38 W.D. Ross, *The Right and the Good* (Oxford, UK: Clarendon Press, 1930).

39 *Draper v. Logan County Public Library*, 403 F. Supp. 2d, 608 (W.D.KY. 2003).

40 *Lemon v. Kurtzman*, 403 U.S. 602 (1971).

41 *McCreary County, Kentucky, et al. v. American Civil Liberties Union of Kentucky et al*, 545 U.S. 844 (2005).

42 Robert Booth Fowler, Allen D. Hertzke, Laura R. Olson, and Kevin R. den Dulk, *Religion and Politics in America: Faith, Culture, and Strategic Choices*, 4th ed. (Boulder, CO: Westview Press, 2011).

43 Bruce Cannon Gibney, *A Generation of Sociopaths: How the Baby Boomers Betrayed America* (New York: Hachette Books, 2017), 313.

44 Ibid., 320–2.

45 *Charles River Bridge v. Warren Bridge* 36 U.S. 420 (1837) and *US v. Carolene Products Company*, 304 U.S. 144 (1938) [property rights in general]; *Heart of Atlanta Motel, Inc. v. US*, 379 U.S. 241 (1964) and *United States v. Morrison*, 529 U.S. 598 (2000) [commerce clause]; *United States v. Butler*, 297 U.S. 1 (1936) [taxing and spending clause]; *Home Building and Loan Assn. v. Blaisdell*, 290 U.S. 398 (1934) [contract clause]; *Lucas v. South Carolina Coastal Council* 505 U.S. 1003 (1992) and *Kelo et al. v. City of New London et al.*, 545 U.S. 469 (2005) [takings clause]; and *Lochner v. New York*, 198 U.S. 45 (1905) [substantive due process].

46 See Paul A. Freund, *The Supreme Court of the United States: Its Business, Purposes, and Performance* (Cleveland, OH: World, 1961); and Alpheus Mason and Donald Stephenson, *American Constitutional Law: Introductory Essays and Selected Cases*, 14th ed. (Englewood Cliffs, NJ: Prentice Hall, 2004).

47 See, for example, John Semonche, *Charting the Future: The Supreme Court Responds to a Changing Society, 1890–1920* (Westport, CN: Greenwood, 1978); and Loren Beth, *The Development of the American Constitution, 1877–1917* (New York: Harper and Row, 1971).

48 Carla T. Main, *Bulldozed: "Kelo," Eminent Domain, and the American Lust for Land* (New York, NY: Encounter Books, 2007).

49 *McCulloch v. Maryland*, 17 U.S. 316 (1819).

50 *Rostker v. Goldberg*, 453 U.S. 57 affirmed a male-only draft, but in *United States v. Virginia*, 518 U.S. 515 (1996) the Court ruled that the Virginia Military Academy's (VMI) ban of female students, and the provision of a "comparable" institution called the Virginia Women's Institute for Leadership (VWIL), did not provide equal or comparable facilities and educational opportunities as did VMI, and thus ordered VMI to accept female students. And in *Craig v. Boren*, 429 U.S. 190 (1976) the Court upheld Oklahoma's drinking age laws that discriminated by allowing a lower drinking age for women.

51 Michelle Alexander, *The New Jim Crow: Mass Incarceration in the Age of Colorblindness* (New York: The New Press, 2012).

52 For example, Maria J. D'Agostino and Helisse Levine, eds., *Women in Public Administration: Theory and Practice* (Sudbury, MD: Jones & Bartlette, 2011); Bruce Cannon Gibney, *A Generation of Sociopaths: How the Baby Boomers Betrayed America* (New York: Hachette Books, 2017), 316–17; Mary E. Guy and Sean McCandless, "Social Equity: Its Legacy, Its Promise," *Public Administration Review* 72 (2012): 5–13; Camilla Stiver, *Gender Images In Public Administration: Legitimacy And The Administrative State* (Thousand Oaks, CA: Sage Publications, 2002).

53 Kenneth Culp Davis, *Administrative Law Text* (St. Paul, MN: West, 1972), 1; see also Julia Beckett and Heidi Koenig, eds., *Public Administration and Law: An ASPA Classic* (Armonk, NY: M.E. Sharpe, 2005).

54 Lief H. Carter, *Administrative Law and Politics: Cases and Comments* (Boston, MA: Little, Brown, 1983), 34.

55 Philip Hamburger, *Is Administrative Law Unlawful?* (Chicago, IL: University of Chicago Press, 2014).

56 Anthony Bertelli and Laurence E. Lynn, Jr., *Madison's Managers: Public Administration and the Constitution* (Baltimore, MN: Johns Hopkins University Press, 2006); Jerry L. Mashaw, *Creating the Administrative Constitution: The Lost One Hundred Years of American Administrative Law* (New Haven, CT: Yale University Press, 2012).

57 The "classic" case review and upholding the "public interest" standard is *Red Lion Broadcasting Co. v. FCC*, 395 U.S. 367 (1969).

58 Kenneth Culp Davis, *Administrative Law Text* (St. Paul, MN: West, 1972).

59 Estes Kefauver and Jack Levin, *A Twentieth-Century Congress* (New York, NY: Essential Books, 1947).

60 Robert LaFollette, "Congress Wins a Victory over Congress," *New York Times Magazine* (August 1946), 4.

61 David H. Rosenbloom, "'Whose Bureaucracy Is This, Anyway?' Congress' 1946 Answer," *PS: Political Science and Politics* 34, no. 4 (December 2001): 774.

62 Ibid., 773–7.

63 Joel Aberbach, *Keeping a Watchful Eye* (Washington, DC: Brookings Institution, 1990).

64 Harrison Fox and Susan Hammond, *Congressional Staffs* (New York, NY: Free Press, 1977).

65 Stephen Bailey, *Congress Makes A Law: The Story Behind the Employment Act of 1946* (New York, NY: Columbia University Press, 1950).

66 Charles Bullock, "House Careerists: Changing Patterns of Longevity and Attrition," *American Political Science Review* 66 (December 1972): 1295–300; Morris Fiorina, *Congress: Keystone of the Washington Establishment*, 2d ed. (New Haven, CT: Yale University Press, 1989); John Hibbing, *Congressional Careers* (Chapel Hill: University of North Carolina Press, 1991).

67 David Rosenbloom, *Building A Legislative-Centered Public Administration: Congress and the Administrative State, 1946–1999* (Tuscaloosa: University of Alabama Press, 2000).

68 *United States Congressional Record: May 24, 1946* (Washington, DC: U.S. Government Printing Office, 1946), 5659.

69 Marshall Dimock, *Law and Dynamic Administration* (New York: Praeger, 1980); David H. Rosenbloom and Rosemary O'Leary, *Public Administration and Law,* 2nd ed. (New York: Marcel Dekker, 1997).

70 Administrative Procedure Act, Section 706(2) (A).

71 For further reading, see Sara Baase, *A Gift of Fire: Social, Legal, and Ethical Issues for Computers and the Internet*, 2nd ed. (Upper Saddle River, NJ: Prentice-Hall, 2003); Bradley Chilton, "'Star Trek' and *Stare Decisis*: Information Technology and Legal Reasoning," *Journal of Criminal Justice and Popular Culture* 8 (2001): 25–36; Bradley Chilton, "Public Interest Ethic," in Allen Kent, ed., *Encyclopedia of Library and Information Science* (New York: Marcel Dekker, 1996), vol. 58, 275–81; Bradley Chilton, "Managing Information Services in the Public Interest Ethic," *Journal of Information Ethics* 2 (1993): 44–52.

72 Cass Sunstein, *Republic.com* (Princeton, NJ: Princeton University Press, 2001).

73 For example, John Sullins, "Information Technology and Moral Values," in N. Zalta, ed., *The Stanford Encyclopedia of Philosophy*, retrieved from https://plato.stanford.edu/archives/spr2016/entries/it-moral-values/; James H. Moor, "Why We Need Better Ethics for Emerging Technologies," in J. van den Hoven and J. Weeker, eds., *Information Technology and Moral Philosophy* (Cambridge, UK: Cambridge University Press, 2008), 26–39.

74 For example, Linda L. Brennan and Victoria E. Johnson, eds., *Social, Ethical and Policy Implications of Information Technology* (Hershey, PA: IGP Press, 2003); Herman T. Tavani, *Ethics and Technology: Ethical Issues in an Age of Information and Communication Technology* (Hoboken, NJ: John Wiley & Sons, 2004).

75 For example, Yu-Che Chen and Michael J. Ahn, eds., *Routledge Handbook on Information Technology in Government* (New York: Routledge, 2017); Kerreth Kernaghan, "Digital Dilemmas: Values, Ethics and Information Technology," *Canadian Public Administration* 57 (#2, June 2014): 295–317.

76 For example, Bradley Chilton, "Managing Information Services in the Public Interest Ethic," *Journal of Information Ethics* 2 (1993): 44–52.

77 Retrieved at www.ethics.iit.edu

78 Retrieved at http://courses.cs.vt.edu/professionalism/WorldCodes/Zimbabwe.Code.html (updated 2005).

79 Retrieved at www.aitp.org/?page=EthicsConduct

80 Retrieved at http://computerethicsinstitute.org/publications/tencommandments.html

81 For example, Terrell Ward Bynum and Simon Rogerson, *Computer Ethics and Professional Responsibility: Introductory Text and Readings* (Oxford, UK: Blackwell, 2004).

82 For example, Richard K. Ghere, "Accountability and Information Technology Enactment: A Cross-National Perspective," in Melvin Dubnick and H. George Frederickson, eds., *Accountable Governance: Problems and Promises* (Armonk, NY: N.E. Sharpe, 2011), 146–64.

83 For example, Sara Baase, *A Gift of Fire: Social, Legal, and Ethical Issues for Computers and the Internet*, 2nd ed. (Upper Saddle River, NJ: Prentice-Hall, 2003).

84 *Yahoo! Inc. v. La Ligue Contre le Racisme et l'antisémitisme (LICRA)*. While the U.S. District Court found in favor of Yahoo! Inc., the 9th Circuit U.S. Court of Appeals later reversed, which simply required that Yahoo! Inc. not allow the Nazi memorabilia to be sold to anyone in France. The U.S. Supreme Court denied any further appellate review of the case in 2006.

85 *U.S. v. Williams* (2008).

86 Under the 2001 Patriot Act, as amended 2010, in title 18 of the United States Code, sections 2339A and 2339B.

87 *Bernstein v. U.S. Department of Commerce* (9th Circuit, 2004).

88 As per the 2016 European Commission, retrieved at http://ec.europa.eu/justice/data-protection/

89 Debbie Elliot, "Gunman Who Ambushed Baton Rouge Officers Searched for Police Home Addresses," (June 30, 2017), retrieved at www.npr.org/sections/thetwo-way/2017/06/30/535093321/gunman-who-ambushed-baton-rouge-officers-searched-for-police-home-addresses

90 For example, Anna Ya Ni, "Protection of Personally Identifiable Information in Government: A Survey of U.S. Regulatory Framework and Emerging Technological Challenges," in Yu-Che Chen and Michael J. Ahn, eds., *Routledge Handbook on Information Technology in Government* (New York, NY: Routledge, 2017), 266–83.

91 *A&M Records v. Napster* (9th Circuit U.S. Court of Appeals, 2001).

92 *University City Studios v. Corley* (2nd Circuit U.S. Court of Appeals, 2001).

93 *Lucent Techs., Inc. v. Lucentsucks.com* (E.D. Va. 2000).

94 *Playboy Publications, Inc. v. Welles* (S.D. Ca. 1998).

95 The coalition known as *Digital Due Process* may be found at https://digitaldueprocess.org/

96 The ECPA may be found at title 18 of the United States Code, section 2510 and following.

97 For example, Anatoly Kucherena. *Time of the Octopus: Based on the True Story of Edward Snowden* (London: Glasgoslav Publications, 2017).

98 Retrieved from https://digitaldueprocess.org/

99 For example, Alfred Tat-Kei Ho, Kate Bender, Julie Steenson, and Eric Roche, "Big Data and Local Performance Management: The Experience in Kansas City, Missouri," in Yu-Che Chen and Michael J. Ahn, eds., *Routledge Handbook on Information Technology in Government* (New York, NY: Routledge, 2017), 95–107.

100 Federal Trade Commission v. CompuCredit Corporation & Jefferson Capital Systems (N.D. Ga. 2008).

101 For example, Jian-Chuan Zhang, Xiao Zhang, and Zhieheng Wang, "Internet of Things for Public Service: Innovative Practice in China," in Yu-Che Chen and Michael J. Ahn, eds., *Routledge Handbook on Information Technology in Government* (New York, NY: Routledge, 2017), 124–36.

102 For example, Isaac Asimov, *I, Robot* (New York, NY: Gnome Press, 1950); Isaac Asimov, *Robots and Empire* (New York, NY: Doubleday Publishing Co., 1985).

103 For example, W. Wallach and C. Allen, *Moral Machines: Teaching Robots Rights from Wrong* (Oxford, UK: Oxford University Press, 2010).

104 For example, Lawrence Lessig, *Code and Other Values of Cyberspace* (New York, NY: Basic Books, 1999).

105 J. Scott McDonald, "Language as a Barrier to Local Government Access: Spanish Language Access to Local Government Websites", government document, NSF 1338471, *Broadband Use Data* (2015), available online at Harvard Dataverse, V1, doi:10.7910/DVN/USCRQN; J. Scott McDonald, Gerald A. Merwin, Keith A. Merwin, Regina K. Morris, and Edris L. Brannen, "Serving Constituents with Limited English Proficiency (LEP) in the US: Challenges and Implications for Local Government Websites," in Ed Downey, Carl Ekstrom and Matthew Jones, eds., *E-Government Website Development: Future Trends and Strategic Models* (Hershey, PA: IGI Global, 2011), 35–53.

106 Mark Warschauer, *Technology and Social Inclusion: Rethinking the Digital Divide* (Cambridge, MA: MIT Press, 2003).

107 For example, Lola Mergel, "Social Media Communication Modes in Government," in Yu-Che Chen and Michael J. Ahn, eds., *Routledge Handbook on Information Technology in Government* (New York, Y: Routledge, 2017), 168–79.

108 For example, Thomas M. Georges, *Digital Soul: Intelligent Machines and Human Values* (Boulder, CO: Westview Press, 2003).

109 For example, Rafay Baloch, *Ethical Hacking and Penetration Testing Guide* (Boca Raton, FL: CRC Press/Taylor & Francis, 2014); Lora Frecks, "Civic Hacking: Citizens Creating New Digital Government Interfaces," in Yu-Che Chen and Michael J. Ahn, eds., *Routledge Handbook on Information Technology in Government* (New York, NY: Routledge, 2017), 196–216.

Applications of the Public Administration Profession

Federalism, States, Communities, and Honesty

"Fully Inform and Advise. Provide accurate, honest, comprehensive, and timely information and advice to elected and appointed officials and governing board members, and to staff members in your organization."
                    —(Code of Ethics, American Society for Public Administration, 2013)

BOX 5.1 | CHAPTER OBJECTIVES

1 Discuss federalism and how managerial decentralization permeates American governance.
2 Overview state and local public administration, policymaking, and reform and reorganization.
3 Summarize important state and local policy, e.g., education, planning and crisis management.
4 Critique the public service ethical issues of honesty, evasion and transparency, especially in states and communities.

Federalism, states, and communities present a common challenge to public administration of balancing, compromising, and getting along in close quarters with those who may be next door. And it is in these close quarters that honesty, lying, and evasion become critically sensitive grounds for conflict—and also for consensus when there is trust, full information, and transparency. Our understanding of public administration would be incomplete without at least a general overview of the federalism interrelationships of states and local communities with one another, as well as with the national government. For example, changes in federalism and intergovernmental relations after events such as 9/11 and Hurricane Katrina provided significant challenges to local and state administrative, political, and nonprofit decision-making officials—especially our first responders—in the areas of communication, coordination, and especially dollars! And problems facing citizens of various states and localities are incredibly diverse, including differences in preparing and responding to natural disasters, coping with reductions in higher education demands or funding, and dealing with the increasing demands and costs of Medicare and Medicaid. Over and over, the question is the same. How are state and local administrators, officials, and nonprofit organizations supposed to balance, compromise, and remain accountable to increasing needs of citizens with dwindling resources? While the question seems the same, the responses are as varied as the streets where we live—from urgent natural disaster crises to mundane nuisances of cracks in the sidewalks on your street. It is in this complexity that the ethics of honesty seem most important. How can states and communities maintain the transparency of advice and information necessary for the trust of all citizens, administrators, and officials to make their responses?

This chapter may be unique in public administration survey textbooks—we include a separate chapter on state and local public administration, as well as their interactions with one another and with the national government. This shortcoming in other textbooks may be due to the pervasive view that states and local communities are the minors, like the minor leagues of baseball, while gossip in the halls of federal office buildings pretends that national government is like the major leagues. Many public administration textbooks give attention to the nature of federalism and intergovernmental relations in a top-down view from the national government to the states and local governments. But few, if any, public administration survey textbooks have a separate chapter on the administrative and policymaking influences of state and local governments and the roles and functions of major **state and local public administrators**. Yet, states and communities differ in their public administration from what we see in national government agencies. And nearly six times as many people work in state and local government civil service as work in national government civil service. Shouldn't these many administrative experiences be important for our systematic understanding of public administration?

The chapter begins, first, with an overview of the concept of federalism and discussion of how managerial decentralization now permeates the relationship between the national and **state governments**. This also sets the stage for the remainder of the chapter's focus on public administration by states and communities. Second, we discuss the importance and meaning of the study of public administration and policymaking in states and communities. Third, we provide a brief historical and conceptual overview of reform and reorganization efforts by state and local governments. Fourth, we explore the roles, functions, and distinctions (as well as constraints) of state and local public administrators and officials, especially as they differ from their national government counterparts. Fifth, we examine various state and local policy issues, including education, **planning** and **zoning**, e-government, and emergency management. Finally, we critique ethical public interests perspectives given throughout the chapter, and end with an ethics case study of honesty, evasion, and transparency.

FEDERALISM

Nowhere is the ambiguity of compromise language more evident in the U.S. Constitution than on the issues of **federalism**. The term originally came from the Latin *foedus*, which means "covenant." The concept dates back to the Torah—or the first five books of the Christian Old Testament—in which a *b'rit* (Hebrew, *contract*), and in later translations *pactum* (Latin, "pact"), was made between God and Noah, Abraham, Moses, David, and others. Similarly, a federal form of government was designed as a contract or pact between the national and state governments and the citizens of the US. The Framers revolted against the weakness of the 1781–1789 Articles of **Confederation,** but also rejected the British model of a **unitary state**. Under the Articles of Confederation, all power was held by the states, even that granted to the national government. America suffered as the states held back authority to provide for national defense, to coin a national currency, or develop a strong national economy. The unitary state of Great Britain, however, placed oppressive power in the centralized hands of Crown and Parliament.

The Framers adopted federalism as a compromise between confederation and the unity state. Federalism is based on a division of powers between states and the national government. Thus, it's technically wrong to call the national government the federal government, although everyone understands what you mean. James Madison declared in *The Federalist Papers No. 46* that the states and national government "are in fact but different agents and trustees of the people, constituted with different powers." The Federal Article, or **Article IV of the Constitution** (see Box 5.2) recognizes the legitimacy and power of the states, requires the states to respect one another, and gives the national government an obligation of admitting new states to the nation and ensuring democratic governance.

In addition, the **10th Amendment**, ratified in 1791, reserved to the states all powers that were not specifically enumerated in the Constitution. The 10th Amendment reads, "The powers not delegated to the United States by the Constitution, nor prohibited by it to the states, are reserved to the states respectively, or to the people." But the ambiguity of the Tenth Amendment has confounded the courts, officials, and administrators for generations. Exactly what is reserved to the states and local governments?

The centralization of federalism became evident early in American history, and later the Civil War fought to finally decide these issues.[1] First, Alexander Hamilton proposed creation of a government bank in 1791 to help raise monies and take care of government business. Secretary of State Thomas Jefferson objected that under a strict construction interpretation of the Constitution a government bank was not listed as a national power, and the 10th Amendment reserved all non-listed powers to the states. Hamilton, who was Secretary of the Treasury, countered that the Constitution was concerned with ends and not means, and under a loose construction interpretation the means of a national bank to achieve ends was not forbidden. President George Washington agreed with Hamilton and a national government bank was created. Jefferson later agreed, as President, that Hamilton was right and used his argument to justify the Louisiana Purchase, the use of military in undeclared war, and so forth.

While the creation of a national government bank by George Washington in 1791 was the first step, the end came in 1819 with the case of *McCulloch v. Maryland* (1819). Maryland taxed all out-of-state banks doing business within the state, including the national government bank branch in Baltimore. McCulloch was the clerk of the Baltimore branch who refused to pay the Maryland tax, because he claimed a state could not tax the national government. Maryland sued McCulloch, arguing that the national government had no constitutionally enumerated power to create a bank; thus, the states reserved that power and Maryland had the power to tax the national bank branch in Baltimore. Luther Martin, lawyer

BOX 5.2 | The Federalism Article: Article IV, U.S. Constitution (1789)

Section 1: Full faith and credit shall be given in each state to the public acts, records, and judicial proceedings of every other state. And the Congress may by general laws prescribe the manner in which such acts, records, and proceedings shall be proved, and the effect thereof.

Section 2: The citizens of each state shall be entitled to all privileges and immunities of citizens in the several states. A person charged in any state with treason, felony, or other crime, who shall flee from justice, and be found in another state, shall on demand of the executive authority of the state from which he fled, be delivered up, to be removed to the state having jurisdiction of the crime. No person held to service or labor in one state, under the laws thereof, escaping into another, shall, in consequence of any law or regulation therein, be discharged from such service or labor, but shall be delivered up on claim of the party to whom such service or labor may be due.

Section 3: New states may be admitted by the Congress into this union; but no new

states shall be formed or erected within the jurisdiction of any other state; nor any state be formed by the junction of two or more states, or parts of states, without the consent of the legislatures of the states concerned as well as of the Congress. The Congress shall have power to dispose of and make all needful rules and regulations respecting the territory or other property belonging to the United States; and nothing in this Constitution shall be so construed as to prejudice any claims of the United States, or of any particular state.

Section 4: The United States shall guarantee to every state in this union a republican form of government, and shall protect each of them against invasion; and on application of the legislature, or of the executive (when the legislature cannot be convened) against domestic violence. ◤

Source: Cornell University Law School, LII/ Legal Information Institute, retrieved from www.law.cornell.edu/constitujtion/constitution.articleiv.html

for the state of Maryland, argued: (1) a national bank wasn't necessary to carry out any of its powers under the Constitution, Article I, Section 8, Clauses 1–18; (2) Congress had no explicit power or right to create a national bank; and (3) the states may thereby tax such a national bank by their Reserved powers under the 10th Amendment. Daniel Webster, lawyer for the national government, argued the reverse: since a bank was helpful to Congress to carry out its explicit powers to collect taxes and care for property, it was necessary and proper under the Constitution, Article I, Section 8, Clause 18. Chief Justice John Marshall agreed with Webster and upheld the power of Congress to create a national bank under the Constitution, arguing that the 10th Amendment did not limit this power of the national government. For Chief Justice John Marshall, the necessary and proper clause gave significant *implied powers* to the national government, as he defined:

> Let the end be legitimate, let it be within the scope of the Constitution, and all means which are appropriate, which are plainly adapted to the end, which are not prohibited, but consist with the letter and spirit of the Constitution, are constitutional.[2]

America continued to struggle with issues of federalism and states' rights, but *McCulloch v. Maryland* (1819) was the beginning of the end for what we refer to as dual federalism. The Civil War and the ending of slavery, racial discrimination, and so forth with the 13th, 14th, and 15th Amendments brought an end to these struggles, at least institutionally—but politically, economically, and certainly culturally and ethically, the battle was just beginning. In order to create and ratify the 1789 Constitution, compromises were made to allow states' rights to slavery. But slavery was ended after changes in a common moral consciousness. The **utility perspective** of the public interests—with its **utilitarian** calculation—was used by many states to legitimate slavery in the early U.S. Republic. It resulted in the tyranny of a majority against the minority African-American slaves in these states and communities. These majoritarian preferences were ended only through positing new **civil rights** ending slavery, giving equality and the right to vote to the former slaves in the 13th, 14th, and 15th Amendments. But the utility perspective remains dominant and is often been criticized for the way in which a tyranny of the majority may impose an injustice upon minorities when it is to the advantage of the majority.

Changing Face of Federalism

What has federalism come to mean today for public administrators? In the first theoretical analysis of federalism to date, Malcolm Feeley and Edward Rubin argue that most discussions of federalism are "remarkably mushy" as a "thinly disguised defense of political conservatism, which is conveniently set aside whenever objectives are better pursued at the national level."[3] Although there is no shortage of scholarly and popular literature about federalism, little to none of it presents a theory of the subject. This may belie the genius of the Framers' use of ambiguous language on federalism to achieve compromise with states' rights confederation supporters, while still achieving a strong, central, national government. Or it may document the pragmatic American as a person who prefers what works to theoretical nicety. For example, when federal district court judges took over the prison systems of 42 states in the 1970s to protect fundamental rights and create constitutionally compliant prisons, why was there no intense political opposition?[4] Of course, there was some scholarly resistance, but why didn't the bar, the press, politicians, and the public oppose or slow down what scholars called a judicial juggernaut? Feeley and Rubin documented that the public never bought in[5] because the cause of rallying around states' rights was empty, that "federalism is no longer an operative principle in the United States. What passes for federalism, we argue, is merely managerial decentralization."[6]

The current **managerial decentralization** of federalism in public administration is characterized by changing models of allocation of authority, a new emphasis on diversity and innovation, and grant-getting (or perhaps games-winning?). First, models for allocation of authority between national and state government have evolved toward disengagement of the national government and greater power and responsibility of the states.[7] The early model of dual federalism or layer-cake theory, from 1789 to 1933, sought to create separate sovereign spheres of power in national, state, and local governments, restricting the national role to powers enumerated in the Constitution. The New Deal of the 1930s and the expansion of national powers to deal with the Great Depression marked the rise of cooperative federalism or marble-cake theory, from 1933 to 1964, characterized by sharing and mutual interdependence of national, state, and local governments.

BOX 5.3 | Models of Federalism

- *Dual federalism/layer-cake theory* (1789–1933): separate sovereign spheres of power for federal, states, and communities, restricted national role to enumerated powers.
- *Cooperative federalism/marble-cake theory* (1933–1964): New Deal expansion of national powers in the 1930s; sharing and mutual interdependence of federal, states, & communities.
- *New federalism/picket-fence federalism* (1964–present): federal, states, communities, and other policy experts cluster with one another, rather than separate by level of government.
- *Coercive/unfunded federalism* (1970s–present): unfunded mandates, entitlements and deregulation limit innovation by states & communities; entitlements are national programs administered by states or communities. Unfunded mandates are individual constitutional rights.

The role of states and local governments became delivery of services funded by the national government. The new federalism is the model which characterizes relations from 1964 to the present time, focused on restoring power and responsibility to states and localities.[8] But, unlike earlier eras, authority within new federalism seems to flow within areas of expertise and not by separate sovereign spheres of national, state, and local governments. For example, former North Carolina Governor Terry Sanford characterized new federalism as picket fence federalism, where national, state, local, and other specialists within each policy area clustered with one another, rather than separate by level of government.[9] (See Figure 5.1.) And the power on each picket may be based in states or localities, with the disengagement of the national government and increasing state and local power responsibility. Second, diffusion and innovation of policy, rather than uniformity, now characterize the managerial decentralization of contemporary federalism. For much of U.S. history, the national government has sought uniformity among the states and localities in policy. The Congress, President, and national courts required uniformity of states and localities in the areas of racial equality, the rights of criminal defendants, interstate commerce, and other policy areas that were brought up to national standards. This is clearly defined in the multitude of civil rights cases, largely dating back to *Plessy v. Ferguson* (1896), and progressing through to *Brown v. Board of Education* (1954), and the enforced desegregation of public schools. While the Congress, President, and national courts have maintained the uniform standards of these prior precedents as a minimum, recent decades have witnessed greater authority given to states and localities in developing ways to conform to these and other constitutional values. Similarly, cities and localities have been freed from the constraints of state control, contrary to the famous **Dillon's Rule**, by which localities possessed only those powers given them by a state. This diversity of innovation has brought with it greater issues of honesty, evasion, and transparency: the more variations of policy implementation, the more variations of lying, evasion, and transparency in policy advising and sharing

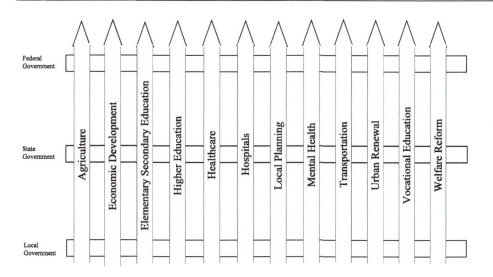

FIGURE 5.1

Picket-Fence Federalism

Source: Terry Sanford, *Storm over the States* (New York, NY: McGraw-Hill, 1967).
Note: Vertical slats represent the intergovernmental connections across three main levels of government.

information. However, we generally prize the unique culture and politics of a state or locality that may be expressed within its policies more fully, more creatively, and with variety. For example, clean government in Wisconsin, individualism in Wyoming, traditionalism in Mississippi, or internationalism in New York City may not be the recipe for Texas, Iowa, or Idaho.

Third, managerial decentralization is also focused on **grant-getting** and the networking of connections to obtain national, state, and private funds for governance. Since 1964, the national government has simplified grant-giving to the states by allocating money to each state. Most grants are categorical grants, provided to states and localities for specific programs and narrow purposes. For example, the U.S. Department of Housing and Urban Development (HUD) houses the Grants Management Center (GMC), which oversees the grant application process for categorical grants. HUD awards the grants on either a competitive or lottery basis. One example is the Housing Choice Voucher program, which provides rental assistance for low-income families who want to find a home in the private market and who, based upon income, could not otherwise do so.[10]

Coercive or Unfunded Federalism

While the managerial decentralization of federalism gives more discretionary power and managerial authority to states and localities—and thus state and local public administrators—the reality of unfunded mandates, entitlements, and deregulation limits innovation. This new reality of unfunded federalism has been called coercive federalism. Entitlements are national programs administered by state or local governments, such as unemployment, public housing, and many

BOX 5.4 | Block Grants and Revenue Sharing

Block grants provide for more general purposes and diverse activities, such as health services, education, and law enforcement. For example, Community Services Block Grant (CSBG) provides states and state-recognized Indian Tribes with funds for programs that try and alleviate causes and conditions of poverty. In addition, block grants are found in the policy area of law enforcement, such as the Local Law Enforcement Block Grant (LLEBG), which provides much-needed funds to state and local law enforcement agencies to fund programs that try and reduce crime and improve public safety.

Revenue-sharing grants, which were effectively outlawed in 1987, allowed states to spend the monies as they like, as long as they did not discriminate by race or other unlawful activities. As you can imagine, conservatives, such as Ronald Reagan, were none too happy to have the national government borrowing money it did not have to provide unchecked to states and local governments for projects that he— and other conservatives—did not believe were necessary (water parks, tennis courts, etc.).

Grants may also be classified by how the national government decides to fund the grant. *Project grants* are funded because a state or locality submitted a proposal that specified the project to be funded. *Formula grants* are funded by simple decision rules based on the state's population, miles of highway, and so forth. *Matching grants* require the state or locality provide some of its own funding which is variously matched by national monies.[11] ◣

health services. While states can redefine eligibility to reduce the number of beneficiaries of entitlements, it is difficult for a state to cut off a person's benefits. Unfunded mandates are individual property interests in public goods or services that are protected by legal rights, including adequate public education, prison and jail conditions, etc. For example, state and local governments complain that they are struggling in a competitive global economy. The federal government imposes laws—well intentioned though they may be—such as the Occupational Safety and Health Act, the Family and Medical Leave Act, and the No Child Left Behind Act of 2001. Each piece of legislation requires states and localities to fund large parts of each program, while at the same time being regulated by the Federal Government. Costs are enormous to state and local governments. Congress responded in 1995 by passing the 1995 Unfunded Mandates Reform Act, which effectively required Congress to double-check itself before imposing any more requirements upon the states and localities. The results are mixed as to whether or not it really made any difference.[12] Some are simply skeptical from the start, and do not believe Congress did much of anything to check itself.[13]

What has happened to states' rights in this era of deregulation? Many have espoused national government deregulation—the process of simplifying, reducing, or removing legal restrictions by the national government on businesses and people to support and develop the market economy. Since the 1980s, deregulation was a states' rights mandate designed give these issues back to the states to regulate how, and if, they saw fit. So, when the national government scaled down enforcement of laws regulating the environment, civil rights, predatory lending, and workplace safety, many states entered into the void. After all, shouldn't states enact laws to protect their people in conformity with their prevailing community standards? Yet, national government has often responded to these creative responses by states and local governments with added uniform protections of individuals, especially minorities. These national-added uniform protections often reflect a distrust of the honesty, full information, and transparency of states and local governments in controversial minorities' rights areas. For example, the national government prohibited heavily polluted California from setting its own standards on greenhouse emissions, blocked states from regulating bankers who caused a meltdown in mortgage lending, and limited state workplace safety regulations for mines or factories.[14] How does honesty, full information, and transparency operate in the relationship of states and local governments with the national government? Why does distrust inevitably bring an end to states' rights? Entitlements, unfunded mandates, and state deregulation by the national government take a greater share of state and local budget dollars and limit states and communities from thinking outside the box in the innovation of new strategies.

STATE AND LOCAL PUBLIC ADMINISTRATION

Thomas P. "Tip" O'Neil, former Speaker of the U.S. House of Representatives, famously quipped, "All politics is local." Perhaps, too, all public administration is state and local. While this is not entirely true, we do contend that administration in the public interests is most often realized at the state and local levels. State and local governments impact our daily lives much more than the federal government does. Every day, you travel a street, drink a glass of water, stop at a stop sign, eat lunch, talk on a cell phone, or pay some kind of state and/or local tax (sales, food, property, etc.). All of these activities, either directly or indirectly, are affected, impacted, or regulated in some way by state and local governments. As an example, take a look at a local economic development and planning controversy.

The development, implementation, and evaluation of public policy are usually seen at the state and local levels of governance. In fact, public administration is far more prevalent at the state and local levels than at the federal level—at least in terms of direct influence or impact upon residents in a variety of ways and policy areas, including tax burden, regulatory policy, economic pressure, education policy, and a host of others. The impact of state and local governments is vital to the continuation of our American political and administrative systems.[15]

Public administration at the state and local level involves the citizenry, engages the public, private, and nonprofit sectors, encompasses a wide range of interests, issues, and policy areas, while at the same time is largely dependent upon the Federal Government for much of the funding that supports state and local endeavors. Before we provide some basic historical and conceptual overview of state and local governments' relationships and autonomy, let's review five basic reasons why we should study public administration at the state and local levels.

Studying state and local communities

Why is the study of public administration in states and communities important? First, if "all politics is local," then the democratic administrative state is best realized at the state and local levels for many important issues of everyday life. One author commented in the early part of the twentieth century that "Public administration in the United States, partly because it is federal, partly because it reflects attitudes of democracy and self-government, is deeply rooted in the local communities."[16] The **9th Amendment** and 10th Amendments to the Constitution and common law history recognize these police powers granted to state and local governments. **Police powers** are government powers over matters that are near and dear and close to the people, such as their health, welfare, education, morality, and general safety. It is from the concept of police powers that state and local governments later created law enforcement forces called police, such as the London Constabulary of Metropolitan Police (first named "bobbies" for founder Robert "Bobby" Peel) in 1829. The constitutional concept of police powers necessitates that state and local governments fiercely maintain governance that is highly local to be immediately responsive to these personal needs. For example, see the study (Box 5.5) on building a new high school.

State legislative control of local municipal charters, for example, was designed to provide significant political input and oversight of local government actions. This action led to less home rule, or governing autonomy on the part of the local governments, but even so cities, which had been in existence long before states came about during the Revolutionary era, were largely and sufficiently self-contained governing and economic units, and so the states did not need to keep close tabs on their actions. That changed with the migration of farmers to the

---

BOX 5.5 | Building a School in Northern Virginia: Can It Really Be This Difficult?

The town of Purcellville and Loudon County, Virginia, entered into a joint planning agreement in 1995 titled the Purcellville Urban Growth Area Management Plan (PUGAMP), which was designed to project future growth needs of the rural western town of Purcellville, including a high school. The County of Loudon, however, which was going to be largely affected by this growth, both in terms of additional residents, demand for services, and most importantly tax growth, wanted equal input into the approval of future projects. One such project was the intended development and construction of a high school in Fields Farm, just north and west of Purcellville. That construction has been delayed by court rulings and judgments. Appeal to the Virginia Supreme Court by the Town will cause further delay.

The need for an additional public high school in Loudon County sounds reasonable enough—doesn't it? Perhaps not, though. Purcellville does not want the additional traffic and congestion that will come with the high school, considering it already has a high school—Loudon Valley High. Proponents of the high school argue that the current high school enrollment is beyond its acceptable capacity and therefore impedes students' ability to learn effectively. Opponents counter that there are plenty of other locations within Loudon County, particularly near the small German settlement of Lovettsville, which is about 10 miles north of Purcellville. But what is really at issue is jurisdictional authority: who—the Town or the County—has the greater control or influence over and in the PUGAMP. At the center of the controversy are a number of local elected and administrative officials including the Loudon County Commission, Purcellville Mayor (Bob Lazaro), Town Council, Loudon County Administrator (Kirby M. Bowers), Purcellville Town Manager (Rob Lohr), Loudon County's Director of Planning (Julie Pastor) as well as her counterpart, Purcellville's Director of Planning (Martha Semmes).

Source: Shannon Sollinger, "County OK's Field Farm's School," *Loudon Times Mirror*, June 6, 2007, www. timescommunity.com

cities, but it also included foreign immigration. For example, city dwellers comprised only half of the U.S. population (46 percent) in 1910.[17] This influx of people to the cities, instigated in large part by the Industrial (and technological) Revolution, put into motion a whole series of events, including **municipal reform** movement (which we will discuss in more detail later) that largely impacted not only state and local politics, but also the administration of both old and new policy areas, such as economic development and local planning.[18]

Second, public administration at the state and local levels is closer to the people than public administration at the national level. And it is in these close quarters that honesty, lying, and evasion become critically sensitive grounds for conflict—and also for consensus when there is trust, full information, and transparency. It is true that about 90 percent of all federal bureaucrats work outside of the Washington, DC, beltway and thus live close to where they work. But they are not as easily accessible to the common citizen living in Mount Pleasant, Iowa; Kootenai County, Idaho; or Spring Township, Illinois, or any number of the thousands of small towns, townships, communities, and counties scattered across the United States as is the town administrator, city manager, parks and recreation director, waste water treatment plant manager, or the town street sweeper (yes, some towns still have one). The people who hold these local government positions are generally required to live within the jurisdiction they work in—sometimes because it is law, but most of the time because they want to live in the community they work in. They want to know and serve their neighbor and community. They want to make and have a lasting impact on their fellow citizens. They want to positively affect the public interests. The downside, of course, is that being too chummy might lead to cronyism and unfair political games based on who you know rather than following legal and administrative guidelines.[19]

Third, an examination of public administration at the state and local levels reveals a greater sense of community and civic understanding, awareness, and practice of civic obligations, i.e., greater pursuit of the public interests. Local government, for

---

BOX 5.6 | Social Capital on the Decline: Bowling Alone

Social capital, a term coined by Robert Putnam (director of the Saguaro Seminar and professor of public policy at Harvard) in his groundbreaking work *Bowling Alone: The Collapse and Revial of American Community*, goes beyond the resources necessary to engage community on a cultural and social level. It suggests that the implications of *not* having social capital means that state and local governments, specifically communities and sub-communities within those jurisdictions, lack the necessary tools capable of a sense of community or togetherness that is vital to the development and continuation of democracy and democratic institutions, and more importantly—or as importantly—deters civic and social *disengagement*. With greater levels of disengagement and a continuing loss of social capital states and local governments see (a) higher crime rates, (b) lower education performance, (c) higher rates of teen pregnancy, (d) lower rates of low-birth-weight babies, and (e) higher infant mortality rates. Thus, the consequences of a decrease in "social capital" can impose policy and administrative difficulties upon various state and local officials. ◤

Source: Bowling Alone, "Bowling Alone," Saguaro Seminar, retrieved from www.bowlingalone.com/

example, attracts some 88 percent of all volunteers as compared with states or national government. Local government managers, both at the county and municipal levels, strongly encourage volunteers and citizen activists.[20] However, this position of civic understanding and community awareness is being challenged. For example, a 2006 study[21] revealed that public and private higher education failed to provide adequate knowledge on American history and government. Since the more a student learns about civics and history, the more they will be an active citizen, the study concluded there is a coming crisis in American citizenship. Similarly, it is getting more difficult to attract and keep young people in positions of public administration—at any level—because of the lure of big money in the private sector. As the level of social capital declines (see Box 5.6), so does our broader sense of community; thus, the less likely that individuals will participate in civic obligations, citizen councils, and initiatives.[22] The reversal of these trends is critical to continuing citizen awareness and involvement in civic activities, and therefore pursuing the public interests.

Fourth, state and local governments are major contributors of public services. The number of state (approximately 5 million) and local (approximately 13 million) government employees is nearly six times the size of the civilian Federal Government workforce (about 3 million). Of the nearly 18 million state and local government employees, over 7 million work in elementary and secondary education, with another 3 million in higher education.[23] Demand is high for various services, including education, medical care, criminal justice, judicial and legal, fire and police protection, state liquor stores, and much more. What does all of this cost? And who pays the bill? This second question is easy to answer: the taxpayer does! In 1998, for example, total state and local taxes, fees, and other revenue-generating means brought in approximately $1.3 trillion; by 2008, that figure increased to $2.4 trillion! This nearly equaled the Federal Government budget in fiscal year (FY) 2008—nearly a whopping $3.0 trillion![24] State and local governments are not only big businesses, but they are vital to America.

Fifth, the states and communities have interesting policy innovations and reforms of administration. Devolving responsibility to the lower levels of government, such as President Reagan advocated in the 1980s, meant that state, municipal, and county governments, as well as **special districts**, assumed greater responsibility for funding and implementing basic public services, including Medicare and Medicaid and education. In recent years, because of 9/11 and **Hurricane Katrina**, more attention is paid to state and local levels to be **first responders**. In addition to greater financial and human resources and commitment, both professional and volunteer, it means that state and local governments must become innovative in policy experiments.

In 1932, U.S. Supreme Court Justice Louis Brandeis argued that citizens serve as a **"laboratory,"** where they "try novel social and economic experiments without risk to the rest of the country."[25] Justice Brandeis and many others have been fascinated with the new and creative policy innovations of states. For example, Michigan, Missouri, and Wisconsin experimented with welfare-to-work policies in the 1980s, which ultimately became the impetus for future national welfare change in the 1990s. Of course, much of the policy innovation in a state may relate to state or local wealth, the presence and impact of interest groups, and general public interests in the topic. U.S. and states' laws and constitutions place even more restrictions on cities, counties, and other localities. But even so, communities often have different freedom to privatize, outsource, and other means to pursue the public interests through policy innovation.[26] For example, *Governing Magazine*, in conjunction with the Ash Institute for Democratic Governance and Innovation, produces several winners each year for "Innovations in American Government." Box 5.7 details three case studies featuring recent winners: San Mateo County, California, worker exchanges; Colorado's mental health monitoring; and Cincinnati, Ohio, listening to employees.

State and Local Government Reforms

In addition to policy innovation, state and local public administrative organizations have undergone significant changes of structure and procedures, more than in the national government. These changes have focused on increasing professionalism, enhancing how work is accomplished (i.e., efficiency, effectiveness, and economy), and past attempts to try (unsuccessfully) to separate administration from politics. The patronage or spoils system was the preferred state and local

---

BOX 5.7 | States and Local Government Innovation

- **Worker Exchanges.** San Mateo County, CA, administers the Management Talent Exchange Program. Participating public managers nominate top-notch applicants for assignments ranging up to three months. They exchange or place them in outside agencies or departments. The applicants/nominees enhance not only their resume, but also their skill set, and in turn organizations benefit by getting projects accomplished that otherwise would have gone undone.

- Monitoring Mental Health. The State of Colorado's Department of Personnel and Administration assesses employees' mental wellness through a two-step process. First, the employee completes a pre-screening questionnaire. Second, the data is coded into a system that identifies individuals who need additional help, beyond what the state can provide. It is a great tool

for determining demographic trends—for example, males were far less likely to seek help than females. The program is expected to serve approximately 6,800 individuals.

- Listening to Employees. The City of Cincinnati opened up a platform whereby city employees' voices and opinions were heard along a variety of issues and topics. One of the key components of the project was to allow city employees to help evaluate the effectiveness of various city programs across various priority areas. Not only were city employees' views expressed, but there was an added benefit of providing employees the opportunity to learn about other city departments and projects.

Source: Mike Maciag, "How Governments are Innovating their Workforces," *Governing Magazine*, August 2013, retrieved July 17, 2017 from www.governing.com/

personnel system until the last century. From the time of President Andrew Jackson (1820s) to the end of the nineteenth century, the spoils system dominated state and local government hiring. Government jobs were exchanged for political party support and allowed the influence of political machines, such as **"Boss" Tweed** of New York and **Tom Pendergast** of Kansas City, to thereby rule state and local government public administration machinery and control delivery of social and welfare services. The corruption of the system was interrupted and derailed from time to time by progressive reformers. Reformers were often civic-minded, socially connected, and moral in their tone. They were known for holding strong civic and religious values that undergirded their belief in and practice of reform, and they eventually succeeded in changing the organizational culture of public administration.[27] We examine two broad examples of reform: local government restructuring and state executive reorganization.

Municipal Reform Efforts American reform efforts at the local level largely began during the scientific management revolution, in which reformers focused on separating administration from politics by emphasizing scientific task analysis and time and motion studies. Many reformers were prompted by Woodrow Wilson's 1887 article advocating a separation of administration from politics. For example, reformer George W. Curtis advocated merit-based hiring systems, Emory Upton spoke for greater professionalism, and Richard S. Childs was the most influential individual in establishing the council-manager form of local government.[28] All focused first on breaking down the strongholds of the political machines in local administrations. Independent organizations and institutions, aimed largely at researching, writing, and activism, sprang up and placed considerable pressure on the political machines. These included the National Municipal League (1894) (now the National Civic League), National League of Cities (1926), National Civic Federation (1900), National Child Labor Committee (1904), and a host of others.[29]

State Executive Reorganizations State executive reorganization efforts made their way onto the political agendas of state governors and legislators sometime before 1920. As early as 1915, Illinois and New York experimented with constitutional changes,[30] to reduce political influence in regulatory agencies and independent commissions with oversight of railroad rates, barbering, and so forth. The goal of state executive reorganizations was to streamline organizations, departments, and agencies by function and place them under central control of the governor. Reorganizations didn't touch the constitutionally defined state offices, such as secretary of state, treasurer, and attorney general. But all others were viable targets. The primary goals of state executive reorganization were to increase economy and efficiency and clarify chains of command. In many instances the changes were as much symbolic or rhetorical as they were substantive. Consolidating agencies by function, such as budgeting or personnel, sounded great, but each individual department still had to make their own budgeting and personnel decisions. A guiding presence may have been helpful, but to eliminate these functions from individual departments or agencies was not realistic. In the end, it was largely more political rhetoric, or symbolism, than helpful.

By the 1930s, state executive reorganization efforts had slowed. Establishment of the "Brownlow Commission" revived the process and continued it for

> ### BOX 5.8 | National League of Cities
>
> The **National League of Cities** (NLC) was formed in 1926. It is the oldest and largest national organization representing municipal governments throughout the United States. Its mission is to strengthen and promote cities as centers of opportunity, leadership, and governance. Working in partnership with the 49 state municipal leagues, the National League of Cities serves as a resource to and an advocate for the more than 19,000 cities, villages, and towns it represents. More than 1,600 **municipalities** of all sizes pay dues to
>
> NLC and actively participate as leaders and voting members in the organization. Since the 1920s, by means of policy statements and research assistance to legislators, it has fought to minimize public spending, serving as a watchdog on government finance and administrative efficiency. It is considered the oldest taxpayers' research organization in the country. ▶
>
> Source: National League of Cities, "About NLC," retrieved from www.nlc.org/INSIDE_NLC/aboutnlc.aspx

40 years.[31] The **Brownlow Commission** was also referred to as the Commissions on Organization of the Executive Branch, or the President's Committee on Administrative Management (1937). It focused on executive reorganization in both the national and state levels and urged greater efficiency, economy, and effectiveness. Results were often disappointing because the organizations defensively protected their power. Yet, reformers continued to pursue the public interests by eliminating waste and fraud, pursuing more efficient and economical delivery of public services, and separating politics from administration.[32]

Administering State and Local Government

State and local governments—especially local communities—are incredibly diverse. The U.S. Constitution contains only sparse details on the states, but no mention of local governments, including municipalities, counties, and special districts. Local governments are constrained by state constitutions and laws. This brief overview of the administration of state and local government outlines their structures, roles, and functions.

State Governments   State government authority and power is given some attention in the Constitution. For example, the bond between the states and the national union is clearly laid out. In 1869, Chief Justice Salmon P. Chase wrote that "The Constitution, in all of its provisions, looks to an indestructible union, composed of indestructible states."[33] The Constitution also provides for states' rights and states' sovereignty in Article IV, in which Section 4 requires the "guarantee of a republican form of government." And the 10th Amendment reserves powers to the states (e.g., police powers). The states, unlike local governments, are guaranteed an administrative and political position in the union by the Constitution.

Theories abound that try and explain the role of state governments in the federal system. First, the capacity thesis contends that the states play a central role in the federal system. Capacity refers to a state government's "ability to respond effectively to change, make decisions efficiently and responsibly, and manage conflict."[34] How well a state is able to muster fiscal and leadership resources is largely

BOX 5.9 | Utah and Virginia Are at the Top of Their Class!

Utah and Virginia both received an "A" for enhancing performance management. In 2005, *Governing* magazine, the trade periodical for state and local administrative managers and administrators, annually ranks states for performance. Utah and Virginia were the only two states to receive an "A." The reason: both states had the fiscal, political, administrative, and technological capacity to perform not only the basic functions of state governments, i.e., collect state income and sales taxes through their highly functional Departments of Revenue, but to also deal with a variety of other issues. For example, Utah's Department of Transportation ran a panel truck around the highways and byways of Salt Lake City soliciting specific questions from citizens regarding

transportation needs of commuters. When the panel truck stopped, commuters stopped as well, swarming the truck and peppering the driver with questions and comments. And in Virginia, for example, the Department of Human Resources implemented a Learning Management System, which is essentially a workforce planning tool to gauge how much time, effort, and fiscal resources will be necessary to plan for future state personnel needs, particularly once the baby boomer generation of civil servants begins retiring in earnest. ◣

Source: Katherine Barrett, Richard Greene, Zach Patton, and J. Michael Keeling, "Grading the States '05: The Year of Living Dangerously," *Governing* (February 2005).

based on how well the administrative agencies perform. So, state governments define good administration by performance management, performance budgeting, and the like. Getting more "bang for the buck," so to speak, is becoming the norm for state governments. This has intensified since the 1980s, with states increasing cooperation among and between states and localities. The bottom line: state capacity is tied to administrative performance on various policy issues.[35]

A second framework is the politics in a comparative approach. The approach here is to compare states along a variety of factors (e.g., population growth, income disparity, ideology, religion) and issues (e.g., education, racial and civil rights, economic development), asking the basic questions. What are the differences between and among states? How are the differences explained? For example, comparative analysis can help understand the key role of state expenditures to prisons to avoid federal district court prison reform litigation and judicial decrees.[36] While less focused on administration, the comparative approach is helpful for studying historical, cultural, constitutional, and political factors associated with states and with roles played by public administrators.

Counties and Parishes Counties or parishes (as they are referred to in Louisiana) are the legal administrative arm of states. Almost all 3,000 counties (and parishes) in the United States have representation in the National Association of Counties through the 53 state associations with 47 states represented (i.e., some states have multiple associations, such as Illinois, which has three). Historically, counties' roots go back the English shire, or political division, nearly 1,000 years ago.[37] When the framers of the U.S. Constitution did not include local governments, and they left that responsibility to the states, counties (as well as municipalities) became the creatures, so to speak, of the states. In other words, counties and municipalities are formed by the states to serve at the behest of the state government.

Prior to the reform movement of the early twentieth century, counties were limited. Beyond being simply the administrative apparatus of the state, counties held no real power. After the reform movement, however, things changed, particularly with the urbanization and later suburbanization of America. Counties, especially urban counties, began to act more like municipalities, trying to cope with city-county consolidation, and the expanding economic and population growth. For example, urban counties, especially, engage the county population with the same basic types of administrative and governmental functions as rural counties do, including law enforcement, courts, road maintenance, and election oversight, but many, such as Loudon and Arlington County, Virginia, or Wake and Mecklenburg, North Carolina, also provide fire, water and sewer, library, and mass transit. Others, such as Orange County, California, also support tourism, airports, sports stadiums, and even pollution control.

Counties are governed in three ways, with many of the administrative responsibilities vested in elected and constitutionally defined officers (e.g., clerk, sheriff). At the same time, however, more and more counties are employing the services of a professional manager. The three forms are: (1) **commission** (32 percent of all counties), with the primary feature being a single body (i.e., commission) performing both the legislative functions, such as enacting ordinances, as well as executive functions, such as establishing budgets; (2) **county administrator** (56 percent of all counties), where the county is run by an appointed manager, who oversees the daily operations of the county; and (3) **elected county executive** (12 percent of all counties),[38] where there is a distinct separation of legislative (i.e., elected council) and executive (i.e., elected county executive) powers. Generally speaking, rural counties embrace the pure commission form, while large urban counties prefer the elected county executive type. Of course, the pressing demands placed upon counties not only to shoulder the typical administrative duties but also to provide input and some oversight with policy issues (such as mentioned above) requires more counties to seriously consider adopting the county administrator/manager model. Harnett County, North Carolina, for example—a somewhat typical rural southern county—embraced the administrator/county type, with Neil Emory as county manager (see Box 5.10). Harnett County is growing and expanding, with Campbell University, new hospitals and medical facilities, and other services, moving in to meet the growing retirement and elderly community. Counties just don't look like their predecessors looked like years ago!

Municipalities Cities, towns, and townships make up the bulk of sub-state administrative and political entities, equaling over 25,000 units alone. They are the epicenter of communities. Even though municipalities and towns are workhorses of local governments, there is really no rhyme or reason, as they say, for planning local governments. Instead they come about, or are incorporated, via migration patterns, economic expansion, citizen demand, interest group pressure, and a variety of other means. Really, no rational reason exists to explain the growth and development of municipalities—other than to note that the state permits them to be created. Therefore, they are what we refer to as creatures of the state.

BOX 5.10 | Neil Emory, Former County Manager, Harnett County

Neil Emory, former county manager of Harnett County, North Carolina, was born in Weaverville, just outside of Asheville, Mr. Emory, who had always had an interest in civil service, attended and graduated from Appalachian State University with undergraduate and master's degrees in political science and public administration, respectively. After spending some time as a county finance director, he landed his first position as county manager with Caswell County. He was only 24. After several county management positions, he landed as the top administrator for Harnett

County in 1992. He believes in his role as public servant. As a public servant he sees his role as twofold. First, it is his objective to measure the priorities of the community, including the civic and moral standards of the community, and what the community wants to be and then help; and second, he believes that government must perform basic functions, such as fire, law enforcement, etc. ◣

Source: Neil Emory, interview with Stephen M. King, June 2005.

Municipalities, including cities and towns, are established via state charters, or a legal and uniform grant of power. City charters spell out what a city or town can or cannot do, and to a great extent determine how a local government entity can be organized. Even though there are various types of charters—including special, classified, optional, and home rule—we will concentrate only on the **home rule charter**, particularly as it differs from the more traditional limited grant of state power that is derived from Dillon's Rule.

Dillon's Rule was established as the result of an 1868 Iowa Supreme Court case opinion written by Judge John Dillon,[39] where he noted that municipalities have only those powers that are: (1) expressly granted by the state (e.g., fiscal power), (2) implied powers (e.g., taxing powers), and (3) indispensable powers (e.g., water and sewer). Any other power that is not expressly defined in the specific state constitution or granted to the municipal corporation by the state is therefore "expressly prohibited" to the municipal corporation.[40] Dillon's Rule is still the most popular, with 31 states operating under it, 10 states not operating under it, 8 having only certain municipalities under it, and 1 (Florida) that has conflicting authority.[41] By far, then, it is the most popular for states, but the most unpopular among local public administrative types, particularly county, city, and town managers. The most popular charter preferred by municipal reformer types is the home rule charter. It permits city residents to choose whatever form of government they desire, but again only within the limits of state legislation. Even though home rule provisions are available in most states, communities have to file formal requests or petition with the state legislature to access these powers. As you can imagine, local public administrators see the infringing power of the state legislature as obtrusive to their ability to fulfill the public interests.

Municipal governments take on one of three basic forms: council-manager, mayor-council, or commission. The commission form developed in the early part of the twentieth century, specifically created in Galveston, Texas, in order to more efficiently deal with the aftermath of a hurricane that killed thousands of people in 1900. The necessity for moving and setting up emergency manpower and

BOX 5.11 | An Ethics Moment: When the County Knows Best—Or Does It?

West Nile virus, an illness transmitted from wildlife to humans by mosquitoes, has made its second appearance in two years in Phoenix, Arizona, resulting in a number of confirmed fatal cases among birds and a growing number of positive cases in humans, reported by hospitals and doctors to the Maricopa County health department's vector control program. In response, the county has tracked the locations of most intense activity, has ramped up its public education program to ask people to be vigilant in draining any stagnant water sources where mosquitoes breed, and advised the public to wear repellent, particularly in the evenings, at night, and early morning, when the insects are most active.

After plotting the outbreaks, the county identified a large "hot zone" of cases and determined that this area— mostly residential neighborhoods—should be fogged with insecticide to reduce the mosquito population. The insecticide of choice is a synthetic pyrethroid called Anvil. According to the EPA (Environmental Protection Agency), "pyrethroids can be used ... without posing unreasonable risks to human health when applied according to the label. Pyrethroids are considered to pose slight risks of acute toxicity to humans, but at high doses, pyrethroids can affect the nervous system."

Maricopa County proceeded with a program to fog an area of about eight square miles in the early morning hours of a Friday; a time when mosquitoes are active, winds are calm, and most people are in their homes asleep.

Maricopa County also made the decision not to notify residents in the affected area in advance that their neighborhood would be fogged.

Many of those homes, however, use evaporative cooling, a process that draws outdoor air into the home. The pesticide fog was also drawn into the homes, and the residents exposed while they slept. Some symptoms of pyrethroid exposure include rashes and breathing difficulties. Persons with lung ailments and small children are susceptible at a lower dosage than the "average" person. Persistent exposure or exposure to large concentrations can cause other health problems. Pyrethroids are a carcinogen.

While it is unknown how many residents of Phoenix were affected by the insecticide, none knew they may have been exposed. Therefore, none knew whether, if they did show symptoms, they should seek medical treatment. I am one who came down with a rash after sleeping with an evaporative cooler running on a night when the county fogged my neighborhood. Evaporative coolers bring in outside air, cooling the air with water. In this case, the water was off, so it was ambient outdoor air being drawn in. I woke up to the smell of it, but had no idea as to the source. I learned a few days later that one of my neighbors saw the trucks on our street at 3:00 A.M. (This was the day I came down with the rash.) ◣

Source: submitted by Thomas Babcock. From Donald Menzel, ed., "Ethics Moment" column, *PA Times* (December 2004).

materials was too much for the weak mayor form of government. It was thought that putting an elected commission in charge of one particular city department— such as police, fire, or water—the level of efficiency would increase. But because there was no chief executive, either in the form of a mayor or manager, the infighting took away from meeting the public interests.[42]

A second form of municipal government evolved that emphasized a professional city manager. The council-manager form of municipal government was first used in Staunton, Virginia, in 1908. It was born out of both the Industrial Revolution and the later reform movement, first as an attempt to incorporate French

---

BOX 5.12 | An Ethics Moment: Should Ethics Exams Be Used to Screen Job Applicants?

Some local governments are requiring job applicants to take an ethics examination as part of their application process, particularly with their police departments. The city council of Monroeville, Pennsylvania, for example, approved in 1997 that an ethics evaluation be conducted of all persons seeking to join the Monroeville Policy Department. The Monroeville Police Department also uses ethics testing in the process for promotion to corporal, sergeant, and lieutenant.

According to City Manager Mary Ann Nau,

A couple of local incidents that reflected unethical thinking impressed me with the idea we needed to know that our officers were ethically thinking people from the start. It

is too late to wait until an officer comes up for promotion to wonder about their standards for dealing with the situations they encounter.

Monroeville's test is called the Defining Issues Test and is administered by the Center for the Study of Ethical Development and the University of Minnesota. The test consists of six stories, each describing a moral dilemma. Respondents must decide what the major actor in each story should do.

Discussion Question: So, should ethics exam be used to screen job applicants? ◤

Source: based on a story published in *Pittsburgh Post Gazette,* February 13, 1997; submitted by Gary Zajac of the University of Pittsburgh. From Donald Menzel, ed., "Ethics Moment" column, *PA Times,* May 1998.

BOX 5.13 | Jim Twombly, Former City Manager, Broken Arrow

Jim Twombly, former **city manager**, arrived in Broken Arrow, Oklahoma, a thriving suburb of Tulsa, in July 2004. Previously he served as City Administrator for Pella, Iowa, corporate home of the world-famous Pella Windows and the May Tulip Festival. Previously he served as assistant to the city manager of Oklahoma City and associate planner. He holds a BA and MA in urban affairs from St. Louis University. He has also attended the Public Executive Institute at the LBJ School of Public Affairs at the University of Texas at Austin. He sees his role as city manager as bringing together all

different groups and integrating many variables in order to serve not only the city, but private and nonprofit interests, as well — in other words, to serve all interests for the "betterment of the city." One of the major projects he is tasked with is the complete renewal and updating of the downtown, using his planning background to help develop a long-range plan, not only for the economic development but also the beautification of the downtown businesses and infrastructure. ◤

Source: interview with Stephen M. King, July 2005.

---

and German methods for incorporating greater tools of efficiency and economy, and second as a means to separate politics from administration. The typical city-manager, who is a trained professional, and who today has a Master's of Public Administration (MPA) degree, is hired by the city council to implement the policies adopted by the city council. However, as one can guess this form of municipal governing is anything but immune from politics. City managers are required to refrain from engaging in partisan politics, but they are certainly part of the policy development process, largely because they are asked by the council members themselves, interested community parties, such as citizens and interest groups, to provide their professional opinion. When this happens, politics is part of the administration process![43] Generally, the city manager form is found in medium-sized cities, anywhere from 10,000 up to 225,000 or so.

Finally, the mayor-council form of government. It is most popular in cities over 250,000 in population, and in small towns with usually under 2,500. Depending upon the size of the city or town, the mayor is weak, where he or she is appointed or voted from among the elected council. The mayor serves at the behest of the council and is largely a figurehead. However, in the large cities, such as San Francisco and Chicago, the mayor is a powerful political and administrative figure, setting the budget, appointing committee heads, and overseeing city regulatory bodies. Unlike its weak mayor counterpart, it is a job filled with political tension, usually between the mayor and council, but also with the rank-and-file merit employees, many of whom are union-based.[44]

Special Districts Special districts are specialized local units of government, such as airport and mass transit authorities like the New York's Metropolitan Transportation Authority, and school districts like Virginia's Loudon County School District, that do just what their title implies: meet a single need, where other forms of local governments cannot or will not meet them. They are generally managed by special governing boards, usually appointed by governors, legislatures, or even local officials, but they can also be elected. They are created in a number of ways, including by special enabling legislation or referendum. Mass transit and education districts are not anywhere close to being the largest special districts as a percentage of function—that status belongs to natural resources and fire protection.[45]

Special districts have exploded in number over the last few decades. Currently, there are some 35,000 special districts spread throughout the United States, with Illinois having the largest number (over 3,000, largely in the Chicago area) and Alaska having the fewest (under 10). School districts, on the other hand, have plummeted in number, from just over 108,000 in the early 1940s to just over 13,000 in 2002—the reason being, of course, the large number of mergers and consolidations beginning in the 1950s. In fact, by the early 1970s the consolidation of school districts bottomed out, with the number of school districts nationwide remaining fairly constant thereafter.[46] Consider, for example, the special utility district in our Ethics Case Study of *NUMADNO v. Holder* (2009) in Chapter 3, and the growth of hybrid organizations special districts. Are these private hybrid organizations subject to accountability and responsibility, as are democratically elected public organizations? Arguments in favor of using special districts are that they coordinate and apply funding and attention to specialized areas that do not generally overlap with municipal boundaries. A drawback, of course, is the nature of special districts, such as school boards or utility boards, and they often lack accountability to the public.

State and Local Policy Issues

What are examples of the nature and influence of state and local governments in the policy process? The following section includes brief overview of five policy areas that confront the state and local government administrator: education, planning and zoning, e-government, and emergency management. This brief overview cannot begin to cover the details of each area and the many state and local responses. Rather, we emphasize aspects of the diversity of issues that face state and local governments, the creativity in responding to these issues, and their policy impact in promoting the public interests. State and local governments have great influence on U.S. public policy. For example:

- State constitutions create rights that may not exist at a national level, e.g., rights to public education, to define marriage, to medicinal marijuana use, to required waiting period before abortion.
- State governments are becoming more dominated by the executive branch.
- Local governments are policy entrepreneurs, in seeking ways around restrictions on raising tax revenue, e.g., by calling it an impact fee.
- Local governments place greater power on managers to act not only as chief administrative officers, but as economic development planners.[47]

▶ **BOX 5.14** | **Case Study: No Child Left Behind: Is It in the Public Interests?**

States spend the largest portion of their money on education, along with welfare, healthcare, and corrections. With regard to education, states pass enabling legislation that provides local school districts with the authority and finances to operate individual school systems. Even though school districts have their own authoritative jurisdictional boundaries, complete with staff, personnel, and finances to run the district, the state is largely in control, determining the funding formulas (e.g., New York ranks highest, at just over $12,000 per pupil; surprisingly, Utah is last in per-pupil spending, at just over $5,000), the number of days a school must stay open, the number of grades to be taught, and a host of other details—most of which should probably be decided at the local level. Nonetheless, despite the state influence in education, the Federal Government is becoming more involved. A great example is the implementation and impact of the 2001 **No Child Left Behind Act (NCLB)**.

NCLB is really an amendment to Title I of the Elementary and Secondary Education Act of 1965. According to NCLB, all states were required to meet certain levels of accomplishment in reading and math measured through regular examination in grades 3–8. The test results are to be published and the test scores are to be categorized according to race, ethnicity, gender, and other factors. The argument for mandatory testing is to ensure that no group of students, regardless of race, gender, or ethnic background, is "left behind." In fact, upon the urging of the First Lady, Laura Bush, reading scores became the primary focus, encouraging all schools to have all students reading by the third grade. Those schools and districts that do not meet the adequate yearly progress (AYP) levels will be scrutinized and ultimately punished (i.e., withholding of federal educational funding). The key public administration officials, i.e., those held accountable for implementing the new federal law, included everyone from the Secretary of the federal Department of Education all the way down to school principals. In between are parents and students, who are generally given very little leeway in determining their educational focus and goals. ◢

Source: Thomas R. Dye and Susan MacManus, *Politics in States and Communities*, 12th ed. (Upper Saddle River, NJ: Prentice-Hall, 2007), 580, 582.

Education Policy   Education policy is a state and local government priority. As early as the mid-seventeenth century (1640s), when the Massachusetts colonial legislature required towns and villages to provide some form of education for their children using public funds, education was understood to be under the purview of the state government and local community. All state constitutions specifically designate public education as a right for their citizens. For example, North Carolina's constitution states in Article IX that "Religion, morality, and knowledge being necessary to good government and the happiness of mankind, schools, libraries, and the means of education shall forever be encouraged." Like most states, North Carolina, in order to meet this goal, requires a uniform system of schools (section 2), a State Board of Education (section 4) that will administer and supervise the free public school system (section 5), and supply much of the funding (section 2).[48] By the late eighteenth century the United States government recognized the importance of public education and, through passage of the Northwest Ordinance of 1787, Congress provided for grants of federal land to states to build public schools. But it was not until the mid-nineteenth century that the first state (Connecticut, in 1850) mandated free and public education. By the turn of the twentieth century most states had compulsory attendance laws. Today, most state constitutions require the provision of an adequate public education as a right, and the issue is not open to a public interests utilitarian calculation of benefits/costs.

State governments and state boards of education, led by state superintendents of instruction or education, provide much of the funding and regulation of public education. Yet, local governments led by independent school districts oversee the daily operations of education policy. The local school districts, led by district superintendents, hire teachers, principals, and staffs, oversee curriculum, and perform basic operational and regulatory functions. As one can imagine, the school districts are extremely diverse in curriculum formation. Many of these issues are viewed as too political and socially divisive, such as teaching about creationism, sex education, and abortion. These and other curricular issues seem to provoke advocates and critics who argue over the proper role of public schools in teaching controversial topics and criticisms.[49]

Planning and Zoning   Planning and zoning is almost entirely a local government policy issue area, usually involving a variety of individual interests, including interest groups, citizen councils, state legislative boards, executive commissions, and others. Planning controversies arise and are usually settled with compromise, balancing, and calculation of interests.[50] With the conclusion of World War II, the suburbs exploded in growth, largely because of returning veterans taking out GI loans to subsidize new homes outside their old towns and cities. Developers sold the new tracts of land with the vision of paradise, hoping that people, whether they could really afford to or not, would move to the other side of the tracks, and thus escape the drudgery of urban life. It worked. Suburbs sprang up like unwanted weeds, from New York to California, and with it came the need for greater local planning than ever before.[51]

Early city planning guidelines, dating back to the late seventeenth century, dictated that cities take the form of grids, with streets running in straight lines north-south and east-west. Parks, buildings, homes and other features were carefully laid out to fit into the grid pattern. This was especially true of most Southern,

BOX 5.15 | Power of Public School Superintendents

Public school superintendents are similar to city and county managers—they are hired by an elected body, the school board, and serve at the discretion of the board. They are hired because of their expertise in educational policy and administration. Like local managers, school superintendents have substantial oversight and input with budget formation, operational oversight, and personnel issues. However, because education is a highly political issue, school superintendents tend to be on the political hot seat more so than city or county managers. Still, their roles are similar: working between an elected board, citizen and local group interests, and trying to meet personnel demands.

The job is certainly not easy; it is physically, mentally, and emotionally demanding, requiring 10- to 12-hour days, more during budget season, and living in a community fish bowl, where their life is not their own. With the imposed national government educational performance measurement standards, the pressure on superintendents to lead their districts to perform at predetermined standards or lose accreditation and standing is multiplied. Some states, such as North Carolina, have reported a failure to reduce the high-school dropout rate and haven't met increased test expectations, even with increases in public funding. School superintendents have a hot seat job, stressed with the pressure to perform. ◢

Source: Karen McMahan, "Standard 'Solutions' Not Remedying Ed Problems," *Carolina Journal* (November 2006): 8.

Midwestern, and Western new towns that sprang up through most of the nineteenth century. However, cities in the East, particularly Boston, Philadelphia, and New York, which were founded and grew long before grid patterns, had to absorb much of the new growth from immigration during the late nineteenth and early twentieth centuries. The large cities became a hodge-podge of housing projects, streets that went nowhere, row after row of tenement housing that did not meet any type of code enforcement, and industrial parks and buildings that provided low-income jobs, but little of anything else substantive to the community. There was no code enforcement largely because there were few, if any, codes to enforce— and very few willing to enforce the few codes that existed.

Later, city planners, most of whom had engineering backgrounds, began to create masterplans, where they followed comprehensive planning guidelines. These included factors such as projected growth rates, transportation development, and even cultural patterns. The masterplans are developed for cities to consider when they expand. City councils do not usually read or review them. Rather, the councils established committees, commissions, and neighborhood councils to exercise oversight of the planning process.[52] Today, planners are highly professionalized, with undergraduate and graduate degrees in planning and development. Many belong to professional associations, such as the American Institute of Planners. The development of planners as professionals spurred the replacement of citizen planning commissions with city and county planners who provided the guidelines and oversight in the planning process of a community.[53]

The Politics of Planning   Today, the professional world of planning is not without its politics. Application of the utility perspective of the public interests in calculating benefits/costs or allowing the market to determine individual preferences may sometimes lead to unacceptable conclusions, such as the suburban sprawl that chokes many urban areas. State **Smart Growth programs**, which first began in Maryland in the 1990s, have spread across the country. Smart growth is a concept that understands growth is inevitable, but believes it is the responsibility of public officials, at both the state and local level, to ensure that this growth is fair and equitable. Many cities and counties, such as Portland, Oregon, and Loudon County, Viriginia, instituted smart growth strategies to control growth by way of strategies such as "urban growth boundaries, preservation of agricultural lands, historic areas, and sensitive environmental regions."[54] Sun Belt cities, such as Charlotte, North Carolina, incorporate mixed-use development with well-planned mass transit offerings to combat suburban sprawl.[55] However, free-market advocates contend that smart growth does not prevent many of the problems it claims it does. In fact, because of increased government regulation at the state and local level, while smart growth increases the cost of available land and houses, its impact on congestion is debatable.[56]

Zoning ordinances are passed by the city council or county commissioners usually at the recommendation of professional planners. Zoning ordinances divide the jurisdiction into specific districts, whether residential, commercial, industrial, or other. Zoning is an attempt to separate residential growth from commercial and industrial uses; the logic being, of course, that property owners don't want to buy or build a house in an area that might allow a tool and die shop to be built next door. Changes to the zoning ordinances come from citizens, developers, builders, and others—anyone who wants to build or buy a piece of property and turn its existing zoning into something else. This requires a variance, or exception, to the zoning ordinance, where the professional planners, the party requesting the zoning change, and the elected body can clash. Planners, who are professionals and who only play an advisory role and cannot dictate planning policy, know the laws and regulations. Council workers and commissioners are elected by the people to meet the public interests. And the individuals requesting the zoning change do so for individual gain. What is best for the community, including town, city, or county? What is in the public interests? Most recommendations of professional planners are accepted as truth, but there are times when a council or commission must listen to the demands of their local constituents and approve a zoning change that does not benefit the whole, but only a narrow interest. For example, the Fields Farm issue described at the beginning of this chapter is a primary example. What is in the public interests: a second high school in western Loudon County, Virginia, in Purcellville? Or a second high school in western Loudon County, Virginia, or somewhere else?

e-Government   What is e-government? And what does it mean for state and local governments, citizens, and the public interests? Electronic-government, or e-government, means that various government entities, departments, and agencies have their own portal and pages that allow citizens to search for information and in fewer instances to interact, such as pay bills or even participate in a live electronic town hall. Few state and local governments provide the latter service, but over 80 percent of all states and communities provide web portals to all citizens to search for information.

At the national level, the President sponsors e-government initiatives encouraging citizens and businesses to access information and use e-tools (e.g., www.whitehouse.gov/omb/egov) to participate in governance. For example, in 2002 the President launched the e-government initiative, introducing E-Government Performance Management and the Federal Enterprise Architecture, which is designed to simplify and unify federal agency work processes. Since then the citizen who has access to the web can gain entrance with three mouse clicks at www.FirstGov.gov and access to all federal, state, and local government websites.[57]

At the state and local level, some governments give e-access to citizens to download and fill out forms, such as hunting and fishing licenses, tax forms, vehicle registration, e-bank transfers, and for paying parking tickets, utility bills, and other fees. Studies also show positive citizen participation and involvement in municipal government affairs by and through the use of websites.[58] The only real drawback to providing more services is the legal liability question and the cost of improving the state and local government's portal. More than states and the Federal Government, local governments are labeled the "nation's e-gov leaders," accounting for some 1,500 different applications, and the number of new digital government applications by local governments is projected to surpass by a factor of three the number of new applications introduced by the federal and state governments by 2020.[59]

Are there any limits to the public interests of open information for all in e-governance? Obviously, there must be some limits on information access to protect national security interests, to prevent libelous falsehoods about innocents from being spread, to protect certain digital property rights, and to prohibit morally unacceptable preferences such as obscenity and illegal pornography. And, we saw in Chapter 4 on duty to the Constitution and laws, certain private information on public employees and others must be protected, e.g., public employee medical records. These information transparency limits seem to be based in the **duty perspective** of the public interests of constitutions and legal values, rather than the calculations of the utility perspective of the public interests.

BOX 5.16 | e-Government's Impact on State and Local Communities

The e-government technology boom means that state and local governments are a 24/7 organization. State and local governments are always open, thanks to the World Wide Web. State and local government presence on the web has exploded. Consider some facts:

- By 2003 over 70 percent of all Americans were online.
- Nearly 200 million people in the United States are online daily.

- The vast majority of states (43) allow citizens to pay some form of their taxes online.
- Nearly all (96 percent) U.S. counties and cities are online, with 84 percent of local government websites searchable by citizens for specific types of information. ▲

Source: Nicholas Henry, *Public Administration and Public Affairs*, 9th ed. (Upper Saddle River, NJ: Pearson-Longman, 2004), 164; David Osborne and Peter Hutchinson, *The Price of Government: Getting the Results We Need in an Age of Permanent Fiscal Crisis* (New York, NY: Basic Books, 2004), 202.

From the perspective of the Universalizability Principle, the administrator's decision habit of listening to all affected persons, what does e-governance mean for the public interests? Certainly e-government promotes the public interests by allowing citizens, businesses, and government agencies to better communicate, organize, and disagree with one another. Others contend that e-government and open information technology has created institutional change in governance with different venues for working together, creating virtual communities, and promoting values of diversity, common-weal, and, of course, performance.[60] Clearly state and local administration in the public interests will not remain the same with increasing e-government technology.[61]

Emergency Management Although shared between federal, state, and local governments,[62] emergency management now arises as a highly important state and local issue, especially after the **Oklahoma City bombing**, 9/11, Hurricane Katrina, Hurricane Sandy, and other disasters. Average citizens now recognize the important role of first responders—such as fire, police, and other emergency officials—in an emergency. Emergency management illustrates an important limit of the utility perspective of the public interests—the utilitarian calculation of benefits/costs is not humanly possible during an emergency. Is there time to stop and calculate when horrible tragedy is all around? Of course not! In defense of the utility perspective of the public interests, we ordinarily rely on common sense, past experiences, and a rule of thumb to guide our actions when a crisis demands immediate response. It is often important that we determine the best possible action, i.e., to save human lives versus saving houses in a flood. But there are times when the tragedy of death and human loss is so great that stopping to calculate benefits and costs is simply not the right thing to do, e.g., just sending in all the first responders after the 9/11 terrorism. In times of crisis, the utility perspective of the public interests may presuppose greater human capacity to predict and control the future than we can deliver, e.g., the failures of federal agencies to act after Hurricanes Katrina. To illustrate state and local policies in emergency management, we briefly overview three disasters—the Oklahoma City bombing, 9/11, and Hurricane Katrina—and focus on the role public servants played during and after each incident, with attention to public interests concerns.

The Oklahoma City bombing struck at 9:02 A.M. on April 19, 1995, with the detonation of a rented Ryder truck loaded with 5,000 pounds of ammonium nitrate fertilizer parked in front of the Murrah Federal Building in downtown Oklahoma City (OKC). The blast killed 168 people, including 19 children.[63] Timothy McVeigh (the primary suspect) and accomplices Terry Nichols and Michael Fortier were all tried and convicted. Nichols received 161 consecutive life sentences, Fortier received a 12-year prison sentence and a $200,000 fine, and McVeigh was executed by lethal injection in June 2001.

Rescue efforts began immediately at the scene of the bombing. The Emergency Medical Services Authority (EMSA) responded to over 1,800 calls to 911. EMSA ambulances, city fire and police, and various civilians immediately responded. Within a half-hour of the bombing, the State Emergency Operations Center (SEOC) was set up, with various members of the State of Oklahoma Departments of Public Safety, Human Services, and others. SEOC was assisted in its efforts by federal, state, local, and nonprofit agencies, including the Civil Air Patrol and the

American Red Cross. Over 12,000 people took part in the next several days and weeks of ongoing rescue operations.

The OKC bombing prompted immediate federal and state legal action, including the Antiterrorism and Effective Death Penalty Act of 1996 and the Victim Allocation Clarification Act of 1997, which provided victims of manmade acts of violence the right to observe trials and offer testimony. In addition, the Federal Government, in conjunction with state and local officials, barricaded all federal buildings in major American cities with what is known as Jersey barriers. Years after the attacks the temporary barriers have been replaced with permanent steel-enforced cement barriers. Deep street setbacks and armed guards are now typical at federal buildings, costing hundreds of millions of dollars.

September 11, 2001, marked one of the deadliest days for civilian deaths on American soil. September 11 (or 9/11) was composed of a series of planned and coordinated attacks by terrorists affiliated with Osama Bin Laden and Al-Qaeda.[64] On the morning of 9/11, four large commercial airliners were hijacked. Each was fully fueled up. American Airlines Flight 111 crashed into the North Tower of the World Trade Center, while the second American Airlines Flight 77 struck the Pentagon. The first United plane, Flight 175, crashed into the South Tower of the WTC, while the second United aircraft, Flight 93, crashed over southwest Pennsylvania, the result of passengers trying to gain control of the plane from the hijackers. Total causalities were nearly 3,000.

In New York City (NYC), rescue and recovery operations began immediately, with city fire, emergency services, and police officers at the command centers established in the lobby of the World Trade Center, on Vesey Street, and in a firehouse in Greenwich Village. Poor communication devices caused outages to occur between commanders and firefighters, many of whom were working their way up the stairs of the two towers looking for victims when the towers collapsed. Hundreds of firefighters were killed. Police, EMTs, and others quickly arrived at the devastating scene. NYC police, Port Authority of New York police, and New Jersey police were killed while in rescue when the towers collapsed. New York City Office of Emergency Management (OEM) was responsible for coordination of the City response. OEM's headquarters had to be moved twice, finally to a pier on the Hudson River. It was here that (then) Mayor Rudolph Giuliani provided press conferences and coordinated over 90 different city, state, and federal rescue and recovery agencies working for months after the disaster.[65]

The after-effects of 9/11 continue. The National Commission on Terrorist Attacks upon the United States (aka the 9/11 Commission) published its findings.[66] Chaired by former New Jersey governor Thomas Kean, the Commission prepared a complete account of the attacks, both before, during, and after with stern rebukes. The findings also commended many civil servants, especially the local NYC police and New Jersey fire, police, and EMS workers, who placed their lives on the line to assist in the rescue and recovery operation. The Inspector General of the Central Intelligence Agency (CIA) completed an internal review of the CIA's involvement in investigating terrorism and specifically Al Qaeda. Even the United States Department of Commerce's National Institute of Standards and Technology (NIST) conducted a thorough investigation of the collapse of the two towers. This led to improved coding and building standards for future commercial construction of high-rise buildings. From these events of 9/11 and follow-up reports came our term *first responders*. First responders are the local and state emergency crews who are the first to respond to tragedies (like 9/11) and continue to resolve these problems. This required new funding and support to meet these and future emergencies.

Hurricane Katrina was the costliest ($81.2 billion) and one of the deadliest (1,836 lives lost) natural disasters in United States history. On August 29, 2005, Hurricane Katrina slammed into New Orleans, Louisiana, with Catastrophic Category 5 damages including winds and flooding, breaching levees around the city. The low-lying city was almost completely engulfed in flood water. The death toll in Louisiana alone was nearly 1,600, with the largest percentage in New Orleans. On August 28, New Orleans mayor Ray Nagin ordered mandatory evacuation. Many of New Orleans' residents, who had no means of transportation out of the city, were encouraged to make their way to various refuges of last resort, such as the Superdome. There was a large-scale breakdown of public order, police out of control, widespread looting, residents stranded on rooftops, bodies floating down flooded streets, and entire parishes destroyed. The aftermath of responses by national, state, and local governments to the Hurricane Katrina disaster was sorely criticized. Did our system of federalism break down? Did political and administrative leadership fail?

Many first responders were sent into New Orleans by national, state, and local government organizations, as well as nongovernmental agencies. But it seems their efforts were hampered by a number of factors: poor communication and coordination between and among government organizations, faulty planning process, the very slow response of the national government, among other problems.[67] Scholars found that administrative breakdowns were rampant in the response to Katrina: little mobilization of resources, personnel problems galore, and an unclear mission and lack of focus plagued national and local agencies.[68] According to recommendations of the National Response Plan, disaster planning and response is first and foremost the responsibility of local government. But when those resources quickly ran out in the face of such a large natural catastrophe, responsibility went directly to state and national governments, requiring additional assistance.[69] Yet, at the national level, the **Federal Emergency Management Agency (FEMA)** seemed bogged down with problem after problem, from logistics to implementation of plans to get trucks and supplies to stranded residents. As a result of poor communication and coordination at FEMA, the Department of Homeland Security (DHS) under the leadership of Michael Chertoff took over all federal, state, and local operations.[70]

While national, Louisiana, and New Orleans governments seemed to falter, incredible rescue efforts came in from other cities around the country, nonprofit and faith-based organizations, and the private sector. Within days of Hurricane Katrina, local governments around the country sent police, fire, and other public safety officers to provide assistance, aiding New Orleans police and fire personnel, many of whom were working in 24-hour shifts. The charitable efforts of these outsider nongovernmental organizations provided much of the temporary shelter, clothing, food, and other necessities for New Orleans evacuees. Nonprofits and faith-based organizations quickly organized and came to the rescue, including the American Red Cross, Salvation Army, Service International, the Southern Baptist Association, and others, raising over $4 billion in contributions to Katrina victims. Private businesses and corporations gave over $400 million in relief aid. Most important, however, is what can be learned from the mistakes in order to prevent this from occurring once again.[71]

ETHICS CASE STUDY | Honesty, Evasion, and Transparency in the Public Interests

John P. Thompson's novel *Without Purpose of Evasion* (2017) paints with prose the daily hot seat of a veteran city manager buffeted by the political winds, all the time wondering, "How can he align his professional responsibilities and personal values with the greater public interest he has sworn to uphold while being mindful of his job security and his family's well-being?"[72] In other words, how can a city manager ethically act without purpose of evasion? Are there times when public administrators should evade the truth with political officials or citizens who oppose a much-needed law, e.g., to help the needy, the homeless, welfare mothers and children . . . or the environmental poisoning of a community? Should public administrators

BOX 5.17 | Ethics Codes and Gambling in North Carolina

North Carolina's former Speaker of the House, Jim Black (Democrat-Mecklenburg), appointed Kevin Geddings as a member of the state's newly established lottery commission. Geddings, a former chief of staff to South Carolina Governor Jim Hodges, and the owner of radio stations and a public relations firm in Charlotte, was the only commissioner with some lottery experience. While in South Carolina, he led the pro-lottery campaign charge that predated a statewide referendum in 2000 that eventually provided for the state's lottery. However, it was not long before ethical considerations, primarily conflict of interest concerns, began to creep into the picture.

In October of 2005, Geddings disclosed he was a close acquaintance with Alan Middleton, vice president for government relations at Scientific Games Corporation, a leading company that provides instant-win tickets and lottery computer software. Scientific Games is one of the leading bidders to be North Carolina's gambling vendor. Even after this public revelation, Geddings said he would distance himself from any potential problems, by recusing himself as a voting commissioner during the process of hiring North Carolina's lottery contractor. However, after statewide news reports, Geddings resigned.

A few days later it was revealed that Geddings resigned from the lottery commission just a few hours before Scientific Games was to have paid him nearly $25,000, including $9,000 the day after he was named to the board. This bit of information was not revealed by Geddings or Scientific Games. As a result of this and other information, North Carolina Attorney General Roy Cooper ordered an investigation into apparent violations of state lobbying laws. ◣

Source: Jim Morrill and Mark Johnson, "Three Face Inquiry over N.C. Lottery," *Charlotte Observer*, November 3, 2005, retrieved from www.charlotte.com/mld/charlotte/news

lie to those whom they question to expose corruption of public funds, or interrogate for a crime? What does it mean to fully inform and advise, as in our ASPA Code of Ethics provision at the start of the chapter? We all sense that these are hard moral decisions. And the old saw "Honesty is the best policy" doesn't seem to grapple with the seriousness of each situation.

If honesty is a virtue of good moral character, then entire areas within public administration are morally wrong, such as investigative interrogation of the civilly and criminally accused, deceptive acts by general inspectors into public corruption, or police officers of undercover operations, and so forth. Aristotle argued that honesty overrides friendship as a virtue—but is the truth subordinate to any other moral good? For example, if a known murderer comes to your door to ask where the intended victim is, must you tell the truth if doing so will certainly result in the victim's death? Should your entire medical history be transparent and freely available online? Or should your grades and teacher's comments from kindergarten through college be transparent and posted online for all to see—even for prospective employers to read about your problems in sleeping during writing time in third grade? Accountability to the greater good seems to necessitate lying or less transparency (privacy?) in these cases and many others, where we balance untruth against a greater evil.

Lying and Moral Development

Others respond that **lying** is an inevitable behavior of all humans, beginning early in life, so get used to it. Yet, moral development psychologists have found that most, but not all, people grow out of lying behaviors. For decades of research by moral development psychologists, 98 percent of parents rated "honesty" as the trait most desired of their children. Other traits, such as good judgment or confidence, don't even come close. In turn, kids seem get the message, as 96–98 percent also said lying is morally wrong. So, why do 98 percent of kids lie? It all begins at a young age—kids start lying at age 2 or 3. Professor Victoria Talwar's research demonstrates that lying is related to intelligence. In order to lie, a child must first understand the truth, then intellectually imagine an alternative reality, and convincingly persuade another person on the imagined reality. By age 4, most children experiment with lying, and use a lie whenever they seek to avoid punishment. Many parents simply dismiss the young child's lying behavior as too young to understand the lie and that they will grow out of it. Instead, kids grow into it, not out of it: by age 4, they lie every 2 hours; by age 6, every 1.5 hours; and by age 7 they are either hooked or not. While many parenting websites and books advise parents to just let lies go and they'll grow out of it, the majority of 6-year-olds are socialized by parents out of lying by age 7 (we guess the parents don't read those books). And, according to the research of child psychologists, the most effective socialization was by parents reading and teaching the worth of honesty and truthfulness, such as reading the children's

(continued)

book *George Washington and the Cherry Tree*. The fear of punishment or negative socialization do not seem to work, such as spanking or reading the children's book *The Boy Who Cried Wolf*, about a boy who was eaten by a wolf. It is the parent as an example that most effectively socializes the child: when they see their parent using lies to avoid conflicts, the child does the same. This was depicted in the 1997 movie *Liar Liar*, in which Jim Carrey portrays a lawyer-father who is under a spell by his son to tell the truth for one day. Thus, a large percentage of 7-year-olds are hooked and keep lying—about once per hour.[73]

Others portend that the normal moral development of children to adults will overcome much of the excesses of lying at a social level. For example, **Lawrence Kohlberg** adapted a psychological theory originally from the Swiss psychologist Jean Piaget,[74] and posited six constructs of **moral development**, each more adequate than the one before. Kohlberg argued that people develop their **moral reasoning through six stages** in three groups, which he labeled pre-conventional morality, conventional morality, and post-conventional morality. That is, most people morally develop from pre-conventional obedience to avoid punishment, to conformity to social norms, and finally to the embrace of universal ethical principles—such as basic rights under a social contract.[75] Other scholars, such as **Carol Gilligan**,[76] add a feminist perspective to Kohlberg's theory of moral development and posit an **ethic of care**—from individualistic survival, to self-sacrificing goodness, and finally to a morality of nonviolence and peace. Both suggest that lying would be moderated at a social level by moral development. This additional perspective to moral development attends to virtue ethics—the ethics of caring—as an aspiration of all persons in their being or moral character, rather than simply rationally following a social contract and universal rules.

Is Honesty Always the Best Policy?

But is honesty always the best policy in the public workplace? Philosopher Immanuel Kant (1724–1804) agreed that every lie was immoral. But he advised that not every untruth—or *falsiloquium*—is a bad lie—or *mendacium*. Kant demonstrated this distinction with an example. If a known murderer comes to your door to ask where the intended victim is, must you tell the truth if doing so will certainly result in the victim's death? No. Thus, he argued, if the truth will be improperly used, you have no moral obligation to speak the truth.[77] This utilitarian ethical reasoning—or the utility perspective—places the consequences of speaking the truth in balance and requires good ethical judgment instead of blind subservience to a rule. How far does moral reasoning about *falsiloquium* work for public administrators? Some scholars apply this widely to various public workplaces, such as police organizations, to argue that "**nonmaleficence**, the avoidance of harm . . . is generally considered to override obligations to be truthful when the two are juxtaposed, justified both the police use of lies and the police use of force."[78] But is every public service provider like the police in confronting crime and evil—and justified in the use of lying and force to accomplish their ends? Are police lies and force justified by the avoidance of harm? Other scholars caution that going too far with these justifications for lying leads to a breakdown of democratic institutions and trust in public servants. The rationale that "the end justifies the means" leads only to more lying and eventual breakdown of the system, especially by police.[79] In the end, the *falsiloquium* moral exception must be nuanced and rarely used, except to avoid overwhelming bad outcomes—such as lying to the murderer who seeks his victim. To apply this to police, for example, we may look closely at the varying motivation of the liar and the recipient of the lie, e.g., lying to hostage takers or kidnapers, lying to spare the feelings of a victim or their loved ones, or lying while undercover.[80]

Transparency and Full Advice

Virtue, utility, and duty ethical perspectives all posit the need for transparency and full advice of public administrators, from micro-level lying to society-wide trust. The legitimacy of democracy depends on transparency of government officials and administrators with the public. Thus, the regime values of transparency are clearly enumerated in laws that require full advice by public administrators, such as statutory amendments to the Administrative Procedure Act of 1946 (APA), including: (1) the Freedom of Information Act, Pub. L. No. 89–487, 80 Stat. 250 (amended to 5 U.S.C. Section 552); (2) the Privacy Act of 1974, Pub. L. No. 93–579, 88 Stat. 1896 (amended to 5 U.S.C. Section 552[a]); (3) the Government in the Sunshine Act of 1976, Pub. L. No. 94–409, 90 Stat. 1241 (codified as amended to 5 U.S.C. Section 552 (b)); and (4) the Electronic Freedom of Information Act of 1996, Pub. L. No. 104–231, 110 Stat. 2422 (amended to 5 U.S.C. Section 552). There are also state law counterparts to each of these laws, such as state freedom of information acts, privacy acts, state and local government sunshine laws, and digital freedom of information. Please feel free to look up your state's laws! The original 1946 Administrative Procedure Act (APA) did little in defining public information beyond previous statutes which required agencies to publicize information about their organization, opinions, orders, and public records in the *Federal Register* since the 1930s. Since the original 1946 APA, the Freedom of Information Act of 1966 amended the APA and required agencies to make available their records and documents to any person requesting them, except under certain exemptions of the statute or other laws. For example, you can't request the medical records of a federal employee (unless it's your personal medical record). The Privacy Act of 1974 protects the right to privacy of individuals, prohibiting agencies from releasing records concerning individuals without their consent, preventing the collection of information that is not relevant and necessary, and allowing individuals to review and seek to correct agency records on themselves. The Government in the Sunshine Act of 1976 requires open meetings by federal agencies, commissions, and boards under most circumstances.

(continued)

> ### ◤ ETHICS CASE STUDY | *Continued*
>
> **Discussion**
> - What does it mean to fully inform and advise—e.g., Commissioner Geddings?
> - What is the moral development of children? How do children learn not to lie?
> - Is honesty always the best policy? When may honesty *not* be the best policy?
> - What constitutional regime values encourage the responsibility of public servants to be honest, transparent, and accountable to the public? ◤

CONCLUSION

Federalism, states, and communities present a common challenge to public administration with people who are local to us, with needs we can see nearby, and who are sometimes in our face. State and local citizens are people on the streets where we live, not like the seemingly invisible people we do not know who benefit from our tax dollars to the national government. As a result, public administration within federalism, states, and communities requires more virtue, utility, and duty to these nearby people. Under these perspectives of the public interests, the ethical public administrator must serve with honesty, transparency, and with full advice, while also protecting the privacy rights of individuals, balancing against evil uses of information and assisting the public to participate in the development, implementation, and assessment of democratically authorized policies and public programs. The timely, transparent, easy-to-understand and complete flow of public information is crucial to the success of the public administrator.

The constitutional structure of federalism has developed over the decades according to the customs of the people and what worked for administration in the public interests. For example, while the Constitution was ambiguous in outlining a dual federalism with neatly divided national and state power, it has come to authorize the marble-cake federalism of today, with a sharing of power and empowerment of states and communities through the reality of managerial decentralization.

In delivery of services under their police powers, states and communities provide much of our safety, welfare, and responsive service to crime, education, health. States and communities must respond to citizen demand for action, interest group complaints, powerful business and corporate lobbies demanding tax credits for possible incoming economic development projects, and every unfilled pothole! From governors to mayors, legislatures to city councils, state bureaucrats to city managers, this is where the buck stops in administration of the public interests. In an age of devolution, transformation, reinvention, and performance management, state and local governments try to change and adapt organizationally to meet the growing need for a wide variety of services.

Two centuries of state and local government reform and reorganization have focused on efficiency, effectiveness, and responsiveness to the public interests. For example, nineteenth-century municipal reformers sought to end the incompetence and corruption of the spoils system, restore the moral value of public service, and reinstill the public trust. Citizens still wanted public services and goods, yes, but they also demanded that government be responsive and listen to an additional level. Due to their proximity to the public, state and local governments—especially local governments—are much better at this than the national government is. Education, planning and zoning, e-government, and **crisis management** are but four policy issue areas of the many that face state and local public administrators. What these four policy areas demonstrate is a commitment by state and local administrators to deliver the public interests. State and local public servants demonstrate an unending resiliency and Job-like patience when dealing with thorny social policy issues.

With aging and retiring baby boomers, current and future generations will be needed to fill many of the vacancies that occur at the state and local levels. For example, the average tenure of a city manager is approximately five years. The average age of a city manager is 56. What does this tell us? Soon there will be a vacuum of empty city manager positions to fill. But with the majority of young people who graduate college moving to the private and nonprofit sectors, who will fill these types of positions? What OKC, 9/11, and Katrina taught us—among other things—is that the need for committed and hard-working young people is required to continue the pursuit of the public interests, if our democracy is to continue.

ACTION STEPS

1. Visit several state and local government websites. Are there similarities? Differences? Use the various options and links available on each website. Were they easy or difficult to follow? Put yourself in the position of a citizen. Does their e-government access help you to be a better citizen, more aware, informed, or active? What about citizens whose first language is Spanish?

2. Interview a state or local public administrator regarding a recent reorganization, reinvention, or organization-wide reform at their workplace. What do they think about the reform? Does it make their job better? Does it even affect how they do their job? Is it rhetoric or results?

3. Critique the utility perspective of the public interests used in the U.S. Supreme Court's ruling in *McCulloch v. Maryland*, 17 U.S. 315 (1819). How may a utility perspective of the public interests tend to result in the centralization of government power? How may it result in the tyranny of a majority against the minority in states and communities? How might you check and balance this tendency to centralize government power? (Hint: use of the duty perspective to the public interests.)

4. Read about local economic protectionism and recycling *C&A Carbone v. Town of Clarkstown*, 511 U.S. 387 (1994). The town of Clarkstown, New York, forbade the use of any out-of-state trash services and required use of one particular (local) private trash company that charged well above the market rates. How may the utility perspective of the public interests be faulted for promoting local economic protectionism? How may this abuse of power and the public interests be reformed?

KEY CONCEPTS AND NAMES

state and local public administrators 178
state governments 178
planning 178
zoning 178
federalism 178
confederation 179
unitary state 179
Article IV, U.S. Constitution 179
10th Amendment 179
McCulloch v. Maryland (1819) 179
utility perspective 181
utilitarian 181
civil rights 181
managerial decentralization 181
picket fence federalism 182
unfunded federalism 182
Dillon's Rule 182
grant-getting 182
block grants 184
revenue-sharing grants 184
9th Amendment 186
police powers 186
municipal reform 187
social capital 187
special districts 188
Hurricane Katrina 188
first responders 188
"laboratories" 188
Worker exchanges 189
"Boss" Tweed 190
Tom Pendergast 190
state executive reorganizations 190
municipalities 191
National League of Cities 191

Brownlow Commission 191
Counties 192
Parishes 192
Commissions 193
county administrators 193
elected county executives 193
home rule charter 194
city manager 196
No Child Left Behind Act (NCLB) 198
education policy 199
city planning 199
public school superintendents 200
Smart Growth programs 201
zoning ordinances 201
duty perspective 202
Oklahoma City bombing 203
September 11, 2001 204
Federal Emergency Management Agency
  (FEMA) 205
lying 207
Lawrence Kohlberg 208
moral development 208
moral reasoning through six stages 208
Gilligan 208
ethic of care 208
falsiloquium 208
mendacium 208
nonmaleficence 208
the end justifies the means 209
motivation 209
full advice 209
Freedom of Information Act 209
crisis management 211

NOTES

1   For an excellent historical discussion, see Sidney M. Milkis and Michael Nelson, *The American Presidency: Origins and Development, 1776–2002*, 4th ed. (Washington, DC: CQ Press, 2003).

2   *McCulloch v. Maryland*, 17 U.S. (4 Wheat.) 316 (1819).

3   Malcolm M. Feeley and Edward L. Rubin, *Federalism: Political Identity and Tragic Compromise* (Ann Arbor: University of Michigan Press, 2008), preface, 2.

4   For example, Bradley S. Chilton, *Prisons Under the Gavel: The Federal Court Takeover of Georgia Prisons* (Columbus: Ohio State University Press, 1991).

5   Malcolm Feeley and Edward Rubin, *Judicial Policy Making & the Modern State* (New York: Cambridge University Press, 1999).

6   Malcolm M. Feeley and Edward L. Rubin, *Federalism: Political Identity and Tragic Compromise* (Ann Arbor: University of Michigan Press, 2008), 4.

7   Carol S. Weissert and Daniel Scheller, "Learning from the States? Federalism and National Health Policy," *Public Administration Review* 68 (#1, December 2008): S162–74.

8   For an excellent overview, even though it is dated, see Morton Grodzins, *American System: A New View of Government in the United States*, ed. Daniel J. Elazar (New Brunswick, NJ: Transaction Publishers, 1984). Also, for a chronological review of federalism and intergovernmental relations, see Kala Ladenheim, "History of U.S. Federalism" (University of South Carolina, 1999), retrieved October 2007 from www.cas. sc.edu/poli/courses/scgov/History_of_Federalism.htm

9   See Terry Sanford, *Storm over the States* (New York, NY: McGraw-Hill, 1967); and Deil S. Wright, "Revenue Sharing and Structural Features of American Federalism," *Annals of the American Academy of Political Social Science* 49 (May 1975): 100–19.

10 Homes and Communities, U.S. Department of Housing and Urban Development, "Categorical Grants," retrieved October 2017 from www.hud.gov/offices/pih/centers/gmc/categorical/index.cfm

11 Peter J. Ferrara, a former Reagan staff member, wrote an attack on revenue sharing. See Peter J. Ferrara, "For Revenue Sharing, Time Has Run Out," *Backgrounder* 417 (March 13, 1985), retrieved October 2007 from www.heritage.org/Research/Budget/bg417.cfm

12 United States General Accounting Office, "Unfunded Mandates: Analysis of Reform Act Coverage" (Washington, DC: U.S. Government Printing Office, 2004), retrieved October 2007 from www.gao.gov/new.items/d04637.pdf

13 David S. Broder, "Those Unfunded Mandates," *Washington Post* (2005, March 16), 42.

14 For example, David Cohen, "What Ever Happened to (the Good Kind of) States' Rights?" *New York Times* (2008, March 23), 4.

15 For example, Glenn Abney and Thomas P. Lauth, eds., *The Politics of State and City Administration* (Albany: SUNY Press, 1986).

16 Leonard D. White, *Introduction to the Study of Public Administration,* 4th ed. (New York, NY: Macmillan, 1955), 25.

17 David R. Berman, *Local Government and the States: Autonomy, Politics, and Policy* (Armonk, NY: M.E. Sharpe, 2003), 55.

18 John Locke Foundation, "Smart Growth," retrieved from www.johnlocke.org/agenda2006/smartgrowth.html; and Samuel R. Staley, "Outsmarting Growth's Impacts in Virginia," *Virginia Viewpoint*, Virginia Institute of Public Policy, retrieved June 2007 from www.virginiainstitute.org/viewpoint/2002_8.html

19 Dennis L. Dresang and James J. Gosling, *Politics and Policy in American States and Communities,* 5th ed. (New York, NY: Pearson-Longman, 2006), 307, 308.

20 Retrieved at https://www.bls.gov/news.release/volun.nr0.htm

21 Intercollegiate Studies Institute, *The Coming Crisis in Citizenship: Higher Education's Failure to Teach America's History and Institutions* (Wilmington, DE: Intercollegiate Studies Institute, 2006).

22 Terry Christensen and Tom Hogen-Esch, *Local Politics: A Practical Guide to Governing at the Grassroots,* 2nd ed. (Armonk, NY: M.E. Sharpe Publishers, 2006), 216–17; and Rosalynn Silva, "Taking Pulse of Neighborhood Councils," *PA Times* (February 2007): 6.

23 Kevin B. Smith, Alan Greenblatt, and John Buntin, *Governing States and Localities* (Washington, DC: Congressional Quarterly Press, 2005), 300.

24 U.S. Federal, State, and Local Government Revenue, FY 1998, 2008, retrieved November 27, 2008 from www.usgovernmentrevenue.com/yearrev2008_0.html#usgs302

25 G. Alan Tarr, "Laboratories of Democracy? Brandeis, Federalism, and Scientific Management," *Publius* 31 (#1, Winter 2001): 38.

26 Kevin B. Smith, Alan Greenblatt, and John Buntin, *Governing States and Localities* (Washington, DC: Congressional Quarterly Press, 2005), 20, 21.

27 Ibid., 316–18. See also Richard J. Stillman II, *Creating the American State: The Moral Reformers and the Modern Administrative World They Made* (Tuscaloosa: University of Alabama Press, 1998).

28 Richard J. Stillman II, *Creating the American State: The Moral Reformers and the Modern Administrative World They Made* (Tuscaloosa: University of Alabama Press, 1998).

29 David R. Berman, *Local Government and the States: Autonomy, Politics, and Policy* (Armonk, NY: M.E. Sharpe, 2003), 62.

30 Leonard D. White, *Introduction to the Study of Public Administration,* 4th ed. (New York, NY: Macmillan, 1955), 175.

31 James W. Fesler and Donald F. Kettl, *The Politics of the Administrative Process* (Chatham, NJ: Chatham House, 1991), 101.

32 For a thorough overview of state executive reorganization, especially looking at empirical data that supports their efforts, see James l. Garnett and Charles H. Levine's "State Executive Branch Reorganization," *Administration and Society* 12 (#3, 1980): 227–76. For a trend-based review of state executive, see Stanley B. Botner's "Recent Trends in State Executive Reorganization in the Midwest," *American Review of Public Administration* 7 (#1, 1973): 25–6.

33 Thomas R. Dye and Susan A. MacManus, *Politics in States and Communities*, 12th ed. (Upper Saddle River, NJ: Pearson-Prentice Hall, 2006), 68.

34 Ann O'M Bowman and Richard C. Kearney, *State and Local Government,* 6th ed. (Boston, MA: Houghton Mifflin, 2005), 4.

35 For example, Arnold Fleishman, *Politics in Georgia,* 2nd ed. (Athens: University of Georgia Press, 2007).

36 For example, Bradley Chilton and David Nice, "Triggering Federal Court Intervention in State Prison Reform," *Prison Journal* 73 (1993): 30–45.

37 For an excellent historical and functional overview of counties, go to the National Association of Counties (www.naco.org) website.

38 Ann O'M Bowman and Richard C. Kearney, *State and Local Government,* 6th ed. (Boston, MA: Houghton Mifflin, 2005), 279.

39 *City of Clinton v. Cedar Rapids and Missouri River Railroad Co.*, 24 Iowa 455 (IA, 1868).

40 Sally Ormsby (chair), *Dillion's Rule: Good or Bad for Local Governments?* (Fairfax County, VA: League of Women Voters of the Fairfax Area Education Fund, 2004), S-1, retrieved April 2007 from www.lwv-fairfax.org/LWV-Dillion-DTP-99041.pdf

41 Ibid., S-4.

42 For example, Delmer D. Dunn and Jerome S. Legge, Jr., "Local Government Managers and the Complexity of Responsibility and Accountability in Democratic Governance," *Journal of Public Administration Research and Theory* 11 (#1, 2001): 73–88.

43 For example, Delmer D. Dunn and Jerome S. Legge, Jr., "Politics and Administration in U.S. Local Governments," *Journal of Public Administration Research and Theory* 12 (#3, July 2002): 401–22.

44 John J. Harrigan and David C. Nice, *Politics and Policy in States and Communities,* 9th ed. (New York: Pearson-Longman, 2006), 129–33.

45 Thomas R. Dye and Susan A. MacManus, *Politics in States and Communities*, 12th ed. (Upper Saddle River, NJ: Pearson-Prentice Hall, 2006), 461.

46 John J. Harrigan and David C. Nice, *Politics and Policy in States and Communities,* 9th ed. (New York: Pearson-Longman, 2006), 125; see also Ann O'M Bowman and Richard C. Kearney, *State and Local Government,* 6th ed. (Boston, MA: Houghton Mifflin, 2005), 275.

47 See David H. Rosenbloom and Robert S. Kravchuk, *Public Administration: Understanding Management, Politics, and Law in the Public Sector*, 6th ed. (Boston: McGraw-Hill,

2005), 89–90; Thomas R. Dye and Susan A. MacManus, *Politics in States and Communities*, 12th ed. (Upper Saddle River, NJ: Pearson-Prentice Hall, 2006), 51.

48 North Carolina State Constitution, retrieved October 2017 from www.ncga.state.nc.us/Legislation/constitution/ncconstitution_whole.html

49 David C. Saffell and Harry Basehart, *State and Local Government: Politics and Public Policies*, 8th ed. (New York: McGraw-Hill, 2005), 325–6.

50 For a good case study account of the development and planning of Chicago's public housing in the late 1940s and 1950s, read Martin Meyerson and Edward C. Banfield, *Politics, Planning, and the Public Interest* (New York: The Free Press, 1955).

51 Dennis R. Judd and Todd Swanstrom, *City Politics*, 9th ed. (New York, NY: Routledge, 2014), 268, 272, 277.

52 David C. Saffell and Harry Basehart, *State and Local Government: Politics and Public Policies*, 8th ed. (New York: McGraw-Hill, 2005), 312, 314.

53 Thomas R. Dye and Susan A. MacManus, *Politics in States and Communities*, 12th ed. (Upper Saddle River, NJ: Pearson-Prentice Hall, 2006), 483.

54 David C. Saffell and Harry Basehart, *State and Local Government: Politics and Public Policies*, 8th ed. (New York: McGraw-Hill, 2005), 314, 315; Kevin B. Smith, Alan Greenblatt, and John Buntin, *Governing States and Localities* (Washington, DC: Congressional Quarterly Press, 2005), 356.

55 Zach Patton, "Back on Track: Sprawling Sun Belt Cities Discover a New Way to Grow." *Governing* (June 2007): 32–8.

56 Randal O'Toole, "The Planning Penalty: How Smart Growth Makes Housing Unaffordable," Public Interest Institute, *Policy Study No. 06-02* (March 2006), 1–48; "The Folly of 'Smart Growth'," *Regulation* (Fall 2001): 20–25; Robert H. Nelson, "If at First You Don't Succeed, Rename Your Program," *Virginia Viewpoint*, no. 2002-5 (February 2002), retrieved October 2017 from www.virginiainstitute.org/viewpoint/2002_5.html

57 David Osborne and Peter Hutchinson, *The Price of Government: Getting the Results We Need in an Age of Permanent Fiscal Crisis* (New York, NY: Basic Books, 2004), 203.

58 James K. Scott, "'E' the People: Do U.S. Municipal Government Web Sites Support Public Involvement?" *Public Administration Review* (May/June 2006): 349.

59 Nicholas Henry, *Public Administration and Public Affairs*, 9th ed. (Upper Saddle River, NJ: Pearson-Longman, 2004), 164–5.

60 Jane E. Fountain, *Building the Virtual State: Information Technology and Institutional Change* (Washington, DC: Brookings Institution Press, 2001).

61 Robert B. Denhardt and Joseph W. Grubbs, *Public Administration: An Action Orientation*, 4th ed. (Belmont, CA: Thomson-Wadsworth, 2003), 435.

62 Viviane E. Foyou, *The Agenda of Disaster Relief Policy in the Post-War Period: Congressional Activities of Disaster Relief: 1947–2005* (Saarbrücken, Germany: VDM Verlag Dr. Müller, 2009).

63 For example, City of Oklahoma City, *Alfred P. Murrah Federal Building Bombing, April 19, 1995: Final Report* (Stillwater, OK: Fire Protection Publications, Oklahoma State University, 1996); Clive Irving, *In Their Name: Oklahoma City: The Official Commemorative Volume* (New York, NY: Random House, 1995). More in-depth detail on the plot, actors, and firsthand accounts, including rescue and government agencies involvement, can be found in Edward T. Linenthal's *The Unfinished Bombing: Oklahoma City in American Memory* (New York, NY: Oxford University Press, 2001). For an up-close look at the investigation of Timothy McVeigh and other perpetrators, see Richard A. Serrano's *One of Ours: Timothy McVeigh and the Oklahoma City Bombing* (New York, NY: W.W. Norton, 1998).

64 For a brief overview of the details of the coordinated attacks on the Twin Towers, the Pentagon, and crash of Flight 93 in western Pennsylvania, see National Commission

on Terrorist Attacks Upon the United States, *The 9/11 Commission Report* (New York, NY: W.W. Norton, 2004).

65 For a critical review of Rudy Giuliani's mayoral leadership, read Wayne Barrett and Dan Collins' *Grand Illusion: The Untold Story of Rudy Giuliani and 9/11* (New York, NY: HarperCollins, 2006).

66 National Commission on Terrorist Attacks Upon the United States, *The 9/11 Commission Report* (New York, NY: W.W. Norton, 2004).

67 Jonathan Walters and Donald Kettl, "The Katrina Breakdown," *Governing* (December 2005): 20–22.

68 Saundra K. Schneider, "Administrative Breakdown in the Governmental Response to Hurricane Katrina," Special Report, *Public Administration Review* 65, no. 5 (September/October 2005): 515–16.

69 Jonathan Walters and Donald Kettl, "The Katrina Breakdown," *Governing* (December 2005): 22.

70 For a critique of the interrelated roles of local, state, and federal governments in a disaster situation, such as Katrina, see Donald F. Kettl, *The States and Homeland Security: Building the Missing Link* (New York, NY: Century Foundation, 2003); and Anne M. Khademian, "Strengthening State and Local Terrorism Prevention and Response," *The Century Foundation*, retrieved October 2017 from www.tcf.org/Publications/HomelandSecurity/4.stateandlocal.pdf

71 Donald F. Kettl, "The Worst is Yet to Come: Lessons from September 11 and Hurricane Katrina," *Fels Government Research Service Report 05-01* (Philadelphia: Penn Arts and Sciences, Fels Institute of Government, 2005), 1–17.

72 John P. Thompson, *Without Purpose of Evasion—A Novel: A Story of Conflict, Conscience, and Real-Life Consequences* (Minneapolis, MN: North Loop Press, 2017), from the back cover.

73 Kang. Lee and Victoria Talwar, *Children and Lying: A Century of Scientific Research* (New York: Wiley/Blackwell Publishers, 2010).

74 Jean Piaget, *The Moral Judgment of the Child* (London: Kegan Paul, Trench, Trubner and Co., 1932).

75 Lawrence Kohlberg, *Essays on Moral Development*, vol. 1, *The Philosophy of Moral Development* (San Francisco, CA: Harper & Row, 1981).

76 Carol Gilligan, *In a Different Voice: Psychological Theory and Women's Development* (Cambridge MA: Harvard University Press, 1982 [2nd ed., 1993]).

77 Immanuel Kant, *Practical Philosophy*, ed. and trans. Mary Gregor (New York, NY: Cambridge University Press, 1986), esp. 425, "On a Supposed Right to Lie from Philanthropy."

78 Carl B. Klockars, "Blue Lies and Police Placebos: The Moralities of Police Lying," *American Behavioral Scientist* 27 (#4, March/April 1984): 529–44.

79 Jerome H. Skolnick, "Deception by Police," *Criminal Justice Ethics* 1 (#2, Summer/Fall 1982): 40–54.

80 For example, Thomas Barker and David L. Carter, "Police Lies and Perjury: A Motivation-Based Taxonomy," in *Police Deviance*, 2nd ed. (Cincinnati, OH: Anderson Publishing Co., 1991), 153–6.

Public Organizations Management and Loyalty

"Promote Ethical Organizations: Strive to attain the highest standards of ethics, stewardship, and public service in organizations that serve the public."
—(Code of Ethics, American Society for Public Administration, 2013)

BOX 6.1 | CHAPTER OBJECTIVES

1 Summarize and critique the variety of open and closed organizational systems.
2 Clarify the nature of the ethics and public interests in public organizations management.
3 Compare and apply the Old Public Administration, New Public Management, and New Public Service.
4 Critique the public service ethical issues of loyalty and whistleblowing in public organizations.

Organizations are the core of society. Whether public or private, organizations strive to meet the needs of individuals, groups, businesses, governments, communities, and fulfill various goals from efficiency to equity. To meet these needs, organizations employ their finances, time, and especially people in positions of leadership, skills, and other activities. The real challenge today is for traditional Weberian-style organizations, with a machine model emphasizing uniformity and control, to face a rapidly changing environment with new forms of organization that are flatter, more task-driven, technology-emphasizing, and people-friendly in seeking to develop creative energy and potential in all. Whether public, private or nonprofit, the twenty-first-century organization will seek to better meet the needs and fulfill the demands of not only its workers, but also the citizen and clientele it serves.

This chapter reviews the history, theory, and evolution of organizations in the public interests. We examine the various and many major authors, ideas, and philosophies as they have had an impact on the development of organization theory, focusing primarily upon the public organization as a means for addressing the need of fulfilling the public interests. Scholars who study organizations categorize organizations in a variety of ways—each with assumptions about the public interests—such as closed versus open models, classical models and ideology, managing the dynamics of organizations, and managerial, political, and legal approaches to studying organizations. Scholars of administration generally agree that organizations evolve, but do not agree, and in many cases do not even address the issue, of what organizations evolve into, or, what their evolutionary pattern evokes, especially in terms of administrative and policy outcome.[1] We contend that the outcome must benefit the public interests.

The chapter is divided into three sections. First, we explore the historical development of closed organizations, including discussion of classical theories. These theories tend to separate politics and administration, reserving discretion in the public interests to politicians. Second, we overview open systems, including the human relations, informal group, decision-making, neoclassical, and systems approaches in organization theory. Open systems generally maintain some level of responsibility to the public interests for all participants. Finally, the chapter applies organizational theories within the contemporary literature of **public management**, including the **New Public Service**. We focus our discussion of public management in the context of **Janet and Robert Denhardt**'s *The New Public Service*. We contrast the *New Public Service* with the *old public administration* and the *new public management* approaches to public administration. We also critique the literature on ethical issues in loyalty and whistleblowing within public organizations.

ORGANIZATIONS

Just as we saw there were many definitions for public administration, so too are there many definitions of organizations. Organizations are usually defined according to specific contexts and perspectives. Some definitions, for example, revolve around the specialization of task and integration of specialists in order to achieve desired ends,[2] while others define organizations as a system of coordinating informal groups with formal ones in order to accomplish a goal.[3] Writers concur that any **formal organization**, and in many cases informal ones as well, are designed to accomplish a goal, and to do it in a structured way.[4] We agree. For our purposes a formal organization is defined as a "group of people coming together for a common purpose, dividing up responsibilities according to tasks, skills, and knowledge, and coordinating and leading these efforts in order to reach the desired goal."[5] Granted, this is a broad definition, and really applies to any formal organizations, such as Microsoft, U.S. Department of Defense, or the Salvation Army, but even in the emergence of **informal organizations**, there are people, they generally have some consensus on why they are informally organized, and they have common goals and objectives. So, even though informal organizations, such as tens of thousands of small nonprofits and faith-based or para-church organizations, are not as large and formalized in terms of structure, rules, lines of communication, and the like, they still represent the core of what organizations are all about: bringing people together to achieve a common goal.[6]

Just like there's no unified theory to explain everything in the universe, there's no single theory to encompass everything about organizations. Instead, there are many theories, each compelling, but each falling short of explaining the totality of organizations. No one theory is able to explain everything about organizations, how they evolve, how people operate within them, what their purpose is, and many other aspects. As one scholar notes, organization theory is a "loosely knit community of many approaches to organizational analysis."[7] Even though the scientific study of modern organization theory is a fairly recent phenomenon, the study and practice of organizations is thousands of years old.[8]

The Ancients and Organizations

Dating back to biblical times the use of tribes, nomads, the formation of Egyptian courts, and Babylonian administrative hierarchies all ascribe to the use and development of organizations to advance common goals—administration in the public interests. For example, during the exodus from Egypt, which is recorded in chapter 18 of *Exodus*, Moses' father-in-law, **Jethro the Midianite**, chastises Moses, God's appointed leader, administrator, and judge, for trying to adjudicate all the cases brought before him. Instead, Jethro wisely advised and Moses established a hierarchy to arrange authority. It was much like nineteenth-century German sociologist Max Weber's ideal type of organization—called a **bureaucracy**—delegating the smaller and less important cases to trusted persons, while Moses heard only the more significant ones. Other biblical accounts of organizational structure and process—which include the descriptions of kings' administrative courts, such as kings David and Solomon, Nehemiah and the rebuilding of the temple, and others—reflect the human need to create, build, and organize.

Sun Tzu's (c. 6th century BCE) *The Art of War* (date unknown) highlighted the need for hierarchy, communication, and planning in successful warfare. Winning a war is not simple; it is costly, administratively nightmarish, and organizationally challenging. Tzu knew that amassing and coordinating a large number of troops, munitions, and material was just the start. Winning the campaign took planning and strategy by top officials, who could confidently pass down orders and expect them to be followed. This was achieved through a formal organization.

The ancient Greeks also emphasized organizational techniques to win their battles with enemies. Philip of Macedon (382–336 BCE) and his son, **Alexander the Great** (356–323 BCE), used a number of modern organizational techniques, such as line and staff, organization by function, standardization, mobility, intelligence, and support services, to achieve a fighting machine unequaled in the known world. In addition to their legions of warfare, which were developed around strict rules, line and staff, delegation of authority, hierarchy, and communication, the Romans built roadways, cities, and aqueducts. All of these achievements were impossible without the formal use of organization.

Aristotle (384–322 BCE), in his *The Politics*, developed a political philosophy that was based on constitutionalism and the rule of law. His philosophy was reflective of organizational principles, such as the specific nature of the chief executive's powers, which was not the same for all states or organizations but ultimately reflected the specific environment. Aristotle relied on the basic belief that people are social creatures and are therefore motivated to form an organization (or state) in order to protect themselves, family, and property. The state (organization) is composed of rules (laws), communication, purpose, and objectives and goals. Each variable is representative of the makeup of modern organizations.

BOX 6.2 | Sun Tzu—*The Art of War*

Sun Tzu was a Chinese general who lived in the state of Wu around the 6th century BCE, and one of the earliest realists in international relations theory. His popular book *The Art of War* was a piece on military strategy, suggesting that winning war is not simple, but can be done with planning, strategy, and coordination of effort and resources. Actually, some believe that Tzu did not even exist, and that the book was written by Chinese philosophers somewhere around the 4th century BCE. Nothing is confirmed, and so the legend and his ideas live on.

Source: "Sun Tzu," *The Columbia Electronic Encyclopedia*, retrieved May 10, 2018, from https://encyclopedia2.thefreedictionary.com/Sun+Tzu

Niccolò Machiavelli (1469–1527), in his book *The Prince,* reflected on the role of the shrewd, practical manager of public goods and services. Machiavelli's description and advocacy of questionable tactics, such as the destruction of enemies when they serve no further purpose, were tempered by practical considerations that any wise administrator in an organization should follow. These included merit as a way of moving up in the ranks of the organization, favoring unity of command, and learning when and how to unseat your foes through cunning (political) craftiness. Although Machiavelli was often accused of violating many fundamental moral principles, he advocated these behaviors so the Prince could be effective within political and organizational limits in achieving the overall public good.

The Americanization of European Designs

The nineteenth and twentieth centuries brought along the integration and organization of the industrial might of American entrepreneurs and their capital, the adoption of European means of Scientific Management Principles, the growth of cities and urban environments, and the influx of millions of immigrant workers, all producing an outflow of products and services never before seen. With this output was the need for sound principles of authority, management, communication, hierarchy, and other basics of organization. As one author noted, organizations changed from "'communal' forms based on the bonds of kinship and personal ties . . . to 'associative' forms based on contractual arrangements among individuals."[9] The modern organization was born.

Late nineteenth-century European means of management and personnel in industry contributed to the need for the modern organization. Two phases of industrialism pressed for new forms of organization: the first began in the early 1800s, marked by the emergence of factories, such as the British textile industry; and the second, which began in the mid-1800s, in which the factory system diversified into clothing, food, engineering, iron, transportation, weapons, and other products. The complexity and precision of industrial organizations made clear the need for new structures and organizations.[10] In order to produce the volume of products and services demanded by the world, the need for rational—meaning efficient, economical, and effective—organizational design grew exponentially. It was during the second major phase that the classical organizational

---

BOX 6.3 | What did Karl Marx say?

The worker becomes all the poorer the more wealth he possesses, the more his production increases in power and range. The worker becomes an ever cheaper commodity the more commodities he creates. With the increasing value of the world of things proceeds in direct proportion to the devaluation of the world of men. Labor produces not only commodities; it produces itself and the worker as a commodity—and does so in the proportion in which it produces commodities generally. ◢

Source: Karl Marx, *Economic and Philosophic Manuscripts* of 1844, trans. Martin Milligan (New York, NY: International Publishers, 1964), 9–56.

---

theorists emerged, advocating a bureaucratic structure and process that would maximize output while at the same time minimizing costs. The demand for economic and industrial growth punctuated the private sector, while at the same time resonating with the need for government to regulate and oversee the tremendous increase in output and urbanization. Similar organizational systems were developed in the world's militaries. Karl Marx and Max Weber, for instance, both from the German school of rational efficiency and technical expertise, believed that bureaucratic structures would contribute to the economic, political, and social development, including new classes of workers, called managers, whose primary responsibility was directing and coordinating resources within the newly minted modern organization for the purpose of achieving predetermined goals.

Mary Jo Hatch, contemporary American organization historian, has compared the industrialism which laid the foundation for producing the classical theories and theorists of organization with the post-industrialism which superseded the industrial state in such a way so as to reinvent, even radically transform, the means, ends, and purposes of not only doing work but in living and interacting in a technology-infused age. For Hatch, the industrial phase marked by nation-states regulating economies, the **routinization** of method, bureaucratic structure, standardization and centralized control and functionalization, stood in contrast with the post-industrialism marked by global competition, **decentralization of authority**, emphasis on speed, timing, and information output, flatter organizational structures, loose boundaries between organizations and functions, diversity and innovation in meeting customer needs, and emphasis on task-based teamwork and organizational learning.[11] **Post-industrial societies required new ways of organizing**, particularly focused on people and means rather than upon structure and function. This laid the groundwork for developing new contemporary theories of organization, such as neoclassical, human relations, and open systems approaches.

The Americanization of designs from Europe and Asia strongly suggests that the seminal works of organization theory, whether from a sociological or management perspective, were adopted to emphasize American industrial might, as well as infusing them into what became the administrative and welfare states. The influence of modern American public administration, from the late nineteenth century, particularly with emphasis on the Scientific Management approach, through the pre-World War II time period, and the strength of F. D. Roosevelt's executive branch co-optation of administrative authority—with the Brownlow

Report—strongly suggests that American influence was directed toward increasing the role and function of government at all levels to address the pressing economic, political, and social needs of society. The following sections examine the ideas and personalities that shaped organization theory and behavior, particularly as they relate to public administration and pursuit of the public interests.

CLOSED SYSTEMS: THE CLASSICAL THEORIES

The academic study of organization is in no way the exclusive province of business management or political science. As a matter of fact, other more diverse disciplines, such as anthropology, sociology, psychology, social psychology, and economics, provided much of the information, questions, and knowledge regarding organizations and organizational behavior that we draw upon today.[12] It is safe to assume, we argue, that rigorous and analytical multidisciplinary investigations of organizations, particularly among industrial psychologists and sociologists, prompting theoretical discussions and empirical hypotheses, did not emerge in earnest before the 1940s.[13] Further, the varieties of organization theory studies focus largely around what several researchers claim are: (1) subject matter, such as individuals, structure, and processes; (2) type of theory, such as systems, public choice, group politics, and personality; and (3) purpose of organization theory as predictive, using empirical research methods and techniques to determine what is knowable and what isn't about organizations.[14] Let's begin our investigation of the various theories of organizations with the classical period.

The **classical school of organization** was the first to develop. The classical school derives its name from the pioneer scholars and practitioners who established working theories and models depicting organizations and their behavior. Classical theorists are as diverse as Adam Smith and his economic theories of the firm, to sociologist Emile Durkheim and his theory of shifting societies, to Max Weber and the definition of bureaucracy. Classical theorists do not emphasize the responsibility of each organizational participant to the public interests; the public interests are of concern only to the elites who set the mandates of the organization. Classical theorists instead emphasize the structural aspects of the organizations, finding that formal organizations are to be almost machine-like, placing preeminence on attaining efficiency, economy, and effectiveness. They contend that there is one best way of doing work in order to achieve the highest rates of productivity, and therefore it is imperative to order the organization's characteristics, such as hierarchy, chain of command, communication, authority, and, ultimately, organizational behavior, accordingly. Further, a major goal of classical organization theory is to reduce performance variation of both human and capital elements of production. Often the metaphor of a machine is chosen, given that the goal is to calibrate work process and **outcomes** within an acceptable error range.

Early Economic Theories of Organizations

In 1776, Scottish economist Adam Smith (1723–1790)[15] theorized that organization of time and personnel was necessary to mass produce manufactured goods, such as the pin factory discussed in his book *The Wealth of Nations*. According to Smith, it is crucial to organize men and material, using specialization of function as the primary measure, to produce the goods necessary to sell and distribute both home and abroad, but to do it in such a way that the individual contributions of one worker is not as important as the multiplied efforts of many workers in the organization. Each worker is trained to do a specialized task, and when those tasks are combined and monitored for efficiency and economy they produce a sum that is greater than its parts. This thinking led to the development and implementation of the factory system, which ultimately contributed to evolution of the Industrial Era by the 1890s.

By the mid- to late 1840s a brilliant German philosopher and economist named Karl Marx (1818–1883) developed his famous theory of capital.[16] Marx believed that labor, or what he termed collective effort, was the social foundation for all societies worldwide. Individual labor was useless unless understood within the larger physical environment of organization, or the function of collective labor. Collective labor, when organized under the political and economic oversight of the state, will produce a more rational and humane treatment of workers than afforded by the capitalists (i.e., bourgeoisie), whose sole intention is to produce profit based off the forced labor of the worker. Capitalists demand more profit and thus impose more controls upon the worker, forcing workers to work more efficiently, and thus increasing the tension between the two groups. Workers organize collectively, such as in unions, to ward off the pressures of capitalists and managers. This antagonistic relationship precipitates the need for intervention from government, a civil form of organization, with authority and power to control the actions of each.

Sociology and Bureaucratic Theory

Even though Emile Durkheim (1858–1917), the French sociologist, expanded Adam Smith's notions of the manufacturing organization to one of industrialization by the late nineteenth century, arguing that all aspects of human society work together like parts of a machine, something he referred to as **sociological functionalism**, and thus contributing greatly to the sociological literature and knowledge of organizations; it was the work of **Max Weber (1864–1920)**, an eminent German sociologist, whose contribution to organizational theory was the formal definition and explanation of the bureaucratic structure.[17] While society and industry expanded during the latter part of the nineteenth century, creating jobs, building cities and towns, and increasing the size and authority of government, there was no formal description and explanation of this organizational phenomenon known as bureaucracy. Weber filled this void by constructing what he termed the "ideal type" of organization, called the bureaucracy. It was not labeled ideal because it was perfect; it was labeled ideal because it was approximation of what Weber believed society *and* individual organizations could evolve into if there were no outside forces restricting their evolution.

Weber's **theory of bureaucracy** imposed rational constraints upon the social environment, or organization, as evidenced in the prescription of several key values:

- *Division of labor*—work is divided according to purpose and type, and there are clear lines of jurisdiction or authority.
- *Specialization of function*—there is no overlap or duplication of functions, providing for greater efficiency of productivity.

- *Hierarchy* is defined as a vertical chain of command, with the orders going down and the responses coming up.
- *Framework of rules and procedures* is designed to enhance greater predictability and stability of routine in the organization.
- *Impersonal relationships*—no person is viewed more important than any other person, thus ensuring that all are provided the same attention.
- *Professionalization* of workers is promoted, where a person's knowledge, skills, and abilities are elevated over name recognition, societal status, and economic background.
- *Record-keeping system* provides that actions are current and consistent with previous actions.

Each element or value—and the combination thereof—was designed to promote greater efficiency, control, and growth of the bureaucracy. Conformity to standards was expected, and deviance from the standards was not tolerated, because it was expected that any movement away from the elements described above would detract from attaining the goals of bureaucracy. This is what many scholars refer to as a closed system of organization.[18]

A great deal of criticism has been heaped upon Weber and his ideal construct; primary among it is that real-world organizations simply do not look like, nor run like, what Weber said they should look and run like! The criticisms are numerous—for example, rules are arbitrary. Informal organizations are numerous and sometimes subvert the formal structures. Individuals are often confused about their roles, primarily because they play numerous roles instead of one. And individuals are motivated for reasons other than rational ones, such as money and promotions—including that they just really like doing their job.[19] We will examine some of these criticisms later, but suffice it to say that Weber's contribution to organization theory became the benchmark for future classical theorists and the foundation upon which innumerable theorists and researchers built.

Engineers, Businessmen, and Scientific Management

A second major theme of the classical school of organizational theory is Scientific Management. It is a broad-ranging stratum of ideas, but its main thesis is directed toward improving organizational efficiency and economy by analyzing tasks and workflow. The key values of Scientific Management are: (1) maximizing efficiency, (2) striving for rationality in work procedures, (3) maintaining high productivity levels, and (4) achieving a profit.[20] The primary spokesperson for the movement was Frederick Winslow Taylor (1856–1915).[21] Taylor and others, like **Frank Gilbreth** (1868–1924) and **Lillian Gilbreth** (1878–1972),[22] emphasized that machine-like efficiency was necessary in order for the organization to achieve full production. This purpose inspired Taylor to advance the idea of *time and motion studies*, a concept that required factory and industry workers to rework their physical motions for carrying out a specific task, such as shoveling coal, hauling pig-iron, or even laying bricks. The belief was that by altering or changing the physical movement necessary to complete a particular task, it would be possible to work more efficiently and thus effectively and economically accomplish the task in less time. Ultimately, Taylor and the Gilbreths celebrated the industrial

BOX 6.4 | Frank Bunker Gilbreth (1868–1924) and Lillian Evelyn Moller (Gilbreth) (1878–1972)

Frank Bunker Gilbreth and Lillian Evelyn Moller (Gilbreth) were made famous by the 1950 movie *Cheaper by the Dozen*. Married in 1904 and the parents of 12 children, they formed a management consulting firm of Gilbreth, Inc., based almost entirely on the application of engineering time and motion studies to management situations, both public and private. They were obsessed with making even the most menial tasks more efficient and effective by the reduction of time and motion to complete the activity. This included everything from improvements in bricklaying to laying out the ideal kitchen for a person with a heart disease (constructing a kitchen so that all parts, from utensil holders to the stove, would be easily and efficiently accessible). After Frank's untimely death, Lillian carried on the work, raising the children, lecturing, and consulting until her death in 1972. ▲

Source: The Gilbreth Network, "Frank and Lillian Gilbreth," retrieved from http://gilbrethnetwork.tripod.com/bio.html

zenith of the day by arguing that humans were dignified by joining the machines as its efficiently designed appendage.

Scientific Management reformers such as Henry Laurence Gantt (1861–1919), who for a time worked for Taylor, emphasized the human aspect of work, arguing, for example, that the physical conditions people work in should be respectable. Nevertheless, the machine-like dehumanizing effect favored by Taylor and the Gilbreths is what most remember of Scientific Management studies. This dehumanizing effect would not be tolerated today, of course, and with good reason. But the industrial system of the early twentieth century relied on the piecework method, and Scientific Management reformers such as Gantt—from whom the **Gantt Chart** is named—devised new visual display charts for scheduling work based on time rather than quantity of work achieved. Such alterations were beneficial for both management and the worker. The worker could produce more and thus be paid more, and management would get more out of the worker and thus achieve a higher production rate and profit.[23]

Scientific Management would have remained an isolated phenomenon, one relegated to the business industry had it not been for **Harrington Emerson** (1853–1931). Emerson was born into a wealthy and prominent New Jersey family, received a European education, and then showed his maverick side by embarking on a journey westward that included stints as a professor in modern languages, banker, land speculator, and all-around entrepreneur. He is best known for his pioneering work in industrial engineering and Scientific Management. He promoted Scientific Management not so much in the workplace, but to mass audiences. He established a successful consulting business, labeled himself as an efficiency engineer, published books on industrial efficiency that described his Emerson Efficiency System, a system that included production routing procedures, standard working conditions, time and motion studies, and worker bonus plans.[24] In effect, Emerson disseminated his ideas of Scientific Management, promoting not only the theory itself, but by default many of its adherents, such as Taylor and the Gilbreths, through lectures, articles, and books.

The Principles Approach

The third stream of thought and practice in the classical tradition of organization theory and behavior is broadly known as the Principles approach, and more specifically as Administrative Management. The Scientific Management adherents attempted to change and rationalize the organization from the bottom up, with changes in the way work is done. The Administrative Management proponents argued that the best way to change the organization is from the top down, emphasizing that managers were the key parts in the organization and therefore various rationalizing principles should direct their administrative functions.[25] One of the best-known proponents of the Principles approach was a Frenchman named **Henri Fayol** (1841–1925).

Fayol, a wealthy French industrialist, wrote in the early part of the twentieth century, but his work was not translated into English until after World War II.[26] After turning around a failing mining company he retired and started a center for the study of administration in order to put into print and practice his ideas.[27] His basic ideas were: (1) to reorganize upper management positions, (2) educate everyone in the organization in management theories, (3) eliminate as much red tape as possible; and (4) establish lateral lines of communication within the organization. To accomplish this he argued that every organization should comprise five essential functions: *plan* (or what many refer to today as strategize), *organize, command, co-ordinate,* and *control.* He even went so far as to identify **14 principles common to all organizations.** Fayol's work set the stage for future studies of management.

Others, like James D. Mooney (1884–1957), along with Alan C. Reiley, substantiated Fayol's work. In 1931, Mooney and Reiley published *Onward Industry: The Principles of Organization and their Significance to Modern Industry* (later republished in 1939 as *The Principles of Organization*).[28] They argued there were four main principles of management, including coordination, scalar chain of command, specialization, and line/staff functional differences. Given that both Mooney and Reiley were General Motor executives in the early 1930s, the bulk of their observations are from private sector experience.[29]

Where Scientific Management placed the emphasis on the workers following simplified and quantified rules and procedures for accomplishing various work

---

BOX 6.5 | Henri Fayol's 14 Principles of Organization[30]

1. Division of labor
2. Balancing authority and responsibility
3. Discipline
4. Unity of command
5. Unity of direction
6. Subordination of individual interest to organizational interests
7. Adequate remuneration
8. Centralization of authority
9. Chain of command
10. Order
11. Fairness
12. Stability of tenure of employees
13. Initiative
14. Promote *esprit de corps* within rank and file of organization

tasks, the Administrative Management theorists argued that management should be the priority item of any organization. Later, others such as **Leonard White** (1891–1958) summarized the previous work of both the Scientific Management and Principles schools. For example, White published the first recognized textbook devoted exclusively to public administration and management, *Introduction to the Study of Public Administration* (1926),[31] where he discussed at some length the belief that management lends itself to a value-free analysis, the emphasis on the intersection of science and technology, the management of organizational resources, and even basic comparisons between the private and public sectors. White also drew heavily upon the politics/administration dichotomy, which most scholars contend is drawn from Woodrow Wilson's 1887 essay,[32] arguing that administration was a science and politics was a craft, and never shall the twain meet. Most contemporary scholars and practitioners understand that administration and policy are anything but separate; however, in the early part of the twentieth century, when the vestiges of the Reform Movement were still evident, there was the need to justify the rational and empirical world of administrative action in comparison to the nonrational and normative world of politics.

The last major contribution to the Principles approach within Administrative Management theory was with the work of Luther Gulick (1892–1993) and Lyndall Urwick (1891–1983).[33] Because of Gulick's ties to President Roosevelt's administration through being a member of the Committee for Administrative Management (aka the Brownlow Committee, named after committee chairman Louis Brownlow [1879–1963]) and consultant to the National Resource Planning Board and his close personal friendship with the President, he had actual experience in the government world. He believed that various rules or principles existed to make every organization, particularly government organizations, run more efficiently and be controlled from the manager's perspective. Again, these principles were not much different from the principles first introduced by Fayol. They included: hierarchy, unity of command, specialization of function, span of control, and rational organizational design. Most importantly to Gulick and Urwick, they believed that the right structural arrangements of management authority had to be discovered and then fill the available positions with the right people in order for the organization to function properly.[34]

Management was the key. The greater the emphasis on management authority, working top-down, the better was the organization. To form a rational construct of management principles, Gulick and Urwick devised an acronym, *POSDCORB*, which described the basic functions of any management system: Planning, Organizing, Staffing, Directing, Coordinating, and Budgeting. But how would this strictly management oriented and administratively driven perspective connect to democratic pluralist values? The answer was to require the administrator to be responsible to the elected official, primarily the president.[35] Thus, management principles summarized in POSDCORB included:

- *Planning*: envision and strategize for the future.
- *Organizing*: plan and systematically align and categorize.
- *Staffing*: meet all personnel and human resource needs.
- *Directing*: develop sound leadership and managerial skills.
- *Coordinating*: bring together all resources for fulfillment of organization goals.

- *Reporting*: develop sound communication means and technology.
- *Budgeting*: control the organization through fiscal planning and accounting.

Closed systems focused on development of machine-like qualities of efficiency, effectiveness, and economy. The primary goal, whether in the private or public sector, was to achieve the greatest output for the least input, while doing so at the least possible cost. Surely there is not much inherent in this philosophy of organization that speaks to fulfilling the public interests. If you said this, you would be mistaken. Fulfilling the public interests is indeed a normative concept, and as such it focuses on meeting the values of fiscal, organizational, and policy economy. Granted, human well-being and fostering interpersonal and organizational relations was not a priority in the closed system, but the common good of recognizing the strengths and weaknesses of large-scale hierarchical organizations was achieved.

OPEN SYSTEMS: MODERN THEORIES

Differing dramatically from the closed systems approach is the open systems approach. The **human relations approach** is a subset or group of a broader open, natural, informal, and even organic model. The basic argument is that unlike the classical approach, which views organizations in a rational and mechanistic fashion, with workers and managers operating largely based on economic means; the open systems model, particularly the human relations subcomponent, contends that workers worked and contributed to the overall organization for non-economic reasons.[36] These reasons may include a sense of responsibility to the public interests shared by each participant within the organization. In addition to the human relations perspective found under the open systems umbrella, we will also look at decision making, neoclassical, systems approach, organizational learning, and organizational culture. Clearly, the human dimension of organizational morality was beginning to take shape, delineating more clearly the focus on pursuit of the public interests.

Informal Organizations

A step or two ahead of her time was **Mary Parker Follett** (1868–1933). As a social psychologist, she balked against the time-honored traditions of the classical school, believing instead that worker satisfaction was a key factor in the development of productive social organizations. Individuals and informal social groups within the larger organization must reconcile their differences and goals. One way was through effective administration, sound communication, and promotion of differences among and between workers. Due to her focus on these less than formal traits of traditional classical organization theory, her ideas of power with the employees rather than power over the employees ushered in the thinking behind the human relations approach, including the famous Hawthorne Studies.[37]

Decision-Making Approach

Others, including **Chester Barnard (1866–1961)**, were highly influential in promoting the informal group concept. Barnard, who was not a scholar but a successful

BOX 6.6 | The Hawthorne Experiments

The Hawthorne experiments were conducted during the late 1920s and early 1930s at Hawthorne Western Electric Plant, located just outside of Chicago. Elton Mayo (1880–1949), who was with the Harvard Business School, and his research associate, Fritz J. Roethlisberger, conducted experiments on worker productivity. Mayo believed that such factors as worker fatigue affected organizational productivity. In order to test this thesis, they conducted several on-site controlled experiments. One such experiment was to divide plant workers into multiple groups, isolating one set of workers from other groups of workers, and controlling or manipulating certain variables, such as the intensity of lighting illumination. In the experiment group, the level of illumination was decreased frequently, while the control group's level of illumination remained unchanged. The researchers expected to find that the level of productivity would decrease in the experiment group, while remaining the same or even increasing in the control group. To their surprise, the productivity levels of both groups increased.

Unsure of why the results turned out the way they did, the researchers actually went to the workers for explanation, and the workers admitted that, despite the varying levels of illumination, they worked just as hard because they were the center of attention. In other words, worker productivity changed not necessarily because of changes in the physical environment but because of changes in the social group environment. Workers encouraged each other to keep up the pace, and continue to work hard despite the physical conditions. This was especially true of female workers. They responded well to the attention given them by the researchers. This became known as the Hawthorne effect.

A second important contribution of the Hawthorne experiments was the **informal group**. Where the formal organization is the organization that is outlined on paper, with boxes, titles, and arrows pointing down, the informal group "is the group formed by employees that exists over and above the formal organization . . . [with] a leadership structure quite apart from the formal organization, and that the group had its own norms with respect to production." In many respects, what Mayo and his associates found was that productivity was more the result of worker-to-worker motivation to produce within the informal group than it was a result of management and the formal organization. Thus, it struck a blow against the classical approach which stressed there was one right way to manage and organize. ◢

Source: F.J. Roethlisberger, *Man-in-Organization: Essays of F.J. Roethlishberger* (Cambridge, MA: Belknap, 1968). For Mayo's own analysis, see Elton Mayo, *The Human Problems of an Industrial Civilization* (New York, NY: Viking, 1933).

businessman and leader with the New Jersey Bell Telephone Company in the 1930s, wrote *The Functions of the Executive* (1938).[38] His book was somewhat of a bridge between the classical and human relations schools, because he saw the organization in human rather than simply structural terms. Still, he recognized that decision making was a key variable to working through the minefield of equilibrium changes or exchanges between workers and management. The manager's job was to "allocate satisfactions or rewards in exchange for the employees' acquiescence to the prescribed behavior; behavior that the organization required to meet its goals and survive."[39] Barnard contended that there were differences between the informal and formal organizations, especially with regard to measuring behavior. He argued "that workers had a social-psychological zone of acceptance, referring to their relative willingness to obey the leader's directives."[40] The best workers, then, were workers who were compatible with management on a variety of factors, including education and personality, not just skill level.

Herbert Simon's (1916–2001) work in the science of administrative decision making built on and went beyond Barnard's work (see Chapter 2) to include a portrayal of "organizational decision-making as a kind of compromise between rational, goal oriented behavior and non-rational behavior."[41] Simon distinguished between facts and values, where administrators give validity to values, weighing means and ends, and ultimately assessing the consequences of action within the parameters of these values.[42] It is the organization that defines what values determine rational over non-rational behavior. Administrators or other decision makers ultimately make decisions regarding these various values, including the laws, rules, and regulations commonly implemented in society. But no decision is based on pure rational thought or behavior; the best the administrator can hope for is to both satisfy and suffice, or what Simon coined satisficing in his book *Administrative Behavior* (1945), for which he was later awarded the 1978 Nobel Prize in Economics. This form of satisficing recognizes that rational behavior is thus bounded by its very administrative environment, including the level and amount of information, skills, and knowledge, both of the administrator and the worker, and of the overall organization itself.[43] Simon's work was critical in learning more about how administrative decisions are made.

Dwight Waldo (1913–2000) challenged the positivist uprising in the social sciences in the late 1940s, in debates with Herbert Simon and others in political science and public administration. He summoned the courage to state unequivocally that individual, group, and institutional morality, fixed within normative philosophy of administration and management, should not be so readily dismissed in the wake of logical positivism and the behavioral outcomes it produces. In his famous tug-of-war with Herbert Simon published in the *American Political Science Review*,[44] Waldo rejected Simon's claim that administrative decisions focused solely on facts as opposed to values were scientifically valid and, thus, moved closer to the overall goal of administrative efficiency. Why? Because, as Waldo so succinctly yet forcefully put it, the administrative world is not the same as the political world. Efficiency by itself is a claim of values—one that is determined by the decision maker.[45]

Neoclassical Approach

The new human relations approach to organization theory focused on methodology—the use of closely empirical research to determine workers' interpersonal relations affecting the overall organization. Similar to the human relations approach, it focuses on the individual and not the organizational structure. However, motivation of the individual, as opposed to informal groups and decision making, within the organization is critical to explaining decisions and productivity. Two theorists are most prominent: Abraham Maslow and Douglas McGregor.

Abraham Maslow (1908–1970) received his PhD in psychology from the University of Wisconsin in 1934 and focused his attention on the theoretical development of humanistic psychology, particularly in the development of the concept of self-actualization and human motivation. Maslow is most well-known for his needs hierarchy, where he argued that humans have five basic needs ordered in a **hierarchy of needs**: physiological, safety, love or affiliation, esteem, and self-actualization.[46]

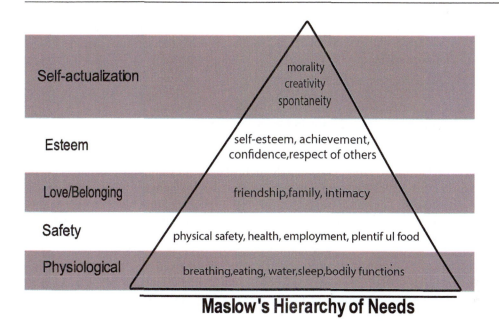

Self-actualization	morality creativity spontaneity
Esteem	self-esteem, achievement, confidence, respect of others
Love/Belonging	friendship, family, intimacy
Safety	physical safety, health, employment, plentif ul food
Physiological	breathing, eating, water, sleep, bodily functions

Maslow's Hierarchy of Needs

FIGURE 6.1
Maslow's Hierarchy of Needs

Each lower need must be met before higher needs emerge in the person's life. A person, for example, must have food for physical nourishment, but once their physical need for food is met they have additional and higher needs, which in turn (when they are met) they advance up the hierarchy, ultimately trying to reach the nirvana of needs: self-actualization. From an administrative point of view, Maslow's theory was not easily adaptable—not until the organizational humanists, such as Douglas McGregor and others, came along to apply Maslow's theory of human needs and motivation into an administrative and organizational setting. Maslow included five levels of human needs in a hierarchy of needs with his book *Motivation and Personality*: biological and physiological needs, safety needs, belongingness and love needs, esteem needs, and self-actualization needs (see Figure 6.1).[47]

Douglas McGregor (1906–1964) earned his PhD from Harvard and argued in his classic book *The Human Side of Enterprise* (1960)[48] that workers could be self-motivated (i.e., Theory Y) as opposed to externally motivated by management (i.e., Theory X). Both theories make assumptions about human motivation and behavior. **Theory X** assumptions are:

- Work is generally not desired, but is done only out of economic necessity.
- Workers like to be closely supervised.
- Workers do not generally assume new responsibilities without having to be told.
- Workers are strictly motivated by money and threat of punishment.

Obviously, these same assumptions of human motivation were the foundation of Scientific Management theory. McGregor; however, perceived that post-World

War II research in industrial psychology, for example, validated another set of assumptions about human need and motivation. He labeled this **Theory Y**. The assumptions included:

- People enjoy work.
- People are self-motivated and controlled.
- People do, in fact, create and innovate.
- People's motivation is largely due in response to rewards, not punishment.

McGregor accepted Maslow's theoretical work and adapted it to management/worker behavior, suggesting that the reason why organizations do not achieve higher levels of performance is because they expect too little out of workers; they don't meet the higher end level of needs, such as esteem and self-actualization.[49] Some contend that McGregor actually modeled his two theories after real-life organizations: Theory X and the military and Theory Y and professional organizations, such as law and medicine.[50] Whether or not this is true is not as relevant as the fact that McGregor's work legitimated the esoteric work of Maslow and other humanistic psychologists as a means to help explain large-scale organizational administrative behavior.

Systems Approach

Systems theory recognizes the importance of both process and outcome within the organization. The systems framework developed after World War II, with an emphasis on interactions and interrelationships between various elements. These elements included: the environment, inputs (i.e., resources), the system itself (processes), **outputs** (product or service of the system or process), and feedback (effects of the outputs on the environment).[51] One advantage of systems theory is its streamlined and linear approach to decision making; equally so, one of its disadvantages is found in its linearity, meaning critics believe it is too simple to fully explain the interaction and interrelationship between organizations in society. Three of the more notable systems theorists are David Easton and Daniel Katz and Robert Kahn.

David Easton (1917–2014) applied the cybernetic or systems model to political science.[52] Easton set forth on an ambitious project: to deal with the empirical and behavioral side of political science, a side that emerged from the institutional cover of bygone days, when the intention of students of politics were focused on the legal and institutional characteristics of government. The Chicago School, as it came to be known, argued for a more exacting science of politics, one whose theory and inquiry were to be strictly scrutinized from a position of interdependence with society. Easton's contribution to this strict scrutiny reinstated the notion that political theory was important, particularly as it helped to explain the behavioral aspects made so prominent in the aftermath of the War. Thus he theorized that political and policy issues, such as women's and civil rights, should be examined through the systems process described above.

Daniel Katz (1903–1998) and Robert Kahn (1918–), both psychology scholars, launched into an open systems perspective of organizations, declaring that organizations were more than simply lines and boxes on a hierarchy chart. Rather organizations were seen as "whole beings, complex and constantly interacting with their environment."[53] Katz and Kahn envisioned the organization as complex, but also as a constantly changing phenomenon; therefore, it is never static, and always changing, depending in large part on the environment it operates within. As some have described, the university setting is a model of the open systems approach as explained by Katz and Kahn.[54]

In addition, the role of smaller groups internal to the larger organization was examined more closely by scholars of **Organizational Development** (OD), as well as related theories of organizational learning and organizational culture. OD is defined as "a planned organization-wide attempt directed from the top that is designed to increase organizational effectiveness and viability through calculated interventions in the active workings of the organization using knowledge from the behavioral sciences."[55] In other words, OD is focused on the role and input of the individual and small group within the larger organization, focusing less on structural aspects of organizations and more on what is referred to as organic or natural aspects of organizations. Kurt Lewin (1890–1947) was recognized as the leading pioneer/guru of OD, as early as the 1940s.[56] OD made its mark in the private sector as well as the public sector, with advocates such as Robert Golembiewski (1932–2016).[57]

Organization Learning

A more recent perspective of the open model approach to organizational behavior is **Organizational Learning (OL).** The key premise of OL is that: (1) organizations are like organisms—they are constantly (or should be) changing in response to their respective external environments; and (2) that organizations will not learn unless individuals within the organizations learn. If organizations (or really individuals) stop learning, or adapting to changes in their respective environments, particularly social, economic, administrative, managerial, and even political, then both individuals and organizations stagnate and cannot function as they are designed to.

According to OL, there are two basic types of learning: adaptive, where there are changes made in reaction to the environment; and proactive, where changes are made on a more deliberate basis. Adaptive learning is (more or less) lower-level learning, i.e., learning by reacting, whereas proactive learning is higher-level learning, i.e., learning by doing, so to speak. Pioneers of OL, such as **Richard Cyert** (1921–1998) and **James G. March** (1928–), argued that OL is mainly an adaptive process; one where goals, Standard Operating Procedures, or what they referred to as attention rules, and search rules are all essentially made to fit the organization, or at least with each other within the organization. Essentially, Cyert and March argued from a behavior approach of the market: the organization, in order to act rationally, focuses on its rules of order and operation in order to perform more efficiently. Reacting positively or initially to changes in the external environment, such as to inflation, recessions, ups and downs in the stock market, were not a part of their thinking as to what an organizational learning environment is all about.[58] Later, March with Johan Olsen (1939–) made a similar argument for institutional learning cycle, which

> involves the selective recollection and interpretation of experiences (the
> usable history), understandings of the rules and identities derived from these

experiences, interpretations of the nature of previous institutional actions and their consequences, and the adaptation of rules and identities based on these interpretations.[59]

Many scholars and researchers have contributed to a better understanding of OL, none probably more influential than **Chris Argyis** (1923–2013), Donald Schon (1930–1997), and Peter Senge (1947–). Argyris built upon systems theory and developed an organizational learning model with organizations as systems, where learning involves the detection and correction of error. He outlined two types of learning that occurred in organizations: single-loop and double-loop learning. The first, single-loop, occurred without asking questions, either about the reason for the issue or how to correct consequences that result because of the issue. For example, President Donald Trump proposes to partially privatize Social Security, by making it possible through tax changes and other means for younger taxpayers to hold back a certain percentage of their pay check and privately invest it. If this proposal were to become law (it hasn't yet), then this would be a form of single-loop or adaptive learning. On the other hand, double-loop learning provides alternative responses to the very issue itself. With President Trump's Social Security proposal example, critics challenge the basic assumption of privatization itself, while also criticizing the President's proposal for implementing privatization. The first form of learning simply reacts to changes in the environment, but the second not only reacts but actually modifies the organization (or, in this case, proposed) basic norms and philosophy. Obviously, for Argyris the double-loop learning is superior, particularly during times of radical change.

Building on Argyris' work is Donald Schon (1930–1997) and his concept of the **learning society**. Schon agrees with Argyris's initial assumption that double-loop learning was superior for organizations, but he took it step further. He posited that organizations should be in a constant state of learning (i.e., double-loop learning), given the changing nature of society and societal institutions, including economic, political, and social. In his key work *Beyond the Stable State* (1973), Schon argued that

> We must . . . become adept at learning. We must become able not only to transform our institutions, in response to changing situations and requirements; we must invent and develop institutions that are "learning systems", that is to say, systems capable of bringing about their own continuing transformation.[60]

So, for Schon, learning is not simply something that is individual; it is also institutional or social. This is critical when public or private organizations are trying to exist, for example, in an ever-changing high-technology world.

Third is Peter Senge (1947–), who was strongly influenced by both Argyris and Schon and credits much of what he understands about modern organizations and institutions from both. However, Senge argues that organizations must be constantly learning and enhancing their capabilities to learn, primarily through development of five specific disciplines he regards as the centerpiece of learning organizations. The five disciplines are: systems thinking, personal mastery, mental models, building shared vision, and team learning. The key discipline, which he explores in *The Fifth Discipline* (1990), is the discipline "that integrates the others, fusing them into a coherent body of theory and practice." Each of the five disciplines is interwoven along three dimensions: practices, or what a person does; principles, a person's guiding ideas and insights; and essences, a high level of being. So, the learning organization is an organization that incorporates all individuals, led by leaders who are designers and teachers and stewards.[61] Developing learning organizations should be the motivation of all managers and administrators, given that learning organizations, as opposed to non-learning organizations, will thrive and change, and thus be higher performing.

Organizational Culture

The **organizational culture** perspective is a departure from the rational, functional approaches to organizations that were part of the classical approach. The organizational culture perspective studies and manages the non-rational cultural elements of organizations, such as symbols or signs, artifacts of human values, language and jargon, rituals and rites, justifications and ideologies, and underlying value assumptions. Professor J. Steven Ott defines the organizational culture perspective in this way:

> Instead of viewing an organization as goal-oriented structure (formal or informal), functions, information systems and decision processes, or groups of members, the organizational culture perspective put on a different set of "lenses" through which to "see" an organization. When we look through these special organization culture lenses, we see a mini-society made up of social constructions . . . As in *all* cultures, *all* facts, truths, realities, beliefs and values are *what the members agree they are*—they are perceptions . . . It is the gestalt—the holistic composite interweaving—of these ways of seeing things, assumptions about the nature of things and relations, patterns of doing things, beliefs, values, and realities that together comprises the identity, or the language of this book, the structure or contents of an organizational culture.[62]

The academic discipline of anthropology has traditionally defined itself by the study of culture. Social anthropologists have studied large-scale organizations to develop a rich understanding of social relationship within these cultural contexts. The empirical theory generated by these studies makes it essential to take into account the ideas and values associated with a cultural context. Culture does have to be a material existence—although physical human-made artifacts may be studied to understand the meanings that people assign to them. The findings of cultural contexts and their meanings are persuasive and have been applied by scholars in a wide variety of social science disciplines, including public administration, business administration, clinical psychology, law, economics, and others.[63]

The organizational culture perspective addresses a major feature of the cultural context in contemporary American public administration: the diverse populations of Hispanics, African Americans, Asian Americans, Native Americans, and other workplace groups of persons by race, ethnicity, gender, religion, sexual orientation, disabilities, and perspectives. We discuss diversity issues in Chapter 7, on human resources management. The realities of diversity require attention to the organizational culture perspective by public administrators to better understand

and work with conflicts, disputes, oppression, and other dynamics of organizational life. Thus, successful application of the organization culture perspective is found in public management of social equity and diversity issues in the public workplace.[64]

Whether described and explained through the development of organizational culture, informal organizations, various means of learning how administrative and organizational decisions are made (i.e., satisficing), the neoclassical or human relations school, behavioralism as evidenced through the output-driven systems approach to decision making, or the more recent organizational learning concepts, the point is clear: fulfilling the public interests is morally justified and sought after through better understanding and clarity of the human dimension of organizations. Organizations are composed of people—people who create informal groups within the larger organization in order to make sense out of their work life and to try and find meaning through the production of widgets and delivery of services that they perform on a daily basis. They are pursuing the public interests, not only for themselves but for their co-workers, families, and secondary relationships (i.e., those who buy goods or use services).

PUBLIC MANAGEMENT

So, how should we manage public organizations? Over the past 30 or so years, much has been written about managing the public sector like a business. The argument goes: running the public sector like a government leads to waste, abuse, inefficiency, unaccountability, and organizational malaise. Thus, the soothsayers coax, we should substitute business thinking, business principles, and market incentives to manage the public sector.

Like Robert Denhardt (1942–) and Janet Denhardt, professors of public administration at the University of Southern California, we contend that this is not what government is or was designed to do. Government is not just another business—contrary to popular thinking. Certainly there are similarities in organization, management, and process between business and government. Government, however, is fundamentally different from business. The purpose of government is to govern; the work of government is to serve; the outcome of government is pursuit of the public interests. The degree of efficiency, effectiveness, and economy of implementing public decisions is certainly important, but the end is pursuit and accomplishment of the public interests. Or, as the Denhardts put it, "What is most significant, and most valuable about public administration is that we serve citizens to advance the common good."[65]

Thus, public management appears to be many things to many people, depending upon the context in which the need for management occurs, i.e., political, legal, administrative, economic, organizational, etc. However, three perspectives have come to dominate approaches to managing public organizations today: **Old Public Administration,** New Public Management, and New Public Service.

Old Public Administration (OPA) reflects the values associated with the advent of the Industrial Revolution and the Progressive Movement—greater efficiency and economy of service delivery, improved mechanization, increasingly effective communications technology, organizational and administrative enhancements, municipal reform, and a growing tendency toward adopting business approaches to non-business ventures, such as government and government reorganization and reform efforts. Of course, the history of public administration is much older than the end of the nineteenth century, but from a modern standpoint this is a good place to begin. At the heart of OPA was a belief in the politics/administration dichotomy. Politics, which was defined as the initiation of policy development, and administration, which was understood to be the implementation of policy, were two separate entities. As we learned earlier, this belief was rooted in the early writings of Woodrow Wilson, which emphasized two key themes: (1) the distinction between politics and administration, and (2) organizations, whether private or public, seek the "greatest possible efficiency . . . through hierarchical structures of administrative management."[66]

New Public Management (NPM) takes the more drastic step to incorporate and apply business techniques to government practices and application, whereas OPA sought to create greater efficiency and economy through organizational hierarchy. This is not really new, but NPM is "a normative model, one signaling a profound shift in how we think about the role of public administrators, the nature of the profession, and how and why we do what we do."[67] NPM's basic purpose is to banish OPM; what its proponents— such as **David Osborne** and **Ted Gaebler**,[68] Osborne and Peter Plastrik,[69] Donald Kettl[70] and others—claim is an outdated, antiquated, and ill-equipped closed organizational system, unprepared to adapt to the management and organizational changes of the twenty-first century. The use of market mechanisms, such as supply and demand, enhanced communication and information technology, outsourcing and privatization, are regarded to be much better for guiding and leading the public sector.[71] Each of these factors is designed to improve output productivity and thus enhance policy outcomes, through greater accountability to customers and clients, redefinition of agency and department missions, and above all in decentralizing the decision-making process in order to include greater input. Although some critics argue **democratic accountability** is missing in NPM,[72] proponents of NPM seem undeterred in efforts to a create streamlined, market-based, entrepreneurial public sector. Responsiveness, accountability, measurability, adaptability, results-oriented, customer-clients, revenue generation, and other buzzwords abound in NPM, but NPM proponents focus on the transformed purpose of public management.

New Public Service (NPS) does not seem easy to define or even readily definable. It is not something that can be earmarked. It is, as we noted above, much more normative and subjective, yet it contains several key characteristics that help to distinguish what it is—and perhaps what it is not. The NPS possesses characteristics (i.e., serving citizens, seeking the public interests, valuing citizenship, thinking strategically, assessing accountability, serving rather than steering, and valuing people not just productivity) that contrast with two other historical and theoretical approaches: OPA and NPM. In this section, we will briefly compare these three approaches (OPA, NPM, and NPS), showing how each marks the wider parameters of public administration generally and public management specifically. We intend to use the Denhardt's New Public Service (NPS) approach to convey the differences between the three, and show how NPS is a better model or approach for: (1) explaining the practice of public management, and (2) placing it within the context of the wider public interests.

What is new about the New Public Service (NPS)? It is not that is so much new as it is a return to understanding and appreciating public service for what is its foundation and source: public and service. It is contrasted with NPM and OPA. The NPS is less empirical and more normative, asking such questions as: How can we define the essential character of what we do? What is the motivating force that propels our actions? What gives us strength and capacity when the trials and turmoil of our work get us down? How can we face complex and intractable problems with very limited resources and a public that often resents and criticizes what we do? The Denhardts' answer is commitment to public service and pursuit of the public interests.[73]

New Public Management

NPM first gained an American audience with the publication of a landmark book: David Osborne and Ted Gaebler's *Reinventing Government* (1992). The authors, one a former city manager and the other a journalist and consultant, spent several years interviewing and researching government officials, primarily at the local and state levels, who adopted NPM techniques, and examined them for similarities. What they discovered unleashed a wave of change throughout all three levels of government, but especially at the federal level. The reinvention of government continues to the present day.[74]

Osborne and Gaebler discovered reinvention principles in their interviews of government officials. These principles of governance seem straight out of a business management text, something that might have been penned by Peter Drucker. The strategies and procedures used by many government officials, they asserted, assisted them to deliver government services in a much more efficient, economic, and effective way. Osborne and Gaebler were clear in their pro-government affirmation: "Our purpose is not to criticize government, as so many have, but to renew it. We are as bullish on the future of government as we are bearish on the current condition of government."[75]

Osborne and Gaebler's principles were quickly put into practice at the federal level. President Clinton appointed Vice President Gore to head the **National Performance Review** (NPR), an ad hoc organization with the mission to implement various elements of NPM into the federal bureaucracy, in order to achieve reduction of waste and overlapping functions. For example, within one year of implementation the NPR federal movement resulted in over 300,000 FTE (full-time equivalent) reductions, regulatory reductions, and other cost-saving measures. In addition, Congress passed the **Government Performance and Results Act** (1993), which required federal managers to establish specific performance standards and to manage for results. The law sought to reduce the level of waste and inefficiency found in Federal Government programs. And, just 10 years later, during President Bush's first administration, the Office of Management and Budget (OMB) instituted the Program Assessment Rating Tool (2001), which was an attempt "to link executive branch budget recommendations to the performance of specific federal programs."[76] One way to achieve this kind and quality of performance in government at all levels was to forge a strong relationship between the forces of **strategic planning** (i.e., not a new thing to government) and performance management (i.e., somewhat of a new thing to government). The results were to prove beneficial, but with some concerns. In order to better understand, let's take a brief look at two tools used by performance managers: strategic planning and performance measurement.

BOX 6.7 | Reinvention Principles of Osborne and Gaebler

- *"Steering rather than rowing"*—where public officials act more like business entrepreneurs, seeking out a wide range of policy possibilities to choose from, "steering" the community toward a variety of options.
- *"Empowering rather than serving"*—where public entrepreneurs shift ownership of public policies and policy initiatives to the community as a whole, "empowering" citizens and neighborhoods.
- *"Injecting competition in service delivery"*—with public entrepreneurs recognizing that governments cannot provide every service at optimal satisfaction levels, and thus increases the use of privatization and contracting-out as two means of achieving higher levels of service quality and policy effectiveness.
- *"Transforming rule-driven organizations"* into mission-seeking, purpose-driven organizations that do not stifle human creativity and ingenuity.
- *"Funding outcomes, not inputs"* becomes the policy thrust of public officials, who believe that government should be directed toward accomplishing policy goals and outcomes as opposed to simply overseeing budget outlays.
- *"Meeting the needs of the customer, not the bureaucracy"*—where the public entrepreneur learns from his private-sector counterpart "that unless one focuses on the customer, the citizen will never be happy."

- *"Earning rather spending"*—where the public official responds to fiscal constraints by finding innovative ways to deal with impending budget shortfalls, rather than simply cutting programs.
- *"Prevention rather than cure"*—where public entrepreneurs believe that preventing public policy problems is better than always trying to deal with the after effects of policy problems, even disasters (both natural and political).
- *"From hierarchy to participation and teamwork"* is the key phrase organizationally, where the public official sidesteps the old hierarchical organizations of the early twentieth century, to embrace a technologically savvy information-based age, one that governments and public managers must embrace in order to meet the current political, administrative, and social problems.
- *"Leveraging change through the market"*: probably the crux of the NPM approach, strongly arguing that market forces, not politics, should govern each government jurisdiction, with the public manager creating the right environment so the market can operate efficiently and effectively. ◣

Source: Janet V. Denhardt and Robert B. Denhardt, *The New Public Service: Serving, Not Steering* (New York, NY: Armonk, NY: M.E. Sharpe, 2003), 18–19.

Strategic Planning Strategic planning is commonly found in private and non-profit sectors, and is certainly a major element of any public manager's job. But strategic planning is different for public managers than in the private sector. Planning is obvious; we all make plans. However, public managers must also connect these plans to measurable performance indicators in the public interests, the government-mandated goals and missions of public organizations. Unlike private sector profit measures, how do we define **performance-based** measures that are in the public interests? Let's begin with some definitions.

Strategic planning is defined as a comprehensive and continuous process that looks toward organization-specific goals and defines the performance to be measured. These organization-specific goals include the public interests, as stated in the **enabling statute** or incorporation mission by which the organization was created. Strategic planning is not the same as long-range planning in several ways. For example, long-range planning is only interested in setting goals, not on how to achieve those goals; long range planning does not take into consideration the specific organizational environment, such as federal, state, or local governments; and long-range planning is often a document that is put together by one or two individuals, usually top-level managers, whereas strategic planning is a bottom-up process that involves several layers of the organization and many people, each contributing their skills, perspectives, and talents to the process of drawing up a strategic plan.[77]

There are several steps in strategic planning.[78] First, the organization must establish its mission. A good place for a public agency to begin is to look at the enabling statute by which a legislature first created the agency. Private and nonprofit organizations often are required to include such a mission statement in their articles of incorporation. A proper enabling statute includes some reference to the specific powers that were delegated from the legislature to the public agency, sometimes on all four corners (in the 1930s, this often meant four examples of what the agency could do). For example, Missouri's Office of Administration (OA) established a four-year (2005–2009) strategic plan based on the statute by which the Missouri state legislature first created the organization, and rearticulated by stating its Vision, Mission, and Values. OA's Vision is to "Ensure initiatives, policies, and services are implemented in a uniform and consistent manner throughout state government." Its Mission is to "provide guidance and assistance to state government entities through the implementation of executive office initiatives, the establishment of uniform procedures and rules as well as providing services to them in a cost-effective manner." The Missouri Office of Administration set out four key values to accomplish in its Vision and Mission: leadership, responsiveness, accountability, and partnership.

Second, the organization must assess the environment in which the strategic plan will be implemented, particularly looking for political, economic, or cultural factors that may affect, negatively or positively, the implementation and impact of the strategic plan. For example, before the city of Vancouver, Washington, initiated its recent strategic plan, it assessed the following environmental variables, noting that each was critical to the success of the strategic plan. To do so it conducted a citizen survey in 2004. The variables included: (1) dealing with population growth; (2) traffic congestion, quality of road systems, and availability of public transportation; (3) fostering a smalltown feel; and (4) ensuring an environment of livability.[79]

Third, the organization must assess its own strengths and weaknesses—not an easy thing to do. Using the information derived from the Citizen Survey in 2004, for example, the City of Vancouver convened many public hearings, listening to the needs of its residents, and heard from its city employees through focus groups to understand how to deal with these various challenges. Fourth, according to Denhardt and Grubbs and others, the fourth step in the strategic planning process is to listen to the leaders of the organization who will be required to implement the plan and direct the organization. For example, the State of Oregon developed a collaborative effort "to enhance watershed health and restore native fish to Oregon waters." To accomplish this goal required the commitment, direction, and leadership, not only of the planning organizers, but of the directors and their staffs of key state regulatory agencies, for example, who were charged with implementing the plan, such as the Oregon Water Resources Department and the Oregon Fish and Wildlife Department.[80] Planning by itself—even strategic planning—that is not tied a performance system that provides accountability measures is simply an event or, worse, just a document. Therefore, it must be tied to performance measurement standards.[81] Some even go so far as to label this process as managing for results.[82]

Performance Management   Performance management uses measurement tools that aim to quantitatively measure the inputs, outputs, and outcomes of public programs for management. Thus, the goal is to provide public managers with more information regarding the efficiency and effectiveness of their programs. Another way to define it is that "performance measurement is government's way of determining whether it is providing a quality product or service at a reasonable cost." This may also be understood as a type of performance measurement system that provides answers to questions such as: What was achieved? How efficiently and effective was the work completed? and How were the citizens aided by the effort?[83]

In 1980, the Federal Government Accounting Standards Board (GASB), based on authority granted it from the Civil Service Reform Act of 1978, defined performance measurement as

> an assessment of an organization's performance, including measures of productivity (quantifying the outputs and inputs of an organization and expressing the two as a ratio—output to input, such as inspections per personnel per day); effectiveness, which determines the relationship of an organization's outputs to the organization's prescribed goals; quality, which examines the accuracy, thoroughness, and complexity of an output; and timeliness, which measures the time involved to accomplish the output.[84]

Today, the categorization of performance measures is fairly routine and accepted. The various categories include:

- *Input measure* (agency level and indicates the quantity and quality of various organizational resources, such as personnel and funding).
- *Process measure* (agency level and indicates how well goods and services are delivered, i.e., the effectiveness measure, such as percentage of tax refunds mailed within 30 days).
- *Output measure* (agency level and indicates the quantity and quality of goods and services produced, such as number of potholes filled, percentage of city households participating in citywide voluntary recycling program, number of foster care homes, etc.).
- *Outcome measure* (agency level and indicates the societal effect of these goods and services, i.e., the output measures, such as impact of voluntary recycling program upon citizen's civic involvement or percentage of training school residents taking the GED test who pass it).[85]

Generally speaking, a sound and working performance measurement system should be, among other things, results-oriented, reliable, valid, quantitative, cost-effective, easy to understand, and comparable. In addition, benchmarks, or baseline data provided for comparative purposes, must be established in order to provide direction and guidance to the organization's performance measurement system. North Carolina's Benchmarking Project, which began in 1995 as an initiative by the University of North Carolina's School of Government, is a good example of how local governments can assess and compare service delivery and costs associated with that service delivery in a variety of areas (e.g, residential refuse collection, police patrols, street maintenance and repair, building inspections, jail operations, foster care) to other localities and municipalities.[86]

Performance-based measurement, coupled with strategic planning tools, has taken the public sector by storm. We have seen that strategic planning is not a new phenomenon in the public sector. All levels of government have engaged in some form of strategic planning, particularly in the area of budgeting,[87] for the last four decades. The problem lies in implementation. Development of a strategic plan is one thing, but implementing it requires some type of accountability system, something that ties goals with results; hence, the need for a performance based measurement system. But more important than simply a performance based measurement system is the movement to performance management. Robert J. O'Neill Jr., executive director of the International City/County Management Association (ICMA), for example, writes that "When used in conjunction with (strategic planning), performance data become(s) part of a larger performance management system to improve quality, productivity, and customer satisfaction."[88] A large and steadily growing literature base strongly advocates the use and effectiveness of performance measurement systems, particularly when coupled with strategic planning tools, in order to accomplish a variety of goals, including the use of better marketing techniques, to promote public service delivery. In fact, some even claim that performance management is one of six trends that are transforming government.[89] Performance management is transforming the public sector. Consider the example in Box 6.8, performance strategic management in Minnesota.

However, are these transformations all for the better? Some disagree. First, the managing for results idea embraced not only an increased emphasis on results, but the managerial authority to achieve such results. After decades of reform, there appears to be a gap between achieving results and increased managerial authority to oversee and govern those results.[90] Second, application of private sector performance measurement variables—based largely on the profit motive—to a public sector system raises various tensions between the competing administrative and political goals and means to accomplish those goals.[91]

Do we give too much attention to performance measurement as to put it on a pedestal and idolize it? Has this rhetoric become an ideology that fails to attend to the public interests? At an empirical level, the performance measurement approach seems to neglect or ignore a basic reality—public servants who attend to the public interests are perceived by the public as more productive.[92] Yet, performance measurement practices continue to ignore the importance of ethical behavior in the public interests. In a recent national survey, only 43 percent of human resources professionals said their performance-based measurements include ethical conduct as part of employees' performance appraisals.[93] Many critics argue that the pursuit of performance-based measurements for public organizations

BOX 6.8 | Performance Management at the Minnesota Pollution Control Agency (MPCA)

The MPCA has developed and carried out strategic plans since the early 1990s, with the primary goal of facilitating quality agency operation and enhancing controls for more effective environmental protection. Originally organized according to categories of air, land, and water, the MPCA realized that by the end of 1999 its organizational structure was not well suited for an outcome-based performance measurement system. Thus the MPCA instituted a three-phase operation: (1) develop program performance measures; (2) add environmental outcome measures to the program performance measures to enhance organizational and program effectiveness; and finally (3) add cost-efficiency to program effectiveness and environmental outcome measures to provide a well-balanced performance measurement system.

As to be expected, there were wrinkles in the system. The MPCA operated within the context of the National Environmental Performance Partnership System (NEPPS), to comply with the U.S. Environmental Performance Agency (EPA). The NEPPS had a contractual relationship with the MPCA to report performance measurement data. The wrinkle was that NEPPS was based largely on outputs, but the MPCA preferred to deal with outcomes. In order to fulfill its contractual obligations with the EPA through the NEPPS, the MPCA institutionalized "periodic reporting as an aid to executive-level decision-making."[94] Today, the MPCA's upper-level management team is focusing on outcome-based measures, something that is more difficult to quantify—yet is politically more desirable. This required a sophisticated data management system, costing MPCA approximately $8 million, but will allow their focus on outcome-based, geographically based, natural ecosystem, and river basin components system.

The result: the MPCA is now up to date with a performance management system. They have redesigned business processes, a fully integrated strategic planning performance measurement system, and a fully revamped public personnel system that will enable the MPCA to meet future performance measurement and strategic planning needs. For example, in order to accomplish these goals the MPCA will institute five-year strategic plans rather than one-year plans, as in the past. This will provide a larger performance database of information to draw from, thus enhancing the MPCA's goal of environmental protection and agency effectiveness.[95]

comes at the expense of democratic values and social justice values, such as social equity, which are not easily quantifiable, but nevertheless essential to democracy.[96] Similarly, the performance measurement movement subordinates "core aspects of democratic constitutionalism to simply achieving results."[97] Finally, there are many who challenge the performance movement and argue that the one-size-fits-all mentality, a panacea to perceived inefficiency, is not the only answer to correcting performance-based ills in a democratic society.[98]

Performance-based measurement is more than likely here to stay, particularly since it plays well to politicians and a citizenry that is demanding wasteful spending to be curtailed. One of the main questions, and ultimately hurdles, to overcome for both the proponents and opponents, however, is to learn how to adapt a highly sterile, quantitative, and results-oriented movement to a dynamic, qualitative, and public-interests-motivated democratic system. Not many argue against program inefficiency and ineffectiveness; not many contend that accountability is passé. It is clear, though, that at least some make valid arguments against the one-size-fits-all mentality that pervades the results-oriented or outcomes-based organizational and program mindset, precisely because it adequately fails to account for non-measurable administrative and policy outcomes, or that seemingly circumvent constitutional values.

Just as performance management has been criticized, the entirety of **New Public Management** (NPM) has been similarly criticized by scholars such as H. George Frederickson, Louis Gawthrop, Gary Wamsley and the Blacksburg scholars, **Charles Goodsell,** and many others,[99] who argued that the characteristics associated with NPM, such as those emphasized by Osborne and Gaebler in their groundbreaking work,[100] were not truly representative of government service and government employees. NPM was not limited to the practicalities of government management. Yet, the New Public Management has swept across the USA, Australia, and New Zealand.[101] Challenging the New Public Management (NPM), Janet and Robert Denhardt have posited a viable democratic alternative with the New Public Service (NPS), focused on "public service, democratic governance, and civic engagement."[102]

New Public Service (NPS)

First, at its core NPS is a normative model for public agency purpose and public management work. Whereas OPA called for a closed model of organization, NPS called for an open model; whereas NPM argued for a market-based system oriented toward customer satisfaction, NPS countered with a return to democratic pluralism and greater citizen input into the decision-making process. Early critics of the OPA model, such as Dwight Waldo and **Robert Dahl,** sought to highlight the need for competing values to efficiency and economy, such as administrative responsibility and democratic pluralism,[103] but their prophetic voices were too early and faint at the time, and the rational man model spawned by Herbert Simon drowned out all others.[104] With questions regarding the exclusive viability of NPM for bringing about greater organizational and individual productivity,[105] and more importantly the wealth of literature and public attention to the need for greater community and citizen involvement in the democratic process,[106] and coupling that with the enhanced community role of public managers,[107] it is clear that neither the OPA nor the NPM approach to public administration and public management is sufficient to explain or describe the contemporary changes and current demands placed upon public official or, more importantly, to explain the importance of the public interests. The NPS model described by the Denhardts is such an attempt.

Second, over the past decade or so there has been a renewed interest in community and civil society. The Denhardts claim that several reasons surface as to why individuals, and especially Americans, are interested in renewing community, including increased alienation in a technological society, social and political dislocations in response to the Vietnam War and the civil rights movement of the 1960s, and even the fear associated with the existence of, and threat to use, weapons of mass destruction.[108] Whatever the reason, people are searching, and the search runs the gamut of society, including education,[109] religion,[110] moral order,[111] and politics.[112] Putnam's analysis, for example, suggests a decrease in the number of Americans who engage in voluntary associations, including bowling

> ## BOX 6.9 | Democracy and the Public Interests
>
> Philosopher Michael Sandel argues that individual interests and choice should be protected by government through enactment of legal and political procedures in order to pursue the public interests. Citizens must look beyond or even set aside their self-interests, which requires a more knowledgeable and active citizenry. Others, such as H. George Frederickson and Jane Mansbridge, claim that there is a need for a "spirit of public administration" and a "public spirit." Frederickson's intent is directed more toward the enhancement of social equity, whereas Mansbridge's emphasizes political and managerial altruism. ◣
>
> Source: Michael Sandel, *Democracy's Discontent* (Cambridge, MA: Belknap, 1996), 30, 5–6; H. George Frederickson, *The Spirit of Public Administration* (Tuscaloosa: University of Alabama Press, 1997); Jane Mansbridge, ed., *Beyond Self-Interest* (Chicago: University of Chicago Press, 1990).

leagues, churches, neighborhood groups, and various civic associations. Because these institutions and organizations are the heartbeat of society, with their decreasing emphasis in the development and order of society, the unencumbered pursuit of individual rights takes precedent. The role that public administrators and managers play is critical to facilitating and directing the discussion of good public policy based on sound administrative and managerial principles, while at the same time listening to and interacting with various interests and the community as a whole.[113]

A third theoretical strand in the development of the NPS is **organizational humanism**. Here, it is our intention to simply highlight a couple of points that figure prominently in the foundation of NPS. First, organizational humanism is not new. It dates back to the 1920s and the work by Harvard organizational theorists Roethlisberger and Dickson at the Hawthorne plant of the **Western Electric Company**, where they discovered that human beings are important components in the workplace.[114] Social psychology and group dynamics was the centerpiece of Kurt Lewin's work in the 1930s, in which, among many other findings, he showed that group commitment was critical to decision making.[115]

Probably most crucial to the development of organizational humanism was the work of psychologist Abraham Maslow, management theorist Douglas McGregor, and organizational behavioralist Chris Argyris.[116] Each was committed to fostering growth in what was becoming known as the human relations school of thought—the stream of research and thought that emphasized the role of the individual *in* the organization rather than the adaptation of the individual's needs *to* the organization. Argyris and Robert Golembiewski took this research to another level, labeling it organizational development, which was contrary to the popular research and thinking of the rational model of administration. Other aspects of organizational humanism were captured in the movement labeled the New Public Administration (not to be confused with NPM), led by such luminaries as H. George Frederickson and Robert Denhardt,[117] where among other critiques they argued against the traditional hierarchical model of bureaucratic organization and some, like Frederickson, argued for even greater administrative discretion on the part of the public manager in order to facilitate social equity in the implementation of public policy.

The fourth theoretical root of the NPS is **postmodern public administration**. Adherents of postmodern public administration contend several things. One, we have lost the capacity to determine what is real and what is not. Using worldviews and scientific theories to describe and explain reality is simply not good enough; there are too many unexplained phenomena. Two, individuals are human, not robots, and they have feelings and emotions. It is difficult to describe such reality in terms of the rationalist model of behavior, and thus the postmodernists advocated interpretive and value-critical approaches or examinations of human behavior and reality. And three, communication in the traditional hierarchical organizational pattern is devoid of what postmodernists refer to as discourse, or "the notion that public problems are more likely resolved through discourse than through 'objective' measurements or rational analysis."[118] Human beings want to talk (including public managers) and they want to talk in a non-rational, goal-oriented way; they simply want to discuss problems, hoping that continued discussion will develop into "negotiation and consensus building."[119]

The four theoretical foundations discussed by the Denhardts account for the primary theoretical differences between NPS and OPA and, especially, NPM. Next, we introduce the reader to seven practical public management differences between the NPS and the other two approaches. The Denhardts readily acknowledge "that differences, even substantial differences, exist in these various viewpoints,"[120] but these capture the heart of the NPS—fulfilling public service in the public interests.

The NPS is not simply a theoretical construct, but it is a management reality. It is where the city and county manager live and work; it is the crux of the state personnel director's job focus; it is where the nonprofit agent interacts with public sector agencies on a daily basis, working for better social service delivery to people in need; and, most importantly, it is where the citizens interact with public officials on a variety of policy and management issues. The NPS is about public service. Elmer Staats (1914–2011), retired Comptroller General of the United States, probably said it best when he paraphrased the British scholar Harold Laski (1893–1950) on what public service is: "It is the discovery that people serve themselves only as they serve others."[121] To truly have this understanding of public service requires a different mindset than either the OPM or the NPM represents.

Serve Citizens, Not Customers   First, the NPS stresses that the focal point of public service is the citizenry, not customers or clients. Certainly, the recipient of a direct transaction of government, such as public daycare for latchkey children, is a customer; or the parent who sends their child to the public school system is a client of that agency (i.e., education), but each one is first a citizen. David Osborne and Ted Gaebler even use the terms *customer* and *citizen* interchangeably. "rather than government managers choosing service providers in a competitive bidding process, it lets each citizen choose his or her service provider. It establishes accountability to customers."[122] But even Osborne and Gaebler acknowledge that citizens are not always the focus of government service; it is the recipient of government contracts, or the beneficiary of government program funding. For example, who is the real customer of the Department of Defense: the citizenry or Boeing? Who are the primary clients or customers of the Department of Education: parents or principals?

The point is that the concepts of citizenry and customers are different. Customers seek to maximize their self-interests and individual benefits, while the citizenry are described as individuals within the common contractual arrangement of a democratic republic who, because of giving up certain private rights to government and government's authorities, gain protection and security from each other and outsiders. Citizens remain citizens even though they reasonably expect the government to deliver services in a convenient, secure, reliable, personal, fair, and fiscally responsible fashion.[123]

Seek the Public Interest   Second, the NPS argues that public managers "have a central and important role in helping citizens to articulate the public interest, and conversely, that shared values and collective citizen interests should guide the behavior and decision making of public administrators." The Denhardts, and others who promote the NPS (or variations thereof),[124] do not necessarily reject the need for performance outcomes of the political process, or that public managers should use substantial discretionary authority to substitute their beliefs for the will of the people, but they do contend that public managers "have a unique and vitally important responsibility to engage with citizens and create forums for public dialogue."[125]

Value Citizenship over Enterpreneurship   The third principle of public management stressed by the Denhardts as being a crucial part of the NPS is citizenship over entrepreneurship. The first of these seven principles stressed the value of citizen over customer; that it is critically important to recognize that governments govern in a political environment, and as such the focus of government programs and service delivery are citizens, not merely customers. Citizen is a political concept; customer is a business concept. Citizens are the heart of a democracy; customers and those who serve the customers (i.e., entrepreneurs) are the center of a market. Thus, it behooves us to briefly explore this third principle, because it is at the heart of what is truly the goal of the NPS: the public interests.

Recall that Osborne and Gaebler stressed that government should be steering rather than rowing, meaning that government generally, and public managers (or

---

BOX 6.10 | Public Interests in the New Public Service (NPS)

For NPS advocates Janet and Robert Denhardt, the search for public interests is found in citizens' search for the needs of the larger community, to look beyond their individual short-term interests, which are often economic and politically based, to a broader public interest that encompasses what Michael Sandel refers to as "a sense of belonging, a concern for the whole, and a moral bond with the community."[126] Of course, the naysayer and cynic is ever present, arguing that there is no such thing as the public interest; that the public interest is simply a procedural or process-oriented concept, one that avails itself to furthering the political and administrative rights of all citizens; or that it is the collection of broad and shared individual and group interests. We contend that the public interest is not simply a procedural concept, but it is a normative concept, even an ethical idea, one that denotes a standard "for evaluating specific public policies and a goal which the political order should pursue."[127]

public entrepreneurs) specifically, are to guide or steer the apparatus and delivery of services to the specific client and/or customer, using, among other means, the market-based system of supply and demand to provide these services in the most efficient and economical way. NPM managers are not so much managers as they are entrepreneurs, or risk-takers. This view sees the public entrepreneur with considerable more discretionary authority than the public manager in the OPA approach. Of course, along with risks for success come risks resulting in failure—leveraging the county employees' retirement funds in high–risk stocks and bonds, and in the end losing everything.

The NPS approach envisions the public manager not as a policy or administrative entrepreneur, but as an enabler, guide, and facilitator. Government is not the be-all and end-all; governance, or the "exercise of public authority,"[128] is the key factor in public management today. Governance is the cooperation between government, nonprofit, and private sources in order to develop and implement public policy.[129] The public manager, thus, becomes a conduit or facilitator in matching resources, infrastructure, citizen groups, and policy objectives in order to meet a desired end. Simply basing one's public management decision on the vagaries of the market is short-sighted at best and detrimental to the democratic governance process at worst. Whereas OPA is bound by laws and regulations, and the public administrator is simply the implementer of politically defined objectives; and where the NPM bases managerial decision making on the externalities of economic and market considerations, it is the NPS that focuses the role of government (or governance) on democracy and social criteria, where the voice of the citizen is necessary and desirable in the public decision-making process, whether it is where to put the new soccer field in Anywhere, USA to whether and/or how Social Security should be changed.[130]

Think Strategically, Act Democratically   The fourth principle embodied in the NPS posits that establishing the vision of a new policy and implementing that new policy is not merely the role of government officials located in Washington, DC, Raleigh, North Carolina, or Polk County, Iowa, but the focus "is to join together all parties in the process of both designing and carrying out programs that will move in the desired direction."[131] To support greater public participation in the policy-making process, as well in the development of the policy, is the focus of the NPS. Among other factors, the desire is to encourage greater civic knowledge and participation. Obviously, not all citizens are interested in participating in policy matters. In fact, most Americans are both unaware and uninterested in political and policy matters. And when Americans do participate, it is usually when they have a vested political or economic self-interest, not because they want to become more aware of the civic and political—to say nothing of the administrative. So, how is this a realistic means to thinking strategically, while acting democratically?

Government (and/or the governance process) is indeed not the only answer, but the answer, or at least part of the answer, lies in the fact that government must create opportunities for igniting citizen action and building community. And this means that government must be perceived to be open and accessible, or being responsive to citizen demands. If the citizens do not believe this, do not perceive this to be true, then regardless of whether or not the government is open, accessible, and responsive; the citizens will not respond.

One tool to enhance citizen involvement in the twenty-first century is to enhance civic knowledge. And one way to do that is to increase awareness and knowledge of information technology and its application to simple government service delivery as well as the governance process. Congress passed the **e-Government Act** in 2002 in order to "enhance the management and promotion of electronic government services and processes" and to "promote the use of the Internet and other information technologies to provide increased opportunities for citizen participation in government." The Act was designed to expand e-government initiatives, such as e-rulemaking, e-records management, e-authentication, such as e-signatures, and other such enhancements. Many of these goals have been reached. Check out any Federal Government website and see what you can do as a citizen!

But e-service delivery is only part, and a small part at that. What about e-town halls or e-citizen complaints and e-government response and/or action to those complaints, all within a much shorter time period than in a non-e-government environment? Virtual town halls are a reality, and much of the success of e-government is taking place outside of the United States. For example, the Barcelona City Council (Spain) has a program that facilitates exchange of information between citizens of Barcelona and its city council members. The city council holds an e-town hall meeting, with different topics covered each month. Also, much work is being done in England to enhance the "potential of e-democracy to empower grassroots civic networks."[132] Here in the United States, the Office of e-Government facilitates upgrading all federal agency sites, and initiating greater use of e-democracy techniques. States and local governments are also moving into e-government. For example, former Minnesota governor Jesse Ventura received up to 13,000 emails a week from citizens, giving him their opinion on a range of state and local issues.[133]

Recognize That Accountability Isn't Simple   Citizen involvement in democratic accountability takes us to the fifth principle of NPS: that all need to recognize and understand that democratic accountability is not as simple as the proponents of the NPM wish us to believe. In fact, as Robert Behn advocates, the OPM approach is actually more dedicated, at least indirectly, to democratic accountability than is the NPM, primarily because the OPM sees accountability in an indirect relationship between citizens and public managers through the check and balance system.[134] Democratic accountability is not an ancient concept, but it is certainly a key variable in the clash between the democratic and administrative states, and between elected officials and public managers.

The question arises as to whom the public officials are accountable, and for what? According to the NPS approach, as opposed to either of the other approaches, accountability is both a legal and moral issue. Public managers are required to respond to their personal conscience, as well as the citizenry consciences and predispositions toward right and wrong, as well as the organizational framework, including rules, regulations, and culture in which they work. OPM contends that public managers are accountable to the organization in which they work, while NPM contends that managers are responsible to the entrepreneurial influence of the market. Second, who are unelected civil servants accountable to? Behn answers this: both process and results.[135]

Answering this question; however, only raises additional ones, such as: "Who decides what results government should be accountable for producing? How are the results determined? How and who determine whether or not the results have been met? Who is responsible for implementing the accountability process? How will this process work?"[136] The NPS response: the public manager is accountable to more than just the organization and hierarchy, more than just the market; the public manager is responsible to a myriad of institutions, laws, groups, norms, values, and processes. Why? Because the NPS contends that at the center of accountability is citizenship and the public interests.[137]

Serve Rather Than Steer   The sixth principle of the NPS approach to public management is the emphasis on using value-based, shared leadership. Under the OPA approach, for example, leadership was concentrated in the hands of top-level officials of the hierarchy, while in the NPM style decision making and leadership is decentralized.

The NPS approach to leadership is threefold: values-based, shared, and servant-oriented. First, values-based leadership is transformational, not simply transactional.[138] James MacGregor Burns describes **transformational leadership** as leadership that unites leaders and followers, rather than envisioning leadership as something that leaders do to followers. Burns' view of leadership is one of purpose and power, where effective transformational leaders are able to successfully use the power of their office for the benefit of the follower, rather than to force the follower into some type of submission. On the other hand, **transactional leadership** is an exchange of values between a leader and a follower, or between what Burns identifies as "initiator and respondent."[139] The transactional leader is one who provides the follower with a reward for meeting the expectations of the leader (i.e., the toddler receives cheers and claps from the parent when she goes to the restroom on her own), whereas transformational leadership is based more on the enduring values of morality, ethics, and the like. Ethical leadership causes both the leader and the follower to respond differently, both toward each other and toward the accomplishment of the goal.[140]

Second, the NPS approach advocates shared leadership. Shared leadership engages the citizenry; it empowers them to be part of the decision-making process. Obviously, not every public management venue is open to shared leadership (I don't think we expected the President to take a vote of the citizens to determine whether or not the United States was to respond militarily to Osama Bin Laden after we learned he was the mastermind of 9/11). However, the decision by the city council to decide whether or not to use a vacant lot for an expansion of the town recreation center or to build one Little League regulation baseball field and two soccer fields is an issue that the town's citizens can, and should, be involved in making. The theory and developing concept of shared leadership has a growing literature base, focusing on networks and the involvement of diverse stakeholders.[141]

Third, the NPS approach promotes serving rather than owning. The NPM approach sees public managers as entrepreneurs, seeking out the best buy for various public services, their delivery and implementation, and evaluation. The Denhardts are quick to point out that results, whether good or bad, of entrepreneurial decision making in the private sector fall squarely on the shoulders of the business owners and investors—a limited group. Entrepreneurial decision-making in the public sector has a much broader effect upon the citizens and not just the recipients of the services provided. Thus, when the decision to privatize jails, for example, does not work, primarily because of poor or no levels of accountability, then the effect is not felt in simply the penal environment, but to the citizenry and taxpayers at large.

Value People, Not Just Productivity   The seventh and final principle associated with the NPS approach is the emphasis on people. People are the centerpiece of the NPS approach to public administration broadly and public management narrowly. Slightly modifying the Denhardts' language we might say that the OPA used control to achieve efficiency, the NPM used incentives to achieve productivity, and the NPS used people to respect the ideal of the public interests. It boils down to this. What is most important? In the OPA approach, the focus was solely on achieving efficiency, and the role of people was simply that of an automaton, one that, according to theorists like Frederick Taylor, were simply cogs in the wheel of efficiency. Management could basically do what it wanted to with the people in order to get them to produce the most number of goods and/or services with the least number of inputs of resources. Under the NPM approach, public managers, or rather public entrepreneurs, use people to meet objectives, reach desired results, using (among other means) contracts to set and enforce the level of results desired. Thus, if you want the person to perform differently or better, then you must entice them with market-based incentives. The NPS approach, however, does not see people as simply cogs in the wheel of commerce, or agents in a principal-agent theory, but as human beings who display values and norms, such as trust, dignity, and service.[142] Of course, for this to happen, argue the Denhardts, government must advance the notion of citizen participation and empowerment, which in turn "build[s] citizenship, responsibility, and trust, and advance[s] the values of service in the public interest."[143]

Leadership in the Public Interests

Warren Bennis and Ben Nanus wrote that there is a major difference between leaders and managers (whether private or public): "Managers are people who do things right and leaders are people who do the right thing." The authors clarified this by noting that "The difference may be summarized as activities of vision and judgment—effectiveness versus activities of mastering routines—efficiency."[144] For the authors, the leaders they interviewed viewed themselves as leaders and not managers. Their perspective of leadership was to concern themselves with basic purposes, general direction, vision, and transformation, not only of the organization they led, but of the culture or environment in which they found themselves and their organization. Managers; however, did not do the same thing as leaders, and thus were not considered leaders. Managers "spend their time on the 'how to's,' the proverbial 'nuts and bolts' of the organization, not with the larger picture."[145] Professor Hal Rainey takes umbrage with Bennis and Nanus's unfair assessment of the lack of substance in the volumes of recent management and leadership literature. In addition, he notes that the authors' own research on 90 leaders in the public, private, and nonprofit sectors, "lack[ed] clarity and convincing validation."[146] This may be true, as well, but in broader terms we simply disagree with Bennis and Nanus's assessment of the supposed differences between what (or who) is a leader and what (or who) is a manager, and more importantly what each do.

Further, Henry Mintzberg sees similarities between what leaders and managers do. He categorized the similarities into four distinct roles, including interpersonal, informational, decisional, and negotiation.[147] Interpersonal roles are largely fig-urehead, liaison, ceremonial, or symbolic, such as when the city manager welcomes dignitaries to the city. Informational roles are when managers act in a broad-sweeping fashion to collect, use, and dissemination information, such as when state department directors of budgeting or even the director of the federal Office of Management Budget gathers, uses, and distributes that information for the purpose of putting together the government's budget. Decisional roles are entrepreneurial based, such as when a county manager or county economic development director searches out prospective business and industry owners for possible relocation. And fourth, managers act as negotiators, such as when personnel directors act as a go-between with employees and the state regulatory board investigating personnel issues.

When we think of leadership we conjure up images of General George Patton riding high in the turret of a tank in World War II, commanding the attention of his troops. Or we see Bill Gates, the quiet billionaire technocrat-leader of Microsoft, musing and mulling over ideas about how to make computer software better, specifically Microsoft software. Or we may remember President George Bush surveying the damage at Ground Zero after 9/11 following the deadliest attack on American soil since Pearl Harbor. Or President Barack Obama issuing the order to hunt down the 9/11 mastermind, Osama Bin Laden. Or President Donald Trump persuading congressional leaders to pass a budget bill to end the continued threat of national government shutdown. But we suspect that the average person does not see the leadership reality of a mid-level federal manager in the Department of Transportation, or envision the world of city managers like Jim Twombly of Broken Arrow, Oklahoma, or Tommy Gonzalez of El Paso, Texas. We contend that each of these public managers is, and must be, considered a leader as well. Perhaps we should refer to them as leader-managers.

So, What is Leadership?   Leadership is many things to many people—trite, but true. Justice Potter Stewart of the U.S. Supreme Court once defined obscenity as "I know it when I see it." Perhaps the same holds true for leadership. Popular images of leaders focus on individual talent and the person who is "self-made." Closer examination of leadership reveals that talent may be overrated compared to the luck of riding a tide of advantages of location, timing, and background. Was Bill Gates a leader due to his talent and genius alone, or was his success due to being born in 1955—just old enough for the PC, but too young to have taken the IBN junior executive track? Of course, Bill Gates had a unique talent, but was his leadership born of genius or from inputs by his family, society, schools, and the uncanny locus and focus of success (luck?).[148] There are many theories of leadership, but there are very few solid definitions of leadership. What is public leadership all about? And are there any similarities with public management?

First, leadership is about people—the people who are leaders, the people who the leaders lead (i.e., followers), and the people who are the recipients, clients, customers, citizens, etc. of the goods or services that are produced and/or delivered by the organizations, both private and public, that the leaders lead in order to produce the good and/or deliver the service. Second, leadership is about relationship—the relationship between the leaders and the followers. Third, leadership is about use of authority to influence—influencing others in the organization in order to achieve a desired goal. Fourth, leadership is about achievement of

BOX 6.11 | Definitions of Leadership

"A leader is one who attempts to exert influence through some form of power that results in gaining compliance from those being led." (Vasu, Stewart, and Garson)

"Leadership is the process of influencing the activities of a group in efforts toward goal attainment in a given situation." (Starling)

"Leadership is the capacity of someone to direct and energize people to achieve goals." (Rainey)

"I know he's a good general, but is he lucky?" (Napoléon Bonaparte)

"Public leadership may thus be defined as an inter-human process of identifying, defining, and carrying out goals using democratically sanctioned norms and behaviors." (Rusaw)

"The new leader . . . is one who commits people to action, who converts followers into

leaders, and who may convert leaders into agents of change." (Bennis)

"Leadership is a concept of owing certain things to the institution. It is a way of thinking about institutional heirs, a way of thinking about stewardship as contrasted with ownership." (DePree)

Source: Michael L. Vasu, Debra W. Stewart, and G. David Garson, *Organizational Behavior and Public Management,* 3rd ed. (New York, NY: Marcel Dekker, 1998), 90; Grover Starling, *Managing the Public Sector,* 5th ed. (San Diego, CA: Harcourt Brace, 1998), 358; Hal G. Rainey, *Understanding and Managing Public Organizations* (New York, NY: Wiley & Sons, 2003), 290; A. Carol Rusaw, *Leading Public Organizations: An Integrative Approach* (Fort Worth, TX: Harcourt College Publishers, 2001), 3–4; Warren Bennis and Burt Nanus, *Leaders: The Strategies for Taking Charge* (New York, NY: Harper and Row, 1985), 3; Max DePree, *Leadership is an Art* (New York, NY: Doubleday, 1989), 12, 148.

BOX 6.12 | City Managers are Leaders, Too

In a recent study of city managers, the author (Stephen King) found that all of the city managers examined exemplified leadership qualities, whether in terms of leading the charge to dedicate a downtown park, to push for increasing the number of businesses and business startups in a downtown economic development enterprise zone, or demonstrating willingness to lead the community by hammering nails in a Habitat for Humanity home on a Saturday morning. City managers lead by example; city managers lead by displaying

administrative discipline in a sometimes volatile political environment; and city managers lead by display of character.

Leadership is not just about getting the job done or even getting it done right; it is about caring for people and projects enough that the public manager does things right so that he or she gets the right things done.

Source: Stephen M. King, "The Moral Manager: Vignettes of Virtue in Virginia," *Public Integrity* 8 (#2, Spring 2006).

goals—goals that are set for the purposes of furthering the mission of the organization. Fifth, leadership is about change—change of the processes, goals, people, relationship, influence, and even the means of achievement in order to accomplish the mission of the organization. People, relationship, influence, achievement, and change—isn't this what public managers do, as well as what generals, presidents, and business icons do? They may do them in different organizational settings and cultures, under different written and unwritten rules, in closer or more distance quarters with the frontline workers, but there are enough similarities to warrant that managers do leadership things and leaders do manager things.

> **ETHICS CASE STUDY** | **Loyalty and Whistleblowing**

A most difficult ethical issue for public administrators is when to put aside loyalty for someone you know and work with—to blow the whistle on their wrongdoing.[149] Perhaps this is why it is a rare event in the worklife of public administrators; we prefer to be loyal to our organizational partners. We think of our childhood moral lessons on loyalty, such as Scout's Law #2, "A Scout is true to his family, Scout leaders, friends, school, and nation" (elsewhere, the 1910 Boy Scouts original oath, "A Scout is Loyal to his King"). Remnants of history have left us with phrases used today in public affairs, such as "the loyal opposition." In 1642, the House of Commons in Great Britain sought to disagree with certain actions of their king, Charles I (1600–1649). King Charles I regarded their complaints as disloyalty. But William Lenthall, Speaker of the Commons, maintained that they were **"loyal to loyalty."** Thus, the right of **the loyal opposition** to disagree with the king, queen, or majority government was created. But what is loyalty? Can it be excessive or a vice? Consider your workplace loyalties in our ethics case study.

Loyal to Loyalty

Loyalty has been defined in public affairs:

> Loyalty [is] taken to refer to a relationship between persons—for instance between a lord and his vassal, between a parent and his children, or between friends. Thus, the object of loyalty is ordinarily taken to be loyalty to a person or group of persons.[150]

For others, loyalty is not to focus on persons, but a cause: "Loyalty is the principle or cause of the idea of loyalty . . . Loyalty is always to a cause, not merely to a person or group of persons."[151] Royce goes on to urge that we be loyal to loyalty: "In choosing and in serving the cause to which you are to be loyal, be, in any case, loyal to loyalty. Loyalty shall mean . . . the willing and practical and thoroughgoing devotion of a person to a cause."[152]

All three major ethical theories deal with the loyalties between persons. With utilitarianism, loyalty may be good because it has good consequences for the individual and for society. With deontology, loyalty is good because it is intrinsically good in-itself for the individual to do. But with **virtue**, loyalty is good for its reflection on good moral character of the individual. For Aristotle, loyalty is excellent moral character, not as an action, but a habit of the heart: "We are what we repeatedly do; excellence, then, is not an act but a habit." Thus, loyalty was a virtue for the ancient Greeks, who sought to possess arete (Greek, excellence) and *eudaimonia* (Greek, "well-being") of their being. Yet, as we have seen throughout this history of public administrators, character virtues may be vague. But the vice-terms are many and useful as antonyms to help understand the virtues. For example, we have seen the vice-terms of *lazy, irresponsible, feckless, inconsiderate, unco-operative, harsh, intolerant, selfish, mercenary, indiscreet, tactless, arrogant, unsympathetic, cold, incautious, unenterprising, feeble, presumptuous, rude, brutal,* and *disloyal.*[153]

Can loyalty be excessive and turn into a vice? Like most acts, too much of a good thing seems to turn to vice. Excessive loyalty seems to invite irre-sponsibility and unthinking behavior to simply follow the leader. Loyalty in excess can be too partisan and unethical because we fail to give good reasons for our moral decisions. Yet we need loyalty in some relations with other persons, e.g., our family, friends, some work-group teams. Without loyalty, these groups would surely fall apart as dysfunctional. Marcia Baron has argued that loyalty is good up to a point, except when it is trumped by other moral goods, such as the demands of equity, benevolence, and justice.[154]

Whistleblowing

Whistleblowing is the action of turning aside loyalties, and informing others about unethical or illegal behaviors at the workplace. The term was associated with Ralph Nader "to categorize those public employees who challenge activities of their own agencies when they deem such activities to be improper."[155] Prominent whistleblowers have been featured on the cover of *Time* magazine as persons-of the year, such as Cynthia Cooper of Worldcom, Coleen Rowley of the FBI, and Sherron Watkins of Enron,[156] and increasing media attention has been given to whistleblowers within the FBI and other national, state, and local public agencies. Usually a person simply informs or makes public disclosure of corruption or illegal wrongdo-ing. But three additional justifications have also been found in analyses of actual instances of whistleblowing: (1) **deviations from ideal bureaucratic procedures**—not necessarily unethical or illegal; (2) **disputes over policy** alleged as inefficient or ineffective; and (3) **morals violations** alleged as unfair or unethical in principle. In a closely empirical study of state and local cor-rections, Mark Hamm found that the latter category, morals violations, was the least likely to succeed—and most often subject to retaliation.[157]

Over the past two decades there has been a marked increase in the num-ber of public employees who have disclosed unethical and even illegal actions within the organization they work in.[158] The whistleblower usually reveals sensitive information about wrongdoing in a public organization or pro-gram—wrongdoing that can include fraud, waste, or some type of employee or financial abuse.[159] According to survey data, the typical whistleblower has been with the particular agency or department for about 7–10 years,

(continued)

ETHICS CASE STUDY | *Continued*

is a male, and is around 45 years of age. Many are in upper-level administrative or professional positions—that is, they have pretty good access to sensitive information, and the inner workings of the organization and/or program they work for or in.[160] The whistleblower usually acts because of the person's position in the organization, the length of tenure spent in the organization, and the desire for alternative employment. In addition, whistleblowers do not really rationally calculate what may occur in terms of retaliation; they tend to rely more on doing what they consider right, holding to a strong sense of individual responsibility, a commitment to absolute moral obligations, and commitment to pursue the public interests.[161] What about the example of Bunnatine Greenhouse, who whistled on Uncle Sam (see Box 6.13)?

BOX 6.13 | Whistling on Uncle Sam

Bunnatine (Bunny) Greenhouse was the principal assistant procurement officer responsible for contracting in the U.S. Army Corps of Engineers. As a civil servant in the sprawling bureaucratic Department of Defense (DOD), she was responsible for awarding multiple billions of dollars to private companies who were hired to assist in the redevelopment of Iraq, including taking care of the homeless and schoolless children, building infrastructure, and other social and community projects.

Some companies—like Halliburton, the large Texas firm that held more than 50 percent of all private contracts in Iraq, and once headed by Vice President Dick Cheney—were getting government contracts without doing any bidding. Are there violations of law, ethics, or other regulations with these private sector companies?

Bunnatine raised the issue, and she was under a great deal of scrutiny and pressure for her whistleblowing. Her boss, Major General Robert Griffin, the Corps' deputy commander, said her performance was poor and as a result she was demoted. She was offered the chance to take another job elsewhere in the Corps or simply retire. She did not accept any of these options, except to do her job as she was hired to do. According to Greenhouse, reliance on her Christian faith was what gave her the courage and strength to press on.

Source: Deborah Hastings, "Faith Sustains Whistle-blower," *News and Observer* (August 7, 2005), 22A.

Is whistleblowing a violation of the *prima facie* duty of loyalty to an employer, to an agency? On the face of it, it seems that in signing employment contracts—even with a public employer—employees promise not to inform or publicly disclose the activities of their employer. Work teams cannot function if there is no loyalty within the work group. Idealists maintain that public employee loyalty is to the cause of the public interests—loyal to loyalty. Social atomists, on the other hand, maintain that loyalty at the workplace is always to other persons or groups. Analyses conclude that loyalty to a department or agency—even a public agency—is misguided, because these organizations are not persons or causes.[162] But where is the line between loyalty and whistleblowing?

Therein lays the rub. We know from analyses that whistleblowing on issues of corruption and illegal actions are most often successfully lodged against an employer or co-employees. And, according to close empirical studies, moral violations seem the least likely to succeed.[163] However, what about all the terrain in between? And what about retaliation against the whistleblower?

We know that **retaliation against the whistleblower** is most certain, even when corruption or illegality is proven in a public forum. Most whistleblowers simply resign and leave, possibly giving up their life-dream careers, such as FBI Special Agent Bassem Youssef, who proved serious misconduct by the FBI Detroit Office investigation of Zacarias Moussaoui, the 19th terrorist in the 9/11/2001 attack on the World Trade Towers and Pentagon. Agent Youssef proved that FBI agents may have stopped the 9/11 attacks if they were not obstructed by misguided FBI supervisors bent on self-careerism rather than the investigation of these terrorists.[164] Yet other whistleblowers seek re-entry or return to their life-dream career, e.g., FBI Special Agent Jane Turner found her career with the FBI was ruined by whistleblowing on supervisors who illegally falsified data from cases with Native American reservations to obtain corrupt payola, as well as FBI promotions and salary bonuses. After re-entry to the FBI, she found that she was forever labeled as a betrayer, even after proving her allegations, and a federal district court reinstated her to her FBI position and awarded her $1.3 million in damages:

> the organization that you blow the whistle on never forgets what they
> see as a betrayal. A whistleblower threatens the internal machinery
> of an organization, which many times have been set up to benefit the
> individuals who are running the organization. That was certainly the
> case at the Minneapolis FBI Office. Managers collected big bonuses
> and big salaries by inflating the number and quality cases in Indian
> Country. They also used false and misleading data from Indian
> Country so they could get bigger titles, and more money.[165]

What are the consequences of retaliation against a whistleblower? Retaliation against the whistleblower includes isolation in the organization, character assassination, demotion, and even firing.[166] According to recent survey data, almost 60 percent of federal whistleblowers reported they lost their jobs. Another 19 percent reported harassment and/or transfer, and still another 15 percent reported that they had their job responsibilities or even their salary reduced as a direct result of their whistleblowing.[167] What can

(continued)

whistleblowers do to legally protect themselves? Up until the 1980s legal protections were few, and therefore whistleblowers were very careful about blowing the whistle, given the consequences mentioned above. With passage of the False Claims Act of 1986 and the Whistleblowers Protection Act of 1989, whistleblowers are now encouraged to whistleblow and can expect protection when they do.[168] These statutory **protections for the virtuous whistleblower** at the public workplace may specify: the various protections of whistleblowers, to whom the protections apply, who may be wrongdoers, types of wrongdoing, how to file a claim against retaliation, processes and time limits of claims against retaliation, confidentiality requirements, and sanctions for false claims.

Deciding to blow the whistle on fellow workers, and especially supervisors, is obviously not an easy decision. The whistleblower must recognize the consequences in doing so, and understand the legal protections available. What is most encouraging about the majority of whistleblowers is that they are doing it because of their personal and professional commitment to moral obligations; that is, they understand that lying, cheating, defrauding, stealing, and other such acts are not only wrong in and of themselves, but they are wrong because they damage the relationship and trust established between the public agency or department and the public they serve. In other words, the illegal and unethical acts damage the fragility of the public interests. As Joe Carson of the Oak Ridge National Laboratory said, "Whistleblowers are thinking of what's good for others, not just looking out for number one."[169]

Discussion

- What is loyalty? What is whistleblowing? Do organizations encourage loyalty?
- What does it mean to be loyal to a person? Loyal to a cause? Loyal to a principle of loyalty?
- For what four reasons may employees usually blow the whistle?
- How do you balance organizational loyalty and your duties to report violations of laws, unethical practices, and inefficiencies? ▲

CONCLUSION

The role and function of organizational theory is critical to the development of a sound public administration practice. Our framework for organization theory, by open and closed systems, is a means to categorize and explain how public organizations function independently and *inter*dependently, along with private and nonprofit sectors, in pursuit of the public interests, for both open and closed systems of organization are designed to achieve the public interests.

Closed systems emphasize structure, rules, and regulations, with the focus on accomplishing efficiency, economy, and effectiveness. Born during a period of economic, technological, political, and social change, closed models such as Weber's focus on directing and administering physical resources toward accomplishing an end task. Human effort and need was acknowledged as a means toward an ends, not an end of itself. Administrative and political values, such as the public interests, were not the focus of these closed systems of organization. Instead, the focus was upon operational administrative principles, manipulated to accomplish the predetermined goals as efficiently and economically as possible.

Open systems suggest something quite different. Theories such as organizational humanism and organizational learning, for example, include formal structure, information organization, individuals, as well as the work or job task. Further, open system theories include the input and responsibility of each organizational participant in working toward the public interests. Individuals give organizations their character, whether in groups—informal or formal—or working independently. From the early work at the Hawthorne Electric plant to Maslow's hierarchy of needs, to McGregor's Theory Y to organizational development, the open models of organization theory and behavior strongly emphasizes the need for human input in administration in the public interests.

Public management differs from private management in several ways. First, public management incorporates the concept of the public interests. We recognize and acknowledge the diversity of opinion regarding the meaning and application of this normative and somewhat subjective concept, but we also understand that the public interests is what public servants talk about when they are asked what it means to them to serve the public, or to do the job they do. Second, public management is situated somewhere in the middle of a continuum ranging from government ownership to private enterprise, depending upon agencies and enterprises that do the serving, to the public that receives the direct and indirect benefit of the services delivered, to the political and administrative influence of public agencies.[170] Third, public management's purpose is simply different from that of private management. Whereas private management is designed to reach the highest performance level in order to make the most profit on the number of widgets sold, public management not only strives for high performance, it also operates under stricter scrutiny, including democratic accountability.

Contemporary approaches to manage public organizations include the Old Public Administration (OPA), New Public Management (NPM), and New Public Service (NPS). Given the criticisms and empirical research against the OPA and NPM approaches, the NPS appears ascendant in how we ought to manage public organizations. Further, the NPS approach emphasizes the roles of citizenship and community as well as organizational humanism and aspects of postmodern public administration—as opposed to strictly efficiency or market approaches of NPM, or formal organizational structures and procedures of OPA. Public management is more than just about rules and hierarchy; it is about people. It is about fulfilling the public interests.

Finally, administration in the public interests also means leadership, because leaders are empowered to establish and reach goals, use resources, set agendas, strategize visions, empower employees and citizens alike, and effectively move the community forward. Leadership is not for the weak at heart. It is tough work, but it is deeply gratifying. It is for those who wish to see beyond the account balance ledgers, who desire to get more out of life than a bonus check at the end of the year for selling the most widgets, and who have a deep-rooted commitment to an ethical organizational culture and pursuing, hopefully, the fulfillment of the public interests.

ACTION STEPS

1. Interview public servants and ask for their definition of leadership and management. Refer to Max De Pree, Warren Bennis and Burt Nanus, Malcolm Gladwell, and Henry Mintzberg to help you discuss your interview responses. Explain any differences and the way you approached the assignment.

2. Go to a governmental agency—in person or via their website. Using Osborne and Gaebler's list of reinventing principles, determine whether or not the agency institutes any or all of the principles. Explain any differences and the way you approached the assignment.

3. Prepare a Gantt Chart of how you anticipate scheduling your time for the semester. Include your time in class, studying, social activities, work schedules, breaks, etc. What do you learn about yourself, your time management skills, or other related factors?

4. Do formal organizational structures dictate particular perspectives of the public interests? Consider the U.S. Supreme Court case of *Wilson v. Seiter*, 501 U.S. 294 (1991), involving prison bureaucracy. In this case, the Court prohibited judicial review of prison organizations, procedures, or conditions unless there was proof those administrators acted with deliberate indifference to inmate injuries or constitutional rights violations. According to the Court, what prison organizational structure is in the public interests?

5. Visit a government agency—in person of via their website. From your personal observation, informal or formal interviewing, and documents analysis, learn how the department uses any or all of Henri Fayol's 14 Principles of Management. Do these classic principles still apply today? What did you learn?

KEY CONCEPTS AND NAMES

Public management 218
New Public Service 218
Janet and Robert Denhardt 218
formal organizations 219
informal organizations 219
Jethro the Midianite 219
bureaucracy 219
Sun Tzu 219
The Art of War 219
Alexander the Great 219
Niccolò Machiavelli 220

The Prince 220
Scientific Management Principles 220
Mary Jo Hatch 221
routinization 221
decentralization of authority 221
post-industrial organizing 221
classical school of organization 222
sociological functionalism 223
Max Weber 223
theory of bureaucracy 223
Frank Gilbreth 224

NOTES

1   Robert Denhardt, Ljubinka Andonoska, and M. Bentley, "An Overview of Organization Theory and Behavior," in Jos C.N. Raadschedlers & Richard J. Stillman, II, eds., *Foundations of Public Administration* (Irvine, CA: Melvin & Leigh, 2016), chapter 9.

2   Victor A. Thompson, *Modern Organization* (New York, NY: Knopf, 1961).

3   Chester I. Barnard, *Functions of the Executive*, 30th anniversary ed. (Cambridge, MA: Harvard University Press, 1968).

4   Harold F. Gortner, Julianne Mahler, and Jeanne Bell Nicholson, *Organization Theory: A Public Perspective,* 2nd ed. (Fort Worth, TX: Harcourt Brace, 1997), 2.

5   See Robert C. Ford, Barry R. Armandi, and Cherrill P. Heaton, *Organization Theory: An Integrative Approach* (New York, NY: Harper and Row, 1988), 3.

6   Ibid., 19.

7   Harold F. Gortner, Julianne Mahler, and Jeanne Bell Nicholson, *Organization Theory: A Public Perspective,* 2nd ed. (Fort Worth, TX: Harcourt Brace, 1997), 5.

8   The discussion of organization theory history is drawn from Jay M. Shafritz and J. Steven Ott, *Classics of Organization Theory,* 5th ed. (Belmont, CA: Wadsworth, 2001), 8–9; Robert C. Ford, Barry R. Armandi, and Cherrill P. Heaton, *Organization Theory:*

An Integrative Approach (New York, NY: Harper and Row, 1988); M. Judd Harmon, *Political Thought: From Plato to the Present* (New York, NY: McGraw-Hill, 1964); and Michael L. Vasu, Debra W. Stewart, and G. David Garson, *Organizational Behavior and Public Management,* 3rd ed. (New York, NY: Marcel Dekker, 1998), 27–30.

9   W. Richard Scott, *Organizations: Rational, Natural, and Open Systems*, 5th ed. (Upper Saddle River, NJ: Prentice-Hall, 2003), 4–5.

10   See Mary Jo Hatch, *Organization Theory: Modern, Symbolic, and Postmodern Perspectives* (New York, NY: Oxford University Press, 1997), 22, 23.

11   Ibid., 25–6.

12   Harold F. Gortner, Julianne Mahler, and Jeanne Bell Nicholson, *Organization Theory: A Public Perspective,* 2nd ed. (Fort Worth, TX: Harcourt Brace, 1997), 7.

13   W. Richard Scott, *Organizations: Rational, Natural, and Open Systems*, 5th ed. (Upper Saddle River, NJ: Prentice-Hall, 2003), 9, 10.

14   Harold F. Gortner, Julianne Mahler, and Jeanne Bell Nicholson, *Organization Theory: A Public Perspective,* 2nd ed. (Fort Worth, TX: Harcourt Brace, 1997), 9, 10.

15   See Adam Smith, *An Inquiry into the Nature and Causes of the Wealth of Nations* (New York, NY: Random House, 1937).

16   The discussion of Marx is drawn from two sources, including Michael Novak, *The Spirit of Democratic Capitalism* (Lanham, MA: Madison Books, 1991); and Mary Jo Hatch, *Organization Theory: Modern, Symbolic, and Postmodern Perspectives* (New York, NY: Oxford University Press, 1997), 28–9.

17   See H.H. Gerth and C. Wright Mills, *From Max Weber: Essays in Sociology* (New York, NY: Oxford University Press, 1946); and Max Weber, *The Theory of Social and Economic Organization* (New York, NY: The Free Press, 1947).

18   See Nicholas Henry, *Public Administration and Public Affairs*, 9th ed. (Upper Saddle River, NJ: Pearson-Longman, 2004), 58.

19   David H. Rosenbloom and Deborah D. Rosenbloom, *Public Administration: Understanding Management, Politics, and Law in the Public Sector*, 4th ed. (New York, NY: McGraw-Hill, 1998), 148.

20   George J. Gordon and Michael E. Milakovich, *Public Administration in America,* 6th ed. (New York, NY: St. Martin's Press, 1998), 121.

21   See Frederick W. Taylor, "Scientific Management," in *Classics of Public Administration,* 5th ed., ed. Jay M. Shafritz, Albert C. Hyde, and Sandra J. Parkes (Belmont, CA: Thomson-Wadsworth, 2004), 43–6. For a more complete description of Taylor's ideas, see Frederick W. Taylor, *Principles of Scientific Management* (New York, NY: Norton, 1911).

22   See Frank G. Gilbreth, *Primer of Scientific Management* (New York, NY: Van Nostrand, 1912).

23   Nicholas Henry, *Public Administration and Public Affairs*, 9th ed. (Upper Saddle River, NJ: Pearson-Longman, 2004), 61.

24   See "Biographical Note," Pennsylvania State University Library, retrieved October 2007 from www.libraries.psu.edu/speccolls/FindingAids/emerson4.html. For a more complete description of Emerson, see Harrington Emerson Papers, 1848–1931, Accession 1964-0002H, Historical Collections and Labor Archives, Special Collections Library, University Libraries, Pennsylvania State University.

25   W. Richard Scott, *Organizations: Rational, Natural, and Open Systems*, 5th ed. (Upper Saddle River, NJ: Prentice-Hall, 2003), 41–3.

26   See Henri Fayol, *General and Industrial Management* (London: Pitman, 1949).

27   Mary Jo Hatch, *Organization Theory: Modern, Symbolic, and Postmodern Perspectives* (New York, NY: Oxford University Press, 1997), 32.

28   James D. Mooney and Alan C. Reiley, *The Principles of Organization* (New York, NY: Harper and Row, 1939).

29 Robert C. Ford, Barry R. Armandi, and Cherrill P. Heaton, *Organization Theory: An Integrative Approach* (New York, NY: Harper and Row, 1988), 33.

30 Henri Fayol, *General and Industrial Management* (London: Pitman, 1949).

31 Leonard D. White, *Introduction to the Study of Public Administration*, 5th ed. (New York, NY: Macmillan, 1955.

32 See Woodrow Wilson, "The Study of Administration," in *Classics of Public Administration*, 5th ed., ed. Jay M. Shafritz, Albert C. Hyde, and Sandra J. Parkes (Belmont, CA: Thomson-Wadsworth, 2004), 22–35.

33 See Luther Gulick, "Notes on the Theory of Organization," in *Classics of Public Administration*, 5th ed., ed. Jay M. Shafritz, Albert C. Hyde, and Sandra J. Parkes (Belmont, CA: Thomson-Wadsworth, 2004), 90–98. For a fuller discussion see Luther Gulick and L. Urwick, *Papers on the Science of Administration* (New York, NY: Institute of Public Administration, 1937).

34 Michael L. Vasu, Debra W. Stewart, and G. David Garson, *Organizational Behavior and Public Management,* 3rd ed. (New York, NY: Marcel Dekker, 1998), 34.

35 Ibid., 35.

36 Nicholas Henry, *Public Administration and Public Affairs*, 9th ed. (Upper Saddle River, NJ: Pearson-Longman, 2004), 63.

37 Michael C. LeMay, *Public Administration: Clashing Values in the Administration of Public Policy* (Belmont, CA: Thomson-Wadsworth, 2004), 119.

38 Chester A. Barnard, *The Functions of the Executive* (New York, NY: Harper & Row, 1938).

39 Michael L. Vasu, Debra W. Stewart, and G. David Garson, *Organizational Behavior and Public Management,* 3rd ed. (New York, NY: Marcel Dekker, 1998), 39.

40 Michael C. LeMay, *Public Administration: Clashing Values in the Administration of Public Policy* (Belmont, CA: Thomson-Wadsworth, 2004), 119.

41 Michael L. Vasu, Debra W. Stewart, and G. David Garson, *Organizational Behavior and Public Management,* 3rd ed. (New York, NY: Marcel Dekker, 1998), 39.

42 Michael C. LeMay, *Public Administration: Clashing Values in the Administration of Public Policy* (Belmont, CA: Thomson-Wadsworth, 2004), 126.

43 Ibid., 126.

44 Herbert A. Simon, Peter Drucker, and Dwight Waldo, "'Development of Theory of Democratic Administration': Replies and Comments," *American Political Science Review* 46 (#2, 1952): 494–503.

45 Dwight Waldo, *The Administrative State: A Study of the Political Theory of American Public Administration*, revised ed. (New York, NY: Holmes & Meier, 1984).

46 Ibid., 122.

47 Abraham H. Maslow, *Toward a Psychology of Being*, 3rd ed. (New York: Wiley, 1998).

48 Douglas McGregor, *The Human Side of Enterprise* (New York, NY: McGraw-Hill, 1960).

49 Michael L. Vasu, Debra W. Stewart, and G. David Garson, *Organizational Behavior and Public Management,* 3rd ed. (New York, NY: Marcel Dekker, 1998), 44.

50 Michael C. LeMay, *Public Administration: Clashing Values in the Administration of Public Policy* (Belmont, CA: Thomson-Wadsworth, 2004), 122.

51 Ibid., 127.

52 David Easton, *The Political System: An Inquiry into the State of Political Science* (New York, NY: Alfred A. Knopf, 1953).

53 See Michael C. LeMay, *Public Administration: Clashing Values in the Administration of Public Policy* (Belmont, CA: Thomson-Wadsworth, 2004), 128; Daniel Katz and Robert L. Kahn, *The Social Psychology of Organizations,* 2nd ed. (New York, NY: John Wiley and Sons, 1978).

54 Michael L. Vasu, Debra W. Stewart, and G. David Garson, *Organizational Behavior and Public Management,* 3rd ed. (New York, NY: Marcel Dekker, 1998), 46, 47.

55 Nicholas Henry, *Public Administration and Public Affairs*, 9th ed. (Upper Saddle River, NJ: Pearson-Longman, 2004), 66–7.

56 Wendell L. French and Cecil H. Bell, Jr., *Organization Development: Behavioral Science Interventions for Organization Improvement* (Englewood Cliffs, NJ: Prentice-Hall, 1973).

57 E.g., Robert T. Golembiewski, *Ironies in Organizational Development*, 2nd ed. (New York, NY: CRC Press, 2002).

58 "Organizational Learning," SFB 504 Glossary, retrieved October 2007 from www.sfb504.uni-mannheim.de/glossary/orglearn.htm; and Robert B. Denhardt, *Theories of Public Organization*, 4th ed. (Belmont, CA: Wadsworth Publishing, 2004), 94–7, 193–5.

59 H. George Frederickson, Kevin B. Smith, Christopher W. Larimer, and Michael J. Licari, *The Public Administration Theory Primer*, 2nd ed. (Boulder, CO: Westview Press, 2012).

60 Mark K. Smith, "Donald Schon: Learning, Reflection, and Change," *Encyclopedia of Informal Education* (2001), retrieved October 2001 from www.infed.org/thinkers/et-schon.htm

61 Mark K. Smith, "Peter Senge and the Learning Organization," *Encyclopedia of Informal Education* (2001), retrieved October 2007 from www.infed.org/thinkers/senge.htm

62 J. Steven Ott, *The Organizational Culture Perspective* (Chicago: The Dorsey Press, 1989), vii–viii.

63 Robert Dingwall and Tim Strangleman, "Organizational Cultures in the Public Services," in Ewan Ferlie, Laurence E. Lynn, Jr., and Christopher Pollitt, eds., *The Oxford Handbook of Public Management* (New York, NY: Oxford University Press, 2007), 468–90; Ralph P. Hummel, *The Bureaucratic Experience*, 2nd ed. (New York, NY: St. Martin's, 1982); Anne Khademian, *Working with Culture: The Way the Job Gets Done in Public Programs* (Washington, DC: CQ Press, 2002); Gareth Morgan, *Images of Organizations*, updated ed. (Thousand Oaks, CA: Sage, 2007); R. Richard Ritti and Steve Levy, *The Ropes to Skip and the Ropes to Know: Studies in Organizational Theory and Behavior*, 8th ed. (New York, NY: Wiley, 2009); Edgar Schein, *Organizational Culture and Leadership*, 4th ed. (San Francisco, CA: Jossey-Bass, 2010).

64 Mitchell F. Rice, "Organizational Culture, Social Equity, and Diversity: Teaching Public Administration Education in the Postmodern Era," *Journal of Public Affairs Education* 10 (2004): 143–54.

65 Janet V. Denhardt and Robert B. Denhardt, *The New Public Service: Serving, Not Steering* (Armonk, NY: M.E. Sharpe, 2003), 4.

66 Ibid., 6, 7.

67 Ibid., 13.

68 David Osborne and Ted Gaebler, *Reinventing Government: How the Entrepreneurial Spirit is Transforming the Public Sector* (Reading, MA: Addison-Wesley, 1992).

69 David Osborne and Peter Plastrik, *Banishing Bureaucracy* (Reading, MA: Addison-Wesley, 1997).

70 Donald F. Kettl, *Reinventing Government: A Fifth-Year Report Card* (Washington, DC: Brookings Institute, 1998); and Donald F. Kettl, "The Transformation of Governance," *Public Administration Review* 6 (#6, 2000): 488–97.

71 An adequate description NPM is presented in Christopher Hood, "A Public Management for All Seasons?" *Public Administration* 69 (Spring 1991): 3–19. See also Michael Barzelay, *The New Public Management: Improving Research and Policy Dialogue* (Berkeley: University of California Press, 2001); and Michael Barzelay, *Breaking Through Bureaucracy: A New Vision for Managing in Government* (Berkeley: University of California Press, 1992).

72 Robert D. Behn, "The New Public Management Paradigm and the Search for Democratic Accountability," *International Public Management Journal* 1 (#2, 1998): 131–64.

73 Janet V. Denhardt and Robert B. Denhardt, *The New Public Service: Serving, Not Steering* (Armonk, NY: M.E. Sharpe, 2003), 3–4.

74 For example, John J. Forrer, James Edwin Kee, and Eric J. Boyer, *Governing Cross-Sector Collaboration* (San Francisco, CA: Jossey-Bass, 2014).

75 David Osborne and Ted Gaebler, *Reinventing Government: How the Entrepreneurial Spirit is Transforming the Public Sector* (Reading, MA: Addison-Wesley, 1992), xxii.

76 Beryl A. Radin, *Challenging the Performance Movement: Accountability, Complexity and Democratic Values* (Washington, DC: Georgetown University Press, 2006), 7.

77 Robert B. Denhardt and Joseph W. Grubbs, *Public Administration: An Action Orientation*, 4th ed. (Belmont, CA: Wadsworth, 2003), 256–7.

78 Ibid., 259. These are identified with Denhardt and Grubbs; however, these particular steps are generally representative of the basic steps for most strategic plans.

79 City of Vancouver, "Strategic Plan: The Importance of Strategic Planning," City of Vancouver, WA, retrieved October 2007 from www.cityofvancouver.us/StrategicPlan. asp?menuid=10462&submenuid=10480&itemID=11418

80 Pat Dusenbury, "Governing for Results and Accountability," Strategic Planning and Performance Measurement series, 4, Urban Institute, retrieved October 2007 from www.urban.org/url.cfm?ID=310259

81 Ibid.

82 Performance Measurement Team, Department of Management and Budget, Fairfax County, VA, "A Manual for Performance Measurement: Fairfax County Measures Up," 11th ed. (2007), 11.

83 Ibid., 4.

84 Citizen-Driven Government Performance, "A Brief Guide for Performance Measurement: Local Government," National Center for Public Productivity, retrieved October 2007 from http://andromeda.rutgers.edu/~ncpp/cdgp/teaching/brief-manual.html

85 Division of Planning, Department of Administration, RI, retrieved October 2007 from www.planning.ri.gov/

86 School of Government, "North Carolina Benchmarking Project," University of North Carolina, retrieved October 2007 from www.iog.unc.edu/programs/perfmeas/index. html. For a more detailed overview of the benchmarking project, specifically when compared to other benchmarking projects, see Charles Coe, "Local Government Benchmarking: Lessons from Two Major Multigovernment Efforts," *Public Administration Review* 59 (#2, March/April 1999): 110–15.

87 Charlie Tyer and Jennifer Willand, "Public Budgeting in America: A Twentieth Century Retrospective," *Journal of Public Budgeting, Accounting and Financial Management* 9 (#2, Summer 1997), retrieved October 2007 from www.ipspr.sc.edu/publication/ Budgeting_in_America.htm

88 Robert J. O'Neill, Jr., "Moving from Performance Measurement to Performance Management," *Public Management* 88 (#3, April 2006): 29–30.

89 For a thin slice of the literature, see Mark Abramson, Jonathan Breul, and John Kamensky, "Six Trends Transforming Government," *Public Manager* 36 (#1, Spring 2007): 3–11; Theodore H. Poister and Gregory Streib, "Elements of Strategic Planning and Management in Municipal Government: Status after Two Decades," *Public Administration Review* 65 (#1, January/February 2005): 45–56; and Philip Kotler and Nancy R. Lee, "Marketing in the Public Sector: The Final Frontier," *Public Manager* 36 (#1, Spring 2007): 12–17.

90 Pat Dusenbury, "Governing for Results and Accountability: Strategic Planning and Performance Measurement," *Urban Institute* (August 2000), retrieved from www. urban.org/sites/default/files/publication/62406/310259-Strategic-Planning-and-Performance-Measurement.PDF

91 Ibid.

92 Donald P. Moynihan, "Managing for Results in State Government: Evaluating a Decade of Reform," *Public Administration Review* 66 (#1, January/February 2006): 77–89.

93 Ronald Simeone, John Carnevale, and Annie Millar, "A Systems Approach to Performance-Based Management: The National Drug Control Strategy," *Public Administration Review* 65 (#2, March/April 2005): 191–202.

94 For example, Willa A. Bruce, "Ethical People Are Productive People," *Public Productivity and Management Review* 17 (1994): 241–52.

95 Ethics Resource Center, "Performance Reviews Often Skip Ethics, HR Professionals Say" (2002), retrieved from http://ethics.org/about-erc/press-releases.asp?aid-1150

96 H. George Frederickson, "Comparing the Reinventing Government Movement with the New Public Administration," *Public Administration Review* 56 (#3, May/June 1996): 263–70.

97 Suzanne J. Piotrowski and David H. Rosenbloom, "Nonmission-Based Values in Results-Oriented Public Management: The Case of Freedom of Information," *Public Administration Review* 62 (#6, November/December 2002): 643–57.

98 See especially Beryl A. Radin, "The Government Performance and Results Act (GPRA): Hydra-Headed Monster or Flexible Management Tool?" *Public Administration Review* 58 (#4, July/August 1998): 307–16; and her book *Challenging the Performance Movement: Accountability, Complexity and Democratic Values* (Washington, DC: Georgetown University Press, 2006).

99 See Janet V. Denhardt and Robert B. Denhardt, *The New Public Service: Serving, Not Steering* (Armonk, NY: M.E. Sharpe, 2003), 22, 23.

100 David Osborne and Ted Gaebler highlighted 10 characteristics. For closer examination of each, see their book, *Reinventing Government: How the Entrepreneurial Spirit is Transforming the Public Sector* (Reading, MA: Addison-Wesley, 1992), or read the summary in Janet V. Denhardt and Robert B. Denhardt, *The New Public Service: Serving, Not Steering* (Armonk, NY: M.E. Sharpe, 2003), 16–19.

101 Christopher Pollitt, *Managerialism and the Public Service*, 2nd ed. (Cambridge, UK: Basil Blackwell, 1993); and Larry D. Terry, "Administrative Leadership, Neo-Managerialism, and the Public Management Movement," *Public Administration Review* 58 (#3, 1998): 194–200; and Christopher Hood, "The 'New Public Management' in the 1980s: Variations on a Theme," *Accounting Organizations and Society* 20 (#2–3, 1995): 93–104.

102 Janet V. Denhardt and Robert B. Denhardt, *The New Public Service: Serving, Not Steering* (Armonk, NY: M.E. Sharpe, 2003), 24. Robert Denhardt and Janet Denhardt, "The New Public Service: Serving Rather than Steering," *Public Administration Review* 60 (#6, 2000): 549–59.

103 Dwight Waldo, *The Administrative State* (New York, NY: John Wiley and Sons, 1948); and Robert A. Dahl, "The Science of Public Administration," *Public Administration Review* 7 (Winter 1947): 1–11; and Robert A. Dahl, *A Preface to Democratic Theory* (Chicago, IL: University of Chicago Press, 1956).

104 Herbert A. Simon, *Administrative Behavior*, 2nd ed. (New York, NY: The Free Press, 1957).

105 See Christopher Hood, "A Public Management for All Seasons?" *Public Administration* 69 (Spring 1991): 3–19.

106 Michael Sandel, *Democracy's Discontent* (Cambridge, MA: Belknap, 1996).

107 John Nalbandian, "Facilitating Community, Enabling Democracy: New Roles for Local Government Managers," *Public Administration Review* 59 (#3, 1999): 187–97.

108 Janet V. Denhardt and Robert B. Denhardt, *The New Public Service: Serving, Not Steering* (Armonk, NY: M.E. Sharpe, 2003), 32, 33.

109 Hillary Rodham Clinton, *It Takes a Village to Raise a Child* (New York, NY: Simon and Schuster, 1996).

110 Marva Mitchell, *It Takes a Church to Raise a Village* (Orlando, FL: Destiny Image Publishers, 2001).

111 Richard John Neuhaus, *America against Itself* (Notre Dame, IN: University of Notre Dame Press, 1992).

112 Robert Putnam, *Bowling Alone* (New York, NY: Simon and Schuster, 2000).

113 John Nalbandian, "Facilitating Community, Enabling Democracy: New Roles for Local Government Managers," *Public Administration Review* 59 (#3, 1999): 187–97.

114 F. J. Roethlisberger, *Management and the Worker, An Account of a Research Program Conducted by the Western Electric Company, Hawthorne Works, Chicago. With the Assistance and Collab. of H.A. Wright*, 10th ed. (Cambridge, MA: Harvard University Press, 1950).

115 Hal G. Rainey, *Understanding and Managing Public Organizations* 5th edition (New York: Wiley/Jossey-Bass, 2014), 36, 37.

116 Ibid., 38, 39.

117 H. George Frederickson, *The New Public Administration* (Tuscaloosa: University of Alabama Press, 1980); and Robert B. Denhardt, *In the Shadow of Organization* (Lawrence: Regents Press of Kansas, 1981).

118 Janet V. Denhardt and Robert B. Denhardt's *The New Public Service: Serving, Not Steering* (Armonk, NY: M.E. Sharpe, 2003) cites O.C. McSwite, *Legitimacy in Public Administration* (Thousand Oaks, CA: Sage, 1997), 41.

119 Ibid., 42.

120 Ibid.

121 Elmer B. Staats, "Public Service and the Public Interest," *Public Administration Review* 48 (#2, March/April 1988): 605.

122 David Osborne and Ted Gaebler, *Reinventing Government: How the Entrepreneurial Spirit is Transforming the Public Sector* (Reading, MA: Addison-Wesley, 1992), 169.

123 Janet V. Denhardt and Robert B. Denhardt *The New Public Service: Serving, Not Steering* (Armonk, NY: M.E. Sharpe, 2003), 61.

124 Although a variation of Denhardt and Denhardt's approach to articulation and application of the NPS, Patricia Ingraham and David Rosenbloom's overview of the macro developments in public personnel policy since 1968 warrant attention. See Patricia Wallace Ingraham and David H. Rosenbloom, "The New Public Personnel and the New Public Service." *Public Administration Review* 48 (#2, March/April 1989): 116–25.

125 Janet V. Denhardt and Robert B. Denhardt *The New Public Service: Serving, Not Steering* (Armonk, NY: M.E. Sharpe, 2003), 78.

126 Michael J. Sandel, "America's Search for a New Public Philosophy," *Atlantic Monthly* (March 1996): 57–74, at 74.

127 Michael J. Sandel, *Democracy's Discontent: American in Search of a Public Philosophy* (Cambridge, MA: Harvard University Press, 1996), 283.

128 Janet V. Denhardt and Robert B. Denhardt, *The New Public Service: Serving, Not Steering* (Armonk, NY: M.E. Sharpe, 2003), 86.

129 For an excellent discussion of governance in the twenty-first century, see Donald Kettl, *Transformation of Governance in the 21st Century* (Baltimore, MD: Johns Hopkins University Press, 2002).

130 Janet V. Denhardt and Robert B. Denhardt, *The New Public Service: Serving, Not Steering* (Armonk, NY: M.E. Sharpe, 2003), 88.

131 Ibid., 103.

132 Stephen Coleman, "The Network-empowered Citizen: How People Share Civic Knowledge Online," Institute for Public Policy Research, retrieved October 2007 from www.ippr.org.uk/uploadedFiles/research/projects/Digital_Society/the_networkempowered_citizen_coleman.pdf

133 Douglas Holmes, *e.gov: e-business Strategies for Government* (London: Nicholas Brealey, 2001), 274, 285.

134 Robert D. Behn, "The New Public Management Paradigm and the Search for Demo- cratic Accountability," *International Public Management Journal* 1 (#2, 1998): 144.

135 Robert D. Behn, "The New Public Management Paradigm and the Search for Demo- cratic Accountability," *International Public Management Journal* 1 (#2, 1998): 142.

136 Ibid., 142, 144, 145, 146.

137 Ibid., 131.

138 Ibid., 145.

139 Ibid., 146.

140 Raymond W. Cox III, "The Profession of Local Government Manager: Evolution and Leadership Styles," in *The Effective Local Government Manager,* 3rd ed., ed. Charldean Newell (Washington, DC: International City/County Management Asso- ciation, 2004), 12.

141 Denhardt and Denhardt draw upon two primary sources. See John Bryson and Bar- bara Crosby, *Leadership for the Common Good* (San Francisco: CA: Jossey-Bass, 1992); and Jeffrey Luke, *Catalytic Leadership* (San Francisco, CA: Jossey-Bass, 1998).

142 Janet V. Denhardt and Robert B. Denhardt, *The New Public Service: Serving, Not Steering* (Armonk, NY: M.E. Sharpe, 2003), 164. For the value of trust, see David G. Carnevale, *Trustworthy Government: Leadership and Management Strategies for Building Trust and High Performance* (San Francisco, CA: Jossey-Bass, 1995).

143 Janet V. Denhardt and Robert B. Denhardt, *The New Public Service: Serving, Not Steering* (Armonk, NY: M.E. Sharpe, 2003), 166.

144 Warren Bennis and Burt Nanus, Leaders: The Strategies for Taking Charge (New York, NY: Harper and Row, 1985), 21.

145 Ibid., 23.

146 Hal G. Rainey, *Understanding and Managing Public Organizations*, 5th ed. (New York, NY: John Wiley & Sons, 2014), 335–381, at 373..

147 Mintzberg is cited in Michael L. Vasu, Debra W. Stewart, and G. David Garson, *Orga- nizational Behavior and Public Management*, 3rd ed. (New York, NY: Marcel Dekker, 1998), 92.

148 For example, Malcolm Gladwell, *Outliers: The Story of Success* (Boston: Little, Brown & Co., 2008).

149 David Hollenback, "Plural Loyalties and Moral Agency in Government," in John C. Haughey, ed., *Personal Values in Public Policy: Conversations on Government Deci- sionmaking* (New York, NY: Paulist Press, 1979), 74–90.

150 John Ladd, "Loyalty," in Paul Edwards, ed., *Encyclopedia of Philosophy* (New York, NY: MacMillan/Free Press, 1967), vol. 5, 97–8.

151 Josiah Royce, "Loyal to Loyalty," in John K. Roth, ed., *The Philosophy of Josiah Royce* (New York, NY: Tomas Y. Crowell, 1971), 289–307.

152 Ibid., 291.

153 Marcia Baron, "The Moral Status of Loyalty," in Daryl Close and Nicholas Meier, eds., *Morality in Criminal Justice: An Introduction to Ethics* (St. Paul, MN: Wad- sworth, 1995), 190–202.

154 Ibid.

155 Mark S. Hamm, "Whistleblowing in Corrections," *Sociological Viewpoint* 51 (1989): 35–45, esp. 36.

156 Richard Lacayo and Amanda Ripley, "TIME Persons of the Year: Coleen Rowley, Cynthia Cooper, Sherron Watkins," *Time Magazine* (December 20, 2002–January 6, 2003): cover, 30–60.

157 Mark S. Hamm, "Whistleblowing in Corrections," *Sociological Viewpoint* 51 (1989): 35–45, esp. 36.

158 Sissela Bok, "Blowing the Whistle," in Joel L. Fleishman, Lance Liebman, and Mark M. Moore, eds., *Public Duties: The Moral Obligation of Government Officials* (Cam- bridge, MA: Harvard University Press, 1981), 204–20.

159 Malcolm Gladwell, *Outliers: The Story of Success* (Boston: Little, Brown & Co., 2008), 143.

160 Nicholas Henry, *Public Administration and Public Affairs*, 9th ed. (Upper Saddle River, NJ: Pearson-Longman, 2004), 263.

161 Philip H. Jos, Mark E. Tompkins, and Steven W. Hays, "In Praise of Difficult People: A Portrait of the Committed Whistleblower," *Public Administration Review* 49 (#6, November/December 1989): 555, 556, 558.

162 For example, Ronald Duska, "Whistleblowing and Employee Loyalty," in Daryl Close and Nicholas Meier, eds., *Morality in Criminal Justice: An Introduction to Ethics* (St. Paul, MN: Wadsworth, 2003), 185–9.

163 For example, Mark S. Hamm, "Whistleblowing in Corrections," *Sociological Viewpoint* 51 (1989): 35–45.

164 Spencer S. Hsu, "FBI Whistleblower Trial Highlights Bureau's Post-9/11 Transformation," *Washington Post* (September 28, 2010), retrieved from www.washingtonpost.com/wp-dyn/content/article/2010/09/28/AR2010092807213.html

165 National Whistleblower Center, "FBI Whistleblower Wins Final Judgment" (August 14, 2007), retrieved from www.whistleblowers.org/index.php?option=com_content&task=view&id=111

166 Philip H. Jos, Mark E. Tompkins, and Steven W. Hays, "In Praise of Difficult People: A Portrait of the Committed Whistleblower," *Public Administration Review* 49 (#6, November/December 1989): 553.

167 Ibid., 554.

168 Henry cites the results of surveys that point not only to successful allegations of whistleblowing, but that more individuals (approximately 50 percent) are willing to blow the whistle than were before the 1989 protection act was passed; Nicholas Henry, *Public Administration and Public Affairs*, 9th ed. (Upper Saddle River, NJ: Pearson-Longman, 2004), 264.

169 "Religion Helped Workers Speak Up," *Washington Times* (August 22, 2005), retrieved from www.washingtontimes.com/news/2005/aug/22/20050822-123631-4900r/?page=all

170 Robert A. Dahl and Charles E. Lindblom, *Politics, Economics, and Welfare* (New York, NY: HarperCollins, 1953); Gary Wamsley and M. N. Zald, *The Political Economy of Public Organizations* (Lexington, MA: Heath, 1973); and Barry Bozeman, *All Organizations are Public: Bridging Public and Private Organizational Theories* (San Francisco, CA: Jossey-Bass, 1987).

Human Resources Management and Diversity

"Strengthen social equity. Treat all persons with fairness, justice, and equality and respect individual differences, rights, and freedoms. Promote affirmative action and other initiatives to reduce unfairness, injustice, and inequality in society."
—(Code of Ethics, American Society for Public Administration, 2013)

BOX 7.1 | CHAPTER OBJECTIVES

1 Identify the historical periods, decision makers, and development of human resources management.

2 Summarize the basic concepts, tasks, and processes of human resources management.

3 Discuss the contemporary issues of public employment unions and collective bargaining.

4 Critique the human resources management ethical issues of diversity, discrimination, affirmative action, and equal opportunity.

For Leonard White, the crux of public administration is the people who serve. The human resources manager directs and manages people with given skills, knowledge, and abilities, coupled with the finances and authority to do the best job possible. But what is the goal of the resources manager: efficiency, economy or effectiveness? Is it equity, fairness, and social justice? Is it performance appraisal and accountability? Or, is it some combination thereof? We contend, of course, it is pursuit of the public interests. Most importantly, who is the proper recipient of the stewardship exercised by the public service employee: interest groups, clientele, recipients, or the public interests?

People are the greatest resource—and usually the highest expense—of the public service. It is people who implement laws, people who oversee the finances, and people who manage programs and other people. In human resources terminology, terms and concepts such as *human capital* or *human resource* are used in a positive sense to denote public-service employees and to describe their importance to the organization overall. But sometimes these terms may be used in a negative sense, reducing a human being to something akin to a tool or file cabinet. We believe that this is not healthy. Employees are not just resources in this manner.

The increasing diversity of people is an important feature of the postmodern era in U.S. public administration. So it is that our precept quoted above, from the 2013 ASPA Code of Ethics, requires ethical treatment of diverse peoples with fairness, justice, and the elimination of inequalities and all forms of discrimination. Traditional orthodox bureaucratic theories and practices paid little attention to these concerns and differences, perhaps assuming everyone was homogeneous in background, ideology, race/ethnicity, and other cultural aspects. These orthodox bureaucratic methods and teachings are no longer compatible with the realities of the times, and must give way to new models for teaching, processing, and understanding that are postmodern.[1] Diverse populations are a major feature in the US today, led by rapidly expanding numbers of **Hispanic, Latina/o** and **Chicana/o,** Asians and Pacific Islanders, African Americans, and other race/ethnicity groups. And diverse people are now found throughout the US. With this increasing multiculturalism in America, the practice of public administration now requires greater attention to social equity, diversity, ethics of justice, and overall competency in multiculturalism. Thus, throughout this chapter and in our ethics case study, we include an extended critique of the ethical issues of diversity, discrimination, affirmative action, and equal opportunity within the public workplace.

In this chapter, we discuss human resources management from philosophical, historical, and contemporary approaches, examining not only the major ideas and trends, but also the many details of people who serve the public interests today, for each of the major systems of personnel selection and steps of human resources management is designed to help achieve the public interests. Most of what we will say is directed toward the public sector, including the state and local, as well as the federal, branches of government. However, we also discuss the impact of human resources issues in the nonprofit and faith-based sectors as well.[2] Finally, we include an extended critique of the ethical issues of diversity, discrimination, affirmative action, and equal opportunity within the public workplace.

DEVELOPMENT OF HUMAN RESOURCES MANAGEMENT

The early period of the nation found the wealthy and politically astute holding governmental positions, usually by virtue of their position rather than their performance, while the end of the nineteenth century and beginning of the twentieth saw the implementation of what is known as the merit system. The Constitution did not mention how to appoint individuals to various and sensitive political positions, but only that the President had the power to appoint various officials, ambassadors, and other consuls, including judges and justices. The early appointments, especially during the beginning of the new nation, represented the President's preference for what made a good civil servant.

Various scholars provide typologies depicting historical phases of human resources management, changes to personnel development, laws, and regulations, and other aspects of human resources management.[3] Without a doubt, however, each draw their understanding of civil service and our democratic processes and institutions from the landmark work of **Frederick Mosher (1913–1990)**.[4] For clarity, conciseness, and historical accuracy we will draw from several scholars, although we will most closely follow **Frederick Mosher's historical typology**, while making two changes.[5] Thus we examine five historical eras of human resources management and show the development of each as it pertains to the public interests: the Guardians (1787–1829), the Spoils Period (1829–1883), the Reform Period (1883–1906), the Management Period (1906–1955), and the Professional Career Period (1955–present).

The Guardians (1787–1829)

George Washington's presidency (1789–1797) actually marked the rudimentary beginnings of the merit system, but this was never to be because of the intense clash of party warfare between the **Federalists** and the **Jeffersonian-Republicans** and the ideological loyalties that ruled the day. Washington was frustrated by the factions and his problems in making appointments to sensitive administrative posts, such as his first four executive office positions: Thomas Jefferson as Secretary of State, Alexander Hamilton as Secretary of Treasury, Henry Knox as Secretary of War, and Edmund Randolph as Attorney General.[6] Washington wanted men of stature, character, intelligence, and above all loyalty, to the new nation. He also appointed men who had in mind the best interests of the new nation, and who were moral and ethical in their outlook on civic and public affairs. Even though this federal personnel phase was highly elitist and ideologically determined, it contained at its core pursuit of the public interests. In addition to demanding loyalty and good moral character, a strong executive was the defining criterion of Washington,[7] and later, too, for John Adams in 1797–1801 and Thomas Jefferson in 1801–1809.[8]

The Spoils Period (1829–1883)

The term *spoils* is attributed to Senator William L. Marcy of New York, who in 1832 commented, "American politicians see nothing wrong in the rule that to the victor belong the spoils of the enemy."[9] With the presidency of Andrew Jackson in 1829–1837 and the advent of a new, more populist democracy came the increased involvement of the common man rather than the wealthy elite who had dominated the public service in the previous phase. Certainly, it is true that Jackson appointed top officials in the manner laid down by George Washington and others, including virtue, honesty, and propriety, but he also advocated the common man.[10]

Jackson himself rued the idea of engaging in administrative detail and appointments. He enjoyed the game of politics, but the necessity for executive administration forced his hand to apply his populist philosophy to the filling of executive posts as well as shaping domestic and foreign policy. Jackson's supporters actually saw this as a reform away from the elitism of the past. But the advent and continuation of political patronage was taken to mean that, since an individual supported a particular presidential candidate, when that candidate won office his supporters should reap the spoils of victory, including "jobs for the boys" in federal service.

Historians posit that Jackson really never actually reached out to the common person as much as we are led to believe; it was more symbolic and linguistic than tangible during his presidency. The spoils system truly came into its own

BOX 7.2 | William L. Marcy

Senator **William L. Marcy**, born December 12, 1786 in Southbridge, Massachusetts, and who died July 4, 1857 in Ballston Spa, New York, graduated from Brown University in 1808, and was admitted to the bar in New York, where he began to practice law in 1810. Throughout his military and civil service career he held many positions, including: as a lieutenant in the War of 1812, a recorder of Troy, New York in 1816, adjutant-general of the New York militia in 1821, comptroller of the state of New York from 1823 to 1829, associate justice of the New York Supreme Court from 1829 to 1831, United States senator from December 1831 to July 1832, governor of New York from 1833 to 1838, Secretary of War under President Polk from 1845 to 1849, and later Secretary of State under Franklin Pierce from 1853 to 1857.

Throughout his long career he made no bones about his Democratic loyalties, and believed that everyone who supported the winning candidate should be rewarded for their loyalty. Therefore, it is no surprise that Senator Marcy is the author of the famous phrase: **"To the victor, go the spoils."** This included, of course, all of the perks surrounding civil service positions, regardless of one's knowledge, skills, and abilities for the particular position.

Source: "William L. Marcy," NNDB, retrieved from www.nndb.com/people/987/000051834/

with John Tyler's presidency in 1841–1845, to President Abraham Lincoln's administration in 1861–1865, and onward through the latter part of the nineteenth century.[11] Office seekers were rampant. Undue and unmerciful political pressure was put upon presidents and other lesser political appointees to make way for the untold numbers of individuals seeking political patronage payback. President Garfield, for example, wrote to his wife in 1877: "I had hardly arrived [in Washington] before the door-bell began to ring and the old stream of office-seekers began to pour in. They had scented my coming and were lying in wait for me like vultures for a wounded bison." Others, like 1885–1888 Secretary of Interior Lucius Q.C. Lamar noted: "I eat my breakfast and dinner and supper always in the company of some two or three eager and hungry applicants for office . . . I have no time to say my prayers."[12]

The Reform Period (1883–1906)

The post-Civil War period saw an increase in the number of patronage positions, and greater graft and corruption, particularly at the state and local levels. Reforms were more out of the desire for a restoration of "wholesome democracy," i.e., the public interests, than for administrative efficiency. The emergence of the party system, complete with its moral decline in political and administrative standards, led to a number of instances involving various financial kickbacks from contractors, skimming of receipts, and other abuses. However, the nation was growing, the economy, especially in the western states, was booming, and the country was not involved in major foreign disputes.[13] Thus, even to the most hardened reformer, the need for civil service reform was not really apparent until the assassination of President James A. Garfield in 1881 by a disgruntled federal government office seeker named Charles Guiteau. This critical incident was the tragic spark that brought attention to the excesses of the spoils system inherent in the corruption of the political parties. Changes were required, and the reformers at all three levels of government were there to see that the changes took place.

Thus, as a result, the 1883 Pendleton Act was signed into law, and with it came administrative oversight of civil servants by the newly formed U.S. Civil Service Commission, and the inclusion of merit examinations. Initiated by Senator George Pendleton, an Ohio Democrat, the intention was to end the spoils system. The primary changes of this legislation included:

- Influence of British civil service action, including competitive examinations and a neutral civil service that was free from political influence.
- Establishment of the U.S. Civil Service Commission, which was to establish and carry out personnel rules and laws.
- Lateral entry rather than only bottom level entry—meaning a person could enter public service at a higher level than the bottom level.
- No special administrative class was established as in Britain—rather, the President was encouraged to appoint high level officials based on political loyalty rather than administrative competence per se.
- Position classification, standard pay schedules, and objective performance appraisals were also developed.
- Personnel selection to be based on practical job-related knowledge, skills, and abilities, rather than general academic ability.
- Due process protections: dismissal for cause and protection from patronage.

However, with each successive administration, the number of merit positions did not automatically increase exponentially. Each president wanted to leave his

---

▶ BOX 7.3 | Assassination that Rocked the Personnel World

On July 2, 1881 President Garfield was feeling good about himself, his short term in office as President of the United States (he had been since March), and although he knew the country was still trying to put the Civil War behind them, he earnestly believed that his own Republican Party was trying to heal the wounds from the 1880 presidential campaign, which saw division within the Republican ranks. He prepared to set off on a vacation before gearing up for what he expected to be difficult political battles ahead. He and his entourage arrived at the Baltimore and Potomac Railroad station and, amid the flurry and hustle of holiday travelers Charles Guiteau, a disgruntled federal office-seeker, appeared out of the crowd, pushed close to President Garfield, and fired two shots, one that delivered the fatal blow of shattering bones and puncturing vital internal organs. He tried escaping, but an alert guard stopped him. The President was whisked away to a hospital and Guiteau off to a local jail. President Garfield later died as a result of complications from the gunshot wound— only the second president to be assassinated while in office. And Charles Guiteau was tried, convicted, and executed for his part in the assassination. ◀

Source: "Charles Guiteau," NNDB, retrieved from www.nndb.com/people/210/000044078; Douglas MacGowan, "July 2, 1881," Crime Library, retrieved from www.crimelibrary.com/terrorists_spies/assassins/charles_guiteau/

mark of loyalty-bearing positions, and so he extended coverage to more employees, who were brought into public service by patronage practices. Many of these individuals were European immigrants and the poor, who lived in urban America toward the end of the nineteenth century and into early part of the twentieth.

Administrative and personnel reforms took place at both the state and local levels, as well as at the federal level. Led by such reform-minded stalwarts as George William Curtis and Dorman B. Eaton, the movement for reform was precipitous, particularly in states such as New York, Massachusetts, Pennsylvania, Wisconsin, and California.[14] In fact, it was this very reform-minded thinking that led Woodrow Wilson to pen his famous "The Study of Administration" article in 1887, advocating the separation of politics from administration, and thus prompting the growth of state and local civil service commissions and the impetus for local administrative reforms such as the use of city managers.

With the reformers on one side, largely consisting of the wealthy industrialists and middle classes, and the immigrants and lower classes on the other, the stage was set for a clash of interests, values, and goals. And it did not take long before we began to see a winner of this clash emerge. The reformers, led by such luminaries as George William Curtis, **Emory Upton**, Frederick W. Taylor, Richard S. Childs, and many others, who believed in promotion of the public interests more than raw and unbridled partisan politics, relished the fact that middle-class, oftentimes Midwestern and Western backgrounds, coupled with their strong family upbringing and religious training and value indoctrination, would help establish the fact that corruption and graft should not win out over moral and efficient government and governing processes.[15] The reformers moved for changes in how government officials were selected to serve in a government position, from one of spoils to merit. The reformers sought to depoliticize the public interests, in particular through the establishment of civil service commissions, including the federal, state, and local levels.[16]

The Management Period (1906–1955)

In 1906, the New York Bureau of Municipal Research (see Chapter 2 for more details) was established and sought to study and apply scientific methods of administration to public administration overall and specifically to human resources management. Bureaus such as this—supported by private philanthropy—were established because the reformers did not see a difference between public and private organizations; only that people worked in both, and management of people was the same in either. Efficiency was manifested through position classification and overall control of public personnel systems. By 1930, for example, over 80 percent of the federal government's nonmilitary personnel were covered by a civil service/merit system. Today, the figure is more than 90 percent.

Franklin D. Roosevelt (FDR) and Dwight D. Eisenhower had an overriding influence in human resources management. FDR, for example, wanted greater authority over his New Deal programs, and the way to do this was to centralize responsibilities and functions. The Committee on Administrative Management (aka Brownlow Committee, 1937) found several key factors that were necessary to meet FDR's goals: (1) challenge the need for specialized and technical employees; (2) blur the distinction between politics and administration; (3) passage of the Hatch Act of 1939 and publication of the results of the First Hoover Commission,

1949, and various "little Hoover commissions" at the state level, which emphasized greater dependence upon management, including close integration of personnel management with general presidential management, establishment of an
Executive Office of President—the core of which was the White House staff and
the budget office, and consolidation of all line agencies, including all regulatory
commissions, into twelve cabinet agencies, the idea being greater centralization of
authority and oversight by the President.[17]

Second, President Eisenhower, who sought to place greater numbers of
Republicans into sensitive and powerful administrative positions long held by
Democrats, ordered a Second Hoover Commission, formed in 1953, and its Second Report in 1955 reinvigorated the politics-administration dichotomy by its
recommendation for 800 more presidential appointees, adding another 3,000
upper-echelon administrative class of civil servants, which was to be called the
Senior Civil Service.[18] This followed the already established practice in Britain. It
did not last, however, and died by the late 1950s, but was resurrected in the 1978
civil service reform legislation, with the advent of the **Senior Executive Service**,
prompting more centralized management of agencies and their personnel.[19]

The Professional Career Period (1955–Present)

Specialized professionalism was established by molding of the civil service system to
one based on the knowledge, skills, and abilities (KSAs) of the person rather than the
position. Professionals like lawyers and scientists became a part of the federal government, but their dislike for politics and political bureaucratic relationships was evident. In the early periods, clerkships and clerical position dominated, where the need
for standards of efficiency and effectiveness were warranted, but during the post-
World War II period, with the advent of technological and communication advances,
came the professionals.[20] The impact of scientists, especially in the health (e.g., NIH),
aerospace (e.g., NASA), and environmental (e.g., EPA) areas, was predominant, but
large numbers of lawyers, physicians, educators, accountants, management specialists, and others filled numerous positions at both the federal and state levels. Local
governments were at first slower to respond to the professional changes, but by the
1970s greater numbers of local officials acquired management degrees (e.g., MPAs),
and more individuals with technical degrees, such as in telecommunications and
computer science, especially in larger cities and counties.[21]

The defining point in the final historical phase of human resources management was the passage of the 1978 Civil Service Reform Act and the inauguration
of a new commitment to civil service.[22] For approximately 100 years the Pendleton Act was the key piece of civil service legislation. However, it became increasingly clear that substantial reform was necessary. One of the main problems was
lack of direction between the President and the Civil Service Commission over
personnel policy at the federal level. President Carter made it clear that change
was necessary and he targeted five problem areas that needed change, including:
rewriting and discarding the overly technical rules and regulations that detailed
every action for recruiting, testing, selecting, and classifying federal civil service
employees; overprotection of employees who deserved to be fired, but could not
be because of the excessive number of rules that protected them from political
action; greater need for management flexibility; more compensation given due
to longevity rather than performance; and trying to reduce the discrimination of

women and racial minorities. The civil service reform act corrected these problems through a series of personnel, organizational, and management changes. The major changes included: (1) creation of the Office of Personnel Management (OPM), which was designed to provide policy leadership, and the Merit Systems Protection Board (MSPB), which was responsible for investigations and appeals. Whereas previously the Civil Service Commission held both responsibilities, the workload would be divided and the old CSC would be abolished; (2) the Senior Executive Service (SES) was formed, and it was created as a separate personnel system for high ranking civil service officials; (3) more flexibility within each agency to deal with their own personnel problems and issues; (4) establish federal based performance appraisal system; (5) create a merit pay system for managers below SES; (6) provide better protection for whistleblowers; (7) combine the work of the Equal Employment Opportunity program within the Equal Employment Opportunity Commission; and (8) finally create a more independent Federal Labor Relations Authority, which was designed to oversee changes in labor-management relations at the federal government level.[23]

With the 1980 election of President Ronald Reagan, a "devolutionary mindset" took hold. This meant that Reagan's federalism philosophy was to devolve or hand responsibility down to states and local governments. For example, in his first administration, former President Reagan appointed good friend and business mogul J. Peter Grace to examine where regulatory waste was located in the national government and offer recommendations for eliminating it. By 1984, the Grace Commission—or the Private Sector Survey on Cost Control—produced nearly 2,800 recommendations that it said would save nearly $425 billion over three years.[24] The effect of such a report led many to believe that big government was "bad" government, and thus, unfortunately, many individuals who worked for the national government felt they were negatively labeled. This may have devalued the contributions of government employees and embraced the stereotype of the private sector as more efficient and effective.

BOX 7.4 | The 1978 Civil Service Reform Act

President Jimmy Carter's 1978 statement on signing the Civil Service Reform Act:

> History will regard the Civil Service Reform Act of 1978 as one of the most important laws enacted by this Congress. In March, when I sent my proposals to Congress, I said that civil service reform and reorganization would be the centerpiece of my efforts to bring efficiency and accountability to the Federal Government ... It puts merit principles into statute and defines prohibited personnel practices. It establishes a Senior Executive Service and bases the pay of executives and senior managers on the quality of performance ... It provides a more sensible method for evaluating individual performance ... The act assures that whistleblowers will be heard, and that they will be protected from reprisal ... Our aim is to build a new system of excellence and accountability. ▲

Source: Jimmy Carter, "Civil Service Reform Act of 1978 Statement on Signing S. 2640 Into Law, October 13, 1978," retrieved from www.presidency.ucsb.edu/ws/index.php?pid=29975

BOX 7.5 | The Grace Commission

In 1982, former President Reagan directed the Grace Commission, named after its executive director, J. Peter Grace, the late industrialist, to "work like tireless bloodhounds to root out government inefficiency and waste of tax dollars." For two years, 161 corporate executives and community leaders led an army of 2,000 volunteers on a waste hunt throughout the Federal Government. Funded entirely by voluntary contributions of $76 million from the private sector, the search cost taxpayers nothing. The Grace Commission made 2,478 recommendations, which according to the report, if implemented, would save $424.4 billion over three years, an average of $141.5 billion a year—all without eliminating essential services. The 47 volumes and 21,000 pages of the *Grace Commission Report* constitute a vision of an efficient, well-managed government that is accountable to taxpayers. ▲

Source: reprinted in part from J. Peter Grace, "President's Private Sector Survey on Cost Control," *A Report to the President*, vol. 1, retrieved from www.uhuh.com/taxstuff/gracecom.htm

Before long, privatization, contracting out, and outsourcing became the rage. The argument was that the private sector could provide public services at lower costs and in more productive ways than could government. This mindset is not new, dating at least as far back as World War II with federally chartered government corporations. In World War II the national government relied on contracting out, as government workers produced only a small share of weapons. However, the 1980s style of contracting out set the stage for a nationwide movement to privatize many aspects of the public sector, with the belief that it would improve delivery of service and the numbers of goods, and lower cost to the taxpayers.

Based on actual requests for fiscal year 2008, the national government spent nearly $530 billion in contractual services with the private, nonprofit, and nongovernmental sectors.[25] The biggest winners in these contracts were in supplies and equipment (around 35 percent) and with general services (at nearly 45 percent). Observers of this phenomenon posited that costs of contracting out generally were more expensive than the federal civilian payroll, and the number of indirect employees, or what some refer to as shadow employees, had grown to over 5.5 million, nearly triple the number of federal civilian employees.[26] In addition, privatization or outsourcing had given rise to an entirely new brand of elite employee: the Washington lobbyist. This was not your ordinary lobbyist. Often he was a former federal official who resigned from government, and who ended up as a high-paid executive or consultant to a company within the same industry that he once regulated or oversaw as a public employee. One study by the **General Accountability Office** (GAO)—an independent, nonpartisan agency that works for Congress—found that nearly one-third of 5,000 former mid- and high-level employees, including military officers, had gone to work for private contractors.[27] This revolving door syndrome, as some refer to it, was certainly impacting the public's negative perception of the greedy former public servant, who gave up their civil service position for a run at the big bucks!

BOX 7.6 | Outsourcing

What is outsourcing? Today, we see even more emphasis on outsourcing. In 1998, Congress passed legislation that required federal agencies to inventory all personnel positions that could possibly be outsourced. This yielded a number at nearly 800,000 positions! President Donald Trump has been a proponent of government outsourcing. Is it good for citizens? Is it effective for provision of public services? Is it the best for the public interests? In a fascinating new book, *New York Times* columnist Thomas Friedman has argued that in the new "flat world," outsourcing in and to the private

sector has been a must, both nationally and internationally. In other words, the pragmatic aspect of outsourcing may outweigh its potentially negative and harmful public effects. As they say, only time will tell. ◤

Source: Stephen W. Hays and Richard C. Kearney, *Public Personnel Administration: Problems and Prospects*, 4th ed. (Upper Saddle River, NJ: Prentice-Hall, 2003), 334; and Thomas L. Friedman, *The World is Flat: A Brief History of the Twenty-First Century* (New York, NY: Farrar, Straus, and Giroux, 2005).

By then, the reinvention of government movement had taken hold, particularly at the local and state levels, and its effects are still felt by personnel experts.[28] Not to be outdone, President Bill Clinton in 1991 initiated the National Performance Review (NPR) project, designed by Vice President Al Gore, Jr.[29] The primary emphasis of the NPR was Reinvention—to streamline government processes in order to achieve more effective outcomes, including deregulating the public personnel process.[30] This was particularly necessary at the federal level, where close to 200,000 jobs and over 2,000 federal field offices were closed—all in the name of making government more accountable.[31] Although the NPR is no longer an active organization in Washington, its effects were long-lasting. For example, the recent hue and cry for greater accountability through performance accountability measures seems to be the next generation of the NPR. What is troubling is that, in the government's marked determination to focus on numbers, accountability, and greater efficiency, we may have lost sight of the greater call for the civil servant: to serve the public interests. The civil service is about people serving people, not programs.

Given all this history, especially at the national government level, what are the basic laws, functions, processes, and policies of human resources management? We survey it all, describing relevant key terms, phrases, and laws, discussing basic functions of human resources management, describing the basic overall process of labor-management relations in the government arena, and highlighting two policy areas directly affected by human resources management changes that impact the public interests.

ELEMENTS OF HUMAN RESOURCES MANAGEMENT

Human resources management is all about serving others! Regardless of the organization, whether it is the Post Office, the city manager's office, the state Department of Transportation (DOT), or the local Salvation Army. The position from CEO to custodian, or the people they serve—everyone: civilians to military, citizens within the city's jurisdiction, the state road system, and those who travel on it, and the self-declared needy—it really just boils down to public servants doing what their title indicates: serving others. And the hope is that, by serving others, we may serve the public interests. It is important, then, to distinguish between the basic tasks of personnel administration (which is much more functional) and human resources management (which is more oriented to the needs of employees).[32]

Personnel Administration Versus Human Resource Management

Personnel administration identifies the basic administration of line and staff functions and the system those functions operate in, such as recruitment, selection, and compensation. The early period of administrative reform sought to change the corrupt and unethical personnel systems of patronage and spoils, such as the urban political machines of Chicago and New York, to one of merit, and to do so meant a wholesale change in the way government was looked at (i.e., organizational and institutional), as well as the way various government functions operated. This change was directed at the entire system, focusing on prioritizing work efficiency and effectiveness, primarily through administrative principles of change and work techniques.

Human resource management, on the other hand, has come to mean something different—at least symbolically, if not substantively as well. Some believe that public personnel has simply expanded its intellectual boundaries by referring to people in public service as resources, implying more than rote knowledge of personnel systems and functions. Others contend that human resource management is more closely aligned with sensitivity to values. Still others simply mean the term places emphasis where emphasis is due: on people. Whereas traditional personnel administration systems emphasized planning, employee acquisition, employee development, and sanction, human resources management is the broader focus of partnering with line agencies to achieve the organization's mission, such as improving the quality of work life for the civil servant, helping to support the change process in the organization, and even contracting out various personnel functions, such as payroll and benefits, if the need arises. In other words, human resources *management*—not personnel administration—seems to imply greater interest in the whole of the person, not just as a number or statistic.[33]

In addition to focusing on the common public administration values of economy, efficiency, and effectiveness, human resources management focuses on how managers, elected officials, and even citizens and citizen groups might influence more traditional political values, such as promoting social equity, enhancing administrative representativeness, fostering employee rights, and promoting the overall well-being of public employees. The latter values, for example, are illustrated in a variety of hot-button political issues associated with employee rights in collective bargaining, affirmative action, and sexual harassment cases, as well as issues of diversity, such as gender equality and sexual orientation. Given the basic differences between personnel administration and human resources management, what are the elements of these administrative operations, and how do they affect the public interests?

Personnel are defined as both the employees and the functional and administrative unit responsible for hiring, firing, promoting, and redirecting.[34] Government is often measured by the number of full-time and part-time employees, with the former referred to as full-time equivalent (FTE) employees. The numbers are large. Total local and state FTEs were 16.4 million in 2007.[35] Total federal non-military personnel numbered approximately 1.8 million in 2008, while military personnel (including reserves) were 3 million.[36] If we count shadow employees—independent contractors hired by the governments—the total number who work directly or indirectly for governments is close to 30 million.

Unfortunately, survey research indicates that the number of top high school and college graduates are thinking less of joining the soon-to-be depleted ranks of government employees,[37] especially at the federal level, where the Office of Personnel Management (OPM) predicts up to a 40 percent attrition rate of current federal employees within the next 10 years based on retirement eligibility.[38] This results from the sizable number of aging baby boomers who are retiring or moving in the later stages of their working life to the private or nonprofit sectors. Attitudes toward the public service are contradictory—for example, although over two-thirds of Americans trust their bureaucrats to do the right thing, fewer and fewer young people want to work for the government. Instead, they are moving to the more short-term lucrative private sector positions.

The merit system is based on knowledge and tenure. As we mentioned earlier, George Washington's guardian class may have de facto been the wealthy and elite of their day, but they were also the most knowledgeable, educated, civic-minded, and career-oriented. So, in one sense, George Washington and his immediate presidential successors actually preferred an early form of merit or civil service system. On the downside, of course, many point out the overemphasis on partisan and social-class loyalty, something that was around for decades later.

The non-civil service system, or spoils system, was based on patronage, where employees are selected on basis of partisan and/or personal loyalty, rather than "knowledge, skills, and abilities" (KSA). Today, some 3,000 political executives are appointed by the President to hold a high-level political position with substantial policymaking powers. Some argue that we have exceeded the saturation point for political executives; that, when compared with other democracies, such as Great Britain, which has about 100, our national bureaucratic system, for example, is top-heavy with too many non-merit-based policymakers who are unaccountable, except to the President alone. So, what are the basic steps and/or functions of hiring a qualified candidate to be represented by the civil service system?

PROCESS OF HUMAN RESOURCES MANAGEMENT

There are several steps or components for dealing with managing people in a public or nonprofit organization. First, position classification "organizes jobs under civil service system into classes based on job descriptions denoting similarity of duty and responsibility, provides for a logical and efficient promotional process, separates authority, sets up chain of command, and details pay scales."[39] General Schedule (GS) and Senior Executive Service (SES) are at the federal level. GS, for example, is a federal system of various levels or grades of pay and job classifications from 1 to 15, established in 1949 by the Classification Act, which was a continuation and enhancement of a 1923 law called the Classification Act that "established the Classification Programs Division of the Office of Personnel Management" in order to group positions into classes on basis of duties and responsibilities (Table 7.1).[40] GS-1 to GS-4 are lower-level positions—typically secretarial and clerical. GS-5 to GS-11 are middle-level positions divided into two

TABLE 7.1

2017 U.S. Government General Schedule (GS) Salary Table ($)

Grade (GS-)	Step 1	Step 2	Step 3	Step 4	Step 5	Step 6	Step 7	Step 8	Step 9	Step 10	Within-Grade Amounts
1	18,526	19,146	19,762	20,375	20,991	21,351	21,960	22,575	22,559	23,171	Varies
2	20,829	21,325	22,015	22,559	22,853	23,525	24,197	24,869	25,541	26,213	Varies
3	22,727	23,485	24,243	25,001	25,789	26,517	27,275	28,033	29,791	29,549	758
4	25,514	26,364	27,214	28,064	28,914	29,764	30,614	31,464	32,314	33,164	850
5	28,545	29,497	30,449	31,401	32,353	33,305	34,257	35,209	36,161	337,113	952
6	31,819	32,880	33,941	35,002	36,063	37,124	38,185	39,246	40,307	41,368	1,061
7	35,359	36,538	37,717	38,896	40,075	41,254	42,433	43,612	44,791	45,970	1,179
8	39,159	40,464	41,769	43,074	44,379	45,684	46,989	48,294	49,599	50,904	1,305
9	43,251	44,693	46,135	47,577	49,019	50,461	51,903	53,345	54,787	56,229	1,442
10	47,630	49,218	50,806	52,394	53,982	55,570	57,158	58,746	60,334	61,922	1,588
11	58,329	54,073	55,817	57,561	59,305	61,049	62,793	64,537	66,281	68,025	1744
12	62,722	64,813	66,904	68,995	71,086	73,177	75,268	77,359	79,450	81,541	2,091
13	74,584	77,070	79,556	82,042	84,528	87,014	89,500	91,986	94,472	96,958	2,486
14	88,136	91,074	94,012	96,959	99,888	102,826	105,764	108,702	111,640	114,578	2,938
15	103,672	107,128	110,584	114,040	117,496	120,952	124,408	127,864	131,320	134,776	3,456

Note: Salary Table 2017 — General Schedule Incorporating the 1.00% General Increase, Effective January 2017

Source: "General Schedule (GS) Payscale Table for 2017," *Federal Pay.org*, retrieved May 17, 2018 at www.federalpay.org/gs/2017

sub-schedules. The first are GS-6, -8, and -10, which are technical, skilled craft, and senior clerical. The second are GS-5, -7, -9, and -11, which are professional career grades, with GS-5 and GS-7 entry-level positions for college graduates. Finally, GS-12 to GS-15 are senior-level positions, just below the SES. The SES replaced the "super-grades" of GS-16 to GS-18, providing the pay-grade link between presidential appointees and normal civilian workers.[41] These current GS levels were established originally by the Civil Service Reform Act of 1978.[42]

States are not covered by the GS or SES classifications, but the Intergovernmental Personnel Act (IPA) of 1970 reinforced the requirement that states have merit features built into their personnel systems.[43] Local governments are less regulated. As of this writing, all states and most local governments have some type of classification system. Several problems still exist despite the reinvention efforts of the 1990s. First, classification systems have grown more complicated, encouraging "classification creep," increasing administrative costs and reducing managerial staffing flexibility (e.g., the average number of job classifications in one state government is around 2,000!). Second, there is an overemphasis of reviews and audits by the OPM or corresponding state/local agency. Third, job classification is quickly becoming outdated as result of changing technology, particularly with the advent and use of the internet and web technology. Fourth, some changes have occurred to assist in the reclassification of many government positions, including broad banding, where managers are "urged to consolidate existing classifications into fewer classes, thus reducing complexity and also increasing flexibility and mobility for employees" and "rank-in person" similar to the military.[44] Another set of changes came from National Performance Review (NPR) and the **National Commission on the State and Local Public Service** (the Winter Commission), which called for reduced complexity of personnel classification systems.[45]

Second, recruitment is the process of advertising job openings and soliciting candidates to apply.[46] There are many challenges in recruiting new applicants to national government. For one there is a shrinking pool of possible candidates, both in terms of "knowledge, skills, and abilities" (KSAs) and, more importantly, the desire to work in government at all. For example, only one in three Americans even want to work for government. Further, of the best students, such as *Phi Beta Kappa* college graduates, only 5 percent rank government as their first career choice, while 34 percent rank the private sector as their first choice.[47] Nonetheless, recruiting individuals to the public sector is more or less largely influenced by who is interested in working in the public sector. More minorities, young people, and Democrats are attracted, as opposed to non-minorities, older individuals, and Republicans. In addition, government needs to increase its use of social media and the internet in the advertising and recruitment process. The third step in hiring is examination. It is a complex process, where written and oral tests are used to determine the level of KSAs of potential employees. Open and competitive examinations are at the heart of a solid and competitive civil service system. Exams are generally the fairest way of determining who is eligible to fill a spot. In order to be fair, exams must be valid[48]—that is, they should measure what they are designed to measure, such as general intelligence (IQ tests)—and be unbiased— that is, the exams should not directly or indirectly be discriminatory against age, race, ethnicity, gender, or other variables. A key method to assess the validity of various forms of examination is adverse impact analysis to identify statistically differential outcomes by race not linked to ability or job performance. Race-norming, where the test givers simply add points to lower scores, especially where the test taker is of a minority race/ethnicity, began in the late 1980s, but was later declared unconstitutional in 1991.[49]

The fourth step in hiring is selection. Choosing the best candidate for an open position is critical to maintaining a strong civil service system. State and local examination processes are generally in place, with many valid and reliable selection methods at the state and local levels. Selecting the best candidate is not always easy, especially in the policy areas of affirmative action, comparable worth, and veterans' preference. Women and minorities are high on the select list for government positions, but all candidates must achieve minimum levels on standardized exams.[50] The certification process means that only a select number of the highest-ranking candidates are deemed eligible for possible selection.[51]

The fifth step in hiring is compensation. How much is a government employee paid? How much should a particular government employee be paid? Compensation levels are set by a combination of law and market forces, assessed through job and salary surveys to assess market-level wages and benefits. In addition, there are other key values in determining compensation decisions, such as market equity, performance or merit, seniority or longevity, cost of living, and social equity or justice. Further, there are different types of compensation systems, such as merit pay, bonuses, and gainsharing, that address the balance between fixed and at-risk compensation systems—each designed to influence employee motivation. The first question is answered dependent upon whether it is a national or sub-national position. The second question is largely dependent upon, not only normative values, but also pragmatic concerns, such as economic necessity and geographical location. As we have mentioned, state and local government employees' compensation varies as widely as California is distant from Vermont. Municipalities and counties base their compensation levels on state legislative mandates to local economic conditions, such as budget restraints or increases. Federal positions are preset according to the General Schedule mentioned above. GS-1 to GS-15 rankings are determined by Congress and published through the Office of Personnel Management.

How much should an employee be paid is dependent upon several factors, such as minimum economic needs. For example, is the employee living in St. Louis, Missouri, or Boston, Massachusetts? If the latter, then the salary levels listed in the GS table (Table 7.1) are adjusted by 16.99 percent, whereas in St. Louis the levels are adjusted by only 11.27 percent. This is known as locality pay adjustments. Locality pay was instituted in 1993 in order to provide employees living in high-cost areas relatively higher salaries than individuals living in lower-cost areas. Generally speaking, entry-level federal employees are paid better than state and local employees, but that is assumed to be the case because of the inclusion of low-paid teachers and criminal justice employees.[52] Since 2010, however, city managers with a large number of years of experience working in large metropolitan areas can expect salaries and benefit packages to exceed $250,000.[53] And municipal and county health administrators and chief law enforcement officials in large metro areas generally have salaries that exceed $150,000.[54]

Another problem facing public sector employees is the pay gap between themselves and private sector employees. Private sector managers that are equivalent to the GS-15 federal employees easily make two and perhaps three times the GS-15 employee. At the state level the difference is not as great, but significant nonetheless. For example, a biologist in the private sector earns approximately $70,500, while his public sector counterpart earns just under $42,000. In 2004, state salaried employees grew only 0.45 percent, while the 2005 increase was roughly 1.19 percent. This kind of increase does not even keep pace with inflation. Certainly the public-private pay gap is real, and it will never be completely narrowed, but great strides by various public organizations are attempting to do so. Federal performance appraisal systems, which were established by the Civil Service Reform Act of 1978, tried to establish some fair method for evaluating how an employee's work performance was measured, but there was less emphasis on how to tie additional pay to enhanced performance. One way was through comparability to the private sector—e.g., the U.S. Pay Comparability Act of 1990 required federal agencies to close the pay gaps between the public and private sectors by up to 20 percent. Changing economic times, fluctuating budgets, and increasing budget deficits (except for a brief interlude during the 1997–2001 Clinton administration) have essentially prevented such reductions in pay gaps.

However, the competition for top-level public employees is high, and this drives up salaries. Further, debates over comparable worth of salaries by gender have had some impact on the salaries of women, but still not gender equality in pay.[55] Relatedly, James Perry and others reviewed 57 empirical studies of the effectiveness of merit pay in the public sector and concluded that performance-related merit pay does not deliver as promised.[56] Similarly, James Bowman reviewed empirical studies of merit performance pay in federal, states, and local government to conclude that the "performance of pay for performance programs . . . is . . . disappointing" and often counterproductive.[57] Yet, Jonathan Walters, in *Governing* magazine,[58] reported that municipal versus state executives are generally better paid. Allen Frank, Chief Information Officer for the City of Philadelphia, earns $190,000; Rhoda Mae Kerr, Fire Chief for the City of Little Rock, AR, takes in $102,000; and Bill Bratton, Chief of Police for Los Angeles, brings in nearly $260,000! Still, with all of the big bucks earned by these local government chief executives, their salaries and benefit packages do not come close to what they could earn in the private sector. For example, Kevin Baum, who is assistant fire chief in Austin, Texas, makes one-third less what his organizational counterparts at Austin-based Dell Computer makes.[59]

The sixth step in hiring is training and development (T&D). Once the employee is recruited, examined, selected, and paid, they need to be continually trained and developed. The **Government Employees Training** Act of 1958 required federal agencies to provide training. Later, in the late 1960s President Johnson instituted the Office of Training and Development and Regional Training Centers, along with the establishment of the Federal Executive Institutive in Charlottesville, Virginia. The institute has graduated thousands of federal managers, chiefly those of the SES variety. State and local governments benefited from grants allocated for T&D, but this was reduced during the cutbacks of the mid-1980s. Forty-six states have training requirements for local government employees, with the majority for police, fire, and emergency personnel. Much training is done in-house or through universities, such as the University of North Carolina's Institute of Government. State governments need better training programs and practices and better assessment of outcomes, such as training being based upon needs assessment, the use of individual development plans (IDPs), and individual learning accounts (ILA).[60]

The seventh step in hiring is **performance appraisal**, or the evaluation of an employee's work performance. It is primarily used for purposes of retention and promotion, as well as to document any disciplinary actions. Performance appraisal is a management technique, used by individual public managers to address the myriad of concerns associated with accounting for how well or how poorly an individual in the public sector does his or her job. The most common methods of performance appraisal include supervisor ratings, where the immediate supervisor rates employees' performances; self-ratings, when employees rate themselves using a standardized form, usually with some type of narrative and documentation to support claims of performance; peer ratings, which, of course, is when fellow employees rate each other; subordinate ratings, where employees rate their supervisor; and, finally, group ratings, where an outside person rates performance of an entire group, unit, or organization based on random interviews, "on the job" (OTJ) visits, or use of performance documentation. Best practices empirical research suggests the elements of clear performance goals and objectives, timely, specific, and behavioral feedback, ongoing employee participation, and the need for clear, detailed and specific performance documentation.[61]

Quality of work life (QOL) is the eighth step. Governments and public sector organizations are extremely aware of the need to provide a solid quality of work life for their employees. Recent adjustments include family-friendly rules and regulations, particularly in areas of flextime, part-time, and health leave; employee wellness programs; and even sponsoring, if not paying for, alcohol abuse treatment centers. The federal legislation Family and Medical Leave Act of 1993 provided up to 12 weeks of unpaid leave per year for a variety of health and personal issues, including childbirth, child-related services, including adoption and childcare, elder care, and other situations.[62]

The eight steps of public human resources management attest to its importance. Further protection of public service employees' rights is our next topic: collective bargaining and unionization.

COLLECTIVE BARGAINING AND UNIONIZATION IN THE PUBLIC SECTOR

Even though collective bargaining and unionization is done on behalf of the employee, it impacts the public interests through indirect and direct economic, social, and political means. Oftentimes referred to as labor-management relations, the centerpiece of such formal relations is to work out economic and work-related differences between labor and management. To a greater extent it is the reordering of power relations between management and labor, something that did not occur during the first half of the twentieth century, but after World War II it became much more active. Of course, the primary historical focus was upon the private sector, particularly in the occupational areas of shipyard workers, truck drivers, dock workers, and other blue-collar employees; the possibility of public labor-management interaction, unionization, and even striking did not begin in earnest until the 1960s.

Historical Precedents

The early movement of labor-management relations began in late 1800s and early 1900s, with passage of the **Lloyd-LaFollette Act** of 1912. This legislation allowed for unionization of public sector employees, particularly postal workers, but restrictions on how they could organize and bargain largely made this law ineffective. The number of public sector unions grew slowly, largely because of several concerns.[63] First, the idea of public sovereignty was considered sacrosanct; public sector unionization was considered to be a usurpation of this sovereignty. Second, government services are considered either necessary (e.g., fire and police) or unprofitable (e.g., mass transportation) and thus the need for public unions is less than in the private sector. Third, government is too varied in occupations and greater geographic dispersion to make unionization doable.

Passage of the Wagner Act of 1935 provided the impetus public employees needed to have the right to bargain collectively. Despite the Wagner Act, the right to negotiate was hampered because of the lack of strong public unions—unions that had the same bargaining power and position as did their private sector counterparts. Several executive and congressional acts have occurred since the mid-1930s to promote public sector labor relations.

In 1962, President Kennedy issued Executive Order 10988 affirming the rights of public sector employees to unionize and to discuss labor issues with management. But the order stopped short of permitting negotiating. Then, in 1969, another executive order, issued by President Nixon, called for a more coherent labor policy at the federal level through establishment of Federal Labor Relations Council (FLRC), slightly expanding the ability and right to bargain collectively, except the main issues of salary and benefits remained outside the bargaining parameters.[64] Then, in 1978, the Civil Service Reform Act (CSRA) was passed, and it provided the needed push that corrected most of the historical shortfalls regarding the inability of public sector employees to unionize and collectively bargain in good faith. It accomplished the following: (1) combined executive orders into one legislative act, thus providing some sense of uniformity; and (2) it replaced the FLRC with the Federal Labor Relations Authority (FLRA).[65]

Process of Labor-Management Negotiations

What happens when the two sides—labor and management—cannot work out their differences in a timely fashion, specifically when one side has made what it considers a fair offer, but the other side rejects it, and vice versa? Various forms of reconciliation are available, such as mediation, fact-finding, and arbitration. **Mediation** involves a third party to help work out a settlement, but a mediator is not allowed to impose his or her own solution. The use of mediation has reached an all-time high, with many lawyers and other trained professionals working as full-time independent mediators. This growth is due largely to the fact that mediation is successful in getting through many labor-management impasses. **Fact-finding** uses the third party more as an informal and non-binding judge, examining evidence on both sides, presenting evidence, and in some cases making specific recommendations for both sides to consider. **Arbitration** is the third technique that both sides use to work through impasses. It is the most stringent of the three methods, where in some cases both parties must make their best offer and then the arbitrator will choose one of the offers, or (as it is in most cases) will make modifications to one or more offers, and then require both parties to accept the modification.[66]

Of course, when all else fails strikes can be effective, but also politically hazardous. In 1970, the Postal Workers Union struck. It began in New York City with some 25,000 postal workers, but soon spread to include nearly 200,000

BOX 7.7 | Strikes Do Not Always Work

A famous public sector strike was the **Professional Air Traffic Controllers Organization** (PATCO) strike in August 1981. With membership of over 90 percent of air traffic controllers, PATCO seemed to have solidarity and political strength—until they pushed President Reagan one step too far. After 95 percent of members rejected the government's $40 million offer in pay/benefits package increases, the union decided to strike. President Reagan declared it an illegal strike, threatening public safety and security, and fired nearly 12,000 striking controllers. PATCO later filed for bankruptcy. ◣

Source: Robert B. Denhardt and Joseph W. Grubbs, Public *Administration: An Action Orientation,* 4th ed. (Belmont, CA: Wadsworth, 2003).

workers. Things were so desperate in the mail business that President Nixon ordered 27,000 National Guardsmen to sort mail. Finally, he broke his own precedent never to negotiate with public sector employees. The government and postal workers reached a settlement, but shortly afterward Congress passed the Postal Reorganization Act, which set up the Post Office as a government corporation and provided the postal employees with the opportunity to bargain.

ETHICS CASE STUDY | Discrimination by Race, Ethnicity, Gender, Religion, Sexuality, Disability

This chapter would not be complete without extended scrutiny of the law of diversity and anti-discrimination that greatly impact human resources management. American history features prominent and constant conflicts over diversity of race, ethnicity, religion, gender, sexuality, physical or mental abilities, and other differences between persons. The Constitution and laws have sought to resolve these disputes with at least the basic respect and dignity each person is owed. And an important duty of all public administrators is to ensure this basic human dignity to all. This extended ethics case study of prominent constitutional language, court decisions, statutes, and public policies on diversity issues in public affairs may belie a pattern or practice of moral decision-making by public administrators in their dealings with diversity conflicts and discrimination. How would you summarize this rule or duty?

John Rawls, Justice as Fairness

Political philosopher John Rawls (1921–2002) of Harvard University, sought to develop universal rules for ethical decision-making based on equality or justice as fairness. You may recall John Rawls from Chapter 3 discussions of rule-utilitarianism. John Rawls believed that we can achieve justice by imaging ourselves in a position of radical equality with all other persons behind a veil of ignorance. He imagined the veil of ignorance as if all persons were gathered together as souls before they were born—a reality in which no one would know their wealth, mental or physical abilities, gender, race/ethnicity, sexuality, religion, or other demographics as they were later born into the world. Behind the veil of ignorance, each individual would come together to make a universal rule of justice that was unbiased, just, and fair for the betterment of all, because no one would not yet know their specific situation in life.[67] According to Rawls, in the veil of ignorance we would logically form a social contract for the betterment of all, based on two universal principles of justice: (1) the **liberty or equality principle**—"each person is to have an equal right to the most extensive basic liberty compatible with a similar liberty for others"; and (2) the **opportunity principle**—"social and economic inequalities are to be arranged so that they are both a) reasonably expected to be to everyone's advantage, and b) attached to positions and offices open to all." If these two universal principles of justice were to conflict, the second must yield to the first and, thus, respect of human dignity, liberty, and equality trumps all other considerations.[68] Rawls' theories of justice as fairness, equality principle, and opportunity principle have been influential in public affairs. His student, U.S. Attorney General Robert Kennedy, thus named the 1961 "Equal Employment Opportunity" (EEO) Executive Order 10925 after Professor Rawls' equality principle and opportunity principle.

A major criticism of Rawls' theory is that it may be more suitably applied to broad social issues, like Jim Crow segregation, and less so to practical public administration issues, such as professionalism in deciding a budget, or human resources hiring concerns.[69] So, what about the ethics of affirmative action and hiring a less qualified applicant who is a member of a disadvantaged group in society? Rawls' justice as fairness theory may be applied in four ways in applications of affirmative action policies: (1) not hiring would further deprive the individual; (2) hiring may bring about the realization of liberty without harming others of their liberty; (3) hiring ensures they are not shut out from any open position; and (4) hiring assures that privileges innate to the office or position will continue to work toward the advantage of all in society and not only a select few.[70] Consider the practical public administration consequences of each possibility.

First, by not hiring, is this person deprived further of freedom or some other value? If an individual is hired who is not qualified to do the job, would that disadvantage all individuals—their co-workers, manager, and public? Would this also deprive the individual hired of a certain measure of self-respect and self-esteem? What if the applicant is instead directed to a job-skill development center, with the promise of a possible future interview and hiring based on their development of specific skills? If there is a later re-interview, I have not deprived the applicant—instead, the applicant may now be in a better position with improved skills and knowledge for

(continued)

better employment opportunities. Second, does hiring someone less skilled over someone more skilled in fact harm the more highly skilled worker? It may give the more-skilled worker the false impression that they have only an equal chance at landing a position as a less-skilled minority candidate. Would this be unjust and deny their opportunity? Third, consider the damage of a false sense of dignity and self-respect. Hiring a person for a job they are not qualified for may only encourage the false belief of their ability to advance in society where the demand for education, skill, and technical knowledge is increasing. In today's fast-moving and highly technologically oriented workplace, it is imperative that all workers, affirmative action hires, and others are encouraged to be as well prepared to enter the job market as possible.

This extended ethics case study of prominent constitutional language, court decisions, statutes, and public policies on diversity issues in public affairs may belie a pattern or practice of moral decision-making by public administrators in their dealings with diversity conflicts and discrimination. Consider John Rawls' rule-utilitarian theory of justice and its application to the many issues of diversity and public administration. Does Rawls' theory play-out to good resolutions in all diversity areas?

Race

Debates over racism in public affairs often focus on **racial profiling**.[71] Profiling is a typical investigation technique that examines behavior patterns of people involved in civil offenses (e.g., tax fraud) and crimes, such as drug traffickers who drive below the speed limit to avoid attracting police attention. Racial profiling is more commonly thought of as a tactic used by police in suspecting a person of crime based on a stereotype about their race or ethnicity, especially African American, Hispanic-Chicanx, Asian, Native American, as well as Muslim religion.[72] But when bureaucrats, police, and other public servants treat African Americans or others differently than they treat white people, they may be denying equal protection of the law under the 14th Amendment. *US v. Armstrong* (1996) was a case alleging racial profiling because U.S. District Attorneys in Los Angeles prosecuted only crack drug crimes because it was the drug of choice among African-American culture; powder cocaine was primarily used by white drug users. The class action lawsuit included 24 black defendants who were convicted of crack drug crimes—but no non-blacks were prosecuted in the jurisdiction for crack possession. Further, the civil rights lawsuit alleged the discriminatory intent of criminal sentences mandated by Congress for possession of crack that were many times than for the same amount of pure cocaine. The Court upheld the convictions and found no civil rights violations by the U.S. District Attorneys or in the sentencing laws. In *Illinois v. Wardlow* (2000), critics believe the U.S. Supreme Court legitimated the use of racial profiling by the Chicago Police Department. Mr. Wardlow, a black man, was convicted as a parolee with an illegal weapon that was uncovered in a police stop-and-frisk search, conducted without a warrant. Wardlow was selected for the stop and frisk only because he was walking home after a night shift from work in a high-crime neighborhood (near his home), he was black, and he ran when police cars converged on him with spotlights and Chicago police came bounding after him with weapons and shouting. Critics argue the police suspected Mr. Wardlow primarily because he was a black man in a high-crime neighborhood (a black neighborhood) late at night. Would police stop-and-frisk a white man in similar circumstances?

Can African Americans really obtain justice through legal systems and courts that once enforced the slavery and still work in segregation? In *Duncan v. Louisiana* (1968), the Court incorporated the **right to a jury trial** in state courts, to protect a black defendant who was denied the right to a jury for a crime punishable by two years in prison. *Batson v. Kentucky* (1986) prohibited the use of peremptory challenges by prosecutors, to remove all blacks from the jury of a black defendant. *Johnson v. California* (2005) re-emphasized the *Batson* decision; while prosecutors normally get to remove 6 to 12 persons during jury selection without giving any reasons (peremptory), the removal of all black jurors in the trial of a black defendant is *prima facie* (at face value) proof of intending unlawful discrimination by race.[73]

Is the system racist if criminal sanctions, including the ultimate sanction of death, are meted out in a discriminatory fashion to African Americans? Four Justices (but not a majority of five) in *Furman v. Georgia* (1972) argued that the **death penalty** was invalid under the 8th Amendment as cruel and unusual punishment, largely for the reason that it was given in overwhelming numbers to black men. Later, in *McCleskey v. Kemp* (1987), the Court accepted the social science research showing that blacks who killed whites were much more likely to be sentenced to death, yet ruled against McCleskey because he did not prove that there was unlawful **race discrimination** by his particular jury or judge. However, in *Johnson v. California* (2005), the Court ended a system of racial segregation in California prisons that was designed to prevent interracial gang violence, requiring the integration of prison cells.[74]

Affirmative action is one of the more intense areas of ethical controversy in human resources management. It has decreased in political and legal strength, but recent cases such as *Grutter v. Bollinger* (2003) uphold affirmative action—although in a companion case, *Gratz v. Bollinger* (2003), the Court struck down a rigid numeric **quota** system used by the University of Michigan in undergraduate admissions.[75] Actually, there is not simply *one* affirmative action policy; there are a myriad of policies. What, then, precisely is affirmative action? And, if at all, does it act in the public interests? It is the term given to represent any number of policies that have at least three common factors, including: (1) a statement affirming the organization's commitment to correct discrimination, (2) some type of analysis of existing practices and their consequences, and (3) a set of goals to improve affirmative

(continued)

action practices.[76] These practices might be quotas, set-aside programs, or timetables for change. In many instances, the policies are not as direct as quotas, but they include desire and/or willingness on the part of human resources managers, admissions directors, and others in positions of personnel responsibility to strongly consider the race and sex of an applicant before making a decision. Some critics of affirmative action policies argue this is reverse discrimination.

Affirmative action's history is tied to the United States' civil rights history. Title VII of the Civil Rights Right Act of 1964 is the most noteworthy example of civil rights legislation that was passed to prohibit discrimination based on "race, color, religion, national origin, or sex [gender]." As early as prior to World War II, however, the Federal Government attempted to address the issue of discrimination, particularly as it affected public sector employment, primarily through the issuance of executive orders. President F.D. Roosevelt issued Executive Order 8802, which essentially banned discrimination on the basis of race, religion, or national origins. It was limited, however, to businesses and industries with Federal Government contracts related to defense production. In 1961, President Kennedy issued Executive Order 10925, which called for the employment of racial minorities, but, as in FDR's order, it did not have enforcement power. In 1965, President Johnson issued Executive Order 11246, which required that all companies and industries that did any kind of business with the Federal Government must take affirmative action in providing equal opportunity to job employment, regardless of race, religion, or national origin. The enforcement came when contracts were severed with companies and industries that refused to abide by the affirmative action statement. Subsequent executive orders added women[77] and sexual orientation[78] to the list of protected categories of persons with government contractors.

What is the Supreme Court's position? In *Regents of the University of California v. Bakke* (1978), the Court declared that rigid numeric quotas by race in medical school admission decisions at the University of California were illegal, but that race could be considered in a **non-quota** fashion, among many other factors. More important, Justice O'Connor convinced her peers that the goal of diversity, rather than redressing past discrimination, was the greater public interest in their decision. Although she conceded that affirmative action schemes are by nature discriminatory, she argued that such a non-numeric, non-quota level of affirmative action was constitutional and was desirable in promoting diversity. But the Court has continued to limit the expansion of affirmative action policies by numeric quotas—for example, forbidding a public sector employer from laying off more senior employees (e.g., who were white and male) in favor of retaining less senior employees (e.g., who were black).[79] The exception is that quotas may be ordered from the judicial bench, when there is evidence of policies of illegal discrimination, in writing or historical practice, such as refusal by the Alabama State Patrol to hire blacks in 1940 to 1972.[80]

With all these case details of a racist system of public affairs, what hope is there for equality of African Americans? Skeptical scholars suggest there is no law in the law; that the law is simply a functioning of extremely conservative ideologies and elite social backgrounds of Justices who will surely strike down human rights for African Americans and other non-whites, such as affirmative action. *Grutter v. Bollinger* (2003) allowed the continued use of non-numeric, non-quota-style affirmative action in state agencies, e.g., the University of Michigan, which did not have the long history of racist discrimination. The U.S. Supreme Court again upheld the use of non-numeric, non-quota-style affirmative action by government agencies in the recent case of *Fisher v. University of Texas at Austin* (2016).

Affirmative action policies are aimed at making the public workplace more diverse and are generally accepted by all.[81] The Court has maintained the constitutional validity of affirmative action in the *Bakke* (1978) case, but has not expanded the application of numeric quotas without proof of past discrimination. Affirmative action programs are here to stay and include all levels of governance.[82] The diversity of the public service now includes greater numbers of minorities by categories of race/ethnicity, gender, religions, and disabilities.[83] The public interests of affirmative action remain focused on Justice O'Connor's goal of social and organizational diversity rather than reparation.

Ethnicity

What is ethnicity? Or, for that matter, what is race? The U.S. Supreme Court formally took Judicial Notice—judicially noted as a matter of fact—of the nature and meaning of the dual concepts of race and ethnicity in 1987. Their judicial notice (the original also cited hundreds of scientific studies):

> There is a common popular understanding that there are three major human races–Caucasoid, Mongoloid, and Negroid. Many modern biologists and anthropologists, however, criticize racial classifications as arbitrary and of little use in understanding the variability of human beings. It is said that genetically homogeneous populations do not exist and traits are not discontinuous between populations; therefore, a population can only be described in terms of relative frequencies of various traits. Clear-cut categories do not exist. The particular traits which have generally been chosen to characterize races have been criticized as having little biological significance. It has been found that differences between individuals of the same race are often greater than the difference between the 'average' individuals of different races. These observations and others have led some, but not all, scientists to conclude that racial classifications are for the most part sociopolitical, rather than biological, in nature.[84]

Asians and Pacific Islanders are U.S. citizens who themselves are from—or their ancestors were from—the Asian Pacific region, such as the Philippines,

(*continued*)

China, Japan, India, Korea, and Vietnam. Like African Americans, many Asian and Pacific Islander Americans have been subjected to segregation—to the extreme measure of *internment* in relocation camps. For many, immigration issues have featured prominently in the U.S. human rights history of Asians and Pacific Islanders. *Korematsu v. US* (1944) illustrates the extreme segregation experience of **Japanese Americans in internment camps** during World War II. The Court officially approved the relocation of Japanese Americans in the internment camps of World War II as justified by the war declared against Japan. The US has since apologized by allowing the victims' claims against the government in 1948, to proclaim U.S. wrongdoing in 1976 by President Ford, and to make reparations by President Reagan in 1988. Other concerns with issues of Immigration may be illustrated in *Nguyen v. INS* (2001), where the son born out of wedlock between a U.S. soldier and a Vietnamese mother was deported from the US because his father would not admit to his paternity.

Hispanic Americans have recently exceeded the number of African Americans and constitute the largest minority group by race/ethnicity in the US, according to the 2010 *Census*. Hispanic is the term most often used by those identifying with this ethnicity, as designed by the U.S. Census Bureau. In 1976, U.S. Congress passed Public Law 94-311, after years of lobbying by Mexican Americans and others, to officially recognize Hispanics as a group. *Hispanic* is an umbrella term like Asian. But most Hispanic adults today do not identify with the government-mandated term, instead preferring to identify with their country of origin. According to a 2012 Pew Research Survey, only 24 percent preferred the term *Hispanic*.[85] The term *Hispanic* doesn't recognize the indigenous roots that most come from and instead focuses on Spanish ancestry. Perhaps this is because, in racist Eurocentric society, the Spanish have more prestige than the indigenous. Thus, some prefer the term *Chicana*/o or *Chicanx*, from the ancient Aztecs, because it does not negate this indigenous heritage. Others, such as Justice Sotomayor, prefer the term *Latina* (or male, *Latino*) to indicate her birth in Puerto Rico and Caribbean culture. Because Hispanic refers to vastly different people with some historic Spanish or Iberian culture or language as a common denominator, Spanish-language issues often feature prominently in the human rights history of Hispanic peoples. *Hernandez v. New York* (1991) illustrates **Spanish-language** issues when the Court upheld the removal of a potential Latino juror in the trial of a Latino defendant, as lawful and race-neutral. In the case, the prosecutor cited language problems in his challenge for cause, to remove all potential jurors who were of the same Latino background as the defendant. In the jury selection process, attorneys may remove an unlimited number during jury selection for cause, such as bias or other problems, if the judge concurs. In *Alexander v. Sandoval* (2001), the Court dismissed a lawsuit contesting Alabama's English-only driver's license testing. Alabama had once allowed drivers' license testing in any of 17 different languages, but under an English-only law had limited the test language to only English. The Court reasoned that this was changed for budget-cutting, economic purposes and was thereby race-neutral—not designed to discriminate against Spanish-language Hispanics. At any rate, it was the business of the U.S. Department of Justice to sue the state of Alabama in such cases—not individual lawsuits.

Hebrews, Arabs, Persians, and other Middle East peoples claim a common ancestor in **Abraham**, as recorded in chapter 25 of the book of Genesis. These Semitic peoples also share a long history of human rights issues in conflicts, persecution, and holocausts. The resulting diaspora of Semitic peoples throughout the world has resulted in ethnic identities focused on common religious-cultural associations, rather than common languages or genetics. The continuing conflicts may be illustrated in the case of *National Socialist Party v. Skokie* (1977), involving the Free Speech rights of Nazis to march in a predominantly Jewish suburb of Chicago, as portrayed in the 1980 movie *The Blues Brothers*. The Court upheld the First Amendment rights of the American Nazis to express their hate and conflicts with Jews, even with survivors of World War II concentration camps. Similarly, the case of *St. Francis College v. Al-Khazraji* (1987), illustrates conflicts and workplace discrimination in which the Court upheld the protection of Middle-Eastern Americans from workplace discrimination by race. The case is also significant for the Court's judicial notice of the concept of race/ethnicity, as quoted above.

Native Americans have been subject to genocide, killings, kidnappings, harassment, dehumanization, and ripoffs by individuals, nonprofits, corporations, and by colonial, federal, state, and local governments in the US. In 2000, Kevin Gover, as Director of the **U.S. Bureau of Indian Affairs** (BIA), admitted that, since its creation in 1825, the BIA participated in the ethnic cleansing of Native Americans. It was the first official apology of its kind by the U.S. government for the genocide of Native Americans. Native Americans now focus attention on gaining civil rights and reclaiming treaty rights, both illustrated in *Morton v. Mancari* (1974), where the Court upheld Bureau of Indian Affairs preferred-employment for Native Americans under treaty law and affirmative action law. And, although *Santa Clara Pueblo v. Martinez* (1978) upheld the sovereignty of tribal courts under the Indian Civil Rights Act (1968), *Nevada v. Hicks* (2001) illustrates the continuing backlash by federal, state, and local governments to limit Native American tribal court jurisdiction and power. In this case, the Court limited the tribal court from any power in dealing with a case where a Nevada state game warden trashed the home of a tribal member on the reservation. Finally, in *City of Sherrill v. Oneida Indian Nation* (2005), the Court recognized that treaty rights were violated by federal, state, and local officials over 200 years in New York land takings. Yet, the Court forbade tribal members the right to buy back their historic and treaty-designated reservation territory in order to reclaim the lands for the tribal reservation (*denying* their tax-free-status

(*continued*)

ETHICS CASE STUDY | *Continued*

as reservation lands under state and local property tax law). Only monetary damages were allowed to the Oneida Indian Nation for the loss of historic reservation properties.

BOX 7.8 | Immigration the the U.S. Constitution

Congress shall have the power . . . to establish an uniform Rule of Naturalization.

(U.S. Constitution, Article I, Section 8, Clause 2) ▲

America is a nation of **immigrants**, and the human rights concerns of many peoples of various ethnicities often focus on immigration visa admissions, status, deportation, naturalization-citizenship, citizenship by birth or soil, and other U.S. citizenship policies. Before 1960, most immigrants to the US were from First World or northern countries. Since 1960, most immigrants to the US tend to come from Third World or southern countries. This change seems to add new problems of hate crime, work discrimination, and other human rights issues for new waves of immigrants, who may have different languages, cultures, cuisine, skills, and ethnicities than immigrants of the previous century. For example, in *Zadvydas v. Davis* (2001), the Court allowed indefinite detention in immigration camps for years in the forced deportation of a refugee immigrant until some country will agree to take him in—but none have. Currently, over **one-half million immigrants** are in **detention** while awaiting deportation.

Gender[86]

Women for most of Western history were considered chattel, like slaves, treated as property and often listed on the property deeds of farms and estates in colonial times. The common law doctrine of *coverture* did not allow a woman, by herself, to own real property, but her ownership was covered by a husband, father, son, brother, or other male guardian. Women were denied the right to own real property, to vote, to make contracts, to be educated, or to work (except in narrowly limited servant roles). Some of the territories, such as Wyoming, sought to attract more women settlers by being the first to offer the right to own property, contract, and vote. With a legal status like slaves, it is no wonder that many abolitionists were women, who lobbied for the 14th Amendment Equal Protection clause to cover women as well as the former slaves—only to have equality for women denied at the last minute. *Bradwell v. Illinois* (1872) illustrates the struggle for **women's rights**, in which the Court allowed the state of Illinois to constitutionally exclude women from admission to the legal profession, reasoning:

Man is, or should be, woman's protector and defender. The natural and proper timidity and delicacy which belongs to the female sex evidently unfits it for many of the occupations of civil life . . . The paramount destiny and mission of woman are to fulfill the noble and benign offices of wife and mother.

Yet, the women's movement was highly successful in mobilizing forces to ratify the 18th Amendment (prohibition) and 19th Amendment (women's right to vote), even without the right to vote in most of the states. Although Congress proposed the *Equal Rights Amendment* in 1972, there was no similar success in getting ratification. But, the US and states governments have passed statutes that grant these human rights, such as *comparable worth* in the Equal Pay Act of 1963, equality of sex as well as race in Title VII of the Civil Rights Act of 1964, the prohibition of gender discrimination in education under Title IX of the Education Amendments of 1972, and many other state and national statutes.

BOX 7.9 | The Framework of Equal Protection

<--->

Minimal	Intermediate	Strict
Scrutiny	Scrutiny	Scrutiny
(e.g., wealth)	(e.g., gender)	(e.g., race/ethnicity)

But the Court and others have begun to distinguish the human rights of women from those of blacks and others. In the 1970s, the Court formulated three tiers of equal protection classifications. Since before World War II, the Court had used a *rational basis test* to determine if a law or public action was unconstitutional in its arbitrary discrimination. The law/action was valid if the purpose behind it was a legitimate one and it was rational (articulable). But, since *Korematsu v. US* (1944), the Court treated race/ethnicity discrimination with *strict scrutiny*; if there is discrimination against race/ethnicity—the law or public action classifying persons must be necessary to achieve a compelling governmental interest. With issues of gender discrimination, the Court developed a middle tier, or **intermediate scrutiny**, that applied to discrimination by gender—the law or public action classifying persons must substantially relate to the achievement of an important governmental interest.

At the extreme end of discriminatory behavior in urban and public affairs, **hate crimes against women** are *not* reported as such by the U.S. Government or the 50 states, under the Hate Crimes Statistics Act of 1990. Crimes in which a woman is victimized because of her gender are reported as hate crimes only if they fall under some other protected hate crime classification. For example, the FBI tabulates hate crime reports to include classifications of male/female victims and assailants under hate crime

(continued)

categories of race/ethnicity, religion, sexual orientation, or disability. But the states and national government have not developed gender as a protected category of hate crimes, although bills are pending before the U.S. Congress at this writing that would change that. *US v. Morrison* (2000) illustrates the limits of the U.S. Congress in the federalization of policies to deal with hate against women, in which the U.S. Supreme Court ruled that Congress had no constitutional authority over rape of women as a hate crime under the commerce clause. Thus, a federal statute protecting women was invalid and the female victim could not sue under the statute against Virginia Tech for a date rape that the state or university would do nothing about. This may be because some crimes against women as females are already enhanced in their sentences under existing state laws. Similarly, in *American Booksellers Association v. Hudnut* (CA7, 1985), the 7th Circuit U.S. Court of Appeal struck down Indianapolis, Indiana, anti-pornography ordinances as unconstitutional, balancing freedom of sexual expression over the need to limit some extreme hate expressions toward women through pornographic subordination. But the reality of hate toward women as females is evident from local, state, and national crime reports in the US. The laws of many other countries have developed special hate crime protections for women—for example, Canada's anti-pornography laws are designed to protect women from extreme anti-women sexual expressions.

Workplace discriminations against women, especially sexual harassment, have become a major source of lawsuits in federal district courts under Title VII of the Civil Rights Act of 1964. In the core provisions of this statute, Title VII, 42 U.S.C. section 2000e-2, defines what is illegal, what employers cannot do. It, thus, defines equality in employment essentially as a negative right, as discussed in the introduction to this chapter. The law does not define directly what employers can do to promote diversity in the workplace. For example, in stating that employers cannot discriminate in regard to terms, conditions, or privileges of employment because of sex, it suggests that employers must not take sex into account, must be gender-blind. Ignoring stereotypes, myths, and biases which have been pervasive in our society and culture has not proven to be an easy task. Interpreting the language and intent of Congress in this regard has fallen to the federal courts. One of the most important cases addressing the meaning of gender neutrality and the question of discriminatory effects or impacts tackles the enduring issue of pregnancy. Significantly, in the case of *General Electric v. Gilbert* (1976), the Supreme Court determined that, since Congress did not expressly define discrimination in *Title VII*, it was appropriate for the Court to look to equal protection caselaw to define discrimination. The case involved an employer's disability coverage which excluded **pregnancy-related disability** for women.

Historically, pregnancy has been a most critical issue in defining the roles of women in society. Pregnancy traditionally had a negative impact on women's careers as they were often simply discharged or found themselves back at entry-level positions. Shortly after the *Gilbert* case, in *Nashville Gas Co. v. Satty* (1977), the Supreme Court upheld an employer's sick-leave policy that excluded pregnancy. Perhaps, because the *Gilbert* case came only shortly after a case addressing essentially the same issue in an equal protection context, the Supreme Court justices felt bound by precedent. Yet, as the dissenters noted in *Gilbert*, the Court was interpreting a statute, not the constitutionality of the statute. In any event, it was the dissenters who perhaps 'got it right' in *Gilbert*; less than two years later, in 1978, Congress amended Title VII to define discrimination "because of sex" as follows:

> The terms "because of sex" or "on the basis of sex" include, but are not limited to, because of or on the basis of pregnancy, childbirth, or related medical conditions; and women affected by pregnancy, childbirth, or related medical conditions shall be treated the same for all employment-related purposes, including the receipt of benefits under fringe benefit programs, as other persons not so affected but similar in their ability or inability to work. This subsection shall not require an employer to pay for health insurance benefits for abortion, except where the life of the mother would be endangered if the fetus is carried to term, or except where medical complications have arisen from an abortion.

Congress may have redefined neutrality to recognize or take into account inherent differences. Yet, incorporating difference, or diversity, into rights remains tied to an equal protection analysis which continues largely to focus on neutrality.

In 1987, the Supreme Court addressed the issue of gender neutrality versus preferences in regard to a California law mandating "special" benefits for women. In the case of *California Federal Savings & Loan v. Guerra* (1987), a female employee alleged that her employer violated California state law in not having her position or a similar alternate position open for her when she sought to return to work following pregnancy disability leave. Her employer challenged the legality of the California law under Title VII, 42 U.S.C. section 2000e-2.

Further, sexual harassment is also a form of employment discrimination based on gender and has great importance for urban and public affairs. Sexual harassment includes any unwelcome sexual advances, requests for sexual favors, and other verbal or physical conduct of a sexual nature when submission to or tolerance of it is made either explicitly or implicitly in a term of employment, or used as the basis for employment decisions, or it unreasonably interferes with one's work and creates a **hostile work environment**. Sexual harassment may be either **quid pro quo** (trading), sexual **favoritism** (for favored status at work), or hostile work environment (see above). Finally, in *Pennsylvania State Police v. Suders* (2004), the Court allowed a more streamlined path to the federal courts for a victim of sexual harassment while working with the Pennsylvania State Police. The Court

(*continued*)

reasoned that because Nancy Drew Suders could prove a "hostile working environment" so intolerable that quitting qualified as a fitting response, she could proceed directly to federal court and ignore the many administrative hearings required by the agency in sexual harassment complaints.

The two types of sexual harassment originally recognized by the courts include hostile work environment and quid pro quo harassment. The latter applies to supervisors who make sexual threats or offers usually tied to sexual acts, such as, "If you don't have sex with me, I will demote you," or "Have sex with me and I will promote you." Compliance with the sexual advances becomes a term of employment. The following question may be posed. Can such conduct ever be truly welcomed? Consider, when a supervisor threatens to fire a single mother (or father, for that matter), who may not have other immediate or favorable job prospects, if they do not have a sexual affair, if this is perhaps not a form of economic and psychological coercion. Such intimidation will influence the behavior of the victim. Nevertheless, where there is harassment by a supervisor, the victim must prove they did not welcome the advances. While the Supreme Court has recognized that a supervisor's conduct may be particularly threatening because of his or her power and authority, to prove this aggravated form of harassment, the plaintiff must also demonstrate that a tangible employment has resulted. In essence, the tangible action corroborates that the supervisor used their power. Thus, today, the Court no longer uses the term *quid pro quo*, referring rather to two types of hostile work environments.

When a plaintiff is unable to prove aggravated harassment by a supervisor, they may still seek to show a **hostile work environment**. Note, such harassment need not impair work performance if it creates an intimidating or hostile environment. The guidelines do not directly address other possible impacts on the victim. Following *Meritor Savings Bank v. Vinson* (1987), the Court first recognized that sexual harassment at the workplace violated the Civil Rights Act of 1964. The Court returned to address workplace sexual harassment in 1993. The case of *Harris v. Forklift Systems* (1993) clarified the issue of impacts as well as the elements necessary to a claim of hostile environment. Harris, a sales manager, quit her job after being subjected to verbal insults and sexual innuendos over a period of two years. She sued the company, claiming a hostile or abusive environment.

Since the *Harris* case, the Supreme Court has more particularly addressed issues of employer liability for a supervisor's actions and under circumstances where the employee quits their job because of the harassment. Lawsuits are rarely brought unless there is a significant probability of success. In discrimination lawsuits, a central question is, who pays? While employees and supervisors may be personally liable in a sexual harassment claim, they generally do not have the 'deep pockets' of an employer. The Equal Employment Opportunity Commission (EEOC) Guidelines define employer liability in regard to the conduct of fellow employees as follows:

an employer is responsible for acts of sexual harassment in the workplace where the employer (or its agents or supervisory employees) knows or should have known of the conduct, unless it can show that it took immediate and appropriate corrective actions.

If an employer promptly takes corrective actions, a victim of harassment is also more likely not to file a charge with the EEOC. Significantly, the standard or test for liability is an objective one.

In cases where there is no tangible action, a hostile environment claim can be presented but the employer may avoid liability by showing an affirmative defense that it exercised reasonable care to prevent and correct promptly the harassment and the employee "unreasonably" failed to take advantage of the preventive or corrective action. Where an employer has an effective sexual harassment policy and complaint process, the failure of an employee to utilize it may, therefore, shield the employer from liability in cases where the harasser is a supervisor or co-employee. The EEOC, however, adds that employee delay in bringing a complaint need not eliminate liability, but it may still limit the plaintiff's monetary damages.

Religion

Within the context of the public interests, **discrimination toward different religions** may be expressed by hate crimes such as vandalism of mosques, synagogues, churches, and so forth. It may also include discrimination at the workplace, by law enforcers, and other public actors. In *Employment Division v. Smith* (1990), Justice Scalia announced a **neutrality test** in dealing with religious discrimination by the government. In the case, the Court ruled that states may criminalize peyote under uniform and evenly applied drug laws, even if it criminalizes sincere religious practices within the Native American Church—infringing upon religious freedoms. Congress responded to the *Smith* decision with the Religious Freedom Restoration Act of 1993 (RFRA) to bolster the protection of religious freedoms. But in *City of Boerne v. Flores* (1997), the Court declared parts of the RFRA were unconstitutional. The Court allowed a City Historic Landmark Commission the power to stop a growing church from building any additions of any sort, because the historic landmark regulations were applied with neutrality, with no intent to specifically discrimination against the church. But the struggle for exceptions and freedom of religion in the US continues. In *Watchtower v. Stratton* (2002), the Court ruled that city administrators and police cannot require soliciting permits of Jehovah's Witnesses in order for them to canvas door to door. Because witnessing is their central religious belief, the city permit requirements were an unconstitutional burden on their free exercise of religion. And while *O'Lone v. Estate of Shabazz* (1987) ruled for the power of a state prison to deny Muslims an exception from uniform, valid regulations (he was denied rest on his holy day in prison work), the Court in *Cutter v. Wilkinson* (2005) upheld the Religious Land Use and Institutionalized

(*continued*)

Persons Act of 2000 (RLUIPA) to require that prisons must accommodate religious exercises, even of non-mainstream religions.[87]

Yet, religious peoples still suffer discrimination and hate from individuals, corporations, and even local, state, and national government agencies. In *Church of Lukumi Babalu Aye v. Hialeah* (1993), the Court stopped the attack by the city of Hialeah, Florida, against a local Santeria church, ruling that city ordinances specifically designed to end the religious practices of the Santeria were unconstitutional. Similarly, the Court invalidated state government actions and protected the hateful religious expressions of the Ku Klux Klan in *Capitol Square v. Pinette* (1995). The Court ruled that the Ku Klux Klan had a right to maintain a burning cross on the lawn of the Ohio state capitol at Christmastime, just as other religious groups could maintain symbols on the capitol grounds. Finally, the Court greatly limited and nearly overruled its decision in *Employment Division v. Smith* (1990) in *Gonzales v. O Centro* (2006). In *O Centro*, the Court invalidated the federal DEA prosecution of the Uniao Do Vegetal Church's sacramental use of hoasca. Hoasca is a tea brewed from Amazon Rainforest plants that contains DMT, a hallucinogen regulated under Schedule I of the Controlled Substances Act. The Court upheld the Religious Freedom Restoration Act of 1993 and protected religious exercises and use of the sacramental tea, even though the Federal Government asserted it was a crime under a uniform, valid, and evenly-applied drug enforcement law.

Of great importance to nonprofit administrators, the Court explicitly declared the religious **exemption** rule for religious nonprofits. In *Hosanna-Tabor Church v. EEOC* (2012), the Court upheld the right of a church organization to make decisions on hiring, firing, and other human resources decisions with ministerial personnel on the basis of compatibility with religious purposes of the church. Similarly, *Burwell v. Hobby Lobby* (2014) ruled that a closely held for-profit private corporation may have a religious exception from a regulation its owners have a religious objection to, if less restrictive means to further the goals of the law are available (i.e., contraceptives and abortion health benefits).

Sexuality

Throughout Western history, homosexuality has been persecuted and reviled as an abomination to God, as were other sexual orientations that differed from heterosexuality, such as bisexuality, transsexuality, bestiality, and intersexuality. With some historical exceptions, such as the classical Greeks, who embraced homosexuality, many Western societies believed that homosexuality was a sin to be punished by the gods or God. Of course, the ancient Judeo-Christian-Muslim laws also taught that other abominations were equally sinful and condemned, e.g., shaving your legs as a woman, shaving your face as a married man, any sort of hair dye or facial makeup, short haircuts for men or women, and many other personal bodily traits or uses that concealed or altered what was evidenced as God's intended creation. While many persons of differing sexuality have made great contributions to Western society, a negative stigma was attached to these differing

---

BOX 7.10 | 1993 Religious Freedom Restoration Act

In 1993, Congress enacted the Religious Freedom Restoration Act (RFRA) in response to the Supreme Court's ruling in *Employment Division v. Smith* (1990). In that ruling, the Court upheld an Oregon law used to deny unemployment benefits to two Native American men who lost their jobs because of their religious use of peyote. The Court determined that neutral, generally applicable laws may be applied to religious practices even when not supported by a compelling government interest.

After Smith, Congress passed RFRA to prevent the government from substantially burdening a person's free-exercise rights unless the burden furthered a compelling government interest and was the least restrictive means of furthering that interest. Section 2000bb-2(1) declared the law applicable to any form of government—federal, state, or otherwise. In applying RFRA to the states, Congress relied on its powers under Section 5 of the 14th Amendment to adopt and enforce laws that protect citizens' due-process and equal-protection rights. It is on this ground that the Supreme Court ruled RFRA unconstitutional as applied to state and local governments.

The Supreme Court's ruling came in 1997 in a case involving a zoning dispute in Texas. In 1995, the Catholic archbishop of San Antonio applied for a building permit to enlarge a church in Boerne (pronounced "Bernie"), Texas. Located in a historic district, the church was no longer large enough for its congregation. The zoning board turned down the archbishop's request, citing historic-preservation laws. The archbishop sued the city, claiming that RFRA required the city to exempt the church from its historic-preservation laws.

The federal district court, however, found that Congress had never had the constitutional authority to enact the law and apply it to the states. The 5th U.S. Circuit Court of Appeals reversed that decision, finding the act constitutional and declaring that the denial of the permit substantially burdened the Catholic diocese's free exercise of religion. City officials appealed to the Supreme Court.

In *City of Boerne v. Flores*, the Court said RFRA exceeded Congress's authority under the 14th Amendment. The Court ruled RFRA was not a proper exercise of Congress's enforcement power under Section 5 of the Amendment because it violated the separation of powers.

Source: reprinted from article by Greg Groninger, "Religious Freedom Restoration Act Analysis," *First Amendment Center*, retrieved from www.firstamendmentcenter.org/analysis.aspx?id=14383

(*continued*)

sexual orientations. For example, the American Psychiatric Association listed homosexuality as a psychiatric disorder until 1974.

Homosexual and other sexual orientations were incorporated into the **English common law crime of sodomy** in the late sixteenth century, making these doctrines of canon law (the code of the church) into the proscribed law of the land, and punishable by public authorities as well.[88] By 1961 in the US, all 50 states and the District of Columbia had criminalized homosexual sodomy. But over recent decades homosexuals and other sexual orientations have become more tolerated; in 1986, only 24 states and the District of Columbia criminalized homosexual sodomy; and today, no states criminalize homosexuality. Yet the hate and discrimination continue and, according to reports to the FBI under the Hate Crime Statistics Act, male homosexuals are often the target of violent hate crimes, most typically some form of extreme intimidation offenses. Scholars and practitioners argue that the numbers are even higher because many hate crimes against homosexuals go unreported. In fact, recent studies have concluded that Lesbian-Gay-Bisexual-Transsexual (**LGBT**) **people** are twice as likely to be targeted for **hate crime** as African Americans, and the rate of hate crime against them has surpassed all other crime rate growth.[89]

Should homosexual and other differing sexual orientations between consenting adults be a civil right protected from the reach of the law? *Bowers v. Hardwick* (1986) denied the right to privacy for consensual adult sexual conduct, upholding Georgia's sodomy statute as it applied to men and women, homosexuals, heterosexuals, and other sexual orientations. But in *Lawrence v. Texas* (2003), the Court overruled *Bowers v. Hardwick* (1986) and struck down a Texas sodomy statute as unconstitutional for focusing only on male homosexuality in sodomy and arbitrary discrimination. The Court also cited European and other comparative examples of laws on the privacy of consensual adult sexual conduct. In the Defense of Marriage Act (1996) (DOMA), U.S. Congress defined marriage for federal purposes as the union of one man to one woman, allowing states to refuse recognition of same-sex marriages of other states. The U.S. Supreme Court ruled the DOMA statute was unconstitutional discrimination in *US v. Windsor* (2013). And in *Obergefell v. Hodges* (2015), the Court ruled all state and local laws prohibiting same-sex marriage were violations of constitutional rights to privacy and equal protection of the laws.

Discrimination and violations of human rights continue against homosexuals and people of differing sexuality. In addition, human rights violations may occur between homosexuals or people of differing sexuality. In *Oncale v. Sundowner Offshore Services* (1997), the Court ruled that sexual harassment at the workplace was *not* limited to rights violations of women by men but may include homosexual harassment between men. From 1993 to 2012, the U.S. military followed a "Don't Ask, Don't Tell" policy to avoid discrimination against sexual orientation at the workplace, and many other state and local public and nonprofit agencies still follow the policy. A series of cases have ruled that homosexuals and those of differing sexual orientations may not violate the 'free speech' rights of others who voice their disapproval of homosexuals or force their way into the associations or public forums of the groups of others who disapprove of homosexuality or alternative sexual orientations. For example, in *Hurley v. Irish American GLIB* (1995), a gay-lesbian-intersexual-bisexual group (GLIB) asked the state of Massachusetts to use its authority to force their entry into a private St. Patrick's Day parade in Boston, Massachusetts. The Court ruled that the state may not require private parade organizers to include groups conveying a message that the organizers do not approve of.

Disability

"Disability Law" is the phrase that Chief Justice Roberts has given to this subject area of the public interests. Discriminations based on abilities or disabilities are legally defined as "arbitrary partiality or prejudice on the basis of a person's physical or mental disability." Over 43 million Americans have one or more disability. Historically, the disabled were segregated, often sterilized and institutionalized, and suffered discrimination in employment, housing, public accommodations, education, transport, communication, recreation, health services, voting, and access to public services.

BOX 7.11 | Federal Statutes on Disability

Significant national legislation in recent decades addresses discrimination by abilities, including:

- *Age Discrimination in Employment Act of 1967* (ADEA) restricts age discrimination in employment.
- *Architectural Barriers Act of 1968* requires greater access to public buildings.
- *Rehabilitation Act of 1973* prohibits employment discrimination against people with disabilities.
- *Comprehensive Employment and Training Act of 1973 (CETA)* created jobs and job training programs for the disabled.
- *Rehabilitation Education Act of 1976 (REA)* develops affirmative action for the disabled.
- *Americans with Disabilities Act of 1990 (ADA)* requires the reasonable accommodation of the disabled.

Issues of physical ability have tended to focus on the Age Discrimination in Employment Act (ADEA) and the Americans with Disabilities Act (ADA). *Gregory v. Ashcroft* (1991) illustrates age discrimination issues in state government, where the state of Missouri required state judges

(*continued*)

to retire by age 70. The Court reasoned that the people of a state could restrict a judge's age in retirement or in taking office, and the federal ADEA or 14th Amendment couldn't restrict the sovereignty of the state in such matters. However, in *Smith v. City of Jackson* (2005), the Court ruled that city police officers alleging age discrimination in a new pay scheme had a valid claim, were not limited by state sovereignty, and could proceed in the federal court. Further, the city police officers could proceed to litigation with use of evidence proof of either disparate treatment (*de jure* or policies by law mandating age discrimination) or disparate impact (*de facto* age discrimination without written policies, but discriminatory as implemented). But the Court added that the police officers had failed to state a sufficiently specific disparate impact claim and seemed to express doubt that they would succeed. *Pennsylvania Department of Corrections v. Yeskey* (1998) illustrates discrimination litigation under the ADA, in which the Court ruled that the ADA was unambiguous in extending its application to state prisons and inmates. The prison must reasonably accommodate all persons with disabilities for all of its programs. So, this inmate with hypertension must be accommodated in a special boot camp program for early release. In *US v. Georgia* (2006), the Court ruled that the ADA was not limited by state sovereignty and could be used by an inmate to sue for monetary damages when a state prison did not reasonably accommodate his disabilities. Tony Goodman, a paraplegic inmate at the Georgia State Prison in Reidsville, was confined to his 12- by 3-feet cell for 23 to 24 hours a day and couldn't even turn his wheelchair around, was unable to use the toilet or shower, and was often forced to sit in his own feces and urine for hours while prison personnel refused to help him. The Court, in a strongly worded Opinion of the Court by conservative Justice Scalia, decried the lack of decency afforded Goodman and ordered a new trial applying the ADA to liability of the Georgia State Prison.

Issues of mental disability typically involve what the Court simply labels as either some type of mental illness or mental retardation. *Heller v. Doe* (1993) illustrates how the Court distinguishes the human rights of the mentally ill from the mentally retarded for determining their involuntary commitment to various institutions for care. The Court ruled that the standard of proof required for commitment of the mentally ill is beyond a reasonable doubt, while commitment of the mentally retarded requires only clear and convincing evidence. The Court also upheld the practice of allowing close family members and guardians the legal status to represent parties in these cases. In *Atkins v. Virginia* (2002), the Court held that the imposition of the death penalty on a severely mental retarded defendant was unconstitutional cruel and unusual punishment violating the 8th Amendment. Similarly, in *Roper v. Simmons* (2005), the Court also found that the imposition of the death penalty on juveniles under the age of 18 was unconstitutionally cruel and unusual punishment, violating the 8th Amendment.

Discussion

- How are values of diversity and anti-discrimination summarized by John Rawls?
- What are the *similarities* in anti-discrimination constitutional regime values by categories of race, ethnicity, gender, religion, sexuality, and disability?
- What are the *differences* in anti-discrimination constitutional regime values by categories of race, ethnicity, gender, religion, sexuality, and disability?
- How would you summarize public values of diversity and anti-discrimination? ▲

CONCLUSION

What are the lessons of human resources management and professionalism for administration in the public interests? Both public personnel administration and human resource management play critical roles in the formulation, development, and evaluation of a sound system of functions and values for enabling and protecting the worth of civil servants, as well as promoting the political and legal rights of offended groups and citizens as a whole. The history of public service selection and human resources management demonstrate the pursuit of the public interests. Developments in the processes of human resources management also reference this attention to public interests values. Sufficient attention is necessary to ensure the future well-being of both the servant and the served. Our example of whistleblowing may help illuminate the complexity of administration in the public interests.

The extended ethics case study of diversity and discrimination, with many examples, was included to illustrate more than just the minimal rules of the game of law as applied to administration in the public interests. These many case examples are grouped by the topical areas of anti-discrimination laws and policies catalogued by the U.S. government: race, ethnicity, religion, sexuality, and disability. These case examples of ordinary disputes with public administrators also illustrate the duty of the public interests—and its attendant deontological duties—in the legal resolution of these disputes. Our extended analysis and ethical critique of discrimination in American public affairs points to the plural nature of the public interests in changing complex ways of delineating the reparation of past injustices and continuation of equal opportunity. We believe developments of the public administration profession recounted throughout this chapter and others points to the ascendance of the public interests as an applied ethics concept.

ACTION STEPS

1. Survey different local governments. Speak with a top-level public official and inquire: if, and how, they apply reinvention of government principles in public employment. What have been the results?

2. Contact a state or local government jurisdiction human resources management department—in person or via the web. Inquire how the basic steps of human resources management are carried out, especially the *compensation* and *training and development* steps.

3. Make the decision—individually or in groups—to hire one of three candidates for a public service agency. Assume each applicant is nearly identical in their background, education, experience, and skills. Choose one for the public service agency position. The pool includes one black and two white applicants. Given the public interests of diversity, should you choose the one black applicant? Why, or why not?

4. Consider the ethics of discrimination in public affairs—by race, ethnicity, gender, religion, sexuality, and disability—and forge a general, universal statement of a duty to diversity in public affairs. Does your rule include both anti-discrimination and affirmative action concepts in one statement?

KEY CONCEPTS AND NAMES

NOTES

1 Mitchell F. Rice, "Organizational Culture, Social Equity, and Diversity: Teaching Public Administration Education in the Postmodern Era," *Journal of Public Affairs Education* 10 (2004): 143–54.

2 See, generally, Stephen E. Condrey, ed., *Handbook of Human Resource Management in Government*, 3rd ed. (San Francisco, CA: Jossey-Bass, 2010).

3 N. Joseph Cayer, *Public Personnel Administration*, 4th ed. (Belmont, CA: Thomson-Wadsworth, 2004), 17–41; Grover Starling, *Managing the Public Sector*, 7th ed. (Belmont, CA: Thomson-Wadsworth, 2005), 454–63; Nicholas Henry, *Public Administration and Public Affairs*, 9th ed. (Upper Saddle River, NJ: Prentice-Hall, 2004), 250–55; and George J. Gordon and Michael E. Milakovich, *Public Administration in America*, 6th ed. (New York, NY: St. Martin's Press, 1998), 254–8.

4 Frederick Mosher, *Democracy and the Public Service* (Cambridge: Oxford University Press, 1968), 53–98.

5 According to Nicholas Henry, Starling attributes the first five periods to Mosher, and the sixth period to Dennis L. Dresang, *Public Personnel Management and Public Policy* (New York, NY: Addison Wesley Longman, 2003). See Grover Starling, *Managing the Public Sector*, 7th ed. (Belmont, CA: Thomson-Wadsworth, 2005), 458–9. The seventh phase is attributable to Henry.

6 See Leonard D. White, *The Federalists: A Study in Administrative History* (New York, NY: Macmillan, 1956), 517–18.

7 Ibid., 3.

8 Ibid., 29. See also Leonard D. White, *The Jeffersonians: A Study in Administrative History: 1801–1829* (New York, NY: Macmillan, 1959), 5.

9 Nicholas Henry, *Public Administration and Public Affairs*, 9th ed. (Upper Saddle River, NJ: Prentice-Hall, 2004), 251.

10 Leonard D. White, *The Jacksonians: A Study in Administrative History* (New York, NY: Macmillan, 1954), 5.

11 Ibid., 310.

12 Leonard D. White, *The Republican Era: A Study in Administrative History, 1869–1901* (New York, NY: The Free Press, 1958), 6.

13 Ibid., 8–14.

14 Ibid., 297.

15 See Richard J. Stillman II, *Creating the American State: The Moral Reformers and the Modern Administrative World They Made* (Tuscaloosa: University of Alabama Press, 1998).

16 David H. Rosenbloom and Robert S. Kravchuk, *Public Administration: Understanding Management, Politics, and Law in the Public Sector*, 6th ed. (Boston: McGraw-Hill, 2005), 209–10.

17 See Grover Starling, *Managing the Public Sector*, 7th ed. (Belmont, CA: Thomson-Wadsworth, 2005), 461.

18 Robert B. Denhardt and Joseph W. Grubbs, *Public Administration: An Action Orientation*, 4th ed. (Belmont, CA: Wadsworth, 2003), 254.

19 Ibid.

20 Robert B. Denhardt and Joseph W. Grubbs, *Public Administration: An Action Orientation*, 4th ed. (Belmont, CA: Wadsworth, 2003), 213.

21 Nicholas Henry, *Public Administration and Public Affairs*, 9th ed. (Upper Saddle River, NJ: Prentice-Hall, 2004), 255.

22 Alan K. Campbell, "Civil Service Reform: A New Commitment," *Public Administration Review* 38 (#2, March/April 1978): 99–103.

23 See Robert B. Denhardt and Joseph W. Grubbs, *Public Administration: An Action Orientation*, 4th ed. (Belmont, CA: Wadsworth, 2003), 214–17; and George J. Gordon and Michael E. Milakovich, *Public Administration in America*, 6th ed. (New York, NY: St. Martin's Press, 1998), 281.

24 Donald F. Kettl and James W. Fesler, *The Politics of the Administrative Process,* 3rd ed. (Washington, DC: CQ Press, 2005), 86.

25 "Agencies Submitting Data to FPDS-NG as of December 11, 2008," The Project on Government Oversite, retrieved December 18, 2008 from www.fpdsng.com/downloads/agency_data_submit_list.htm

26 Nicholas Henry, *Public Administration and Public Affairs*, 9th ed. (Upper Saddle River, NJ: Prentice-Hall, 2004), 334.

27 Ibid., 337.

28 Steven W. Hays and Richard C. Kearney, "Anticipated Changes in Human Resource Management: Views from the Field," *Public Administration Review* 61 (#5, September/October 2001): 585–97.

29 National Performance Review, *From Red Tape to Results: Creating a Government that Works Better and Costs Less* (Washington, DC: U.S. Government Printing Office, 1993).

30 Ibid., 20–26.

31 Steven W. Hays and Richard C. Kearney, "Anticipated Changes in Human Resource Management: Views from the Field," *Public Administration Review* 61 (#5, September/October 2001): 217.

32 For example, W. David Patton, Stephanie L. Witt, Nicholas Lovrich, and Patricia J. Fredericksen, *Human Resource Management: The Public Service Perspective* (Boston: Houghton Mifflin, 2002).

33 Ibid.

34 Michael C. LeMay, *U.S. Immigration: A Reference Handbook* (Santa Barbara, CA: ABC-CLIO, 2004), 186.

35 United States Census Bureau, "2007 Census of Governments," retrieved December 18, 2008 from www.census.gov/Press-Release/www/releases/archives/employment_occupations/012797.html

36 Bureau of Labor Statistics, "Federal Government Excluding Postal Service," updated March 12, 2008, retrieved December 18, 2008.

37 Nicholas Henry, *Public Administration and Public Affairs*, 9th ed. (Upper Saddle River, NJ: Prentice-Hall, 2004), 257. Henry also cites the following: U.S. Merit Systems Protection Board, "Are New College Grads Landing Government Jobs?", *Issues of Merit* (September 2002): 4–5; Philip E. Crewson, "Are the Best and the Brightest Fleeing Public Sector Employment? Evidence from the National Longitudinal Survey of Youth," *Public Productivity and Management Review* 20 (#4, 1997): 363–71.

38 U.S. Office of Personnel Management, "Executive Branch Retirement Statistics: Fiscal Years 2007–2016," February 2017, retrieved May 17, 2018 from www.opm.gov/policy-data-oversight/data-analysis-documentation/federal-employment-reports/reports-publications/executive-branch-retirement-statistics-fy2006-2015.pdf

39 Michael C. LeMay, *U.S. Immigration: A Reference Handbook* (Santa Barbara, CA: ABC-CLIO, 2004), 189.

40 Nicholas Henry, *Public Administration and Public Affairs*, 9th ed. (Upper Saddle River, NJ: Prentice-Hall, 2004), 256.

41 Office of Personnel Management. "About the SES," retrieved December 18, 2008 from www.opm.gov/ses/about_ses/history.asp

42 See "Salary Table 2004-ES: Rates of Basic Pay for Members of the Senior Executive Service, Effective January 2004," U.S. Office of Personnel Management, retrieved October 2007 from www.opm.gov/oca/04tables/pdf/es.pdf

43 For a summary of the law, see "SL 60001.675 *Intergovernmental Personnel Act of 1970*," Social Security Administration, retrieved July 2005 from www.ssa.gov/policy/poms.nsf/lnx/1960001675?opendocument

44 George J. Gordon and Michael E. Milakovich, *Public Administration in America*, 6th ed. (New York, NY: St. Martin's Press, 1998), 1998, 262. For an extensive survey of results on the use of broad-banding, see Human Resources Management Panel, "Broadband Pay Experience in the Public Sector," *National Academy of Public Administration* (August 2003): 1–39, retrieved October 2007 from http://71.4.192.38/NAPA/NAPAPubs.nsf/17bc036fe939efd685256951004e37f4/0e93d959629dffd385256d9d004dbe30/$FILE/BroadbandPayPublic-03-07.pdf

45 National Commission on the State and Local Public Service, *Hard Truths/Tough Choices: An Agenda for State and Local Reform* (Albany, NY: Nelson A. Rockefeller Institute of Government, 1993).

46 Michael C. LeMay, *U.S. Immigration: A Reference Handbook* (Santa Barbara, CA: ABC-CLIO, 2004), 191.

47 Nicholas Henry, *Public Administration and Public Affairs*, 9th ed. (Upper Saddle River, NJ: Prentice-Hall, 2004), 257, 258. See also Gregory B. Lewis and Sue A. Frank, "Who Wants to Work for the Government?" *Public Administration Review* 62 (#4, July/August 2002): 395-404.

48 John Nalbandian, "The U.S. Supreme Court's 'Consensus' on Affirmative Action," *Public Administration Review* 49 (#1, January/February 1989): 38–45. Nalbandian examines how the Court analyzed *Griggs* and other affirmative action cases in order that it might justify the public employer to consider race in personnel actions and decisions.

49 Nicholas Henry, *Public Administration and Public Affairs*, 9th ed. (Upper Saddle River, NJ: Prentice-Hall, 2004), 280.

50 George J. Gordon and Michael E. Milakovich, *Public Administration in America*, 6th ed. (New York, NY: St. Martin's Press, 1998), 265.

51 Most merit systems, whether at the national or sub-national levels, require the top three candidates. (Note: In many instances this rule has expanded to include more than just the top three candidates.) As you can imagine, this *rule of three* is controversial because it can be used to discriminate against women and ethnic minorities. Veterans also are able to receive additional points in the overall ranking system—simply because they are veterans. Other methods are becoming more acceptable, including web-based advertising and recruiting.

52 George J. Gordon and Michael E. Milakovich, *Public Administration in America*, 6th ed. (New York, NY: St. Martin's Press, 1998), 257-8.

53 Grover Starling, *Managing the Public Sector*, 7th ed. (Belmont, CA: Thomson-Wadsworth, 2005), 489.

54 See Evelina R. Moulder, "Salaries of Municipal Officials, 2000," in *The Municipal Yearbook 2001*, ed. International City/County Management Association (Washington, DC: ICMA, 2001), 91–114; and Evelina R. Moulder, "Salaries of County Officials, 2000," in *The Municipal Yearbook 2001*, ed. International City/County Management Association (Washington, DC: ICMA, 2001), 115-35.

55 For example, Paula England, *Comparable Worth: Social Institutions and Social Change* (New York, NY: Routledge, 1993); Barbara J. Nelson, *Leadership and Diversity: A Case Book* (Los Angeles: UCLA Press, 2004); Norma M. Riccucci, *Women, Minorities and Unions in the Public Sector* (New York, NY: Praeger, 1990); Norma M. Riccucci and Katherine C. Naff, *Personnel Management in Government: Politics and Process*, 6th ed. (New York, NY: Routledge, 2007).

56 James L. Perry, Trent Engbers and So Yun Jun, "Back to the Future? Performance-Related Pay, Empirical Research, and the Perils of Persistence," *Public Administration Review* 69 (#1, 2009): 1–31.

57 James S. Bowman, "The Success of Failure: The Paradox of Performance Pay," *Review of Public Personnel Administration* 30 (#1, 2010): 70–88.

58 Jonathan Walters, "Worth the Money?", *Governing* (July 2004): 34–7.

59 Even within public sector employees there are gaps. Consider the State of North Carolina's pay system for its top officials in the UNC system compared with counterparts in similar or the same non-educational-based positions. According to the *Raleigh News and Observer*'s reporting of a 2004 study, the average salary for lawyers at the three largest universities and the UNC system was $165,594, well above the norm for the state. UNC-Chapel Hill's top attorney, Leslie Strohm, for example, makes $230,000, which is more than double that of State Attorney General Roy Cooper. David McCoy, the state budget director, makes about $125,000, while Charles Leffler, the vice chancellor for finance and business at North Carolina State University, makes $203,000. In addition, the average salary for UNC chancellors was nearly $191,000, while cabinet members and Council of State secretaries drew a paltry $102,264. "Something is wrong in Denmark," paraphrasing a famous saying. Some discussion has been made by states and localities at offering merit pay—and some in fact do offer some type of performance pay—but the number of extra dollars to award the best employees is usually limited, given that it is dictated by tight budgets, compounded by lean revenues and high expenditures. Beyond these complications, the question of pay tied to performance is problematic. How does a state agency or municipal department award performance pay? How is the performance measured? And how is the performance pay apportioned?

60 George R. Gray and others, "Training Practices in State Government Agencies," *Public Personnel Management* 26 (#2, Summer 1997): 187–202.

61 Michael C. LeMay, *U.S. Immigration: A Reference Handbook* (Santa Barbara, CA: ABC-CLIO, 2004), 196–7.

62 Grover Starling, *Managing the Public Sector*, 7th ed. (Belmont, CA: Thomson-Wadsworth, 2005), 234.

63 The following ideas are drawn from Robert B. Denhardt and Joseph W. Grubbs, *Public Administration: An Action Orientation*, 4th ed. (Belmont, CA: Wadsworth, 2003), 229–31.

64 Ibid., 231.

65 Some of the important public unions are the American Federation of State, County, and Municipal Employees (AFSCME), National Education Association (NEA), American Federation of Teachers (AFT), National Federation of Federal Employees, National Treasury Employees Union, Postal Workers Union, and the National Association of Letter Carriers. Each union is designed to promote and defend its members' positions, both economically and professionally. In addition, public labor unions are becoming more of a political force to be reckoned with, particularly at the state level, where some 43 states have comprehensive labor-relations laws, most of which are favorable toward unions than similar federal laws.

66 Robert B. Denhardt and Joseph W. Grubbs, *Public Administration: An Action Orientation*, 4th ed. (Belmont, CA: Wadsworth, 2003), 233.

67 Debra W. Stewart, "Theoretical Foundations of Ethics in Public Administration: Approaches to Understanding Moral Action," *Administration and Society* 23, no. 3 (November 1991): 362.

68 John Rawls, *A Theory of Justice* (Cambridge, MA: Harvard University Press, 1971).

69 Debra W. Stewart, "Theoretical Foundations of Ethics in Public Administration: Approaches to Understanding Moral Action," *Administration and Society* 23 (#3, November 1991): 363.

70 This problem comes from Nicholas Henry, *Public Administration and Public Affairs*, 9th ed. (Upper Saddle River, NJ: Pearson, 2004), 440.

71 For example, Mario A. Rivera and James D. Ward, "Toward an Analytical Framework for the Study of Race and Police Violence, *Public Administration Review* 77 (#2, 2017): 242–50; Mario A. Rivera and James D. Ward, *Institutional Racism, Organizations & Public Policy* (New York, NY: Peter Lang, 2014); James Ward, "Race, Ethnicity, and Law Enforcement Profiling: Implications for Public Policy," *Public Administration Review* 62 (#6, 2002): 726–35.

72 Michael D. Reisig and Robert J. Kane, eds., *The Oxford Handbook of Police and Policing* (New York, NY: Oxford University Press, 2014).

73 Martha A. Myers and Susette M. Talarico, *The Social Contexts of Criminal Sentencing* (New York, NY: Springer, 1987).

74 Ibid.

75 Grover Starling, *Managing the Public Sector*, 7th ed. (Belmont, CA: Thomson-Wadsworth, 2005), 472.

76 Robert B. Denhardt and Joseph W. Grubbs, *Public Administration: An Action Orientation*, 4th ed. (Belmont, CA: Wadsworth, 2003), 240.

77 Nicholas Henry, *Public Administration and Public Affairs*, 9th ed. (Upper Saddle River, NJ: Prentice-Hall, 2004), 277.

78 Ibid., 278.

79 *Firefighters Local Union #1784 v. Stotts* (1984).

80 *U.S. v. Paradise*, 480 U.S. 149 (1987).

81 Nicholas Henry, *Public Administration and Public Affairs*, 9th ed. (Upper Saddle River, NJ: Prentice-Hall, 2004), 288, cites a survey done by Charlotte Steeh and Maria Krysan, "The Polls—Trends: Affirmative Action and the Public, 1970–1995," *Public Opinion Quarterly* 60 (Spring 1996): 144–5.

82 Nelson C. Dometrius and Lee Sigelman, "Assessing Progress Toward Affirmative Action Goals in State and Local Government: A New Benchmark," *Public Administration Review* 44 (#3, 1984): 241–6.

83 Sylvester Murray and others, "The Role Demands and Dilemmas of Minority Public Administrators: The Herbert Thesis Revisited," *Public Administration Review* 54 (#5, September/October 1994): 409–17; James D. Slack, "Affirmative Action and City Managers: Attitudes Toward Recruitment of Women," *Public Administration Review* 47 (#2, March/April 1987): 199–206; and Pan Suk Kim and Gregory B. Lewis, "Asian Americans in the Public Service: Success, Diversity, and Discrimination," *Public Administration Review* 54 (#3, May/June 1994): 285–90.

84 Justice White, *St. Francis College v. Al-Khazraji* 481 U.S. 604 (1987), fn. 1.

85 Anthony LaRose, *Juarez: Seeds in the Desert* (Tampa, FL: Pumpkin Publishing, 2015).

86 We sincerely appreciate the advice and editing of Susan Lentz, PhD, JD, in this section on gender issues of diversity. For further reading, see, for example, Maria J. D'Agostino and Helisse Levine, eds., *Women in Public Administration:Theory and Practice* (Sudbury, MD: Jones & Bartlette, 2011); Bruce Cannon Gibney, *A Generation of Sociopaths: How the Baby Boomers Betrayed America* (New York, NY: Hachette Books, 2017), 316–17; Mary E. Guy and Sean McCandless, "Social Equity: Its Legacy, Its Promise," *Public Administration Review* 72 (2012): 5–13; Camilla Stiver,

Gender Images In Public Administration: Legitimacy and the Administrative State (Thousand Oaks, CA: Sage Publications, 2002).

87 Mary K. Stohr and Anthony Walsh, *Corrections: From Research, to Policy, to Practice* (Los Angeles, CA: Sage Publications, 2018).

88 Bradley S. Chilton, "Cliobernetics, Christianity, and the Common Law," *Law Library Journal* 83 (1991): 355–62.

89 Haeyoun Park and Iaryna Mykhayalyshyn, "LGBT People Are More Likely to Be Targets of Hate Crimes Than Any Other Minority Group," *New York Times* (June 16, 2016), retrieved from www.nytimes.com/interactive/2016/06/16/us/hate-crimes-against-lgbt.html

Public Financial Management and Corruption

Each State Party shall, in accordance with the fundamental principles of its legal system, develop and implement or maintain effective, coordinated anti-corruption policies that promote the participation of society and reflect the principles of the rule of law, proper management of public affairs and public property, integrity, transparency and accountability.

—(United Nations Convention Against Corruption (2003)[1]

BOX 8.1 | CHAPTER OBJECTIVES

1 Survey the underlying assumptions of political economy and critique neoliberal economic theory.

2 Summarize public financial management by the history, steps, and processes of public budgeting.

3 Overview public financial management concepts of public finance, taxation, and deficit issues.

4 Discuss the impact of public financial management practices on the public interests.

5 Critique the public service ethics issues of corruption, especially within public financial management.

The **2003 United Nations Convention Against Corruption** is the only legally binding universal anti-corruption instrument. This multilateral treaty takes a broad mandate to the global problem of public corruption by upholding the rule of law, requiring express appropriate rules for public financial and property management, transparency, accountability, and integrity. Most United Nations Member State Parties have agreed to the Convention, including the US in 2003. Surprisingly, the 2013 ASPA Code of Ethics doesn't mention the word *corruption*, or specifically reference the related ethical concepts of conflicts of interests, bribery, **embezzlement,** and other dishonest use of authority for personal benefit. Yet, public corruption is the topic of greatest focus in legislation on ethics for public administrators.[2]

This chapter addresses the pivotal issue of corruption in public service, especially in federal public service. The 2017 U.S. Congress Joint Economic Committee reported that "Over the past six months, the Office of Government Ethics has received 39,105 inquiries—up more than 5,000 percent over the comparable period leading up to President Obama's 2012 election and first months in office."[3] While many today want change, no one wants live in corruption, moral myopia, or sociopathic upheaval of public bureaucrats. We normally read about corruption, graft, and similar unethical practices as part of developing countries. Many scholars in public administration don't see the relevance of ethics or anti-corruption for U.S. public service—these are problems for the Third World. Particularly with financial resources management, scholars perceive few problems of ethics or corruption. If public corruption or mal-accounting are exposed here by the media, it's dismissed as the action of a "bad apple" or individual crime. And the response seems to be "it isn't my job to fix" such an aberration, "I'm just the public bookkeeper." Are we so advanced in public management theory, so removed from reality, that we fail to see what practitioners and the public sees—the corruption of the public service? This may explain why the ascendant Public Management Research Association (PMRA) provides almost no attention at their academic conferences to corruption, administrative evil, transparency, and ethics (only 0.58 percent of PMRA panels). In contrast, the traditional American Society for Public Administration (ASPA) seeks out the membership and input of practitioners and provides a high level of attention to these topics.[4]

Jesse Burkhead's classic book *Government Budgeting* laid out a primary **historical purpose** of budgeting, public finance, and financial management practices— to **limit corruption,** graft, treasury raids, pilfering, boss-rule, and irresponsible wasteful expenditure.[5] Not only in a distant past to control some king's treasury raid or pilfering, but also our contemporary U.S. constitutional experience. The Constitution provided that "No money shall be drawn from the treasury, but in consequence of appropriation made by law; and a regular statement and account of the receipts and expenditures of all public money shall be published from time to time."[6] In the first century of constitutional budgeting, it was the mal-accounting of surpluses that was seen as the cause of public corruption and vice: "The remarkable thing is not that the system breeds corruption, but that it should work at all."[7] Urban reformers, such as the New York Bureau of Municipal Research, proposed budgeting-by-law systems in the cities, because "'boss rule,' graft, and corruption had proceeded to the point where it was extremely difficult to carry on transactions with governments on a rational basis."[8] This antipathy toward graft and corruption in the cities also contributed to reform of national government budgeting, leading to the eventual passage of the 1921 Budget and Accounting Act.[9] With rapid growth of budget expenditures and deficit spending, the vices of mal-accounting brought new responsibilities for public administrators to anticipate, audit, police, and administer all aspects of budgeting responsibility and accountability, such as controlling the influence of lobbyists, gift-giving, embezzlement, and other corruption.[10] Today, public administration programs now include extensive curricula and research on **fraud, waste, abuse,** and corruption in public organizations, with public agencies incorporating techniques of digital forensics and forensic accounting to take control of mal-accounting, corruption, and other financial vices.[11]

When Donald Trump submitted his first U.S. budget bill as President in 2017, the message emblazoned on the cover of the proposed budget read: "America

First: A Budget Blueprint to Make America Great Again." We should not take for granted that this budget bill and the scrutinized **budget process** documents precisely the kind of proper management of public finances and property urged by the 2003 U.N. Convention Against Corruption. The very structures, tools, and processes of financial management have been designed to fulfill the public interests without corruption—without betraying the trust of the citizens who paid these monies—in these public financial resources management.

Public **financial management** is not an exact science; neither is it purely politics where only your political connections rule; the decision is political, but the execution is somewhat scientific. What is true today—much more so than it was prior to the beginning of the twentieth century—is the increased involvement of mayors, governors, presidents, and other chief executives in the formation, allocation, and development of financial management. The role of chief executives in the budgeting process is enhanced largely because of the perceived need for greater executive oversight, management, and political checks and balance with the legislative branch. Financial management is about making tough philosophical choices about public funds in an open environment of participants.

The chapter begins, first, with a survey of the political economy of public financial management, including neoliberal economic theories that are currently popular with both Democrats and Republicans. Second, from these economic assumptions, we analyze the two basic elements of public financial management—public budgeting and public finance—and how each is put to use to administer public interests. Some argue that public budgeting is simply the allocation of goods and resources, based largely upon individual and/or group perspectives—the public interests are simply relational. So, too, are those who argue public finance is merely the allocation of who pays—with no public interests goals in mind. We contend that the patterns of behavior in public budgeting and public finance belie the reality of the operation of administration in the public interests—that the whole is more than simply the sum of the parts. Finally, we include an ethics case study of corruption and financial management. In the end, should financial management be about utility, duty, or virtue—the best use of public dollars to benefit the greatest number, to give to each their fair share, or to support the vision of the leader?

POLITICAL ECONOMY

John Maynard Keynes proclaimed that:

> The ideas of economists and political philosophers, both when they are
> right and when they are wrong, are more powerful than is commonly
> understood. Indeed the world is ruled by little else. Madmen in authority,
> who hear voices in the air, are distilling their frenzy from some academic
> scribbler of a few years back.[12]

By "madmen in authority," Keynes was referring to Adolf Hitler, the Nazis, and others who used the powerful ideas of Fredrich Nietzsche to justify global domination, the end of traditional ethics, and the beginning of a new era of ethical egoism and sociopathy. Nietzsche was made the official philosopher of the

Third Reich. But it was political economists like Keynes and many others who challenged this with an approach to utilitarianism that reduced utility—the greatest good for the greatest number—to economic indicators that were calculated and manipulated for the public interests and commons.

The term *economics* is derived from *oeconomicus* (*Greek*, "estate economics").[13] When applied in the 1600s to the administration of national households, it became political economy, from the Greek, *polis* (city-state) and *oeconomicus*. We use *political economy* because it is far more descriptive than the adjective-less modern term, *economics*. All economics are political economics, the "shuffling of money to the preferences of those in charge."[14] From the estate management of ancient philosophers, political economy was developed in the sixteenth to eighteenth centuries as an alternative to mercantilism, which posited strong governmental economic control of trade with colonies and others to benefit the mother-country. Americans rebelled against the mercantilism of England in the Revolutionary War. Political economy was attractive to the American colonists, emphasizing the role of individuals over the state. **Adam Smith**'s (1723–1790) book, *An Inquiry into the Nature and Causes of the Wealth of Nations* (1776), outlined the first comprehensive system of political economy. He argued that individuals acting in their own interests in an open marketplace advanced the interests of society as if guided by an invisible hand. It became known as **liberalism** for its focus on individual freedoms and free trade local and global markets, versus the **protectionism** and state control of mercantilism. Influenced by Thomas Hobbes, John Locke, and others, political economy was a holistic study of markets, society, individuals, governments, and morals. **David Ricardo** (1772–1823) expanded on free trade ideas in liberalism with the concept of **comparative advantage**; states should export goods they produced more cheaply and import cheap goods by others. Utilitarian ethical thinkers Jeremy Bentham, James Mill, and John Stuart Mill combined **economic cost-benefit analysis** with utility and the expansion of democracy.[15] Yet others focused on the **laissez-faire** of the market and the evil of government intervention, such as Austrian American **Ludwig von Mises**: "the task of the state consists solely and exclusively in guaranteeing the protection of life, health, liberty, and private property against violent attacks. Everything that goes beyond that is an evil."[16]

Critics of liberal political economy arose, including German-American economist **Friedrich List** (1789–1836), who argued Smith's "cosmopolitical" system didn't deal with the reality of national borders and the need for the **protectionism** of mercantilism. President Donald Trump now seems to advocate these ideas, with his proposals to impose tariffs on imports to protect U.S. steel and other industries, to reject international trade agreements with China and North American Free Trade Agreement (NAFTA). But may there be unforeseen consequences, i.e., global cuts on U.S. crops and other exports? **Karl Marx** (1818–1883) argued Smith's liberalism was unscientific, ignoring class-based conflicts and the oppression of the workers by the bourgeois classes. He proffered **communism**, with state or common ownership of the means of production and equal distribution of wealth to all or by need. Vladimir Lenin (1870–1924) and Joseph Stalin (1878–1953) applied Marx's communist theory to Russia and the former USSR, with greater state powers of totalitarianism. Mao Zedong (1893–1976) and Fidel Castro (1926–2016) applied communism to China and Cuba, respectively, emphasizing the state-led revolution of agrarian peasants. **Alfred Marshall** (1842–1924) rejected political economy and urged a new economic science.

Economics should be objective and value-free, he argued, like the physics of Sir Isaac Newton (1642–1727).

John Maynard Keynes (1883–1946) posited, in *The General Theory of Employment, Interest, and Money* (1936), an inverse relationship between unemployment and inflation. He transformed liberalism by arguing government must manipulate fiscal policy and expand welfare to balance the economy. His ideas influenced FDR and the rise of the **welfare state** in the 1930s Great Depression. His economic ideas changed the meaning of liberalism—away from Adam Smith's passive state, individualism, and invisible hand capitalist marketplace. But it was the expansions of World War II, not Keynesianism, which spurred the US out of the Great Depression and into a postwar boom economy. Yet, Keynes' ideas dominated the world after World War II, and inspired the creation of the International Monetary Fund (IMF) and World Bank.

Today, the dominant approach to economics in America has taken the path of Alfred Marshall's **value-free economic science**. And the focus of economic science is now on **monetarism** as the primary factor in economic growth by control of the supply of money, rather than fiscal policy or welfare funds. **Keynesianism** was marked as a failure with the contradiction of **stagflation** of the 1970s—simultaneous high inflation and unemployment.[17] University of Chicago economist **Milton Friedman** (1912–2006) posited monetarism as a replacement and argued for a revival of classical liberalism—which he labeled **neoliberalism**—in which government should once again take a more passive, limited role in economic and trade controls, divest government-owned industries, promote global free trade, and privatize the public service. In the 1980s, President Ronald Reagan and British Prime Minister Margaret Thatcher were proponents of neoliberalism. House Speaker Paul Ryan claims allegiance to neoliberalism, which he finds compatible with his favorite author, Ayn Rand, of *Atlas Shrugged* (1957) and *The Virtue of Selfishness* (1961). Remember from Chapter 2, on ethical egoism? Prominent economists have banded together to form associations to fight for this new laissez-faire, such as the Mont Pelerin Society, founded by prestigious economists Friedrich Hayek[18] and Milton Friedman—and has included eight Nobel Prize winners in economics. Charles Koch, a billionaire supporter of the conservative movement in America, is a member. However, neoliberals themselves struggle to define their doctrine and the term has been used variously from different perspectives. As one economist critic explains:

> The term has been slippery, operating as a sort of economic Rorschach blob that reveals more about its viewer than itself. For many Leftists, "neoliberal" is just a polite term for capitalism rampant, a doctrine that leads straight from Ronald Reagan to the dystopia of Blake's satanic mills, operated by enslaved child laborers and belching soot and inequality. For the Right, it is simply a label with no content, as the various subgroups prefer to organize themselves as "Austrians" (after the country that produced Hayek, von Mises, and others) or "Chicago School" (the home of Milton Friedman, et al.), etc. These divisions have the convenient effect of allowing any failures of the neoliberal enterprise to be pinned on a heterodox subgroup but never the core ideas themselves.[19]

Thus, **neoliberalism** is ambiguously defined as a new form of liberalism favoring **free-market capitalism**.[20] More empirical comparative approaches to neoliberalism include **public choice** theory, defined as a "body of theory developed by James Buchanan and Gordon Tullock to try to explain how public decisions are made. It involves the interaction of the voting public, the politicians, the bureaucracy, and political action committees."[21] **Rational choice** theorists model individual behavior based on assumptions of rationality—rather than culture, background, ideology, or other variables—by use of micro-economic statistical tools, econometrics, and game theory to predict and control decisions.[22] Critics of neoliberalism include current approaches to political economy, such as **International political economy** (IPE) or **global political economy** (GPE); a global application of economics, political science, and public administration to issues such as development, globalization, international finance, and other problems.[23] And **critical political economy** is an application of Marxist or neo-Marxist class-conflict economic theory to critique public policies created by elites (e.g., neoliberalism) and the oppression or repression of the masses in policy, e.g., taxes.[24]

Critics argue that neoliberalism is facetious as a value-free science, and that it turns a blind eye to many negative and destructive aspects of free markets. While neoliberalism is ostensibly a positivist, value-free science, it strongly implies an **ethical assumption of utility**—that decisions or policies that are good for the greatest number are preferable. Further, neoliberals and their critics go back and forth on the destructive versus beneficial impacts of free markets. For example, with the North American Free Trade Agreement (NAFTA) in 1994,[25] neoliberals have emphasized how NAFTA has saved U.S. consumers billions on goods from Mexico and Canada, while developing strong trade partners in these neighboring countries.[26] Critics point out the U.S. cities and industries that have been decimated by NAFTA, harm to the environment, and harm to local cultures in Mexico.[27] Given the complexity of political economy, how do neoliberals (e.g., Paul Ryan) comport a limited role of government with public budgeting processes?

WHAT IS PUBLIC BUDGETING?

One view of **budgets** may be as a means to track or monitor income and outflow, revenues and expenses, and, hopefully, in the end the two sides balance each other. When they do not, the result may be a deficit (i.e., expenses exceed revenues), a surplus (i.e., revenues exceed expenses), or corruption. Over recent decades, especially at the federal level—particularly during the Reagan administration—the U.S. Government ran excessively high budget deficits. By the end of the 1990s and briefly into the first year of the twenty-first century, the Federal Government actually experienced surpluses: 1999 ($70 billion), 2000 ($127 billion), and 2001 ($236 billion). The Congressional Budget Office even once projected a stunning $5.6 trillion in surpluses by 2010![28] This, of course, was predicted before the year 2000, Iraqi Freedom War, and the financial market meltdown in 2008—but it never came to pass, alas.

A more complete definition of public budgeting fulfills several perspectives and roles: politics, where it is a tool for advancing a public policy agenda; economics, where budgeting is a pseudo-scientific process, concerned with establishing guidelines and factors for raising and spending revenues; and public managers, where the concern is on spending these dollars in the most efficient, effective, and competent way feasible. We contend, however, that a more intense discussion of the public interests is missing in much of the public administration and specifically public budgeting literature. The need to raise revenues and expend public dollars is critically important to maintaining or even advancing the greater common good or public interests. This is especially true with the police powers of state and local government efforts in dealing with our health, safety, welfare, education, and morals.[29] A larger picture of the **history of public budgeting** will help explain our position.

HISTORY OF PUBLIC BUDGETING

Public budgeting is not a new practice. It did not begin in some dusty file cabinet in the early part of twentieth century. Budgeting has been practiced whenever and wherever public administrators and political officials have accounted for the raising and expenditure of revenues. Pre-Sumerian clay tablets detail the budgets of ancient kings over 4,000 years ago. However, our historical background begins roughly at the founding period in America, acknowledging that many British customs and traditions preceded this time. For example, the very term *budget* itself was used to describe the leather bag carried by the king's treasurer, who was later titled the Chancellor of the Exchequer.[30] Earlier political and financial struggles between the English Crown and Parliaments had an impact on the colonies in their struggle with England and, after American Independence, between the President and Congress.[31]

The Colonial Period

British use of the political economy of mercantilism largely defined the economic relationship between itself and the colonies, where the colonies were required to provide cash crops, thus earning enough to purchase goods, including slaves. With an infusion of cash and outflow of tobacco, cotton, and other goods, the colonies became a formidable trading partner, not only with Britain but with France and other countries. But this economic activity did not alleviate them from enduring political intrusion, particularly in the area of greater taxation without representation. In addition, the colonialists assumed strong parliamentary and financial influence over the royal governors, even to the point of setting their salaries. Even though the governors had fairly extensive political and fiscal powers, the colonialists established some semblance of budgetary authority and power in order to audit and control their own finances, but in terms of modern-day budgeting practices it was far from it.

After defeat of the British in 1775, the independent colonies did not trust nor respect strong executives, and thus placed most budgetary authority in the hands of state legislative bodies. Yet, the Articles of Confederation were established in order for the colonies to exercise considerable influence over both the executive and congressional institutions. National taxation levies, for example, were collected from each state as a state (and usually not paid in the waning years under the Articles!). Still, something was needed to be done to control the escalating war debt, estimated by Thomas Jefferson to be over $140 million. But, with operating budgets less than $500,000 each year between 1784 and 1788, where was the revenue coming from? The government took the easy solution: issue bills of credit. The Articles provided that any revenue raised was done in accordance with a property tax levied in proportion to the value of land within the various states, limiting how much Congress could raise and spend. As you may imagine, this system was rife with waste, fraud, and corruption.

After the Articles were discarded in favor of the new Constitution, the founders, who were Federalists, led by Alexander Hamilton and George Washington, favored a stronger executive to counterbalance an already strong legislative branch. The new nation looked to the new Constitution as the primary means for determining fiscal balance and solvency. For example, the Constitution was quite clear on which branch of government could and could not spend tax revenue, how money was to be withdrawn from the **U.S. Treasury**, and how all expenditures should be directed toward the benefit of the public interests. Article I, Section 8, of the Constitution established the foundation of congressional budgetary authority, among many other powers of Congress. It was Hamilton who was in favor of strengthening the role of the executive branch, believing in and achieving the establishment of a national bank, national credit system, accrual of previous war debts, and imposition of a system of taxation to pay debts.[32] Of course, not all of the founders believed as strongly in a centralized government to oversee the fiscal and budgetary needs of the new nation.

Thomas Jefferson and James Madison—the latter being an important architect of the new Constitution—vehemently disagreed over the role of the national government and specifically the President's place in the development and

---

BOX 8.2 | Role of the United States Treasury

The United States Treasury history began in somewhat difficult times—beginning during the American Revolution. The financing of a war is no easy task now, but consider trying to do it with no central agency overseeing the budgeting and financial matters related to public revenues and expenditures! Because of the Articles of Confederation, the Congress, of course, had no powers to "lay or collect" taxes. All of this authority lay with the colonies.

In 1775, the Continental Congress gave the authority to oversee and administer the fledging government finances to two men: George Clymer and Michael Hillegas. By 1776 a Treasury Office of Accounts, which consisted of one Auditor General and several clerks, was set up to keep track of public accounts. Finally, after signing the Declaration of Independence in July of 1776, the new nation was able to borrow money from countries abroad.

Between 1778 and 1781, the Treasury Office was reorganized several times and eventually the "continental dollars" devalued so rapidly that by May of 1781 public outcry was heard and Robert Morris was tabbed the Superintendent of Finance. Morris stayed on through 1784 and then resigned, but not before he brought stability to the devaluing dollar.

Finally, the First Congress of the US met in March of 1789 and by September it had created a "Department of Treasury." Alexander Hamilton served as the first Secretary of Treasury from 1789 to 1795. His first order of business was to insist upon a "dollar for dollar" repayment of the nation's nearly $75 million debt. He wrote, "The debt of the United States . . . was the price of liberty. The faith of America has been repeatedly pledged for it, and with solemnities that give peculiar force to the obligation." In other words, it is the right and ethical thing to do.

Source: "History of the Treasury: Introduction," United States Department of Treasury, retrieved from www.treas.gov/education/history

implementation of fiscal powers. Their conflict went to the point of Alexander Hamilton resigning from his post of Secretary of Treasury in 1794. Despite their disagreements, both believed that the new nation and the new government could not survive without a strong fiscal force, particularly in the areas of domestic and foreign policy. What was more problematic was determining the type of relationship that was to be forged between the President and Congress. How was the Secretary of Treasury to interact—if at all—with the Congress, especially the future House Ways and Means Committee? The former was really seen as working for the latter, given the oversight role that the House had in appropriations matters. For all intents and purposes Hamilton acted more as an emissary of the House, given that there was not an executive budgeting system in place. This did not take place until 1921, with the passage of the Budget Act.

The first appropriations bill was passed in 1789, with personnel items totaling 45 percent, defense 21 percent, and entitlements nearly 15 percent.[33] Jeff McCaffery, budgeting expert at the Naval Postgraduate School, noted that the sums listed in a 1790 appropriations bill were listed in general terms, not identifying specific items. Later, by 1792, Congress began itemizing the appropriation bills. By the early part of the nineteenth century the size of the U.S. House of Representatives grew, and the need for a permanent or standing committee on appropriations became apparent. In addition, the role and function of the Secretary of Treasury became increasingly seen as executive branch and not as a member of the Congress. This contributed to disagreements and clashes between the two branches.[34]

The Nineteenth Century

The nineteenth century was marked by the continuation of the philosophical clash between Hamilton and Jefferson. Both believed in the ideals of the new nation, but disagreed over how it should be politically constructed. Hamilton believed the nation should follow the prior British mercantile system, while Jefferson believed in the independence of common workers and farmers as the social and economic backbone of America. While Hamilton advocated the use of a stronger executive government, Jefferson insisted on a deeper division and separation of powers, especially between the executive and legislative branches, with Congress playing the dominant role. Jefferson's ideas and ideals won out, at least for approximately the first 40 or so years of the nineteenth century. It was not until the continuing controversies between the northern and southern states over the issue of slavery came to a head in the Civil War did Hamilton's beliefs begin to take root. Then a strong national government emerged, led by charismatic and courageous President Lincoln, as increasingly necessary to lead the nation into financial prosperity and around economic adversity. Still, even with increased federal spending during the major nineteenth century American wars, including the War of 1812, the Mexican-American War of the 1840s, and the Civil War (1861–1865),[35] the national government's responsibility was limited, largely because of limited internationalization of goods and services and pre-industrialization of technology and business innovations. Taxes were minimal, fees and charges were cheap, and customs low. Thus, government budgets and the commons, including both national and state, were small. But the Industrial Revolution and the related political and economic changes of the nineteenth and twentieth centuries changed everything.

The Twentieth Century

The twentieth century identified the beginning of the Progressive Reform Movement and expanding definitions of the commons. Science and technology advanced business innovations. Agriculture was slowly losing dominance over the American economy, while industry appropriated the use of machines and scientific management principles to build a new economic dynamo that would require the national government to catch up with the changes or be left behind. Progressives[36] pressed for civil and moral changes, including various labor laws. The Federal Government responded by passing the Federal Trade Commission Act of 1914, which regulated working hours and conditions, as well as protected consumers from unfair business practices.[37] Progressives were similar to socialists in that they demanded immediate political changes, but unlike socialists they did not advocate the use of authoritarian government and control of the major means of production. They did, however, advocate strong, influential government leadership, particularly at the local level. One very important way of providing this municipal leadership was through study and evaluation of the budgetary process through organizations such as the National Municipal League (1899) and the New York Bureau of Municipal Research (1906). The New York Bureau is credited for advocating budgetary reform at the local level,[38] such as the use of an object classification budget for the New York City Department of Health. Later efforts emphasized the use of line-item or object budgeting, and by the 1920s scholars were systematically studying public budgeting.[39]

Despite all of these advances, prior to 1921, federal government agencies still accepted the Jeffersonian ideals as gospel: preparing their expenditure estimates, passing them on to Treasury, who in turn passed them on to Congress. Congress rarely considered new items of spending. Rather it maintained the status quo, not really looking to use the budget as a policy tool. This all changed with the publication of President Taft's 1910 Commission on Economy and Efficiency's report titled "Need for a National Budget." The Commission, which was chaired by Frederick Cleveland, highlighted the need for greater executive administrative power, particularly in the areas of budgetary guidance and direction. Naturally

---

BOX 8.3 | Budget and Accounting Act of 1921

Passage of the Budget and Accounting Act of 1921 had connections back to President Taft's Commission on Economy and Efficiency (1910–1912), which called for an increased role by the President in the development of a federal budget. However, because the Commission's report did not mention the role of the legislature it languished in Congress. By 1919, however, Congress held hearings and made recommendations for presidential involvement in the federal budgetary process. President Wilson actually vetoed the original bill "because of concern with the constitutionality of a provision involving his removal power over the new office of Comptroller General." President Harding signed the bill into law in 1921. ◢

Source: Joint Committee on the Organization of Congress, "The Executive Budget Movement and the Budget and Accounting Act of 1921," Organization of the Congress, 103rd Congress, 1st session, 1993, retrieved from www.rules.house.gov/archives/jcoc2w.htm

Congress resisted for political and power reasons, but shortly after the conclusion of World War I, Congress passed the Budget and Accounting Act of 1921.[40] The act, for the first time, centralized the formation of the federal budget in the executive office, specifically in the newly created Bureau of the Budget (BOB), which was to report to the treasury secretary. The BOB's first director, Charles G. Dawes, initiated technical innovations including mandating reserves and using scientific management principles to ensure greater efficiency and economy in the budgetary process. The Act also created the **General Accounting Office** (GAO), which was to report to Congress.[41] Thus, the budgetary process had two major changes: strong executive directing and more checks and balances.

FDR AND THE BROWNLOW COMMITTEE

President Franklin D. Roosevelt's influence was evident when he initiated a variety of changes aimed at centralizing executive power, including budgets. His 1937 Committee on Administration Management (i.e., the Brownlow Committee, named after its chairman, Louis Brownlow) recommended increasing BOB's authority. By 1939 Congress passed the Reorganization Act, which established the Executive Office of the President and effectively transferred BOB from the Department of Treasury to this new office—directly under the authority of the President. BOB became the budgetary right hand of the President,[42] and gave him the power to initiate budgets and guide policy thereby. By the end of World War II, Congress extended the BOB's function to include government corporations, oversight of agencies, regulation of travel allowances, adoption of a performance budget, and to update accounting systems.[43]

Planning and Programming

In the 1960s with war being waged on two fronts—the domestic war on poverty and a foreign war on communism—and the escalating costs to fight each, the need for more sophisticated ways of budgeting seemed apparent. President Lyndon Baines Johnson's Task Force on Governmental Reorganization in 1964 recommended a more scientific approach to policy analysis, applying economic theory and operations research to the linkage of inputs and outputs. The new budgeting system formed out of such an arrangement was called Planning-Programming-Budgeting System (PPBS).[44] This new style of budgeting was concerned with inputs, outputs, effects, and alternatives. It was the first truly management-based budgeting system, where it was designed to explain management decisions and, ultimately, the spending of hundreds of millions of dollars. Drawn from the private sector, specifically General Motors and Ford Motor Company, PPBS was both a president's dream and nightmare. It provided extensive information, but it required reams of information and data in order to be successful. To minimize the nightmare aspect, in 1961, President Johnson lured a young, bright, and energetic **Robert McNamara** away from Ford to become Secretary of Defense, and implement PPBS, thus bringing about a centralized budget and management system, complete with a strong executive focus.

PPBS was a multidisciplinary budgeting concept, designed to incorporate a more rational rather than incremental data-gathering and analysis process. The intention is for the budget analyst to set goals and then determine cost/benefit ratios in order to choose the best decision for allocation of revenues. President Johnson demanded greater financial accountability and program effectiveness, especially in waging the Vietnam War. He sought to enlist the most sophisticated quantitative techniques of budgeting and program management possible, in order to justify the spending of billions of dollars weekly on the war effort. PPBS was such a system. One way to accomplish this monumental task was to centralize the authority and control of military spending; this was done through the PPBS.

McNamara hired his "**Whiz Kids,**" who were bright, computer-savvy, and mathematically oriented types, drawing them largely from the private sector, to enter the brave new world of government bureaucracy and military jargon, specifically to install a budgeting system that would not only count and keep track of guns, bullets, and dead soldiers, but monitor the costs of doing so. President Johnson was so enthralled that, in 1965, he ordered all government agencies to conform to such a system. The system was too complicated and complex to be effective in non-military departments, such as the Departments of Agriculture and Interior, that upon entering office in 1969 President Nixon ordered an immediate cease and desist, all but effectively declaring the system dead on arrival by the early 1970s. By 1970, the BOB became the Office of Management and Budget (OMB), with the focus on management, not necessarily quantifying and analyzing the effective use of resources. Although no longer used extensively at the federal level, PPBS is still used at some state and local levels.

The 1970s Reforms

Before we discuss further iterations of budgeting methods, we need to provide a brief overview of the significant changes that took place in federal budgeting practices during the mid-1970s, specifically as a result of the Congressional

---

BOX 8.4 | Robert McNamara (1916–2009) and his "Whiz Kids"

Robert McNamara and his "Whiz Kids" brought to the Department of Defense in the 1960s sophisticated policy analytical techniques, including program budgeting and policy evaluation tools, and computer information systems technology that was to revolutionize the way government engaged in public management and policy analysis. The "Whiz Kids" were young, bright, and computer-knowledgeable. Many came with McNamara from the private sector, including Ford Motor Company, where McNamara had been company president in 1960. Based upon these modern techniques for system management, McNamara restructured the military, moving

from strict reliance on nuclear technology to a combination of nuclear and traditional military strategy. His disdain for military career officials in favor of business and non-military types irritated Pentagon officials, many members of Congress, and, of course, the anti-war protestors. He resigned as Secretary of Defense in 1967 and became President of the World Bank, lasting from 1968 to 1981. He continued to write and lecture until his death in 2009.

Source: "Robert S. McNamara," *Answers.com*, retrieved from www.answers.com/topic/robert-s.mcnamara

Budget and Impoundment Control Act of 1974 (i.e., the Congressional Budget Act). (We will later exam these reforms as they affected deficits and deficit controls.) This act was designed to bring some sense of congressional control and oversight back to the public budgeting process. Birthed out of an anti-executive movement, largely associated with the political fallout of Watergate, the act sought to reestablish congressional influence, including the making and implementation of federal budgets. This was necessary for a number of reasons, including the fact that neither the House or the Senate had specific permanent committees designated for: (1) reviewing and critiquing the President's budget requests; or (2) implementing a process to follow for determining what effects the executive budget might have on the total economy; or (3) extending the budgetary review process to a biennial time frame versus an annual one; or (4) restricting the President from impounding funds that appropriated for policies and programs he did not approve of; or (5) establishing an adequate staff to analyze the President's budget requests, while developing specific and reliable alternatives.

First, the act created House and Senate Budget Committees, permanent standing committees, whose jurisdiction was responsible for deciding which program requests were legitimate and realistic among the many funding requests made each year. Second, the act required Congress as a whole body to vote twice per year (i.e., congressional budget resolutions) on spending priorities. Third, it established a time table requiring Congress to schedule various actions to take place (i.e., authorization and appropriate passages, etc.). Fourth, it created the Congressional Budget Office (CBO) as a counter-agency to the Office of Management Budget (OMB). Fifth, so-called backdoor-spending appropriations were eliminated as was the President's unconstitutional power to impound or stop the appropriation of funds to particular areas of political and ideological disagreement between the President and Congress.

Congress fully intended to slow down the executive federal budget decision-making juggernaut without completely doing away with it. For example, the CBO's responsibility was to:

- Establish a **concurrent resolution** by setting expenditure and revenue targets for a fiscal year.
- Provide multiple types of costs estimates.
- Establish fiscal, inflation, and mandate criteria for evaluating when and how to spend dollars.
- Place limits on presidential impoundment power through inclusion of deferrals and rescissions. A deferral is a temporary technique used by the President to defer spending because of administrative functions that save money. Deferrals run out at the end of the fiscal year but can be renewed. A **rescission** is a more controversial and permanent method for reducing spending, where the President or Congress can impound funds out of ideology or dislike for a program.[45]
- Provide an annual report on federal budget options.[46]

Of these five significant changes to the federal budgeting process, impoundment of funds by the President and the establishment of concurrent resolutions by the Congress standout. With regard to the President's power to impound funds, the President could still delay spending using a deferral, unless the Congress overrode the deferral. In *INS v. Chada* (1983), the Supreme Court ruled that a legislative veto of executive agency decisions (delegated to them by Congress) by one house was a violation of the separation of powers doctrine. Instead, Congress could only take back the power it delegated to the agency by a law passed by both houses of Congress and signed by the President. Thereafter, Congress reduced presidential deferrals; otherwise, if not the President would have unlimited veto power.[47]

With Congress in concurrent resolutions, the President submits a budget in February for the fiscal year that begins each October 1. Congress then has several options, including: (1) adopting the budget resolutions; (2) passing appropriation bills; and (3) passing other budget-related legislation, such as authorization legislation, reconciliation bills, various tax-related changes, modifications of various entitlement programs, and even debt limit adjustments. The resolution is concerned with listing total spending, program allocations, and "reconciliation instructions," or the means by which the House and Senate committees "report legislation conforming spending, revenue, or debt-limit levels under existing law to current budget policies."[48] Thus, Congress is better able to check the budgetary actions of the President, by inspecting the spending patterns of each of the 13 executive departments, and by passing individual authorization and appropriation bills.

BUDGETING STYLES AND TECHNIQUES

The intention of each style or technique of **public budgeting** was to institute better means of control over spending habits, but not completely restrict executive freedom to provide various expenditure options. These styles or techniques provided new means of budgeting public funds.

Management by Objectives

By the beginning of the second Nixon administration, the White House and OMB encouraged a new approach to budgeting: **Management By Objectives** (MBO). The idea was for agency heads to establish program and funding objectives and then require a process toward accomplishing those objectives. As one public administration scholar notes, MBO "has a managerial orientation that stresses . . . common sense."[49] Perhaps this was its undoing: too much discretionary fiscal authority in the hands of mid-level managers! Although it was extensively and generally successfully used in the private sector, it failed to generate much political support. It was similar to performance budgeting in that it was concerned with inputs, outputs, and effects, but unlike performance-based budgeting it did not stress the use of alternatives. For example, there is a key question for department and agency officials to ask. How effective are X dollars for meeting Y objectives? Intended to be a decentralized approach to budget decision making, the manner in which it was used in the Nixon administration left much to be desired. Instead of having lower-level bureaucratic input into what objectives should be set and how they should be accomplished, given the limited allocation of revenues available, the Nixon administration instituted top-down control. Further, agency goals were often displaced because of the overemphasis of measurable quantitative goals over qualitative and non-measurable aspects of a program. Although it is still an effective tool, it is not used at the federal level. Its greatest use is at the state and local levels, where, for example, some 47 percent of all U.S. cities in 1993 and nearly two-thirds of all states use some form of MBO.[50]

Zero-Base Budgeting

Zero-base budgeting (ZBB) was originally used by the Texas Instruments Corporation under the direction and leadership of **Peter Pyhrr**, who later assisted Jimmy Carter to implement it when Carter was governor of Georgia.[51] President Carter then brought it with him into the U.S. government during the late 1970s, but that is as far as it went—it left just as quickly as it came. ZBB is based on the theory that incremental decision making is purely political and does not advocate true budgetary reform. Therefore, it features zero-base analysis, where each agency and department must justify its spending from scratch, or the zero-base, using decision packages, with each package of budget proposals ranked in order of priority. The lowest-level packages do not get funded. Supposedly this system is designed to place all programs on equal footing at the beginning of each fiscal year, which theoretically happens. But in reality the wheel that squeaks loudest receives the most grease. In addition, it is counterproductive in many ways, because it consumes significant time, effort, and paper on the part of the various agencies to justify why they want the same level of appropriations.

Target-Based Budgeting

History tells us that President Reagan was driven to change Federal Government as no other president had before (and since). He advocated the reduction of government spending, accomplishing this through the reform and reduction of federal taxes and tax restructuring. In order to accomplish his ideological task he required a public budgeting system, such as target-based budgeting (TBB), that was aimed at top-down control of agency budgets, generally by the director of the OMB, who at the time was David Stockman. In all fairness to the Reagan proposal, the agency heads had discretion to spend their allocated dollars, but only within the limits imposed by the OMB director. Further, they were expected to demonstrate that they in fact achieved their goals set forth the year prior for the next year's budget request. Thus, the idea was to target certain goals, such as the reduction of federal education spending, and mandating that states and localities pick up more of the educational tab, while at the same time redirecting funds to other targeted areas, such as defense spending. So, instead of the agency heads sending their requests to Congress and/or the budget director, the latter forwarded their allotted amounts to the department and agency heads, informing them what was available to them for expenditure purposes. As you can guess, there was considerable discretion in the spending habits and patterns of departments and agencies.

Return to Performance Budgeting

Fueled in large part by the New Public Management revolution—which was in stark contrast to the New Public Service paradigm (see Chapter 6)[52]—performance budgeting gained its impetus through publication and dissemination of David

Osborne and Ted Gaebler's book *Reinventing Government*,[53] and through President Clinton's charge to Vice President Al Gore, Jr., to establish the National Partnership for Reinventing Government, which was designed to direct government and government action to be results-oriented, including the budgeting system. Several types of budgets were highlighted by Osborne and Gaebler, including mission-driven budgeting, output budgeting (i.e., a budget system that focuses on the output of services), **outcome budgeting** (i.e., budget that focuses on the quality of services produced), and customer-driven budgeting.[54] Each of these budgeting types were similar with regard to the larger picture: to make government run more efficiently through control of inputs and outputs. This type of budgeting, as you can well imagine, is similar to performance budgeting—in that it is heavily weighted toward management and incremental decision making—but differs in that it is more participatory and decentralized in nature.[55]

Osborne and Gaebler provided hundreds of examples and illustrations of results oriented government, and it was with this impetus for change that President Clinton chose Vice President Gore to head up the new commission, whose primary responsibility would be not only to find ways to save taxpayer dollars, but to make government work better by working more efficiently and economically. When Congress passed the Government Performance and Results Act of 1993, it dedicated itself to exploring ways toward "mission-driven, results-oriented budgets."[56] So how successful is performance-based and/or results-oriented budgeting? Although they are not exactly the same, they are similar enough to justify the following statement: performance budgeting has a semi-long track record, one that is somewhat difficult to assess, especially at the federal and local levels, while at the state level 47 of 50 states have some aspect of performance budgeting inherent in their budgeting and financial management systems,[57] but one that is generally positive toward performance-based systems.[58]

BOX 8.5 | Performance-Based Budgeting Gains Prominence

Performance-based budgeting drew great attention from states and municipalities. The National Governors Association (NGA) published *An Action Agenda to Redesign State Government* (1993), calling for "performance based state government," complete with measurable goals and outcomes. Not to be outdone, the National Conference of State Legislatures (NCSL) published its own study in 1994, titled *The Performance Budget Revisited: A Report on State Budget Reform.* Now states began jumping on the performance-based-budgeting bandwagon, including Oregon, Minnesota, Montana, Iowa, Texas, Idaho, Ohio, Florida, and many others. Despite the fact that there was still a lack of credibility, time, and resource constraints, and political hurdles to overcome, performance-based budgeting took off. The public demand to validate spending of public tax dollars was great. Even greater was the need to show quantitative evidence that the tax dollars were (1) actually spent on the items indicated, and (2) that there were measurable outputs and outcomes to justify the tax revenue and expenditures. Government, public officials, and public administrators were on a short public relations leash! ◣

Source: Reprinted from Charlie Tyer and Jennifer Willand, "Public Budgeting in America: A Twentieth Century Retrospective," *Journal of Public Budgeting, Accounting and Financial Management* 9 (#2, Summer 1997), retrieved from www.ipspr.sc.edu/publication/Budgeting_in_America.htm

The driving force, of course, is results. What is government getting for its expenditures? All parties involved claim to want to know where, what, and how public funds are being spent: politicians, public administrators, customer-citizens, and clientele groups. This is performance- and/or outputs-based budgeting—the latest in a long list of historical approaches to itemize, manage, document, and otherwise know where, when, how, and, perhaps, why public funds are being spent in the way they are spent.[59]

The various budgeting types reflect the range of human nature factors: pluralistic, controlling, but always changing. The basic responsibility elected and administrative officials have toward securing and protecting public funds is a tremendous burden, but it is one that identifies the need to fulfill the public interests. Politics of budgeting certainly plays a significant role in the budgeting process, given that Democrats and Republicans want to control the public purse strings so as to push their policy agenda. However, pursuit of the public interests regarding public spending, deficit control, and other matters related to public budgeting should take precedent. Whether it does or not is questionable.

BOX 8.6 | The Limits on Performance Budgeting

First it cannot solve or avert a financial crisis. No matter how many benchmarks, performance measures, etc. a city, state, or federal agency set prior to 9/11, it could not have anticipated nor adequately adapted to the financial problems that resulted because of 9/11, the war in Iraq, or the aftermath of Hurricane Katrina.

Second, try as they might, some proponents for performance budgeting who think politics can be eliminated from the equation are simply wrong. They even lay out their own multi-point plan on the use of political strategies or principles for igniting the fire for performance-based budgeting.

Third, performance budgeting cannot reduce the influence of interest groups, which are trying to get all the benefits they can from the *very* political process of public budgeting.

Fourth, performance budgeting does not make poor managers suddenly good managers. It can offer tools and techniques for tying goals to budget outlays, for example, but it cannot make a square peg fit in a round hole. For instance, if local managers believe that continual local recycling programs do not work, despite the evidence to the contrary, then there is not much that performance budgeting can do to help.

And, fifth, performance budgeting cannot redirect the priorities of citizens. Citizens are not looking at the city manager's detailed performance-based report of the exceptional productivity of the city's street-sweeping operation, especially not when, for example, the police department is under fire for not handling a youth gang incident. Their eyes are on their neighborhoods, their elected representatives, and, in the case of a city, upon the political promises of the mayor, not the quantitative criteria offered by performance or outcome budgeting in a department that does not elicit as much political notoriety.

Performance budgeting has its positive benefits, particularly evident in a cultural outcry of doing more with less. But that cry is not new. ▲

Sources: Janet M. Kelly and William C. Rivenbark, *Performance Budgeting for State and Local Government* (Armonk, NY: M.E. Sharpe Press, 2003), 10–11; David Osborne and Peter Hutchinson, *The Price of Government: Getting the Results We Need in an Age of Permanent Fiscal Crisis* (New York, NY: Basic Books, 2004), 328–9; and David N. Ammons and William C. Rivenbark, "Using Benchmark Data to Improve Services: Local Impact of a Municipal Performance Comparison Project," *Southeastern Conference of Public Administration*, October 5–8, Little Rock, Arkansas.

PUBLIC FINANCE: TAXES, REVENUES, AND SPENDING

Before we can discuss financial management processes, we need to overview public finance: taxes, revenues, and spending powers of governments. *The commons* are often defined by taxing and tax spending. Taxes are as old as written history. However, let's take just a brief walk through time and examine some of the major changes that took place in the history of U.S. government public finance.

Brief History of U.S. Public Finance

During the early years of our nation's founding, citizens had little contact with the national government, given that almost all of the national government's revenue came in the form of excise taxes, tariffs on imported goods, and custom duties. The Articles of Confederation (1781–1789) were abandoned by the founders largely because of the failure of the central government to levy taxes. The founders included the tax power in Article I of the U.S. Constitution (the Article on Congress) that permitted Congress to "lay and collect taxes, duties, imposts, and excises, pay the Debts and provide for the common Defense and general Welfare of the United States." However, despite this authority and the need to pay off many debts, the U.S. government did not impose taxes on individual personal income. Instead, it imposed excise taxes and custom duties at higher and higher levels to raise revenues.

By the Civil War, the U.S. government finally enacted a personal income tax, but the rate was only about 3 percent on annual incomes above $800. Of course, it all changed with the 16th Amendment in 1913, allowing Congress a permanent personal income tax system. Beginning with World War I and continuing through the next decade, Congress passed successive revenue acts that raised the tax rates. Since WWII, the increase in taxes was generally related to crises, such as the Korean War, Vietnam War, and President Johnson's War on Poverty. The Economic Recovery Tax Act of 1981 made a basic change in the taxing structure, with a 25 percent reduction in most individual tax brackets. The 1997 Taxpayer Relief Act gave tax benefits to families with children. The 2001 **Economic Growth and Tax Relief and Reconciliation Act** reduced the top tax rate to 33 percent, and relief for families with children.[60]

Why Taxes?

Public funds, or revenue, are mostly gathered through taxes (or fees), but there are other means as well. Why taxes? Before the government can engage in distributing or providing a service or program, such as highway maintenance, police protection, or Medicare, it has to have funding. So taxes are established and collected. The result is what we call revenue. Government revenue is further categorized in several ways that will help us understand the commons and the extent of government's influence. First, taxes raised are either direct or indirect. Direct revenue comes mainly from personal and corporate income tax, whereas indirect revenue comes from sales or value-added taxes. Second, public revenue can come through transfers, which are grants of money provided from one level of government, usually the national, to other levels of government, usually state and local governments. Third, government revenue is acquired through borrowing on public bonds and loans. And, fourth public revenue is gathered from "profits from government enterprises, franchising and licensing, and even savings and investment earnings.[61] Before we examine the expenditure side of the public ledger, let's look briefly at the types and kinds of taxes.

One way to categorize taxes is based on their impacts on members of a society: regressive, progressive, or proportional. Regressive taxes, such as sales on goods and services, are taxes that tax individuals with lower incomes at a proportionally higher rate than those with higher incomes. For example, the single parent with multiple children who works three jobs and makes a combined income of $25,000 and the business executive who makes $250,000 both pay the same sales tax on the $250 grocery bill, but in this scenario the tax is regressive, taking about 1 percent of the family's income, while in the second case the impact is one-tenth of that! That is a substantial difference, particularly when many individuals are working to make ends meet. On the other hand, a progressive tax takes a larger share the higher one's income in tax (e.g. the executive making $250,000 will pay the top federal income tax rate of nearly 40 percent, while the single parent working three jobs and making $25,000 will be taxed less than half that amount). The liberal moral argument is that the more one makes, the more the individual should be required to be taxed, while the conservative moral argument claims that it is unfair to tax someone at a higher rate simply because they make more money, causing a disincentive to earn more money, something that it is antithetical in a free-market economy. Finally, a proportional tax is where all individuals—both the executive and the single parent—are taxed at the same rate. For example, if a proportional tax rate of 20 percent is applied to both cases—the executive and the single parent—the government takes $5,000 versus $50,000, while the rate is the same. Proponents of the proportional rate claim that total revenue will actually go up (i.e., simply because fewer deductions are permitted), and the filing process is far simpler. Opponents are largely against such a plan, because they contend it is simply ethically wrong to tax all income groups at the same rate (see Table 8.1).

Types of taxes differ depending upon the level of government. First, at the national or federal level there are two primary types of taxes: individual and corporate. As we noted in our historical survey, individual taxes were used but once prior to the turn of the twentieth century (i.e., for a short period during and after the Civil War). Based on the progressive nature of personal income taxes, politicians, depending upon political and ideological persuasion, battle over whether and when to raise such taxes, especially when it is connected to the wealthy.

Individual income taxes account for the largest percentage of federal revenue. Table 8.1 depicts the increasing dependency of the Federal Government on individual income taxes compared to other forms of revenue. In 1934, the Federal Government took in only $420 million in personal income taxes; by 2008, that number had grown to just over $1 trillion, which accounts for just short of 50 percent of total receipts. Even though most advanced industrial nations use an individual income tax to fund the lion's share of their programs and expenditures, there is still great debate as to equity of a progressive tax system, prompting politicians (e.g., Steve Forbes) and pundits (e.g., Rush Limbaugh) to consider major revisions in the current tax system, including examination of some type of proportional system.

TABLE 8.1

Comparison of U.S. Government Receipts by Source in Selected Increments (Millions of $)

Year	Individual Income Tax	Corporate Income Taxes	Social Insurance Receipts	Excise Taxes	Other	Total Receipts
1934	420 (14%)	364 (12.1%)	30 (1%)	1,354 (4.5%)	788 (2.6%)	2,956
1944	19,705 (45%)	14,838 (33.9%)	3,473 (7.9%)	4,759 (10.8%)	972 (2.2%)	43,747
1954	29,542 (42.3%)	21,101 (30.2%)	7,208 (10.3%)	9,945 (14.2%)	1,905 (2.7%)	69,701
1964	48,697 (43.2%)	23,493 (20.8%)	21,963 (19.5%)	13,731 (12.1%)	4,731 (4.2%)	112,615
1974	118,952 (45.1%)	38,620 (14.6%)	75,071 (28.5%)	16,844 (6.3%)	13,737 (5.2%)	263,224
1984	298,415 (44.7%)	56,893 (8.5%)	239,376 (35.9%)	37,361 (5.6%)	34,440 (5.16%)	666,485
1994	543,055 (43.1%)	140,385 (11.1%)	461,475 (36.6%)	55,225 (4.3%)	58,581 (4.6%)	1,258,721
2004	808,959 (43%)	189,371 (10%)	733,047 (38.9%)	69,855 (3.7%)	78,687 (4.1%)	1,879,919
2008	1,219,661 (48.4%)	345,336 (13.7%)	910,125 (36.1%)	68,835 (2.7%)	−22,782 (−0.9%)	2,521,175
2009	915,308 (43.5%)	138,229 (6.6%)	890,917 (42.3%)	62,483 (3%)	98,052 (4.7%)	2,104,989
2010	898,549 (41.5%)	191,437 (8.8%)	864,814 (40%)	66,909 (3.1%)	140,997 (6.5%)	2,162,706
2011	1,091,473 (47.4%)	181,085 (7.9%)	818,792 (35.5%)	72,381 (3.1%)	139,375 (6.1%)	2,303,106
2012	1,132,206 (46.2%)	242,289 (9.9%)	845,314 (34.5%)	79,061 (3.2%)	151,120 (6%)	2,449,990
2013	1,316,415 (47.4%)	273,506 (9.9%)	947,820 (34.2%)	84,007 (3.3%)	153,367 (5.5%)	2,775,115
2014	1,394,568 (46.2%)	320,731 (10.6%)	1,023,458 (33.9%)	93,368 (3.1%)	189,366 (6.3%)	3,021,491
2015	1,540,802 (47.4%)	343,797 (10.6%)	1,065,257 (32.8%)	98,279 (3%)	201,752 (6.2%)	3,249,887
2016	1,546,805 (47.3%)	299,571 (9.2%)	1,115,065 (34/1%)	95,026 (2.9%)	212,224 (6.5%)	3,268,691

Source: "Historical Tables: Table 2.1, Receipts by Source: 1934–2022," *Office of Management and Budget*, retrieved from www.whitehouse.gov/omb/budget/Historicals

Corporate income taxes, the second type of income tax, are also a progressive tax, but their controversy stems from the fact that it is considered a double tax by some, meaning corporations pay income taxes on net corporate income, and then the shareholders are taxed again on the dividends.[62] As of 2004, they accounted for only about 10 percent of total receipts (see Table 8.1).

State and local levels of government primarily collect revenues by sales, excise, and property taxes. Instead of concentrating on income, sales taxes impact consumption, meaning they are based on how much an individual buys. The more one purchases, the greater the tax burden. But, as we mentioned above, it is also a regressive tax. Only five states do not have a sales tax (Alaska, Delaware, Montana, New Hampshire, and Oregon), with the average rate among the remaining 45 states at 5.8 percent; the lowest, 2.9 percent (Colorado); and the highest, 7 percent, shared by four states (Mississippi, New Jersey, Rhode Island, and Tennessee). Excise taxes are taxes placed on items such motor fuel, cigarette, and other tobacco products (e.g., chewing tobacco), distilled spirits (i.e., liquor), wine, and beer. Sometimes referred to as sin-taxes, excise taxes could be placed on any legal item that is traded, purchased, or otherwise exchanged between individuals. In addition to the revenues they raise on their own, state and local governments also receive substantial revenue from the Federal Government. It comes to them in the form of an **intergovernmental transfer.** It can be a loan or a grant. Total intergovernmental revenue for all state and local governments in 2004–2005, for example, equaled over $438 billion. For example, with regard to education, some of this federal money is provided directly to citizens of the various states (e.g., student loans), but much of it is transferred to the state and local governments, who in turn distribute it to K-12 and universities and colleges (see Table 8.2).[63]

Where state income and sales taxes are the mainstay of state revenue, property taxes are the backbone of local government revenue. Property tax is not very popular—not by citizens or local officials who have to administer it. There are several reasons, including the fact that no one can agree completely on how to valuate property, i.e., whether it is assessed value or market value or some other means. Even the technical means to figure property tax is somewhat complicated. Based on a benchmark measure called mills, which is equal to $1 for $1,000 of assessed value, a $200,000 piece of property assessed at 30 percent of the market value would yield $6,000. (The formula is *market value* x *assessment rate* x *mills = yield*.)[64] However, sometimes the millage rate may change, depending upon action of the General Assembly. As in the case of the state of Iowa, for example, at the time the millage rate was used property was assessed at 27 percent of its market value, whereas the millage rate was applied at 100 percent of the market rate. Therefore, the millage rate had to be adjusted down to 27 cents per $1,000 of assessed value. So, for example, this explains why some Iowa property tax levies are in multiples of 27 cents. In addition, local governments are given authority by the state to levy property taxes for any number of policy or functional areas, including counties, cities, education, township, and others.[65] Confusing, huh! No wonder no one really likes the property tax as a means of collecting local revenue.

Expenditures: Where Does It All Go?

So where does all of this revenue go? At the federal level, spending is divided into two broad categories: mandatory and discretionary. Mandatory items are

TABLE 8.2

State and Local Revenue Sources, 2014

Revenue Source	State/Local ($)	S/L (%)	State ($)	State (%)	Local ($)	Local (%)
Total Revenue	3,633,773,979		2,361,473,724		1,772,052,516	
Inter-governmental	602,230,223	16.57%	550,560,842	23.31%	551,421,642	31.12%
Taxes	1,490,815,697	41.03%	867,177,496	36.72%	623,638,201	35.19%
Charges/Misc.	665,068,920	18.30%	322,003,389	13.64%	262,983,316	14.84%
Utility	160,586,462	4.42%	14,310,794	0.61%	146,275,668	8.25%
Liquor Store	8,502,864	0.23%	7,179,065	0.30%	1,323,799	0.07%
Insurance Trust	706,569,813	19.44%	600,242,138	25.42%	106,327,675	4

Source: "Table 1. State and Local Government Finances by Level of Government and by State: 2014," *U.S. Census Bureau*, retrieved from www.census.gov/govs/estimate/0500ussl_1.html. NOTE: May not add up to 100% due to misc. revenues.

items legislated by Congress and thus required or mandated areas where federal revenue must go. The largest of these areas are entitlement programs, such as Medicare and Medicaid, which are largely means-tested, indicating that Congress sets eligibility requirements and rules to enforce those requirements. Then the amount to be appropriated is determined by the demand for the service. Mandatory spending makes up about two-thirds of federal spending, with Social Security making up about one-third of mandatory spending. Discretionary items are items that Congress has the option of whether or not to spend in this area. Congress has the authority to directly set the spending limits on those items it wants to spend money on, or not. It can increase or decrease at its discretion, so to speak. For example, national defense is a discretionary item, given that Congress has the constitutional power and political authority to add to or take away from the military's budget as it deems appropriate. But, during time of war, even though Congress has the constitutional power to control military appropriations, Congress will generally not refuse to appropriate funds. The war in Iraq is a perfect illustration. The George W. Bush administration asked for and received numerous supplemental appropriations (i.e., appropriations over and beyond the Department of Defense's [DOD] original budget request). The latest in those installments is $93.4 billion for 2007, and $141.7 billion for 2008. The fiscal year 2008 DOD request is $481.4 billion. Obviously, even though national defense is technically a discretionary item, during wartime it is no longer discretionary (see Table 8.3).

At the state and local levels, spending is varied, but the primary areas are education, public welfare, health, prisons/criminal justice, highways and public works, and parks/natural resources. Education spending dominates the local level, with nearly $500 billion spent and less than $200 billion at the state level. Social welfare programs are predominantly administered and funded by the states. However, states spend nearly 70 percent more than local governments (e.g., $317

TABLE 8.3

Federal Discretionary and Mandatory Spending by Sources, FY 2009

Sources	Discretionary	Sources	Mandatory
National Defense	58%	Social Security	35%
Education, Training, Employment, and Social Services	7%	Income Security	19%
Other (Energy, Agriculture, Commerce and Housing Credit, Community and Regional Development, General Government, and Medicare and Social Security)	5%	Net Interest on Debt	10%
Health	5%	Medicare	21%
Income Security	5%	Health (i.e., Medicaid)	12%
Administration of Justice	4%	Veterans' Benefits and Services	3%
Veterans' Benefits and Services	4%		
Transportation	2%		
Natural Resources and Environment	3%		
General Science, Space, and Technology	3%		
International Affairs	4%		

Source: "Proposed Discretionary Budget 2009," *National Priorities Project,* retrieved from www.nationalpriorities.org/node/6916

to $44 billion, respectively). Public health and public safety programs loom large at the local level.[66] About 77 percent of state expenditures are in the following areas: intergovernmental transfers (27 percent), education (13 percent), public welfare (22 percent), utilities (7 percent), insurance trust (8 percent), and hospitals (3 percent), while 70 percent of local expenditures are in education (38 percent), utilities (10 percent), police (5 percent), general administration (5 percent), hospitals (5 percent), interest on the debt (4 percent), and housing/community development (3 percent) (see Table 8.4).

THE PROCESS OF FINANCIAL MANAGEMENT

The process of public financial management has become more complex, there is no doubt. More of everything, including people and governments' needs and wants, necessitates a more complex process of accounting for the increased revenue and expenditures to meet these demands. The National Advisory Council on State and Local Budgeting contends that public financial management is all about good public budgeting, and "Good budgeting is a broadly defined process that has political, managerial, planning, communication, and financial dimensions." Public budgeting at any government level is strategic in nature, with its overall

TABLE 8.4

State and Local Expenditures, 2014

Expenditures	State/Local ($)	State/Local (%)	State ($)	State (%)	Local ($)	Local (%)
Total Expenditures	3,633,773,979		2,048,405,642		1,722,749,379	
Intergovernmental	3,389,399	0.09%	496,878,801	24.26%	16,086,033	0.93%
Education	904,309,998	24.89%	227,543,672	11.11%	620,584,476	36.0%
Public Welfare	542,569,109	14.93%	489,993,868	23.92%	52,575,241	3.05%
Hospitals	165,588,547	4.56%	70,199,198	3.43%	95,389,349	5.54%
Health	89,733,631	2.47%	44,260,066	2.16%	45,473,565	2.64%
Employment Security Administration	4,400,029	0.12%	4,359,890	0.21%	40,139	0.00%
Veterans' Services	1,059,763	0.03%	1,059,763	0.05%	–	
Highways	162,152,041	4.46%	96,440,652	4.71%	65,711,389	3.81%
Police	101,944,943	2.81%	14,052,212	0.69%	87,892,731	5.10%
Fire	44,140,260	1.21%	–		44,140,260	2.56%
Corrections	74,749,653	2.06%	47,819,958	2.33%	26,929,695	1.56%
Natural Resources	27,723,882	0.76%	18,971,299	0.93%	8,752,583	0.51%
Parks and Recreation	37,400,530	1.03%	4,877,732	0.24%	32,522,798	1.89%
Housing	49,944,951	1.37%	8,975,882	0.44%	40,969,069	2.38%
Sewage	51,400,083	1.41%	909,473	0.04%	50,490,610	2.93%
Solid Waste Management	23,100,889	0.64%	1,053,085	0.05%	22,047,804	1.28%
Governmental Administration			53,425,201	2.61%	75,164,470	4.36%
Interest on Debt	107,401,149	2.96%	45,487,467	2.22%	61,913,682	3.59%
Utilities	219,579,491	6.04%	26,285,268	1.28%	193,294,223	11.2%
Liquor Store	6,883,862	0.19%	5,705,110	0.28%	1,178,752	0.07%
Insurance Trust	324,791,548	8.94%	278,323,820	13.59%	46,467,728	2.70%

Source: "Table 1. State and Local Government Finances by Level of Government and by State: 2014," *U.S. Census Bureau,* retrieved from www.census.gov/govs/estimate/0500ussl_1.html. NOTE: may not add up to 100% due to misc. expenditures.

mission to assist political and managerial decision makers make sound, informed decisions about the distribution of financial resources to accomplish goals.[67]

Federal Budgeting

Federal budgeting is certainly a political process, but it has much broader implications, including promoting the public interests. **Aaron Wildavsky**, the dean of the classical approach to the politics of the budgetary process, contends that budgeting has multiple meanings, largely depending upon the context and actors involved.[68] At the most basic level, a budget is simply a prediction. It is used by decision makers to guess about revenue intake, expenditure outflow, and how to balance the difference. How much will it cost to defeat the insurgents in Iraq? In the early stages of the war, President Bush asked for $80 billion to cover the costs of the war for several months. Later, he asked for and received $70 billion—to cover the costs of the war through mid-2009, putting the total cost at over $875 billion.[69] But that was at best a guess—an educated guess, but a guess nonetheless. Budgeting, then, is a prediction about what it will cost to defeat the enemy, pay for prescription drugs, defeat crime, keep the bad guys in prison, and so on.

From a fiduciary-trust concept of the public interests, public budgeting is regarded as a contract between the governed and the government. Presidential and congressional election campaigns are filled with promises. The public is promised that the elderly will receive prescription drug assistance; teacher interest groups are promised higher pay and better working conditions; high tech companies are promised millions of dollars in tax incentives and tax breaks; and local citizen activist groups are promised the new recreation center will be built. Whether or not the promise is kept is one thing, but when the budget is put into action the contractual arrangement is under way.

BOX 8.7 | Aaron Wildavsky (1930–1993)

Aaron Wildavsky was the son of Ukrainian immigrants, grew up in Brooklyn, New York, and attended Brooklyn College. He served in the U.S. Army and in 1958 received his PhD in political science from Yale. From 1962 to his death in 1993, he was professor of political science at the University of California at Berkeley, also served as chair and founding dean of the Graduate School of Public Policy. He wrote over 35 books and hundreds of articles, ranging from presidential politics, budgeting process politics, policy analysis, regulatory policy, and Moses. Those who knew him, like Lawrence Chickering, remember his dynamic personality and engaging sense of wit and wisdom. Chickering wrote about Wildavsky's book on Moses as a political leader: "There is more Wildavsky than Moses in the book; but then, of course, Wildavsky was more interesting than Moses."

Source: A. Lawrence Chickering, "Aaron Wildavsky, RIP—Tribute to the Late Conservative Author, Policy Analyst and Professor—Editorial," *National Review* (October 4, 1993).

Budget Actors and Goals

Who are the primary actors in the U.S. budgeting process and what are their major goals? First is, of course, the President. As a result of the changes in executive budgeting practices beginning in the 1920s, the President became the chief **agenda setter** of budget priorities. However, this role is highly unpredictable, given the propensity for individuality. President George W. Bush, for example, was elected as a Republican and a conservative, but his spending record is anything but conservative. His fiscal management strategy is directed to lowering taxes even during periods of economic uncertainty, including high budget deficits. On the other hand, former President Bill Clinton reduced dramatically the level of defense spending during a time of peace, and increased domestic spending in areas such as AmeriCorps, welfare reform, and environmental protections. In contrast, presidents George W. Bush, Barack Obama, and Donald Trump have increased the level of defense spending with continued military activity in the Middle East.

Second is Congress. Members of Congress are largely motivated by re-election; some are noble in their approach, and are thus moved by fulfilling the public interests. Others regard re-election in a way that the budget process is one of manipulating the appropriations bills to exact as much pork for their constituents as possible. Former Republican Senator Ted Stevens of Alaska, a convicted felon, was regarded as the "King of Pork," because of his avaricious appetite for securing state and local pet projects. Others, like former Republican Representative Steve Largent of Oklahoma, saw their role as one of impacting their state and their constituency with the goal of securing a better and higher quality of life for all citizens. For example, Largent consistently sought increases in appropriations in social and human services, including greater access to healthcare for the elderly. These did not register high on the pork scale, but they were effective in securing a better quality of life for many Oklahomans.[70]

Third are bureaucratic agencies. Agencies are really the driving force in the budgeting process. They are the front-line stakeholders who not only implement the laws, but who actively seek to have their personal and agency goals placed on the President's agenda. To do this they must provide accurate and reliable information to the OMB (Office of Management Budget) when requested. They must be trustworthy, honest, and responsive not only to their respective clientele groups, but to all of the other actors discussed in this section, especially the President and Congress. The role of the agency head, deputy director, program coordinator, and other public administrators is not only to maximize their budget, but also to achieve many public values. These public values may very well weaken their budget maximization claims, including agency autonomy, professionalism, program loyalty, and chain of command.[71]

The Federal Budgetary Process

The federal budgetary process was transformed by the impact of the 1974 reforms (see Figure 8.1). The way Congress establishes taxing and spending legislation is guided by specific procedures set out in the **Congressional Budget and Impoundment Control Act** of 1974 (see "The 1970s Reforms" above), where a greater degree of balance is established between the President and Congress.[72] The key requirement is that Congress constructs a budget resolution setting spending and tax cut limits. There are four basic steps.

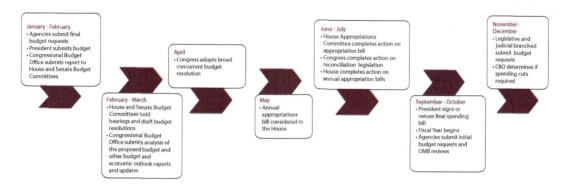

FIGURE 8.1

The Federal Budget Process Calendar

Source: retrieved from http://guides.library.columbia.edu/usgd/budget

Step 1: Presidential Budget Request This begins in February, and is when the President submits to Congress a detailed budget request for the upcoming fiscal year.[73] Developed by the President's Office of Management and Budget (OMB) it does several things: (1) determines the amount of money the Federal Government will direct toward various public purposes; (2) estimates the total amount of revenues needed; and (3) anticipates the deficit (or, in rare circumstances, a surplus) of the Federal Government, reserving to itself the right and responsibility to raise the government's debt limit if necessary. The President's budget request lays out policy priorities. For this purpose the request is specific and lists recommended funding levels for various programs or accounts. The President's budget indicates to Congress the spending and tax changes the President seeks. While most of the federal tax code is permanently set in statute, such as nearly two-thirds of all spending programs, including Medicare, Medicaid, and Social Security, the President does need to request funding for annual discretionary programs that fall under the authority of the House and Senate Appropriations Committees. This type of funding is not permanent, such as defense.

Step 2: Congressional Budget Resolution This provides Congress the authority to establish its own budget priorities. Both the House and Senate Budget Committees hold hearings, listening to and asking senior administration officials and others questions about their various budget requests. After the hearings are complete, the two committees draft a budget resolution, which goes to the respective floors for debate, where it can be amended by majority vote. Finally, it proceeds to both the joint conference committee, composed of members from both houses, where a joint or concurrent budget resolution is passed. The budget resolution is not like a normal piece of legislation—it only requires a majority vote, a filibuster cannot be raised in the Senate to stop it, and the President cannot veto it. A budget resolution is composed of spending categories or functions that list all authorized spending levels for all programs and functions. The difference between what Congress says it can spend (i.e., authority or authorization) and what Congress actually spends (i.e., outlay or appropriation) is usually sizable. It must be noted that the spending totals outlined in the budget resolution are not the same as the authorizing legislation produced by congressional committees. Authorizing legislation only provides a basis for understanding what Congress *might* spend, not what it is required to spend. That is accomplished through a specific appropriations bill. This bill is usually much less than the original authorization legislation.

Step 3: Appropriation Stage   This begins with appropriation bills, and their amendments, and must agree with the numbers from a table called the 302(a) allocation, which is a table representing the total spending limits laid out by budget function in the corresponding budget resolution, distributing them by respective congressional committees. Any additional tax or entitlement bills must also fit within the budget resolution's overall spending limit for the specific committee. The Congressional Budget Office (CBO), which is the fiscal and budget management arm of Congress, tallies the cost and measures it against a budgetary baseline, which projects revenue.[74]

Step 4: Budget Reconciliation   This begins with a single piece of legislation that Congress may use to instruct various committees to produce legislation by a certain date that meets spending and/or tax targets. The budget committees put all of these reconciliation bills together and present them on their respective floors for a "yes" or "no" vote. Reconciliation bills have the advantage of lumping together spending demands, but are usually limited by imposition of the Byrd Rule, named after Senator Byrd of West Virginia, which essentially says that any provision to the reconciliation bill that is deemed out of the ordinary to the general purpose of the law is liable to have a point of order thrown at it. Unless 60 senators vote for the amendment in question, it is stripped from the bill. This is designed to render non-germane amendments ineffective. Finally, the 1974 Act provides for a scorekeeping process to play out. This is where the congressional scorekeepers (i.e., the House and Senate Budget Committees) essentially measure the effects of current and enacted legislation, while assessing its impact on the overall budget plan, which is the budget resolution. Scorekeeping keeps congressional members informed, but it also makes them accountable to their constituents and to each other.[75]

Before explaining how Congress and the President deal with deficits and deficit spending, we turn to a brief explanation of the state and local budget processes.[76] Both are different and will be covered separately.

Example: The Budget Process, Fiscal Year 2016[77]

The last budget resolution passed by Congress was in May 2015, the first budget resolution passed in over five years—or since. Former President Obama transmitted a budget proposal to Congress on February 2, 2015 for Fiscal Year 2016—from October 1, 2015 to September 30, 2016. However, Congress was expected to oppose his budget requests because the proposed level for discretionary spending was 7 percent over the budget caps specified in the Budget Control Act of 2011, and large tax increases on corporations and the wealthy were proposed to fund programs in education and infrastructure maintenance.

Yet, Congress passed a budget resolution in May 2015, the first in over five years. To be sure, congressional budget resolutions are non-binding and symbolic; actual spending levels are specified later in appropriations bills. Congress passed a budget resolution, but envisioned increased military spending and decreased social programs and a balanced budget by 2025. After passing the budget resolution, it went to budget reconciliation procedures. Congressional Republicans hoped to later repeal the Affordable Care Act with a simple majority vote, and expected Obama's presidential veto.

Congressional Republicans sought to stop funding bills that didn't defund Planned Parenthood, that would reauthorize the Export-Import Bank, increase the debt limits, change defense or non-defense spending caps, allow the Iran nuclear deal, or keep the Highway Trust Fund from going broke. However, on September 30, 2015, they passed the 2016 Continuing Appropriations Resolution to keep the Federal Government from completely shutting down, as it had in October 2013. The resignation of Speaker of the House John Boehner (Republican, Ohio) triggered the passage of the continuing resolution to fund the government. However, on October 23, 2015, the House of Representatives passed the 2015 Restoring Americans' Healthcare Reconciliation Act under the budget reconciliation process, to prevent the possibility of a filibuster in the Senate. The bill repealed parts of the 2010 Patient Protection and Affordable Care Act (i.e., employer mandates and taxes on Cadillac medical plans) and defunded Planned Parenthood for one year. It was the 61st effort in five years by House Republicans to repeal the 2010 Patient Protection and Affordable Care Act.

Just before midnight on October 26, 2015, Congress passed the 2015 Bipartisan Budget Act, by a vote of 266–167 in the House of Representatives (one-third of Republicans voted for the budget), and 64–35 in the Senate (35 Republicans voted against). Republican and Democratic leaders also agreed to: increase the budget caps of the Budget Control Act of 2011; temporarily suspend the debt limit until March 2017; make changes in Medicare and Social Security disability insurance; and repeal part of the Patient Protection and Affordable Care Act, requiring larger businesses to enroll new employees automatically in a health plan. Speaker John Boehner said the compromise was to "clean out the barn" before Paul Ryan was Speaker. Obama signed the budget on November 2, 2015.

The U.S. Treasury estimated the U.S. government would run out of funding, so Congress passed a five-day extension of the continuing resolution on December 11, 2015, and a bipartisan appropriations bill was passed on December 15, 2015, entitled the 2016 Consolidated Appropriations Act. The government did not shut down. Meanwhile, the House 2015 Restoring Americans' Healthcare Reconciliation Act was amended by the Senate and a final compromise version passed by Congress on January 6, 2016. It was vetoed, as expected, by the President on January 8, 2016 (only the sixth veto of his presidency). The House failed to get a two-thirds supermajority vote to override the President's veto, with a vote of only 241–186.[78]

State Budgeting

State governments face different challenges and problems than the federal government. A similar challenge is to balance budgets; however, that is made easier because unlike the federal government most state constitutions require state and local governments to balance their budgets.[79] Unlike the federal government, most states, including Texas, prepare two-year or biennial budgets. The general process entails five steps:

1. *Budget instructions* are provided by the governor and his budget office to the various executive departments by asking them for their basic requests, but also placing broad policy limits on those requests.
2. *Department requests* are to be submitted some six to twelve months earlier. During this timeframe, the departments prepares spending priorities, including placing these priorities within their specific departmental plans as well as the broader capital improvement plans of the states.
3. *Gubernatorial review* occurs when the governor and his budget office examine and critique these requests and plans for spending, hold public hearings, and then provide instructions to the departments and agencies for revision in requests. It is the job of the governor, then, to determine which programs to pursue, which are politically viable, where reductions need to be made, and where tax increases or decreases can be made.
4. *General Assembly* enters the process and converts the submitted gubernatorial budget requests into an appropriation bill, which then follows the normal path of any bill, including committee scrutiny, further public hearings, and legislative tinkering. It must pass in both Houses before it can be sent to the governor for his signature.
5. *The governor's **line-item veto*** power allows the chief executive to change specific aspects of the bill, primarily for political advantage. Governor veto powers vary greatly between states.[80]

Local Budgeting

Local budgeting is different from both state and federal budgeting. Whereas federal budgeting is a "vast, sprawling enterprise comprised of a variety of organizations," and state budgeting is politically and technically driven, local budgeting is motivated by the public organization, not just political faces and personalities. Local budgets must balance, i.e., revenues must equal expenditures. In other words, there is not room for backdoor spending and program-driven policy agendas that so often make up federal and state budget processes.[81] Local budgeting—specifically municipal budgeting—is about solving problems, generally through accepting the reforms that work, and rejecting the reforms that failed, all for the general purpose of promoting the public interests.[82]

The local budgeting process generally begins with what local public administrators refer to as the chart of accounts.[83] It is updated annually, and the main function is to classify budget data and other useful information of financial transactions. Each financial activity of the local government entity is recorded in the chart of accounts. Generally, this activity is reserved for performance budget measures.

Local governments examine the various fund accounts, trying to determine somewhat precisely where their revenue is coming from, such as government funds, which "focus primarily on the sources, uses, and balances of current financial resources," including the general fund, special revenue funds, capital projects funds, debt service funds, and permanent funds; proprietary funds, which "focus on the determination of operating income, changes in net assets, financial position, and cash flow, including the two most prominent proprietary funds enterprise and internal service"; and fiduciary funds, which "focus on net assets and changes in net assets from assets held in trustee or agency capacity for others, which cannot be used to support general government spending. These include pension funds, investment trust funds, private-purpose trust funds, and agency funds."[84]

A second major similarity among local governments is to establish a **budget calendar** for directing the budget preparation process. One example is the initial revenue forecast. After this forecast is constructed—usually by the city or county manager's office—it is presented to the city council or county commissioners for their review and feedback. If and when the elected officials approve the forecast, it is put into operation. An illustration is that of Sauk Village, Illinois, where the budget calendar lays out the basic steps and procedures inherent in the local government organization.

A third similarity for local government budgeting is funding on a cash basis; that is, spend only when the dollars are actually in the coffer, not when revenue is promised (i.e., through forecasted revenues, such as in federal grant dollars).[85] Whereas the Federal Government engages in deficit spending, neither state nor local governments are constitutionally allowed to. This places a major emphasis on solid revenue forecasting—that is, trying to determine future revenue, and, most importantly, matching that revenue with anticipated expenditures.[86] Departments and other agencies are required to fill out budget worksheets, where they must anticipate future spending based in large part on itemization and previous budgetary history.[87] Some contend that unless state and local governments stay the course with new performance budgeting, and its emphasis on inputs, outputs, and effectiveness, the age of the permanent fiscal crisis will be upon us.

The process of public budgeting is complex—there is no doubt. But the basic premise is simple: prepare a fiscal plan that describes and diagrams how public dollars are to be spent. Inherent in this process is (or should be) the natural

---

BOX 8.8 | The Basic Steps of Local Budgeting for Small Towns in Indiana

- *First,* county auditor submits a certificate which verifies the assessed value of county's political subdivisions, shows average growth or loss of value, tax estimates, etc.

- *Second,* two publications of public budget (first one ten days before first public hearing, second one three days before first public hearing) by the county government.

- *Third,* somewhere near the end of the year budget work sheets are distributed to the various department heads, and by January (but no later than February), the departments have completed their strategic planning and submitted their requests.

- *Fourth,* public hearings are held and taxpayers have the no more than seven days to object to the budget, including tax levy, tax rate, etc.

- *Fifth,* local governments submit budgets to the County Auditor and County Tax Adjustment Board (TAB) and they make adjustments as needed. Taxpayers may object to adjustments.

- *Sixth,* towns have until February 1 to adopt new budgets. ◢

Source: Budget Division, *Local Government Budget Manual: A Guide Through the Process of Indiana Local Government* Budgeting (Indianapolis: State of Indiana, August 2011).

inclination of elected, appointed, and merit-civil-service public officials to care for and protect public dollars. This is primarily how public budgeting influences or pursues the public interests. Whether it the Federal Government's $2.9 trillion 2008–2009 budget,[88] the state of Virginia's $36.9 billion spending plan,[89] or Dunn, North Carolina's $8.7 million local budget,[90] the point is the same: governments prepare plans to spend the citizens' money.

Deficits and Deficit Spending

What happens when spending outdistances revenue? State and local governments are generally restricted from overspending, either (or both) by constitutional amendment or statutory guidelines. The national government, however, is not so restricted. Several times throughout history, Congress has attempted to deal with spending and overspending. More often than not it becomes a political battle between the President and Congress, along with countless private and public interests groups, lobbyists, and many others. The 1974 reforms placed fairly strict controls on federal spending; however, it did not stop Congress from spending more than it takes in; thus, it could still engage in deficit spending.

A **deficit** is the yearly amount of money a government unit spends beyond what it takes in each year. Accumulated deficits are a large part of the federal **debt**, or the total amount of money the government owes beyond what it has the means to pay. The entire decade of the 1980s, and into the early part of the 1990s, the deficit reached unprecedented heights. According to some figures, the deficit increased four times, from roughly $74 billion to nearly $300 billion. By the end of President H.W. Bush's only term, the deficit reached nearly $400 billion, which was approaching nearly 8 percent of the nation's Gross Domestic Product (GDP). Congress acted to deal with the increasing federal deficits and overall debt.

However, for the first time in nearly three decades the Federal Government reached a **budget surplus** (i.e., taking in more revenue than it expended), to the tune of $70 billion. By 2000, the surplus was $127 billion, and in 2001 it was $236 billion. Then everything changed on September 11, 2001, when terrorists attacked on U.S. soil. President Bush pledged a war on terror—globally, in Iraq, Afghanistan—which greatly increased the federal budget. As a result of these actions, coupled with President Bush's 10-year $1.3 trillion tax cuts and increased federal spending, federal deficits skyrocketed.

ETHICS CASE STUDY | Corruption

As we discussed at the beginning of the chapter, a primary historical purpose of precise and detailed lawful budgeting, public finance, and financial management practices was to limit corruption, graft, treasury raids, pilfering, boss-rule, and irresponsible wasteful expenditure,[91] both historically and in our contemporary constitutional experience. This primary purpose of public financial resources administration continues in the US and globally today with a growing concern for corruption.[92] Public financial management practices must be designed to uphold the 2003 United Nations Convention against Corruption multilateral treaty, with **anti-corruption safeguards** to uphold the rule of law, requiring rules for public financial and property management, transparency, accountability, and integrity.

Corruption exacts a tremendous annual cost in financial terms, in addition to human costs in careers, retirements, organizational time, and lives. In 2016, the International Monetary Fund (IMF) estimated the monetary costs of corruption as follows:

> the annual cost of bribery alone [is] at about $1.5 to $2 trillion (roughly 2 percent of global GDP). The overall economic and social costs of corruption are likely to be even larger, since bribes constitute only one aspect of the possible forms of corruption.[93]

America saw a record increase in 2017 of **ethics complaints** to the U.S. Office on Government Ethics alleging corruption. Consider U.S. Senator Martin Heinrich's report of the U.S. Congress Joint Economic Committee 2017:

> Over the past six months, the Office of Government Ethics has received 39,105 inquiries—up more than 5,000 percent over the comparable period leading up to President Obama's 2012 election and first months in office. Corruption is not a concept we are used to discussing in the context of the contemporary American economy. Many of the most informative studies on corruption are from developing countries, which shows just how much President Trump has begun to undermine the norms and institutions that enable not only our democracy to function, but also our economy.[94] Corruption has been generally defined as "the abuse of position or power—a violation of the public trust—often for personal gain by an individual or institution in the public or private sector."[95]

Corruption in public administration has been defined as the use of a position of trust of public servants for dishonest gain. It may be a transfer to better oneself or for one or more citizens. But when the gain is received without regard to due process and public interest, it raises serious ethical concerns on the capability of a democratic government to serve all citizens.[96]

The English word *corrupt* comes from the Latin *corruption*, meaning "to mar, destroy, contaminate, or putrefy." In Middle English, the word *corrupt* was used to refer to physical or moral contamination or destruction. Within contemporary public administration, corruption is used to mean some action or decision that is antithetical to the basic purposes of public service.[97] Sometimes it is used to refer generally to the failure of public organizations or as an unethical betrayal of the essential professional ethic of public administrators to serve the public "honestly and disinterestedly as trustees of the public interest."[98] The history of public administration in the US has been a series of reforms to guard against corruption.[99] Efforts to prevent corruption in public administration usually focus on accountability, responsibility,

(continued)

and integrity of public servants.[100] The 2013 ASPA Code of Ethics doesn't mention the word *corruption*, or specifically reference the related ethical concepts of conflicts of interests, bribery, embezzlement, and other dishonest use of authority for personal benefit. Public corruption is the focus of legislation on ethics for public administrators.[101]

Corruption is also associated with public scandals, which have been the fodder for the sale of newspapers, TV time, and web space for so long that we have come to call it yellow journalism. Corruption, sex, abuse of power, and other vices of individuals in the public service are regularly paraded on display by the media to excite, titillate, and outrage the consumer—and destroy careers. You may have seen it—for example, the news story on a prison guard who had sex with an inmate, a cop who took a bribe to ignore the drug dealer, a city manager who had a street crew blacktop their driveway for free, or even the Senator who was convicted on seven counts of bribery charges. We talk about the cycle of scandal because it never seems to go away. A scandal seems to keep dredging up over and over again to brand individuals, groups, or organizations who can never escape a mark of shame.[102]

Classifications of Corruption

Corruption may be classified as criminal or civil, and petty or grand within criminal corruption. Petty criminal corruption is classified in most states if the amount of money or property taken was less than $100 (as in the common law). Injury to persons is not considered petty. Grand criminal corruption is classified for over $100 money or value, and any injury to persons. Civil corruption is more difficult to define and may involve token amounts of money or value received, often within the context of common practices in the workplace and with conflicting opinions on ethics, e.g., holiday gifts at office. For example, Dallas County, Texas, judges and staff had received gift boxes of cookies, turkeys, or hams from local law firms for holidays as long as . . . no one could remember. But it may be interpreted as a violation of state ethics law. Local lawyer Mike Brown thought it ludicrous to think of this as corrupt: "Any implication that a cookie could curry a law firm more favor is ridiculous." But District Judge Jay Patterson decided no cookies, even at the risk of being considered on the Grinchy side: "I don't want to sound silly about this. I think the integrity of the judge has to be without blemish, for all the obvious reasons."[103]

Corruption laws may be classified by the specific occupational sector in the public service. For example, general anti-corruption laws may simply refer to all publicly elected officials and bureaucrats. For example, prohibitions against soliciting or offering bribery usually include public service in general. However, certain forms of anti-corruption laws target police who are influenced not to report drug sales, other vice crimes, or prostitution. Other specific anti-corruption laws may focus only on judges, lawyers, educators, or school administrators, or within labor unions.

Finally, corruption may be classified by the number of people involved. Personalistic or individual corruption is often called the "bad apple" theory, e.g., a lone police officer takes a bribe to ignore a ticket. Corruption is caused by one bad individual; thus, better recruitment is the remedy to avoid hiring the one bad apple. Many public ethics codes at the workplace apply this perspective and assume that individuals simply make bad choices when corruption occurs. However, close empirical studies of police and corrections officers reject this individualistic theory of corruption; instead, corruption reflects the "values which are habitually practiced and accepted," and those officers who resist the "code" are the "goofs" or deviant apples.[104] **Institutional corruption** includes all members of an organization who share a set of habitually accepted values, e.g., a majority of correctional officers in a state prison provide illegal boxes of cigarettes to inmates based on an accepted rate. A further example: most convenience stores that are openly nightly have "police cups" behind the counter to give free coffee or soft drinks to officers who stop at the store, thus, institutionalizing "the gift" to encourage a police presence. The remedy usually proposed is more bureaucratization and accountability, e.g., body cameras on all police while on duty. Finally, systemic corruption exists when society-wide conflicts may impose immoral behavior as a job expectation, e.g., past department-wide shakedowns of merchants by the New York Police Department in the 1960s and 1970s for "protection money" or for the "widows' and orphans' fund." This also relates to corruption of noble cause—the loss of the moral commitment to protect, honor, and serve by police in decaying urban settings, or by military soldiers imprisoning terrorists in Abu Ghraib Prison in Iraq in 2004–2005, or in Cuba at Guantanamo Bay Prison in 2004 to the present. The remedy proffered has usually included intensive efforts at greater professionalization.

Methods of Corruption

The methods of corruption include the variety of behaviors, actions, or inactions that may be proscribed as corruption. While early attempts to categorize the varieties of corruption focused only on types and means of political graft,[105] all states, local governments, and the Federal Government have now formulated ethics codes and laws to deal with the wide variety of corruption behaviors.[106] The categories below are a brief list of some of the major types of corrupt activities.

Bribery developed from the common law crime of **extortion**—the corrupt collection of excessive or unauthorized fees/taxes/monies by a public official acting under color of office. Bribery, however, involved the voluntary giving of something of value to influence performance of official duty. While ancient laws punished only corrupt public officials, modern statutes punish the briber (bribe-giver) as well. English laws also limited application of the offense to the bribery of judicial officers, while American statutes include judges and nearly all other public officials, public employees, and even many commercial or occupational supervising employers. Related offenses include

(continued)

misconduct in office, accepting unlawful gratuities, compounding a crime, conspiracy, extortion, and even embracery—the voluntary giving of something of value to influence the official performance of a juror.

Official **misconduct in office** refers to the corrupt intentional behavior of a public official while exercising their duties under color of office. Logically, a public official may engage in misconduct in office by **nonfeasance** (failure to perform), **malfeasance** (wrongful performance), and **misfeasance** (improper performance). Acting under color of office simply means within the proper and usual scope of duties of the public officials. Intentional violation of a citizen's civil rights constitutes a federal crime. Relatedly, current statutes define **obstruction of justice** to include all unlawful acts intentionally designed to hinder or stop the administration of civil or criminal administration of the laws. Many forms of corruption activities by public servants may constitute obstruction of justice by intentionally avoiding the dutiful execution of the laws. The historic common law crime protected only judicial institutions. Obstruction of justice today may include many civil liabilities, as well as criminal acts such as refusing to obey a court order, harboring known fugitives, failing to report or falsely reporting a crime, hindering police officers in the performance of their duties, and intimidating or influencing jurors, witnesses, or litigants.

Embezzlement is the fraudulent conversion of the personal property of another by a person entrusted with the property. Created by modern statutes, this crime is often associated with public officials—as well as bank employees, lawyers, and others who, in the course of their lawful activities, come into possession of property owned by others. Embezzlement converts property to one's own use.

False pretenses is knowingly and designedly obtaining the property of another person by false representations with the intent to defraud the victim. Public servants may engage in false pretenses in knowingly misrepresenting to the public the laws or demanding payments not required by law. Benjamin Franklin quipped, "a fool and his money are soon parted." Criminal false pretenses involve making falsehoods designed to obtain another person's money or goods; sometimes known as a confidence game or con. While larceny requires a taking, and embezzlement a conversion, false pretenses requires an act of fraud. It is difficult to prove, as many people misunderstand or misstate things.

Extortion or blackmail involve the illegal taking of money by anyone who employs threats or other illegal use of fear or coercion in order to obtain the money, and whose conduct falls short of the threat to personal safety required for robbery (which includes threat of immediate harm). At common law, extortion was the illegal collection of an excessive fee or taxes by a corrupt public official. Public servants may still be charged with extortion for illegal use of their public office powers to coerce others to obtain monies or something of value. Today, extortion is more akin to robbery, except the timing of the threat of force is not so immediate. Some statutes require that the defendant actually begin to carry out the threat before the behavior constitutes the crime of extortion.

Receiving or concealing stolen property involves obtaining and having control over property (for however short a time) known to be stolen, with the intent of permanently depriving its rightful owner. The *mens rea*, or intent to deprive, may be inferred from circumstances surrounding the receipt of the property (e.g., purchasing a new mink fur coat from a salesman's car trunk for $20). Public servants may knowingly receive or conceal property they know to be stolen, using their public office powers, e.g., to store stolen cars from another in the city garage, or store stolen guns from another in a city warehouse.

Many modern statutes consolidate bribery, larceny, and all other crimes of misappropriation and deprivation into one crime simply called **theft**: "Conduct denominated theft in this article constitutes a single offense embracing the separate offenses heretofore known as larceny, embezzlement, false pretenses, extortion, blackmail, fraudulent conversion, receiving stolen property and the like."[107] Note that the consolidated theft statutes do not include the crime of robbery.

Forgery offenses are rising among public administrators. It is the making of false legal documents or the altering of existing documents, such as checks, property titles, stocks, bonds, or money orders. The crime requires the criminal act of a false writing or material alteration with the intent to defraud others. Related offenses include uttering (passing bad checks or false legal documents to others) and counterfeiting (a treasonous crime against the US; the creating of false currency).

Contempt is a civil liability or crime from the ancient English equity or chancery courts that were separate of the common law or common pleas courts for many centuries. The U.S. Constitution brought them together in federal courts (the states followed). For these ancient equity courts, acts disrespecting the courts or judicial processes, which also obstructed the administration of justice, were punishable as criminal contempt by fines or incarceration by the discretion of the judge. Today, civil contempt is an offense against a party for whom a court order was issued. Direct contempt occurs in the immediate presence of a court while in session. Constructive contempt occurs outside the court's presence by failing or refusing to obey the court's lawful order. Modern statutes have incorporated this equitable power into law and give great discretionary power to judges in determining what, when, where, and whom may be found in contempt. Like the ancient chancery courts, some jurisdictions allow judges to find and punish contempt on the spot, without a right to hearings or arguments.

Conflicts of Interest

Conflicts of interest have greatly increased in use for civil law liability and ethical reviews in both public and private sectors worldwide. Corruption Watch of South Africa defines conflicts of interest as

(*continued*)

ETHICS CASE STUDY | *Continued*

> Any financial or other private interest or undertaking that could
> directly or indirectly compromise the performance of the public
> servant's duties or the reputation of a public servant's department in
> its relationship with its stakeholders. A situation in which a public
> official has a private interest which influences, or appears to influence
> a public decision.[108]

Conflicts of interest may include:

- Holding public office as well as private business interests and using
  your public position to benefit your private interests.
- Influencing government tender processes so that your family members
  and friends are awarded state contracts.
- Abusing your position within a government department to ensure
  your friends and family members are hired into the same department.
- Accepting bribes in order to disclose confidential information about
  the government department that you work for.
- Tendering for a municipal contract when you are an employee of the
  municipality.[109]

However, a conflict of interest is difficult to identify and prove. For example,
is it a conflict of interest for a city employee to meet their state governor as a
guest speaker at a city management conference? Monitoring and preventive
resolution of conflicting interests is even more challenging. How effective at
controlling conflicting interests are the quarterly forms requiring that city
employees report any meeting with executive or legislative officials? Conflict
of interest by public servants requires more specific strategies for preventing
conflicting interests.[110]

Equally vague are related workplace ethics codes prohibiting the
"appearance of impropriety." This language was standard in state judicial
codes of ethics until recently, but this ambiguous language has been tossed
aside in past decades by state judges' associations, bar associations, and
other professional ethics code associations. It seems too vague and ambiguous to be enforced without arbitrariness and discrimination. Yet, public
organizations, such as the U.S. Department of Housing and Urban Development, may still use similar language as the basis for terminating employment
of its staff. In *Wild v. US* (6th Cir. U.S. Ct.App., 1982), Judge Richard Posner
of the 6th Circuit U.S. Court of Appeals upheld the dismissal of Lawrence
A. Wild, an employee of the U.S. Department of Housing and Urban Development (HUD) in Chicago, Illinois. He had violated the Department's code
prohibiting the "appearances of official impropriety." Wild's specific offense,
according to Judge Posner, was allowing the apartment buildings he owned
to "deteriorate so badly it did not escape newspaper comment." Mr. Wild
argued the HUD code was so "vague as to provide inadequate notice" as to

what kind of "off-duty conduct places [an official's] job on the line." Judge Posner disagreed and applied the "appearance standard"—he was culpable for what it reasonably appeared to be, not what he actually did.[111] Can conflict of interest and appearance of impropriety ethics complaints take the form of a "witch hunt" to simply attack others of conflicting personalities or diverse cultures? When is an ethics violation too vague or ambiguous as to violate constitutional due process of law?

Transparency, RICO, and Citizen Engagement

What to do about corruption? Of course, corruption may be reduced or prevented by the old standby approaches of external and internal controls, as we've discussed throughout this book. More recently, policy makers, managers, and practitioners have come to focus on transparency, financial disclosure, and similar procedures to remedy corruption. Transparency involves openness, accessibility, accountability, and honesty in government and public sector organizations sharing information with the public. Increasingly, the emphasis is on accessibility, as in freely available online to those who seek access. Financial disclosure specifically refers to sharing of financial and accounting information to the public. However, there are few studies of the impact of U.S. public sector transparency and financial disclosure—and with little evidence of the success of transparency in reducing corruption.[112]

Civil and criminal sanctions specially designed to help attack public corruption exist in federal courts and 33 state jurisdictions. The 1970 Racketeer Influenced and Corrupt Organizations Act, often simply called RICO, 18 U.S.C. sections 1961–1968, enabled the lawful seizure by federal prosecutors of monies, real estate, and other properties of racketeering organizations. Passed with the 1970 Organized Crime Control Act, it extends criminal and civil remedies against the leaders of criminal organizations involved in racketeering, including public sector officials, judges, and others. Racketeering is generally defined as carrying on illegal business that involves crime, and legally defined to include any act, orders, assistance, or threat involving a predicate offense of treason, piracy, and counterfeiting—as well as state criminal offenses such as murder, kidnaping, gambling, arson, robbery, bribery, extortion, dealing in obscene materials, controlled substance or listed chemicals, and so forth. RICO statutes have greatly expanded the list of criminal offenses that federal courts may now prosecute. RICO requires proof of a pattern of racketeering activities, with continuity of two or more racketeering activities within a 10-year timeframe and continuing relationships. Louisiana Commissioner of Agriculture & Forestry Gil Dozier was convicted in federal court of extortion and RICO racketeering in 1980 for compelling companies doing business with his department to give him campaign contributions. Pennsylvania state judge Mark Ciavarella was convicted in 2011 under federal RICO in a "kids for cash" kickback scheme to assign housing of juveniles with a private organization, Pennsylvania Child Care. President Donald J. Trump was named in a RICO case filed in 2013

(*continued*)

for misrepresenting Trump University "to make tens of millions of dollars" but delivering "neither Donald Trump nor a university." The case was scheduled for federal RICO hearings on November 28, 2016. However, just after Trump won the presidential election, he settled for $25 million without any admission of wrongdoing. Has RICO deterred or otherwise reduced corruption in the public sector? Many scholars have criticized that it has added to corruption, as RICO is administered in a racist discriminatory pattern, RICO has allowed significant distortion and discarding of due process rights under the Constitution, and RICO has contributed to neglect of homicide

BOX 8.9 | Mini-Case Study in Corruption

In 2005, Kevin Geddings resigned from his position as the Commissioner for the State Lottery in North Carolina. Hours after his resignation, the Scientific Games Corp. (a scratch-off supplied), which was bidding to supply scratch-offs for North Carolina, reported that they had used Kevin Geddings' former employer, a public relations firm, before Geddings' appointment as commissioner and paid him for services performed. Geddings, however, did not report this connection to North Carolina's Board of Ethics prior to becoming commissioner. Since the commission was looking for new suppliers, Geddings' past connection posed obvious concerns of fraud. After his resignation and the Scientific Games Corp.'s announcement, Geddings was charged with nine counts of fraud, including both mail and wire fraud. Three counts were thrown out before the three-week trial started.

During the trial, Geddings' defense argued that he was not guilty because he resigned from the public relations firm before joining the commission and because he didn't realize that he had to tell the Ethics Board about the connection. Geddings did testify that he "was not as precise" as necessary on the state ethics disclosure form. Both the governor and the House speaker testified that they did not know about the connection when they appointed him.

After a three-week trial and six hours of jury deliberation, Geddings was found guilty of five counts of mail fraud and innocent of one count of wire fraud. Each count carried a potential 20-year sentence, although everyone associated with the case doubted he would receive such a steep sentence.

After the trial, Geddings moved to St. Augustine, Florida to await sentencing. He began serving a four-year sentence in 2007, but was released in 2010 when the U.S. Supreme Court determined that mail and wire fraud crimes had to be intentional. Geddings' fraud was not deemed intentional and, on August 27, 2010, his sentenced was vacated, which effectively means the crime, trial, and sentencing never occurred. Geddings currently works at a marketing consulting firm that he started in St. Augustine, GLK Consultants LLC, which deals with advertising, marketing, and public relations.

and violent crime, because police focus only on RICO-related drug offenses and ignore cases in homicide crimes.[113]

Citizen engagement offers greater hope for preventing corruption in public administration. Close empirical research has documented the success of various citizen engagement strategies within public administration for improved accountability and prevention of corruption. However, much of this research is comparative or area field studies outside the US.[114] For example, the implementation of democratic policing organization reforms of national police seems associated with citizen perceptions of reduced corruption in their governments. Democratic policing, similar to community policing in the US,[115] structures regular police-citizen interactions as part of daily law enforcement routines, facilitates citizen co-production of order in neighborhood watches, and takes police organizations street-level to the people. For example, democratic policing moves police offices from a central downtown location to store-front locations throughout the city, moves police within grade schools and high schools in Drug Abuse Resistance Education (DARE) program, and puts police on bicycles and on walking beats within neighborhoods.[116] Empirical studies document that, in settings such as Turkey, Hong Kong, Mexico, South Africa, and others, there is a significant increase in quality of living and human rights scores (i.e., as measured by Freedom House and others) associated with the citizen engagement accompanying the organizational reforms of democratic policing.[117] Would the radical organizational reform of policing work in the US to infuse citizen engagement into public life? How would citizen engagement be introduced into other government, nonprofit, and hybrid-private public service organizations?

Discussion

- What is corruption? How extensive is the problem?
- What does the 2003 UN Convention Against Corruption mandate of governments to control it?
- How is corruption classified: by petty/grand/civil? by occupation? by numbers?
- What are the methods of corruption?
- How may corruption be controlled? Conflicts of Interest? Avoid the appearance of impropriety? Transparency? RICO? Citizen engagement? ▲

CONCLUSION

The structures, tools, and processes of public financial management have been designed to fulfill the public interests with accuracy, honesty, comprehensiveness, and timely details on these basic symbols of policy and public administration services and goods. As overviewed in our discussion of political economy and the history of budgeting, public financial management is not only a fiscal and monetary resources tool, but it may be a political measure of the various and often conflicting components of the public interests. Yes, budgeting reflects distinct political wants and needs; we recognize this, but it also reflects the greater public interests; which is establishing a firm financial foundation for future generations. And this will take our elected leaders and civil servants to make difficult and unpopular decisions regarding how to spend our money.

Thus, public financial management requires the virtues of prudence in decision making, as well as honesty, trustworthiness, respect, fairness, and dedication to pursuing and fulfilling the public interests. Yet ethical breakdowns frequently occur with corruption, conflicts of interest, the appearance of impropriety, and other ethics crises. There seem to be many factors involved in these conflicts: the increasing pressure from interest groups; the cyclical nature of politics itself; the changing economic, fiscal, and monetary dynamics of the national economy; and the short-term mindset of elected officials offset with the long-term outlook of merit-based agency officials. It is a wonder how public financial management succeeds in this complex political reality, intertwined with internal bureaucratic interests and besieged with competing external interests.

ACTION STEPS

1. Research state and local government agencies, in person or on the web. Ascertain by interview or internet report how each agency uses performance-based budgeting. How are results measured? To what degree do these results dictate future goals, missions, and planning for each agency?

2. Examine a simple line-item municipal budget. What is the total budget allocation amount? How many different revenue sources are accounted? Describe what a line-item budget does for the public administrator, elected official, local interest group, and general public.

3. Do the public interests empower judges in the budgetary process? Consider the case of a federal judge who ordered new taxes to desegregate public schools in *Missouri v. Jenkins*, 495 U.S. 33 (1990). The new taxes were upheld even though voters had rejected a new tax three times in public referendums.

4. Look up the corruption laws in your state statutes, either online or in hard copies. What civil and criminal corruption prohibitions do you find? Are there specific corruption prohibitions for particular occupations, such as police, educators, or judges? Does your state have laws on conflict of interest by public servants and officials? Do these laws seem too vague or ambiguous to you—or are they clearly written?

KEY CONCEPTS AND NAMES

NOTES

1 United Nations Convention Against Corruption (2003), Chapter II. Preventive measures, Article 5. Preventive anti-corruption policies and practices, Section 1. Retrieved from www.unodc.org/documents/treaties/UNCAC/Publications/Convention/08-50026_E.pdf

2 For example, National Conference of State Legislators (NCSL), "Penalties for Violations of State Ethics and Public Corruption Laws," retrieved from www.ncsl.org/research/ethics/50-state-chart-criminal-penalties-for-public-corr.aspx

3 Senator Martin Heinrich, "The Costs of Corruption to the American Economy" (May 2017), *U.S. Congress Joint Economic Committee*, retrieved from www.jec.senate.gov/public/_cache/files/c6be7b7d-cb39-499a-b6d6-d5b3d65368c8/the-costs-of-corruption-to-the-american-economy-final.pdf

4 Kaifeng Yang, "From Administration to Management," in Mary E. Guy and Marilyn M. Rubin, eds., *Public Administration Evolving: From Foundations to the Future* (New York: Routledge, 2015), 103–22.

5 Jesse Burkhead, *Government Budgeting* (New York: John Wiley, 1956), see, chapter 1, "The Development of Modern Budgeting," 2–30.

6 U.S. Constitution, Article I, Section 9.

7 Henry Jones Ford, *The Cost of Our National Government* (New York: Columbia University Press, 1910), 60—alleging the national government mal-accounting of the surpluses from US tariffs.

8 Jesse Burkhead, *Government Budgeting* (New York, NY: John Wiley, 1956), 15.

9 Ibid., 21.

10 For example, Paul H. Douglas, *Ethics in Government* (Cambridge, MA: Harvard University Press, 1952).

11 For example, Fraud Examination and Financial Forensics at CUNY-John Jay College, Department of Public Management, retrieved from www.johnjay.cuny.edu/fraud-examination-and-financial-forensics

12 John Maynard Keynes, *The General Theory of Employment, Interest, and Money* (New York, NY: Macmillan 2007 reprint of 1936 original), 383–4.

13 Xenophon, "The Oeconomicus," (about 362 BCE) in *Xenophon IV: Memorabilia, Oeconomicus, Symposium, Apology*, E.C. Marchant and O.J. Todd, trans. (Cambridge, MA: Harvard University Press/Loeb Classical Library, 1923), 362–525.

14 Bruce Cannon Gibney, *A Generation of Sociopaths: How the Baby Boomers Betrayed America* (New York, NY: Hachette Books, 2017), 132.

15 See, generally, William J. Barber, *A History of Economic Thought* (New York, NY: Penguin Books, 1967); Robert Heilbroner, *The Worldly Philosophers: The Lives, Times and Ideas of the Great Economic Thinkers*, 7th ed. (New York, NY: Touchstone Press, 1999).

16 Ludwig von Mises, *Liberalism: In the Classical Tradition*, (Auburn, AL: Ludwig von Mises Institute, 1927), retrieved from mises.org/library/liberalism-classical-tradition/html/p/30

17 João Ricardo Faria, and F.G. Carneiro, "Does High Inflation Affect Growth in the Long and Short Run?" *Journal of Applied Economics* 4 (#1, 2001): 89–105.

18 See, Eugene F. Miller, *Hayek's The Constitution of Liberty: An Account of Its Argument* (London: Institute of Economic Affairs, 2011).

19 Bruce Cannon Gibney, *A Generation of Sociopaths: How the Baby Boomers Betrayed America* (New York, NY: Hachette Books, 2017), 102.

20 Jeffrey A. Tucker, "What is 'Neoliberalism' Anyway?" (May 17, 2017), *Foundation for Economic Education*, retrieved from https://fee.org/articles/what-is-neoliberalism-anyway/

21 Thayer Watkins, "Public Choice Theory" (2017), *San Jose State University Economics Department*, retrieved from www.sjsu.edu/faculty/watkins/publicchoice.htm

22 Laurence J. O'Toole, Jr., "Rational Choice and Policy Implementation: Implications for Interorganizational Network Management," *American Review of Public Administration*, 25 (#1, 1995): 43–57.

23 Benjamin Cohen, *International Political Economy: An Intellectual History* (Princeton, NJ: Princeton University Press, 2008).

24 Gary Browning and Andrew Kilmister, *Critical and Post-Critical Political Economy* (New York, NY: Palgrave Macmillan, 2006).

25 Thomas D. Lynch and Jered B. Carr, "Public Administration Implications of the North American Free Trade Agreement," *International Journal of Public Administration* 19 (#9, 1996): 1555–95.

26 Free exchange, "In Defence of NAFTA: NAFTA Has Been a Disappointment But Its Benefits Are Underappreciated" (February 2, 2017), *The Economist*, retrieved from www.economist.com/news/finance-and-economics/21716033-nafta-has-been-disappointment-its-benefits-are-underappreciated-defence

27 Gerardo Otero, "Neoliberal Globalization, NAFTA, and Migration: Mexico's Loss of Food and Labor Sovereignty," *Journal of Poverty* 15 (2011): 384–402.

28 Nicholas Henry, *Public Administration and Public Affairs*, 9th ed. (Upper Saddle River, NJ: Prentice Hall, 2004), 243.

29 David C. Nice, *Public Budgeting* (Boston: Cengage, 2001).

30 Robert W. Smith and Thomas D. Lynch, *Public Budgeting in America*, 5th ed. (Upper Saddle River, NJ: Prentice Hall, 2004), 71.

31 See Leonard D. White, *Introduction to the Study of Public Administration*, 4th ed. (New York, NY: Macmillan, 1954), 239, 240; Leonard D. White, *The Federalist: A Study in Administrative History* (New York, NY: Macmillan, 1956), 323; and Jerry L. McCaffery, "The Development of Public Budgeting in the United States," in *A Centennial History of the American Administrative State,* ed. Ralph Clark Chandler (New York, NY: The Free Press), 349–53.

32 Jerry L. McCaffery, "The Development of Public Budgeting in the United States," in *A Centennial History of the American Administrative State,* ed. Ralph Clark Chandler (New York, NY: The Free Press), 355.

33 Ibid., 357.

34 Ibid., 358, 359.

35 Allen Schick, *The Federal Budget: Politics, Policy, Process* (Washington, DC: Brookings Institution, 2000), 12.

36 Richard J. Stillman II, *Creating the American State: The Moral Reformers and the Modern Administrative World They Made* (Tuscaloosa: University of Alabama Press, 1998). See discussion of Frederick Cleveland, Frank J. Goodnow, and W.F. Willoughby in Aaron Wildavsky and Naomi Caiden, *The New Politics of the Budgetary Process*, 5th ed. (New York, NY: Pearson Longman, 2004), 37.

37 Janet M. Kelly and William C. Rivenbark, *Performance Budgeting for State and Local Government* (Armonk, NY: M.E. Sharpe, 2003), 22.

38 For an extensive historical overview of municipal budgeting, see Irene S. Rubin, *Class, Tax, and Power: Municipal Budgeting in the United States* (Chatham, NJ: Chatham House, 1998), 31–60.

39 Smith and Lynch claim that, in 1929, A.E. Buck, staff personnel of the New York Bureau, was the first to document and write the first text on budgeting; *Public Budgeting in America*, 5th ed. (Upper Saddle River, NJ: Prentice Hall, 2004), 76.

40 Janet M. Kelly and William C. Rivenbark, *Performance Budgeting for State and Local Government* (Armonk, NY: M.E. Sharpe, 2003), 27.

41 Nicholas Henry, *Public Administration and Public Affairs*, 9th ed. (Upper Saddle River, NJ: Prentice Hall, 2004), 216.

42 Robert W. Smith and Thomas D. Lynch, *Public Budgeting in America*, 5th ed. (Upper Saddle River, NJ: Prentice Hall, 2004), 78.

43 Ibid., 78, 79.

44 Janet M. Kelly and William C. Rivenbark, *Performance Budgeting for State and Local Government* (Armonk, NY: M.E. Sharpe, 2003), 31.

45 David Nice, *Public Budgeting* (Belmont, CA: Thomson-Wadsworth, 2002), 108, 110.

46 Robert W. Smith and Thomas D. Lynch, *Public Budgeting in America*, 5th ed. (Upper Saddle River, NJ: Prentice Hall, 2004), 95, 96.

47 Aaron Wildavsky and Naomi Caiden, *The New Politics of the Budgetary Process*, 5th ed. (New York, NY: Pearson Longman, 2003).

48 Ibid., 96, 97.

49 Nicholas Henry, *Public Administration and Public Affairs*, 9th ed. (Upper Saddle River, NJ: Prentice Hall, 2004), 221.

50 Ibid., 222.

51 George J. Gordon and Michael E. Milakovich, *Public Administration in America*, 6th ed. (New York, NY: St. Martin's Press, 1998), 316.

52 Janet V. Denhardt and Robert B. Denhardt, *The New Public Service: Serving, Not Steering* (Armonk, NY: M.E. Sharpe, 2003).

53 David Osborne and Ted Gaebler, *Reinventing Government: How the Entrepreneurial Spirit is Transforming the Public Sector* (Reading, MA: Addison-Wesley, 1992).

54 Ibid., 162–3.

55 For a more extensive analysis of "budgeting outcomes" and performance budgeting see David Osborne and Peter Hutchinson, *The Price of Government: Getting the Results We Need in an Age of Permanent Crisis* (New York, NY: Basic Books, 2004), 65–93.

56 Nicholas Henry, *Public Administration and Public Affairs*, 9th ed. (Upper Saddle River, NJ: Prentice Hall, 2004), 236.

57 Janet M. Kelly and William C. Rivenbark, *Performance Budgeting for State and Local Government* (Armonk, NY: M.E. Sharpe, 2003), 36–41.

58 David Osborne and Peter Hutchinson, *The Price of Government: Getting the Results We Need in an Age of Permanent Crisis* (New York, NY: Basic Books, 2004), 84–7.

59 Charlie Tyer and Jennifer Willand, "Public Budgeting in America: A Twentieth Century Retrospective," *Journal of Public Budgeting, Accounting and Financial Management* 9 (#2, Summer 1997), retrieved October 2007 from www.ipspr.sc.edu/publication/Budgeting_in_America.htm

60 This brief historical overview of the U.S. tax system was drawn from Fact Sheets, "History of the U.S. Tax System," U.S. Department of the Treasury, retrieved October 2007 from www.treas.gov/education/fact-sheets/taxes/ustax.shtml. For additional information, see Alan O. Dixler, "Direct Taxes Under the Constitution: A Review of the Precedents," Tax Analysts, November 20, 2006, retrieved October 2007 from www.taxhistory.org/thp/readings.nsf/ArtWeb/2B34C7FBDA41D9DA852573080006 7017?OpenDocument; and "A Brief History of U.S. Law on the Taxation of Americans Abroad," American Citizens Abroad, retrieved October 2007 from www.aca.ch/hisustax.htm

61 Michael C. Lemay, *Public Administration: Clashing Values in the Administration of Public Policy* (Belmont, CA: Wadsworth, 2002), 269.

62 Jeffrey D. Greene, *Public Administration in the New Century: A Concise Introduction* (Belmont, CA: Wadsworth), 259.

63 Robert B. Denhardt and Joseph W. Grubbs, *Public Administration: An Action Orientation*, 4th ed. (Belmont, CA: Wadsworth, 2003), 167–8.

64 Ibid., 261.

65 Susan Crowley, "Legislative Guide to Local Property Tax," Iowa Legislative Service Agency, Legal Services Division (December 2007): 1, 2.

66 "Table 1. State and Local Government Finances by Level of Government and by State: 2004–2005," U.S. Census Bureau, www.census.gov/govs/estimate/0500ussl_1.html (accessed October 2007).

67 National Advisory Council on State and Local Budgeting, *Recommended Budget Practices: A Framework for Improved State and Local Government Budgeting* (Chicago, IL: Government Finance Officers Association, 1998), 3.

68 Aaron Wildavsky and Naomi Caiden, *The New Politics of the Budgetary Process*, 5th ed. (New York, NY: Pearson Longman, 2003), 2–3.

69 CNN, "Bush Spells out $70 Billion War-Funding Request," retrieved December 18, 2008 from www.cnn.com/2008/POLITICS/05//02/war.funding/index.html

70 For an interesting overview of both the positive and negative sides of congressional spending, see the series of articles in *Extensions: A Journal of the Carl Albert Congressional Research and Studies Center* (Spring 2007), titled "Congress and Money."

71 Irene S. Rubin, *The Politics of Public Budgeting: Getting and Spending, Borrowing and Balancing*, 5th ed. (Washington, DC: CQ Press, 2006), 13.

72 The following discussion is drawn from Martha Coven and Richard Kogan, "Introduction to the Federal Budget Process," Center on Budget and Policy Priorities (2004), www.allhealth.org/recent/audio_02-11-05/3-7-03.cbpp.budget-process.pdf; Robert Keith, "A Brief Introduction to the Federal Budget Process," *Congressional Research Service Report for Congress* (1996), retrieved October 2007 from www.house.gov/rules/96-912.htm; and Allen Schick, *The Federal Budget: Politics, Policy, Process* (Washington, DC: Brookings Institution, 2000).

73 Robert Keith, "A Brief Introduction to the Federal Budget Process," *Congressional Research Service Report for Congress* (1996), retrieved October 2007 from www.house.gov/rules/96-912.htm

74 Martha Coven and Richard Kogan, "Introduction to the Federal Budget Process," Center on Budget and Policy Priorities (2004), www.allhealth.org/recent/audio_02-11-05/3-7-03.cbpp.budget-process.pdf, 5.

75 Robert Keith, "A Brief Introduction to the Federal Budget Process," *Congressional Research Service Report for Congress* (1996), retrieved October 2007 from www.house.gov/rules/96-912.htm

76 Much of the information presented is drawn from Janet M. Kelly and William C. Rivenbark's excellent in-depth account of the state and local government budgeting process; *Performance Budgeting for State and Local Government* (Armonk, NY: M.E. Sharpe, 2003). Other sources include: David Osborne and Peter Hutchinson's scathing account of the current fiscal crisis and methods for addressing this crisis in state and local governments in *The Price of Government: Getting the Results We Need in an Age of Permanent Fiscal Crisis* (New York: Basic Books, 2004); and Thomas R. Dye and Susan A. MacManus, *Politics in States and Communities*, 11th ed. (Upper Saddle River, NJ: Prentice Hall, 2003), for an excellent overall perspective of the state and local budgeting process.

77 Center on Budget and Policy Priorities, "Policy Basic: An Introduction to the Federal Budget Process" (February 2, 2016), retrieved from www.cbpp.org/research/policy-basics-introduction-to-the-federal-budget-process

78 Ibid.

79 Thomas R. Dye and Susan A. MacManus, *Politics in States and Communities*, 11th ed. (Upper Saddle River, NJ: Prentice Hall, 2003), 279.

80 Edward J. Clynch and Thomas P. Lauth, eds., *Governors, Legislatures, and Budgets: Diversity Across the American States* (Santa Barbara, CA: ABC/CLIO, 1991); Edward J. Clynch and Thomas P. Lauth, eds., *Budgeting in the States: Institutions, Processes and Politics* (New York, NY: Praeger, 2006).

81 Gerasimos A. Gianakis and Clifford P. McCue, *Local Government Budgeting: A Managerial Approach* (Westport, CT: Quorum, 1999), 3, 4.

82 Irene S. Rubin, *Class, Tax, and Power: Municipal Budgeting in the United States* (Chatham, NJ: Chatham House, 1998), 2.

83 *Performance Budgeting for State and Local Government* (Armonk, NY: M.E. Sharpe, 2003), 48. The majority of the discussion is taken from Kelly and Rivenbark's account

of local budgeting process. Although no local government's budgeting process is the same as every other local government's process, there are similarities.

84 Ibid., 50.

85 Janet M. Kelly and William C. Rivenbark cite Robert J. Freeman and Craig D. Shoulders, *Governmental and Nonprofit Accounting,* 5th ed. (Upper Saddle River, NJ: Prentice-Hall, 1996).

86 For example, J. Scott McDonald and Emeka O.C. Nwagwu, "Windfall Revenues: New Experiences For Cut-Back Managers," *International Journal of Public Administration* 24 (#4, 2001): 355–62.

87 Janet M. Kelly and William C. Rivenbark cite Robert J. Freeman and Craig D. Shoulders, *Governmental and Nonprofit Accounting,* 5th ed. (Upper Saddle River, NJ: Prentice-Hall, 1996), in their *Performance Budgeting for State and Local Government* (Armonk, NY: M.E. Sharpe, 2003), 58.

88 Office of Management and Budget, "FY 2009 Summary Tables," retrieved December 18, 2008, form www.whitehouse.gov/omb/budget/fy2009/summary table.html

89 Virginia Department of Planning & Budget, "2009 Executive Budget Document: Part B: Executive Budget 2008–2010 biennium: Total FY 2009," www.dpb.state.va.us/budget/buddoc09/index.cfm Accessed December 19, 2008.

90 City of Dunn, North Carolina, "Budget Adopted June 5 2008," retrieved December 19, 2008 from www.dunn-nc.org/finance/downloads/Budget%20FY%202008-2009.PDF

91 Jesse Burkhead, *Government Budgeting* (New York, NY: John Wiley, 1956), see chapter 1, "The Development of Modern Budgeting," 2–30.

92 For example, Abraham D. Benavides, Adira M. Fierro-Villa, and Eduardo Cobian Aguayo, "Public Service and Good Governance vs. Corruption and Self-Promotion: MPA Programs in Mexico," *Journal of Public Affairs Education* 19 (#4, Fall 2013): 615–34; Joel L. Fleishman, "Self-Interest and Political Integrity," in Joel L. Fleishman, Lance Liebman, and Mark M. Moore, eds., *Public Duties: The Moral Obligations of Government Officials* (Cambridge, MA: Harvard University Press, 1981), 52–92.

93 Fiscal Affairs and Legal Departments, "Corruption: Costs and Mitigating Strategies" (May 2016), *International Monetary Fund SDN/16/05,* retrieved from www.imf.org/external/pubs/ft/sdn/2016/sdn1605.pdf

94 Senator Martin Heinrich, "The Costs of Corruption to the American Economy" (May 2017), *U.S. Congress Joint Economic Committee,* retrieved from www.jec.senate.gov/public/_cache/files/c6be7b7d-cb39-499a-b6d6-d5b3d65368c8/the-costs-of-corruption-to-the-american-economy-final.pdf

95 James S. Bowman and Jonathan P. West, *Public Service Ethics: Individual and Institutional Responsibilities* (Los Angeles: Sage/CQ Press, 2015), 169.

96 Rod Erakovich, William Carroll, Chelsea Smith, Tunde Campbell, and Leo Wright, "Corruption, Ethics and Accountability: A Normative Approach to Control," *PA Times* (November 2013), retrieved from http://patimes.org/corruption-ethics-accountability-normative-approach-control/

97 Walter Lipmann, "A Theory about Corruption," in Arnold J. Haidenheimer and Michael Johnston, eds., *Political Corruption: Concepts and Contexts,* 3rd ed. (New York, NY: Routledge, 2001), 294–7; Jonathan Rose, "The Meaning of Corruption: Testing the Coherence and Adequacy of Corruption Definitions," *Public Integrity* 20 (#3, 2018): 220–33.

98 H. Whitton, "The Rediscovery of Professional Ethics for Public Officials: An Australian Review," in N. Preston, ed., *Ethics for the Public Sector: Education & Training* (Sydney: Federation Press, 1994).

99 Frank Anechiarico and James B. Jacobs, "Visions of Corruption Control and the Evolution of American Public Administration," *Public Administration Review* 54 (#5, September/October 1994): 465–73.

100 Frank Anechiarico and James B. Jacobs, *The Pursuit of Absolute Integrity: How Corruption Control Makes Government Ineffective* (Chicago, IL: University of Chicago Press, 1998).

101 For example, National Conference of State Legislators (NCSL), "Penalties for Violations of State Ethics and Public Corruption Laws," retrieved from www.ncsl.org/research/ethics/50-state-chart-criminal-penalties-for-public-corr.aspx

102 For example, John P. Crank and Michael A. Caldero, *Police Ethics: The Corruption of Noble Cause* (Cincinnati, OH: Anderson Publishing, 2000).

103 Terri Langford, "County Courts Divided Over Cookie Control: Judges Have Different Opinions on How to Handle Law Firms' Sweet Charity," *Dallas Morning News* (December 22, 2000): 31A, 39A.

104 For example, Edwin M. DeLattre, *Character and Cops: Ethics in Policing*, 2nd ed. (Washington: AEI Press, 1994); Michael Johnston, "Police Corruption," in *Political Corruption and Public Policy in America* (Monterrey, CA: Books/Cole Publishing, 1982), 72–107; Bernard J. McCarthy, "Patterns of Prison Corruption," in Daryl Close and Nicholas Meier, eds., *Morality in Criminal Justice: An Introduction to Ethics* (Belmont, CA: Wadsworth, 2003); Ellwyn R. Stoddard, "The Informal 'Code' of Police Deviancy: A Group Approach to 'Blue-Coat' Crime," *Journal of Criminal Law, Criminology, and Police Science* 59 (1968): 201–13.

105 For example, V.O. Key, "Techniques of Political Graft," in Arnold J. Haidenheimer and Michael Johnston, eds., *Political Corruption: Concepts and Contexts*, 3rd ed. (New York, NY: Routledge, 2001), 46–53.

106 For example, National Conference of State Legislators (NCSL), "Penalties for Violations of State Ethics and Public Corruption Laws," retrieved from www.ncsl.org/research/ethics/50-state-chart-criminal-penalties-for-public-corr.aspx

107 American Law Institute, *Model Penal Code: Official Draft and Explanatory Notes* (Philadelphia: American Law Institute, 1985), section 223.1, 147, retrieved May 18, 2018 from www.icla.up.ac.za/images/un/use-of-force/western-europe-others/UnitedStatesofAmerica/Model%20Penal%20Code%20United%20States%20of%20America%201962.pdf

108 Corruption Watch, "Conflict of Interest" (Johannesburg, South Africa: Corruption Watch, 2017), retrieved from www.corruptionwatch.org.za/wp-content/uploads/2015/06/Corruption-Watch-Conflict-of-interest.pdf

109 Ibid.

110 Gordon Boyce and Cindy Davids, "Conflict of Interest in Policing and the Public Sector: Ethics, Integrity and Social Accountability," *Public Management Review* 11 (#5, 2009): 601–40.

111 Andrew Stark, "The Appearance of Official Impropriety and the Concept of Political Crime," *Ethics* 105 (#2, January 1995): 326–51.

112 Luca Ettera, "Can Transparency Reduce Corruption? Evidence from Firms in Peru and Mali on the Impact of the Extractive Industries Transparency Initiative (EITI) on Corruption," paper presented at Doing Business Conference, Georgetown University, Washington, February 20–21, 2014, retrieved from https://eiti.org/document/can-transparency-reduce-corruption; Archon Fung, Mary Graham, and David Weil, *Full Disclosure: The Perils and Promise of Transparency* (New York, NY: Cambridge University Press, 2007).

113 For example, William L. Anderson and Candice E. Jackson, "Law as a Weapon: How RICO Subverts Liberty and the True Purpose of Law," *The Independent Review: A Journal of Political Economy* 9 (#1, 2004): 85–97; Robert Blakey and Brian Gettings, "Racketeer Influenced and Corrupt Organizations (RICO): Basic Concepts—Criminal and Civil Remedies," *Temple Law Quarterly* 53 (1980): 1009–48; Jordan Blair Woods, "Systemic Racial Bias and RICO's Application to Criminal Street and Prison Gangs," *Michigan Journal of Race and Law* 17 (#2, 2012): 303–57.

114 For example, Expert Meeting Group, *Preventing Corruption in Public Administration: Citizen Engagement for Improved Transparency and Accountability* (New York, NY: United Nations Department of Economic and Social Affairs, 2012); Davide Torsello, ed., *Corruption in Public Administration: An Ethnographic Approach* (Cheltenham, UK: Edward Elgar Publishing, 2016)—this edited volume includes closely empirical studies of corruption and its remedies in Italy, Hungary, Bosnia, Russia, Kosovo, and Turkey.

115 Many think of community policing as a Japanese invention brought to the US. However, it was the invention of the US Army occupation forces in Japan after World War II—for example, Paul P. Chwialkowski, "Japanese Policing: An American Invention," *Policing: An International Journal of Police Strategies & Management* 21(#4, 1998): 720–31.

116 Trent Ikerd and Samuel Walker, *Making Police Reforms Endure* (Washington, DC: U.S. Department of Justice, Office of Community Oriented Policing Services, Center for Problem-Oriented Policing, 2010).

117 For example, Salih Hakan Can, Izzet Lofca, and Bradley Chilton, "A Comparative Analysis of Democracy, Respect for Human Rights, and Democratic Policing Reforms in Turkey & Fourteen Nations," *Asia Pacific Journal of Policing & Criminal Justice* 7 (2009): 69–94.

Nonprofits and Faith-Based Organizations

"Nonprofit executives and board members also should be willing to ask uncomfortable questions: Not just 'Is it legal?' but also 'Is it fair?' 'Is it honest?' 'Does it advance societal interests or pose unreasonable risks?' and 'How would it feel to defend the decision on the evening news?'"

—(Deborah L. Rhode and Amanda K. Packel)[1]

BOX 9.1 | CHAPTER OBJECTIVES

1 Distinguish the roles of nonprofits and faith-based organizations in public services delivery.

2 Understand the historical influences, and developments of nonprofits and faith-based organizations.

3 Clarify the partnership collaborative roles of governments, nonprofits, and faith-based organizations.

4 Critique the public service ethical issues of conflicts and interplay of religious and spiritual values in the public administration profession.

Our chapter's introductory ethics quote is not an ethics precept or code, but rather is intended to put nonprofit administrators and board members on the hot seat. So, how would you feel to defend your ethical decisions on the evening news? In the face of moral myopia,[2] we continue our application of ethics and the public interests to these nonprofit organizations, including **faith-based organizations**.

Since 1996, the Federal Government, along with many state and local governments, have worked to meet the public's demand for social and welfare services by coordinating with these nonprofits and faith-based organizations, such as parachurches (religious organizations without worship components) and church ministries, funded in part through grants made available by the Federal Government. The United States has moved from an intergovernmental to an intersectoral[3] or interorganizational[4] administrative and policy system, one where the working relations between units of government are no longer sufficient to meet increasing societal and citizen demands for service delivery. It requires that government agencies, departments, and organizations work with various private, nonprofit, and faith-based organizations to effect policy changes and deliver vital public services. By sailing more often and more deeply into the waters of public service, nonprofits and faith-based organizations have become a more significant part of the puzzle of the public administration profession. The public interests are no longer the sole domain of government: "Over the last several decades, the Federal Government's work has increasingly been carried out through an elaborate network of contracting, intergovernmental grants, loans and loan guarantees, regulations, and other indirect administrative approaches."[5]

The purpose of this chapter is to give greater attention and clarity to the place of nonprofits and faith-based organizations in the public sector today. In many ways, this chapter is a necessary reality check, because many public administration surveys and texts seem to omit or neglect nonprofit and faith-based organizations. In order to accomplish this task, the chapter is divided into the following sections. First, we outline the definition, scope, and impact of nonprofit organizations. We also discuss theoretical influences of nonprofit organizations, and overview the history of nonprofits and faith-based organizations (FBOs). Second, we analyze the influence of FBOs, particularly as they differ from nonprofits. And finally, our ethics case study reviews implications for the changing partnerships of governments, nonprofits and FBOs—and the conflicts and interplay of religious and spiritual values in the public administration profession.

NONPROFIT ORGANIZATIONS

Nonprofit organizations have contributed significantly to the governance process over the past several decades or so. However, depending upon how one defines and examines nongovernmental organizations, their influence goes back much farther. Theda Skocpol argues that voluntary associations, particularly those with a civic focus, date to the nation's founding.[6] **Marvin Olasky** contends that the use of religious faith—especially Christianity—predated what we term faith-based organizations, extending back to the pilgrims landing at Plymouth. In short, the *Mayflower* was a voluntary faith-based experiment. Olasky's argument is that reaching out to others—which is what nonprofits and faith-based organizations are supposed to be all about—is centered not in organizations, per se, but with individual human desires to help others.[7] Lester Salamon, a recognized authority on the role of nonprofits in American society, concurs: "Like the arteries of a living organism, these organizations carry a life force that has long been a centerpiece of American culture—a faith in the capacity of individual action to improve the quality of human life."[8] Suffice it to say that the contributions of people, resources, and ideas, whether voluntarily associated or professionally organized, such as in today's nonprofit and faith-based arenas, is significant to governance and the public administration profession.

Scope and Growth of Nonprofits

Defining Terminology   First, we need to clarify the use of terminology. The term *nongovernmental organization (NGO)* is generally associated with internationally based organizations that have global economic and social agendas. However, in this book, and specifically this chapter, we do not use the term this way. We refer to nongovernmental organizations as those organizations that are not particularly authoritative and directly linked or defined by governmental jurisdiction, legal status, or constitutional definition, such as nonprofits and faith-based organizations. Over the years various and diverse titles have been used, including the *tax-exempt sector*, the *civil society sector*, the *commons*, the *charitable sector*, the **voluntary sector**, the *nonproprietary sector*, and the *nonprofit sector*.[9] According to Peter Frumkin, it was not until the 1950s and 1960s that the term *nonprofit* surfaced and over time replaced the more commonly used and understood term that referred to those organizations that are not directly within the jurisdictional and legal umbrella of national and subnational governments. But as we will later learn, this rather broad distinction includes a hefty number of charitable and voluntary organizations that contribute substantially to the political, social, and economic life of most Americans.[10] For the purposes of this chapter we will use the terms *nonprofits* and *faith-based organizations* when referring generally to nongovernmental organizations.

Nonprofit organization   The definition of nonprofit organization includes those private organizations "that are prohibited from distributing any profits they may generate to those who control or support them."[11] Nonprofits are not like their private sector counterparts, which exist for the sole purpose of generating profits for their shareholders, but neither are they like the public sector agency, which is controlled by political, regulatory, and constitutional influences. Instead, nonprofits, including faith-based organizations, straddle both areas. They are private organizations, so it is important that they engage in administrative and management actions promoting efficiency, effectiveness, and economy, but they also exist

---

BOX 9.2 | Marvin Olasky

Marvin Olasky, born June 12, 1950, authored *The Tragedy of American Compassion*, a book that inspired President George W. Bush's emphasis on the use of faith-based organizations for the delivery of social services. Olasky was born into a Jewish family in Boston, Massachusetts; became an avowed atheist and Marxist in high school; and then, while attending undergraduate school at the University of Michigan in the 1970s, he had a spiritual awakening, dissociating himself from his atheistic and Marxist beliefs, and embraced Christianity. He was baptized into the Presbyterian Church in 1976. *The Tragedy of American Compassion* argued that the social ills of today are rooted in the countercultural revolution of the 1960s.

Only until churches, para-church organizations, or what has become known as faith-based organizations, become more involved in the delivery of social and welfare services, will there be a lasting effect in society. When Texas Governor George Bush became President G.W. Bush in 2001, Olasky saw his ideas become public policy with the creation of the White House Office of Faith-Based and Community Initiatives. Olasky is currently the Distinguished Chair in Journalism and Public Policy and Professor of Journalism at Patrick Henry College, Purcellville, Virginia. ◢

Source: "Marvin Olasky," NNDB, retrieved from www. nndb.com/people/325/000058151/

to meet public needs. They must be flexible to meet the challenges of the market, while continuing to focus on the needs of the public clientele and citizenry they were chartered to serve. For the purposes of this chapter, we will focus on non-profits that serve the public interests.

Why do nonprofits—and, as we will later see, faith-based organizations—even exist? What is their purpose (or purposes)? What do they do that government agencies and organizations cannot (or will not) do? They are designed to first and foremost serve the public interests. Gita Gulati-Partee, Program Director, Public Policy, at the North Carolina Center for Nonprofits, writes: "A non-profit organization is a private corporation that works for the *public's benefit* but is separate and independent from government."[12] Further, the **National Council of Nonprofit Associations**, which is a network of nearly 40 state and regional associations representing 22,000 nonprofits, strives to see that nonprofits work "together for the public good."[13] And Lester Salamon contends that nonprofits are "dedicated to mobilizing *private initiative for the common good.*"[14]

Another major reason for nonprofits' existence is the motivation inherent in the nonprofit workers. They are motivated to pursue goals that benefit society, to help children, the elderly, and the homeless. As Paul Light notes, nonprofit workers are "motivated primarily by the chance to do something worthwhile, savoring the chance to make decisions on its own, take risks, and try new things."[15] Where government agencies cannot do the job, where they are unable to reach beyond their regulated boundaries, the nonprofit community is able to meet the social, welfare, or economic needs of the public. Nonprofits exist for the good of all, not the select interests of a few. How far-reaching are nonprofits? How expansive is this sector?

Nonprofits and the Law   Nonprofits are designated by the Internal Revenue Service (IRS) as an organization that does not distribute profits to shareholders (see Table 9.1). The National Center for Charitable Statistics, a research subsidiary of the Urban Institute, divides nonprofit organizations into three groups: 501(c)(3) public charities, 501(c)(3) private foundations, and "other" nonprofit organizations. Public charities, which account for more than 60 percent of all registered nonprofit organizations, include education, healthcare organizations, and other human services organizations. Private foundations are generally established by the philanthropic endeavors of a family or individual. Their primary purpose, therefore, is to fund other nonprofits. Finally, the "other" category includes everything from trade associations and labor unions to social and recreational clubs. The largest number of nonprofits, over 876,000, falls into the first category, as do the nation's approximately 350,000 religious congregations.[16]

The number and revenue generation of nonprofits is staggering. By most accounts, the total number of nonprofits increased from 1.1 million in 1995 to 1.6 million in 2015, a 45 percent change.[17] By 2015, public charities reporting to the IRS declared revenues of over $1 trillion (a 56 percent increase adjusted for inflation since 1995) and assets equaling nearly $2 trillion (an 84 percent increase adjusted for inflation since 1995).[18] Private charitable contributions reached over $295 billion in 2006, an increase of nearly 30 percent in current dollars (but only 10 percent in constant dollars) since 2000. Approximately one-third of private giving in 2006 went to congregations and other religious organizations (what we call "para-church" organizations). Finally, foundation giving exceeded $36 billion in 2005, which was a 142 percent increase since 1995, adjusted by inflation.[19]

The number of volunteers rose dramatically over the next seven years—largely because of the 9/11 effect—to approximately 15 million, with nearly 13 billion volunteer hours logged.[20] Even when broken down by paid and volunteer workers, the Johns Hopkins University Center for Civil Society Studies reports that, as of mid-2004, U.S. nonprofits had 9.4 million paid workers and another 4.7 million "full-time equivalent" volunteers, for a total workforce of 14.1 million.[21] This equates to over 8 percent of the wages and salaries paid in the US.[22] Thus, growth of the nonprofit world is staggering.

Social Impact of Nonprofits   What is the impact of nonprofits upon society today? Clearly, without the number, size, and growth of nonprofits, including faith-based organizations, which we will examine in more detail later in the chapter, the swath of human services delivered would be negatively affected. Nonprofits

---

TABLE 9.1

Internal Revenue Service (IRS) Designation of Exempt Organizations

Section of 1986 Code	Description of Organization	General Nature of Activities	Application Form No.	Annual Return Required to be Filed	Contributions Allowable
501(c)(1)	Corporations Organized under Act of Congress (Including Federal Credit Unions)	Instrumentalities of the United States	No Form	None	Yes, if made for exclusively public purposes
501(c)(2)	Title holding corporation for exempt organization	Holding title to property of an exempt organization	1024	990 or 990EZ	No
501(c)(3)	Religious, Educational, Charitable, Scientific, Literary, Testing for Public Safety, to Foster National or International Amateur Sports Competition, or Prevention of Cruelty to Children or Animals Organizations	Activities of nature implied by description of class of organization	1023	990 or 990EZ, or 990-PF	Yes, generally
501(c)(4)	Civic Leagues, Social Welfare Organizations, and Local Associations of Employees	Promotion of community welfare; charitable, educational or recreational	1024	990 or 990EZ	No, generally

arise where government agencies are oftentimes ill-suited to meet the service need. Many nonprofits are locally born and bred, so to speak. Because various cultural factors in society are influential to the initiation and development of nonprofits, including family, church, and school,[23] many nonprofits contribute back, and are thus part—if not the heart—of the community they exist in. Habitat for Humanity in Erwin, North Carolina, for example, exists to meet the living needs of many low-income residents in Harnett County, without which services many would not have suitable living accommodations. Donations to Habitat for Humanity in central Harnett County, as in the many thousands of other locations around the country, come from individuals, educational organizations, church congregations, and para-church ministries.

A second major impact is establishing partnerships with public sector organizations to meet public needs. At the University of North Carolina-Chapel Hill's School of Government, for example, much work is being done by researchers to examine the partnering relationship mentioned by national scholars, like Lester Salamon,[24] Margaret Henderson, Gordon P. Whitaker, and others who make up the project team for the Project to Strengthen Nonprofit-Government Relationships. Much of their work is directed toward discovering how and why municipal and county governments in North Carolina interact (or not interact) with nonprofits. Too often collaboration on issues is infrequent or even nonexistent. This is not because the two entities fail to realize the various problems are readily apparent. It is often because of obstacles, such as having different perceptions as to what the problem is, lacking understanding concerning each other's work, dealing with the economic effects and different cultural bases of a county, town, or community, or working with an unbalanced political and organizational power arrangement.[25] Each of these obstacles can be overcome through more frequent and accurate communication, which in turn establishes greater trust by the recipients of services in both the public agency and the nonprofit organization (Figure 9.1).[26]

The extent of partnering increases with the various needs identified, whether it is to house a 47-year-old recovering alcoholic, or giving a former welfare mother the needed information technology type skills, in order for them to land jobs and succeed in the evolving information-driven economy. But in order to further examine this relationship, or partnering, we need to establish and discuss theoretical reasons for the existence of nonprofit organizations. For this we turn to the work of Lester M. Salamon.

Explaining Nonprofit Organizations: Theoretical Dimensions

As an observer of nonprofit management noted, nonprofit organizations are important for larger reasons than simply issues surrounding "management capacity, fundraising strategies, and public relations campaigns." They are important because they arise "as an institutional response to societal disquiet and need."[27] They are institutional actors in an American pluralistic society; a society that relishes diversity, freedom, and order, but a society that also requires commitment and sacrifice on the part of its citizenry in order to secure these values. Nonprofit organizations are a historical part of the fabric of American society.[28] We will briefly examine the historical development of nonprofits in the next section. For now we need to establish a theoretical basis for the existence and importance of nonprofits, particularly in the delivery of social services.

NTEE Major Group

A. Arts, Culture, and Humanities
B. Education
C. Environmental Quality, Protection, and Beautification
D. Animal-Related
E. Health
F. Mental Health, Crisis Intervention
G. Diseases, Disorders, Medical Disciplines
H. Medical Research
I. Crime, Legal Related
J. Employment, Job Related
K. Food, Agriculture & Nutrition
L. Housing & Shelter
M. Public Safety, Disaster Preparedness & Relief
N. Recreation & Sports
0. Youth Development
P. Human Services
Q. International, Foreign Affairs & National Security
R. Civil Rights, Social Action & Advocacy
S. Community Improvement & Capacity Building
T. Philanthropy, Voluntarism & Grantmaking Foundations
U. Science & Technology
V. Social Science
W. Public & Societal Benefit
X. Religion-Related
Y. Mutual & Membership Benefit
Z. Unknown

FIGURE 9.1

National Taxonomy of Exempt Entities (NTEE) Major Groups, A to Z

Theories of Nonprofits Lester M. Salamon, Director for Civil Society Studies, the Johns Hopkins University, asks "What is the role of the nonprofit sector and its relationship with government?" Scholars have too often described the role of nonprofits in society, and even detailing their relationship with governments in delivering services; however, they do not do a good job of *explaining* this relationship.[29] Salamon presents plausible theoretical explanations that we would like to discuss.

We have described that the nonprofit sector is immense and contains numerous organizations, particularly in the social service sector, like **American Red Cross, Catholic Relief** Services, Girl Scouts, and many others, that work to meet the avalanche of human needs on a daily basis. Partially as a result of its size, and partially as a result of the sheer need to compete with the private sector for clientele base, the nonprofit sector is morphed into something it is not, or at least was not intended to be: a highly professional, organized, revenue-driven institution, competing for customers in an extremely volatile market environment. At the same time, though, when nonprofit organization partners with a government

BOX 9.3 | Social Capital

Robert Putnam, the Peter and Isabel Malkin Professor of Public Policy, John F. Kennedy School of Government, Harvard University, argues for greater attention on what he calls social capital. The public is enhanced when society invests in the various forms of capital— physical, financial, human, and, of course, social—that provide the basis for greater civic and social engagement:

Students of social capital have only begun to address some of the most important questions that this approach to public affairs suggests. What are the actual trends in different forms of civic engagement? Why communities differ in the stocks of social capital? What *kinds* of civic engagement seem most likely to foster economic growth or community effectiveness? Must specific types of social capital be matched to different public problems? Most important of all, how is social capital created and destroyed? What strategies for building (or rebuilding) social capital are most promising? How can we balance the twin strategies of exploiting existing social capital and creating it afresh? ◣

Source: Robert D. Putnam, "Social Capital and Public Life," *American Prospect* (#13, Spring 1993), retrieved from http://epn.org/prospect/13/13putn.html

entity—such as when New York City and the American Red Cross teamed with each other as well as worked in concert with thousands of other nonprofit and government agencies in the wake of the September 11 tragedy—the result is generally one of need overshadowed by distrust and uncertainty. Why? Because, as Salamon notes, the prevailing theories of the welfare state and the voluntary sector are diametrically opposed, proffering different and even disparate explanations for explaining social policy making.

Theory of the Welfare State   Let's describe these prevailing theories and then offer Salamon's solution—which is only one solution, we acknowledge—to offering a better theory to help explain government and nonprofit relations. The first theory is that of the welfare state. It focused on the expansion of government, especially the Federal Government, particularly since the New Deal (i.e., the 1930s), but with some impetus for welfare expansion dating to the Progressive Era, moving through and including the **Great Society** programs of the 1960s. It called for government organizations, such as the Department of Health, Education, and Welfare (HEW— now HHS), which were hierarchical in structure, governed by reams of rules and regulations that took on the social problems of the day. The problems seemed too much: crime and drugs out-of-control, homelessness, single-parent families, low educational levels, racial/ethnic bias in employment, and (most of all) poverty. Perhaps you know or have seen this level of hopelessness in Chicago's low-income housing projects, English literacy programs for Hispanic and other immigrants in south-central Los Angeles, or public health and job-training programs in rural Appalachia. Further, the Federal Government established **Medicare** and **Medicaid** programs for the elderly and poor and disabled to receive some basic type of health insurance and healthcare needs; created Aid to Families with Dependent Children (AFDC) to meet monthly living expenses, while all the time requiring state and local governments to assume more responsibility of the implementation, administration, and financial co-responsibility of these programs. According to the welfare state model, the government was to provide "professionalized public service [in] an integrated state administrative apparatus" with a bent toward currying political favor with the clientele it served.[30] This model did not include the voluntary sector as a direct and co-partner in meeting and/or alleviating this human needs and suffering.

Theory of Market Failure/Government Failure   According to Salamon, the prevailing theories of the voluntary sector, which included market/government failure and contract failure, did not provide the necessary linkages between government and the voluntary sector. In fact, as Salamon notes, "the existing theories of the voluntary sector (likewise) leave little room to expect effective cooperation between nonprofit organizations and the state." He continues that "it was to get away from such blurring of the boundaries between the public and private sectors that the concept of the private nonprofit sector was invented."[31] So, it was the voluntary sector, composed of the nonprofit organizations—and more recently the faith-based organizations—that targeted specific areas of need that were either overlooked by government agencies or failed to deliver adequate services, such as the area of inmate rehabilitation.[32]

Contract Failure Theory   The second broad theory or model explaining the existence of the voluntary sector is contract failure. According to Salamon, the primary focus is that, for goods and services directed toward a certain age or other demographic group, such as the elderly, "the purchaser is not the same as the consumer," and thus "the normal mechanisms of the market, which involved consumer choice on the basis of adequate information, do not obtain." Some type of proxy therefore has to be created to offer the purchaser a certain level of assurance that the services meet minimum standards of quality. The nonprofit organization provides that assurance, given that they are in business not to make

---

BOX 9.4 | Nonprofits' Real Worth

The basic argument is that neither the market nor the government could produce these goods or services in sufficient quantity to be of worth. The market cannot produce these goods that voluntary associations produce because the market demand is low. Government can tax its citizens to produce the good—called the free rider problem—but even then, the government has problems. For example, the government will only produce the goods that receive majority support, which leaves certain groups without goods simply because they cannot convince the majority of the citizenry and/or community to adopt their same views as to what is needed.

Therefore, so goes the argument, in order to meet this demand for collective goods, that the voluntary sector was established. It "supplies a range of 'collective goods' desired by one segment of a community but not by a majority. From this it follows that the more diverse the community, the more extensive the nonprofit sector it is likely to have."

Source: Lester M. Salamon, *Partners in Public Service: Government-Nonprofit Relations in the Modern Welfare Estate* (Baltimore, MD: Johns Hopkins University Press, 1995), 39; Lester M. Salamon, *America's Nonprofit Sector: A Primer*, 2nd ed. (Baltimore, MD: Johns Hopkins University Press, 1999), 12–13.

to a profit but to meet charitable needs.[33] Thus, nonprofits would more likely be able to be trusted than would the private sector (i.e., because of the profit motive) or government sector (i.e., for partisan positioning).

Theory of Third-Party Government This third theory capitalizes on the shortcomings of the previous theories. The welfare state theory, for example, fails to account for the diverse and complex intergovernmental relations, usually called **New Federalism,** and its various derivations, that sprang to life in the early to mid-1970s. It advocated devolution (or giving away authority) to lower levels of government—states, counties, and municipalities—for the administration and in many cases increased funding of programs, such as Medicare and Medicaid. In addition to governmental agencies and organizations, it abdicated responsibility to a variety of other entities, such as research and development (universities), healthcare administration (hospitals), and social service delivery (faith-based organizations).[34] In addition, the market-based theories (i.e., market and contract theories) failed to take into account the vast number of individuals with needs that were not adequately being met through a demand and supply relationship, one that measures success through accumulation of profit and meeting a bottom line. Thus, as Salamon notes, "The result is an elaborate system of 'third-party government' [where] government shares a substantial degree of its discretion over the spending of public funds and the exercise of public authority with third-party implementers."[35]

In fact, Salamon, like others mentioned above, including contemporaries such as Theda Skocpol, and historical figures such as Alexis de Tocqueville, contend that voluntary associations exist among other reasons for the benefit of pluralistic freedom and pursuit of the public good or interest. He refers to this as the stakeholder theory, where the "central argument is that a need for nonprofit organizations is not sufficient to ensure that such organizations are created."[36] Rather, people form voluntary associations made up of others who have a passion for seeing the hurting made well, for the homeless to find shelter, or for weary to find rest. They do not have a political stake as much as a social or even religious stake, in seeing that community and even national needs are met, in spite of the failed government and market and contract systems. They recognize they will not make huge profits; they will not establish bureaucracies in order to lay claim to sacred turf, but what will happen is that someone's needs will be met, all because like-minded individuals formed a 501(c)(3) or (c)(4) organization, raised funds, instituted some basic rules for governing, and went about to meet the need.

Voluntary Failure What happens when nonprofit organizations cannot meet the need? Was the American Red Cross able to meet every human need on that fateful day in September 2001? The answer, of course, was no. Can faith-based, or even secular social service, organizations meet all shelter, medical, job skill development, rehabilitation, alcohol and drug recovery, and a myriad of other human needs without government assistance? The answer is, again, no. In other words, there are substantive as well as financial needs that government—not the voluntary sector—has and should provide to fill in the gaps left by the voluntary sector. But we know that governments do not act without the problem becoming a formal issue, being placed on the institutional agenda, collecting majorities to support government action; laws are then written, rules are made, and the

> ### BOX 9.5 | Clara Barton and the American Red Cross
>
> While traveling in Europe during the post-Civil War years, Clarissa "Clara" Harlowe Barton (1821–1912) learned of the Swiss-inspired International Red Cross Movement, and upon her return to the United States struggled to found a Red Cross Society in 1881. She was the head of the American Red Cross for nearly a quarter of a century. The Red Cross has been a symbol of aid and comfort during time of war, natural disasters, and other upheavals that require a healing touch. During both of the world wars, it grew at a tremendous rate, with chapters jumping from 107 in 1914 to 3,864 in 1918, and in World War II it employed over 100,000 nurses and shipped more than 300,000 tons of supplies overseas. During 9/11 it was at or near Ground Zero, providing much-needed assistance, and with the onslaught of Hurricane Katrina it was in the middle of New Orleans assisting those most in need. It is the shining star of many shining stars in the nonprofit movement, aiding and assisting where government cannot. ▲
>
> Source: American Red Cross Museum, "A Brief History of the American Red Cross," *American Red Cross*, retrieved from www.redcross.org/museum/history/brief.asp

governmental machinery rumbles into action. It is slow, ponderous, and time-consuming. Voluntary responses, on the other hand, are like Edmund Burke's little platoons, where individuals and community interests realize that they are often the first line of defense (or offense, for that matter) to meet the need for addressing, for example, neighborhood crime through the formation of watch groups. Salamon acknowledges that "government involvement is less a substitute for, than a supplement to, private nonprofit action." Further, he concludes that "this reformulation of the market failure theory does a far better job of making sense of the fundamental reality of extensive government-nonprofit ties."[37]

Thus, the answer is what Salamon defines and advocates as public-private partnerships. Public and private entities, such as the nonprofit organizations, must not exclude each other; rather they must partner together to address or manage, if not solve, many of the social ills we have mentioned. Some critics have questions about these various theories,[38] but the point remains that partnering between government and nonprofit organizations is not only at the heart of secular voluntary organizations, but is being pushed politically by U.S. Presidents from George W. Bush, to Barack Obama, to Donald Trump—through faith-based initiatives and programs, instituted since 2001. Next, we briefly describe the history of voluntary organizations, including the development of faith-based organizations.

Historical Development of the Voluntary Sector

The bulk (some 90 percent) of nonprofit organizations have come into existence since the close of World War II.[39] With the millions of GIs returning to civilian life, the drain on government resources increased, especially educational services, and by the 1960s under President Johnson's Great Society programs more and more nonprofit activity took place, particularly in the area of social and health services. All of these areas were strongly influenced by the presence of nonprofit organizations. However, the history of nonprofit or voluntary associations does not begin in 1945, at the turn of the twentieth century, or during or after the Civil War. No, the antecedents of voluntary associations, whether for membership or public service, dates to pre-Colonial days.[40]

Public and Private Merger Unlike today, where the distinction between public and private is somewhat notable—although some scholars claim a **blurring effect** exists between the two institutions[41]—the distinction between private and public institutions was less noticeable more than three centuries ago. This was particularly true with the institutions of Church and State. From Jamestown to Plymouth, and forward to the colonization of America from the early to late eighteenth century, church, civic government, family, education, philanthropy, and other social capital endeavors moved and merged from the same philosophical and institutional foundation: civic justice and human governance. Instead of voluntary activities and commitments on the part of individuals, civil governments required public service of their citizens, whether in the form of road building, militia training, educational service, or care for family members.[42] As Theda Skocpol argues, the relationship of government with civil society organizations, such as veterans' associations, was strong, and thus the idea that civil organizations, or voluntary associations, such as what we label today as nonprofit organizations, was strong, too, leading to what she contends was the enhancement of democracy and democratic institutions. As she notes, the voluntary associations "aimed to gather good men or women … into vast, encompassing associations that mirrored—and had the power to influence—the democratic republic of which they were a part."[43] But, she argues, this is not the case today, where many of the proponents of voluntary associations are also opponents of any connection with government and politics.[44] The de-emphasis of voluntary associations cripples the complete fulfillment of the public interests.

The Influence of Religion Beginning in the mid-eighteenth century the United States experienced an unprecedented religious movement called the **Great Awakening** from 1740 to 1760. It was social and political as well as religious in nature, sweeping evangelicals and other Christians into not only the pews but positions of civic and economic influence. This religious transformation of colonial America laid the foundation for civic freedom organizations, such as the Sons of Liberty, which assumed leadership toward resisting British rule.[45] Organizational power became the starting point for civic freedom. Whenever colonists banded together to resist what they perceived was British tyranny, through the formation of such groups as Benjamin Franklin's secret Freemasons, the members realized how much potential there was in a company of many like-minded folks. Other founding fathers, such as Thomas Jefferson, feared that, just like unchecked civil government, unchecked voluntary associations held the recipe for abuse of power. Government-sponsored charters of corporations was a partial solution, but it was not until Jefferson supported the government's responsibility for higher education—and thus the establishment of his beloved **University of Virginia**—did the state begin to take a more active role in controlling the burgeoning influence of voluntary associations, especially those affiliated with religious meaning, intention, and instruction.

According to Peter Hall, one of the more famous struggles taking place between the Jeffersonians and Federalists at the beginning of the nineteenth century was over the incorporation of Dartmouth College, a private college, by the state of New Hampshire. In *Dartmouth College v. New Hampshire* (1819), the U.S. Supreme Court denied the state the power to seize a privately incorporated college. Rather than rule the incorporation document was a political tool of the state, the Court ruled that the power of incorporation was a "private contract protected from government interference."[46] This ruling, however, did not apply to state restriction of charities.

Alexis de Tocqueville's classic book *Democracy in America* (1835) romantically painted a picture of a free and unencumbered nation filled with private voluntary organizations, separate from state dominance. Although this may have been true in the Northeast, it was less so in the West and South, where public institutions held sway. Not until the Civil War did additional opportunities for what Hall refers to as "further advancing the claims of private eleemosynary enterprise[s]" emerge. The damage caused to the social and civic soul of the United States by the Civil War set the tone for the next half-century, with private and voluntary associations of power, especially in the areas of social, religious, and legal leading the way.[47] By the late 1880s, a philosophical shift in social thinking took place: the advent of rationalization.

The Scientific Management of Giving   The Industrial Revolution dramatically altered how industry did business, how universities established their curriculum, how governments provided services, and how charities doled out assistance. The age of philanthropy arose with the tycoons of business: Andrew Carnegie, J.P. Morgan, and Cornelius Vanderbilt. These three and others, but especially Carnegie, raised the level and attitude of professional giving to new heights. Carnegie believed it was the responsibility of those who engineered the economic and business success of the United States who should contribute in a rational and organized fashion their talents and money to assist those less fortunate, so they developed the foundation and the professional staff to administer the foundation—an institutionalized means for giving financially in the present in order to meet the needs of the future. And, while foundation money was set aside for charity, foundations for academic and public policy purposes were also established, foundations such as the Brookings Institution, the Social Science Research Council, and the National Bureau of Economic Research.[48] It was believed that research and study by these types of organizations would be beneficial toward finding ways to alleviate the social and economic maladies of the poor.

Government, too, bought into the rationalization philosophy. Efficiency, effectiveness, and economy were the lynchpins of a scientifically managed public administration. The ideal bureaucracy of Weber, the scientific management principles of Fayol and Taylor, and the management philosophy of Gulick, all had influence upon the centralization of the Federal Government and development of the welfare state beginning in 1932, but also in the Progressive Reform movement of municipalities and states as early as the turn of the twentieth century. Each of these philosophical ideas regarding the scientific management of government administration and policy translated into pragmatic concerns for city planning, economic development, housing of homeless, and treating the mentally ill.

Historical Overview of Nonprofit Action

Of course, in retrospect the past does not lie. The use of government institutions in the early part of the twentieth century, especially in the care for the homeless and mentally ill, was an abysmal failure, resulting in *poor houses* and *insane asylums* that came nowhere close to solving the problems. If anything, they only perpetuated the misery. But, as Lester Salamon notes, "the task of responding to the poverty and distress created by the massive urbanization and industrialization in the late nineteenth and early twentieth centuries was left largely to local governments and private, charitable groups."[49]

New Deal Era   President Roosevelt's New Deal combined a centralization approach to planning and decision making at the federal level, with "a formalization of the voluntaristic and associational relationships between business, charity, and government that (former Secretary of Commerce) Herbert Hoover had built during the 1920s."[50] According to Peter Hall, President Herbert Hoover's book *American Individualism* (1922) chronicled the great inequalities and injustices caused by modern industry, and believed that equality of opportunity, combined with an ethos of service and cooperation, could lead to a new social and economic order.[51] Hoover believed in the concept of community, a concept that really never became popular until some three to five decades later. He believed that the thrust of charitable giving, assistance, and respect was to come from voluntary associations, with the role of the national government being something akin to an umpire, encouraging the voluntary organizations through less burdensome rules and laws to apply their knowledge, skills, and abilities to the social ills at hand. Roosevelt supposedly seized on the idea of government sponsorship of voluntary associations, but, with the depth of the economic depression created by the stock market crash of 1929 looming, he emphasized central government control of social and economic rebuilding through the alphabet agencies and programs spawned by his vision of New Deal policy. Despite Roosevelt's best intentions, state and local governments continued to dominate the field. State and local welfare spending outdistanced Federal Government spending clear into the 1960s.[52]

The 1960s and 1970s   Voluntary associations, which now take on the title of nonprofit organizations, received the lion's share of their income from government dollars. For example, beginning in the 1940s, government contributions to private universities, especially through grants, the GI Bill, and the **National Defense Education Act,** became the single largest source of higher education revenue.[53] Coming out of the 1950s era of Federal Government investigation into the tax-exempt status of charitable giving, and trying to determine whether or not large philanthropic organizations (such as the Ford, Carnegie, and Rockefeller Foundations) were fronting communistic alliances and relationships by funneling millions of dollars into anti-American organizations, charities, foundations, and other voluntary associations became more cognizant of their reporting procedures and revenue-generating methods, particularly in light of increased Federal Government oversight and regulation.[54] A softening tone came from **John D. Rockefeller III.** His call "for a public-private partnership in the drafting policies affecting 'private initiative in the public interest' acknowledged the complexities and uncertainties of the relationship between government and the private sectors that had developed since the war,"[55] which included understanding the effects of tax policy upon private giving. It was economist Martin C. Feldstein who, after surveying the field of philanthropy, "found strong connections between tax incentives and giving and suggested a compelling and credible rationale for the tax treatment of nonprofits."[56]

Feldstein's work was accentuated by the results of the blue-ribbon **Commission on Private Philanthropy and Public Needs**, chaired by John Filer, then chairman of Aetna Life & Casualty Co. The **Filer Commission**, as it was known, surveyed the role of nonprofits, considered the regulatory and tax issues affecting them, urged that private sector financial assistance be expanded, and called for a permanent commission on nonprofits. In its 1975 report, then, it concluded that society was indeed composed of a third or independent sector, one that dominated American life in all aspects and one that could not be overlooked any further.[57] What happened next—the election of Ronald Reagan and the imposition of his ideologically defined devolution of authority—drastically altered the playing field of nonprofits.

The Reagan Revolution   There is no doubt that the 1980s saw substantial change directed toward nonprofit giving—economically, politically, and socially. Most noticeable at the federal level was the implementation of the Economic Recovery Tax Act of 1981, which among other factors provided an across the board tax cut of 25 percent over three years, a reduction in the maximum tax rate from 70 to 50 percent, and increased depreciation expense levels.[58] Because 62 percent of nonprofit organizations report that over 41 percent of their revenues come from the Federal Government in the form of grants and aid, and that fees and service charges (28 percent) and private giving (approximately 20 percent) account for the balance, the end result of the tax cuts was a large reduction of the Federal Government's involvement in social services, human resource training, and other areas.[59]

BOX 9.6 | A Thousand Points of Light

The phrase, "a thousand points of light," was coined by former President G.H.W. Bush in his inaugural address, January 20, 1989. The primary message of the address focused on encouraging the American people to engage their community, to serve their neighbors and friends, and to set a tone for serving that had not been seen in generations. Here is part of that address:

> The old solution, the old way, was to think that public money alone could end these problems. But we have learned that is not so. And in any case, our funds are low. We have a deficit to bring down. We have more will than wallet; but will is what we need ... We will turn to the only resource we have that in times of need always grows—the goodness and the courage of the American people. I am speaking of a new engagement in the lives of others, a new activism, hands-on and involved, that gets the job done. We must bring in the generations, harnessing the unused talent of the elderly and the unfocused energy of the young ... I have spoken of a thousand points of light, of all the community organizations that are spread like stars throughout the Nation, doing good. We will work hand in hand, encouraging, sometimes leading, sometimes being led, rewarding.

Source: Avalon Project, "Inaugural Address of George Bush," *Yale Law School*, retrieved from www.yale.edu/lawweb/avalon/presiden/inaug/bush.htm

Philosophically, the intention of the Reagan administration was to: reduce the level and size of Federal Government through restructuring the tax system; engage in a major devolution to give authority and responsibility to state and local governments, particularly in the area of health and social services; and commit to greater voluntary and private action. Presidents Reagan and George H.W. Bush tried to encourage private and voluntary giving to nonprofit organizations through the Task Force on Private Initiatives and Thousand Points of Light initiatives.[60] Realistically, however, according to the critics like Lester Salamon and others, Reagan's tax cut and devolutionary federalism transformation proved to be a lost opportunity to develop public and private partnerships, which in turn devastated the nonprofit industry by a reversal of what was intended. Using extensive survey data and employing sophisticated statistical methodology, Salamon and his associates at Johns Hopkins University concluded that:

- Between 1977 to 1982, inflation-adjusted federal social services spending dropped 31 percent.
- Federal levels of education spending were down 36 percent by 1989.[61]
- Private charitable giving was reduced by approximately $10 billion between1981 to 1984.[62]

According to the critics, then, what was intended for good turned into disaster for the nonprofit industry. The 1990s, however, saw a change. With the election of Bill Clinton in 1992, Congress moved to restore federal spending in human and social service areas, including Medicaid. Despite a failed attempt in 1993 to overhaul the private insurance industry with a nationalistic model, the Clinton administration believed that greater Federal Government involvement was needed, and the result was that between 1989 and 1994 areas such as health (5 percent), income assistance (13 percent), and housing (12 percent) all increased.[63] The nonprofit sector response is mixed, with overall nonprofit revenues up nearly 96 percent compared to similar figures in the late 1970s and early 1980s, but toward the latter part of the 1980s and early part of 1990s that growth slowed, with the greatest slowdown in the health-related services sector. Civic (up over 200 percent) and social services (up nearly 120 percent) organization revenue was up dramatically between 1977 and 1996, with the largest share of revenue dollars coming from increased fee income (1980s) and revived Federal Government income (early to mid-1990s). During the same time period, private giving was only up about 4 percent.[64]

Finally, as nonprofit organizations began moving into other areas once dominated by the for-profit industry (i.e., day care and home healthcare), they encountered unprecedented competition for services and revenues. What was once viewed as the domain of nonprofit or voluntary organizations soon began to be viewed as territory ripe for for-profit picking! Giving and receiving suddenly took on a different dimension—moving from a Mom and Pop corner store mentality to a multi-billion-dollar-per-year Walmart superstore mentality. The nonprofit sector would never be the same.

Next, we examine the burgeoning area of faith-based organizations (FBOs). What effect have FBOs had upon the voluntary nonprofit sector and public service delivery? What challenges are unique to FBOs? And what relationships or partnering with governments and public administration exist, especially at the state and local levels?

FAITH-BASED ORGANIZATIONS

Seek the welfare of the city … for in its welfare you will find your welfare.

(Jeremiah 29:7)

Let each of you look not to your own interests, but to the interests of others.

(Philippians 2:4)

What we mean by *maslaha* [public interest] is the preservation of the objective of the Law, which consists of five things: the protection of religion, life, intellect, lineage, and property. Whatever ensures the protection of these five principles is *maslaha*.

(Al-Ghazali, d. 1111)

These quotes are from the perspective of diverse world religions on "the welfare of the city," "the interests of others," and the "maslaha [public interest] is the preservation of the objective of the Law," each illustrate the broader cultural context of administration in the public interests. These examples of Judeo, Christian, and Islamic values have transformed the world over the millennia with numbers that have grown to over 4.5 billion adherents today and growing. And it connects public administrators to the substantial global support of nongovernmental actors now operating in areas thought to be the exclusive province of government. These actors, including many hybrid-private, nonprofit and faith-based organizations, are increasing in numbers and influence. Many public services are now delivered through such nongovernmental organizations, especially nonprofits.[65] For example, nonprofits and faith-based organizations provide social services such as bill payment assistance, food assistance, and job training programs. And, within criminal justice, nonprofits and faith-based organizations provide crime prevention programs[66] and assist as intermediaries in community policing.[67]

The world of faith-based organizations (FBOs) is much overlooked by public administration scholars. The role of FBOs has come to the forefront of national attention since President George W. Bush created the White House Office of Faith-Based and Community Initiatives in 2001. FBOs are at work in every state, working with state and local government organizations to mollify a myriad of social and welfare services problems. Yet, very little serious public administration scholarly work is done on FBOs. Regardless of the reason why this is the case, this section explores and describes the role, function, challenges, and future of FBOs as part of the nonprofit network.

FBOs are similar to more traditional and largely secular-oriented nonprofit organizations in that they are privately organized, governed, and led in order to meet many unmet needs in the areas of social services. They are also dissimilar, because their explicit faith mission and purpose is to address these individual and social needs through a framework of values centered on religion. In fact, the term *faith* is favored over *religion*, because faith is regarded as less institutional-sounding and rules-defining. Faith is broader in context and definition than religion, with the world's three major religious institutions, including Christianity,

Judaism, and Islam, able to incorporate various and diverse parts of their faith foundations into a working framework supporting service delivery, without necessarily and purposely trying to win over adherents. FBOs are able to retain their basic religious and faith foundational commitments, but they are not allowed to purposely and effectively evangelize their faith doctrines in most organizations while under the use of federal funding.[68]

In fact, some depict the differences between secular and faith-based nonprofit organizations in terms of outputs and values. Peter Frumkin of the **Hauser Center for Nonprofit Organizations** at Harvard distinguishes between instrumental and expressive outputs. The former depicts nonprofits that "focus on operational details as part of the process of becoming an ever more efficient purveyor of

---

BOX 9.7 | Battle Lines Over Government Funding: What Are the Public Interests?

The battle lines are drawn over whether or not government funding is appropriate and constitutional. The opposition—led by such critics as Barry Lynn, executive director of **Americans United for Separation of Church and State**; shock organizations such as Ethical Atheist (at ethicalatheist.com) and TheocracyWatch.org; and research organizations, like the Cato Institute—contend for a variety of reasons that government funding of FBOs is clearly unconstitutional and is a deliberate breach of the wall of separation of Church and State.

On the other hand, the proponents strongly disagree, including Presidents Donald Trump, Barack Obama, George W. Bush, Bill Clinton, and luminaries such as: Louis P. Sheldon, founder and chairman of the Traditional Values Coalition; John J. DiIulio, Jr., former assistant to the president and first director of the White House Office of Faith-Based and Community Initiatives; Marvin Olasky, professor at Patrick Henry College, founder of *World Magazine*, and author of *The Tragedy of American Compassion* (1992); and the previously mentioned Lewis D. Solomon, among many others. They argue that public funding of FBOs—as long as it follows strict federal and state guidelines regarding Church-State separation—is not only constitutional, but essential to the amelioration of social and economic decay.

Not all of the proponents agree on what is or is not allowable. However, their basic argument is that FBOs are critical to the moral re-transformation of American society through the development and implementation of social service delivery via faith-based values and means. ◣

Sources: Barry W. Lynn, "Pro: Is Bush Violating Separation of Church and State?" *Wichita Eagle* (January 7, 2003), retrieved from www.kansas.com/mld/eagle/news/editorial/4886899.htm; Ethical Atheist, "Faith-Based Funding," retrieved from www.ethicalatheist.com/docs/faith_based_funding.html; Theocracy Watch, "Faith-Based Initiative," *Center for Religion, Ethics, and Social Policy at Cornell University*, retrieved from www.theocracywatch.org/faith_base.htm; Michael Tanner, "Corrupting Charity: Why Government Should Not Fund Faith-Based Charities," *Cato Institute: Briefing Papers* 62 (#22, March 2001), retrieved October 2007 from www.cato.org/pubs/briefs/bp62.pdf; George W. Bush, "Executive Order: Establishment of White House Office of Faith-Based and Community Initiatives," *Press Release, Office of the Press Secretary* (January 29, 2001), retrieved from www.whitehouse.gov/news/releases/2001/01/print/20010129-2.html; Louis P. Sheldon, "Con: Is Bush Violating Separation of Church and State?" *The Wichita Eagle* (January 7, 2003), retrieved from www.kansas.com/mld/eagle/news/editorial/4886897.htm; John J. DiIulio, Jr., "Compassion in Truth and Action: How Sacred and Secular Places Serve Civic Purposes, and What Washington Should and Should No Do To Help," *Pew Forum*, retrieved from www.pewforum.org/publications/speeches/diiulio0307.htm; Marvin Olasky, *The Tragedy of American Compassion* (Wheaton, IL: Crossway, 1992); Lewis D. Solomon, *In God We Trust? Faith-Based Organizations and the Quest to Solve America's Social Ills* (Lanham, MD: Lexington Books, 2003), 7.

programs," while the latter "holds that only by centering its activity on the expression of important private values and commitment [such as religious faith—author] the nonprofit sector remain vibrant and innovative."[69] FBOs are expressive and value-driven, working toward an end that favors the inclusion and even integration of religious faith principles in the development and implementation of service delivery. Lewis D. Solomon, Professor of Law at George Washington University, ordained rabbi, and author of *In God We Trust* (2003), argues that FBOs are the foundation for moral regeneration in the United States. Solomon claims that "The public interest in FBOs is not a product of heightened religiosity; instead it derives from the public's exasperation with secular social services, whether offered by a governmental unit or a nonprofit provider."[70]

FBOs raise the standard for social service delivery to a new and different level. They not only demarcate the areas in society most ravaged by the lack of governmental attention, but they do so by pointing out that issues ranging from low-income single mothers with several children and no appreciable job skills, to the homeless, widowed, and orphaned, require attention that perhaps nonprofits will not address. The relationship between FBOs and governments is not new, but the ever-increasing attention and influence that is in part given to FBOs through government funding is new. The final section of this chapter will address serious questions over not only the influence of FBOs, but also government funding.

The Basics of FBOs

Numbers FBOs are numerous. However, there are no reliable data on their total number, primarily because the National Center for Charitable Statistics does not classify FBOs separately from nonsectarian organizations.[71] Based upon recent survey information, John E. Seley and Julian Wolpert report, conservatively, that some 37 percent of total nonprofit organizations may be religious in nature.[72] The percentages in the Bible Belt region of the United States (mainly southern states) may be even higher. However, tentatively, the actual percentage of faith-based human service providers may only be in the 18–20 percent range, placing the total number of FBOs, excluding churches that provide human services, between 6,500 and 8,000.

Definition of Faith-Based What is a faith-based human service provider? Robert Wuthnow, Director of the **Center for the Study of Religion at Princeton**, defines an FBO as a private nonprofit organization affiliated with faith or religion to provide faith-based social services. Faith-based social services "are a complex array of activities ... that often differ little from the activities of nonsectarian organizations ... by contributing positively to the functioning of civil society."[73] Lewis D. Solomon characterizes FBOs in several ways: (1) they are often small, parochial groups, (2) while at the same time defying any specific religious affiliation, given that FBOs are Protestant, Catholic, Jewish, Islamic, and even other faiths; (3) they are found in the inner city and suburbs; (4) they are distinctly ethnically diverse; (5) they provide a wide array of human services; and (6) they present their faith dimension in some way, either directly or indirectly.[74] Notice that FBOs are similar to nonsectarian nonprofit organizations in that they attempt to provide human services where and when government can or does not do so, and in doing so they further try and reverse the decline in civil society organizations.

BOX 9.8 | Faith-Based Organizations Engage in Public Service Delivery

Faith-based organizations are entities tied to the religious community, whether Christian or non-Christian, including congregations, national networks, such as Catholic Charities, and "freestanding religious organizations, that because of their spiritual roots and impact are being called upon to play a greater role in implementing, administering, and managing certain public services." It is clear that faith-based organizations are becoming a larger part of the community development movement, one that tries to build upon the existing social and religious structure that is part of the community. At the least, faith-based organizations help to provide greater social and economic stability in America's many and diverse communities. ◤

Source: Office of Policy and Development, "Faith-based Organizations in Community Development," *U.S. Department of Housing and Urban Development*, retrieved from www.huduser.org/publications/commdevl/faithbased_execsum.html

However, as we have noted they are strikingly dissimilar because they focus the purpose and goal of service delivery around religious faith.

Differences Between FBOs and Secular Nonprofits   FBOs take on a couple of different guises: churches and para-church organizations. Churches, or congregations, provide thousands of opportunities to meet the needs of the widows and orphans, the poor and needy, and individuals in other classes too numerous to mention. Approximately 87 percent of all churches—and some estimates place the number of Christian Protestant congregations around 350,000, which does not include Catholic parishes—engage in human service provision, including recreation, youth camps, meal services, homeless shelters, day care, teenage pregnancy programs, and many more.[75] Para-church, or faith-affiliated, organizations include large nonprofit service organizations such as Catholic Charities, Lutheran Social Services, the Salvation Army, and many smaller organizations that provide shelter to the homeless, food pantries, clothing banks, and even work skills development programs.

Whether the programs are congregation or para-church-based, the faith element is extremely important to the development and implementation of the service provision. In an important 2002 study, depicting the faith-based service provision of FBOs in 15 states, political scientists John C. Green and Amy Sherman found that faith dimensions range from extremely direct, which they labeled "Mandatory," to completely indirect, which they labeled as "Not Relevant." Interestingly enough, when FBOs were asked, "Which of the following best describes the faith dimension of your organization's social service programs," less than 1 percent said mandatory, while 20 percent said they were not relevant.[76] The largest percentage (45 percent) of both non-congregation FBOs, which Green and Sherman labeled "nonprofits," listed their faith dimension as passive, meaning the organizations showed their faith through action rather than invitation to listen to or partake in their religious beliefs. In a 2003 study of five different types of welfare-to-work programs in the urban area of Los Angeles County, the researchers found that the FBOs—as opposed to government-run, for-profit, and nonsectarian nonprofit organizations—were most effective in increasing clients' hope and optimism for the future, based in large part upon the FBOs' message of faith.[77] Therefore, faith is an integral component of FBOs; it is the thing that separates them from their nonsectarian nonprofit counterparts.[78]

Brief History of Faith in Human Services Delivery

The role of faith and religion is no stranger when it comes to supporting human welfare and social services delivery in the United States. Beginning with Jamestown Colony in 1607 and continuing through the nineteenth century, Americans have responded to the needs of the poor, orphaned, homeless, and others who required some type of financial or other assistance. From ministers such as Cotton Mather, Charles Chauncey, to Thomas Bacon and John Wesley, to charitable aid societies such as **New York's Society for the Relief of Poor Widows with Small Children,** the Massachusetts Charitable Fire Society, and Richmond, Virginia's Charitable Association of Young Men, the seventeenth and eighteenth centuries were filled with thousands of examples of human compassion, reaching out to the needs at hand, and conducted largely without government assistance.[79]

The nineteenth century was no less active, with human intervention to alleviate and/or mollify human suffering. Irishman Thomas Chalmers' church-based savings banks and work exchanges were designed to aid the poor and down-and-out without government involvement. In the early 1800s, New York City inhabitants

---

BOX 9.9 | Charles Loring Brace

Charles Loring Brace (1826–1890) was born in Connecticut in June of 1826. He was raised and educated for the clergy and later ordained as a Methodist minister. In 1852, however, he became the head of the newly formed Children's Aid Society of New York. It became his life's work and ministry. He did not sit in an office, poring over books or only praying—although he did much of that, as well. Mr. Loring walked the streets of New York City, getting to know the people he wanted to help, especially the children. As a knowledgeable critic of society, he realized and understood that unless the children were given a chance to make something of their lives, then society itself would tumble into the abyss of social and economic decay.

Taking the children off the street was one thing, but it was not the best. He believed that children needed a family. And so, to this end, he removed homeless children from New York City and sent them on trains to the far reaches of the western prairies and beyond, where many would be taken into solid family settings, given the chance to live a life of hard work and hope. The trains that took the children were known as the Orphan Trains. He died in 1890, and the Orphan Trains came to an end in the 1920s, but largely because of changing laws against child labor and because of shifting attitudes toward families staying together. For nearly a half a century, Charles Loring Brace and the Children's Aid Society brought aid and comfort where government could not or would not. ▶

Source: Dave Jackson and Neta Jackson, "Charles Loring Brace: The Founder of the Orphan Trains," *Trailblazer Books,* retrieved October 2007 from www.trailblazer-books.com/books/roundup/Roundup-bio-html

saw the establishment of two organizations: the Society for the Prevention of Pauperism and the New York Association for Improving the Condition of the Poor. Both were dedicated to dividing the city into sections, with individual society members assigned to oversee the individuals living in the districts, assess their needs, and minister to them what was necessary, and when.[80]

Charles Loring Brace and the Orphan Train   The mid- to late 1800s saw the likes of Charles Loring Brace (1826–1890), a Yale graduate, who believed in the worth of children, to seize the opportunity to change the dead-end lives of New York City's orphan population. Combining character development, Bible training, and room and board, he formed the New York Children's Aid Society in 1853. Realizing that this was more short-term than long-term success, he formed what became known as the Orphan Trains, an attempt to link up orphan children with families living in the West, who were in need of part-time workers. Granted, there were many instances of abuse, but at the same time many children escaped a dreary future in the slums of New York City to live and work on a farm or ranch in a state like Kansas or South Dakota. The program existed through the early 1890s, and over time stipulations were made that host families should treat the children right and that they receive Bible and Christian training.[81]

By the early twentieth century, governments worked more closely with private charities. What was believed to be too large for private charities to handle on their own, including church congregations and church organizations, was pinpointed by promoters of government welfare, such as Reverend R.M. Newton, as a means to assist and direct government aid to the most needy. Publications such as *The Christian Century* believed that reformation of the mind was as important as restoration of the soul and spirit, and that reason and rationalism were essential to the building of a new society, one that saw the need, not only for philosophical and higher theological changes, but pragmatic and administrative ones as well.[82] Eventually the progress of FDR's New Deal policies became the norm, eclipsing what had been for three centuries the primary domain of families, private charities, including churches, church organizations, and faith-based societies: serving the needs of the poor. The welfare state had begun.

Connection with Government and Public Administration

FBOs regained strength with passage of the 1996 **Personal Responsibility and Work Opportunity Reconciliation Act** (PRWORA), also known as the 1996 Welfare Reform Act, which included Section 104, or the Charitable Choice (CC) amendment. The CC amendment, which was written by then Senator John Ashcroft (Republican, Missouri), called for nondiscrimination and equal access of federal funding, primarily with regard to state and federal Temporary Assistance for Needy Families (TANF) funds toward religious or religiously affiliated organizations that provided human welfare or social services. It was expanded to include welfare-to-work grants program, the Community Services Block Grant, and some substance abuse and mental health services program.[83] Despite their success, one of the major drawbacks of FBOs is their alleged violation of the Church-State principle, and particularly prominent is the CC's provision that prohibits government from stopping FBOs hiring employees based on their (the FBOs') religious preference.[84] The argument from the FBOs' perspective is that, unless they are able to hire individuals who hold to their (the FBOs') religious and theological/doctrinal viewpoint, then the organization is ultimately defeating itself by not providing a unified front in the service delivery. The opponents' position, of course, is that the process is unconstitutional: government funds should not be spent on unlawful acts of hiring discrimination.

What acts are constitutional and what are not? This is not the proper place to attempt to answer this question to the fullest degree it deserves. Suffice it to say; however, the role of religion and government are not and should not be understood to be diametrically opposed. Constitutional scholar John Witte, Jr. wrote in defense of the use of FBOs:

> It is one thing to prevent government officials from delegating their
> core police powers to religious bodies, quite another thing to prevent
> them from facilitating the charitable services of voluntary religious and
> nonreligious associations alike ... To press separationist logic too deeply
> into "unessentials" not only "trivializes" the place of religion in public and
> private life ... [It] also trivializes the power of the Constitution, converting
> it from a coda of cardinal principles of national law into a codex of petty
> precepts of local life.[85]

What is an essential versus an unessential act—the display of the Ten Commandments on a courthouse lawn? Is it constitutional for the government to fund a homeless shelter that displays on its walls biblical scripture, and provides free of charge the clients with a Gideon New Testament Bible? Does this violate the 1st Amendment prohibition against the establishment of religion by government? Does this interfere with the free exercise of religious believe by an individual, i.e., the homeless guest? Or does the government funding of the religious-base homeless shelter promote the public interests? These and related questions continue to hound the ordinary reality of faith-based organizations (FBOs).

What is legal and what is not? A 2002 comprehensive legal survey of government partnerships with faith-based organizations found several major findings: (1) direct financial support to FBOs is now permitted by federal constitutional law, but that such support must be limited to secular activity; (2) indirect financial support of FBOs, such as education vouchers, is also permitted, as long as recipients have choices between FBOs and secular counterparts; (3) many state constitutions restrict financial support of FBOs; (4) FBOs are generally exempt from federal prohibition on religious discrimination in employment; (5) FBOs may retain their religious identity while receiving federal funds; and (6) with very few exceptions, contracts between states and FBOs are silent on the subject of rights and responsibilities to FBOs.[86]

The Politics and Administration of Faith-Based Organizations

Former President George W. Bush promised in 2001 that faith-based organizations could compete on level ground and for equal opportunity to federal funding with any other nonprofit organizations servicing clientele. So, in January 2001, in an executive order, he noted that "Faith-based and other community organizations are indispensable in meeting the needs of poor Americans and distressed neighborhoods. Government cannot be replaced by such organizations, but it can and should welcome them as partners. The paramount goal is compassionate results."[87] With this executive order the White House Office of Faith-Based and Community Initiatives was formed. Before Jim Towey assumed the directorship, former President Bush turned to an academic who had experience and knowledge of the role of faith in affecting human problems—John DiIulio.

John J. DiIulio, Jr. (1958–), then professor of Public Affairs at Princeton University (now at the University of Pennsylvania), accepted the President's offer to be the first Director of the White House Office of Faith-Based and Community Initiatives, or "Faith Czar." He also served as a special assistant to the president. DiIulio intended to serve six months, but actually stayed nine. DiIulio's charge was threefold: first, to boost charitable giving, both in terms of human and financial; second, to form centers and conduct program audits in several cabinet agencies; and, three, to create a higher-octane approach to civic society awareness through "greater government solicitude for faith-based and community organizations."[88] DiIulio's real purpose was to give speeches and promote the faith-based centers. He was an academic, not a politician or administrator. The President understood this, but DiIulio's academic background and scholarly work, especially in the area of prison and prisoner-reform methods and programs, and his commitment to both Evangelical and Catholic observance, provided legitimacy to the argument that faith was invaluable to addressing the human service problems plaguing America.

With the Federal Government, cabinet-level agencies that have faith-based centers include: education, justice, labor, health and human services, housing and urban development, and labor. How is faith initiated in programs located in these various departments? The Department of Education, using the No Child Left Behind Act of 2001 as its poster child, is motivated to encourage greater awareness of opportunities that can assist in strengthening children's and youths' education. Opportunities include FBOs offering mentoring services to children to help lower the dropout rate, partnering with local schools in various programs, such as the Even Start Family Literacy Program, integrating literacy training for low-income students and parents. The U.S. Department of Housing and Urban Development's Office of Community Planning and Development has a long history of working with FBOs in such areas as Housing for the Elderly or supportive services such as HUD's HOPE VI program, which is geared toward revitalizing run-down low-income housing projects. And, of course, the U.S. Department of Justice's Office of Justice Program houses many of the FBOs that provide services in the areas of faith-based prison services, intermediate work-release centers, and families, victims, and drug-related issues.[89]

State and local governments are prime breeding grounds for FBOs to exist. In our modern federal system of government (more like managerial decentralization), state and local governments are the lynchpins between federal programs and federally *funded* programs. State governments administer the funds, qualify federal rules or make rules of their own, and the local governments, including municipalities and counties, administer the programs. It is at the state and local levels where the proverbial rubber meets the road. As most officials and policy advocates understand, collaboration is the key to success for FBOs. As we have seen, Federal Government, and more and more state governments, is (and more than likely always will be) the primary factor in the funding and delivering of human social services. However, without the input of state and local governments and, as we have noted, an increasingly important role of FBOs, the much-needed services would not be distributed. Study after study has consistently shown the overwhelming use, efficacy, and extent of FBOs throughout the 50 states and in thousands of communities across America.[90]

ETHICS CASE STUDY | Religion and Spirituality in the Public Interests

Our ethics case study for this chapter is different. We include two mini-case-studies, on the ethics of religion and spirituality in public administration, mixed in with discussions from the public administration literature. Throughout the chapter, discussion of nonprofits and faith-based organizations, the underlying tension for public administrators is the recognition of nongovernmental religion and spirituality perspectives on the public interests. To be sure, the use of religion and spiritual revelation in administrative ethics is widely practiced. But this dominant approach to administrative ethics is often misunderstood and controversial in a diverse society. This is especially true in criticism of the Abrahamic tradition of Judeo-Christian-Islamic believers.[91] Yet, many have shown there is an "empirical connection between individual spirituality and participation in public service."[92] Why do some express phobia toward religion and spirituality in public administration? It seems that something that has been so successful for so many millennia in the area of ethics and morality would be of help in our public administrative problems, especially as it affects the public interests.[93] But the primary purpose, definitions, descriptions, and moral values of such a religious tradition, being both absolutist and monotheistic, seems to prompt most administrative scholars and ethicists to distance themselves from overt displays of religion and its application to public organizations and institutions. Yet, public administration scholar Jeff Greene notes that "Public administrators can look back over several thousand years of philosophical and religious discussion about ethics. The literature contains a rich source of ethical principles."[94] The dean of public administration theorists, Dwight Waldo, argued that religion had much to offer and was relevant to public organizations through "extrapolation and application."[95] And former ASPA President Don Menzel believes that spiritual values should receive greater treatment in graduate-level ethics courses.[96] So, how can we apply religious principles or ideas to public administration and administrative ethics? Consider Box 9.10, on teaching spirituality.

Of course, as Jeff Greene writes, there is no doubt that ethical philosophers were greatly influenced by theologians—including Augustine, Thomas Aquinas, and others—who argued that a right relationship with God was necessary to make behavior ethical, and for entrance into the heavenly kingdom.[97] The question before us is not how Christian ethics monitors individual Christians' lives, or even establishes a Christian ethic through a renewed interest in ethics and a "community ethic of being,"[98] but how religion in general, whether Judaism, Christianity, or Islam (these three being

(continued)

ETHICS CASE STUDY | *Continued*

BOX 9.10 | Mini Case Study: Should Spirituality Be Taught in Public Administration?

Public administration professionals, both practitioners and educators, have long taken pride in their ability to be objective, analytical, fair, and competent in carrying out their duties. Values, especially those associated with religious or spiritual belief systems, are widely regarded as taboo in the context of the work and mission of one's public agency or employer. Moreover, the historical Church-State separation upon which America was founded reinforces this outlook.

After all, public administrators serve a collective clientele, not individuals with specific needs of body and soul. Or do they? Are social agencies and social workers, for example, committed to serving those whose needs are objectively defined and measured (e.g., food, shelter, abuse)? Or, should they serve the needy in a more holistic, even spiritualistic way?

Some observers contend that professional social workers can and should treat only the afflictions of the body, not the mind or soul. Others are not so pure and even suggest that social workers in practice have no choice but to treat the afflictions of mind and body. This is particularly so, says Professor Edward R. Canada of the University of Kansas, when there is "a crisis or occasion of grief and loss."

The challenge of treating mind and body in professional social work has reached the stage where there are now 50 accredited university social work programs that offer courses on spirituality and social work. This educational need is driven by what many believe is the reality of practicing spirituality in one's work. For example, a 1999 survey of members of the National Association of Social Workers found that 71 percent of the respondents said they "help clients consider the spiritual meaning and purpose" of their current life situation and 63 percent said they help clients develop spiritual or religious rituals as part of their treatment. Surveys also show that many social workers pray for their clients, often without their permission.

Discussion Questions

- Is there a place for teaching religion and spirituality in public administration programs?
- Does this cross over-the line of acceptable professional education?

Source: D.W. Miller, "Programs in Social Work Embrace the Teaching of Spirituality," *Chronicle of Higher Education* (May 18, 2001); Donald Menzel, "Ethics Moment" column, *PA Times* (September 2001).

the three largest monotheistic world religions), or spirituality in particular, has an impact upon social and organizational ethical dimensions as well as individual decisional patterns.[99] Obviously, each monotheistic religion perceives itself in a battle for God against forces of evil and oppression around the world, both from a communal (i.e., organizational to institutional) to an individual perspective, i.e., spirituality. The three monotheistic religions offer what each believes to be necessary and fundamental to meet the spiritual needs of individuals and organizations, without falling prey to various modern or postmodern challenges to their core values.[100]

Separation of Religion from State

The separation of religion and State seems to be the central concern to those who oppose the use of religious ethics in the practice of public administration. They may fear that public administrators will impose their religion or spiritual beliefs upon them, force them to agree to beliefs in exchange for public service, or require them to support a religion that isn't their own. The notion of a "wall of separation" began with an 1802 letter by President Thomas Jefferson to his Baptist friends. Baptists believed in strict-separation of Church and State as a theological doctrine to keep government out of the Church, to keep secular decay and corruption away from Christianity. Jefferson wrote that he shared their belief that there should be a "wall of separation" between Church and State, but admitted that neither the 1789 U.S. Constitution nor the 1792 Bill of Rights created this wall. Instead, the supreme law of the land prevented the national government from creating one national religion, and protected the exercise of individual religious beliefs. Thus, the wall of separation is not found in the Constitution, the Bill of Rights, or elsewhere in statutes, treaties, or the supreme law of the land. Not until *Everson v. Bd. of Education* (1947) did the Supreme Court first use the phrase, only to decide it was constitutional for New Jersey to direct public tax dollars to benefit all by bussing children to church-schools.[101]

Of course, public administrators commonly find the foundations of their ethics within religion, and don't usually impose their religion upon others. But there have been times in history when public administrators did impose their religious beliefs upon citizens who opposed those beliefs. For example, in *US v. Reynold* (1879), the Court upheld the arrests and convictions of Latter Day Saints (LDS, Mormons) in Utah for the common law crime of polygamy. More recently, the Court in *Bob Jones University v. US* (1983) upheld the end of federal-tax-exempt status for a Baptist college that sincerely believed their faith required separation of students by race in classrooms, the cafeteria, sidewalks, work-study, the library, and in dating or social events. Most readers would object to a public administrator imposing a religion or spiritual belief that conflicted with theirs. What are we to do about the imposition of conflicting views between the thousands of radically different theological belief systems in Christian, Muslim, Jewish, and other religions? Or what about imposing the theological doctrines and beliefs of one dominant or powerful Christian religion upon all other religious peoples, or "noners" (people whose religion is "none of the above")?[102] To require or even suggest that Christian ethics should be the primary moral guidebook for all individuals and organizations is simply not constitutional,

(*continued*)

ETHICS CASE STUDY | *Continued*

BOX 9.11 | Mini Case Study: Ethics and Religious Expression in the Workplace

You are the Chief of the State Division of Vehicular Licensing with 1,250 employees located at six district offices. The Director of District 2 approaches you about a thorny problem: what to do about providing employees who are Muslims suitable times of the day to worship. The problem began on October 30, when the state shifted from Central Daylight Time to Central Standard Time. As it turns out, the fall back of the clock pulled the Muslim sunset prayer back into work hours.

A group of Muslim co-workers requested that the District office allow them to conduct their sunset prayer at 5:00 p.m. The District office closes at 6 p.m. The group said that they would be willing to work from 6:00 p.m. to 7:00 p.m. to make up for the time lost.

The Director is unsure of what other Districts have done and does not know if state law requires public agencies to accommodate employees' religious beliefs. It is, of course, clear to all that public agencies cannot promote religious beliefs and practices, but this is not quite the same thing.

As the Division Chief, you inform the Director that other District offices have not faced this issue before. Moreover, state law is reasonably clear: employers (public and private) must accommodate employees' religious beliefs as long as the requests are reasonable and do not create a hardship.

Discussion Questions

- Is the request by the workers reasonable?

- Would shifting the sunset prayer hour to 5 P.M. create a hardship for the District Office of Vehicular Licensing? (Remember that the primary work of the District Office is to issue licenses to the public on a first-come, first-served basis.)

- Would agreeing to the request be viewed as favoritism toward one group of employees? If so, would this create morale problems?

- What recommendation should I make to the District Director? ▲

Source: Donald Menzel, "Ethics Moment," *PA Times* (February 2006).

since all individuals are guaranteed protection of free exercise of religious beliefs and against the establishment of religion under the 1st Amendment. Otherwise, it may result in riot, rout, civil insurrection, and at the least it would not be ethical or workable in a diverse and pluralistic society.

However, many ethical philosophers find in Christian ethics a set of moral concepts that are widely accepted by those in Abrahamic traditions and society in general—broad enough in scope that Christian New Testament scripture can be used to define and frame an ethics for all.[103] Many prominent public administration scholars recognize the teachings of Jesus as being highly appropriate for normative guidance in public administrative ethics. Lance deHaven-Smith argues:

> Public administration is not just a subfield of administration in general, or of the study of bureaucratic organizations. Public administration includes the study of ethics, politics, political theory, and public policy. It is more than mere managerial effectiveness; it is also a search, in theory and practice, for good government in the broadest sense of the term.[104]

In other words, we would argue, it is a search for the public interests in whatever place they be found. Other public administration writers specifically contend that "The Judeo-Christian tradition establishes the moral barometer of right and wrong behavior, and to exclude its functional as well as ethical utility is to do a philosophical injustice to the study of administrative ethics."[105] Willa Bruce argues that religion and spirituality, which she defines as "an individual search for meaning, purpose and values which may or may not include God," are one of the core elements of defining and shaping moral action. Morality and administrative action, whether examined in an individual administrator's decision making or through an agency's position on a policy issue, are influenced by the role of religion and spirituality.[106] Still others argue that biblical proverbs should be used as guiding principles of public decision making.[107] Suffice it to say, religion and religious and spiritual values have some type of influence upon ethical issues and ethical decision making.[108]

Discussion

- Why is there a phobia against religion and spirituality in public administration?
- Should spirituality and religious ethics be taught in public administration?
- How have theologians influenced the development of ethical philosophy?
- Are there Judeo-Christian-Islamic ethics that may be widely accepted in society? ▲

CONCLUSION

With collaboration or partnering come challenges to successful partnerships between government and the nonprofit sector, including FBOs. There is a need to strengthen these relationships, primarily because of the nature of a secular society and government that has not, until recently, recognized and embraced the role of private values, including religion and faith, in the mix of effecting change, especially in the social and healthcare services network. How long must we despise ourselves and ignore these enduring and very real aspects of life? Shouldn't the public interests include the reality of all of life? In response, many have called for reform,[109] some have argued for a resilient nonprofit sector,[110] and some have called for a stronger lobbying voice for the nonprofit sector.[111] Salamon, for example, argues that the challenges include fiscal, greater competition with the for-profit sector, need for greater effectiveness, increasing use of technology, enhanced need for policy legitimacy, and human resource development. At the same time; however, he believes that increased opportunities for the nonprofit sector (and, to some extent, FBOs) await as well, including changing demographic and social shifts, new pools of money for private philanthropy, greater visibility and salience in the eyes of government officials and the restless public, and, of course, increased government social welfare spending.[112]

There remains a tension with the introduction of personal, religious, and spiritual values into the public sector with nonprofits and faith-based organizations. While religious ethical teachings have had the greatest impact on the morality of individuals in society, there may be unacceptable sectarian bias introduced with public sector services by individuals in nonprofits and faith-based organizations. Yet, public sector employees, volunteers, and contractors cannot be expected to leave their religious values at the office door. Religion has a legitimate place in the public square and a protected place in the lives of individuals—even public servants. Clearly, we have not solved the problems of the interplay of religious values and public service. But the reality is that we continue to provide public services by the means of nonprofits, faith-based organizations, and individuals with religious and spiritual values.

The time for greater awareness, and for public administrators to think outside of the governmental box regarding how to address the policy issues revolving around social and human services, is not for the future—it is for now. As Donald Kettl has so aptly stated, we live in a transformed society, one in which the old engines of the past will no longer drive the vehicles of the present and future. Government alone is not, nor ever was, the sole answer. It must work in tandem or partnership, as many declare, with the nexus of private nonprofit and faith-based organizations in order to meet the challenges surrounding many of society's perplexing problems.

ACTION STEPS

1. Visit a local nonprofit or faith-based organization. Talk to the workers, volunteers, and clientele. For the workers and olunteers, ask how they like doing what they do. Why do they do it? What benefits do they personally derive from their work or volunteering? For clientele, ask when they

first started coming, why they still come, what benefits they get from the nonprofit or faith-based organization?

2. Contact a local nonprofit and ask about their mission, vision and purpose, and how they perform their duties. What theory of nonprofits seems to fit the local nonprofits you contacted?

3. Do a literature search of the four types of nonprofit organizations—*funding agencies, member-serving, public-benefit,* and *faith-based*—and acquire some basic empirical information, such as total number, types, membership, location throughout the United States, type of services provided, etc. Put your information into a spreadsheet or Word table format, giving a brief explanatory narrative for each section.

4. Do the public interests impose limits upon faith-initiatives in the provision of public services? Reflect on the case of *Santa Fe School District v. Doe,* 530 U.S. 290 (2000), where the U.S. Supreme Court declared unconstitutional the student-led, student-initiated prayer at a public high school football game.

5. Suppose you are the new "Faith Czar" for a president, governor, mayor, or agency. Detail how you would answer the question put to the first US Faith Czar, John J. DiIulio, Jr.: "Do you know if you are going to heaven?" How would you answer this, and faithfully act in the public interests without regard to religious identity or sectarian bias? How did John DiIulio (i.e., *Godly Republic*) answer this?

KEY CONCEPTS AND NAMES

NOTES

1 Deborah L. Rhode and Amanda K. Packel, "Ethics and Nonprofits," *Stanford Social Innovation Review* 7 (#3, Summer 2009): 28–35 (esp. 35).

2 Ibid., 35.

3 Nicholas Henry, *Public Administration and Public Affairs*, 9th ed. (Upper Saddle River, NJ, 2004), 331, 360.

4 Robert B. Denhardt and Joseph W. Grubbs, *Public Administration: An Action Orientation*, 4th ed. (Belmont, CA: Thomson-Wadsworth, 2004), 106.

5 Donald F. Kettl, *The Transformation of Governance: Public Administration for Twenty-First Century America* (Baltimore, MD: John Hopkins University Press, 2002), 129.

6 Theda Skocpol, *Diminished Democracy: From Membership to Management in American Civic Life* (Norman: University of Oklahoma Press, 2003), 12.

7 Marvin Olasky, *The Tragedy of American Compassion* (Wheaton, IL: Crossway, 1992), 6.

8 Lester M. Salamon, *The Resilient Factor: The State of Nonprofit America* (Washington, DC: Brookings Institution, 2003), 1–2.

9 Peter Frumkin, *On Being Nonprofit: A Conceptual and Policy Primer* (Cambridge, MA: Harvard University Press, 2002), 10.

10 Ibid., 15.

11 See Lester M. Salamon, *The Resilient Factor: The State of Nonprofit America* (Washington, DC: Brookings Institution, 2003), 7–8.

12 Gita Gulati-Partee, "A Primer on Nonprofit Organizations," *Popular Government* 66 (#4, Summer 2001): 31, retrieved October 31, 2007 from www.publicintersection.unc.edu/pdf/aprimer-gita.pdf; emphasis added.

13 National Council of Nonprofit Associations, "Nonprofit Agenda: A Blueprint for Action" (July 1, 2004), retrieved from www.ncna.org/_uploads/documents/live/bluprint_pdf.pdf

14 See Lester M. Salamon, *The Resilient Factor: The State of Nonprofit America* (Washington, DC: Brookings Institution, 2003), 2; emphasis in original.

15 Paul C. Light, "The Content of their Character: The State of the Nonprofit Workforce," *Nonprofit Quarterly* 9 (#3, Fall 2002): 6.

16 Amy Blackwood, Kennard T. Wing, and Thomas H. Pollak, *The Nonprofit Sector in Brief* (Washington, DC: Urban Institute Press, 2008), 1.

17 Ibid., 2.

18 Ibid., 2.

19 Ibid., 3, 4, 5–6.

20 Amy Blackwood, Kennard T. Wing, and Thomas H. Pollak, *The Nonprofit Sector in Brief* (Washington, DC: Urban Institute Press, 2008), 6.

21 Charles Storch, "Illinois Has the Fifth-Largest Non-Profit Workforce in U.S.," *Chicago Tribune* (December 28, 2006), section 5, 4.

22 The Urban Institute, "Quick Facts about Nonprofits," *National Center for Charitable Statistics*, retrieved October 13, 2008 from www.ncces.urban.org/statistics/quickfacts.cfm

23 Jon Van Til, "Nonprofit Organizations and Social Institutions," in Robert D. Herman, ed., *The Jossey-Bass Handbook of Nonprofit Leadership and Management* (San Francisco, CA: Jossey-Bass, 1994), 47.

24 Lester M. Salamon, *Partners in Public Service: Government-Nonprofit Relations in the Modern Welfare Estate* (Baltimore, MD: Johns Hopkins University Press, 1995).

25 Lydian Altman-Sauer, Margaret Henderson, and Gordon P. Whitaker, "Strengthening Relationships between Local Governments and Nonprofits," *Popular Government* 66 (#2, Winter 2001): 33–9, retrieved from www.iog.unc.edu/pubs/electronicversions/pg/pgwin01/article4.pdf. Also see Gordon P. Whitaker and Rosalind Day, "How Local Governments Work with Nonprofit Organizations in North Carolina," *Popular Government* 66 (#2, Winter 2001): 25–32, retrieved from www.sog.unc.edu/pubs/

electronicversions/pg/pgwin01/article3.pdf; and Margaret Henderson, Gordon P. Whitaker, and Lydian Altman-Sauer, "Establishing Mutual Accountability in Nonprofit-Government Relationships." *Popular Government* 69 (#1, Fall 2003), retrieved from www.sog.unc.edu/pubs/electronicversions/pg/pgfal03/article3.pdf

26 Lydian Altman-Sauer, Margaret Henderson, and Gordon P. Whitaker, "Strengthening Relationships between Local Governments and Nonprofits," *Popular Government* 66 (#2, Winter 2001): 38, retrieved from www.iog.unc.edu/pubs/electronicversions/pg/pgwin01/article4.pdf.

27 See Jon Van Til, "Nonprofit Organizations and Social Institutions," in Robert D. Herman, ed., *The Jossey-Bass Handbook of Nonprofit Leadership and Management* (San Francisco, CA: Jossey-Bass, 1994), 62.

28 See Theda Skocpol, *Diminished Democracy: From Membership to Management in American Civic Life* (Norman: University of Oklahoma Press, 2003).

29 See Lester M. Salamon, *Partners in Public Service: Government-Nonprofit Relations in the Modern Welfare Estate* (Baltimore, MD: Johns Hopkins University Press, 1995), 35; Salamon notes the real problem is "a weakness in theory." He further notes "Both students of the voluntary sector and students of the welfare state have failed to appreciate or come to terms with the reality of extensive government-nonprofit relationships until relatively recently because of faults in the conceptual lenses through which they have been examining this reality."

30 Ibid., 37.

31 Ibid., 38.

32 See Charles Colson, *Justice That Restores* (Washington, DC: Prison Fellowship Ministries, 2001).

33 See Lester M. Salamon, *Partners in Public Service: Government-Nonprofit Relations in the Modern Welfare Estate* (Baltimore, MD: Johns Hopkins University Press, 1995), 40.

34 Ibid., 41.

35 Ibid., 41.

36 Ibid., 14.

37 Ibid., 44.

38 See Estelle James, "Commentary," in Charles T. Clotfelter, ed., *Who Benefits from the Nonprofit Sector?* (Chicago, IL: University of Chicago Press, 1992), 250–55.

39 Peter Dobkin Hall, "Historical Perspectives on Nonprofit Organizations," in Robert D. Herman, ed., *The Jossey-Bass Handbook of Nonprofit Leadership and Management* (San Francisco, CA: Jossey-Bass, 1994), 3.

40 Ibid., 4.

41 See Hal G. Rainey, *Understanding and Managing Public Organizations*, 3d ed. (San Francisco: Jossey-Bass, 2003), 59.

42 See Peter Dobkin Hall, "Historical Perspectives on Nonprofit Organizations," in Robert D. Herman, ed., *The Jossey-Bass Handbook of Nonprofit Leadership and Management* (San Francisco, CA: Jossey-Bass, 1994), 5.

43 See Theda Skocpol, *Diminished Democracy: From Membership to Management in American Civic Life* (Norman: University of Oklahoma Press, 2003), 6, 7.

44 She cites several prominent sociologists and other intellectuals that voluntary associations are best defined and developed separate from government. See Robert D. Putnam, *Bowling Alone: The Collapse and Revival of American Community* (New York: Simon and Schuster, 2000); and Michael Sandel, *Democracy's Discontent: American in Search of a Public Philosophy* (Cambridge, MA: Harvard University Press, 1996).

45 See Peter Dobkin Hall, "Historical Perspectives on Nonprofit Organizations," in Robert D. Herman, ed., *The Jossey-Bass Handbook of Nonprofit Leadership and Management* (San Francisco, CA: Jossey-Bass, 1994), 6.

46 Ibid., 10.

47 Ibid., 12, 13.

48 Ibid., 15, 17.

49 Lester M. Salamon, *America's Nonprofit Sector: A Primer*, 3rd ed. (New York: Foundation Center, 2012), 56–7.

50 See Peter Dobkin Hall, "Historical Perspectives on Nonprofit Organizations," in Robert D. Herman, ed., *The Jossey-Bass Handbook of Nonprofit Leadership and Management* (San Francisco, CA: Jossey-Bass, 1994), 18.

51 Ibid., 17.

52 See Lester M. Salamon, *America's Nonprofit Sector: A Primer*, 3rd ed. (New York: Foundation Center, 2012), 59.

53 See Peter Dobkin Hall, "Historical Perspectives on Nonprofit Organizations," in Robert D. Herman, ed., *The Jossey-Bass Handbook of Nonprofit Leadership and Management* (San Francisco, CA: Jossey-Bass, 1994), 21.

54 Ibid., 22–4.

55 Ibid., 24–5.

56 Ibid., 26.

57 Ibid. See also Lester M. Salamon, *Partners in Public Service: Government-Nonprofit Relations in the Modern Welfare Estate* (Baltimore, MD: Johns Hopkins University Press, 1995), 150.

58 Lester M. Salamon, *Partners in Public Service: Government-Nonprofit Relations in the Modern Welfare Estate* (Baltimore, MD: Johns Hopkins University Press, 1995), 167.

59 Ibid., 161.

60 As invoked in his inaugural president address by George H.W. Bush in 1989, retrieved May 21, 2018, from www.youtube.com/watch?v=SQhbEh8AeSA

61 See Lester M. Salamon, *America's Nonprofit Sector: A Primer*, 3rd ed. (New York: Foundation Center, 2012), 64, 65.

62 See Lester M. Salamon, *Partners in Public Service: Government-Nonprofit Relations in the Modern Welfare Estate* (Baltimore, MD: Johns Hopkins University Press, 1995), 155.

63 See Lester M. Salamon, *America's Nonprofit Sector: A Primer*, 3rd ed. (New York: Foundation Center, 2012), 67.

64 Ibid., 67–70.

65 Donald F. Kettl, *The Transformation of Governance: Public Administration for Twenty-First Century America* (Baltimore, MD: John Hopkins University Press, 2002), 127–9.

66 Edmund F. McGarrell, G. Brinker, and D. Etindi, *The Role of Faith-Based Organizations in Crime Prevention and Justice* (Indianapolis, IN: Welfare Policy Center, Hudson Institute, 1999).

67 John J. DiIulio, Jr., *Living Faith: The Black Church Outreach Tradition* (New York: Manhattan Institute for Policy Research, 1998, No. 98-3); C. Winship and J. Berrien, "Boston Cops and Black Churches," *Public Interest* 136 (1999): 52–68.

68 Ira C. Lupu and Robert W. Tuttle, *Government Partnerships with Faith-Based Service Providers: State of the Law* (Albany, NY: The Roundtable on Religion and Social Welfare Policy, 2002), 1.

69 Ibid., 124, 125.

70 Lewis D. Solomon, *In God We Trust? Faith-Based Organizations and the Quest to Solve America's Social Ills* (Lanham, MD: Lexington Books, 2003), 7.

71 Robert Wuthnow, *Saving America? Faith-Based Services and the Future of Civil Society* (Princeton, NJ: Princeton University Press, 2004), 140.

72 Ibid., 141.

73 Ibid., 6–7.

74 See Lewis D. Solomon, *In God We Trust? Faith-Based Organizations and the Quest to Solve America's Social Ills* (Lanham, MD: Lexington Books, 2003), 73.

75 Ibid., 74; see also Robert Wuthnow, *Saving America? Faith-Based Services and the Future of Civil Society* (Princeton, NJ: Princeton University Press, 2004), 28.

76 John C. Green and Amy L. Sherman, *Fruitful Collaborations: A Survey of Government-Funded Faith-Based Programs in 15 States* (Charlottesville, VA: Hudson Institute, 2002), 18.

77 Stephen V. Monsma and J. Christopher Soper, *What Works: Comparing the Effectiveness of Welfare-to-Work Programs in Los Angeles* (Philadelphia: University of Pennsylvania, Center for Research on Religion and Urban Civil Society, 2003), 5.

78 For example, Gary E. Roberts, *Servant Leader Human Resource Management: A Moral and Spiritual Perspective* (New York, NY: Palgrave Macmillan, 2015).

79 See Marvin Olasky, *The Tragedy of American Compassion* (Wheaton, IL: Crossway, 1992), 10–16.

80 Ibid., 25–7.

81 See Lewis D. Solomon, *In God We Trust? Faith-Based Organizations and the Quest to Solve America's Social Ills* (Lanham, MD: Lexington Books, 2003), 50.

82 See Marvin Olasky, *The Tragedy of American Compassion* (Wheaton, IL: Crossway, 1992), 136.

83 Rachel M. Haberkern, "Implementing Charitable Choice at the State and Local Levels," *Welfare Information Network: Issue Notes* 6 (#5, July 2002), retrieved from www.welfareinfo.org/implementingcharitablechoiceIN.htm

84 Gretchen M. Griener. "Charitable Choice and Welfare Reform: Collaboration between State and Local Governments and Faith-Based Organizations," *Welfare Information Network: Issue Notes* 4 (#12, September 2000), retrieved from www.financeprojectinfo.org/Publications/issuenotecharitablechoice.htm

85 John Witte, Jr, *Religion and the American Constitutional Experiment: Essential Rights and Liberties* (Boulder, CO: Westview Press, 2000), 183–4.

86 See Ira C. Lupu and Robert W. Tuttle, *Government Partnerships with Faith-Based Service Providers: State of the Law* (Albany, NY: The Roundtable on Religion and Social Welfare Policy, 2002), 1–2.

87 George W. Bush, "Executive Order: Establishment of White House Office of Faith-Based and Community Initiatives," *Press Release, Office of the Press Secretary* (January 29, 2001), retrieved from www.whitehouse.gov/news/releases/2001/01.htm

88 James Q. Wilson and John J. DiIulio, *American Government*, 8th ed. (Boston: Houghton Mifflin, 2001), 5–6.

89 Gail A. Caputo, *Intermediate Sanctions in Corrections* (Denton: University of North Texas Press, 2004).

90 Byron R. Johnson with Ralph Brett Tompkins and Derek Webb, "Objective Hope: Assessing the Effectiveness of Faith-Based Organizations: A Review of the Literature" (Philadelphia, PA: University of Pennsylvania Center for Research on Religion and Urban Civil Society, 2002); Mark Ragan, Lisa M. Montiel, and Daniel J. Wright, "Scanning the Policy Environment for Faith-Based Social Services in the United States: Results of a 50-State Study," *Rockefeller Institute of Government* (Albany, NY: State University of New York, 2007), retrieved from www.rockinst.org/WorkArea/showcontent.aspx?id=8894; and John L. Saxon, "Faith-Based Social Services: What Are They? Do They Work? Are They Legal? What's Happening in North Carolina?" *Popular Government* 70 (#1, Fall 2004), retrieved from http://ncinfo.iog.unc.edu/pubs/electronicversions/pg/pgfal04/article1.pdf

91 Stephen M. King, "Toward a New Administrative Ethic: An Understanding and Application of the Judeo-Christian Tradition to Administrative Issues." *Public Integrity* 2 (#1, Winter 2000): 17–28.

92 For example, David J. Houston and Katherine E. Cartwright, "Spirituality and Public Service," *Public Administration Review* 67 (#1, January/February 2007): 88.

93 Robert T. Golembiewski, *Men, Management, and Morality: Towards a New Organizational Ethic* (New York, NY: Routledge, 1988), 56–75.

94 Jeffrey D. Greene, *Public Administration in the New Century: A Concise Introduction* (Belmont, CA: Thomson-Wadsworth, 2005), 369.

95 Dwight Waldo, *The Enterprise of Public Administration* (Novato, CA: Chandler and Sharp, 1988), 110.

96 Donald C. Menzel, "Spiritual Values in the PA Curriculum: Why or Why Not?" *Public Administration Times* (July 2005): 8.

97 See Jeffrey D. Greene, *Public Administration in the New Century: A Concise Introduction* (Belmont, CA: Thomson-Wadsworth, 2005), 370.

98 Stanley J. Grenz, *The Moral Quest: Foundations of Christian Ethics* (Westmont, IL: InterVarsity Press, 1999).

99 Stephen M. King, "Religion, Spirituality, and the Workplace: Challenges for Public Administration" *Public Administration Review* 67 (#1, 2007): 103–14.

100 Karen Armstrong, *The Battle for God* (New York, NY: Ballantine Books, 2000).

101 Robert Booth Fowler, Allen D. Hertzke, Laura R. Olson, and Kevin R. den Dulk, *Religion and Politics in America: Faith, Culture, and Strategic Choices*, 4th ed. (Boulder, CO: Westview Press, 2011).

102 Alister E. McGrath, "In What Way Can Jesus Be a Moral Example for Christians?" *Journal of Evangelical Theological Society* 34 (#3, September 1991): 289–98.

103 Lisa Sowle Cahill, "The New Testament and Ethics: Communities of Social Change," *Interpretation* 44 (October 1990): 383–95; and Stephen Charles Mott, "The Use of the New Testament, Part I," *Transformation* 1 (#2, April/June 1986): 21–6; Reinhold Niebuhr, "The Ethics of Jesus," *An Interpretation of Christian Ethics* (New York: Seabury Press; 1979 reissue of 1934 book).

104 "Jesus and Public Administration," in Thomas D. Lynch and Todd J. Dicker, eds., *Handbook of Organization Theory and Management: The Philosophical Approach* (New York: Marcel Dekker, 1998), 57–68.

105 See Stephen M. King, "Toward a New Administrative Ethic: An Understanding and Application of the Judeo-Christian Tradition to Administrative Issues." *Public Integrity* 2 (#1, Winter 2000): 21.

106 Willa Bruce, "Teaching Morality in Graduate Public Administration," paper prepared for presentation at the *Conference on Teaching Public Administration* (Tempe, AZ, February 4–5, 2001), 4, 5.

107 Stephen M. King, "A Proverbial Approach to Public Administration," *Public Voices* 7 (#2, 2005): 28–40.

108 For example, Richard A. McCormick, "Does Religious Faith Add to Ethical Perception?" in John C. Haughey, ed., *Personal Values in Public Policy: Conversations on Government Decisionmaking* (New York, NY: Paulist Press, 1979), 155–73.

109 Paul C. Light, *Making Nonprofits Work: A Report on the Tides of Nonprofit Management Reform* (Washington, DC: Brookings Institution Press, 2011); and Paul C. Light, "The Content of their Character: The State of the Nonprofit Workforce," *Nonprofit Quarterly* 9 (#3, Fall 2002).

110 See Lester M. Salamon, *The Resilient Factor: The State of Nonprofit America* (Washington, DC: Brookings Institution, 2003).

111 See Jeffrey M. Berry with David F. Arons, *A Voice for Nonprofits* (Washington, DC: Brookings Institution Press, 2005).

112 See Lester M. Salamon, *The Resilient Factor: The State of Nonprofit America* (Washington, DC: Brookings Institution, 2003), 15–34, 35–47.

Epilogue
The Public Administration Profession

"Advance Professional Excellence: Strengthen personal capabilities to act competently and ethically and encourage the professional development of others."
—(Code of Ethics, American Society for Public Administration, 2013)

Thomas Friedman, the celebrated *New York Times* columnist and author of the bestseller *The World is Flat*,[1] has argued that the world is "flattening." Due to technological and telecommunication advances, the business and economic world is shrinking, enabling more and more countries worldwide to enter the global market. His message is essentially one of economic materialism, where the economic forces of the world combine to determine our destinies: those who recognize this fact will jump on board and prosper, and those that do not recognize it or fail to act will suffer the consequences.

However, Friedman's image of a flat world is an empty metaphor—all flash and no substance—for it fails to recognize the human side of it all. As one reviewer wrote:

> In the last few years—really ever since the Internet bubble burst and terror struck—most Americans have become well aware of what Friedman does not recognize: that no matter how beneficial or fascinating the IT revolution may be, the history of the twenty-first century will not begin and end with Global Crossing and Geek Squads. Peace and politics, war and friendship, democracy and tyranny, poetry and song, love and commitment, parenting and virtue, morals and devotion and God himself—all these have yet to be digitized. For the most important things, our world, like a vintage record album, is still analog, still round.[2]

The same is true for the public administration profession. There is, as Douglas McGregor once wrote, "a human side of enterprise." We in the public administration profession can get caught up in the flashing changes of economic cycles, globalization, information technology, cultural and demographic shifts, telecommunications revolutions, or performance management in a world of permanent fiscal crisis, disaggregated, and fragmented and disarticulated among other academic jargon. But the public administration profession is mainly about values, policies, and people. It is about public servants promoting and fulfilling the public interests.

The challenges for the public administration profession are in keeping up with and exemplifying ethical behavior in today's society.[3] What are ethical leaders in the field doing? How should the public administrator know about new ethical challenges based on new technologies, new social demographics, and changing politics? We have suggested pursuit of the public interests and three guiding ethical philosophies as foundations for the path of the public administrator in this quest to do what is right and good and competent. First, the public interests are the cornerstone of public service; they are the public in public administration. We've outlined perspectives on what the public interests are based on good moral character, cost-benefit or preferences calculations, and constitutional regime values. Second, we've refined these perspectives of the public interests as applications of ethical philosophies. The ethic of deontology guides us to seek out that action or decision which possesses intrinsic goodness. Utilitarianism guides us to seek a rule of thumb or calculation of preferences that possesses the highest probability of delivering social utility and the greatest good for the greatest number. Virtue ethics guides us to be the best that we can be in mind, heart, body, and soul—and, as a consequence, our decisions and actions will be right and good.

ETHICAL DIRECTIONALITY MODEL

From the beginning of this book, we've emphasized the plural nature of the public interests and ethical theories. It's all of the above—it's not just one and not the other, on or off, one of the above. The practice of ethical public administrators belies the use of multiple perspectives of public interests, and multiple uses of ethical philosophies. It's a matter of degree, of context, and of responsiveness. This may seem as dynamite to the purist, who seeks the formal logic of one ultimate approach universally applied to all persons, all decisions, and all behavior. But close empirical study of public interests and ethics in the public administration profession reveals the plurality in doing the good and the right.[4]

A model of this phenomenon, which we call the "Ethical Directionality Model," is illustrated in Figure E.1. We use "ethical directionality" because our purpose is to provide illumination, guidance, and direction in the wise choice of an ethical theory or approach to decision making in administrative decisions, based on perceptions of the level of consequences or impact, as well as level of intrinsic evil or harm in itself. It's an idea-model, rather than an interval or ratio data model where you can measure precisely with a ruler. Our purpose is to suggest a relationship between the four basic ethical theories as discussed throughout our book, and their overlapping nature or usage/response to basic variations in context or environment that may be predicted.

First, our four basic ethical theories have included:

- Ethical egoism
- Utility
- Deontology
- Virtue.

Each of our basic ethical theories has been represented in the model with a circle, which is labeled. The four circles all overlap one another, just as our four ethical theories overlapped one another throughout our book, on close empirical study of the ethics of public administrators.

Second, variations in the context or environment of ethics are illustrated with a horizontal X axis and a vertical Y axis, each representing variations. The

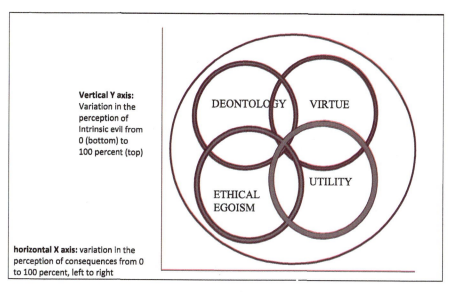

Vertical Y axis: Variation in the perception of Intrinsic evil from 0 (bottom) to 100 percent (top)

DEONTOLOGY VIRTUE

ETHICAL EGOISM

UTILITY

horizontal X axis: variation in the perception of consequences from 0 to 100 percent, left to right

FIGURE E.1
Ethical Directionality Model

horizontal X axis represents the variation of teleological consequences in ethical phenomena, from 0 to 100 percent. The vertical Y axis represents the variation of non-teleological intrinsic evil in ethical phenomena, from 0 to 100 percent. Thus, variations include:

- The horizontal X axis is labeled *variation in perception of consequences*—from 0 to 100 percent.
- The vertical Y axis is labeled *variation in perception of intrinsic evil*—from 0 to 100 percent.

Third, the four basic ethical theories are arranged as they predictably relate to, or respond to, the basic variations in context or environment of the X axis and Y axis. Thus, the ethical directionality model predicts that:

- the *less intrinsic evil*, the more likely ethical egoism or utilitarianism is appropriately preferred in ethical decision making or actions;
- the *fewer consequences*, the more likely ethical egoism or deontology are appropriately preferred in ethical decision-making or actions;
- the *more consequences*, the more likely utilitarianism or virtue are appropriately preferred in ethical decision making or actions; and the *more intrinsic evil*, the more likely deontology or virtue are appropriately preferred in ethical decision making or actions.

This model may help to illustrate the four overlapping quadrants of ethical theories (as discussed throughout this book), as well as help to predict and give guidance and direction on appropriate emphasis between the ethical theories and perspectives for public administrators. Under this model, if an ethical problem seems to have consequences only for only you, and presents little or no harm or intrinsic evil to anyone other than yourself, then *ethical egoism* may be an appropriate source for ethical decision making. For example, when you work alone from your home office, you may feel morally justified to decorate it as you wish: since it's up to you, no one else will see it, it's in your home, you have certain privacy rights at home. On the other hand, if ethical problems may have consequences for many people and the public—but little potential intrinsic evil or harm—*utility ethical* decision making may be a morally appropriate direction for ethical decision making. For example, you may want to consult with others in your public service organization, and perhaps the public you serve, before deciding to change the design and color of your organization's logo. These small examples are simply meant as an illustration of the cleavages and directionality of ethical philosophies to perceptions of variations in the context of intrinsic evil/harm and consequences. How would you use the model to predict more serious issues in ethical directionality in the decision making of public administrators?

A CONCLUSION

We have explored history and our times, which may be in crisis in the ethics of public administration. We have touched on the realities of some politicians who flaunt their narcissism, lack of empathy, and disregard for the facts. But, more so, we have documented with rich empirical detail the pursuit of the public interests by public servants in public agencies, nonprofits, faith-based organizations, and hybrid organizations. We hope that our book, *The Public Administration Profession*, may posit a corrective vision of public service focused on ethics and public interests prescriptions, such as those from the American Society for Public Administration (ASPA) Code of Ethics[5] and elsewhere. Our empirical overview of the public administration profession in America has illustrated the plural concept of public interests—including the commons, regime values, ethics of caring, and moral readings of the Constitution. This may not be your parents' concept of a singular "public interest," which was discarded by skeptics for imposition of the will to power with one right answer to the issues of public goods and services. Instead, this is a return to the original meaning, from the etymological roots of the public interests, which was always plural for others: *pubes + koinon* (Greek, "to be mature and take care of others"). This is also a new pluralistic theory of the public interests emerging from close empirical scholarship by many others, which belies the reality of shared meanings of public goods and service, but with varieties of answers. While we still may use the singular public interest here and there, we imply a plural meaning and seek to use the public interests (emphasis added) to make our points. Further, we document that public administration has woven ethics into its heart. Rather than pushed into a back compartment of public life, we have documented how ethics is fully integrated, area by area, chapter by chapter, with all the institutions, processes, concepts, persons, history, and typologies to be found in public administration. We have prominently featured one precept per chapter from the ASPA Code of Ethics—as well as other ethical sources—with full discussion, examples, analysis, and applications with professional enforcement mechanisms. Further, we have expanded coverage of public administration to include new high-tech information technology, nonprofit organizations, faith-based organizations, hybrid-private organizations, contracting out and collaborations, and paid more attention to public service at the state and local government levels. We hope that you may have found our end-of-chapter ethics case studies useful, together with the lists of key concepts and persons, and local community action steps—plus appendices on writing papers, personal career management, and professional ethics codes in applying these lessons. And perhaps our book has been helpful to some of you to monitor your pre- and post-integration of ethics as both an introduction and a capstone in undergraduate or graduate higher education, helping to shape a future public administration profession.

Richard Stillman posited that American public administration rests on the fulcrum that balances the three values: administration, political efficacy, and public interests.[6] Perhaps this is another way of describing what we mean by the public administration profession. Americans demand efficiency and economy in the administration of public goods and services; they expect equity, equality, and justice when a wrong is committed, when they are defrauded, or when the good or service promised or delivered fails to meet their legal or even ethical expectations; and, finally, Americans assemble in political interest groups, battling each other in order gain the government's attention to administer the goods and services they believe they deserve. The point made by Richard Stillman is that these values cannot be fulfilled to their maximum. What kind of world would we live in if life was centered around some perfect utopian world of efficiency, political efficacy, or the commons? Would we even want this?

The answer is a resounding "No!" Thus, there is the need for political and administrative discretion; there is the need for public officials, including public administrators, to make decisions that do not necessarily balance all three values. The exercise of this administrative discretion is the justice we seek for our context. It is simply necessary to have public administrators that somehow, some way, address the demands of all three values, consider the implications and consequences of not meeting each, and finally come to a decision, be it regarding the making of budgets, the establishing of regulation standards, and myriad other difficult choices.

In the end, professionalism in the public administration profession is about more than memorizing the ASPA Code of Ethics, filling out its *Workbook and Assessment Guide*,[7] or even reading this book. It's about a moral commitment to a noble cause: being an ethical public servant. We are all vulnerable to the corruption or neglect that comes with political and administrative power, whether President Nixon's White House staffers in Watergate in 1974 or King David's dalliance with Bathsheba in 1200 BCE.[8] No one is immune; the temptation to do wrong is always there, be it in one's personal, family, or professional life. When an immoral or unethical act is committed by an elected public official, the trust that is given by the people under the Constitution is damaged. The same is true with the public administrator. Although not elected directly by the people, they are nonetheless accountable for their actions, whether personal or professional, particularly as those actions impinge upon their ability to carry out their public duties. Living in this glass house of public scrutiny isn't easy, but it's a responsibility that goes with the job. Personal character, full disclosure in decisions, and lawful behavior are required of political and civil servants for carrying out their duties in the public interests. Professionalism in the public sector requires accountability and responsibility to citizens in the glass house of public scrutiny.

In the years to come, future generations will face seemingly unprecedented crises, such as terrorism (both domestic and global), disasters (natural and man-made), and economic stresses. It is our hope that, in the face of such overwhelming future tragedy, the public interests and the support of the public will add up to more than the sum of the parts and help public managers to make it so.

NOTES

1   Thomas L. Friedman, *The World is Flat: A Brief History of the 21st Century* (New York: Farrar, Straus and Giroux, 2005).

2   David Hazony, "David Hazony on *The World is Flat: A Brief History of the Twenty-First Century*," *Policy Review* (August/September 2005), retrieved June 2007 from www.printthis.clickability.com/pt/cpt?action=cpt&title=His+World+is+Flat&expire. Other reviews of Friedman's book include Clayton Jones, "Thomas Friedman Wants the Wired World to Let in the Other Half of Humanity," *Christian Science Monitor* (April 5, 2005), retrieved June 2007 from www.csmonitor.com/20050405/p15s01-bogn.html; George Scialabba, "Zippie World!" *The Nation* (June 13, 2005), www.thenation.com/doc/20050613/scialabba (accessed June 2007); Noel Malcolm, "Holy Cow! We're Shrinking," *Telegraph* (August 5, 2005), retrieved June 2007 from www.telegraph.co.uk/core/Content; Roberto J. Gonzalez, "Falling Flat: As the World's Boundaries Are Worn Smooth, Friedman Examines Changing Horizons," *SFGate* (May 15, 2005), retrieved June 2007 from www.sfgate.com/cgi-bin/article.cgi?file; and Michael Langan, "On the Level: Technology Has Created a Faster, Smaller, 'Flat' World," *Boston* (April 3, 2005), retrieved June 2007 from www.boston.com/ae/books/articles/2005/04/03/on_the_level?mode=PF

3   Melvin Dubnick and Barbara Romzek, *American Public Administration: Politics and the Administration of Expectations* (Upper Saddle River, NJ: Prentice Hall, 1991), 388; Robert Denhardt and Joseph Grubbs, *Public Administration: An Action Orientation*, 4th ed. (Belmont, CA: Wadsworth, 2003), 439; David Rosenbloom and David Kravchuk, *Public Administration: Understanding Management, Politics and Law in the Public Sector*, 6th ed. (New York: McGraw Hill, 2005), 552; and David Schuman and Dick W. Olufs III, *Public Administration in the United States*, 2nd ed. (Lexington, MA: D.C. Heath and Co., 1993), 506.

4   For example, James Svara, *The Ethics Primer for Public Administrators in Government and Nonprofit Organizations*, 2nd ed. (Burlington, MA: Jones & Bartlett, 2015), 78–80.

5   James H. Svara, "Who Are the Keepers of the Code? Articulating and Upholding Ethical Standards in the Field of Public Administration," *Public Administration Review* 74 (#5, 2014): 561–9.

6   Richard Stillman, *Public Administration: Concepts and Cases*, 9th ed. (Belmont, CA: Wadsworth, 2009), 343.

7   Ethics and Standards Implementation Committee, *Implementing the ASPA Code of Ethics: Workbook and Assessment Guide* (Washington, DC: American Society for Public Administration, November 22, 2015), retrieved from www.aspanet.org/ASPA-Docs/Resources/Ethics_Assessment_Guide.pdf

8   J. Claude Evans, "'. . . and Nathan Said to David': A Watergate Parallel," *Christian Century* (June 27, 1973): 706.

APPENDIX A: SOURCES OF ETHICS

ASPA Code of Ethics and Review Process
ICMA Code of Ethics with Guidelines
Code of Ethics, U.S. Government Executive Branch
Standards of Conduct, U.S. Department of Defense
Model Ethics Policy for Texas State Agencies

ASPA CODE OF ETHICS AND REVIEW PROCESS

The American Society for Public Administration (ASPA) advances the science, art, and practice of public administration. The Society affirms its responsibility to develop the spirit of responsible professionalism within its membership and to increase awareness and commitment to ethical principles and standards among all those who work in public service in all sectors. To this end, we, the members of the Society, commit ourselves to uphold the following principles:

1. *Advance the Public Interest.* Promote the interests of the public and put service to the public above service to oneself.
2. *Uphold the Constitution and the Law.* Respect and support government constitutions and laws, while seeking to improve laws and policies to promote the public good.
3. *Promote Democratic Participation.* Inform the public and encourage active engagement in governance. Be open, transparent and responsive, and respect and assist all persons in their dealings with public organizations.
4. *Strengthen Social Equity.* Treat all persons with fairness, justice, and equality and respect individual differences, rights, and freedoms. Promote affirmative action and other initiatives to reduce unfairness, injustice, and inequality in society.
5. *Fully Inform and Advise.* Provide accurate, honest, comprehensive, and timely information and advice to elected and appointed officials and governing board members, and to staff members in your organization.
6. *Demonstrate Personal Integrity.* Adhere to the highest standards of conduct to inspire public confidence and trust in public service.
7. *Promote Ethical Organizations.* Strive to attain the highest standards of ethics, stewardship, and public service in organizations that serve the public.
8. *Advance Professional Excellence.* Strengthen personal capabilities to act competently and ethically and encourage the professional development of others.

Members of ASPA commit themselves to support the Code of Ethics and may be sanctioned for their failure and refusal to uphold the Code.

ASPA CODE OF ETHICS REVIEW PROCESS

As part of its commitment to advance and implement the Code of Ethics, ASPA provides a review process with four elements:

1. Responding to inquiries from members about ethical standards and handling ethical dilemmas.
2. Reviewing requests for help from members who have been penalized for upholding the Code and providing support to them.
3. Recognizing members whose actions exemplify the Code.
4. Reviewing and seeking to resolve complaints about a member whose actions may have violated the Code of Ethics.

The complaints process covers only ASPA members and is confidential. Neither the person named in a complaint nor the person making the complaint is publicly identified at any time. The Ethics Committee will defer its own review of a complaint until any other bodies reviewing the actions (courts of law, legislative bodies, agencies, or other organizations involved) have completed their work, and will then determine if future evaluation is required.

The review of a complaint goes through the following stages:

1. A complaint about an ASPA member can be submitted by a member or non-member through ethics@aspanet.org or by mail to the address listed at the end of this page. Complaints must be related to actions occurring after May 1, 2016—the date the current process was initiated. Complaints must specifically reference the tenet of the Code the complainant feels has been violated.
2. The Ethics and Standards Implementation Committee (Ethics Committee) will assess the complaint to determine whether the action is a violation of the Code. If it is deemed not to be a violation, the complaint will be dismissed with explanations to the complainant.
3. If it is judged that the action, if verified, is a violation of the Code, the Ethics Committee will then work with the ASPA Executive Committee to determine if further steps should be taken.
4. Should the Executive Committee authorize the Ethics Committee to get involved in the issue, the Ethics Committee will discuss the complaint with the member and encourage voluntary corrective action. At no point are the names of those involved disclosed to members.

This is intended to be a constructive process that helps members understand how the Code is applied to specific situations. Issues identified in complaints may be used—in generic terms—in the Ethics Committee's educational activities to help raise awareness of ethical challenges and expectations.

Question about the review process can be sent to ethics@aspanet.org or to:
ASPA Ethics Review Questions
1730 Rhode Island Ave., NW, Suite 500
Washington, DC 20036

ICMA CODE OF ETHICS WITH GUIDELINES
International City/County Management Association, 2015

The ICMA Code of Ethics was adopted by the ICMA membership in 1924, and most recently amended by the membership in April 2015. The Guidelines for the Code were adopted by the ICMA Executive Board in 1972, and most recently revised in June 2015. The mission of ICMA is to create excellence in local governance by developing and fostering professional local government management worldwide. To further this mission, certain principles, as enforced by the Rules of Procedure, shall govern the conduct of every member of ICMA, who shall:

Tenet 1. Be dedicated to the concepts of effective and democratic local government by responsible elected officials and believe that professional general management is essential to the achievement of this objective.

Tenet 2. Affirm the dignity and worth of the services rendered by government and maintain a constructive, creative, and practical attitude toward local government affairs and a deep sense of social responsibility as a trusted public servant.

GUIDELINE
Advice to Officials of Other Local Governments.   When members advise and respond to inquiries from elected or appointed officials of other local governments, they should inform the administrators of those communities.

Tenet 3. Be dedicated to the highest ideals of honor and integrity in all public and personal relationships in order that the member may merit the respect and confidence of the elected officials, of other officials and employees, and of the public.

GUIDELINES
Public Confidence.   Members should conduct themselves so as to maintain public confidence in their profession, their local government, and in their performance of the public trust.

Impression of Influence.   Members should conduct their official and personal affairs in such a manner as to give the clear impression that they cannot be improperly influenced in the performance of their official duties.

Appointment Commitment.   Members who accept an appointment to a position should not fail to report for that position. This does not preclude the possibility of a member considering several offers or seeking several positions at the same time, but once a bona fide offer of a position has been accepted, that commitment should be honored. Oral acceptance of an employment offer is considered binding unless the employer makes fundamental changes in terms of employment.

Credentials.   An application for employment or for ICMA's Voluntary Credentialing Program should be complete and accurate as to all pertinent details of education, experience, and personal history. Members should recognize that both omissions and inaccuracies must be avoided.

Professional Respect.   Members seeking a management position should show professional respect for persons formerly holding the position or for others who might be applying for the same position. Professional respect does not preclude honest differences of opinion; it does preclude attacking a person's motives or integrity in order to be appointed to a position.

Reporting Ethics Violations.   When becoming aware of a possible violation of the ICMA Code of Ethics, members are encouraged to report the matter to ICMA. In reporting the matter, members may choose to go on record as the complainant or report the matter on a confidential basis.

Confidentiality.   Members should not discuss or divulge information with anyone about pending or completed ethics cases, except as specifically authorized by the Rules of Procedure for Enforcement of the Code of Ethics.

Seeking Employment.   Members should not seek employment for a position having an incumbent administrator who has not resigned or been officially informed that his or her services are to be terminated.

Tenet 4. Recognize that the chief function of local government at all times is to serve the best interests of all of the people.

GUIDELINE
Length of Service.   A minimum of two years generally is considered necessary in order to render a professional service to the local government. A short tenure should be the exception rather than a recurring experience. However, under special circumstances, it may be in the best interests of the local government and the member to separate in a shorter time. Examples of such circumstances would include refusal of the appointing authority to honor commitments concerning conditions of employment, a vote of no confidence in the member, or severe personal problems. It is the responsibility of an applicant for a position to ascertain conditions of employment. Inadequately determining terms of employment prior to arrival does not justify premature termination.

Tenet 5. Submit policy proposals to elected officials; provide them with facts and advice on matters of policy as a basis for making decisions and setting community goals; and uphold and implement local government policies adopted by elected officials.

GUIDELINE
Conflicting Roles.   Members who serve multiple roles—working as both city attorney and city manager for the same community, for example—should avoid participating in matters that create the appearance of a conflict of interest. They should disclose the potential conflict to the governing body so that other opinions may be solicited.

Tenet 6. Recognize that elected representatives of the people are entitled to the credit for the establishment of local government policies; responsibility for policy execution rests with the members.

Tenet 7. Refrain from all political activities which undermine public confidence in professional administrators. Refrain from participation in the election of the members of the employing legislative body.

GUIDELINES

Elections of the Governing Body. Members should maintain a reputation for serving equally and impartially all members of the governing body of the local government they serve, regardless of party. To this end, they should not participate in an election campaign on behalf of or in opposition to candidates for the governing body.

Elections of Elected Executives. Members shall not participate in the election campaign of any candidate for mayor or elected county executive.

Running for Office. Members shall not run for elected office or become involved in political activities related to running for elected office, or accept appointment to an elected office. They shall not seek political endorsements, financial contributions, or engage in other campaign activities.

Elections. Members share with their fellow citizens the right and responsibility to vote. However, in order not to impair their effectiveness on behalf of the local governments they serve, they shall not participate in political activities to support the candidacy of individuals running for any city, county, special district, school, state or federal offices. Specifically, they shall not endorse candidates, make financial contributions, sign or circulate petitions, or participate in fund-raising activities for individuals seeking or holding elected office.

Elections Relating to the Form of Government. Members may assist in preparing and presenting materials that explain the form of government to the public prior to a form of government election. If assistance is required by another community, members may respond.

Presentation of Issues. Members may assist their governing body in the presentation of issues involved in referenda such as bond issues, annexations, and other matters that affect the government entity's operations and/or fiscal capacity.

Personal Advocacy of Issues. Members share with their fellow citizens the right and responsibility to voice their opinion on public issues. Members may advocate for issues of personal interest only when doing so does not conflict with the performance of their official duties.

Tenet 8. Make it a duty continually to improve the member's professional ability and to develop the competence of associates in the use of management techniques.

GUIDELINES

Self-Assessment. Each member should assess his or her professional skills and abilities on a periodic basis.

Professional Development. Each member should commit at least 40 hours per year to professional development activities that are based on the practices identified by the members of ICMA.

Tenet 9. Keep the community informed on local government affairs; encourage communication between the citizens and all local government officers; emphasize friendly and courteous service to the public; and seek to improve the quality and image of public service.

Tenet 10. Resist any encroachment on professional responsibilities, believing the member should be free to carry out official policies without interference, and handle each problem without discrimination on the basis of principle and justice.

GUIDELINE
Information Sharing. The member should openly share information with the governing body while diligently carrying out the member's responsibilities as set forth in the charter or enabling legislation.

Tenet 11. Handle all matters of personnel on the basis of merit so that fairness and impartiality govern a member's decisions, pertaining to appointments, pay adjustments, promotions, and discipline.

GUIDELINE
Equal Opportunity. All decisions pertaining to appointments, pay adjustments, promotions, and discipline should prohibit discrimination because of race, color, religion, sex, national origin, sexual orientation, political affiliation, disability, age, or marital status.

It should be the members' personal and professional responsibility to actively recruit and hire a diverse staff throughout their organizations.

Tenet 12. Public office is a public trust. A member shall not leverage his or her position for personal gain or benefit.

GUIDELINES
Gifts. Members shall not directly or indirectly solicit, accept, or receive any gift if it could reasonably be perceived or inferred that the gift was intended to influence them in the performance of their official duties; or if the gift was intended to serve as a reward for any official action on their part.

The term "Gift" includes but is not limited to services, travel, meals, gift cards, tickets, or other entertainment or hospitality. Gifts of money or loans from persons other than the local government jurisdiction pursuant to normal employment practices are not acceptable.

Members should not accept any gift that could undermine public confidence. De minimus gifts may be accepted in circumstances that support the execution of the member's official duties or serve a legitimate public purpose. In those cases, the member should determine a modest maximum dollar value based on guidance from the governing body or any applicable state or local law.

The guideline is not intended to apply to normal social practices, not associated with the member's official duties, where gifts are exchanged among friends, associates, and relatives.

Investments in Conflict with Official Duties. Members should refrain from any investment activity which would compromise the impartial and objective performance of their duties. Members should not invest or hold any invest-ment, directly or indirectly, in any financial business, commercial, or other private transaction that creates a conflict of interest, in fact or appearance, with their official duties.

In the case of real estate, the use of confidential information and knowl-edge to further a member's personal interest is not permitted. Purchases and sales which might be interpreted as speculation for quick profit should be avoided (see the guideline on "Confidential Information"). Because personal investments may appear to influence official actions and decisions, or create the appearance of impropriety, members should disclose or dispose of such investments prior to accepting a position in a local government. Should the conflict of interest arise during employment, the member should make full disclosure and/or recuse themselves prior to any official action by the govern-ing body that may affect such investments.

This guideline is not intended to prohibit a member from having or acquiring an interest in, or deriving a benefit from, any investment when the interest or benefit is due to ownership by the member or the member's family of a de minimus percentage of a corporation traded on a recognized stock exchange even though the corporation or its subsidiaries may do business with the local government.

Personal Relationships.   Members should disclose any personal relationship to the governing body in any instance where there could be the appearance of a conflict of interest. For example, if the manager's spouse works for a devel-oper doing business with the local government, that fact should be disclosed.

Confidential Information.   Members shall not disclose to others, or use to advance their personal interest, intellectual property, confidential informa-tion, or information that is not yet public knowledge, that has been acquired by them in the course of their official duties.

Information that may be in the public domain or accessible by means of an open records request, is not confidential.

Private Employment.   Members should not engage in, solicit, negotiate for, or promise to accept private employment, nor should they render services for private interests or conduct a private business when such employment, service, or business creates a conflict with or impairs the proper discharge of their official duties.

Teaching, lecturing, writing, or consulting are typical activities that may not involve conflict of interest, or impair the proper discharge of their official duties. Prior notification of the appointing authority is appropriate in all cases of outside employment.

Representation.   Members should not represent any outside interest before any agency, whether public or private, except with the authorization of or at the direction of the appointing authority they serve.

Endorsements.   Members should not endorse commercial products or ser-vices by agreeing to use their photograph, endorsement, or quotation in paid or other commercial advertisements, marketing materials, social media, or other documents, whether the member is compensated or not for the member's support. Members may, however, provide verbal professional references as part of the due diligence phase of competitive process or in response to a direct inquiry.

Members may agree to endorse the following, provided they do not receive any compensation: (1) books or other publications; (2) professional development or educational services provided by nonprofit membership organizations or recognized educational institutions; (3) products and/or services in which the local government has a direct economic interest.

Members' observations, opinions, and analyses of commercial products used or tested by their local governments are appropriate and useful to the profession when included as part of professional articles and reports.

CODE OF ETHICS
United States Government Executive Branch
Principles of Ethical Conduct for Government Officers and Employees

1. Public service is a public trust, requiring employees to place loyalty to the Constitution, the laws, and ethical principles above private gain.
2. Employees shall not hold financial interests that conflict with the conscientious performance of duty.
3. Employees shall not engage in financial transactions using nonpublic Government information or allow the improper use of such information to further any private interest.
4. An employee shall not, except pursuant to such reasonable exceptions as are provided by regulation, solicit or accept any gift or other item of monetary value from any person or entity seeking official action from, doing business with, or conducting, activities regulated by the employee's agency, or whose interests may be substantially affected by the performance or nonperformance of the employee's duties.
5. Employees shall put forth honest effort in the performance of their duties.
6. Employees shall make no unauthorized commitments or promises of any kind purporting to bind the Government.
7. Employees shall not use public office for private gain.
8. Employees shall act impartially and not give preferential treatment to any private organization or individual.
9. Employees shall protect and conserve Federal property and shall not use it for other than authorized activities.
10. Employees shall not engage in outside employment or activities, including seeking or negotiating for employment, that conflict with official Government duties and responsibilities.
11. Employees shall disclose waste, fraud, abuse, and corruption to appropriate authorities.
12. Employees shall satisfy in good faith their obligations as citizens, including all just financial obligations, especially those—such as Federal, State, or local taxes—that are imposed by law.
13. Employees shall adhere to all laws and regulations that provide equal opportunity for all Americans regardless of race, color, religion, sex, national origin, age, or handicap.
14. Employees shall endeavor to avoid any actions creating the appearance that they are violating the law or the ethical standards promulgated pursuant to this order.

U.S. Office of Government Ethics, Washington, DC, 2005

STANDARDS OF CONDUCT, U.S. DEPARTMENT OF DEFENSE

DoDD 5500.7, U.S. Department of Defense, October 18, 2016

DoDD 5500.7, *Standards of Conduct*, provides guidance to military personnel on standards of conduct and ethics. Violations of the punitive provisions by military personnel can result in prosecution under the Uniform Code of Military Justice (UCMJ). Violations of the punitive provisions by civilian personnel may result in disciplinary action without regard to the issue of criminal liability. Military members and civilian employees who violate these standards, even if such violations do not constitute criminal misconduct, are subject to administrative actions, such as reprimands. The use of the term "DoD Employee" in this article includes civilian employees and military members. *All information derived from AFPAM36–2241V1.*

Ethical Values Ethics are standards by which one should act based on values. Values are core beliefs such as duty, honor, and integrity that motivate attitudes and actions. Not all values are ethical values (integrity is; happiness is not). Ethical values relate to what is right and wrong and thus, take precedence over non-ethical values when making ethical decisions. DoD employees should carefully consider ethical values when making decisions as part of official duties. Primary ethical values include:

> **Honesty.** Being truthful, straightforward, and candid are aspects of honesty. Truthfulness is required. Deceptions are usually easily uncovered. Lies erode credibility and undermine public confidence. Untruths told for seemingly altruistic reasons (to prevent hurt feelings, to promote good will, etc.) are nonetheless resented by the recipients. Straightforwardness adds frankness to truthfulness and is usually necessary to promote public confidence and to ensure effective, efficient conduct of operations. Truths presented in such a way as to lead recipients to confusion, misinterpretation, or inaccurate conclusions are not productive. Such indirect deceptions can promote ill-will and erode openness, especially when there is an expectation of frankness. Candor is the forthright offering of unrequested information. It is necessary according to the gravity of the situation and the nature of the relationships. Candor is required when a reasonable person would feel betrayed if the information were withheld. In some circumstances, silence is dishonest; yet in other circumstances, disclosing information would be wrong and perhaps unlawful.

> **Integrity.** Being faithful to one's convictions is part of integrity. Following principles, acting with honor, maintaining independent judgment, and performing duties with impartiality help to maintain integrity and avoid conflicts of interest and hypocrisy.

> **Loyalty.** Fidelity, faithfulness, allegiance, and devotion are all synonyms for loyalty. Loyalty is the bond that holds the nation and the Federal Government together and the balm against dissension and conflict. It is not

blind obedience or unquestioning acceptance of the status quo. Loyalty requires careful balancing of various interests, values, and institutions in the interest of harmony and cohesion.

Accountability. DoD employees are required to accept responsibility for their decisions and the resulting consequences. This includes avoiding even the appearance of impropriety.

Accountability promotes careful, well-thought-out decision making and limits thoughtless action.

Fairness. Open-mindedness and impartiality are important aspects of fairness. DoD employees must be committed to justice in the performance of their official duties. Decisions must not be arbitrary, capricious, or biased. Individuals must be treated equally and with tolerance.

Caring. Compassion is an essential element of good government. Courtesy and kindness, both to those we serve and to those we work with, help to ensure individuals are not treated solely as a means to an end. Caring for others is the counterbalance against the temptation to pursue the mission at any cost.

Respect. To treat people with dignity, to honor privacy, and to allow self-determination are critical in a government of diverse people. Lack of respect leads to a breakdown of loyalty and honesty within a government and brings chaos to the international community.

Promise keeping. No government can function for long if its commitments are not kept. DoD employees are obligated to keep their promises in order to promote trust and cooperation. Because of the importance of promise keeping, DoD employees must only make commitments within their authority.

Responsible Citizenship. It is the civic duty of every citizen, and especially DoD employees, to exercise discretion. Public servants are expected to engage (employ) personal judgment in the performance of official duties within the limits of their authority so that the will of the people is respected according to democratic principles. Justice must be pursued and injustice must be challenged through accepted means.

Pursuit of Excellence. In public service, competence is only the starting point. DoD employees are expected to set an example of superior diligence and commitment. They are expected to be all they can be and to strive beyond mediocrity.

Ethics and Conflict of Interest Prohibitions   DoD policy is that a single, uniform source of standards on ethical conduct and ethics guidance be maintained within DoD. Each DoD agency will implement and administer a comprehensive ethics program to ensure compliance.

Bribery and Graft. All DoD employees are directly or indirectly prohibited from giving, offering, promising, demanding, seeking, receiving, accepting, or agreeing to receive anything of value to influence any official act. They are prohibited from influencing the commission of fraud on the United States, inducing commitment or omission of any act in violation of a lawful duty, or from influencing testimony given. They are prohibited from accepting anything of value for, or because of, any official act performed or to be performed. These prohibitions do not apply to the payment of witness fees authorized by law or certain travel and subsistence expenses.

Compensation from Other Sources. All DoD employees are prohibited from receiving pay or allowance or supplements of pay or benefits from any source other than the United States for the performance of official service or duties unless specifically authorized by law. A task or job performed outside normal working hours does not necessarily allow employees to accept payment for performing it. If the undertaking is part of one's official duties, pay for its performance may not be accepted from any source other than the United States regardless of when it was performed.

Additional Pay or Allowance. DoD employees may not receive additional pay or allowance for disbursement of public money or for the performance of any other service or duty unless specifically authorized by law. Subject to certain limitations, civilian DoD employees may hold two distinctly different Federal Government positions and receive salaries of both if the duties of each are performed. Absent specific authority, however, military members may not do so because any arrangement by a military member for rendering services to the Federal Government in another position is incompatible with the military member's actual or potential military duties. The fact that a military member may have leisure hours during which no official duty is performed does not alter the result.

Commercial Dealings Involving DoD Employees. On or off duty, a DoD employee shall not knowingly solicit or make solicited sales to DoD personnel who are junior in rank, grade, or position, or to the family members of such personnel. In the absence of coercion or intimidation, this does not prohibit the sale or lease of a DoD employee's non-commercial personal or real property or commercial sales solicited and made in a retail establishment during off-duty employment. This prohibition includes the solicited sale of insurance, stocks, mutual funds, real estate, cosmetics, household supplies, vitamins, and other goods or services. Solicited sales by the spouse or another household member of a senior-ranking person to a junior person are not specifically prohibited but may give the appearance that the DoD employee is using public office for personal gain. If in doubt, consult an ethics counselor. Several related prohibitions in this area include:

- Holding conflicting financial interests.
- Engaging in off-duty employment or outside activities that detract from readiness or pose a security risk, as determined by the member's commander or supervisor.

- Engaging in outside employment or activities that conflict with official duties.
- Receiving honoraria for performing official duties or for speaking, teaching, or writing that relates to one's official duties.
- Misusing an official position, such as improper endorsements or improper use of nonpublic information.
- Certain post-government service employment.

Gifts from Foreign Governments. DoD policy requires all military and civilian personnel, as well as their dependents, to report gifts from foreign governments if the gift, or combination of gifts at one presentation, exceeds a U.S. retail value of $285. This requirement also includes gifts recipients desire to retain for official use or display. Failure to report gifts valued in excess of $285 could result in a penalty in any amount, not to exceed the retail value of the gift plus $5,000.

Contributions or Presents to Superiors. On an occasional basis, including any occasion on which gifts are traditionally given or exchanged, the following may be given to an official supervisor by a subordinate or other employees receiving less pay:

- Items, other than cash, with an aggregate market value of $10 or less.
- Items such as food and refreshments to be shared in the office among several employees.
- Personal hospitality provided at a residence and items given in connection with personal hospitality, which is of a type and value customarily provided by the employee to personal friends.

A gift appropriate to the occasion may be given to recognize special, infrequent occasions of personal significance, such as marriage, illness, or the birth or adoption of a child. It is also permissible upon occasions that terminate a subordinate-official supervisor relationship, such as retirement, separation, or reassignment. Regardless of the number of employees contributing, the market value of the gift cannot exceed $300. Even though contributions are voluntary, the maximum contribution one DoD employee may solicit from another cannot exceed $10.

Federal Government Resources. Federal Government resources, including personnel, equipment, and property, shall be used by DoD employees for official purposes only. Agencies may, however, permit employees to make limited personal use of resources other than personnel, such as a computer, calculators, libraries, etc., if the use:

- Does not adversely affect the performance of official duties by the employee or other employees.
- Is of reasonable duration and frequency and is made during the employee's personal time, such as after duty hours or during lunch periods.
- Serves a legitimate public interest, such as supporting local charities or volunteer services to the community.

- Does not reflect adversely on the DoD.
- Creates no significant additional cost to the DoD or Government agency.

Communication Systems. Federal Government communication systems and equipment including telephones, fax machines, electronic mail, and Internet systems shall be used for official use and authorized purposes only. Official use includes emergency communications and when approved by commanders in the interest of morale and welfare, may include communications by DoD employees deployed for extended periods away from home on official DoD business. Authorized purposes include brief communication made by DoD employees while traveling on Government business to notify family members of official transportation or schedule changes. Also authorized are personal communications from the DoD employee's usual workplace that are most reasonably made while in the workplace, such as checking in with a spouse or minor children; scheduling doctor, auto, or home repair appointments; brief internet searches; and emailing directions to visiting relatives when the agency designee permits. Many restrictions do, however, apply.

Gambling, Betting, and Lotteries. While on federally owned or leased property or while on duty, a DoD employee shall not participate in any gambling activity except:

- Activities by organizations composed primarily of DoD employees or their dependents for the benefit of welfare funds for their own members or for the benefit of other DoD employees or their dependents, subject to local law.
- Private wagers among DoD employees if based on a personal relationship and transacted entirely within assigned Government living quarters and subject to local laws.
- Lotteries authorized by any state from licensed vendors.

Dissident and Protest Activities

Military commanders have the inherent authority and responsibility to take action to ensure the mission is performed and to maintain good order and discipline. This authority and responsibility include placing lawful restriction on dissident and protest activities. Military commanders must preserve the service member's right of expression to the maximum extent possible, consistent with good order, discipline, and national security. To properly balance these interests, commanders must exercise calm and prudent judgment and should consult with their SJAs.

Possessing or Distributing Printed Materials. Military members may not distribute or post any printed or written material other than publications of an official Government agency or base-related activity within any Military installation without permission of the installation commander or that commander's designee. Members who violate this prohibition are subject to disciplinary action under Article 92 of the UCMJ.

Writing for Publications. Military members may not write for unofficial publications during duty hours. An unofficial publication, such as an "underground newspaper," may not be produced using Government or unappropriated fund property or supplies. Any publication that contains language, the utterance of which is punishable by the UCMJ or other Federal laws, may subject a person involved in its printing, publishing, or distribution to prosecution or other disciplinary action.

Off-Limits Action. Action may be initiated under AFJI 31–213, *Armed Forces Disciplinary Control Boards and Off-Installation Liaison and Operations*, to place certain establishments off limits. An establishment runs the risk of being placed off limits if its activities include counseling service members to refuse to perform their duties or to desert, or when it is involved in acts with a significant adverse effect on health, welfare, or morale of military members.

Prohibited Activities. Military personnel must reject participation in organizations that espouse supremacist causes; attempt to create illegal discrimination based on race, creed, color, sex, religion, or national origin; advocate the use of force or violence, or otherwise engage in the effort to deprive individuals of their civil rights. Active participation, such as publicly demonstrating or rallying, fundraising, recruiting and training members, organizing or leading such organizations, or otherwise engaging in activities the commander finds to be detrimental to good order, discipline, or mission accomplishment, is incompatible with military service and prohibited. Members who violate this prohibition are subject to disciplinary action under Article 92, UCMJ.

Demonstrations and Similar Activities. Demonstrations or other activities within an Air Force installation that could result in interfering with or preventing of the orderly accomplishment of a mission of the installation or which present a clear danger to loyalty, discipline, or morale of members of the Armed Forces are prohibited and are punishable under Article 92, UCMJ. Military members are prohibited from participating in demonstrations when they are on duty, when they are in a foreign country, when they are in uniform, when their activities constitute a breach of law and order, or when violence is likely to result. Such activities constitute a breach of law and order, or when violence is likely to result.

MODEL ETHICS POLICY FOR TEXAS STATE AGENCIES

Pursuant to Section 572.051(d) of the Texas Government Code, the Office of the Attorney General (OAG) has developed the following model ethics policy. The following state entities may use this policy in order to satisfy the legal requirement that each entity adopt an ethics policy by January 1, 2008:

(1) a department, commission, board, office, or other agency that is in the executive branch of state government, has statewide authority, and was created by the Texas Constitution or a statute of this state;

(2) a public university system or a public institution of higher education, other than a junior college; and

(3) a river authority created under the Texas Constitution or a statute of this state.

However, no state entity is required to utilize the model ethics policy when developing and/or adopting its own policy. The OAG developed the model ethics policy to function as a general policy that can be used as a guide for minimum levels of ethical requirements for state employees. Noting the many differences among state entities, the OAG recommends that each entity develop an ethics policy that addresses their unique situation and organizational needs.

THE [STATE AGENCY'S] ETHICS POLICY

I. Overview

Pursuant to Section 572.051(c) of the Texas Government Code, the [agency] promulgates the following ethics policy. This ethics policy prescribes standards of conduct for all [agency] employees. This ethics policy does not supersede any applicable federal or Texas law or administrative rule. All [agency] employees must familiarize themselves with this ethics policy. All [agency] employees must abide by all applicable federal and Texas laws, administrative rules, and [agency] conduct policies, including this ethics policy. An [agency] employee who violates any provision of the [agency's] conduct policies is subject to termination of the employee's state employment or another employment-related sanction. An [agency] employee who violates any applicable federal or Texas law or rule may be subject to civil or criminal penalties in addition to any employment-related sanction.

II. Standards of Conduct

A. An [agency] employee shall not:

(1) accept or solicit any gift, favor, or service that might reasonably tend to influence the employee in the discharge of official duties, or that the employee knows or should know is being offered with the intent to influence the employee's official conduct;

(2) intentionally or knowingly solicit, accept, or agree to accept any benefit for having exercised his or her official powers or performed his or her official duties in favor of another;

(3) disclose confidential information, information that is excepted from public disclosure under the Texas Public Information Act (Tex. Gov't Code Ann. ch. 552), or information that has been ordered sealed by a court, that was acquired by reason of the employee's official position, or accept other employment, including self-employment, or engage in a business, charity, nonprofit organization, or professional activity that the employee might reasonably expect would require or induce the employee to disclose confidential information, information that is excepted from public disclosure under the Texas Public Information Act, or information that has been ordered sealed by a court, that was acquired by reason of the employee's official position;

(4) accept other employment, including self-employment, or compensation or engage in a business, charity, nonprofit organization, or professional activity that could reasonably be expected to impair the employee's independence of judgment in the performance of the employee's official duties;

(5) make personal investments, or have a personal or financial interest, that could reasonably be expected to create a substantial conflict between the employee's private interest and the public interest;

(6) utilize state time, property, facilities, or equipment for any purpose other than official state business, unless such use is reasonable and incidental and does not result in any direct cost to the state or [agency], interfere with the employee's official duties, and interfere with [agency] functions;

(7) utilize his or her official position, or state issued items, such as a badge, indicating such position for financial gain, obtaining privileges, or avoiding consequences of illegal acts;

(8) knowingly make misleading statements, either oral or written, or provide false information, in the course of official state business; or

(9) engage in any political activity while on state time or utilize state resources for any political activity.

B. An [agency] employee shall:

(1) perform his or her official duties in a lawful, professional, and ethical manner befitting the state and [agency]; and

(2) report any conduct or activity that the employee believes to be in violation of this ethics policy to [agency designee].

The following requirements are only statutorily applicable to employees or former employees of "regulatory agencies." Tex. Gov't Code Ann. § 572.054(b). However, Subsection III(3) of this policy does not statutorily apply to an agency regulating the operation or inspection of motor vehicles or an agency charged with enforcing the parks and wildlife laws of this state. Tex. Gov't Code Ann. § 572.055(c). Furthermore, other law that restricts the representation of a person before a particular state entity by a former employee of that entity will prevail over the revolving door policy found in Subsection III(2). Tex. Gov't Code Ann. § 572.054(e); Op.Tex.Ethics Comm 275 (1995).

III. REGULATORY AGENCIES

(1) Definitions.
   (a) "Participated" means to have taken action through decision, approval, disapproval, recommendation, giving advice, investigation, or similar action. Tex. Gov't Code Ann. § 572.054(h)(1).
   (b) "Particular Matter" means a specific investigation, application, request for a ruling or determination, rulemaking proceeding, contract, claim, accusation, charge, arrest, or judicial or other proceeding. Tex. Gov't Code Ann. §572.054(h)(2).
   (c) "Business entity" means any entity recognized by law through which business for profit is conducted, including a sole proprietorship, partnership, firm, corporation, holding company, joint stock company, receivership, or trust. Tex. Gov't Code Ann. § 572.002(2).
   (d) "Regulatory Agency" means and department, commission, board, or other agency, except the secretary of state and the comptroller of public accounts, that:

   (i)   is in the executive branch of state government;
   (ii) has authority that is not limited to a geographical portion of this state;
   (iii) was created by the Texas Constitution or a statute of this state; and
   (iv) has constitutional or statutory authority to engage in regulation.

Tex. Gov't Code Ann. § 572.002(8).

(2) A former employee of the [agency], who was compensated, as of the last date of state employment, at or above the amount prescribed by the General Appropriations Act for step 1-salary group A17 of the position classification salary schedule, may not represent any person or entity, or receive compensation for services rendered on behalf of any person or entity, regarding a particular matter in which the former employee participated during the period of state service or employment, either through personal involvement or because the case or proceeding was a matter within the employee's official responsibility.

   (a) Subsection III(2) of this policy does not apply to a rulemaking proceeding that was conducted before the employee's service or employment ceased.
   (b) In Subsection III(2), the secretary of state and the comptroller of public accounts are not excluded from the definition of "regulatory agency."

(3) An association or organization of employees of the [agency] may not solicit, accept, or agree to accept anything of value from a business entity regulated by the [agency] and from which the business entity must obtain a permit to operate that business in this state or from an individual directly or indirectly connected with that business entity.

APPENDIX B: CAREER MANAGEMENT

For excellent overview of cover letters, 1-page resumes, interviewing, and the Federal Resume process, see:

"Federal Resume Guide: What You Should Know When Applying for a Federal Career," National Archives and Record Administration (Washington, DC), retrieved from www.archives.gov/files/careers/jobs/forms/resume-guide.pdf

APPENDIX C: WRITING IN PUBLIC ADMINISTRATION

> **Introduction**
> C.1—APA Citation/Reference Style
> C.2—Briefing a Case (Judicial Opinion)
> C.3—Writing a Book Review
> C.4—Writing a Literature Review Paper
> C.5—Writing a Term Paper (Empirical/Research)

INTRODUCTION

No matter what one is writing, there are a few basic rules to follow to produce more successful student papers.

First, *follow instructions* regarding permissible subject(s), parameters—length, style, and other technical matters, for example, submission—due dates and mode of delivery (paper or electronic), and anything else you or your professor thinks is important. Second, *if in doubt—ask questions*. Third, producing a first-rate paper, like any project takes *planning*. Fourth, closely related to planning is *scheduling*—making certain one has the time needed to do a good job. Fifth, part of planning and scheduling is to *expect the unexpected*—allow a little fudge-factor. Sixth—*think, think, think!!!* Seventh, is *review—proofread and edit*. Finally, *submit on-time*.

Let's look at each of these steps in a little more detail. Many otherwise good papers have received significant deductions in scores because *authors did not follow instructions*. In public administration and public policy, following rules and guidelines is especially important. To do otherwise may result in a grant being rejected, a lawsuit, or some other unpleasant outcome.

Questions—most instructors don't mind them and most like it when a student is engaged in her/his learning. A couple of issues are in order with regard to questions. You may have heard, *there's no such thing as a bad question*. Sorry, but this isn't true. Public administrators are expected to know their stuff, i.e., to listen and read carefully. Don't ask a question that is answered in, say, the written instructions for a paper. Also, don't wait until the last minute. If a paper is assigned for submission in the 12th week of the semester, don't wait until the week before it's due before asking an important question. This may alert a professor that the paper is going to be a rush job.

Planning almost always leads to better outcomes than undertakings that lack strategic thinking. This is certainly the situation with class papers. For a paper, we ask ourselves, what resources are needed to complete the project successfully. First, comes scheduling because time is our most critical resource.

Developing a *realistic schedule* is an essential skill for anyone involved in managing complex tasks. Most of us face deadlines—the ominous due date. We know how much time we have available, or do we? Let's say an assignment is due in 12 weeks, we probably don't have the entire 12 weeks to complete the project, we have other commitments—say a test in another course, maybe another paper, reading for each course, social engagements, a job, you name it. Bottom line here— keep a calendar. If we have a portion of the 12 weeks, planning will enable us to schedule out the task, i.e., what has to be completed by when? When NASA faced the task of landing a human on the moon by the end of 1969, they created interim goals, benchmarks that would enable them to meet the deadline. And guess what happened: they encountered unforeseen circumstances that required rescheduling, so don't be overoptimistic, include some contingency time in case problems arise. Most of us with experience schedule backwards from the due date. The first thing we schedule is a little contingency time, say a week or so. Then we schedule time for what is often overlooked by beginning students—time for proofreading and editing. We then continue our backwards scheduling with the time for writing the paper, researching the subject, outlining, and developing a thesis statement. And don't forget: build in time for thinking and making adjustments as you go. *Only a fool continues to execute a plan she/he knows isn't working.* We must be willing and able to adjust and shift the plan as events dictate. But that in no way means the plan was a failure—planning is important—it is the foundation upon which we build and develop our paper.

Let's return to the most important part of any project—*THINKING!!!* Our thinking is what separates us from others. Executing blindly is a minimal skill, low outcome endeavor. Managers and administrators need to be able to make adjustments, to think, to interpret, to convey ideas in a creative manner. What does that mean for us doing a course paper? Plain and simple, it's not sufficient to spit back what others have said or done before us. We must be thinking constantly about what we are reading, seeing, and hearing—does this new information make sense? How does this information fit with information from elsewhere? Have circumstances changed? Do the author's circumstances fit those that I'm research-ing? We must be able to analyze and interpret, find and communicate the meaning of what others said and did. Then we can make conclusions and recommenda-tions. But, we must never mistake thinking with opinion. An opinion is a view or judgment formed about something, not necessarily based on fact or knowledge. The killer point here is "not necessarily based on fact or knowledge"—we base our well-reasoned conclusions and recommendations on fact and knowledge. In short, we produce a defensible argument to justify our conclusions and recom-mendations.

At the end of any writing project, it's essential to leave time for clean-up, fix-up. First, any paper with obvious typos, grammar errors, punctuation mistakes, or formatting problems loses credibility for itself and the author. Great work poorly presented usually yields less than optimal outcomes; in the case of a student paper— a less than optimal grade. Additionally, as a writing assignment grows more com-plex, the likelihood increases that the parts won't fit together perfectly. This is where time invested in editing and rewriting is time well spent. If at all possible, employ an outside reader, someone knowledgeable is ideal, but not absolutely necessary. But the reader must have a good handle on compositional skills, to identify errors. The reader must be someone who will be honest with you, not someone who doesn't want to hurt your feelings. While a bad review stings and sometimes makes us defensive, honest assessment that all or a portion of the paper falls short is highly valuable. This is what your professor does when she/he reviews a paper. So, getting feedback from an outside source prior to submitting a paper for a grade is a good idea. If we're going to proof and edit our own work, it's essential to let it cool a couple of days. For some reason, most of us can't do a good job reviewing something we've just written—and this includes most of your professors. All of this reviewing, proofing, and editing does little good unless we have sufficient time to produce a quality final draft.

One last point in all of this—professors assessing student work. The authors of this book have accumulated more than 100 years of helping students with papers and assessing those papers. We've reviewed thousands of papers and we, and the vast majority of our colleagues, have a single intent when we review a student's paper—to help that student improve her/his skills, to develop into the best writer, analyst, thinker possible. A review by a professor is not a personal judgment on the person who wrote the paper; it is a professional assessment on how well the paper communicates and the reasoning that went into the paper. In our experience, almost every professor we have encountered shares these values.

TABLE A.C1
Writing Skills–Selected Websites

Site	Description
www.wikihow.com/Improve-Your-Writing-Skills	Four ways to improve one's writing
http://grammar.about.com/od/developinge ssays/a/quicktips.htm	10 quick tips
www.smashingmagazine.com/2009/06/28/50-free-resources-that-will-improve-your-writing-skills/	50 free resources
http://michaelhyatt.com/improve-writing.html	Seven "tricks"
www.bristol.ac.uk/arts/exercises/grammar/grammar_tutorial/	University of Bristol, grammar rules
http://web.mit.edu/me-ugoffice/communication/technical-writing.pdf	MIT technical writing slide show
https://owl.english.purdue.edu/owl/section/4/16/	Purdue University, Owl—technical writing
https://owl.english.purdue.edu/owl/section/4/18/	Purdue University, Owl—social science writing
http://weber.ucsd.edu/~keferree/Writing%20 a%20Good%20Social%20Science%20Paper.htm	"Writing a good social science paper"
http://harrisschool.uchicago.edu/sites/default/files/files/writing.pdf	University of Chicago, writing public policy slide show
http://gsrc.ucla.edu/gwc/resources/writing-in-public-affairs.html	UCLA, writing resources for public affairs
www.hks.harvard.edu/var/ezp_site/storage/fckeditor/file/pdfs/degree-programs/teaching/Case-Writing-Tips-July-2009.pdf	Harvard University, Kennedy School, tips on writing public policy cases

Table A.C1 lists several websites with wonderful guidance and advice on writing in general, as well as writing specific types of papers.

C.1—APA CITATION/REFERENCE STYLE

There are many citation/reference styles out there—we present the *American Psychological Association (APA)* citation/reference style in this Appendix. Other styles are designed for two levels of reading and learning, such as this textbook with endnotes for survey reading to introduce a field, and a second level of in-depth reading by examining the endnotes. APA style is designed for quick inspection of your paper's literature sources. It is often used in student papers because the reader (your *instructor*) can quickly tell what literature you are citing with internal citations in the body of your text. It's also useful for journal articles, so researchers can quickly tell whom is being cited and how. The APA style is very straight-forward and there's a lot of information available on how to do APA. In this section we'll briefly review the APA citation style. You first goal is to master the APA style with your first paper—it's not a big deal, just a few rules to keep in mind. It's always tragic if you get a lower grade for APA errors.

Why is a citation or reference style important? Essentially, it's our paper trail, the evidence that supports our case, the arguments we're presenting. Additionally, it enables us to document others' ideas without concern of accusation that an idea was stolen from another and presented as our own. In short, we give credit where credit is due. Without citations, a reader would not know if the author of a paper is asserting this or that piece of information or if, in fact, that piece of information exists elsewhere. A citation enables a reader to verify that information. Since most of us are not perjurers, we generally accept that the reference is accurate and supports the point or fact being presented. Finally, at a practical level, your correct use of the APA citation/reference style demonstrates to your reader (the *instructor*) that you know what you are doing, you're a contentious student and your argument is sound.

The BASIC PROBLEMS: (1) *when and when not to cite* a piece of information, and (2) *how to present information.* Of course, your skills will develop with experience. It's impossible to lay out a set of iron clad rules in just a couple of paragraphs, so please consider the following information as guides.

First off, better safe than sorry, so when in doubt—CITE! What facts to cite is somewhat of a judgment call, but here's a pretty good rule. If something is common knowledge—don't cite. For example, *the sky is blue*—no citation needed, we all know this. If we state, *the sky is blue because sunlight reaches Earth's atmosphere and is scattered in all directions by the gases and particles in the air. Blue is scattered more than other colors because it travels as shorter, smaller waves* (NASA, 2017), this is *not* common knowledge, and ought to be cited.

Second, theft of another's ideas or information, and presenting it as our own, is plagiarism. Plagiarism is as close to a capital crime as we have in the academic community. Politicians, journalists, authors, and corporate CEOs have lost positions, suffered lawsuits, or been shamed by plagiarism. And humble students, depending on the rules governing their program and institution, have suffered reductions in assignment scores, reductions in course grades, and/or dismissals from their institution. We rely on honor as the primary enforcement mechanism against plagiarism. Additionally, education plays a role—we learn as we go. Citations are our primary defense against plagiarism, so use them freely. It's better to be criticized for having too many citations than run the risk of a charge of plagiarism.

Third, the manner in which we present information is a key to an argument's persuasiveness and a paper's success. There are three basic ways to present pieces of information in a paper: quoting, paraphrasing, or summarizing. Each has its strengths and places where it's most appropriate. First off, a quote is a when one verbatim borrows from another writer. For example:

> With malice toward none, with charity for all, with firmness in the right as
> God gives us to see the right, let us strive on to finish the work we are in,
> to bind up the nation's wounds, to care for him who shall have borne the
> battle and for his widow and his orphan, to do all which may achieve and
> cherish a just and lasting peace among ourselves and with all nations.

This item, selected from Lincoln's second inaugural address, is quoted because of the powerful and unique way that Lincoln stated his points. That's why we quote— *when an author's own words are particularly important or poignant* in getting his/ her idea across. In APA this requires us to cite. Quotes are particularly powerful and ought not to be overused. Otherwise, we place an author's statements in our own words, we paraphrase or summarize. When we paraphrase someone's statement, we simply put it into our own words. We summarize an author's words by going beyond paraphrasing and stating the key aspects and/or importance of what the author said. In either case—summarizing or paraphrasing—we cite.

Let's get down to nuts and bolts. APA style requires two components to complete an attribution to an author, an *in-text citation* and a *reference page*. The in-text citation within APA, is probably the simplest of any style,

(author, date)

So, in the case of our Lincoln quote,

(Lincoln, 1865)

We complete the attribution by including the author and her/his work in a literature cited or reference page. The details of how to cite a particular source and how to construct a reference page are laid out in the APA Style Manual and a vast number of websites. Just make certain the source you use for APA help, is up-to-date. The style changes over time. Table A.C2 lists several websites with guidance on the APA style.

C.2—BRIEFING A CASE (JUDICIAL OPINION)

Because public administration is founded in the rule of law, many courses/seminars include readings of judicial case opinions for analysis of public administration. In some courses/seminars you may be required to submit briefs of cases, usually including these elements. A *case* is a legal conflict in the process of legal interpretation by courts. It calls for a *judicial decision and reasoning* to support that decision. These decisions and reasons are sometimes recorded in written form as *judicial opinions*. Judicial opinions are usually written by *judges or justices of a higher appellate court* under powers of review that are *discretionary* (e.g., *Writ*

TABLE A.C2	
APA Style on the World-Wide Web	
University of Wisconsin—Madison Writing Center	http://writing.wisc.edu/Handbook/DocAPA.html
American Psychological Association	www.apastyle.org/
Purdue Owl	https://owl.english.purdue.edu/owl/resource/560/01/
Cornell University	www.library.cornell.edu/resrch/citmanage/apa
University of Illinois	www.cws.illinois.edu/workshop/writers/citation/apa/
Penn State University	www.libraries.psu.edu/psul/lls/students/apa_citation.html
University of Washington	www.lib.washington.edu/help/guides/43APA.pdf

of Ceriorari) or *mandatory* (e.g., *Writ of Appeal*). For the U.S. Supreme Court, an *OPINION OF THE COURT* (often called the *majority opinion*) is the official judicial opinion of the Court resolving a particular case. If there is no majority vote, the official judicial opinion of the Court is then called the *JUDGMENT OF THE COURT*. A Justice who agrees with the decision, but not the reasons contained in the official opinion of the Court, may state their reasoning in a separate *CONCURRING OPINION*. If a Justice on the Court disagrees with the decision and the reasoning of the official opinion of the Court, they may write a *DISSENTING OPINION*.

Case-briefing is a standard technique used in public administration, law schools, and law-related education to analyze these written judicial opinions. By reducing the judicial opinion to basic elements of the case, you can learn the law, legal process, and how to "think like a judge." For educational applications, case briefs typically include at *least four (4) basic elements (F-I-R-E)*:

F *Facts*: often found in the *case syllabus* or summary at the beginning of most cases, as well as the beginning paragraphs of judicial opinion, these are the *people and chain of events of legal relevance* to the dispute or legal conflict before the court.

I *Issue(s)*: arising from facts of the case, the *legal question(s) resolved by the Court in the case* narrows the facts down and sets them within the *elements of law(s)*. Sometimes the judge or justice will write out the issues or use them to outline their judicial opinions.

R *Reasoning*: after answering issues with a yes-or-no *holding*, the judge or justice will write an opinion focused on the essence of the decision, as distinct from unnecessary points of the case opinion. In addition, there may be *concurring* or *dissenting opinions*.

E *Effect*: or the *action* of the court, includes the further interpretation of a case decision as well as who won by the votes cast and an outcome or result: *affirming* (accepting) or *reversing* (rejecting and setting aside) the judgment of the court below. When reversing, the court will often *remand* (send back) a case to a lower court for specific further action.

C.3—WRITING A BOOK REVIEW

In public administration courses/seminars, the book review paper is a short (three pages or more) summary and critique of a relevant academic treatise. Each instructor usually has a unique format, to ensure the book review paper was written for their class. At a minimum, the book review paper includes three elements: (1) *What did the book say?*—an overview summary of the contents of the book; (2) *How does the book relate to ideas/concepts of the course/seminar?* These are usually found in the topical themes of the syllabus, or as directed by the instructor; and (3) *What critique do you have of the book?* How you agree or disagree with the ideas, evidence, or arguments made in the book. Your critique of evaluation of a book is where you show-your-stuff as a student. You must generally discuss the soundness of the author's argument(s), not just repeat what the author said. In your critique, it is good form to try to be impartial by reading sympathetically with the author, acknowledging your opinions on the subject. According to Mortimer Adler, in *How to Read a Book* (1940; 1973)[1], there are usually four ways in which we make a general criticism of the *soundness* of the author's argument(s):

- *The author is uninformed*: the author lacks some vital relevant information.
- *The author is misinformed*: the author asserts what is not the case.
- *The author's analysis is incomplete*: the author hasn't solved all problems as set out.
- *The author is illogical*: there is a fallacy in the author's reasoning—for example:
  - *non sequitur*: a conclusion doesn't follow the given reasons
  - inconsistency: two or more statements are inconsistent
  - cogency: the author reasons poorly from otherwise good grounds.

Thus, a *book review paper summarizes, analyzes, and evaluates a book*. The evaluation is more important than the analysis, which is more important than the summary. Stated another way, telling a reader what's in a book is less important than telling the reader how this work fits into the greater subject area, which is less important than assessing the value of the book for readers interested in a particular field or subfield. Here, again, we're fortunate—there's a lot written on how to write a book review. Table A.C3 outlines some key components to a review. It is a generic overview, so make certain to follow any guidelines or instructions that your professor provides.

C.4—WRITING A LITERATURE REVIEW PAPER

A literature review is a report of information found in the literature related to a selected issue. The review should describe, summarize, evaluate, and clarify the literature. As a section within a major term paper or thesis, it provides the foundation upon which the current research is built. In its most basic sense, a literature review can be a standalone. Usually, a literature review is an essential component of a greater paper. A literature review provides the intellectual, theoretical, and factual foundation to direct the current study. You may find relevant literature by

TABLE A.C3
Some Components of a Book Review Paper

1. Summary	A *brief* overview of what the book covers. This will be painted broadly with detail only as you think it's important for our audience to have. This may be the least important portion of the review, as it contains the information that a reader might find in any number of sources. *No blah, blah, blah!!!*
2. Context	Background: what do we know regarding the author, the approach to the subject matter, or other relevant information? For example, is the author knowledgeable in this area or qualified to write this book?
3. Key Issues/Lessons	What are the most important things a reader should get out of this book? Unlike the summary, here the review author focuses only on the most important points and goes at these in a bit more detail. This is a key part of any good review.
4. Value	The reviewer will interpret who is (are) the key audience(s) for this book, and what particular value the book may have to them or others.
5. Strengths	We spring off of value and set forth the particular strengths of the book. If space permits, it's a good idea to provide a little detail regarding each strength.
6. Weaknesses	All work has some weakness or shortcoming. This discussion might be very brief or contain numerous points, but it is important to note that the reviewer is alert to weaknesses, and we detail any we find.
7. Other Information	Usually there's some important information not captured in the above sections—place it here.
8. Recommendation(s)	This is particularly important—the reviewer puts his/her reputation on the line in that he/she sums up the strengths and weaknesses, pros and cons, and makes one or more recommendations to readers. Recommendations may be general or to a specific audience. Our recommendations ought to include some general statements and some specific to our peers in this course. This section may be a bit redundant with Value, Strengths, and Weaknesses, but in this section we pull it together.

researchers, professors, practitioners, public managers, and public policy analysts in journals and books in libraries in the stacks, by online journals and books, and by inter-library loan. In reading and summarizing these scholarly works, develop your literature review in an essay style, with paragraphs and themes, not just an annotated bibliography summary of one scholarly work at a time. Consider the following when you write your literature review critique:

1. What does the specific work say?
2. How does the content of the specific work relate to the topic of your paper?
3. What do you think of the author's arguments?

In your critique, generally discuss how you agree or disagree with the author by engaging in a dialogue with the author, not just repeating what the author said. In your critique, try to be impartial by reading sympathetically with the author, acknowledging your opinions on the subject.

So, a literature review is similar to a book review (or article review) yet broader and more inclusive. Before continuing, let's discuss three ways to present literature: bibliography, annotated bibliography, and literature review.

A *bibliography* is nothing more than a *list of the literature for a subject or paper*. APA has clear guidelines for developing and presenting a bibliography. It consists of one entry for each article, book, report, website, or other item included in the paper.

An *annotated bibliography* is a *bibliography with an annotation for each entry*. Usually an annotation is a paragraph or two that describes the entry and may include the subject matter, scope, focus, and methods. Unlike a book review, an annotation seldom includes and assessment or evaluation of the entry.

A good *literature review is greater than the sum of its parts*. Unlike a bibliography or annotated bibliography organized by each entry, *a literature review is organized thematically*. The reviewer must identify the key or important themes that provide the best or most meaningful way(s) to summarize, assess, and evaluate the literature. For example, a reviewer might want to trace the history of a subject identifying key developments. The reviewer may opt to identify the key themes. Or she/he might discuss the research methods that prior scholars employed to analyze and understand the issue. Usually a literature review summarizes, assesses, and evaluates along multiple dimensions, say the development of key themes and identification of important research methods used by others. In a way, a literature review is a lot like a prosecutor building a case—she/he establishes the facts and then provides meaning and interpretation to them. And, like any prosecutor, a good reviewer seeks an airtight case. Like a weaver who uses stands of yarn to make a blanket, a reviewer takes the separate stands of the literature to construct and overview of the present knowledge regarding a particular subject.

C.5—WRITING A TERM PAPER (EMPIRICAL/ RESEARCH)

There are a *wide variety of types of term papers*. This makes following instructions particularly important. Is the assignment for a literature review, a policy analysis, or an assessment of some issue in the field? Does the assignment call for original research, i.e., that the author goes out and gathers data from the field, e.g. interviews with public officials? Make certain you're clear regarding the instructor's expectations; otherwise, you won't be able to plan and schedule.

All term papers feature a *style of paper-writing that is organized, focused on a narrow subject, and documents the sources* of all borrowed ideas, quotes, and materials. Term papers usually include:

- *Title Page*: with the full title, author's name (you), and other information in APA style.

- *Executive Summary* or *Abstract*: short summary (less than 200 words) of your paper on a separate page, following the APA-style.
- *Body*: including introduction, literature review, findings, and conclusion in APA-style.
- *Internal Citations*: consistent use throughout the body of the term paper of APA-style internal citations to credit the things you borrow.
- *References*: at the end of the paper, a separate page titled "References," with APA-style reference citations for all cited works within your term paper.

Oftentimes an instructor leaves it up to a student to *select the subject matter of a term paper*. Many students will jump on the subject they feel will be easiest. This is not usually the best tactic. We've done a lot of research in our time and read thousands of student papers, and without a doubt we know that if a researcher is interested or curious about a subject the likelihood of producing an excellent product increases. And, the process will be much more enjoyable and pleasant. Ease is not the best foundation for selecting a topic—interest is. *Learning about something you're interested in is always easier in the long term and generally produces better results.*

Let's go into a little more depth regarding the research process, as frequently a term paper requires answering some question or questions. The authors suggest posting these questions in an obvious place. One of this text's authors posts these questions above his workspace so that they're always there and he sees them frequently. Generally an assignment is stated in general terms—this is to provide the student researcher-author with a little wiggle room, so that the student has some discretion in how she/he approaches the assignment. In this situation, it's particularly important that the author put into writing the research questions. What questions must be answered in order to adequately address the assignment? For instance, if the assignment were for a literature review, an *obvious question might be*: Who are the *big thinkers* in the subject? *Other questions might be*: What are the key issues in the subject area? How has the subject developed over time? What types of data are used? and Where is the field heading?

A term paper, like any good administrative product, requires *thinking*. We've found that thinking is what moves a technically sound, *pretty good* paper to an *excellent* paper. And the more thinking that takes place early in the research process, the better. Early thinking and organizing can save a lot of wasted energy and time, energy and time that can be focused more precisely on the important issues to be addressed in the paper. More precise focus usually results in a better paper, one that does not beat around the topic while never actually getting to the heart of the matter. Thinking helps us to determine what the key issues are and how we can best focus on them. Also, thinking early on will help us to determine if our subject is too broad or too narrow. A subject that's too broad will result in our producing a superficial paper or the need to cut some of the text along with the prior investment of time and energy. A subject too narrow may result in a trivial paper and/or the urgent need to scramble and expand the subject.

Finally, when the paper is complete and submitted, we have one final activity. Smart authors organize their research and file it away—this includes both hard and digital copies. While a student never submits the same paper twice, he/she may draw on prior research as they develop future papers.

FINAL COMMENTS

First, let's review some *basic points on writing in public administration*:

1. Make sure you understand each part of the paper in entirety—ask your instructor if you don't know.
2. Use quotation marks when directly quoting from a source and underline or italicize court case titles.
3. Run the spell-checking on your computer, but note that you still need to proofread because spell checking will not catch all mistakes (e.g., *its* and *it's*, *trail* and *trial*, there and *their*)
4. Use short, simple sentences with effective verbs to make your writing more persuasive.
5. Organize the overall structure of your paper, making each sentence, paragraph, and subsection a logical part of your argument.
6. Don't procrastinate!
7. Proofread your paper again!
8. Revise, revise, and then revise again!

Of course, another way to remember these points on writing is to think about *grading*. How will your instructor grade your case brief, book review paper, literature review, or term paper? We suggest three basic areas for your punch-list before turning your paper in.

First, does your paper *follow the directions* and is it *complete*?

- Did you pick an accepted topic, as instructed in the course?
- Did you write an original paper, or was it plagiarized?
- Did your paper include the basic components—for example, title page, citations, and references?
- Did your paper properly use APA-style internal citations and references?

Second, does your paper include any *misstatements* and *misinformation*:

- Did your paper misstate any important idea(s) in its presentation and/or writing style?
- Did your paper misinform or confuse the reader as to what is not the case?

Finally, is your paper *cogent* or effective, and persuasive in communicating your ideas.

So: Follow Directions, Be Complete, Be Clear, Be True!

Our discussion on writing in public administration is not comprehensive—*there's a lot more to developing writing and esearch skills than can be imparted in a few pages*. Written communication is one of your most important skills as a public administrator, whether a brief memo or a major report. Most public administration, public policy, and public management programs place considerable emphasis on the development of your writing skills. Most of the effort rests with you. You must work diligently to develop this skill with instruction, criticism, and encouragement from your instructors. Outside of class, there's much you can do to build your writing skills.:

- A desire to improve and a willingness to put in the requisite effort are fundamental to becoming a better writer.
- Reading, reading, and more reading of the works of good writers, both nonfiction and fiction. Seeing how others do it is instructive in and of itself.
- Most universities have assistance available to help students—writing centers and workshops. Using these resources and building their suggestions into future papers may help a good deal.
- Seeking criticism and help from instructors and others is a good idea.

Bottom line: no matter how good a writer we are when we begin our program, each of us can improve. And, improved writing skills often pay dividends in the workplace with faster promotions and higher salaries.

NOTES

1   Mortimer Adler, *How to Read a Book: The Classic Guide to Intelligent Reading*, revised ed. (New York: Touchstone Books, 1972).

INDEX